Family Living™

Our Best Cookbook
COLLECTION

Death by Chocolate, p. 45

928 RECIPES

for Quick Meals, Side Dishes, Salads, Simple Suppers, Chicken, Family Feasts, Party Fare, Sweets, Gift Mixes, Desserts, and Cookies.

ISBN-13: 978-1-60900-141-4

928 recipes to satisfy every taste!

*Whatever you're hungry for, there's a recipe here that's sure to please: **cookies** of all kinds, **desserts** to top off your meals with sweetness, easy recipes for casual **everyday meals**, ready-to-fix **gift mixes**, **party appetizers** and drinks, and **complete menus for family gatherings**! This big 12-in-1 cookbook collection also presents our all-time favorite recipes for **smart suppers** you can fix fast, **treats** to satisfy every sweet tooth, **side dishes** to spice up lunch and dinner, **salads** for the freshest and healthiest meals, **cakes and pies** for ending meals on a sweet note, and a variety of flavorful **chicken** recipes. You'll use this treasury again and again!*

Leisure Arts, Inc.
Little Rock, Arkansas

Cream Cheese-Topped Chocolate Cake, p. 16

Mocha Almond Bars, p. 66

Our Favorite Desserts
Page 11

72 Recipes to Top Off Your Meals with Sweetness

• Cakes
• Pies
• Puddings
• Fruit salads
• More!

Our Favorite Cookies
Page 57

78 Recipes for All the Tastes You Love!

• Crunchy
• Chewy
• Moist
• Flaky
• Unforgettable!

Pumpkin Spice Cake, p. 26

Candy Bar Pizzas and Butterscotch Chewies, p. 67

Pistachio-Coconut Mousse Mix, p. 108

Chicken Chutney Salad, p. 177

Our Favorite Gift Mixes
Page 103

*91 Ready-To-Fix Recipes
to Pack and Present!*

- Cookies
- Fudge
- Coffees
- Creamers
- Breads
- Soups
- More!

Our Favorite Simple Suppers
Page 149

*69 Recipes for
Casual Everyday Meals*

- Casseroles
- Pasta
- Chili
- Soups
- Salads
- Breads

Chocolate Biscuit Mix, p. 134

*Pumpkin Bread with
Orange Sauce, p. 194*

Spiced Apple Punch, p. 222

Eggnog Custard Pie, p. 254
Coconut-Orange Cake, p. 255

Our Favorite Party Fare
Page 195

106 Recipes for
Munching and Sipping

• Savory bites
• Creamy dips
• Crisp wafers
• Cool sips
• Fireside warmers

Our Favorite Family Feasts
Page 241

62 Recipes—From Soup to Dessert!

• Family Feast
• Yuletide Reunion
• Home for the Holidays
• Dashing Through the Snow
• Ski Lodge Supper
• Cozy Little Buffet

Fruit Wreath with
Sweet Cheese Dip, p. 197

Roasted Red Pepper Soup, p. 256

Ham-Pecan-Blue Cheese Pasta Salad, p. 322

BLT Chicken Salad, p. 334

Hooray for Quick Meals
Page 287

75 Easy Recipes for Family Favorites You Can Fix Fast!

• Smart shortcuts
• Full-meal menus
• Kid pleasers
• So much more!

Hooray for Chicken
Page 333

75 Easy Recipes for Delicious, Family-Pleasing Variety!

• Comfort food
• From the oven
• Off the grill
• So much more!

Mexican Chef Salad, p. 301

Dijon Chicken with Pasta, p. 345

Fresh Corn Pudding, p. 408

Apple-Apricot Salad, p. 469

Hooray for Side Dishes
Page 379

*75 Easy Recipes for Spicing Up
Your Lunch and Dinner!*

• Fresh combos
• Creamy casseroles
• Grilled delights
• So much more!

Hooray for Salads
Page 425

*75 Easy Recipes for the Freshest
and Healthiest Meals!*

• Crisp greens
• Fruit medleys
• Perfect pastas
• So much more!

*Vegetable-Rice Toss, p. 406
Red Cabbage and Apple Slaw, p. 407*

*Caesar Salad with Tortelleni and
Asparagus, p. 426*

Chocolate Dream Pie, p. 506

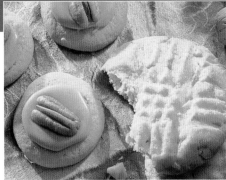

Brown Sugar-Pecan Cookies, p. 532
Texan-Size Almond Crunch Cookies, p. 531

Hooray for Desserts
Page 471

75 Easy Recipes for Ending
Meals on a Sweet Note!

- Moist cakes
- Creamy pies
- Fruity favorites
- So much more!

Hooray for Sweets
Page 517

75 Easy Recipes for Satisfying
Every Sweet Tooth!

- Chewy cookies
- Crunchy snacks
- Rich brownies
- So much more!

Banana Pudding, p. 507

Candy Bar Brownies, p. 557

Our Favorite DESSERTS

Nothing highlights a delicious meal better than a sweet surprise at the end. Whether your tastes run to velvety chocolate pies and rich, moist pound cakes or luscious, fruity treats and refreshingly tart sauces, the recipes in this extravagant collection are sure to satisfy. The hardest part will be deciding which to try first!

Death by Chocolate, p. 45

MEXICAN CHOCOLATE ANGEL FOOD CAKE

1³/₄ cups sifted confectioners sugar, divided
1 cup sifted all-purpose flour
¹/₄ cup sifted cocoa
2¹/₄ teaspoons ground cinnamon, divided
1¹/₂ cups egg whites (10 to 12 large eggs)
1¹/₂ teaspoons cream of tartar
1 teaspoon vanilla extract
1 cup granulated sugar
Sugared grapes to garnish

Preheat oven to 350 degrees. Sift 1¹/₂ cups confectioners sugar, flour, cocoa, and 2 teaspoons cinnamon 3 times into a medium bowl.

In a large bowl, beat egg whites, cream of tartar, and vanilla with an electric mixer until soft peaks form. Gradually add granulated sugar, 2 tablespoons at a time, and beat until stiff peaks form.

Sift about ¹/₄ of confectioners sugar mixture over egg white mixture; fold in gently by hand. Continue to sift and fold in confectioners sugar mixture in small batches. Lightly spoon batter into an ungreased 10-inch tube pan and place on lower rack of oven. Bake 40 to 45 minutes or until top springs back when lightly touched. Remove from oven and invert pan onto neck of a bottle; cool completely. Remove cake from pan, placing bottom side up on a serving plate.

To decorate, combine remaining ¹/₄ cup confectioners sugar and ¹/₄ teaspoon cinnamon in a small bowl. Place a 10-inch round paper doily on top of cake and lightly sift confectioners sugar mixture over doily. Carefully remove doily. Garnish with sugared grapes.

Yield: about 12 servings

FUDGE POUND CAKE

¹/₂ cup butter or margarine, softened
1³/₄ cups granulated sugar
2 teaspoons vanilla extract
3 eggs
1³/₄ cups all-purpose flour
²/₃ cup cocoa
2 teaspoons baking powder
¹/₂ teaspoon baking soda
1 cup sour cream

Preheat oven to 325 degrees. In a large mixing bowl, cream butter, sugar, and vanilla. Beat in eggs.

In a small bowl, combine flour, cocoa, baking powder, and baking soda. Stir flour mixture into butter mixture, alternating with sour cream. Pour into a greased 9 x 5 x 3-inch loaf pan. Bake 1 hour 20 minutes or until a toothpick inserted in center comes out clean. Cool 10 minutes in pan; remove from pan and cool completely.

Yield: 12 to 14 servings

Deliciously light in fat and calories, Mexican Chocolate Angel Food Cake is a divine completion for Christmas dinner. Its lacy decoration is created by sprinkling cinnamon and confectioners sugar over a paper doily.

COCONUT POUND CAKE

CAKE
- 1½ cups butter or margarine, softened
- 3 cups sugar
- 6 eggs
- 3 cups all-purpose flour
- ¼ teaspoon baking soda
- 1 container (8 ounces) sour cream
- 1 teaspoon coconut extract
- 1 teaspoon rum extract
- 1 cup flaked coconut

SYRUP
- 1 cup water
- 1 cup sugar
- 1 teaspoon almond extract

Preheat oven to 325 degrees. For cake, cream butter and sugar in a large bowl. Add eggs, 1 at a time, beating well after each addition. Sift flour and baking soda into a medium bowl. Alternately beat dry ingredients, sour cream, and extracts into creamed mixture. Stir in coconut. Spoon batter into a greased 10-inch fluted tube pan. Bake 1¼ to 1½ hours or until a toothpick inserted in center of cake comes out clean. Cool cake in pan 15 minutes.

For syrup, combine water and sugar in a medium saucepan. Stirring frequently, cook over medium-high heat 5 minutes. Remove from heat and stir in almond extract. Before removing cake from pan, brush about one-third of warm syrup on cake. Invert cake onto a serving plate. Brush remaining syrup on cake. Allow cake to cool completely. Store in an airtight container.

Yield: about 16 servings

OLD-FASHIONED POUND CAKE

- 2 cups margarine, softened
- 3 cups granulated sugar
- 1 teaspoon vanilla extract
- 1 teaspoon almond extract
- 1 teaspoon imitation butter flavoring
- 6 eggs
- 4 cups all-purpose flour (sifted three times)
- ¾ cup milk

Preheat oven to 325 degrees. In large mixing bowl, cream margarine, gradually adding sugar. Beat in extracts and butter flavoring. Beat in eggs one at a time, beating well after each addition. Beginning and ending with flour, alternately add flour and milk, beating well after each addition. Pour batter into ten greased 5 x 3 x 1½-inch loaf pans. Bake 40 to 45 minutes, or until a toothpick inserted into a cake comes out clean.

Yield: 10 small cakes

APPLE SPICE CAKE

CAKE
- 1 package (18.25 ounces) spice cake mix
- 1 cup apple juice
- $1/3$ cup applesauce
- 3 eggs
- $1/3$ cup vegetable oil
- 1 teaspoon maple flavoring
- 2 cups cored, unpeeled, and chopped Granny Smith apples (about 2 apples)

TOPPING
- $1/2$ cup applesauce
- $1/3$ cup firmly packed brown sugar
- $1/4$ cup butter or margarine

Preheat oven to 325 degrees. For cake, combine cake mix, apple juice, eggs, applesauce, oil, and maple flavoring in a large bowl. Beat at low speed of an electric mixer 30 seconds. Beat at medium speed 2 minutes. Stir in apples. Pour batter into a greased 9 x 13-inch baking dish. Bake 40 to 45 minutes or until a toothpick inserted in center of cake comes out clean. Place baking dish on a wire rack while making topping.

For topping, combine all ingredients in a small saucepan over medium-high heat. Stirring frequently, bring to a boil; reduce heat and cook until thickened. Serve warm cake with topping.

Yield: about 16 servings

COFFEE BREAK CAKE

- 1 cup crushed chocolate-covered graham crackers
- 1 cup chopped pecans
- 2 teaspoons ground cinnamon
- 1 package (18.25 ounces) yellow cake mix
- $1^{1}/4$ cups water
- 3 eggs
- $1/3$ cup vegetable oil
- $1/2$ cup sifted confectioners sugar
- 2 teaspoons milk
- 1 teaspoon vanilla extract

Preheat oven to 350 degrees. In a small bowl, combine cracker crumbs, pecans, and cinnamon. In a large bowl, combine cake mix, water, eggs, and oil. Beat at low speed of an electric mixer 30 seconds. Beat at medium speed 2 minutes. Pour two-thirds of batter into a greased 10-inch tube pan. Sprinkle one-half of cracker crumb mixture over batter. Pour remaining batter over crumbs. Sprinkle remaining crumb mixture on top. Bake 40 to 45 minutes or until a toothpick inserted in center of cake comes out clean. Cool in pan 15 minutes. Remove from pan and cool completely on a wire rack.

In a small bowl, combine confectioners sugar, milk, and vanilla; stir until smooth. Drizzle glaze over cake.

Yield: about 16 servings

Guests will find Cream Cheese-Topped Chocolate Cake delicious!

CREAM CHEESE-TOPPED CHOCOLATE CAKE

- 1 package (18.25 ounces) devil's food cake mix
- 2 eggs
- 1/2 cup butter or margarine, softened
- 2 eggs
- 3 1/2 cups sifted confectioners sugar
- 1 package (8 ounces) cream cheese, softened

Preheat oven to 350 degrees. In a large bowl, combine cake mix, 2 eggs, and butter; beat 2 minutes. Spread batter in a greased and floured 9 x 13-inch glass baking dish. In a small bowl, beat 2 eggs, confectioners sugar, and cream cheese until smooth. Spread over cake batter. Bake 35 to 40 minutes or until cake begins to pull away from sides of pan. Cool completely on a wire rack. Store in an airtight container.

Yield: about 12 servings

MOCHA PUDDING CAKE

1 cup all-purpose flour
³/₄ cup granulated sugar
¹/₄ cup plus 2 tablespoons cocoa, divided
1¹/₂ teaspoons baking powder
¹/₄ teaspoon salt
¹/₂ cup skim milk
2 tablespoons vegetable oil
1 teaspoon vanilla extract
1 cup firmly packed brown sugar
1³/₄ cups boiling strongly brewed coffee
9 tablespoons reduced-fat frozen whipped topping, thawed

Preheat oven to 350 degrees. Combine flour, granulated sugar, 2 tablespoons cocoa, baking powder, and salt in a 9-inch square baking pan. Add milk, oil, and vanilla; whisk until smooth. In a small bowl, combine brown sugar and remaining ¹/₄ cup cocoa; sprinkle over batter. Pour coffee over batter (do not stir). Bake 40 to 45 minutes or until a toothpick inserted in cake portion comes out clean. Cool cake in pan 5 minutes. Top each serving with 1 tablespoon whipped topping.

Yield: 9 servings

Mocha Pudding Cake is a chocolate lover's heaven!

APRICOT-NUT CAKES

- 1 package (18½ ounces) yellow cake mix
- 4 eggs
- ¾ cup apricot nectar
- ¾ cup vegetable oil
- 1 jar (4 ounces) apricot baby food
- 1 cup finely chopped pecans, toasted
- 1 cup confectioners sugar
- ¼ cup apricot brandy
- 4 teaspoons freshly squeezed lemon juice

Preheat oven to 325 degrees. Grease three 3½ x 7½-inch loaf pans, line bottoms with waxed paper; grease waxed paper. In a large bowl, combine cake mix, eggs, apricot nectar, oil, and baby food; beat until well blended. Stir in pecans. Pour batter into prepared pans. Bake 40 to 45 minutes or until a toothpick inserted in center of cake comes out clean. Cool in pans 10 minutes on a wire rack. Remove from pans and place on a wire rack with waxed paper underneath.

In a small bowl, combine confectioners sugar, brandy, and lemon juice; stir until smooth. Spoon glaze over warm cakes. Allow cakes to cool completely. Store in an airtight container in refrigerator.

Yield: 3 small cakes

RING OF GOLD APRICOT CAKE

CAKE
- 1 cup butter or margarine, softened
- 2 cups sugar
- 5 eggs
- ½ cup apricot jam
- ½ cup sour cream
- 1 teaspoon vanilla extract
- 2 cups all-purpose flour
- 1 teaspoon baking soda
- ½ teaspoon salt
- 2 cups flaked coconut
- 1 cup finely chopped pecans
- 1 package (8 ounces) dried apricots, finely chopped

GLAZE
- ½ cup apricot jam
- 2 tablespoons apricot nectar

Preheat oven to 350 degrees. For cake, cream butter and sugar in a large bowl until fluffy. Add eggs, 1 at a time, beating well after each addition. Stir in jam, sour cream, and vanilla. Sift flour, baking soda, and salt into a medium bowl. Stir dry ingredients into creamed mixture. Fold in coconut, pecans and apricots. Pour batter into a greased and floured 10-inch springform pan with fluted tube insert. Bake 45 to 55 minutes or until a toothpick inserted in center of cake comes out clean. Cool in pan 10 minutes; turn onto a wire rack to cool completely.

For glaze, combine jam and nectar in a small saucepan over medium heat; stir until well blended. Pour evenly over top of cake. Store in an airtight container.

Yield: about 20 servings

Sour cream and apricot jam give our Ring of Gold Apricot Cake a rich flavor and moist texture.

APPLE-PEAR SKILLET CAKE

1 cup firmly packed brown sugar
6 tablespoons butter or margarine, cut into pieces
1 medium unpeeled baking apple, cored and sliced
1 medium unpeeled pear, cored and sliced
1⅓ cups all-purpose flour
1 cup granulated sugar
2 teaspoons ground cinnamon
1¼ teaspoons baking soda
½ teaspoon salt
2 eggs
½ cup sour cream
2 tablespoons vegetable oil
1 teaspoon vanilla extract

Preheat oven to 350 degrees. Place brown sugar and butter in a 10½-inch cast-iron or ovenproof skillet. Place skillet in oven about 5 minutes or until butter melts. Remove skillet from oven and whisk brown sugar mixture until well blended. Arrange fruit slices over brown sugar mixture. In a medium bowl, combine flour, granulated sugar, cinnamon, baking soda, and salt. In a small bowl, whisk eggs, sour cream, oil, and vanilla; beat into flour mixture. Pour batter over fruit; bake 30 to 35 minutes or until a toothpick inserted in center of cake comes out clean. Remove from oven and place on a wire rack to cool 10 minutes. Run knife around edge of cake; invert onto a serving plate. Serve warm.

Yield: about 12 servings

PEANUT BUTTER CAKE

CAKE
1 package (18½ ounces) butter-recipe yellow cake mix
1 container (8 ounces) sour cream
⅓ cup vegetable oil
⅓ cup smooth peanut butter
3 eggs, separated
1 teaspoon vanilla extract

ICING
¼ cup smooth peanut butter
2 tablespoons butter or margarine, softened
1 teaspoon vanilla extract
3 cups confectioners sugar
4 to 5 tablespoons milk

Preheat oven to 350 degrees. For cake, combine cake mix, sour cream, oil, peanut butter, egg yolks, and vanilla in a large bowl; beat until well blended. In a small bowl, beat egg whites until stiff; fold into batter. Pour batter into a greased 9 x 13-inch baking pan. Bake 30 to 35 minutes or until a toothpick inserted in center of cake comes out clean. Allow cake to cool completely.

For icing, combine peanut butter, butter, and vanilla in a medium bowl; beat until smooth. Add confectioners sugar and gradually add milk; beat until smooth. Ice top of cake.

Yield: 12 to 15 servings

PEANUT BUTTERSCOTCH CAKE

 1/3 cup smooth peanut butter
 1 package (18.25 ounces) white
     cake mix
 1 package (3.5 ounces)
     butterscotch pudding mix
 1 cup water
 4 eggs
 1/4 cup vegetable oil

Preheat oven to 350 degrees. Stirring frequently, melt peanut butter in a small saucepan over medium heat. Remove from heat. In a large bowl, combine cake mix, pudding mix, water, eggs, and oil. Beat at low speed of an electric mixer 30 seconds. Beat at medium speed 2 minutes. Add 1 1/2 cups batter to peanut butter. Pour remaining batter into a greased 10-inch tube pan. Spoon peanut butter mixture over batter. Bake 50 to 55 minutes or until a toothpick inserted in center of cake comes out clean. Cool in pan 15 minutes. Remove from pan and cool completely on a wire rack.

Yield: about 16 servings

EASY FRUITCAKES

 1 package (14 ounces) graham
     cracker crumbs
 2 cups chopped walnuts
 2 cups chopped pecans
 1 package (8 ounces) chopped dates
 1 package (7 ounces) sweetened
     shredded coconut
 1 jar (10 ounces) red maraschino
     cherries, drained and chopped
 1 jar (6 ounces) green maraschino
     cherries, drained and chopped
 1 can (14 ounces) sweetened
     condensed milk
 1 package (10.5 ounces) miniature
     marshmallows

Combine first 7 ingredients in a large bowl or roasting pan. Combine sweetened condensed milk and marshmallows in a heavy large saucepan over low heat. Stir occasionally until marshmallows melt; remove from heat. Pour over fruit mixture; stir until blended. With lightly greased hands, firmly press mixture into four 3 1/4 x 6-inch loaf pans lined with plastic wrap. Chill overnight. Remove from loaf pans and wrap tightly in plastic wrap. Store in refrigerator.

Yield: 4 mini fruitcakes

WHITE FRUITCAKE

 1 package (18.25 ounces) white
     cake mix
 2/3 cup vegetable oil
 1/2 cup sweetened condensed milk
 2 egg whites
 1 1/2 cups chopped candied fruit
 1 1/2 cups chopped pecans

Preheat oven to 350 degrees. In a large bowl, beat cake mix, oil, condensed milk, and egg whites on low speed of an electric mixer until moistened; increase to high speed for 2 minutes. Stir in fruit and pecans. Spoon batter into 2 greased and floured 5 x 9-inch baking pans. Bake 40 to 45 minutes or until a toothpick inserted in center of cake comes out clean. Cool in pans 10 minutes. Remove from pans and cool completely on a wire rack. Store in an airtight container.

Yield: 2 loaves fruitcake

Topped with a citrusy glaze, Easy Lemon Cake is quick to whip up using cake mix and instant lemon pudding mix.

EASY LEMON CAKE

1 package (18.25 ounces) yellow cake mix
4 eggs
³/₄ cup water
³/₄ cup vegetable oil
1 package (3.4 ounces) lemon instant pudding mix
1 cup sifted confectioners sugar
¹/₃ cup frozen lemonade concentrate
2 tablespoons butter or margarine
Lemon slices to decorate

Preheat oven to 350 degrees. In a large bowl, combine cake mix, eggs, water, oil, and pudding mix. Beat at low speed of an electric mixer 30 seconds. Beat at medium speed 2 minutes. Pour batter into a greased 10-inch springform pan with fluted tube insert or a 10-inch fluted tube pan. Bake 40 to 45 minutes or until a toothpick inserted in center of cake comes out clean. Cool in pan 15 minutes; remove sides of pan. Invert onto a serving plate. Use a wooden skewer to poke holes about 1 inch apart in top of warm cake. Combine confectioners sugar, lemonade concentrate, and butter in a heavy small saucepan over medium-high heat. Bring to a boil; remove from heat. Slowly pour glaze over warm cake; cool completely. Place lemon slices around bottom of cake to decorate.

Yield: about 16 servings

VIENNA TORTE

CAKE

- 2 cups granulated sugar
- 2 cups all-purpose flour
- 1 teaspoon baking soda
- 1 cup butter or margarine
- 1 cup water
- ½ cup cocoa
- ½ cup buttermilk
- 2 eggs, lightly beaten
- 2 teaspoons vanilla extract

FROSTING

- 2 cups whipping cream
- 1½ cups sifted confectioners sugar
- 3 tablespoons green crème de menthe liqueur
- 2 tablespoons white crème de cacao liqueur

Preheat oven to 400 degrees. For cake, combine sugar, flour, and baking soda in a large mixing bowl; set aside. In a sauce pan, combine butter, water, and cocoa; bring to a boil. Add the chocolate mixture to the flour mixture and stir until well blended. Beat in buttermilk, eggs, and vanilla. Pour into a greased and floured 15 x 10 x 1-inch jellyroll pan. Bake 20 to 25 minutes or until cake springs back when touched in center. Allow cake to cool in pan.

For frosting, combine whipping cream, confectioners sugar, and liqueurs; beat until stiff peaks form.

Invert cake onto the back of another jellyroll pan. Cut cake crosswise into four equal sections. Placing layers on a serving plate, spread frosting evenly between layers and on top of cake; do not frost sides. Chill torte until ready to serve.

Yield: 10 to 12 servings

European-style Vienna Torte is a light chocolate cake with a crème de menthe filling.

GERMAN CHOCOLATE CHEESECAKE

CRUST

1 1/2 cups chocolate graham cracker crumbs
6 tablespoons butter or margarine, melted
1/4 cup sugar

FILLING

3 packages (8 ounces each) cream cheese, softened
1 1/4 cups sugar
2 tablespoons all-purpose flour
4 eggs
1 package (4 ounces) German baking chocolate, melted
1/4 cup whipping cream
1 teaspoon vanilla extract

TOPPING

3/4 cup sugar
3/4 cup whipping cream
2 egg yolks
6 tablespoons butter or margarine
1 cup flaked coconut
1 cup chopped pecans

Preheat oven to 325 degrees. For crust, combine cracker crumbs, melted butter, and sugar in a small bowl. Firmly press into bottom and 1/2 inch up sides of a lightly greased 9-inch springform pan.

For filling, beat cream cheese and sugar in a large bowl until fluffy. Beat in flour. Beat in eggs, 1 at a time, just until combined. Stir in melted chocolate, whipping cream, and vanilla. Pour over crust. Bake 1 hour or until center is almost set. Cool in pan 1 hour. Loosen and remove sides of pan. Cool completely.

For topping, whisk sugar, whipping cream, and egg yolks in a medium saucepan until well blended. Whisking constantly, add butter and cook over medium heat until mixture is thickened and bubbly. Reduce heat to low; cook 2 minutes longer. Remove from heat and stir in coconut and pecans. Transfer topping to a heat-proof bowl. Let cool 20 minutes or until thick enough to spread on cooled cheesecake. Store in an airtight container in refrigerator.

Yield: about 16 servings

BLACKBERRY SWIRL CHEESECAKE

1/2 cup seedless blackberry jam
4 packages (8 ounces each) cream cheese, softened
1 cup sugar
4 eggs
2 tablespoons freshly squeezed lemon juice
1 tablespoon vanilla extract

Preheat oven to 350 degrees. In a small saucepan, melt jam over low heat; set aside. Wrap aluminum foil under and around outside of a 9-inch springform pan. In a large bowl, beat cream cheese and sugar until fluffy. Add eggs, 1 at a time, beating well after each addition. Beat in lemon juice and vanilla. Pour 2 cups batter into prepared pan. Drizzle 3 tablespoons jam over batter. Repeat layers 2 more times, ending with 2 tablespoons jam on top. Use a knife to swirl jam through batter. Place springform pan in a larger baking pan.

Pour hot water into larger pan to a depth of $^1/_2$ inch. Bake 1 hour or until top is lightly browned and cheesecake is firm around edges. Remove springform pan from water. Cool completely on a wire rack. Cover and chill 2 hours before serving. Remove sides of pan. Serve chilled.

Yield: about 16 servings

ORANGE CHEESECAKES

      12 vanilla wafers
    $1^1/_2$ cups (12 ounces) fat-free cream
              cheese, softened
       1 cup fat-free sour cream
    $^1/_2$ cup sugar
    $^1/_2$ cup egg substitute
       2 tablespoons all-purpose flour
       2 teaspoons orange extract
       1 can (11 ounces) mandarin
              oranges, well drained
       2 tablespoons orange marmalade

Preheat oven to 350 degrees. Place 1 vanilla wafer into bottom of each paper-lined cup of a muffin pan. In a medium bowl, beat cream cheese until fluffy. Add sour cream, sugar, egg substitute, flour, and orange extract; beat until smooth. Spoon cheese mixture over vanilla wafers, filling each cup full. Bake 18 minutes. Turn oven off and leave in oven 2 minutes. Leaving oven door ajar, leave in oven 15 minutes longer. Cool completely in pan.

In a small bowl, combine oranges and marmalade. Spoon orange mixture on top of each cheesecake. Loosely cover and store in refrigerator. Serve chilled.

Yield: 1 dozen cheesecakes

FUZZY NAVEL CAKES

       1 package (18.25 ounces) yellow
              cake mix
       4 eggs
    $^3/_4$ cup peach schnapps
       1 package (6 ounces) instant vanilla
              pudding mix
    $^1/_2$ cup vegetable oil
    $^1/_2$ cup orange juice
    $^1/_2$ teaspoon orange extract
       1 cup peach schnapps
       2 tablespoons orange juice
       3 cups confectioners sugar, sifted

Preheat oven to 350 degrees. Combine first 7 ingredients in mixing bowl and blend well. Pour into 10 greased and lightly floured 1-cup metal gelatin molds, filling half full. Bake 25 to 30 minutes or until cake springs back when lightly touched. Combine 1 cup peach schnapps, 2 tablespoons orange juice, and confectioners sugar. While cakes are still warm in molds, poke holes in cakes; pour liqueur mixture over. Allow cakes to cool in molds at least 2 hours before removing.

Yield: 10 small cakes

25

PUMPKIN SPICE CAKE

CAKE
- ³/₄ cup butter or margarine, softened
- 2 cups sugar
- 1 can (15 ounces) pumpkin
- 4 eggs
- 1 teaspoon vanilla extract
- 3 cups all-purpose flour
- 2¹/₂ teaspoons ground cinnamon
- 2 teaspoons baking soda
- 1¹/₂ teaspoons ground cloves
- ¹/₂ teaspoon salt
- 1 cup chopped walnuts
- 1 cup raisins

ICING
- ¹/₂ cup butter or margarine
- 1 cup sugar
- 1 can (5 ounces) evaporated milk
- ¹/₄ cup maple syrup
- ¹/₄ teaspoon vanilla extract

Preheat oven to 350 degrees. For cake, cream butter and sugar in a large bowl until fluffy. Add pumpkin, eggs, and vanilla; beat until well blended and smooth. In a medium bowl, combine flour, cinnamon, baking soda, cloves, and salt. Add dry ingredients, 1 cup at a time, to creamed mixture; beat until well blended. Stir in walnuts and raisins. Spoon batter into a greased 10-inch fluted tube pan. Bake 55 to 65 minutes or until a toothpick

A thick, buttery icing kissed with maple syrup crowns moist Pumpkin Spice Cake. It's hard to resist this scrumptious dessert!

inserted in center of cake comes out clean. Cool in pan 10 minutes. Invert onto a serving plate. Cool completely.

For icing, melt butter in a heavy medium saucepan over medium-high heat. Stir in sugar, evaporated milk, and maple syrup. Stirring constantly, bring mixture to a boil; boil 6 minutes. Remove from heat. Stir in vanilla. Pour into a medium bowl and cool 10 minutes. Beat 8 to 10 minutes or until thick and creamy. Spread icing over top of cake.

Yield: about 16 servings

TUNNEL CAKE

This yummy chocolate Tunnel Cake has a double surprise inside—a rich cream cheese filling loaded with miniature chocolate chips!

FILLING
- 11 ounces cream cheese, softened
- 1/3 cup sugar
- 1 egg
- 1 cup semisweet chocolate mini chips

CAKE
- 3 cups all-purpose flour
- 2 cups sugar
- 1/2 cup cocoa
- 2 teaspoons baking soda
- 1 teaspoon salt
- 2 cups water
- 2/3 cup vegetable oil
- 2 tablespoons white vinegar
- 1 tablespoon vanilla extract

Preheat oven to 350 degrees. For filling, combine cream cheese, sugar, and egg in a small bowl; beat until well blended. Stir in chocolate chips; set aside.

For cake, combine flour, sugar, cocoa, baking soda, and salt in a large bowl. Add water, oil, vinegar, and vanilla; beat until well blended. Pour half of batter into a well-greased 10-inch fluted tube pan. Spread filling over batter; top with remaining batter. Bake 50 to 55 minutes or until toothpick inserted in center of cake comes out clean. Cool in pan 10 minutes. Remove cake from pan and cool on a wire rack.

Yield: about 16 servings

CREAMY CHOCOLATE PECAN PIE

1 package (8 ounces) cream cheese, softened
3/4 cup sugar
3 eggs
3/4 cup light corn syrup
1/3 cup cocoa
2 tablespoons all-purpose flour
1 teaspoon vanilla extract
1/2 teaspoon salt
1 1/2 cups chopped pecans
1 unbaked deep-dish 9-inch pie crust

Preheat oven to 350 degrees. In a medium bowl, beat cream cheese and sugar until fluffy. Add eggs, corn syrup, cocoa, flour, vanilla, and salt; beat until well blended. Stir in pecans. Pour into pie crust. Bake 55 to 60 minutes or until a knife inserted near center comes out clean. If edge of crust browns too quickly, cover with a strip of aluminum foil. Cool on a wire rack. Cover and chill 2 hours. Serve chilled.

Yield: about 8 servings

BLACK BOTTOM PIES

1 package (3.9 ounces) instant chocolate pudding and pie filling mix
3 1/2 cups cold milk
2 9-inch purchased chocolate crumb pie crusts
1 package (3.4 ounces) instant vanilla pudding and pie filling mix
1 container (12 ounces) frozen non-dairy whipped topping, thawed
1/2 cup mini chocolate chips, divided

In a medium bowl, beat chocolate pudding mix and 1 3/4 cups milk for 1 minute. Pour one-half of chocolate pudding into each crust. Place crusts in refrigerator to chill. In a medium bowl, beat vanilla pudding mix and remaining 1 3/4 cups milk for 1 minute. Pour vanilla pudding over chilled chocolate pudding. Chill for 10 minutes. Spread whipped topping evenly over pies. Sprinkle 1/4 cup chocolate chips over each pie. Cover and store in refrigerator.

Yield: two 9-inch pies

NUTTY FUDGE PIE

1 cup sugar
1/2 cup butter or margarine, melted
1/2 cup all-purpose flour
1/2 cup chopped pecans
2 eggs
3 tablespoons cocoa
1 teaspoon vanilla extract
Ice cream and chopped pecans to serve

(Note: Recipe was tested in a 750-watt microwave.) In a medium bowl, combine sugar, butter, flour, pecans, eggs, cocoa, and vanilla; beat until well blended. Pour batter into a greased 9-inch microwave-safe pie plate. Microwave on medium power (60%) 10 to 12 minutes or until almost set in center (do not overbake). Serve warm with ice cream and pecans.

Yield: about 8 servings

CHOCOLATE-BUTTERSCOTCH PIE

1 can (5 ounces) evaporated milk
1 egg yolk
1 package (6 ounces) semisweet
    chocolate chips
1 cup butterscotch chips
1 container (8 ounces) frozen non-
    dairy whipped topping, thawed
1 purchased vanilla wafer crumb
    pie crust (6 ounces)
  Chopped pecans and chocolate
    sprinkles to garnish

Whisk evaporated milk and egg yolk in a heavy medium saucepan over medium-low heat. Whisking constantly, cook 5 to 6 minutes or until mixture becomes hot and slightly thickened. Reduce heat to low. Add chocolate and butterscotch chips; stir until melted and smooth. Cool to room temperature; fold in whipped topping. Spoon into crust. Garnish with pecans and chocolate sprinkles. Cover and freeze until firm enough to slice.

Yield: about 8 servings

EASY SWEET POTATO PIE

1/4 cup butter or margarine, softened
2/3 cup sugar
1 can (16 ounces) cut sweet
    potatoes in syrup, drained
1 can (5 ounces) evaporated milk
2 eggs
1 teaspoon pumpkin pie spice
1 9-inch unbaked deep-dish
    pie crust
  Whipped cream and pumpkin pie
    spice to garnish

Preheat oven to 375 degrees. Cream butter and sugar in a medium bowl until fluffy. Add sweet potatoes, evaporated milk, eggs, and pumpkin pie spice. Pour into crust. Bake 40 to 45 minutes or until center is set and crust is lightly browned. Cool on a wire rack. Garnish with whipped cream and pumpkin pie spice. Store in an airtight container in refrigerator.

Yield: about 8 servings

PEANUT BUTTER PIE

3/4 cup smooth peanut butter
2/3 cup dark corn syrup
2/3 cup firmly packed brown sugar
3 eggs
3 tablespoons butter or margarine,
    melted
2 teaspoons vanilla extract
1/8 teaspoon salt
1 9-inch unbaked pie crust
1 cup coarsely chopped peanuts

Preheat oven to 400 degrees. Combine peanut butter, corn syrup, brown sugar, eggs, melted butter, vanilla, and salt in a large bowl; beat until well blended. Pour into crust. Sprinkle peanuts over filling. Bake 10 minutes. Reduce oven to 350 degrees and bake 35 to 40 minutes or until center is set. Transfer to a wire rack to cool. Store in an airtight container in refrigerator.

Yield: about 8 servings

Light and airy, Creamy Strawberry Pie is quick to whip up with frozen fruit, melted marshmallows, and a dash of strawberry liqueur.

A chocolate cookie crumb crust is a delicious base for Peppermint Pie. The filling has a texture similar to frozen custard.

CREAMY STRAWBERRY PIE

1 package (10 ounces)
   marshmallows
1 package (16 ounces) frozen
   whole strawberries, thawed and
   drained
3 tablespoons strawberry liqueur *or*
   strawberry juice
1 cup whipping cream, whipped
1 purchased large graham cracker
   pie crust (9 ounces)
   Fresh strawberries to garnish

Place marshmallows in a medium microwave-safe bowl. Microwave on high power (100%) 1½ to 2 minutes or until marshmallows melt, stirring every 30 seconds. Beat in strawberries and liqueur. Fold in whipped cream. Spoon into crust. Cover and chill. Garnish with strawberries.

Yield: about 10 servings

PEPPERMINT PIE

CRUST
2 cups chocolate cookie crumbs
½ cup granulated sugar
⅓ cup butter, melted

FILLING
24 large marshmallows
10 ounces white chocolate
½ cup milk
1 teaspoon peppermint extract
1 cup whipping cream, whipped

For crust, combine all ingredients and press into bottom of an ungreased 9-inch springform pan. For filling, combine marshmallows, white chocolate, and milk in the top of a double boiler over simmering water. Stir constantly until mixture melts and is smooth. Remove from heat. Cool to room temperature. Fold peppermint extract and whipped cream into white chocolate mixture. Pour mixture into crust. Cover and freeze overnight.

Yield: 8 to 10 servings

EGGNOG PIES

1 quart prepared eggnog, chilled
2 packages (one 5.1-ounce and one 3.4-ounce) vanilla instant pudding and pie filling mix
3 tablespoons bourbon
1 teaspoon vanilla extract
1/4 teaspoon ground nutmeg
2 purchased graham cracker pie crusts (6 ounces each)

In a large bowl, combine eggnog, pudding mixes, bourbon, vanilla, and nutmeg; beat just until well blended. Spoon filling into pie crusts; cover and chill overnight. Store in refrigerator. (**Note:** Pies can be frozen; thaw slightly before serving.)

Yield: two 9-inch pies, about 8 servings each

APRICOT-ORANGE CHIFFON PIE

CRUST

1 1/4 cups all-purpose flour
1/2 teaspoon salt
1/2 teaspoon grated orange zest
1/3 cup vegetable shortening
3 to 4 tablespoons cold orange juice

FILLING

1 can (15 1/4 ounces) apricot halves in heavy syrup
1 package (3 ounces) apricot gelatin
1/2 teaspoon orange extract
1/4 teaspoon salt
1 cup half and half
1 package (3.4 ounces) vanilla instant pudding mix
1 container (8 ounces) frozen non-dairy whipped topping, thawed

Preheat oven to 400 degrees. For crust, combine flour, salt, and orange zest in a medium bowl. Using a pastry blender or 2 knives, cut in shortening until mixture resembles coarse meal. Sprinkle with orange juice; mix until a soft dough forms. On a lightly floured surface, use a floured rolling pin to roll out dough. Transfer to a 9-inch pie plate and use a sharp knife to trim edge of dough. Flute edge of dough. Prick bottom of crust with a fork. Bake 15 to 18 minutes or until golden brown. Cool completely on a wire rack.

For filling, drain apricots, reserving syrup. Place reserved apricot syrup (about 3/4 cup) in a small saucepan. Stirring constantly, add gelatin and cook over medium-low heat about 8 minutes or until gelatin dissolves. Transfer to a large bowl; cool at room temperature 30 minutes.

Process drained apricots, orange extract, and salt in a food processor until apricots are puréed. Add to gelatin mixture. In a small bowl, combine half and half and pudding mix; beat according to package directions. Add to fruit mixture; beat until smooth. Fold in whipped topping. Spoon filling into crust. Cover and chill about 2 hours or until firm. Serve chilled.

Yield: about 8 servings

SOUTHERN PECAN PIE

CRUST
- 1¼ cups all-purpose flour
- ¼ teaspoon salt
- 7 tablespoons butter, chilled and cut into pieces
- 3 tablespoons ice water

FILLING
- 4 eggs
- 1¼ cups granulated sugar
- ½ cup light corn syrup
- ¼ cup butter or margarine
- 1 cup pecan halves

Preheat oven to 350 degrees. For crust, sift flour and salt into a mixing bowl. Using a pastry blender or two knives, cut butter into flour until mixture resembles coarse meal. Sprinkle ice water over dough, mixing quickly just until a soft dough forms. On a lightly floured surface, use a floured rolling pin to roll out dough. Place the dough in an ungreased 9-inch pie pan. Trim and crimp edges of dough.

For filling, place eggs in a medium mixing bowl and beat well by hand. In a saucepan, combine sugar, corn syrup, and butter. Bring mixture to a boil. Beating constantly by hand, gradually add sugar mixture to eggs. Stir in pecan halves. Pour mixture into pie shell. Bake 40 to 45 minutes or until a knife inserted in the center comes out clean.

Yield: about 8 servings

BLUEBERRY-LEMON TARTS

- 1 can (14 ounces) sweetened condensed milk
- 1 can (6 ounces) frozen lemonade concentrate, thawed
- 1 container (8 ounces) frozen non-dairy whipped topping, thawed
- 4 packages (4 ounces each) of 6 individual-serving graham cracker pie crusts
- 1 can (21 ounces) blueberry pie filling, chilled
- Lemon zest strips to garnish

In a medium bowl, combine sweetened condensed milk and lemonade concentrate. Fold in whipped topping. Spoon about 3 tablespoons lemon mixture into each crust. Cover and chill. To serve, top each tart with 1 heaping tablespoon chilled pie filling. Garnish with lemon zest.

Yield: 2 dozen tarts

Chocolate Fudge Pie is a decadent treat packed with chocolate chips and rich pecan bits. Edible chocolate hearts add a fun finish.

CHOCOLATE FUDGE PIE

- 1   unbaked 9-inch pie crust
- 1/2   cup butter or margarine
- 1   package (6 ounces) chocolate chips, divided
- 1   cup sugar
- 3   tablespoons all-purpose flour
- 3   eggs
- 1   cup finely chopped pecans
- 1   teaspoon vanilla extract

Preheat oven to 400 degrees. Bake pie crust 5 minutes. Remove from oven; reduce temperature to 325 degrees.

In a heavy medium saucepan, melt butter and 3/4 cup chocolate chips over low heat. In a medium bowl, combine chocolate mixture, sugar, and flour; beat until well blended. Add eggs, 1 at a time, beating well after each addition. Stir in pecans and vanilla. Pour filling into pie crust. Bake 40 to 50 minutes or until filling is firm. Transfer to a wire rack to cool.

Line a baking sheet with aluminum foil; grease foil. In a heavy small saucepan, melt remaining 1/4 cup chocolate chips over low heat. Pour melted chocolate onto prepared baking sheet. Chill 30 minutes or until chocolate hardens. Use a 1 1/8-inch-wide heart-shaped cookie cutter to cut out chocolate hearts. Chill hearts about 5 minutes or until firm. Place chocolate hearts on warm pie; cool. Store in an airtight container in refrigerator.

Yield: about 8 servings

CHOCOLATE-COVERED CHERRY PIE

1 box (8 ounces) chocolate-covered cherries, quartered
1 quart vanilla ice cream, softened
1 9-inch purchased chocolate crumb pie crust
8 maraschino cherries with stems (undrained) and chocolate sprinkles to garnish

In a medium bowl, stir chocolate-covered cherries into ice cream. Spoon ice cream mixture into crust. Dip maraschino cherries in chocolate sprinkles and place on pie to garnish. Add additional chocolate sprinkles to pie as desired. Place in freezer until firm.

Yield: about 8 servings

Fast and easy to make, our Chocolate-Covered Cherry Pie is served in a ready-made chocolate crust. Maraschino cherries and chocolate sprinkles top off the cool confection.

LUSCIOUS LEMON MERINGUE PIE

FILLING

1²/₃ cups sugar
¹/₂ cup cornstarch
¹/₄ teaspoon salt
1³/₄ cups water
¹/₂ cup freshly squeezed lemon juice
4 egg yolks, beaten
3 tablespoons butter or margarine
1 tablespoon grated lemon zest
1 baked 9-inch pie crust

MERINGUE

4 egg whites
¹/₂ teaspoon cream of tartar
¹/₈ teaspoon salt
³/₄ cup confectioners sugar
¹/₂ teaspoon lemon extract

For filling, combine sugar, cornstarch, salt, water, lemon juice, and egg yolk in a heavy large saucepan. Stirring constantly, cook over medium heat until mixture boils and thickens. Continue stirring and boil 1 minute. Remove from heat; stir in butter and lemon zest. Spoon into pie crust.

Preheat oven to 350 degrees. For meringue, beat egg whites, cream of tartar, and salt in a large bowl until foamy. Gradually add confectioners sugar, beating until stiff peaks form. Beat in lemon extract. Spread meringue over hot filling, sealing to edge of crust. Bake 12 to 14 minutes or until meringue is golden brown. Cool on a wire rack. Store in an airtight container in refrigerator.

Yield: about 8 servings

KEY LIME PIE

CRUST

1¹/₂ cups all-purpose flour
¹/₂ teaspoon salt
¹/₂ cup vegetable shortening
¹/₄ cup cold water

FILLING

4 egg yolks
1 can (14 ounces) sweetened condensed milk
¹/₃ cup freshly squeezed lime juice (juice of about 3 limes)
    Green food coloring (optional)

MERINGUE

4 egg whites
¹/₂ teaspoon cream of tartar
¹/₂ cup granulated sugar

Preheat oven to 450 degrees. For crust, sift flour and salt together in a medium bowl. Using a pastry blender or 2 knives, cut in shortening until mixture resembles coarse meal. Sprinkle water over; mix until a soft dough forms. On a lightly floured surface, use a floured rolling pin to roll out dough to ¹/₈-inch thickness. Transfer to a 9-inch pie plate and use a sharp knife to trim edges of dough. Prick crust with a fork. Bake 8 minutes. Cool completely on a wire rack.

Reduce oven temperature to 325 degrees. For filling, combine egg yolks, condensed milk, and lime juice in a medium saucepan over low heat. Cook, stirring constantly, until mixture reaches 160 degrees (about 10 minutes). Remove from heat. If desired, tint green.

For meringue, beat egg whites and cream of tartar in a large bowl until foamy using highest speed of an electric mixer. Gradually add sugar; beat until stiff peaks form.

Pour filling into crust. Spread meringue evenly over filling. Bake 25 to 30 minutes or until meringue is brown. Cool completely on a wire rack. Cover and refrigerate until ready to present.

Yield: 8 to 10 servings

GRAHAM TOFFEE PIE

- 8 graham crackers (2¹/₂ x 5 inches each)
- ¹/₃ cup firmly packed brown sugar
- ¹/₃ cup butter
- 4 egg whites
- 1 cup plus 2 tablespoons granulated sugar, divided
- 1 teaspoon vanilla extract
- ¹/₂ teaspoon cream of tartar
- ¹/₈ teaspoon salt
- 1 cup chopped pecans, toasted
- 1 cup whipping cream

Preheat oven to 350 degrees. Place crackers in a single layer on a 10¹/₂ x 15¹/₂-inch jellyroll pan. In a heavy small saucepan, combine brown sugar and butter. Stirring constantly, cook over medium heat until sugar dissolves and mixture begins to boil. Without stirring, boil 3 minutes. Pour syrup evenly over crackers, spreading to cover crackers. Bake 5 to 7 minutes or until syrup is bubbly and crackers are slightly browned around edges. Cool completely in pan. Break crackers into small pieces.

Reduce oven to 325 degrees. In a medium bowl, beat egg whites until foamy. Gradually add 1 cup granulated sugar, vanilla, cream of tartar, and salt; continue beating until stiff peaks form. Fold in cracker pieces and pecans. Spoon mixture into a greased and lightly floured 9-inch pie plate. Bake 40 to 50 minutes or until filling is set and top is lightly browned. Cool on a wire rack.

Beat whipping cream until frothy. Gradually add remaining 2 tablespoons granulated sugar; beat until stiff peaks form. Spread whipped cream over top of pie. Store in an airtight container in refrigerator.

Yield: 8 to 10 servings

EASY PEACH COBBLER

- ¹/₂ cup butter or margarine, cut into pieces
- 1 cup sugar
- 1 cup all-purpose flour
- 2 teaspoons baking powder
- ¹/₂ teaspoon salt
- ¹/₂ teaspoon apple pie spice
- ³/₄ cup milk
- 1 teaspoon almond extract
- 1 can (21 ounces) peach pie filling

Preheat oven to 350 degrees. Place butter pieces in a 7 x 11-inch baking dish. Heat in oven 3 minutes or until butter melts. In a medium bowl, combine sugar, flour, baking powder, salt, and apple pie spice. Add milk and almond extract; stir until well blended. Pour batter over melted butter; do not stir. Spoon pie filling over batter; do not stir. Bake 40 to 45 minutes or until a toothpick inserted in center of cobbler crust comes out clean. Serve warm or transfer to a wire rack to cool.

Yield: about 8 servings

Mocha Brownie Pies are a luscious blend of brownie mix, instant coffee, and cream cheese. This time-saving recipe is doubly pleasing because there's enough for two pies—one to give and one to keep!

MOCHA BROWNIE PIES

  ½ cup plus 2 tablespoons hot water
1½ tablespoons instant coffee
     granules
  1 package (21.6 ounces) brownie
     mix
  ¼ cup vegetable oil
  1 egg
  2 purchased chocolate graham
     cracker pie crusts (6 ounces
     each)
  1 package (8 ounces) cream cheese,
     softened
  ½ cup sifted confectioners sugar

Preheat oven to 350 degrees. In a small bowl, combine hot water and coffee granules; set aside. In a large bowl, combine brownie mix, oil, ½ cup coffee mixture, and egg. Mix until dry ingredients are moistened. Spread half of batter in bottom of each pie crust. In a medium bowl, combine cream cheese and confectioners sugar; beat until smooth. Beat in remaining 2 tablespoons coffee mixture. Spoon cream cheese mixture evenly over brownie batter in pans. Carefully swirl with a knife. Bake 28 to 31 minutes (do not overbake). Cool 10 minutes before serving. Serve warm or cool completely on a wire rack. Store in an airtight container in refrigerator.

Yield: 2 pies, about 8 servings each

CARIBBEAN BANANA SAUCE

- 1 cup firmly packed brown sugar
- 1½ tablespoons cornstarch
- 1 cup water
- ¼ cup butter or margarine
- ¼ cup dark rum
- 3 bananas, sliced
  Crepes, cake, or ice cream to serve

Combine brown sugar and cornstarch in a heavy medium saucepan. Stirring constantly over medium-high heat, gradually add water. Bring mixture to a boil; cook 3 minutes or until mixture begins to thicken. Add butter; stir until butter melts. Remove from heat. Stir in rum and banana slices. Serve warm over crepes, cake, or ice cream. Store in an airtight container in refrigerator.

Yield: about 2⅔ cups sauce

BUTTER-PECAN SAUCE

- ½ cup sugar
- 1 tablespoon cornstarch
- 1 cup boiling water
- ½ cup chopped pecans
- 1 tablespoon butter
  Dash of salt
- 1 teaspoon vanilla-butter-nut flavoring
  Ice cream or cake to serve

Combine sugar and cornstarch in a heavy medium saucepan. Stirring constantly over medium heat, gradually add boiling water. Add pecans, butter, and salt; cook about 4 minutes or until mixture thickens. Remove from heat. Stir in vanilla-butter-nut flavoring. Serve warm over ice cream or cake. Store in an airtight container in refrigerator.

Yield: about 1¼ cups sauce

A warm tropical pleaser, Caribbean Banana Sauce (left) is laced with dark rum. Wake up ordinary desserts with Butter-Pecan Sauce.

RASPBERRY-PLUM SAUCE

- 2 tablespoons cold water
- 4 teaspoons cornstarch
- 2 packages (12 ounces each)
  frozen raspberries, thawed
- 1¹/₃ cups red plum jelly

In a small bowl, combine water and cornstarch; set aside. Combine raspberries and jelly in a large saucepan over medium-high heat. Bring to a boil, stirring constantly. Blend cornstarch mixture into raspberry mixture. Stirring constantly, cook 3 minutes or until sauce thickens; cool. To remove seeds, place sauce in a fine-mesh strainer and push the sauce through the strainer with the back of a spoon. Discard seeds. Store sauce in an airtight container in refrigerator. Serve warm.

Yield: about 4 cups sauce

PEPPERMINT STICK SAUCE

- 1¹/₂ cups finely crushed
  peppermint candies
- 1¹/₂ cups whipping cream
- 1 jar (7 ounces) marshmallow
  creme

In a medium saucepan, combine candies, whipping cream, and marshmallow creme. Stirring constantly with a wooden spoon, cook over medium heat until smooth. Remove from heat. Pour into an airtight container and refrigerate. Serve chilled over ice cream or cake.

Yield: about 2 cups sauce

FUDGE SAUCE

- 1 package (12 ounces)
  semisweet chocolate chips
- 1 cup butter or margarine
- 4 cups (1 pound) confectioners
  sugar
- 2²/₃ cups evaporated milk
- 2¹/₂ teaspoons vanilla extract
- ¹/₈ teaspoon salt

Combine chocolate chips and butter in a large saucepan over low heat. Stir constantly until melted. Gradually add sugar and evaporated milk, blending well. Increase heat. Stirring constantly, bring to a boil and cook 8 minutes. Remove from heat. Stir in vanilla and salt. Store in an airtight container in refrigerator. Serve warm.

Yield: about 5¹/₂ cups sauce

LEMON FRUIT DIP

1 package (3 ounces) cream cheese, softened
1 container (8 ounces) lemon yogurt
2 tablespoons sifted confectioners sugar
2 tablespoons lemon juice
1 container (8 ounces) frozen non-dairy whipped topping, thawed
  Lemon slice and fresh berry leaves to garnish
  Fresh fruit slices to serve

In a medium bowl, beat cream cheese until fluffy. Add yogurt, confectioners sugar, and lemon juice; beat until well blended. Fold in whipped topping. Garnish with lemon slice and berry leaves. Serve with fruit slices. Store in an airtight container in refrigerator.

Yield: about 4 cups dip

CHERRY CREAM CHEESE DESSERT

1 package (8 ounces) cream cheese, softened
1 can (14 ounces) sweetened condensed milk
1/3 cup lemon juice
1 teaspoon vanilla extract
1 can (21 ounces) cherry pie filling
  Toasted slivered almonds to garnish

In a large bowl, beat cream cheese until fluffy. Beat in sweetened condensed milk, lemon juice, and vanilla. Lightly swirl pie filling into cream cheese mixture.

Spoon into serving dishes. Cover and chill. Garnish with almonds.

Yield: about 6 servings

FROZEN PINEAPPLE SALAD

1 can (20 ounces) crushed pineapple, drained
1 1/2 cups softened vanilla ice cream
1 1/2 cups sugar
1 cup sour cream
1 cup chopped walnuts
2 tablespoons freshly squeezed lemon juice
1 can (8 ounces) pineapple chunks, drained to garnish

In a large bowl, combine pineapple, ice cream, sugar, sour cream, walnuts, and lemon juice. Spoon salad evenly into 8 custard cups, cover, and freeze 8 hours or until firm. Before serving, place in refrigerator 1 hour. Garnish with pineapple chunks. Serve chilled.

Yield: 8 servings

Baked Caramel Apples are sweet, tender perfection! A mix of oatmeal cookie crumbs and caramel ice cream topping is baked inside.

BAKED CARAMEL APPLES

6 large red baking apples (we used Rome Beauty apples)
2¼ cups oatmeal cookie crumbs, divided
¾ cup caramel ice cream topping
¼ cup apple juice

Preheat oven to 350 degrees. Core each apple almost to bottom of apple, leaving bottom intact. Using a vegetable peeler, remove a small strip of peel from top of each apple to prevent splitting. Place apples in an ungreased 7 x 11-inch baking dish. Combine 1½ cups cookie crumbs and caramel topping in a small bowl. Spoon cookie crumb mixture into center of each apple. Sprinkle remaining ¾ cup cookie crumbs over tops of apples. Pour apple juice into baking dish. Bake 35 to 40 minutes or until apples are tender. Serve warm.

Yield: 6 servings

COOKIE PIZZAS

Vegetable cooking spray
1 package (18 ounces) refrigerated peanut butter cookie dough
1 jar (10 ounces) maraschino cherries, drained and halved
1 cup peanuts
1 package (6 ounces) semisweet chocolate chips
8 ounces vanilla candy coating, melted

Use the bottom of an 8-inch round cake pan as a pattern to draw 4 circles on cardboard; cut out and set aside. Preheat oven to 350 degrees. Spray 8-inch round cake pan with vegetable spray until well coated. Divide cookie dough into fourths. With floured hands, press one fourth of dough into cake pan. Bake 8 to 10 minutes. Carefully remove from pan and cool on a wire rack. Repeat with remaining cookie dough.

Place cookies on cardboard circles. Place cherries, peanuts, and chocolate chips on cookies. Drizzle candy coating over cookies; let harden. Store in an airtight container.

Yield: 4 cookie pizzas, 6 servings each

Use your imagination to top tasty Cookie Pizzas with a variety of nuts, candies, and icing. The giant treats make pleasing gifts.

ULTIMATE CHOCOLATE PUDDING

- 3 ounces semisweet baking chocolate, coarsely chopped
- 3 ounces unsweetened baking chocolate, coarsely chopped
- 1/4 cup butter or margarine
- 3 cups milk
- 1 1/4 cups sugar, divided
- 2 eggs
- 4 egg yolks
- 1/2 cup cocoa
- 2 teaspoons cornstarch
- 2 cups whipping cream, divided
- 1 teaspoon vanilla extract
- 1 tablespoon finely chopped bittersweet baking chocolate and fresh mint leaves to garnish

In top of a double boiler over simmering water, melt chocolates and butter, stirring until well blended. Remove from heat and allow to cool. In a heavy large saucepan over medium heat, whisk milk, 1 cup sugar, eggs, and egg yolks. Attach a candy thermometer to pan, making sure thermometer does not touch bottom of pan. Stirring constantly, cook until mixture reaches 180 degrees on candy thermometer or begins to thicken. Strain custard through a fine-mesh strainer into a large bowl. In a heavy small saucepan, sift cocoa and cornstarch into 1 cup whipping cream. Stirring constantly, bring mixture to a boil; cook until slightly thickened. Add chocolate mixture, cornstarch mixture, and vanilla to custard; stir until well blended. Pour into individual serving dishes; cover and chill.

To serve, chill a small bowl and beaters from an electric mixer in freezer. In chilled bowl, beat remaining 1 cup whipping cream and remaining 1/4 cup sugar until stiff peaks form. Spoon mixture into a pastry bag fitted with a large star tip. Pipe whipped cream mixture onto pudding. Garnish with chopped bittersweet chocolate and mint leaves.

Yield: 8 to 10 servings

CRANBERRY-LEMON TRIFLE

- 2 packages (4.4 ounces each) custard mix
- 5 cups milk
- 1 purchased pound cake loaf (16 ounces)
- 1/4 cup crème de cassis
- 1 jar (11 1/4 ounces) lemon curd
- 2 cans (16 ounces each) whole berry cranberry sauce
  Lemon slice and fresh cranberries to garnish

In a large saucepan, prepare custard mix with milk according to package directions. Cover and chill about 30 minutes.

Cut pound cake into 1/4-inch slices. Place slices on a baking sheet. Sprinkle crème de cassis over slices. Fold lemon curd into custard. Place a layer of custard mixture in a 3 1/2-quart trifle bowl. Place a layer of cake over custard. Spoon a layer of cranberry sauce over cake. Repeat layers, ending with custard on top. Garnish with lemon slice and fresh cranberries. Cover and store in refrigerator.

Yield: about 18 servings

DEATH BY CHOCOLATE
(Shown on front cover and page 11)

1 package (21.2 ounces) brownie
    mix
1/2 cup vegetable oil
2 eggs
1/4 cup water
1/4 cup coffee-flavored liqueur or
    4 tablespoons strongly brewed
    coffee and 1 teaspoon sugar
3 packages (3.9 ounces each)
    chocolate instant pudding mix
6 cups milk
1/2 teaspoon almond extract
1 container (12 ounces) frozen
    non-dairy whipped topping,
    thawed
1 package (9 ounces) snack-size
    chocolate-covered toffee candy
    bars, crushed and divided
    Chocolate curls to garnish

Preheat oven to 350 degrees. Prepare brownie mix with oil, eggs, and water in a large bowl according to package directions. Spread batter into a greased 9 x 13-inch baking pan and bake 24 to 26 minutes. Use a wooden skewer to poke holes about 1 inch apart in top of warm brownies; drizzle with liqueur. Cool completely.

Prepare pudding mixes with milk in a large bowl according to package directions; set aside. In a medium bowl, fold almond extract into whipped topping; set aside. In a 4-quart serving bowl, break half of brownies into bite-size pieces. Sprinkle half of crushed candy bars over brownies. Spread half of pudding over candy pieces. Spread half of whipped topping mixture over pudding layer. Repeat layers, ending with whipped topping mixture. Cover and chill. Garnish with chocolate curls.

Yield: about 20 servings

CHOCOLATE-PEANUT BUTTER BARS

1 package (18.25 ounces)
    chocolate cake mix
1/4 cup vegetable oil
1/4 cup smooth peanut butter
1/4 cup water
1 egg
1 teaspoon vanilla extract
1 cup sugar
1/3 cup butter or margarine
1/3 cup milk
1 cup peanut butter chips
1 cup chopped lightly salted
    peanuts

Preheat oven to 350 degrees. In a medium bowl, combine cake mix, oil, peanut butter, water, egg, and vanilla. Spread mixture into bottom of a 9 x 13-inch baking pan lined with lightly greased waxed paper. Bake 20 to 25 minutes or until edges are lightly browned.

In a heavy medium saucepan, combine sugar, butter, and milk. Stirring constantly, bring mixture to a boil over medium-high heat; boil 1 minute. Remove from heat and add peanut butter chips; stir until smooth. Stir in peanuts. Spread hot topping over warm baked mixture. Cool 2 hours in pan or until firm enough to cut. Cut into 1 x 2-inch bars. Store in an airtight container.

Yield: about 4 dozen bars

Irresistible Strawberry Cheesecake Bars are quickly prepared using a packaged mix, jam, and a few other simple ingredients.

STRAWBERRY CHEESECAKE BARS

1 package (18¼ ounces) strawberry cake mix with pudding in the mix
1 cup chopped pecans, toasted
¾ cup butter or margarine, melted
2 packages (8 ounces each) cream cheese, softened
1 cup sugar
⅓ cup strawberry jam

Preheat oven to 350 degrees. In a medium bowl, combine cake mix and pecans. Drizzle melted butter over mixture; stir until well blended. Press mixture into bottom of a greased 9 x 13-inch baking pan. In a medium bowl, beat cream cheese and sugar until smooth. Spread cream cheese mixture over crust. Process jam in a food processor until smooth. Spoon into a resealable plastic bag. Snip off 1 corner of bag. Pipe lengthwise lines of jam about 1 inch apart. Refer to Fig. 1 and use knife to pull jam from side to side through cream cheese mixture at 1-inch intervals. Bake 18 to 23 minutes or until edges begin to brown and center is set. Cool in pan on a wire rack. Cover and chill 2 hours or until firm.

Fig. 1

Cut into 1 x 2-inch bars. Store in an airtight container in refrigerator.

Yield: about 4 dozen bars

CINNAMON-ORANGE STICKY BUNS

2 cans (11.5 ounces each) refrigerated cinnamon rolls with icing
1/2 cup orange marmalade
3 tablespoons chopped pecans
1 cup firmly packed brown sugar
1/3 cup butter or margarine, melted

Preheat oven to 350 degrees. In a small bowl, combine icing from cinnamon roll cans, marmalade, and pecans; spread into bottom of a greased 10-inch fluted tube pan. Place brown sugar in another small bowl. Dip each roll into melted butter and roll in brown sugar. Stand rolls on ends in pan. Sprinkle with remaining brown sugar. Bake 35 to 40 minutes or until golden brown. Cool in pan 5 minutes. Invert onto a serving plate. Serve warm.

Yield: 16 sticky buns

Cinnamon-Orange Sticky Buns are drenched in a buttery brown sugar topping enhanced with orange marmalade and pecans.

CHOCOLATE BREAD PUDDING WITH CARAMEL SAUCE

BREAD PUDDING

 1 can (10 biscuits) refrigerated buttermilk biscuits, baked according to package directions
 2 cups milk
 2 eggs
 2 tablespoons butter or margarine, melted
 2 teaspoons vanilla extract
 $3/4$ cup sugar
 $1/4$ cup cocoa
 $1/2$ cup semisweet chocolate chips

CARAMEL SAUCE

 $1/2$ cup butter or margarine
 $1/2$ cup firmly packed brown sugar
 $1/2$ cup granulated sugar
 $1/2$ cup evaporated milk
 1 tablespoon vanilla extract

Preheat oven to 350 degrees. For bread pudding, tear baked biscuits into bite-size pieces. In a large bowl, combine biscuits and milk; set aside. In a medium bowl, beat eggs, melted butter, and vanilla until well blended. Add sugar and cocoa; beat until well blended. Stir in chocolate chips. Add chocolate mixture to biscuit mixture; stir until well blended. Pour into a greased 8-inch square glass baking dish. Bake 55 to 60 minutes or until set in center and edges pull away from sides of pan.

For caramel sauce, combine butter, sugars, and milk in a medium saucepan. Stirring constantly, cook over low heat until butter melts and sugars dissolve. Increase heat to medium and bring to a boil. Stirring constantly, boil about 9 minutes or until thickened. Remove from heat; stir in vanilla. Cut warm bread pudding into squares and serve with warm sauce.

Yield: about 9 servings

CINNAMON ROLL BREAD PUDDING

BREAD PUDDING

 6 to 8 large day-old cinnamon rolls, torn into small pieces (about 12 cups)
 $1/3$ cup raisins
 $1/3$ cup chopped pecans
 1 quart milk
 5 eggs
 1 cup sugar
 1 teaspoon vanilla extract
 $1/4$ cup butter or margarine, sliced

VANILLA SAUCE

 $1^1/3$ cups whipping cream
 $1/2$ cup sugar, divided
 4 egg yolks
 1 teaspoon vanilla extract

For bread pudding, place cinnamon roll pieces in a greased 9 x 13-inch baking dish. Sprinkle raisins and pecans over rolls. In a large bowl, beat milk, eggs, sugar, and vanilla until well blended; pour over rolls. Cover and chill overnight.

Preheat oven to 350 degrees. Dot mixture with butter slices. Place dish in a roasting pan; fill pan with hot water halfway up sides of baking dish. Bake 40 to 45 minutes or until bread pudding is set in center.

For vanilla sauce, heat whipping cream and ¼ cup sugar in the top of a double boiler over simmering water. Combine egg yolks and remaining ¼ cup sugar in a small bowl; beat until well blended. Stir some of hot cream mixture into egg mixture; return egg mixture to double boiler. Stirring constantly, cook 8 to 10 minutes or until mixture thickens slightly and coats a spoon. Remove from heat; stir in vanilla. Serve warm sauce over bread pudding.

Yield: about 15 servings

PINEAPPLE UPSIDE-DOWN CINNAMON ROLLS

1   can (15¼ ounces) crushed
     pineapple, drained
1   cup firmly packed brown sugar
3   tablespoons butter
1   can (11.5 ounces) refrigerated
     cinnamon rolls
     Maraschino cherry halves to
     garnish

Preheat oven to 375 degrees. In a 10½-inch heavy ovenproof skillet, combine drained pineapple, brown sugar, and butter. Place in oven 10 minutes or until butter melts. Remove pan from oven; stir pineapple mixture to blend. Place rolls on top of pineapple mixture. Bake in lower half of oven 16 to 18 minutes or until rolls are lightly browned. Immediately invert onto a serving plate. Garnish with cherry halves. Serve warm.

Yield: 8 cinnamon rolls

ALMOND-LIME BREAD

1   package (3 ounces) lime-flavored
     gelatin, divided
3   cups buttermilk baking mix
½   cup granulated sugar
¾   cup sour cream
½   cup milk
2   eggs
1   cup sliced almonds, divided
2   tablespoons hot water
1   cup sifted confectioners sugar
¼   teaspoon almond extract

Preheat oven to 350 degrees. Reserve 1 teaspoon lime gelatin for glaze. Combine baking mix, granulated sugar, and remaining gelatin in a medium bowl. Add sour cream, milk, and eggs; beat until well blended. Stir in ¾ cup almonds. Spoon batter into 2 greased and floured 4 x 8-inch loaf pans. Bake 40 to 45 minutes or until a toothpick inserted in center of bread comes out clean. Cool in pans on a wire rack 10 minutes. Remove bread from pans and transfer to a wire rack with waxed paper underneath.

For glaze, combine reserved 1 teaspoon gelatin and hot water in a small bowl; allow to stand 5 minutes. Add confectioners sugar and almond extract to gelatin mixture; stir until smooth. Drizzle glaze over warm bread. Sprinkle remaining ¼ cup almonds over glaze. Allow glaze to harden. Store in an airtight container.

Yield: 2 loaves bread

A classic confection, Microwave Rocky Road Fudge whips up fast using only a handful of ingredients.

MICROWAVE ROCKY ROAD FUDGE

4^1/$_2$ cups sifted confectioners sugar
^{1}/$_2$ cup butter or margarine
^{1}/$_3$ cup cocoa
^{1}/$_4$ cup milk
^{1}/$_4$ teaspoon salt
^{1}/$_2$ cup chopped pecans
^{1}/$_2$ cup miniature marshmallows
1 teaspoon vanilla extract

Line an 8-inch square baking pan with aluminum foil, extending foil over 2 sides of pan; grease foil. In a large microwave-safe bowl, combine confectioners sugar, butter, cocoa, milk, and salt. Microwave on high power (100%) 2 to 2^1/$_2$ minutes or until butter is melted. Add pecans, marshmallows, and vanilla; stir until well blended. Pour into prepared pan. Chill about 1 hour or until firm. Use ends of foil to lift candy from pan. Cut into 1-inch squares and store in an airtight container.

Yield: about 1^1/$_2$ pounds fudge

PEANUT BUTTER FUDGE

1 cup granulated sugar
1 cup firmly packed brown sugar
1 cup evaporated milk
^{1}/$_4$ cup light corn syrup
^{1}/$_8$ teaspoon salt
1 cup large marshmallows, cut into pieces
^{1}/$_2$ cup smooth peanut butter
2 tablespoons butter
1 teaspoon vanilla extract

Butter sides of a medium saucepan. Combine sugars, milk, corn syrup, and salt in pan. Stirring constantly, cook over medium-low heat until sugar dissolves. Using a pastry brush dipped in hot water, wash down any sugar crystals on sides of pan. Attach a candy thermometer to pan, making sure thermometer does not touch bottom of pan. Increase heat to medium and bring to a boil. Cook, without stirring, until mixture reaches soft-ball stage (234 to 240 degrees). Test about ^{1}/$_2$ teaspoon mixture in ice water. Mixture will easily form a ball in ice water but will flatten when removed from water. Add marshmallows, peanut butter, and butter; stir until smooth. Stir in vanilla. Using medium speed of an electric mixer, beat until fudge thickens and begins to lose its gloss. Pour into a buttered 8-inch square pan. Cool completely. Cut fudge into 1^1/$_2$-inch squares, then cut in half diagonally to form triangles. Store in an airtight container or see Chocolate-Dipped Variation, on next page.

Yield: 1 pound, 10 ounces fudge or about 50 triangles

CHOCOLATE-DIPPED VARIATION

    3 ounces chocolate candy
         coating, melted
  1/2 cup chopped pecans, finely
         ground

Using half of fudge pieces, dip edges into melted chocolate, then into pecans. Place on waxed paper to let chocolate harden. Store in an airtight container.

FUDGE SURPRISE

    4 pounds confectioners sugar
    1 cup cocoa
    3 cups chopped pecans
    1 pound pasteurized process
         cheese, cut into pieces
    2 cups butter or margarine, cut into
         pieces
    1 tablespoon vanilla extract

Sift confectioners sugar and cocoa into a very large bowl; stir in pecans. Stirring frequently, melt cheese in the top of a large double boiler over simmering water. Add butter to melted cheese, stirring until butter melts; stir in vanilla. Add melted cheese mixture to sugar mixture; stir until well blended. Press into a 10 1/2 x 15 1/2-inch jellyroll pan. Cover and chill until firm. Cut into 1-inch squares. Store in an airtight container in a cool place.

Yield: about 12 1/2 dozen pieces fudge

CREAMY WHITE FUDGE

    3 cups sugar
    1 cup sour cream
  1/3 cup light corn syrup
    2 tablespoons butter or margarine
  1/4 teaspoon salt
    2 teaspoons vanilla extract
    1 cup chopped walnuts

Butter a 7 x 11-inch baking pan. Butter sides of a large heavy saucepan or Dutch oven. Combine sugar, sour cream, corn syrup, butter, and salt in pan. Stirring constantly, cook over medium-low heat until sugar dissolves. Using a pastry brush dipped in hot water, wash down any sugar crystals on sides of pan. Attach a candy thermometer to pan, making sure thermometer does not touch bottom of pan. Increase heat to medium and bring to a boil. Cook, without stirring, until mixture reaches soft-ball stage (approximately 234 to 240 degrees). Test about 1/2 teaspoon mixture in ice water. Mixture should easily form a ball in ice water but flatten when held in your hand. Place pan in 2 inches of cold water in sink. Add vanilla; do not stir until mixture cools to approximately 200 degrees. Remove from sink. Using medium speed of an electric mixer, beat until fudge thickens and begins to lose its gloss. Stir in walnuts. Pour into prepared pan. Cool completely. Cut into 1-inch squares. Store in an airtight container in refrigerator.

Yield: about 5 dozen pieces fudge

HONEY-PEANUT BUTTER DIPS

- ²/₃ cup smooth peanut butter
- 3 tablespoons honey
- 1 package (12 ounces) butter-flavored crackers
- 22 ounces chocolate candy coating

In a small bowl, combine peanut butter and honey. Place half of crackers on waxed paper. Spoon peanut butter mixture into a pastry bag fitted with a large round tip. Pipe about 1 teaspoon peanut butter mixture onto each cracker. Top with remaining crackers; gently press together. In a heavy medium saucepan, melt candy coating over low heat. Remove from heat. Place each cookie on a fork and dip into candy coating until covered. Place on waxed paper and allow candy coating to harden.

Yield: about 4 dozen sandwich cookies

Butter-flavored crackers are sandwiched with a mixture of peanut butter and honey for Honey-Peanut Butter Dips. The cookies are coated with chocolate for a taste your family will never tire of!

Packed with fluffy cream filling, these chewy chocolate sandwich cookies are an old-time favorite.

SCOOTER PIES

- 1 package (19.8 ounces) fudge-brownie mix
- 1/2 cup water
- 1/3 cup vegetable oil
- 1 egg
- 3 tablespoons all-purpose flour
- 2 egg whites
- 4 tablespoons heavy cream
- 2 teaspoons vanilla extract
- 4 cups confectioners sugar, divided
- 1 1/2 cups vegetable shortening

Preheat the oven to 350 degrees. In a medium mixing bowl, combine the first five ingredients, stirring just until blended. Drop by rounded tablespoonfuls onto foil-lined baking sheet. Bake 12 to 15 minutes, or until set when lightly pressed with finger. Remove from pan and cool on wire rack.

For filling, combine egg whites, cream, vanilla, and 2 cups sugar, beating until smooth. Add shortening and remaining sugar, beating until fluffy.

Spread a generous amount of filling on bottom of one cookie and place another cookie on top of filling. Store in refrigerator in airtight container.

Yield: about 10 cookies

53

GINGERBREAD BROWNIES

BROWNIES
- ½ cup butter or margarine, softened
- 1 cup sugar
- 2 eggs
- 1 package (6 ounces) semisweet chocolate chips, melted
- ¾ cup hot water
- ¾ cup molasses
- 2½ cups all-purpose flour
- 2 teaspoons ground ginger
- 2 teaspoons baking soda
- ½ teaspoon salt
- 1 cup finely chopped walnuts

ICING
- 1 cup sifted confectioners sugar
- 4 tablespoons milk

Preheat oven to 350 degrees. For brownies, cream butter and sugar in a large bowl until fluffy. Add eggs; beat until smooth. Add chocolate chips, water, and molasses; stir until well blended. Sift flour, ginger, baking soda, and salt into a medium bowl. Add dry ingredients to creamed mixture; stir until well blended. Stir in walnuts. Pour batter into a greased 10½ x 15½-inch jellyroll pan. Bake 30 to 35 minutes or until a toothpick inserted in center of brownies comes out clean. Cool in pan on a wire rack.

For icing, combine confectioners sugar and milk in a medium bowl; stir until smooth. Ice brownies. Allow icing to harden. Cut into 2-inch squares. Store in an airtight container.

Yield: about 3 dozen brownies

PEANUT BUTTER BROWNIES

- ¼ cup butter or margarine, melted
- ½ cup granulated sugar
- ½ cup firmly packed brown sugar
- 2 eggs
- 1 teaspoon vanilla extract
- ½ cup all-purpose flour
- ½ teaspoon baking powder
- ½ teaspoon salt
- ½ cup extra-crunchy peanut butter

Preheat oven to 350 degrees. In a medium bowl, combine butter and sugars. Add eggs and vanilla; beat until smooth. In a small bowl, combine flour, baking powder, and salt. Add dry ingredients to creamed mixture; stir just until dry ingredients are moistened. Stir in peanut butter. Spread batter in a greased 8 x 11-inch baking pan. Bake 20 to 25 minutes or until set in center. Cool completely in pan. Cut into 2-inch squares.

Yield: about 1½ dozen brownies

MINT LAYERED BROWNIES

- ½ cup butter or margarine
- 2 ounces unsweetened baking chocolate
- 1 cup sugar
- 1 teaspoon vanilla extract
- 2 eggs
- ¾ cup all-purpose flour
- ½ teaspoon baking soda
- ¼ teaspoon salt
- 1 dozen 1½-inch-diameter chocolate-covered mint candies

Preheat oven to 350 degrees. In a medium saucepan, melt butter and chocolate over low heat. Remove from heat; transfer to a large bowl. Add sugar and vanilla; beat until smooth. Add eggs, 1 at a time, beating well after each addition. Sift flour, baking soda, and salt into a medium bowl. Add dry ingredients to chocolate mixture; stir until well blended. Pour half of batter into a greased 8-inch square baking pan. Arrange mint candies evenly on batter. Top with remaining batter. Bake 30 to 35 minutes or until set in center. Cool completely in pan. Cut into 1½-inch squares. Store in an airtight container.

Yield: about 2 dozen brownies

RASPBERRY FUDGE BROWNIES

- ½ cup butter or margarine, softened
- 1 cup sugar
- 3 eggs
- 1 jar (12 ounces) raspberry jam, divided
- 18 chocolate wafer cookies (2-inch diameter), finely ground
- ½ cup all-purpose flour
- 1 cup (6 ounces) semisweet chocolate chips
- 1 cup chopped walnuts

Preheat oven to 350 degrees. In a large bowl, cream butter and sugar until fluffy. Add eggs and ½ cup jam, beating until smooth. Add ground cookies and flour; mix well. Pour batter into a greased 8 x 11-inch baking dish. Sprinkle chocolate chips evenly over batter. Bake 35 to 40 minutes or until a toothpick inserted in center comes out clean. In a small saucepan, melt remaining jam over low heat, stirring constantly. Stir in walnuts. Pour jam mixture over brownies. Cool completely in pan. Cut into 2-inch squares. Store in an airtight container.

Yield: about 1½ dozen brownies

KITCHEN TIPS

MEASURING INGREDIENTS

Liquid measuring cups have a rim above the measuring line to keep liquid ingredients from spilling. Nested measuring cups are used to measure dry ingredients, butter, shortening, and peanut butter. Measuring spoons are used for measuring both dry and liquid ingredients.

To measure flour or granulated sugar:

Spoon ingredient into nested measuring cup and level off with a knife. Do not pack down with spoon.

To measure confectioners sugar:

Sift sugar, spoon lightly into nested measuring cup, and level off with a knife.

To measure brown sugar:

Pack sugar into nested measuring cup and level off with a knife. Sugar should hold its shape when removed from cup.

To measure dry ingredients equaling less than $1/2$ cup:

Dip measuring spoon into ingredient and level off with a knife.

To measure butter, shortening, or peanut butter:

Pack ingredient firmly into nested measuring cup and level off with a knife.

To measure liquids:

Use a liquid measuring cup placed on a flat surface. Pour ingredient into cup and check measuring line at eye level.

To measure honey or syrup:

For a more accurate measurement, lightly spray measuring cup or spoon with cooking spray before measuring so the liquid will release easily from cup or spoon.

SOFTENING BUTTER OR MARGARINE

To soften 1 stick of butter, remove wrapper and place butter on a microwave-safe plate. Microwave on medium-low power (30%) 20 to 30 seconds.

SOFTENING CREAM CHEESE

To soften cream cheese, remove wrapper and place cream cheese on a microwave-safe plate. Microwave on medium power (50%) 1 to $1/2$ minutes for one 8-ounce package or 30 to 45 seconds for one 3-ounce package.

MELTING CANDY COATING

To melt candy coating, place in the top of a double boiler over hot, not boiling, water or in a heavy saucepan over low heat. Stir occasionally with a dry spoon until coating melts. Remove from heat and use for dipping as desired. To flavor candy coating, add a small amount of flavored oil. To thin coating, add a small amount of vegetable oil, but no water. If necessary, coating may be returned to heat to remelt.

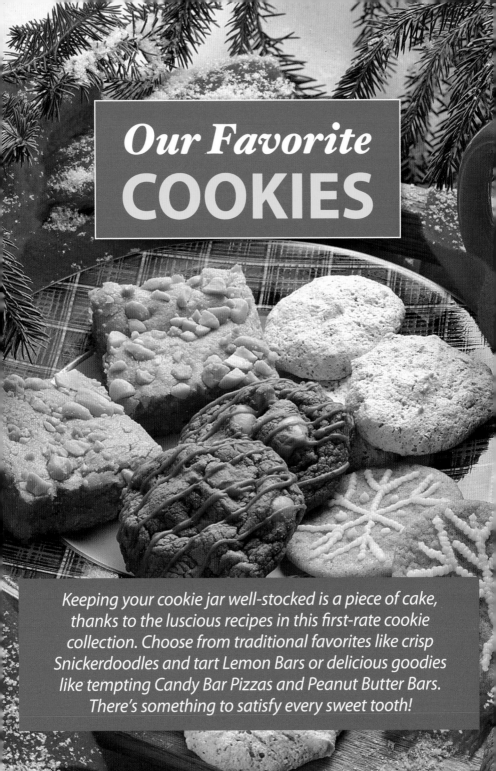

Our Favorite COOKIES

Keeping your cookie jar well-stocked is a piece of cake, thanks to the luscious recipes in this first-rate cookie collection. Choose from traditional favorites like crisp Snickerdoodles and tart Lemon Bars or delicious goodies like tempting Candy Bar Pizzas and Peanut Butter Bars. There's something to satisfy every sweet tooth!

A Tempting Assortment, pp. 60-62

PECAN CRISPIES

1 cup butter or margarine, softened
1 cup firmly packed brown sugar
1 cup granulated sugar
2 eggs
1 teaspoon vanilla-butter-nut
   flavoring
1½ cups all-purpose flour
½ teaspoon baking soda
½ teaspoon baking powder
2 cups quick-cooking oats
1½ cups crispy rice cereal
1 cup finely chopped toasted pecans

In a large bowl, cream butter and sugars until fluffy. Add eggs and vanilla-butter-nut flavoring; beat until smooth. In a small bowl, combine flour, baking soda, and baking powder. Add dry ingredients to creamed mixture. Stir in oats, cereal, and pecans. Shape dough into four 8-inch-long rolls. Wrap in plastic wrap and chill 2 hours.

Preheat oven to 325 degrees. Cut dough into ¼-inch slices. Place 2 inches apart on a greased baking sheet. Bake 8 to 10 minutes or until bottoms are lightly browned. Transfer cookies to a wire rack to cool. Store in a cookie tin.

Yield: about 8 dozen cookies

CHOCOLATE-NUT CHEWIES

1½ cups butter or margarine,
   softened
2 cups granulated sugar
½ cup firmly packed brown sugar
2 eggs
1½ teaspoons vanilla extract
2¼ cups all-purpose flour
¾ cup cocoa
2 teaspoons baking soda
1½ cups finely chopped toasted
   pecans
   Granulated sugar

In a large bowl, cream butter and sugars until fluffy. Add eggs and vanilla; beat until smooth. In a medium bowl, combine flour, cocoa, and baking soda. Add dry ingredients to creamed mixture; stir until a soft dough forms. Stir in pecans. Divide dough into fourths. Wrap in plastic wrap and chill 2 hours.

Preheat oven to 375 degrees. Using one fourth dough at a time, shape into 1-inch balls and roll in granulated sugar. Place balls 3 inches apart on a lightly greased baking sheet. Bake 5 to 7 minutes or until edges are firm. Cool cookies on pan 3 minutes; transfer to a wire rack to cool completely. Store in an airtight container.

Yield: about 10 dozen cookies

Refrigerated and then sliced and baked, Pecan Crispies (from top left, page 59) get their texture from crisp rice cereal. Bits of toasted pecans add a pleasantly nutty flavor to Chocolate-Nut Chewies. Sealed with a kiss of honey, Peanut Butter Postcards (bottom left; recipe on page 60) are topped with yummy icing and colorful "addresses."

PEANUT BUTTER POSTCARDS *(Shown on page 59)*

COOKIES

- 3/4 cup butter or margarine, softened
- 1 cup smooth peanut butter
- 1 cup firmly packed brown sugar
- 3/4 cup granulated sugar
- 2 eggs
- 2 tablespoons honey
- 1 1/2 cups whole-wheat flour
- 1 cup all-purpose flour
- 1/2 teaspoon salt

ICING

- 4 1/2 cups sifted confectioners sugar
- 1/4 cup plus 2 to 2 1/2 tablespoons milk, divided
- 3 tablespoons butter or margarine, softened
- 2 tablespoons honey
- 1 teaspoon clear vanilla (used in cake decorating)
- Black and red paste food coloring

Preheat oven to 350 degrees. For cookies, cream butter, peanut butter, and sugars in a large bowl; beat until fluffy. Add eggs and honey; beat until smooth. In a medium bowl, combine flours and salt. Add dry ingredients to creamed mixture; stir until a soft dough forms. Divide dough in half. Line a 10 1/2 x 15 1/2-inch jellyroll pan with aluminum foil; grease foil. Press half of dough into bottom of prepared pan. Bake 12 to 14 minutes or until lightly browned. Cool in pan 5 minutes. Lift from pan using ends of foil. Cut into nine 5 x 3 1/4-inch cookies while warm. Transfer cookies to a wire rack with waxed paper underneath to cool. Repeat with remaining dough.

For icing, combine confectioners sugar, 1/4 cup plus 1 tablespoon milk, butter, honey, and vanilla in a medium bowl; beat until smooth. Place 3 tablespoons icing in a small bowl. Tint black. Spoon black icing into a pastry bag fitted with a small round tip. Add 1 tablespoon milk to white icing; add additional milk, 1/2 teaspoon at a time, for desired consistency. Place 3 tablespoons white icing into a small bowl. Tint red. Spoon red icing into a pastry bag fitted with a small round tip. Spread white icing over cookies. Allow icing to harden. Use red icing to make lines for postmark. For hearts, squeeze 2 dots of red icing side by side and use tip to pull icing down and together to form a heart. Pipe "addresses" with black icing. Allow icings to harden. Store in single layers between waxed paper in an airtight container.

Yield: 18 cookies

HAZELNUT MACAROONS
(Shown on page 57 and back cover)

- 3 egg whites
- 1/2 teapoon vanilla extract
- 1/2 teaspoon cream of tartar
- 1 cup sugar
- 1 2/3 cups finely ground hazelnuts

Preheat oven to 300 degrees. In a medium bowl, beat egg whites until soft peaks form. Add vanilla and cream of tartar. Gradually add sugar, beating until mixture is very stiff. Gently fold hazelnuts into egg white mixture. Drop teaspoonfuls of mixture 2 inches apart onto a baking sheet lined with parchment paper. Bake 17 to 20 minutes or until edges are lightly browned. Transfer cookies to a wire rack to cool. Store in an airtight container.

Yield: about 5 1/2 dozen cookies

CINNAMON-BROWN SUGAR SNOWFLAKES
(Shown on page 57 and back cover)

- ³/₄ cup butter or margarine, softened
- 1¼ cups firmly packed brown sugar
- 1 egg
- 1 teaspoon vanilla extract
- 1³/₄ cups all-purpose flour
- 1½ teaspoons ground cinnamon, divided
- 1 teaspoon baking powder
- 2 tablespoons granulated sugar
- Purchased white decorating icing to decorate

Preheat oven to 375 degrees. In a large bowl, cream butter and brown sugar until fluffy. Add egg and vanilla; beat until smooth. In a small bowl, combine flour, 1 teaspoon cinnamon, and baking powder. Stir dry ingredients into creamed mixture. Drop teaspoonfuls of dough 3 inches apart onto an ungreased baking sheet. In a small bowl, combine granulated sugar and remaining cinnamon. Flatten cookies with a glass dipped in sugar mixture. Bake 4 to 6 minutes or until edges are very lightly browned. Transfer cookies to a wire rack to cool. Use icing to pipe desired snowflake designs onto cookies. Allow icing to harden. Store in an airtight container.

Yield: about 8 dozen cookies

NUTTY PEANUT BUTTER BROWNIES
(Shown on page 57 and back cover)

- ³/₄ cup smooth peanut butter
- ½ cup butter or margarine, softened
- 1½ cups firmly packed brown sugar
- 2 eggs
- 2 teaspoons vanilla extract
- 1½ cups all-purpose flour
- 1½ teaspoons baking powder
- ⅛ teaspoon salt
- ½ cup chopped peanuts

Preheat oven to 375 degrees. In a large bowl, cream peanut butter, butter, and brown sugar until fluffy. Add eggs and vanilla; beat until smooth. In a small bowl, combine flour, baking powder, and salt. Add dry ingredients to creamed mixture; stir until well blended. Line a 9 x 13-inch baking pan with aluminum foil, extending foil over ends of pan; grease foil. Spread batter in prepared pan; sprinkle peanuts over top. Bake 15 to 18 minutes or until edges are lightly browned. Cool in pan 10 minutes. Use ends of foil to lift brownies from pan. Cut warm brownies into 2-inch squares; cool completely. Store in an airtight container.

Yield: about 2 dozen brownies.

(Shown on page 57 and back cover) A mug of cocoa and these tempting sweets will chase the chill from a wintry day! Topped with lots of crunchy peanuts, Nutty Peanut Butter Brownies (clockwise from left) are moist and chewy. Ground hazelnuts make Hazelnut Macaroons unforgettable melt-in-your-mouth treats. Crispy Cinnamon-Brown Sugar Snowflakes are decorated with frosty icing patterns. Rich macadamia nuts and a drizzling of fruity icing bring a pleasing flavor combination to soft Raspberry Chocolate Chip Cookies (recipe on page 62).

RASPBERRY CHOCOLATE CHIP COOKIES

(Shown on page 57 and back cover; caption on page 61)

COOKIES

2 packages (10 ounces each) semisweet chocolate chips, divided
³/₄ cup butter or margarine, softened
¹/₂ cup granulated sugar
¹/₂ cup firmly packed brown sugar
2 eggs
1 teaspoon vanilla extract
2¹/₂ cups all-purpose flour
³/₄ teaspoon baking soda
³/₄ teaspoon baking powder
¹/₂ teaspoon salt
1 cup coarsely chopped macadamia nuts

ICING

1 cup sifted confectioners sugar
3 tablespoons raspberry-flavored liqueur
Burgundy paste food coloring

Preheat oven to 375 degrees. For cookies, place 1 package of chocolate chips in a small microwave-safe bowl. Microwave on medium-high power (80%) 1 minute; stir. Microwave 1 minute longer; stir until melted. In a large bowl, cream butter and sugars until fluffy. Add eggs and vanilla; beat until smooth. Stir in melted chocolate. In a medium bowl, combine flour, baking soda, baking powder, and salt. Add dry ingredients to creamed mixture; stir until a soft dough forms. Stir in remaining package of chocolate chips and macadamia nuts. Drop tablespoonfuls of dough 2 inches apart onto an ungreased baking sheet. Bake 7 to 9 minutes or until bottoms are lightly browned. Transfer cookies to a wire rack with waxed paper underneath to cool.

For icing, combine confectioners sugar and liqueur in a small bowl; stir until smooth. Tint burgundy. Spoon icing into a pastry bag fitted with a small round tip. Pipe icing onto cookies. Allow icing to harden. Store in an airtight container.

Yield: about 7 dozen cookies

RASPBERRY THUMBPRINT COOKIES

¹/₂ cup butter or margarine, softened
¹/₄ cup firmly packed brown sugar
¹/₄ cup granulated sugar
1 teaspoon vanilla extract
¹/₂ teaspoon salt
1¹/₂ cups all-purpose flour, sifted
2 tablespoons milk
¹/₃ cup miniature semisweet chocolate chips
Raspberry preserves

Preheat oven to 375 degrees. In a medium mixing bowl, cream butter, sugars, vanilla, and salt until light and fluffy. Blend in flour and milk. Stir in chocolate chips. Shape dough into 1-inch balls and place on ungreased baking sheets. Make a small indentation with thumb in the top of each ball. Use a teaspoon to place a small amount of raspberry preserves in each indentation. Bake 10 to 12 minutes. Remove from sheets and cool on wire racks.

Yield: about 3 dozen cookies

Sprinkled with confectioners sugar, Cherry-Topped Chocolate Cookies are moist, chewy treats that are made using cake mix and sour cream.

CHERRY-TOPPED CHOCOLATE COOKIES

1 jar (10 ounces) maraschino cherry halves
1 package (18.25 ounces) devil's food cake mix
½ cup sour cream
1 egg
2 tablespoons confectioners sugar

Preheat oven to 375 degrees. Drain cherries; place on a paper towel and pat dry. In a large bowl, beat cake mix, sour cream, and egg with an electric mixer until light in color (batter will be stiff). Use greased hands to shape dough into 1-inch balls and place 2 inches apart on a greased baking sheet. Press 1 cherry half into center of each cookie. Bake 8 to 10 minutes or until edges are set. Cool cookies on pan 2 minutes; transfer to a wire rack to cool completely. Sift confectioners sugar over cookies.

Yield: about 5 dozen cookies

BUTTERY PECAN COOKIES

    1 cup butter or margarine, softened
    2/3 cup firmly packed brown sugar
    1 teaspoon vanilla extract
    2 cups all-purpose flour
    3/4 cup chopped pecans, toasted and
         coarsely ground
    1/2 teaspoon salt

In a medium bowl, cream butter, brown sugar, and vanilla until fluffy. In a small bowl, combine flour, pecans, and salt. Add dry ingredients to creamed mixture; stir until a soft dough forms. Divide dough in half; shape each half into an 8-inch-long roll. Wrap in plastic wrap and chill 1 hour.

Preheat oven to 350 degrees. Cut each roll into 1/4-inch slices and place 1 inch apart on an ungreased baking sheet. Bake 10 to 12 minutes or until edges are lightly browned. Transfer cookies to a wire rack to cool. Store in an airtight container.

Yield: about 4 dozen cookies

COWBOY COOKIES

    1 cup butter or margarine, melted
    1 cup granulated sugar
    1 cup firmly packed brown sugar
    2 eggs
    1 teaspoon vanilla extract
    2 cups all-purpose flour
    1 teaspoon baking powder
    1 teaspoon baking soda
    1/2 teaspoon salt
    2 cups quick-cooking oats
    1 package (12 ounces) semisweet
         chocolate chips
    3/4 cup chopped pecans

Preheat oven to 350 degrees. In a large bowl, beat butter and sugars until creamy. Add eggs and vanilla; beat until smooth. In a small bowl, combine flour, baking powder, baking soda, and salt. Add dry ingredients to creamed mixture; stir until a soft dough forms. Stir in oats, chocolate chips, and pecans. Drop tablespoonfuls of dough 2 inches apart onto a lightly greased baking sheet. Bake 9 to 11 minutes or until edges are lightly browned. Transfer cookies to a wire rack to cool. Store in an airtight container.

Yield: about 5 1/2 dozen cookies

OATMEAL FAMILY FAVORITES

    1 3/4 cups granulated sugar, divided
    1 cup firmly packed brown sugar
    1 cup vegetable oil
    3 eggs
    1 teaspoon vanilla extract
    1 cup all-purpose flour
    1 teaspoon baking soda
    1/2 teaspoon salt
    4 cups quick-cooking oats
    1 cup sweetened shredded coconut
         Granulated sugar

Preheat oven to 350 degrees. In a large bowl, combine 1 cup granulated sugar, brown sugar, and oil; beat until well blended. Add eggs and vanilla; beat until smooth. In a small bowl, combine flour, baking soda, and salt. Add dry ingredients to sugar mixture; stir until a soft dough forms. Stir in oats and coconut until well blended. Shape dough into 1-inch balls and roll in remaining 3/4 cup granulated

sugar. Place balls 2 inches apart on a greased baking sheet; flatten with bottom of a glass dipped in granulated sugar. Bake 8 to 10 minutes or until edges are lightly browned. Cool cookies on pan 3 minutes; transfer to a wire rack to cool completely. Store in an airtight container.

Yield: about 8 dozen cookies

These Oatmeal Family Favorites are just as good as you remember! Add to the nostalgia by serving them in a wooden Shaker box decorated with homespun fabric and buttons.

MOCHA-ALMOND BARS

Mocha-Almond Bars (shown on page 4) will perk up your day. Semisweet chocolate and instant coffee, combined with the subtle flavor of almonds, give the bars their rich charm.

- 1 cup butter or margarine, softened
- 1 cup firmly packed brown sugar
- 1 teaspoon almond extract
- 2 cups all-purpose flour
- 2 tablespoons instant coffee granules
- $1/2$ teaspoon baking powder
- $1/4$ teaspoon salt
- 1 package (6 ounces) semisweet chocolate chips
- $3/4$ cup sliced almonds, toasted and coarsely chopped

Preheat oven to 350 degrees. In a large bowl, cream butter, brown sugar, and almond extract until fluffy. In a small bowl, combine flour, coffee granules, baking powder, and salt. Add dry ingredients to creamed mixture; stir until a soft dough forms. Stir in chocolate chips and almonds. Press mixture into an ungreased $10^1/2$ x $15^1/2$-inch jellyroll pan. Bake 15 to 20 minutes or until lightly browned on top. Cool in pan 5 minutes. Cut into 1 x 2-inch bars while warm; cool completely in pan. Store in an airtight container.

Yield: about 5 dozen bars

CHOCOLATE-CARAMEL CHEWIES

- $3/4$ cup butter or margarine, softened
- $1/2$ cup firmly packed brown sugar
- 2 eggs
- 1 teaspoon vanilla extract
- $1^1/2$ cups all-purpose flour
- $1/4$ teaspoon baking soda
- $1/4$ teaspoon salt
- $1^1/2$ cups chopped pecans
- 1 cup milk chocolate chips
- 22 caramel candies, quartered

Preheat oven to 350 degrees. In a medium bowl, cream butter and brown sugar until fluffy. Add eggs and vanilla; stir until smooth. In a small bowl, combine flour, baking soda, and salt. Add dry ingredients to creamed mixture; stir until a soft dough forms. Stir in pecans, chocolate chips, and caramel pieces. Drop tablespoonfuls of dough 2 inches apart onto a greased baking sheet. Bake 8 to 10 minutes or until edges are lightly browned. Allow cookies to cool slightly on pan; transfer to a wire rack to cool completely. Store in an airtight container.

Yield: about 4 dozen cookies

CANDY BAR PIZZAS
(Shown on page 4)

CRUST
    2 cups quick-cooking oats
  1/2 cup firmly packed brown sugar
  1/3 cup light corn syrup
    2 tablespoons butter or margarine,
         melted
    2 tablespoons chunky peanut butter
  1/2 teaspoon vanilla extract

FILLING
   26 caramels (about 1/2 of a
         14-ounce package)
    2 tablespoons water
    1 package (6 ounces) semisweet
         chocolate chips
  1/3 cup chunky peanut butter
    2 teaspoons vegetable shortening
  1/2 cup salted peanuts

Preheat oven to 350 degrees. For crust, combine oats, brown sugar, and corn syrup in a large bowl. Add melted butter, peanut butter, and vanilla; stir until well blended. Press mixture into bottoms of two 9-inch round cake pans. Bake 10 to 12 minutes or until lightly browned. Cool in pans 10 minutes.

For filling, microwave caramels and water in a medium microwave-safe bowl on high power (100%) 2 minutes, stirring after 1 minute. Spread evenly over crusts. Microwave chocolate chips in a medium microwave-safe bowl on medium-high power (80%) 2 minutes, stirring after 1 minute. Add peanut butter and shortening; stir until well blended. Stir in peanuts. Spread filling over caramel layers. Chill 30 minutes or until chocolate is firm. Cut into wedges to serve.

Yield: two 9-inch pizzas, 16 servings each

BUTTERSCOTCH CHEWIES
(Shown on page 4)

  2/3 cup butter or margarine, softened
 1 1/2 cups firmly packed brown sugar
    2 eggs
    1 teaspoon vanilla extract
 1 1/2 cups all-purpose flour
  1/4 teaspoon baking soda
    1 package (10 or 12 ounces)
         butterscotch chips
    1 cup chopped pecans

Preheat oven to 375 degrees. In a large bowl, cream butter and brown sugar until fluffy. Add eggs and vanilla; beat until smooth. In a medium bowl, combine flour and baking soda. Add dry ingredients to creamed mixture; stir until a soft dough forms. Stir in butterscotch chips and pecans. Drop tablespoonfuls of dough 2 inches apart onto a greased baking sheet. Bake 7 to 9 minutes or until bottoms are lightly browned. Transfer cookies to a wire rack to cool. Store in single layers between sheets of waxed paper in an airtight container.

Yield: about 4 dozen cookies

TRIPLE CHIP COOKIES

1/2 cup butter or margarine,
    softened
1/4 cup granulated sugar
1/4 cup firmly packed brown sugar
1 egg
1/2 teaspoon vanilla extract
1 1/4 cups all-purpose flour
1/2 teaspoon baking soda
1/4 teaspoon salt
1/2 cup plain granola cereal
    (without fruit and nuts)
1/3 cup semisweet chocolate chips
1/3 cup milk chocolate chips
1/3 cup vanilla baking chips

Preheat oven to 375 degrees. In a large bowl, cream butter and sugars until fluffy. Add egg and vanilla; beat until smooth. Sift flour, baking soda, and salt into a small bowl. Stir in cereal. Add dry ingredients to creamed mixture; stir until a soft dough forms. Fold in chips. Drop heaping teaspoonfuls of dough 2 inches apart onto a greased baking sheet. Bake 8 to 10 minutes or until edges are brown. Transfer cookies to a wire rack to cool completely. Store in an airtight container.

Yield: about 3 1/2 dozen cookies

CHOCOLATE-OATMEAL-RAISIN COOKIES

1 package (16 ounces) pound cake
    mix
3/4 cup vegetable oil
2 eggs
1 teaspoon vanilla extract
1/2 teaspoon ground cinnamon
1 cup quick-cooking oats
3/4 cup (about 6 ounces) chocolate-
    covered raisins

Preheat oven to 375 degrees. In a large bowl, combine cake mix, oil, eggs, vanilla, and cinnamon; beat with an electric mixer until smooth. Stir in oats and raisins. Drop tablespoonfuls of dough about 2 inches apart on an ungreased baking sheet. Bake 8 to 10 minutes or until edges are light brown. Transfer to a wire rack to cool completely. Store in an airtight container.

Yield: about 4 dozen cookies

RAISIN-NUT CHEWIES

2 egg whites
1/2 cup sugar
2 1/2 cups raisin bran cereal
1/3 cup chopped pecans, toasted and
    coarsely ground

Preheat oven to 200 degrees. In a medium bowl, beat egg whites until soft peaks form. Gradually add sugar, beating until mixture is very stiff. Fold in cereal and pecans. Drop teaspoonfuls of mixture 1 inch apart onto a baking sheet lined with parchment paper. Bake 1 hour or until bottoms are lightly browned. Transfer cookies to a wire rack to cool.

Yield: about 3 1/2 dozen cookies

Ever so simple to prepare, Chocolate-Oatmeal-Raisin Cookies begin with pound cake mix and contain a sweet surprise—chocolate-covered raisins!

WHITE CHOCOLATE CHUNK MACADAMIA COOKIES

- 1 cup butter or margarine, softened
- 1 cup firmly packed light brown sugar
- 1/2 cup granulated sugar
- 2 eggs
- 1 teaspoon vanilla extract
- 2 1/4 cups all-purpose flour
- 1 teaspoon baking soda
- 1 teaspoon salt
- 1 cup macadamia nuts, coarsely chopped
- 2 cups white chocolate *or* almond bark, broken into bite-size pieces

Cream butter and sugars until light and fluffy. Beat in eggs and vanilla. Combine flour, baking soda, and salt; gradually add to creamed mixture. Stir in macadamia nuts and chocolate. Drop by heaping teaspoonfuls onto greased baking sheets. Bake in a preheated 350-degree oven 10 to 12 minutes. Cool slightly before removing from baking sheets.

Yield: about 6 dozen cookies

ORANGE CHIP COOKIES

- 1 cup butter or margarine, softened
- 1 1/4 cups sugar
- 1 egg
- 1 tablespoon grated orange zest
- 2 teaspoons orange extract
- 2 1/4 cups all-purpose flour
- 3/4 teaspoon baking soda
- 1/2 teaspoon salt
- 1 package (12 ounces) white baking chips
- 1 cup chopped walnuts, toasted

Preheat oven to 350 degrees. In a large bowl, cream butter and sugar until fluffy. Add egg, orange zest, and orange extract. Beat until well blended. In a medium bowl, combine flour, baking soda, and salt. Add dry ingredients to creamed mixture; stir until a soft dough forms. Stir in baking chips and walnuts. Drop tablespoonfuls of dough onto a greased baking sheet. Bake 8 to 10 minutes or until edges are lightly browned. Transfer cookies to a wire rack to cool. Store in an airtight container.

Yield: about 4 1/2 dozen cookies

LEMON-POPPY SEED TEA CAKES

1/2 cup butter or margarine, softened
1 cup sugar
1 egg
1 tablespoon poppy seed
1 teaspoon lemon extract
1 teaspoon vanilla extract
2 cups all-purpose flour
2 teaspoons baking powder
1/2 teaspoon salt

In a medium bowl, cream butter and sugar until fluffy. Add egg, poppy seed, and extracts; beat until smooth. In a small bowl, combine flour, baking powder, and salt. Add dry ingredients to creamed mixture; stir until a soft dough forms. Divide dough into fourths. Wrap in plastic wrap and chill 1 hour or until firm.

Preheat oven to 400 degrees. On a lightly floured surface, use a floured rolling pin to roll out one fourth of dough to 1/8-inch thickness. Use a 1 3/4-inch-diameter fluted-edge cookie cutter to cut out cookies. Place 2 inches apart on a lightly greased baking sheet. Bake 4 to 6 minutes or until edges are lightly browned. Transfer cookies to a wire rack to cool. Repeat with remaining dough. Store in an airtight container.

Yield: about 8 dozen cookies

LEMON BARS

2 1/4 cups all-purpose flour, divided
2 1/4 cups confectioners sugar, divided
1 cup butter or margarine, melted
2 cups granulated sugar
4 eggs, slightly beaten
1 teaspoon baking powder
2 cups coconut
1/4 cup plus 3 to 4 tablespoons lemon juice, divided

Combine 2 cups flour and 1/2 cup confectioners sugar. Add melted butter; mix well. Spread mixture in a greased 13 x 9 x 2-inch baking pan. Bake in a preheated 350-degree oven 20 to 25 minutes.

Stir granulated sugar and eggs together. Combine baking powder and remaining 1/4 cup flour; add to sugar mixture. Stir in coconut and 1/4 cup lemon juice. Pour over baked crust. Return to oven and bake 30 minutes; cool.

Combine remaining 1 3/4 cups confectioners sugar and remaining 3 to 4 tablespoons lemon juice; pour over baked mixture. Cut into bars.

Yield: about 2 dozen bars

NUTTY BROWN SUGAR BARS

FILLING
- ½ cup butter or margarine
- ½ cup firmly packed brown sugar
- ½ cup evaporated milk
- 1 cup graham cracker crumbs
- 1 cup flaked coconut
- ½ cup chopped pecans
- 15 graham crackers (2½ x 5 inches each)

ICING
- 1 cup firmly packed brown sugar
- 3 tablespoons evaporated milk
- 2 tablespoons butter or margarine
- 1 cup confectioners sugar
- 1 teaspoon vanilla extract

For filling, combine butter, brown sugar, and evaporated milk in a heavy medium saucepan. Stirring constantly over medium-high heat, bring to a boil and boil 1 minute. Remove from heat. Stir in cracker crumbs, coconut, and pecans. Line bottom of a 9 x 13-inch baking pan with half of graham crackers. Pour filling over crackers. Cover filling with remaining graham crackers, pressing to make crackers level.

For icing, combine brown sugar, evaporated milk, and butter in a heavy medium saucepan. Stirring constantly over medium-high heat, cook until mixture begins to boil (about 3 minutes). Remove from heat. Add confectioners sugar and vanilla; stir until smooth. Quickly spread icing over graham crackers. Cool in pan. Cut into 1 x 2-inch bars. Store in an airtight container.

Yield: about 4 dozen bars

CHOCOLATE GINGERBREAD

- ½ cup butter or margarine, softened
- ¾ cup firmly packed dark brown sugar
- ½ cup dark corn syrup
- ¼ cup molasses
- 1 egg
- 3 cups all-purpose flour
- ½ cup cocoa
- 1 teaspoon ground ginger
- 1 teaspoon ground cloves

Cream butter, brown sugar, corn syrup, and molasses. Add egg and beat until well blended. Add flour, cocoa, and spices; stir until blended, adding more flour if necessary to make a stiff dough. Cover and chill at least 1 hour.

On a lightly floured surface, use a floured rolling pin to roll out dough to ⅛-inch thickness. Cut out with desired cookie cutters and place on ungreased baking sheets. Bake in a preheated 325-degree oven 8 to 12 minutes. Cool and remove from baking sheets.

Yield: about 3 dozen cookies

CHOCOLATE GINGERSNAPS

1½ cups butter or margarine, softened
2¾ cups sugar, divided
 2 eggs
½ cup molasses
 4 cups all-purpose flour
¼ cup plus 2 tablespoons cocoa, divided
 2 teaspoons baking soda
 2 teaspoons ground cinnamon
 2 teaspoons ground cloves
 2 teaspoons ground ginger

Preheat oven to 375 degrees. In a large bowl, cream butter and 2 cups sugar until fluffy. Add eggs and molasses; beat until smooth. In a medium bowl, combine flour, ¼ cup cocoa, baking soda, cinnamon, cloves, and ginger. Add dry ingredients to creamed mixture; stir until a soft dough forms. In a small bowl, combine remaining ¾ cup sugar and 2 tablespoons cocoa. Shape dough into 1-inch balls; roll in sugar mixture. Place balls 3 inches apart on a lightly greased baking sheet. Flatten balls into 2-inch-diameter cookies with bottom of a glass dipped in sugar mixture. Bake 5 to 7 minutes or until bottoms are lightly browned. Transfer cookies to a wire rack to cool. Store in an airtight container.

Yield: about 10 dozen cookies

OLD-FASHIONED GINGERSNAPS

1½ cups butter or margarine, softened
2¾ cups sugar, divided
 2 eggs
½ cup molasses
 4 cups all-purpose flour
 2 teaspoons baking soda
 2 teaspoons ground cinnamon
 2 teaspoons ground cloves
 2 teaspoons ground ginger
 Sugar

Preheat oven to 375 degrees. In a large bowl, cream butter and 2 cups sugar until fluffy. Add eggs and molasses; beat until smooth. In a medium bowl, combine flour, baking soda, cinnamon, cloves, and ginger. Add dry ingredients to creamed mixture; stir until a soft dough forms. Shape dough into 1-inch balls and roll in remaining ¾ cup sugar. Place balls 3 inches apart on a lightly greased baking sheet; flatten with bottom of a glass dipped in sugar. Bake 5 to 7 minutes or until bottoms are lightly browned. Transfer cookies to a wire rack to cool. Store in an airtight container.

Yield: about 10 dozen cookies

BUTTERSCOTCH BROWNIES

1/2 cup butter or margarine, softened
2 cups firmly packed brown sugar
2 eggs
1 1/2 teaspoons vanilla extract
1 3/4 cups all-purpose flour
1 1/2 teaspoons baking powder
1/2 teaspoon baking soda
1/4 teaspoon salt
1 cup chopped pecans, toasted

Preheat oven to 350 degrees. In a large bowl, cream butter and brown sugar until fluffy. Add eggs and vanilla; beat until smooth. In a small bowl, combine flour, baking powder, baking soda, and salt. Add dry ingredients to creamed mixture; stir until well blended. Stir in pecans. Spread batter into a lightly greased 9 x 13-inch baking pan. Bake 25 to 30 minutes or until brownies start to pull away from sides of pan. Cool in pan 15 minutes. Cut warm brownies into 2-inch squares; cool completely in pan. Store in an airtight container.

Yield: about 2 dozen brownies

PEANUT BUTTER-CINNAMON BROWNIES

1/4 cup butter or margarine, melted
1/2 cup granulated sugar
1/2 cup firmly packed brown sugar
2 eggs
1 teaspoon vanilla extract
1/2 cup all-purpose flour
1 teaspoon ground cinnamon
1/2 teaspoon baking powder
1/2 teaspoon salt
1/2 cup extra-crunchy peanut butter

Preheat oven to 350 degrees. In a medium bowl, combine butter and sugars. Add eggs and vanilla; beat until smooth. In a small bowl, combine flour, cinnamon, baking powder, and salt. Add dry ingredients to butter mixture; stir just until dry ingredients are moistened. Stir in peanut butter. Spread batter into a greased 7 x 11-inch metal baking pan. Bake 20 to 25 minutes or until set in center. Cool completely in pan. Cut into squares to serve.

Yield: about 2 dozen brownies

SINLESS BROWNIES

1 1/2 cups sugar
1 cup all-purpose flour
1/3 cup cocoa
1/2 teaspoon baking powder
1/4 teaspoon salt
1/4 cup egg substitute
1/4 cup water
1 egg white
2 tablespoons reduced-calorie margarine, softened
1 tablespoon vanilla extract
Vegetable cooking spray

Preheat oven to 350 degrees. In a medium bowl, combine sugar, flour, cocoa, baking powder, and salt. Add egg substitute, water, egg white, margarine, and vanilla; stir until well blended. Spoon batter into an 8-inch square baking pan sprayed with cooking spray. Bake 25 to 30 minutes or until dry on top and set in center. Cut into 2-inch squares.

Yield: about 16 brownies
1 serving (one 2-inch square brownie):
97 calories, 1.0 gram fat, 1.5 grams protein, 22.3 grams carbohydrate

MISSISSIPPI MUD BROWNIES

BROWNIES
- 1 package (19.8 ounces) fudge brownie mix
- 1/2 cup water
- 1/3 cup vegetable oil
- 1 egg
- 1/4 cup all-purpose flour
- 1 1/2 cups miniature marshmallows

FROSTING
- 1 3/4 cups confectioners sugar
- 1/2 cup semisweet chocolate chips, melted
- 1/3 cup milk
- 2 tablespoons butter or margarine, softened
- Purchased tubes of red and green decorating icing (optional)

Preheat oven to 350 degrees. For brownies, combine brownie mix, water, oil, egg, and flour in a medium mixing bowl; stir just until blended. Pour batter into a lightly greased 10 x 8 x 2-inch baking pan. Bake 25 to 30 minutes or until center is set. Top with marshmallows and bake 2 minutes longer.

For frosting, combine confectioners sugar, melted chocolate chips, milk, and butter. Beat until smooth and spread over brownies. Cut into bars.

If desired, use decorating icing to pipe small red and green bows onto tops of brownies.

Yield: about 20 brownies

CHOCOLATE MOCHA BROWNIES

- 1 cup firmly packed brown sugar
- 3/4 cup butter or margarine
- 2 tablespoons instant coffee granules
- 1 tablespoon hot water
- 2 eggs
- 2 teaspoons vanilla extract
- 2 cups all-purpose flour
- 2 teaspoons baking powder
- 1/2 teaspoon salt
- 4 ounces semisweet baking chocolate, broken into small pieces
- 4 ounces white chocolate, broken into small pieces

In a medium saucepan, melt sugar and butter over medium-low heat. Dissolve coffee in hot water and stir into butter mixture. Cool to room temperature.

Preheat oven to 350 degrees. Beat eggs and vanilla into butter mixture. In a large bowl, sift together next 3 ingredients. Stir butter mixture into dry ingredients. Fold in chocolate pieces. Pour batter into a greased 8 x 11-inch baking pan. Bake 25 to 30 minutes or until light brown. Cool in pan. Cut into 1 1/2-inch squares.

Yield: about 3 dozen brownies

PINEAPPLE JUMBLES

1/2 cup butter or margarine, softened
1/2 cup granulated sugar
1/2 cup firmly packed brown sugar
1/2 cup sour cream
1 egg
1 teaspoon vanilla extract
1 1/4 cups all-purpose flour
1/4 teaspoon baking soda
1/4 teaspoon salt
1 cup sweetened shredded coconut
1 cup coarsely chopped walnuts
1 cup finely chopped candied
    pineapple

Preheat oven to 375 degrees. In a large bowl, cream butter and sugars until fluffy. Add sour cream, egg, and vanilla; beat until smooth. In a small bowl, combine flour, baking soda, and salt. Add dry ingredients to creamed mixture; stir until a soft dough forms. Stir in remaining ingredients. Drop tablespoonfuls of dough 2 inches apart onto a greased baking sheet. Bake 10 to 12 minutes or until edges are lightly browned. Transfer cookies to a wire rack to cool. Store in an airtight container.

Yield: about 4 dozen cookies

Pineapple Jumbles (left, page 76) offer a tropical surprise in every bite. Candied pineapple and cherries combine with chopped pecans and a sweet glaze to create pretty Stained Glass Cookies, diamond-shaped shortbread tidbits that are sure to dazzle.

STAINED GLASS COOKIES

1	cup butter or margarine, softened
1 1/2	cups sugar
1	egg
1	teaspoon vanilla extract
2 3/4	cups all-purpose flour
1/4	teaspoon salt
1	pound mixed candied fruit, coarsely chopped
2	cups chopped pecans
1/4	cup light corn syrup

Preheat oven to 375 degrees. In a large bowl, cream butter and sugar until fluffy. Add egg and vanilla; beat until smooth. In a medium bowl, combine flour and salt. Add dry ingredients to creamed mixture; stir until a soft dough forms. Line a 10 1/2 x 15 1/2-inch jellyroll pan with heavy aluminum foil, extending foil over ends of pan; lightly grease foil. Press dough into bottom of prepared pan. In a medium bowl, combine candied fruit and pecans. Sprinkle fruit mixture over dough; lightly press into dough. Bake 22 to 24 minutes or until edges are lightly browned. Lift from pan using ends of foil; allow to cool.

In a small saucepan, bring corn syrup to a boil. Boil 1 minute. Brush corn syrup over top of cookies; cool completely. Cut into diamond-shaped bars or cut into bars. Store in an airtight container.

Yield: about 4 dozen cookies

GUMDROP COOKIES

3	tablespoons vegetable oil
1/2	cup sugar
1/4	cup egg substitute (equivalent to 1 egg)
1	tablespoon grated orange zest
1	teaspoon vanilla extract
1 1/3	cups all-purpose flour
1/2	teaspoon baking powder
1/4	teaspoon salt
	Vegetable cooking spray
4	ounces small spiced gumdrops

In a large bowl, beat oil and sugar until well blended. Add egg substitute, orange zest, and vanilla; beat until smooth. In a small bowl, combine flour, baking powder, and salt. Add dry ingredients to sugar mixture; stir until a soft dough forms. Cover and chill 1 hour.

Preheat oven to 350 degrees. Lightly spray hands and baking sheet with cooking spray. Shape dough into 1-inch balls and place 1 inch apart on prepared pan. Press a gumdrop in center of each cookie. Bake 7 to 9 minutes or until bottoms are lightly browned. Transfer cookies to a wire rack to cool. Store in an airtight container.

Yield: about 3 dozen cookies

SNOWY DAY COOKIES

- 1 cup butter or margarine, softened
- 2 cups sifted confectioners sugar, divided
- 1 teaspoon almond extract
- 1/2 teaspoon vanilla extract
- 2 1/4 cups all-purpose flour
- 1/4 teaspoon salt
- 1 cup slivered almonds, toasted and coarsely ground

Preheat oven to 350 degrees. In a large bowl, cream butter and 1/2 cup confectioners sugar until fluffy. Stir in extracts. In a medium bowl, combine flour and salt. Add dry ingredients to creamed mixture; stir until a soft dough forms. Stir in almonds. Shape dough into 1-inch balls and place 2 inches apart on an ungreased baking sheet. Bake 15 to 20 minutes or until bottoms are lightly browned. Roll warm cookies in remaining 1 1/2 cups confectioners sugar, reserving remaining sugar. Transfer cookies to waxed paper; cool completely. Roll in confectioners sugar again. Store in an airtight container.

Yield: about 4 1/2 dozen cookies

CHOCOLATE SNOWBALL COOKIES

- 1 1/2 cups (9 ounces) semisweet chocolate chips
- 1 package (8 ounces) cream cheese, cut into small pieces
- 1 1/2 teaspoons vanilla extract
- 3 cups finely ground chocolate wafer cookies (about 64 cookies)
- 1 cup finely ground pecans
  Confectioners sugar, sifted

In a large saucepan, melt chocolate chips over low heat, stirring constantly. Add cream cheese and vanilla, stirring until smooth. Remove from heat. Stir in cookie crumbs and pecans. Shape into 1-inch balls; roll in confectioners sugar. Cover and refrigerate 8 hours or until firm.

Roll balls in confectioners sugar again. Store in an airtight container in refrigerator.

Yield: about 6 dozen cookies

SNOWBALL COOKIES

- 3 cups finely shredded coconut
- 1 package (18 ounces) vanilla candy coating
- 1 package (16 ounces) chocolate sandwich cookies

Spread coconut on waxed paper. Melt candy coating in a heavy medium saucepan over low heat. Remove from heat. Place each cookie on a fork and dip into candy coating until covered; roll in coconut. Place cookies on waxed paper and allow candy coating to harden.

Yield: about 3 1/2 dozen cookies

CHOCOLATE CRINKLE COOKIES

1/2 cup butter or margarine, softened
2 cups granulated sugar
6 ounces semisweet baking chocolate, melted
4 eggs
2 teaspoons vanilla extract
2 cups all-purpose flour
2 teaspoons baking powder
1/2 teaspoon salt
1 cup sifted confectioners sugar

In a large bowl, combine butter, granulated sugar, and melted chocolate; beat until well blended. Add eggs, 1 at a time, beating well after each addition. Add vanilla, continuing to beat until smooth. In a small bowl, combine flour, baking powder, and salt. Add dry ingredients to creamed mixture; stir until well blended. Cover dough and chill 4 hours.

Preheat oven to 350 degrees. Place confectioners sugar in a small bowl. Drop teaspoonfuls of dough into confectioners sugar. Shape into 1-inch balls, using sugar to keep dough from sticking to hands. Place balls 3 inches apart on a baking sheet lined with parchment paper. Bake 7 to 9 minutes or until edges are firm. Transfer cookies to a wire rack to cool. Store in an airtight container.

Yield: about 7 1/2 dozen cookies

BITE-SIZE SNOWBALL MACAROONS

1 1/4 cups sugar, divided
1/2 cup all-purpose flour
1/4 teaspoon salt
2 1/2 cups flaked coconut
4 egg whites
1/2 teaspoon vanilla extract

Preheat oven to 325 degrees. In a medium bowl, combine 1/4 cup sugar, flour, and salt. Stir in coconut; set aside. In another medium bowl, beat egg whites until soft peaks form; add vanilla. Gradually add remaining 1 cup sugar; continue to beat until mixture is very stiff. Gently fold coconut mixture into egg white mixture. Drop half teaspoonfuls of mixture onto a lightly greased baking sheet. Bake 9 to 11 minutes or until bottoms are lightly browned. Transfer to a wire rack to cool. Store in an airtight container.

Yield: about 10 dozen macaroons

Fun to make, these Tasty Christmas Wreaths are almost too pretty to eat! Fashioned from braided dough, the dainty cookies are embellished with a garland of icing and holly sprinkles.

TASTY CHRISTMAS WREATHS

COOKIES

- 1/3 cup butter or margarine, softened
- 1/3 cup firmly packed brown sugar
- 1/2 cup sifted confectioners sugar
- 1 egg
- 2 tablespoons grated lemon zest
- 1/2 teaspoon vanilla extract
- 1 1/4 cups all-purpose flour
- 1/4 cup cornstarch
- 1/2 teaspoon ground cardamom
- 1/4 teaspoon baking powder

ICING

- 1 cup sifted confectioners sugar
- 2 tablespoons milk
  Holly mix sprinkles to decorate

For cookies, cream butter and sugars in a large bowl until fluffy. Add egg, lemon zest, and vanilla; beat until smooth. In a small bowl, combine flour, cornstarch, cardamom, and baking powder. Add dry ingredients to creamed mixture; stir until a soft dough forms. Place dough on plastic wrap and shape into four 6-inch-long rolls. Chill 2 hours.

Preheat oven to 400 degrees. Cut each roll into 12 equal pieces. On a lightly floured surface, roll each piece into a 6-inch-long rope. Twist 2 ropes of dough together. Place on a greased baking sheet. Shape into wreaths and press ends together to seal. Bake 6 to 8 minutes or until bottoms are lightly browned. Transfer cookies to a wire rack with waxed paper underneath to cool.

For icing, combine confectioners sugar and milk; stir until smooth. Spoon icing into a pastry bag fitted with a small round tip. Pipe icing onto wreaths; place holly sprinkles on icing. Allow icing to harden. Store in an airtight container.

Yield: 2 dozen cookies

CREAM CHEESE PRESERVE COOKIES

- 1 package (8 ounces) cream cheese, softened
- 1 cup unsalted butter, softened
- 2 cups all-purpose flour
  Grated rind of 1/2 lemon *or* dash of lemon juice
  Blackberry, apricot, and strawberry preserves

Beat cream cheese and butter together until well blended. Add flour and lemon rind; mix well. Shape into four balls of equal size; wrap in plastic wrap and refrigerate until firm.

Roll out one ball at a time between two sheets of plastic wrap to 1/4-inch thickness. Cut out with 2 1/2-inch round scalloped-edge cookie cutter. Place cookies on ungreased baking sheets. On one half of each cookie, use a 1-inch-wide heart-shaped cookie cutter to cut out heart 1/4 inch from edge. Place a small amount of preserves on the other half of each cookie. Fold each cookie in half and press edges together. Bake in a preheated 375-degree oven 15 to 20 minutes or until slightly puffed and just beginning to brown. Cool slightly before removing from baking sheets.

Yield: about 4 dozen cookies

CRUNCHY PECAN COOKIES

- 1 cup butter or margarine, softened
- 1 cup granulated sugar
- 1 cup firmly packed brown sugar
- 1 cup vegetable oil
- 1 egg
- 1 teaspoon vanilla extract
- $3\frac{1}{2}$ cups all-purpose flour
- 1 teaspoon baking soda
- $\frac{1}{2}$ teaspoon salt
- 2 cups finely crushed corn flake cereal
- $1\frac{1}{2}$ cups chopped pecans

Preheat oven to 350 degrees. In a large bowl, cream butter and sugars until fluffy. Beat in oil, egg, and vanilla. In a medium bowl, combine flour, baking soda, and salt. Add dry ingredients to creamed mixture; stir until a soft dough forms. Stir in cereal crumbs and pecans. Drop tablespoonfuls of dough 2 inches apart onto a greased baking sheet. Using a fork dipped in water, make a crisscross design on each cookie. Bake 10 to 12 minutes or until edges are light brown. Transfer to a wire rack to cool completely. Store in an airtight container.

Yield: about 7 dozen cookies

CHEWY PECAN SQUARES

CRUST
- 1 package ($18\frac{1}{4}$ ounces) yellow cake mix
- 1 egg
- $\frac{1}{3}$ cup vegetable oil

FILLING
- 1 cup sugar
- 4 eggs
- $\frac{1}{2}$ teaspoon salt
- 1 cup dark corn syrup
- $\frac{1}{4}$ cup butter or margarine, melted
- 1 teaspoon vanilla extract
- 2 cups chopped pecans

Preheat oven to 350 degrees. For crust, combine cake mix, egg, and oil in a medium bowl. Press mixture into bottom of a greased 9 x 13-inch baking pan. Bake 20 minutes.

For filling, beat sugar, eggs, and salt in a large bowl until well blended. Beat in corn syrup, melted butter, and vanilla. Stir in pecans. Pour over hot crust. Bake at 350 degrees 30 to 35 minutes or until brown around edges and center is set. Cool completely. Cut into $1\frac{1}{2}$-inch squares. Store in an airtight container.

Yield: about 3 dozen squares

CHUNKY CHOCOLATE COOKIES

1 cup butter or margarine, softened
3/4 cup firmly packed brown sugar
1/2 cup granulated sugar
1 egg
1 teaspoon vanilla extract
1 3/4 cups all-purpose flour
1/4 cup cocoa
1/2 teaspoon baking powder
1/2 teaspoon baking soda
1/2 teaspoon salt
1 package (10 ounces) milk chocolate chunks
1/2 cup chopped pecans

Preheat oven to 375 degrees. In a large bowl, cream butter and sugars until fluffy. Add egg and vanilla; beat until smooth. In a small bowl, combine flour, cocoa, baking powder, baking soda, and salt. Add dry ingredients to creamed mixture; stir until a soft dough forms. Stir in chocolate chunks and pecans. Drop tablespoonfuls of dough 2 inches apart onto an ungreased baking sheet. Bake 6 to 8 minutes or until cookies are set and bottoms are lightly browned. Transfer cookies to a wire rack to cool. Store in an airtight container.

Yield: about 4 1/2 dozen cookies

PEANUT BUTTER-FUDGE COOKIES

1 cup chunky peanut butter
2 tablespoons vegetable oil
2 eggs
1 package (21.5 ounces) fudge brownie mix
1/2 cup water
1 package (6 ounces) semisweet chocolate chips
1 cup chopped unsalted peanuts

Preheat oven to 350 degrees. In a large bowl, beat peanut butter, oil, and eggs. Add brownie mix and water; stir until moistened. Stir in chocolate chips. Drop tablespoonfuls of dough onto an ungreased baking sheet. Place 1/2 teaspoon peanuts on each cookie. Bake 12 to 14 minutes or until fingertip leaves a slight indentation when center of cookie is touched. Transfer to a wire rack to cool completely. Store in an airtight container.

Yield: about 5 dozen cookies

PEANUT BUTTER BITES

- ½ cup butter or margarine, softened
- ½ cup granulated sugar
- ½ cup firmly packed brown sugar
- ¾ cup crunchy peanut butter
- 1 egg
- ½ teaspoon vanilla extract
- 1⅓ cups all-purpose flour
- ½ teaspoon baking soda
- ½ teaspoon baking powder
- ¼ teaspoon salt

Preheat oven to 375 degrees. In a large bowl, cream butter and sugars until fluffy. Add peanut butter, egg, and vanilla; beat until well blended. In a small bowl, combine flour, baking soda, baking powder, and salt. Add dry ingredients to creamed mixture; stir until a soft dough forms. Shape dough into balls slightly larger than ½-inch and place 2 inches apart on an ungreased baking sheet. Flatten balls in a crisscross pattern with a fork dipped in flour. Bake 6 to 8 minutes or until bottoms are lightly browned. Transfer cookies to a wire rack to cool. Store in an airtight container.

Yield: about 8 dozen cookies

PEANUT BUTTER BARS

- 1 package (16 ounces) confectioners sugar
- 1½ cups graham cracker crumbs
- 1 cup smooth peanut butter
- 1 cup butter or margarine
- 8 chocolate-covered caramel, peanut, and nougat candy bars, chopped (2.07 ounces each)
- 1 tablespoon milk

Combine confectioners sugar and graham cracker crumbs in a large bowl. In a medium microwave-safe bowl, combine peanut butter and butter. Microwave on medium-high power (80%) 2 minutes or until mixture melts, stirring after each minute. Pour peanut butter mixture over graham cracker mixture; stir until well blended. Press mixture into bottom of an ungreased 9 x 13-inch baking dish. Place candy bar pieces and milk in a medium microwave-safe bowl. Microwave on medium power (50%) 3 minutes or until candy melts, stirring after each minute. Spread melted candy mixture over peanut butter mixture. Cool 20 minutes or until candy mixture hardens. Cut into 1-inch squares.

Yield: about 8 dozen bars

Rolled in cinnamon and sugar before baking, Snickerdoodles are sweet treats that you can make in a jiffy with ingredients on hand. A heart-shaped cookie jar tag says your cookies are baked with love!

SNICKERDOODLES

   1   cup butter or margarine, softened
1^1/$_2$ cups sugar, divided
   2   eggs
   1   teaspoon vanilla extract
2^1/$_2$ cups all-purpose flour
1^1/$_2$ teaspoons ground cinnamon, divided
   1   teaspoon cream of tartar
   1   teaspoon baking soda
 ^{1}/$_4$ teaspoon salt

Preheat oven to 375 degrees. In a large bowl, cream butter and 1^1/$_4$ cups sugar until fluffy. Add eggs and vanilla; beat until smooth. In a medium bowl, combine flour, ^{1}/$_2$ teaspoon cinnamon, cream of tartar, baking soda, and salt. Add dry ingredients to creamed mixture; stir until a soft dough forms. In a small bowl, combine remaining ^{1}/$_4$ cup sugar and 1 teaspoon cinnamon. Shape dough into 1-inch balls and roll in sugar mixture. Place balls 2 inches apart on a lightly greased baking sheet. Bake 6 to 8 minutes or until bottoms are lightly browned. Transfer cookies to a wire rack to cool. Store in an airtight container.

Yield: about 7 dozen cookies

PECAN SANDIES

- 3/4 cup butter or margarine, softened
- 3/4 cup sifted confectioners sugar
- 1/4 cup firmly packed brown sugar
- 1 egg
- 1 1/2 teaspoons vanilla extract
- 2 1/4 cups all-purpose flour
- 1/2 cup chopped pecans, toasted and finely ground
- 1/4 teaspoon salt

In a large bowl, cream butter and sugars until fluffy. Add egg and vanilla; beat until smooth. In a medium bowl, combine flour, pecans, and salt. Add dry ingredients to creamed mixture; stir until a soft dough forms. Divide dough in half. Wrap in plastic wrap and chill 1 hour.

Preheat oven to 350 degrees. On a lightly floured surface, use a floured rolling pin to roll out half of dough to 1/4-inch thickness. Use a 3 1/2 x 2 3/4-inch seashell-shaped cookie cutter to cut out cookies. Transfer to an ungreased baking sheet. Bake 7 to 9 minutes or until bottoms are lightly browned. Transfer cookies to a wire rack to cool. Repeat with remaining dough. Store in an airtight container.

Yield: about 2 1/2 dozen cookies

PECAN-CINNAMON COOKIES

- 1/2 cup vegetable shortening
- 1/4 cup butter or margarine, softened
- 1 cup firmly packed brown sugar
- 1/4 cup light corn syrup
- 1 egg
- 1 tablespoon vanilla extract
- 2 cups all-purpose flour
- 2 teaspoons ground cinnamon
- 1 teaspoon baking soda
- 1/2 teaspoon salt
- 1 1/2 cups chopped pecans, toasted

Preheat oven to 350 degrees. In a medium bowl, cream shortening, butter, and brown sugar until fluffy. Add corn syrup, egg, and vanilla; beat until smooth. In a small bowl, combine flour, cinnamon, baking soda, and salt. Add dry ingredients to creamed mixture; stir until a soft dough forms. Stir in pecans. Drop tablespoonfuls of dough 2 inches apart onto a greased baking sheet. Bake 8 to 10 minutes or until bottoms are lightly browned. Allow cookies to cool on pan 5 minutes; transfer to a wire rack to cool completely. Store in an airtight container.

Yield: about 4 dozen cookies

MOM'S SUGAR COOKIES

- ³/₄ cup vegetable oil
- 2 eggs
- 2 teaspoons vanilla extract
- 1 cup sugar
- 2 cups all-purpose flour
- 1 teaspoon baking powder
- ¼ teaspoon salt
- Sugar

Preheat oven to 400 degrees. In a large bowl, beat oil, eggs, and vanilla until well blended. Add 1 cup sugar; beat until smooth. In a small bowl, combine flour, baking powder, and salt. Add dry ingredients to egg mixture; stir until a soft dough forms. Drop teaspoonfuls of dough 2 inches apart onto an ungreased baking sheet. Flatten cookies with bottom of a glass dipped in sugar. Bake 5 to 7 minutes or until bottoms are lightly browned. Transfer cookies to a wire rack to cool. Store in a cookie tin.

Yield: about 5 dozen cookies

MEXICAN SUGAR COOKIES

- ³/₄ cup vegetable oil
- 2 eggs
- 1¹/₂ teaspoons vanilla extract
- 1¹/₄ cups sugar, divided
- 2 cups all-purpose flour
- 1 teaspoon baking powder
- ¼ teaspoon salt
- 1¹/₂ teaspoons ground cinnamon

Preheat oven to 400 degrees. In a large bowl, beat oil, eggs, and vanilla until well blended. Add 1 cup sugar; beat until smooth. In a small bowl, combine flour, baking powder, and salt. Add flour mixture to oil mixture; stir until a soft dough forms. In a small bowl, combine remaining ¹/₄ cup sugar and cinnamon. Drop teaspoonfuls of dough into cinnamon-sugar mixture; roll into balls. Place balls 2 inches apart on a greased baking sheet. Flatten cookies with bottom of a glass dipped in cinnamon-sugar mixture. Bake 4 to 6 minutes or until bottoms are lightly browned. Transfer cookies to a wire rack to cool. Store in a cookie tin.

Yield: about 4¹/₂ dozen cookies

SPICED PUMPKIN COOKIES

COOKIES

- ½ cup butter or margarine, softened
- 1½ cups firmly packed brown sugar
- ¾ cup canned pumpkin
- 1 egg
- 1 tablespoon grated orange zest
- 1¼ cups all-purpose flour
- 1¼ cups whole-wheat flour
- 1 teaspoon pumpkin pie spice
- 1 teaspoon baking soda
- ¼ teaspoon salt
- 2 cups chopped walnuts

ICING

- ½ cup butter or margarine
- 1 cup firmly packed brown sugar
- ¼ cup whipping cream
- 1 tablespoon light corn syrup
- 1 cup sifted confectioners sugar

For cookies, cream butter and brown sugar in a large bowl until fluffy. Add pumpkin, egg, and orange zest; beat until smooth. In a medium bowl, combine flours, pumpkin pie spice, baking soda, and salt. Add dry ingredients to creamed mixture; stir until a soft dough forms. Stir in walnuts. Wrap in plastic wrap and chill 4 hours.

Preheat oven to 375 degrees. Drop tablespoonfuls of dough 2 inches apart onto a greased baking sheet. Bake 10 to 12 minutes or until bottoms are lightly browned. Transfer cookies to a wire rack to cool.

For icing, melt butter in a heavy medium saucepan over medium heat. Stirring constantly, add brown sugar, whipping cream, and corn syrup; cook until mixture comes to a boil. Boil 1 minute. Remove from heat; pour into a heat-resistant medium bowl. Add confectioners sugar and beat until smooth. Ice cookies. Allow icing to harden. Store in an airtight container.

Yield: about 5 dozen cookies

HAIRY MONSTERS

- ½ cup butter or margarine
- ¾ cup sugar
- 1 egg
- 1 cup chopped dates
- 2 cups fruit-flavored crispy rice cereal
- 1 cup salted peanuts, coarsely chopped
- 1 teaspoon vanilla extract
- 1⅓ cups finely shredded sweetened coconut

Whisking constantly, combine butter, sugar, and egg in a heavy medium skillet over medium heat. Add dates to butter mixture. Continue to cook and whisk mixture about 10 minutes, mashing as dates soften. Remove from heat; stir in cereal, peanuts, and vanilla. When mixture is cool enough to handle, use greased hands to shape into 1-inch balls; roll in coconut. Cool. Store in an airtight container.

Yield: about 4 dozen cookies

ORANGE SLICE COOKIES

- 3/4 cup butter or margarine, softened
- 1 cup granulated sugar
- 1/2 cup firmly packed brown sugar
- 1 egg
- 1 teaspoon vanilla extract
- 1 3/4 cups all-purpose flour
- 1/2 teaspoon baking powder
- 1/2 teaspoon salt
- 2 cups (about 1 pound) orange slice gumdrop candies, quartered

In a large bowl, cream butter and sugars until fluffy. Add egg and vanilla; beat until smooth. In a small bowl, combine flour, baking powder, and salt. Add dry ingredients to creamed mixture; stir until a soft dough forms. Stir in candy pieces. Shape dough into three 9-inch-long rolls. Wrap in plastic wrap and chill 3 hours or until firm enough to handle.

Preheat oven to 375 degrees. Cut dough into 1/4-inch slices. Place 1 inch apart on a lightly greased baking sheet. Bake 6 to 8 minutes or until edges are lightly browned. Transfer cookies to a wire rack to cool. Store in an airtight container.

Yield: about 6 dozen cookies

Brew up some Halloween treats for your guests with a batch of Orange Slice Cookies. They're made with sliced gumdrop candies for a delicious surprise!

BANANA-NUT COOKIES

- 1/2 cup butter or margarine, softened
- 1 cup granulated sugar
- 1/2 cup firmly packed brown sugar
- 1 1/2 cups mashed bananas (about 3 large bananas)
- 2 eggs
- 1 teaspoon vanilla extract
- 2 1/2 cups all-purpose flour
- 2 teaspoons baking powder
- 1 teaspoon ground cinnamon
- 1/2 teaspoon baking soda
- 1/2 teaspoon salt
- 2 cups coarsely chopped walnuts

Preheat oven to 375 degrees. In a large bowl, cream butter and sugars until fluffy. Add bananas, eggs, and vanilla; beat until smooth. In a medium bowl, combine flour, baking powder, cinnamon, baking soda, and salt. Add dry ingredients to creamed mixture; stir until a soft dough forms. Stir in walnuts. Drop teaspoonfuls of dough 3 inches apart onto a greased baking sheet. Bake 8 to 10 minutes or until edges are lightly browned. Transfer cookies to a wire rack to cool. Store in an airtight container.

Yield: about 7 dozen cookies

WALNUT SPICE BARS

CRUST

- 1 package (18.25 ounces) spice cake mix
- 1/3 cup vegetable oil
- 1/3 cup applesauce
- 1 egg
- 1 teaspoon vanilla extract

TOPPING

- 1 cup sugar
- 1/3 cup butter or margarine
- 1/3 cup milk
- 1 cup butterscotch chips
- 1 cup chopped walnuts

Preheat oven to 350 degrees. For crust, combine cake mix, oil, applesauce, egg, and vanilla in a medium bowl. Spread mixture into bottom of a 9 x 13-inch baking pan lined with lightly greased waxed paper. Bake 20 to 25 minutes or until edges are lightly browned. While crust is baking, prepare topping.

For topping, combine sugar, butter, and milk in a heavy medium saucepan over medium-high heat. Stirring constantly, bring mixture to a boil and boil 1 minute. Remove from heat and add butterscotch chips; stir until smooth. Stir in walnuts. Spread hot topping over warm crust. Cool in pan. Cut into 1 x 2-inch bars. Store in an airtight container.

Yield: about 4 dozen bars

NUTTY COCONUT BARS

CRUST
- 1 cup all-purpose flour
- 1/2 cup butter or margarine, softened

FILLING
- 1 3/4 cups firmly packed brown sugar
- 1 1/2 cups chopped pecans
- 1/2 cup sweetened shredded coconut
- 2 eggs
- 1 tablespoon butter or margarine, melted
- 1/4 teaspoon baking powder

ICING
- 1/2 cup sifted confectioners sugar
- 2 teaspoons milk
- 1/2 teaspoon vanilla extract

Preheat oven to 350 degrees. For crust, combine flour and butter in a small bowl until well blended. Line a 9 x 13-inch baking pan with a double layer of aluminum foil, extending foil over ends of pan; grease foil. Press dough into bottom of prepared pan. Bake 15 minutes.

For filling, combine brown sugar, pecans, and coconut in a medium bowl. In a small bowl, whisk eggs, butter, and baking powder until well blended. Add to brown sugar mixture; stir until well blended. Spread over hot crust. Bake 18 to 20 minutes or until center is set. Place pan on a wire rack to cool.

For icing, combine all ingredients in a small bowl; stir until smooth. Drizzle icing over top. Allow icing to harden. Lift from pan using ends of foil. Cut into 1 x 2-inch bars. Store in an airtight container.

Yield: about 4 dozen bars

CHOCOLATE CHIP BARS

- 1 package (7 ounces) bran muffin mix
- 1/2 cup butter or margarine, melted
- 1/4 cup firmly packed brown sugar
- 2 eggs
- 1 cup semisweet chocolate mini chips
- 1 cup chopped pecans

Preheat oven to 325 degrees. Combine muffin mix, melted butter, brown sugar, and eggs in a medium bowl; stir until well blended. Stir in chocolate chips and pecans. Spread mixture into a greased 7 x 11-inch baking pan. Bake 25 to 30 minutes or until lightly browned. Cool in pan on a wire rack. Cut into 1 x 2-inch bars.

Yield: about 2 1/2 dozen bars

GERMAN CHOCOLATE COOKIES

- 1 package (18.25 ounces) German chocolate cake mix with pudding mix
- 1 container (8 ounces) vanilla-flavored yogurt
- 1 egg
- 1 can (about 15 ounces) coconut-pecan ready-to-spread frosting

Preheat oven to 350 degrees. In a large bowl, combine cake mix, yogurt, and egg; beat until smooth. Drop teaspoonfuls of dough 2 inches apart onto a greased baking sheet. Bake 10 to 12 minutes or until bottoms are lightly browned. Transfer cookies to a wire rack; ice warm cookies. Store in a single layer in an airtight container.

Yield: about 6 dozen cookies

HONEY-NUT DROPS

1/2 cup butter or margarine, softened
3/4 cup firmly packed brown sugar
1/2 cup honey
1 egg
1/2 teaspoon vanilla extract
2 cups all-purpose flour
1 teaspoon baking powder
1/4 teaspoon salt
1 cup coarsely chopped toasted
   pecans
Granulated sugar

Preheat oven to 350 degrees. In a large bowl, cream butter and brown sugar until fluffy. Add honey, egg, and vanilla; beat until smooth. In a small bowl, combine flour, baking powder, and salt. Add dry ingredients to creamed mixture; stir until a soft dough forms. Stir in pecans. Drop teaspoonfuls of dough 2 inches apart onto a lightly greased baking sheet; flatten with bottom of a glass dipped in granulated sugar. Bake 6 to 9 minutes or until bottoms are lightly browned. Transfer cookies to a wire rack to cool. Store in a cookie tin.

Yield: about 6 1/2 dozen cookies

CHERRY-OAT-NUT SQUARES

3/4 cup butter or margarine, softened
1 cup firmly packed brown sugar
1 1/2 cups quick-cooking oats
1 1/4 cups all-purpose flour
1/2 teaspoon baking soda
1/4 teaspoon salt
1 can (21 ounces) cherry pie
   filling
1 package (3 ounces) cream
   cheese, softened
1 egg
1 1/2 cups sifted confectioners sugar
1 teaspoon vanilla extract
1/2 teaspoon ground cinnamon
1/8 teaspoon ground nutmeg
1 cup finely chopped toasted
   pecans

Preheat oven to 350 degrees. In a medium bowl, cream butter and brown sugar until fluffy. In a small bowl, combine oats, flour, baking soda, and salt. Add dry ingredients to creamed mixture; stir until well blended. Reserving 1/2 cup oat mixture, firmly press remainder of mixture into bottom of a lightly greased 9 x 13-inch baking pan. Spread cherry pie filling over crust. In a medium bowl, beat cream cheese and egg. Add confectioners sugar, vanilla, cinnamon, and nutmeg; beat until smooth. Stir in pecans. Spread cream cheese mixture over cherries. Crumble reserved oat mixture over cream cheese mixture. Bake 40 to 45 minutes or until center is set and top is lightly browned. Cool in pan. Cut into 1 1/2-inch squares. Store in an airtight container in refrigerator.

Yield: about 4 dozen squares

Honey-Nut Drops (in basket) are bursting with nutty goodness. Cherry-Oat-Nut Squares are moist sweets that are created with cherry pie filling, cream cheese, and nuts.

FORGOTTEN COOKIES

- 1 cup chopped pecans
- 4 egg whites
- 1/2 teaspoon cream of tartar
- 1 cup sifted confectioners sugar
- 2 teaspoons vanilla extract

Preheat oven to 350 degrees. Spread pecans evenly on an ungreased baking sheet. Stirring occasionally, bake 10 to 15 minutes. Remove from oven; cool to room temperature.

Reduce oven temperature to 200 degrees. In a large bowl, beat egg whites until foamy. Add cream of tartar; beat until soft peaks form. Gradually add sugar, beating until stiff peaks form. Stir in vanilla. Fold in pecans. Drop by tablespoonfuls onto a waxed paper-lined baking sheet.

Bake 2 hours 30 minutes to 2 hours 40 minutes or until golden yellow. Cool completely on baking sheet. Carefully peel away waxed paper. Store in an airtight container.

Yield: about 3 1/2 dozen cookies

COCOA PECAN MERINGUES

- 4 egg whites
- 1 1/2 teaspoons vanilla extract
- 1/4 teaspoon cream of tartar
- 1/8 teaspoon salt
- 1 cup granulated sugar
- 1/2 cup cocoa
- 1 cup finely ground pecans
  Pecan halves

Preheat oven to 200 degrees. Beat egg whites, vanilla, cream of tartar, and salt at high speed until soft peaks form. Beat in sugar, a few tablespoons at a time, until meringue is stiff and shiny. Sift cocoa on top of meringue and carefully fold into mixture. Fold in ground pecans. Drop by heaping teaspoonfuls onto ungreased baking sheets. Place a pecan half on top of each meringue. Bake 1 1/2 hours or until firm and dry. Remove from sheets and cool on wire racks.

Yield: about 3 dozen cookies

MERINGUE DELIGHTS

- 1 egg white
- 3/4 cup firmly packed dark brown sugar
- 1 tablespoon all-purpose flour
  Pinch of salt
- 1 cup pecans, chopped

Beat egg white until stiff. Add brown sugar and beat until blended. Stir in flour, salt, and pecans. Drop teaspoonfuls of mixture 2 inches apart onto greased baking sheets. Bake in a preheated 325-degree oven 10 minutes. Cool slightly before removing from baking sheets.

Yield: about 3 dozen cookies

MARGUERITES

1 cup sugar
1/3 cup water
1/8 teaspoon salt
1 egg white
1/2 cup finely chopped pecans
35 to 40 saltine crackers

In a heavy medium saucepan, combine sugar, water, and salt. Stirring constantly, cook over medium-low heat until sugar dissolves. Using a pastry brush dipped in hot water, wash down any sugar crystals on sides of pan. Attach a candy thermometer to pan, making sure thermometer does not touch bottom of pan. Increase heat to medium and bring to a boil. Cook, without stirring, until syrup reaches soft-ball stage (approximately 234 to 240 degrees). Test about 1/2 teaspoon syrup in ice water. Syrup will easily form a ball in ice water but will flatten when held in your hand. Remove from heat. In a medium bowl, beat egg white until stiff. Beating constantly, slowly pour syrup over beaten egg white. Continue beating 1 to 2 minutes (mixture will be thick and glossy). Stir in pecans.

Preheat oven to 325 degrees. Place crackers on an ungreased baking sheet. Spread a heaping tablespoonful of mixture on top of each cracker. Bake 8 to 10 minutes or until tops are set. Transfer cookies to a wire rack to cool. Store in an airtight container.

Yield: 35 to 40 cookies

MAPLE-NUT WREATHS

1 cup butter or margarine, softened
1/2 cup sugar
1 egg
1 teaspoon vanilla extract
2 1/2 cups all-purpose flour
2 cups chopped pecans, toasted and finely ground
1/2 cup maple syrup

Preheat oven to 350 degrees. In a large bowl, cream butter and sugar until fluffy. Add egg and vanilla; beat until smooth. Add flour; stir until a soft dough forms. Place 1/2 cup dough in a small bowl; set aside. Place remaining dough in a cookie press fitted with a star plate. Press dough into 4-inch lengths onto a baking sheet lined with parchment paper. Join ends of each dough length to form a wreath. Add pecans and maple syrup to reserved dough; stir until well blended. Place 1 teaspoon pecan mixture in center of each wreath. Bake 10 to 15 minutes or until bottoms are lightly browned. Transfer cookies to a wire rack to cool. Store in an airtight container.

Yield: about 5 dozen cookies

S'MORE CHOCOLATE BARS

- 1 package (21.1 ounces) brownie mix
- $\frac{1}{2}$ cup vegetable oil
- $\frac{1}{2}$ cup water
- 1 egg
- 7 graham crackers (2½ x 5-inch rectangles), coarsely crumbled
- $1\frac{1}{2}$ cups semisweet chocolate chips
- 3 cups miniature marshmallows

Preheat oven to 350 degrees. In a large bowl, combine brownie mix, oil, water, and egg; stir until well blended. Pour into a greased 9 x 13-inch baking pan. Sprinkle cracker crumbs over batter. Bake 20 minutes. Sprinkle chocolate chips over brownies; top with marshmallows. Bake 8 to 10 minutes longer or until marshmallows begin to brown. Cool in pan on a wire rack. Use an oiled knife to cut into 1 x 2-inch bars. Store in an airtight container.

Yield: about 4 dozen bars

PEANUTTY S'MORE BARS

- 6 graham crackers (2½ x 5-inch rectangles)
- 2 jars (7 ounces each) marshmallow creme
- $\frac{2}{3}$ cup plus 1 tablespoon crunchy peanut butter, divided
- 1 package (6 ounces) semisweet chocolate chips

Coarsely crumble crackers into a lightly greased 9 x 13-inch baking pan. Stirring frequently, melt marshmallow creme and $\frac{2}{3}$ cup peanut butter in a medium saucepan over medium-low heat. Immediately pour marshmallow mixture over cracker pieces, spreading with a spatula if necessary. Stirring frequently, melt chocolate chips and remaining 1 tablespoon peanut butter in a small saucepan over low heat. Drizzle over marshmallow mixture. Chill 2 hours or until firm. Cut into 1 x 2-inch bars. Store in an airtight container in a single layer in refrigerator.

Yield: about 4 dozen bars

NO-BAKE BROWNIES

- 1 can (14 ounces) sweetened condensed milk
- 1 box (12 ounces) vanilla wafer cookies, finely crushed
- $\frac{1}{2}$ cup chopped walnuts
- 1 ounce unsweetened chocolate, melted
- $\frac{1}{2}$ cup semisweet chocolate chips, melted

In a large bowl, mix first 4 ingredients together until well blended using lowest speed of an electric mixer. Spread mixture evenly into a greased 9-inch diameter cake pan. Spread melted chocolate chips over top. Cover and refrigerate 1 hour or until firm. Cut into wedges to serve. Store in an airtight container in refrigerator.

Yield: about 10 to 12 brownies

MOCHA CRUNCH COOKIES

- ¹/₂ cup butter or margarine, softened
- ¹/₄ cup vegetable shortening
- ¹/₂ cup plus 2 tablespoons granulated sugar, divided
- ¹/₂ cup firmly packed brown sugar
- 1 egg yolk
- 1¹/₂ teaspoons vanilla extract
- 1³/₄ cups all-purpose flour
- 1 tablespoon instant coffee granules
- ¹/₄ teaspoon baking powder
- ¹/₄ teaspoon baking soda
- ¹/₄ teaspoon salt
- ¹/₂ cup semisweet chocolate mini chips

Preheat oven to 375 degrees. In a large bowl, cream butter, shortening, ¹/₂ cup granulated sugar, and brown sugar until fluffy. Add egg yolk and vanilla; beat until smooth. In a small bowl, combine flour, instant coffee, baking powder, baking soda, and salt. Add dry ingredients to creamed mixture; stir until a soft dough forms. Stir in chocolate chips. Shape dough into 1-inch balls; place 2 inches apart on an ungreased baking sheet. Flatten cookies with bottom of a glass dipped in remaining 2 tablespoons granulated sugar. Bake 10 to 12 minutes or until edges are lightly browned. Allow cookies to cool on pan 2 minutes; transfer cookies to a wire rack to cool completely. Store in an airtight container.

Yield: about 4 dozen cookies

CHOCOLATE-KISSED COOKIES

- 1 package (20 ounces) refrigerated sugar cookie dough
- 1 package (14 ounces) milk chocolate candies with almonds

Preheat oven to 350 degrees. Drop 1 teaspoon cookie dough into each cup of an ungreased miniature muffin pan. Press chocolate candies into dough. Bake 8 minutes or until edges are lightly browned. Cool cookies in pan 5 minutes; transfer to a wire rack to cool completely. Store in an airtight container.

Yield: about 5 dozen cookies

EASY PUDDING COOKIES

- 1 cup buttermilk baking mix
- 1 package (3.4 ounces) instant chocolate pudding and pie filling mix
- ¹/₃ cup vegetable oil
- 1 egg, beaten
- ¹/₄ cup English toffee bits
- 2 tablespoons sugar

Preheat oven to 350 degrees. In a large bowl, combine baking mix, pudding mix, oil, and egg; stir until a soft dough forms. Stir in toffee bits. Drop teaspoonfuls of dough 2 inches apart onto a greased baking sheet. Flatten with the bottom of a glass dipped in sugar. Bake 5 to 7 minutes or until edges are lightly browned. Transfer cookies to a wire rack to cool. Store in an airtight container.

Yield: about 3¹/₂ dozen cookies

CHEWY SPICE COOKIES

COOKIES

1 cup sugar
1 cup molasses
$1/4$ cup applesauce
$1/4$ cup skim milk
2 tablespoons vegetable oil
1 teaspoon rum flavoring
$3^1/2$ cups all-purpose flour
$1^1/2$ teaspoons ground ginger
1 teaspoon baking soda
$1/2$ teaspoon ground cloves
$1/2$ teaspoon ground nutmeg
$1/4$ teaspoon ground allspice
$1/8$ teaspoon salt
Vegetable cooking spray

ICING

4 cups sifted confectioners sugar
4 tablespoons plus 1 teaspoon skim milk
2 tablespoons lemon juice
2 tablespoons grated lemon zest

Preheat oven to 375 degrees. For cookies, beat sugar, molasses, applesauce, milk, oil, and rum flavoring in a large bowl until well blended. In a medium bowl, combine flour, ginger, baking soda, cloves, nutmeg, allspice, and salt. Add dry ingredients, one third at a time, to sugar mixture; stir until a soft dough forms. Spray hands with cooking spray. Shape teaspoonfuls of dough into balls and flatten slightly with fingers. Place 2 inches apart on a baking sheet lightly sprayed with cooking spray. Bake 6 to 8 minutes or until bottoms are lightly browned. Transfer cookies to a wire rack with waxed paper underneath to cool.

For icing, combine all ingredients in a medium bowl; stir until smooth. Ice cookies. Allow icing to harden. Store in an airtight container.

Yield: about 6 dozen cookies

CHOCOLATE-OAT BARS

$1/4$ cup vegetable oil
$3/4$ cup firmly packed brown sugar
$1/3$ cup granulated sugar
2 egg whites
2 teaspoons vanilla extract
$1^1/2$ cups all-purpose flour
1 cup quick-cooking oats
$1/2$ teaspoon baking soda
$1/8$ teaspoon salt
Vegetable cooking spray
$1/2$ cup semisweet chocolate mini chips

Preheat oven to 375 degrees. In a large bowl, beat oil and sugars until well blended. Add egg whites and vanilla; beat until smooth. In a small bowl, combine flour, oats, baking soda, and salt. Add dry ingredients to sugar mixture; stir until well blended. Press dough into a 9 x 13-inch baking pan lightly sprayed with cooking spray. Sprinkle chocolate chips over top; press into dough. Bake 10 to 12 minutes or until lightly browned. Cool in pan. Cut into 1 x 2-inch bars. Store in an airtight container.

Yield: about 4 dozen bars

For the old-fashioned taste of gingerbread without all the calories, try Chewy Spice Cookies (bottom) topped with a zesty lemon icing. Wonderfully delicious Chocolate-Oat Bars (top) are made with only a drizzling of oil.

99

HAWAIIAN LUAU COOKIES

1/2 cup butter or margarine, softened
1/2 cup granulated sugar
1/2 cup firmly packed brown sugar
1 egg
1/2 teaspoon vanilla extract
1 can (8 ounces) crushed pineapple, drained
2 cups all-purpose flour
1 teaspoon baking powder
1/2 teaspoon baking soda
1/4 teaspoon salt
1 cup macadamia nuts, toasted and coarsely chopped
1 cup sweetened shredded coconut

Preheat oven to 375 degrees. In a large bowl, cream butter and sugars until fluffy. Add egg and vanilla; beat until smooth. Stir in pineapple. In a small bowl, combine flour, baking powder, baking soda, and salt. Add dry ingredients to creamed mixture; stir until a soft dough forms. Stir in macadamia nuts and coconut. Drop tablespoonfuls of dough 2 inches apart onto a lightly greased baking sheet. Bake 8 to 10 minutes or until edges are lightly browned. Transfer cookies to a wire rack to cool. Store in an airtight container.

Yield: about 4 dozen cookies

TROPICAL KEY LIME BARS

CRUST
3/4 cup slivered almonds, toasted
1 1/4 cups all-purpose flour
3/4 cup sweetened finely shredded coconut
1/2 cup sifted confectioners sugar
1 cup butter or margarine, softened

FILLING
1 3/4 cups sugar
4 eggs, beaten
1/3 cup key lime juice
1 drop liquid green food coloring
1/4 cup all-purpose flour
1/4 teaspoon baking powder

Preheat oven to 350 degrees. For crust, place almonds in a food processor; process until almost finely ground. Add flour, coconut, and confectioners sugar; pulse process until well blended. Add butter; continue to process until a soft dough forms. Spread into bottom and 1/4 inch up sides of a greased 9 x 13-inch baking pan. Bake 20 minutes.

For filling, combine first 4 ingredients in a medium bowl; whisk until well blended. In a small bowl, combine flour and baking powder. Add dry ingredients to sugar mixture; whisk until well blended. Pour mixture over crust. Return to oven and bake 25 to 30 minutes or until filling is set. Cool in pan. Cut into 1 x 2-inch bars. Store in a single layer in an airtight container.

Yield: about 4 dozen bars

COOKIE TIPS

BAKING TIPS

Chilling dough: To speed up chilling of dough, place in freezer about 20 minutes for each hour of chilling time indicated in recipe. If dough is to be rolled out into a rectangle or circle, shaping it into that form before chilling will make rolling out the dough much easier.

Eggs: Recipes were tested using large eggs.

Butter: Recipes were tested using salted butter, unless otherwise specified in recipe. When softening butter in the microwave, be careful not to let it melt, as melted butter results in a flatter cookie. If margarine is used, use one labeled "margarine" instead of "spread." Corn oil margarines will make a softer dough, which will increase chilling time.

Dutch Process Cocoa: A richer, darker cocoa, Dutch process cocoa is available in the baking section of most supermarkets and is a refined cocoa that has a more mellow flavor. Regular cocoa can be substituted, but the flavor will be slightly different.

Greasing baking sheets and pans: Use a thin coating of vegetable shortening to grease baking sheets.

Cooling baking sheets: Cool baking sheets between batches so cookies will keep their shape.

Baking batches of cookies: Bake one batch of cookies at a time on the center rack of a preheated oven. If baking two batches at a time, space racks evenly in oven. Allow 1 to 2 inches of space around baking sheet for good air circulation.

Testing for doneness: Use recipe instructions to test for doneness. Since oven temperatures may vary, always check cookies 1 minute before the earliest time stated in recipe to prevent overbaking.

Cooling cookies: Immediately remove cookies from pan unless otherwise stated in recipe. Use a spatula to transfer cookies to a wire rack. If cookies cool and stick to pan, return pan to a warm oven for a few minutes to allow cookies to soften.

Lining pans: When recipe says to line a pan with foil or waxed paper, grease pan first to help keep foil or waxed paper in place. Then grease foil or waxed paper if stated in recipe.

Using a plastic bag to decorate: When you need to drizzle a small amount of icing or melted chocolate and you do not have a pastry bag, use a resealable plastic bag. After filling bag half full of icing or chocolate, seal the bag and cut off a small tip of one corner. Make your first snip small, as you can always cut off more if needed.

Spacing cookies on baking sheet: Leave enough space between cookies to allow them to spread. Most recipes will give you the number of inches.

STORAGE TIPS

• Cookies should be completely cooled before storing.

• Store each kind of cookie separately to prevent flavors from blending. Soft cookies will cause crisp cookies to become soft.

• Store soft cookies in an airtight container. Use waxed paper between layers to prevent cookies from sticking together.

• Store crisp cookies in a tin or container with a loose-fitting lid. In humid areas, the lid will need to be tighter so cookies will stay crisp.

• Store bar cookies in the pan covered with foil or remove from pan and store in an airtight container.

• If soft cookies have dried out, place a slice of apple or bread with cookies for a few days in an airtight container.

• Most cookies (except meringues) can be frozen up to six months. Freeze in plastic freezer bags or plastic containers with tight-fitting lids. Freeze iced cookies between layers of waxed paper after icing has hardened, or wait and ice cookies when thawed and ready to eat. To serve, unwrap and allow cookies to thaw 15 minutes.

MAILING TIPS

Soft, moist cookies and bar cookies are suitable for mailing. Line a sturdy box with waxed paper, aluminum foil, or plastic wrap. Place a layer of crumpled waxed paper or paper towels in bottom of box. Depending on type of cookie, wrap back-to-back if they are flat, in small groups in plastic bags, or individually.

Pack crumpled waxed paper or paper towels snugly between cookies to prevent them from shifting. Tape box securely closed.

HELPFUL FOOD EQUIVALENTS OR SUBSTITUTIONS

$1/2$ cup butter	=	1 stick butter
1 square baking chocolate	=	1 ounce chocolate
1 cup chocolate chips	=	6 ounces chocolate chips
$2^1/4$ cups packed brown sugar	=	1 pound brown sugar
$3^1/2$ cups unsifted confectioners sugar	=	1 pound confectioners sugar
2 cups granulated sugar	=	1 pound granulated sugar
4 cups all-purpose flour	=	1 pound all-purpose flour

Our Favorite GIFT MIXES

Forget the ties and bath products! This year wrap up a gift that your friends, family, and co-workers will really enjoy—a scrumptious, ready-to-fix mix. Our recipes offer a wide selection of goodies like zesty seasonings, savory soups, flavorful beverages, yummy cookies, and more, so you're sure to find something for everyone on your list.

Seasoned Bean Soup Mix, p. 143

The popular county-fair favorite is a breeze to prepare with this mix. A funnel "hat" on the gift bag will come in handy for the cook!

FUNNEL CAKE MIX

- 1¼ cups all-purpose flour
- 2 tablespoons nonfat dry milk powder
- 1 tablespoon sugar
- 1 teaspoon baking powder
- ⅛ teaspoon salt

In a medium bowl, combine flour, dry milk, sugar, baking powder, and salt. Store in an airtight container in a cool place. Give with serving instructions.

Yield: about 1½ cups mix

To serve: Heat about ½ inch vegetable oil in a large skillet over medium heat. In a medium bowl, combine mix, 1 cup lemon-lime soft drink, and 1 egg; beat until well blended. Cover end of funnel with finger. Hold funnel over skillet and pour about ½ cup batter into funnel. Remove finger from funnel and, beginning in center of skillet, release batter in a circular motion toward outside of skillet. Using 2 spatulas to turn, fry funnel cake about 1 minute on each side or until golden brown. Drain cake on paper towels. Sprinkle with confectioners sugar. Repeat with remaining batter. Serve warm.

Yield: about 7 funnel cakes

Layer the ingredients in a jar, top with a doily, and tuck into a coordinating bag. Don't forget to include the baking instructions!

DOUBLE CHIP COOKIE MIX

1 cup plus 2 tablespoons all-purpose flour
¼ teaspoon baking powder
⅛ teaspoon salt
½ cup chopped pecans
½ cup white baking chips
½ cup semisweet chocolate chips
6 tablespoons firmly packed brown sugar
6 tablespoons granulated sugar

In a small bowl, combine flour, baking powder, and salt; stir until well blended. Spoon flour mixture into a wide-mouth 1-quart jar with lid. Layer pecans, white baking chips, chocolate chips, brown sugar, and granulated sugar in jar. Cover with lid. Give with baking instructions.

Yield: about 3½ cups cookie mix

To bake: Preheat oven to 350 degrees. Pour cookie mix into a medium bowl and stir until ingredients are well blended. In a small bowl, combine ¼ cup vegetable oil, 1 egg, 2 tablespoons milk, and ½ teaspoon vanilla extract; beat until blended. Add oil mixture to dry ingredients; stir until a soft dough forms. Drop rounded teaspoonfuls of dough 2 inches apart onto a greased baking sheet. Bake 8 to 10 minutes or until edges are lightly browned. Transfer to a wire rack to cool. Store in an airtight container.

Yield: about 3 dozen cookies

105

SUGAR COOKIE MIX

- 1 cup butter or margarine, softened
- 1/2 cup vegetable shortening
- 6 cups all-purpose flour
- 1 tablespoon baking powder
- 1 tablespoon salt

In a small mixing bowl, combine butter and shortening. In a large mixing bowl, combine flour, baking powder, and salt. Using a pastry blender or 2 knives, cut shortening mixture into flour mixture until mixture resembles fine meal. Store in airtight container in refrigerator up to 4 weeks. Give with baking instructions.

Yield: 8 cups of mix

To make Sugar Cookies: Combine 2 cups Sugar Cookie Mix, 2/3 cup granulated sugar, 1 teaspoon vanilla extract, 2 tablespoons milk, and 1 egg. Stir until well blended. On a floured surface, use a floured rolling pin to roll out dough to 1/8-inch thickness. Cut out dough using desired cookie cutters. Sprinkle with colored sugar and place on lightly greased baking sheet. Bake in preheated 400 degree oven 5 to 8 minutes, or until very lightly browned around edges. Remove from pan and cool on wire rack.

Yield: about 3 1/2 dozen 2 1/2" long cookies

OATMEAL-RAISIN COOKIE MIX

- 1 1/4 cups all-purpose flour
- 1/2 teaspoon baking powder
- 1/4 teaspoon salt
- 1 cup quick-cooking oats
- 1 cup raisins
- 1/2 cup flaked coconut
- 1/2 cup firmly packed brown sugar
- 1/2 cup granulated sugar

In a small bowl, combine flour, baking powder, and salt; stir until well blended. Spoon flour mixture into a wide-mouth 1-quart jar with lid. Layer oats, raisins, coconut, brown sugar, and granulated sugar into jar. Cover with lid. Give with baking instructions.

Yield: about 4 cups cookie mix

To bake: Preheat oven to 350 degrees. Pour cookie mix into a large bowl and stir until ingredients are well blended. In a small bowl, combine 1/3 cup vegetable oil and 2 eggs; beat until blended. Add oil mixture to dry ingredients; stir until a soft dough forms. Drop teaspoonfuls of dough 2 inches apart onto a greased baking sheet or shape dough into 1-inch balls and roll in granulated sugar. Place balls 2 inches apart on a greased baking sheet; flatten with bottom of a glass dipped in granulated sugar. Bake 8 to 10 minutes or until bottoms are lightly browned. Transfer to a wire rack to cool. Store in an airtight container.

Yield: about 4 dozen cookies

COOKIE STARTER

4½ cups all-purpose flour
2 cups granulated sugar
2 cups firmly packed brown sugar
1½ cups nonfat dry milk
1 tablespoon plus 1 teaspoon salt
1½ cups shortening

In a very large bowl, combine first 5 ingredients. Using a pastry blender or 2 knives, cut in shortening until mixture resembles coarse meal. Store in an airtight container in refrigerator. Mix may be stored up to 6 months in the freezer. Give with recipes for Granola, Chocolate Chip, and Peanut Butter Cookies.

Yield: about 11½ cups cookie starter

GRANOLA COOKIES

1 cup Cookie Starter
1 cup granola cereal
1½ teaspoons ground cinnamon
1 egg
1 teaspoon vanilla extract
½ cup raisins

Preheat oven to 350 degrees. In a large bowl, mix together first 3 ingredients. Add egg and vanilla; stir until smooth. Fold in raisins. Drop by teaspoonfuls onto a greased baking sheet. Bake 10 to 12 minutes or until brown. Cool completely on a wire rack. Store in an airtight container.

Yield: about 2½ dozen cookies

CHOCOLATE CHIP COOKIES

½ cup butter or margarine, softened
1 egg
1 teaspoon vanilla extract
3 cups Cookie Starter
1 cup (6 ounces) semisweet chocolate chips
½ cup chopped pecans

Preheat oven to 350 degrees. In a large bowl, beat butter until fluffy. Add egg and vanilla; beat until smooth. Add Cookie Starter; stir until a soft dough forms. Fold in chocolate chips and pecans. Drop by teaspoonfuls onto a greased baking sheet. Bake 8 to 10 minutes or until brown. Cool completely on a wire rack. Store in an airtight container.

Yield: about 3 dozen cookies

PEANUT BUTTER COOKIES

1 cup crunchy peanut butter
1 egg
1 tablespoon water
1 teaspoon vanilla extract
1½ cups Cookie Starter

Preheat oven to 375 degrees. In a large bowl, combine first 4 ingredients; beat until smooth. Add Cookie Starter; stir until a soft dough forms. Drop by teaspoonfuls onto a greased baking sheet. Bake 10 to 12 minutes or until brown. Cool completely on a wire rack. Store in an airtight container.

Yield: about 3 dozen cookies

This light and creamy dessert has an irresistible topping of crunchy nuts and toasted coconut.

PISTACHIO-COCONUT MOUSSE MIX

MOUSSE MIX

  1 box (3½ ounces) instant coconut
      cream pudding mix
  1 box (3½ ounces) instant
      pistachio pudding mix
  2 envelopes (one 2.6-ounce box)
      whipped topping mix

TOPPING

  ⅔ cup flaked coconut, toasted
  ⅓ cup chopped pistachio nuts

For mousse mix, combine all ingredients in a large bowl. Place mixture in airtight container or resealable plastic bag. For topping combine coconut and nuts; place in a small jar. Give with serving instructions.

Yield: about 2 cups of mix and 1 cup of topping

To serve: Combine 1 cup mix with 1¼ cups milk in a large bowl. Beat with an electric mixer at high speed until fluffy, about 3 to 4 minutes. Serve immediately or store covered in refrigerator up to 2 hours. Sprinkle with topping before serving.

Yield: about 4 servings

Friends on your gift list will love how easy it is to prepare this yummy treat: simply add water and pop into the microwave.

MAGIC FUDGE MIX

3 1/2 cups confectioners sugar
1/2 cup cocoa
3 tablespoons non-dairy powdered creamer
1/4 teaspoon salt
1/2 cup butter or margarine, cut into pieces

In a large bowl, combine confectioners sugar, cocoa, creamer, and salt. Using a pastry blender or 2 knives, cut in butter until mixture is well blended. Store in an airtight container in refrigerator. Give with serving instructions.

Yield: about 4 1/2 cups fudge mix

To serve: (*Note:* Recipe was tested in a 750-watt microwave.) Line an 8-inch square baking pan with aluminum foil, extending foil over 2 sides; grease foil. Combine fudge mix and 1/4 cup water in a large microwave-safe bowl. Microwave on high power (100%), stirring every 30 seconds, until mixture is smooth (about 3 minutes). Pour into prepared pan. Chill 1 hour or until firm. Use ends of foil to lift fudge from pan. Cut into 1-inch pieces. Store in an airtight container.

Yield: about 4 dozen pieces fudge

EASY COBBLER MIX

4 cups all-purpose flour
4 cups sugar
3/4 cup dry buttermilk powder
3 tablespoons baking powder
2 teaspoons salt
4 cans (21 ounces each) fruit pie
    filling to give with mixes

In a large bowl, combine flour, sugar, buttermilk powder, baking powder, and salt. Place 2 cups plus 3 tablespoons cobbler mix in each of 4 resealable plastic bags. Store in refrigerator. Give each bag of cobbler mix with 1 can of pie filling and serving instructions.

Yield: about 8¾ cups mix (4 gifts)

To serve: Preheat oven to 350 degrees. Melt ½ cup butter in a 7 x 11-inch baking dish. Spoon pie filling over melted butter. In a medium bowl, combine mix and ¾ cup water. Pour over pie filling (do not stir). Bake 38 to 43 minutes or until crust is golden brown and a toothpick inserted in center of crust comes out clean. Serve warm.

Yield: 6 to 8 servings

INSTANT BROWNIE MIX

4 cups all-purpose flour
6 cups granulated sugar
3 cups cocoa
4 teaspoons baking powder
3 teaspoons salt
2 cups vegetable shortening

Combine first five ingredients and mix well. Using a pastry blender or two knives, thoroughly cut in shortening. Store in an airtight container in a cool, dry place. Give with baking instructions.

Yield: 16 cups of mix, enough for 8 batches of brownies

To bake: Combine 2 cups brownie mix, 2 eggs, 1 teaspoon vanilla extract, and ½ cup chopped nuts (if desired). Stir just until all ingredients are moistened. Spread in a lightly greased 8-inch square baking pan. Bake in a preheated 350 degree oven 20 to 25 minutes, or until set in center. Cut into 2-inch squares.

Yield: 16 brownies

This spicy cookie mix gives busy folks a shortcut for filling their homes with the aroma of holiday baking.

CHOCOLATE-ORANGE-SPICE COOKIE MIX

8 cups all-purpose flour
2¹/₂ cups granulated sugar
2¹/₂ cups firmly packed brown sugar
1 cup cocoa
1 tablespoon dried orange peel
2 teaspoons ground cinnamon
2 teaspoons ground ginger
1¹/₂ teaspoons baking soda
1 teaspoon salt
2³/₄ cups chilled butter or margarine, cut into pieces

In a very large bowl, combine flour, sugars, cocoa, orange peel, cinnamon, ginger, baking soda, and salt. Using a pastry blender or 2 knives, cut in butter until mixture resembles coarse meal. Divide mix evenly into 4 resealable plastic bags (about 4¹/₂ to 5 cups mix per bag). Store in refrigerator. Give with baking instructions.

Yield: about 18 cups cookie mix

To bake: Bring cookie mix to room temperature before mixing. Preheat oven to 375 degrees. In a medium bowl, combine cookie mix, 1 egg, 2 tablespoons milk, and 2 teaspoons vanilla extract; beat with an electric mixer until a soft dough forms. Divide dough in half. On a heavily floured surface, use a floured rolling pin to roll out half of dough to slightly less than ¹/₈-inch thickness. Use a 4-inch-wide x 3¹/₂-inch-high reindeer-shaped cookie cutter to cut out cookies. Transfer to a lightly greased baking sheet. Bake 4 to 6 minutes or until bottoms are lightly browned. Transfer cookies to a wire rack to cool. Repeat with remaining dough. Store in an airtight container.

Yield: about 5 dozen cookies

HAZELNUT MOCHA MIX

1 package (1 pound, 9.6 ounces)
   nonfat dry milk powder
1 package (16 ounces)
   confectioners sugar, sifted
1 package (15 ounces) chocolate
   mix for milk
1 jar (11 ounces) non-dairy
   powdered creamer
2 jars (8 ounces each) hazelnut-
   flavored non-dairy powdered
   creamer
$1/2$ cup cocoa
$1/4$ cup instant coffee granules

In a very large bowl, combine dry milk, confectioners sugar, chocolate mix, creamers, cocoa, and coffee granules; stir until well blended. Store in resealable plastic bags. Give with serving instructions.

Yield: about $18\frac{1}{4}$ cups mocha mix

To serve: Pour 6 ounces hot water over 3 tablespoons mix; stir until well blended.

FIERY ICED COFFEE MIX

1 cup instant coffee granules
1 cup non-dairy powdered creamer
$1/2$ cup sugar
1 teaspoon ground cinnamon
$1/2$ teaspoon ground nutmeg
$1/2$ teaspoon ground red pepper
$1/4$ teaspoon ground cardamom

Process all ingredients in a food processor until well blended. Store in an airtight container. Give with serving instructions.

Yield: about 2 cups mix

To serve: Pour 8 ounces boiling water over 2 tablespoons mix; stir until well blended. Cool and serve chilled over ice.

MOCHA-NUT COFFEE MIX

1 can (30 ounces) instant hot cocoa
   mix
$1\frac{1}{4}$ cups instant coffee granules
$2\frac{1}{2}$ teaspoons vanilla-butter-nut
   flavoring

In a medium bowl, combine all ingredients until well blended. Store in an airtight container. Give with serving instructions.

Yield: about 6 cups coffee mix

To serve: Stir 3 rounded teaspoons coffee mix into 6 ounces hot water.

NIGHTCAP COFFEE MIX

$2/3$ cup nondairy powdered coffee
   creamer
$1/3$ cup instant coffee granules
$1/3$ cup granulated sugar
1 teaspoon ground cardamom
$1/2$ teaspoon ground cinnamon

Combine all ingredients in a medium bowl; stir until well blended. Store in an airtight container.

To serve, spoon 1 heaping tablespoon coffee mix into 8 ounces of hot water. Stir until well blended.

Yield: about $1\frac{1}{3}$ cups coffee mix

SPIRITED COFFEE MIX

- 4 cups firmly packed brown sugar
- 2 cups coffee-flavored liqueur
- 1½ cups non-dairy powdered creamer
- 1½ teaspoons ground cinnamon
- 1 teaspoon ground allspice

In a large bowl, combine brown sugar, liqueur, creamer, cinnamon, and allspice using lowest speed of an electric mixer. Cover and chill overnight. Give with serving instructions.

Yield: about 4 cups of coffee mix

To serve: Spoon 1 tablespoon coffee mix into a mug. Stir in 6 ounces desired hot beverage such as coffee, cocoa, or milk. Store coffee mix in an airtight container in refrigerator.

CAPPUCCINO COFFEE MIX

- ½ cup instant coffee granules
- ½ teaspoon dried orange peel
- 1 cup non-dairy powdered creamer
- ¾ cup sugar
- ½ teaspoon ground cinnamon

Process coffee and orange peel in a food processor until finely ground. Add creamer, sugar, and cinnamon; process until well blended. Store in an airtight container. Give with serving instructions.

Yield: about 1⅔ cups coffee mix

To serve: Pour 6 ounces hot water over 2 heaping teaspoons coffee mix; stir until well blended.

CHOCOLATE-ALMOND COFFEE MIX

- 1 cup nondairy powdered coffee creamer
- 1 cup granulated sugar
- ½ cup instant coffee granules
- ½ cup cocoa
- 1 teaspoon almond extract

In a blender or food processor, finely grind all ingredients until well blended. Store in an airtight container. Give with serving instructions.

Yield: about 2 cups coffee mix

To serve: Stir about 2 heaping teaspoons coffee mix into 6 ounces hot water.

SPICED COFFEE MIX

- 1 cup instant coffee granules
- ⅔ cup firmly packed brown sugar
- 2 teaspoons ground cinnamon
  Cinnamon sticks to garnish

Combine coffee granules, brown sugar, and cinnamon in a food processor; process until well blended. Store in an airtight container. Give with serving instructions.

Yield: about 1½ cups coffee mix

To serve: Stir 1 teaspoon coffee mix into 6 ounces hot water. Garnish with a cinnamon stick.

Our instant mix, flavored with chocolate, cinnamon, and nutmeg, makes it easy to enjoy the rich flavor of this Italian beverage.

INSTANT CAPPUCCINO MIX

1 cup powdered chocolate milk mix
³/₄ cup powdered non-dairy creamer
¹/₂ cup instant coffee granules
¹/₂ teaspoon ground cinnamon
¹/₄ teaspoon ground nutmeg

In a medium bowl, combine all ingredients. Store in an airtight container. Give with serving instructions.

Yield: about 2¹/₄ cups of mix

To serve: Place 1 heaping tablespoon mix in a cup or mug. Add 1 cup boiling water and stir.

This yummy beverage starter combines powdered milk with nondairy creamer, chocolate milk mix, and cinnamon.

CINNAMON MOCHA MIX

1 jar (16 ounces) non-dairy
   powdered creamer
1 package (16 ounces) chocolate
   mix for milk
1 package (16 ounces)
   confectioners sugar
6 cups nonfat dry milk powder
½ cup cocoa
¼ cup instant coffee granules
2 teaspoons ground cinnamon

In a very large bowl, combine creamer, chocolate mix, confectioners sugar, dry milk, cocoa, coffee granules, and cinnamon. Store in an airtight container. Give with serving instructions.

Yield: about 14 cups mix

To serve: Pour 6 ounces hot water over 2½ heaping tablespoons mocha mix; stir until well blended. Serve hot.

RICH HAZELNUT COFFEE CREAMER

1 jar (8 ounces) hazelnut-flavored
   non-dairy powdered creamer
2 tablespoons cocoa
1 teaspoon vanilla-butter-nut
   flavoring

Process creamer and cocoa in a small food processor until blended. Sprinkle vanilla-butter-nut flavoring over creamer mixture; process until well blended. Store in an airtight container in a cool place. Give with serving instructions.

Yield: about 1^2/$_3$ cups creamer

To serve: Stir 1^1/$_2$ tablespoons creamer into 8 ounces hot coffee; stir until well blended.

BAVARIAN MINT COFFEE CREAMER

^{3}/$_4$ cup non-dairy coffee creamer
^{1}/$_2$ cup Dutch process cocoa (we
   used Dorste brand)
^{3}/$_4$ cup confectioners sugar
^{1}/$_2$ teaspoon peppermint extract

Combine all ingredients in a container with a tight-fitting lid. Shake well to blend. Store in airtight container. Give with serving instructions.

Yield: 15 servings

To serve: In a mug, combine 2 tablespoons of creamer with 6 ounces of coffee.

MOCHA CREAMER

1 jar (6 ounces) non-dairy
   powdered creamer
1 cup chocolate mix for milk
^{1}/$_2$ teaspoon ground cinnamon

In a medium bowl, combine creamer, chocolate mix, and cinnamon. Store in an airtight container. Give with serving instructions.

Yield: about 2^1/$_2$ cups creamer

To serve: Stir 1 tablespoon creamer into 6 ounces of hot coffee.

AMARETTO COFFEE CREAMER

^{3}/$_4$ cup non-dairy coffee creamer
1 teaspoon almond extract
1 teaspoon ground cinnamon
^{3}/$_4$ cup confectioners sugar

Combine all ingredients in a container with a tight-fitting lid. Shake well to blend. Store in airtight container. Give with serving instructions.

Yield: 12 servings

To serve: In a mug, combine 2 tablespoons of creamer with 6 ounces of coffee.

CHOCOLATE-MALT COFFEE CREAMER

2 cups instant hot cocoa mix
2/3 cup nondairy powdered coffee creamer
2/3 cup malted milk mix
1/2 teaspoon ground cinnamon

Combine all ingredients in a large bowl; stir until well blended. Store in an airtight container. Give with serving instructions.

Yield: about 3 cups creamer

To serve: Stir 2 heaping teaspoonfuls into 8 ounces hot coffee.

MOCHA SUGAR

1 1/4 cups granulated sugar
3 tablespoons coffee-flavored liqueur
1/2 teaspoon ground cinnamon

In a small bowl, stir all ingredients together until well blended. Store in an airtight container. Give with serving instructions.

Yield: about 1 cup sugar

To serve: Stir desired amount of sugar into coffee.

CHERRY-FLAVORED SUGAR

1 1/2 cups sugar
1 package (0.13 ounce) unsweetened cherry-flavored soft drink mix

In a medium bowl, combine sugar and soft drink mix. Store in an airtight container. Give with serving instructions.

Yield: about 1 1/2 cups flavored sugar

To serve: Stir 2 teaspoons flavored sugar into 6 ounces hot tea; stir until well blended.

CHOCOLATE-COVERED COFFEE SPOONS
Spoons should be given the day they are made.

WHITE CHOCOLATE SPOONS
Vegetable cooking spray
6 ounces white chocolate, chopped
1/2 teaspoon amaretto-flavored oil (used in candy making)
Red and green heavyweight plastic spoons

MILK CHOCOLATE SPOONS
Vegetable cooking spray
1 plain milk chocolate candy bar (7 ounces), chopped
1/2 teaspoon raspberry-flavored oil (used in candy making)
Red and green heavyweight plastic spoons

Line a jellyroll pan with waxed paper; spray with cooking spray. Combine white or milk chocolate and flavored oil in the top of a double boiler. Place over simmering water until chocolate melts. Dip spoons into mixture, shaking off excess chocolate. Place spoons on prepared pan with handles on rim and spoons level. Allow chocolate to harden. Cover and store in a cool place.

Yield: 15 to 20 spoons of each flavor

ALMOND COCOA MIX

1 cup butter
1 cup granulated sugar
1 cup firmly packed brown sugar
2/3 cup cocoa
2 cups softened vanilla ice cream
2 1/2 teaspoons almond extract

In a medium saucepan, combine butter, sugars, and cocoa over low heat. Stirring frequently, cook until butter melts. Transfer mixture to a medium bowl. Add ice cream and almond extract; beat until smooth. Store in an airtight container in refrigerator. Give with storage and serving instructions.

Yield: about 4 cups cocoa mix

To serve: Store cocoa mix in refrigerator until ready to serve. Pour 3/4 cup boiling water or hot coffee over 1/4 cup cocoa mix; stir until well blended.

Handy when someone needs a winter warmer, this delectable drink mix gets its creamy goodness from vanilla ice cream.

A blend of dry ingredients, this mix makes it easy to transform boiling water into hot cocoa.

INSTANT COCOA WITH MARSHMALLOWS

8½ cups (25.6-ounce package) nonfat dry milk
3 cups (16-ounce package) instant chocolate drink mix for milk
1½ cups confectioners sugar
1½ cups miniature marshmallows
1½ cups (6-ounce jar) non-dairy coffee creamer

In a large bowl, combine all ingredients. Store in airtight container. Give with serving instructions.

Yield: 16 cups of mix, enough for 32 servings

To serve: Stir ½ cup cocoa mix into 9 ounces hot water.

CHERRY COCOA MIX

6¼ cups nonfat dry milk powder
1 jar (16 ounces) non-dairy powdered creamer
1 package (16 ounces) chocolate mix for milk
1 package (16 ounces) confectioners sugar
½ cup cocoa
2 packages (0.13 ounces each) unsweetened cherry-flavored soft drink mix
  Whipped cream and maraschino cherries with stems to garnish

In a very large bowl, combine dry milk, creamer, chocolate mix, confectioners sugar, cocoa, and soft drink mix. Store in an airtight container in a cool place. Give with serving instructions.

Yield: about 15 cups cocoa mix

To serve: Pour 6 ounces hot water over about 2½ heaping tablespoons cocoa mix; stir until well blended.

VANILLA-BERRY COCOA MIX

6 cups nonfat milk powder
2 jars (8 ounces each) French vanilla-flavored non-dairy powdered creamer
1 package (16 ounces) confectioners sugar
1 package (15 ounces) chocolate mix for milk
1 package (0.15 ounce) unsweetened raspberry-flavored soft drink mix
½ teaspoon salt

In a very large bowl, combine milk powder, creamer, confectioners sugar, chocolate mix, soft drink mix, and salt. Store in an airtight container in a cool place. Give with serving instructions.

Yield: about 13 cups cocoa mix

To serve: Pour 6 ounces hot water over about 2½ heaping tablespoons cocoa mix; stir until well blended.

AMARETTO COCOA MIX

1 package (25.6 ounces) nonfat dry milk powder
4 cups sifted confectioners sugar
2 jars (8 ounces each) amaretto-flavored non-dairy powdered creamer
1 package (1 pound) chocolate mix for milk
1 jar (11 ounces) non-dairy powdered creamer
½ teaspoon salt

In a very large bowl, combine all ingredients; stir until well blended. Store in an airtight container. Give with serving instructions.

Yield: about 19 cups cocoa mix

To serve: Stir 3 heaping tablespoons cocoa mix into 6 ounces hot water.

HOT CHOCOLATE MIX

Make each cup of hot chocolate to order!

6¼ cups nonfat milk powder
1 jar (16 ounces) non-dairy
    powdered creamer
1 package (16 ounces)
    confectioners sugar
1 container (15 ounces)
    chocolate mix for milk
½ cup cocoa

In a very large bowl, combine all ingredients. Store in an airtight container. Give with serving instructions.

Yield: about 14 cups mix

To serve: Pour 6 ounces hot water or hot coffee over 2½ heaping tablespoons chocolate mix; stir until well blended. If desired, add one or more of the following variations to each cup of hot chocolate.

VARIATIONS:
Flavored syrups
Christmas-shaped marshmallows
Ground cinnamon
Flavored coffee creamers

TRIPLE CHOCOLATE-MINT COCOA MIX

Candies can be ground with a coffee mill or crushed with a hammer.

6 cups nonfat milk powder
1 package (16 ounces) confectioners
    sugar
2 jars (8 ounces each) Swiss
    chocolate-flavored non-dairy
    powdered creamer
1 package (15 ounces) chocolate
    mix for milk
1 package (7½ ounces) round
    peppermint candies, finely
    ground
¼ cup unsweetened cocoa
    powder
1 teaspoon salt

In a very large bowl, combine milk powder, confectioners sugar, creamer, chocolate mix, ground candies, cocoa, and salt. Store in an airtight container in refrigerator. Give with serving instructions.

Yield: about 13½ cups cocoa mix

To serve: Pour 6 ounces hot water over 3 tablespoons cocoa mix; stir until well blended.

CANDIED TEA STIRRERS

Make each batch with a different fruit-flavored candy.

Vegetable cooking spray
34 pieces fruit-flavored hard candy (about 1-inch diameter), crushed
2 tablespoons light corn syrup
Heavyweight plastic spoons

Line a jellyroll pan with waxed paper; spray with cooking spray. In a small heavy saucepan, combine crushed candies and corn syrup over low heat. Stirring frequently, heat until candies melt. Spoon candy into bowl of each spoon. Place spoons on prepared pan with handles on rim and spoons level. Allow candy to harden. Store in an airtight container.

Yield: about 24 spoons

CARIBBEAN TEA MIX

2 cups unsweetened powdered instant tea
2 packages (3 ounces each) orange-pineapple-flavored gelatin
1 cup sugar
3/4 teaspoon coconut extract

In a food processor, combine all ingredients. Process until well blended. Store in an airtight container. Give with serving instructions.

Yield: about 3 cups tea mix

To serve: Stir 2 level tablespoons tea mix into 6 ounces hot water.

ORANGE-NUTMEG TEA MIX

1 cup unsweetened powdered instant tea
1 cup granulated sugar
1 package (0.15 ounces) unsweetened orange-flavored soft drink mix
1 teaspoon ground nutmeg

In a small bowl, combine all ingredients; stir until well blended. Store in an airtight container. Give with serving instructions.

Yield: about 1 2/3 cups tea mix

To serve: Stir 2 tablespoons tea mix into 6 ounces hot or cold water.

Refreshing Mint Tea Mix mingles the citrusy bouquet of dried orange peel and the spicy flavor of whole cloves with mint leaves.

MINT TEA MIX

1¹/₂ cups loose tea leaves
1 jar (0.25 ounces) dried mint
    leaves
2 tablespoons dried orange peel
2 tablespoons whole cloves

Combine all ingredients in a medium bowl; stir until well blended. Store in an airtight container. Give with serving instructions.

Yield: about 1³/₄ cups tea mix

To serve: For 1 cup of tea, place 1 teaspoon tea mix in an individual tea infuser. Pour 1 cup boiling water over tea mix. Allow tea to steep 3 to 5 minutes. Remove infuser; serve hot.

For 1 quart of tea, place 2 tablespoons tea mix in a teapot. Pour 1 quart boiling water over tea mix. Allow tea to steep 3 to 5 minutes. Strain tea; serve hot.

FORGET-ME-NOT TEA

- 1 jar (15 ounces) instant orange breakfast drink mix
- 1 cup granulated sugar
- 1 cup unsweetened instant tea mix
- 1/2 cup presweetened lemonade mix
- 1 package (0.14 ounces) unsweetened cherry-flavored soft drink mix
- 2 teaspoons ground cinnamon
- 1 teaspoon ground nutmeg

In a large bowl, combine all ingredients; mix well. Store in an airtight container. Give with serving instructions.

Yield: about 4 cups tea mix

To serve: Stir 2 heaping tablespoons tea mix into 8 ounces hot or cold water.

PEACH TEA MIX

- 1 cup instant tea mix
- 1 box (3 ounces) peach-flavored gelatin
- 2 cups granulated sugar

Combine all ingredients in a large bowl; mix well. Store in an airtight container. Give with serving instructions.

Yield: about 3 1/2 cups tea mix

To serve: Stir about 2 teaspoons tea mix into 8 ounces hot water.

STRAWBERRY TEA MIX

- 3 cups unsweetened powdered instant tea
- 1 package (0.14 ounces) unsweetened strawberry-flavored soft drink mix

In a small bowl, combine tea and soft drink mix. Store in an airtight container. Give with serving instructions.

Yield: about 3 cups tea mix

To serve: Stir 1 tablespoon tea mix into 8 ounces hot or cold water. Sweeten to taste.

CHERRY-ALMOND TEA MIX

2¼ cups artificially sweetened
     instant tea mix
2 packages (0.14 ounces each)
     unsweetened cherry-flavored
     soft drink mix
2 teaspoons almond extract

Place all ingredients in a food processor; process until well blended. Store in an airtight container. Give with serving instructions.

Yield: about 1½ cups tea mix

To serve: Stir 2 teaspoons tea mix into 8 ounces hot or cold water.

CHERRY TEA MIX

1 package (0.14 ounces)
     unsweetened cherry-flavored
     soft drink mix
1¼ cups sugar-free instant tea mix
     (artificially sweetened)

Combine all ingredients in a small bowl; stir until well blended. Store in an airtight container. Give with instructions for serving.

Yield: 1¼ cups tea mix

To serve: Stir 2 teaspoons tea mix into 8 ounces hot or cold water. Stir until dissolved.

APRICOT-MINT TEA MIX

2 cups unsweetened powdered
     instant tea
2 packages (3 ounces each) apricot
     gelatin
1½ cups sugar
½ teaspoon peppermint extract

Process ingredients in a food processor until well blended. Store in an airtight container. Give with serving instructions.

Yield: about 2⅔ cups tea mix

To serve: Pour 6 ounces hot water over 1 level tablespoon tea mix; stir until well blended.

FIESTA PUNCH MIX

1 bottle (33.8 ounces) margarita
   mix
1 can (6 ounces) frozen orange
   juice concentrate, thawed
½ cup freshly squeezed lime juice
   Lime and orange slices

In a large container, combine margarita mix, orange juice, and lime juice. Cover and store in refrigerator. Add fruit slices and give with serving instructions.

Yield: about 5¾ cups punch mix

To serve: For punch, combine entire recipe of punch mix with 6 cups chilled lemon-lime soft drink. Serve chilled.

For a variation, combine entire recipe of punch mix with 8 ounces tequila and a dash of salt. Serve over ice.

HOLIDAY WINE PUNCH

1 bottle (1.5 liters) white wine
1 bottle (32 ounces) cranberry juice
   cocktail
1 can (12 ounces) frozen pineapple
   juice concentrate
1 can (12 ounces) frozen pink
   lemonade concentrate

In a large container, combine wine, cranberry juice cocktail, and concentrates; cover and chill. Give with serving instructions.

Yield: 13 cups wine mixture

To serve: For each 6½ cups of wine mixture, combine chilled wine mixture and 3 cups chilled lemon-lime soda.

Yield: about twelve 6-ounce servings

HOT SPICED APPLEJACK

6 cups apple cider
1 can (6 ounces) frozen lemonade
   concentrate, thawed
⅓ cup applejack (apple brandy)
⅓ cup dark rum
2 tablespoons firmly packed brown
   sugar
1 teaspoon ground cinnamon
½ teaspoon ground nutmeg

Place all ingredients in a 2-quart container; stir until well blended.

Yield: about nine 6-ounce servings.

To serve: Heat drink mixture and serve hot.

HOT SPICED WINE MIX

¾ cup firmly packed brown sugar
2 teaspoons ground cinnamon
1 teaspoon ground cloves
½ teaspoon grated lemon peel
½ teaspoon grated orange peel
1 teaspoon ground allspice
½ teaspoon ground nutmeg

Combine all ingredients in a small bowl. Place mix in an airtight container. Give with serving instructions.

Yield: about ¾ cup mix

To serve: Combine ¼ cup mix with 1 cup red wine and ¼ cup water. Bring to a boil over medium heat; reduce heat and simmer 5 minutes.

Yield: 1 serving

This flavorful mix is simply stirred into hot apple cider.

HOT BUTTERED DRINK MIX

2³/4 cups firmly packed brown sugar
1 cup unsalted butter, softened
3 tablespoons maple syrup
2 tablespoons ground cinnamon
2¹/2 teaspoons ground cloves
³/4 teaspoon ground nutmeg

In a medium bowl, combine all ingredients with an electric mixer until well blended.

Store in an airtight container in refrigerator. Give with serving instructions.

Yield: about 3 cups mix

To serve: Stir 1¹/2 teaspoons drink mix into 6 ounces of hot apple cider or other juices. For hot buttered rum, add 1 ounce rum to cider mixture.

BAYOU POPCORN SPICE

- 3 tablespoons paprika
- 1 tablespoon garlic powder
- 2 teaspoons onion powder
- 1½ teaspoons ground red pepper
- 1 teaspoon dried thyme leaves
- 1 teaspoon dried oregano leaves
- 1 teaspoon brown sugar
- 1 teaspoon ground black pepper
- ½ teaspoon ground nutmeg
  Microwave popcorn to give

In a small bowl, combine all ingredients until well blended. Store in an airtight container. Give with popcorn and serving instructions.

Yield: about 7 tablespoons mix

To serve: Microwave a 3½-ounce bag of microwave popcorn according to package directions. Open bag carefully to avoid steam. Sprinkle ½ to 1 teaspoon seasoning mix, or more to taste, over popcorn. Hold top of bag closed and shake until popcorn is coated.

WHOLE GRAIN BREAD MIX

- 1½ cups all-purpose flour
- ½ cup whole-wheat flour
- ¼ cup old-fashioned oats
- 2 tablespoons yellow cornmeal
- 2 tablespoons wheat germ
- 2 tablespoons unprocessed bran
- 2 tablespoons firmly packed brown sugar
- 1 teaspoon salt
- 1 package quick-rise dry yeast

Combine all ingredients in a large bowl; stir until well blended. Store in an airtight container in a cool place. Give with baking instructions.

Yield: about 2½ cups bread mix, makes 1 loaf bread

To bake bread: Place bread mix in a large bowl. In a small saucepan, heat 1 cup milk and 2 tablespoons vegetable oil until very warm (120 to 130 degrees). Add to bread mix; stir until a soft dough forms. Turn onto a lightly floured surface and knead 5 minutes or until dough becomes smooth and elastic. Cover and allow dough to rest 10 minutes. Shape dough into a loaf and place in a greased 4½ x 8½-inch loaf pan. Spray top of dough with cooking spray, cover, and let rise in a warm place (80 to 85 degrees) 50 minutes or until doubled in size.

Preheat oven to 375 degrees. Brush top of loaf with a beaten egg. Bake 25 to 30 minutes or until bread is golden brown and sounds hollow when tapped. Serve warm or transfer to a wire rack to cool completely. Store in an airtight container.

EYE-OPENER FRUITY OATMEAL

1 package (about 7 ounces) desired dried fruit, coarsely chopped
1 container (18 ounces) quick-cooking oats
1 jar (3 ounces) non-dairy powdered creamer
1/2 cup granulated sugar or firmly packed brown sugar
1/2 cup desired chopped nuts
1 teaspoon salt

Place dried fruit in a food processor; process until finely chopped. Add remaining ingredients and process until well blended. Store in an airtight container. Give with serving instructions.

Yield: about 7 1/2 cups mix, about 15 servings

To serve: Stir 2/3 cup boiling water into 1/2 cup oatmeal mix until well blended. Let stand until thickened.

VARIATIONS
Apple-Cinnamon-Walnut
Follow basic recipe using dried apples, brown sugar, and walnuts and adding 2 teaspoons ground cinnamon.

Creamy Peach
Follow basic recipe using dried peaches, amaretto-flavored powdered creamer, and granulated sugar and omitting nuts.

Date-Nut
Follow basic recipe using chopped dates, brown sugar, and pecans.

QUICK OATMEAL MUFFIN MIX

4 cups all-purpose flour
1 3/4 cups sugar
1/2 cup dried buttermilk powder
1 1/2 tablespoons baking powder
1 teaspoon salt
1 teaspoon ground cinnamon
1/2 teaspoon ground nutmeg
4 packets (about 1.2 ounces each) fruit and cream instant oatmeal (we used peaches and cream)
1 1/4 cups chilled butter or margarine, cut into pieces

In a large bowl, combine flour, sugar, buttermilk powder, baking powder, salt, cinnamon, and nutmeg. Stir in instant oatmeal mix. With a pastry blender or 2 knives, cut in butter until mixture resembles coarse meal. Divide mix into 2 resealable plastic bags (about 5 1/2 cups mix in each bag). Store in refrigerator. Give each bag of mix with baking instructions.

Yield: about 11 cups muffin mix

To bake: Store muffin mix in refrigerator until ready to bake. Preheat oven to 400 degrees. In a medium bowl, combine bag of muffin mix, 1 cup water, and 1 beaten egg; stir just until moistened. Fill greased muffin cups about three-fourths full. Bake 15 to 20 minutes or until edges are lightly browned and a toothpick inserted in center of muffin comes out clean. Serve warm.

Yield: about 1 dozen muffins

With this yummy muffin mix, just add sour cream and bake.

CHRISTMAS CRANBERRY MUFFINS

 2 cups all-purpose flour
 1 cup sugar
 1 teaspoon baking soda
 $^1/_2$ teaspoon salt
 $^1/_2$ cup chilled butter, cut into pieces
 1 cup sweetened dried cranberries, chopped
 $^1/_2$ cup chopped pecans, toasted
 $1^1/_2$ teaspoons grated orange zest

In a medium bowl, combine flour, sugar, baking soda, and salt. Using pastry blender, cut butter into dry ingredients until mixture resembles coarse meal. Stir in cranberries, pecans, and orange zest.

Divide mix into 2 resealable plastic bags. Store in refrigerator. Give with baking instructions.

Yield: 2 bags muffin mix, about $2^1/_2$ cups each

To bake: In a medium bowl, combine 1 cup sour cream and 1 bag muffin mix ($2^1/_2$ cups); stir just until moistened. Fill paper-lined muffin cups full of batter. Sprinkle with granulated sugar. Bake in a 400-degree oven 18 to 20 minutes or until a toothpick inserted in center of muffin comes out clean and tops are golden brown.

Yield: about 6 muffins

A hearty breakfast is minutes away when you start with this mix.

OATMEAL-RAISIN MUFFIN MIX

  1 cup old-fashioned oats
  ¹/₂ cup sugar
  ¹/₂ cup all-purpose flour
  ¹/₄ cup whole-wheat flour
  2 tablespoons dry buttermilk
      powder
  1 teaspoon baking powder
  1 teaspoon dried orange peel
  ¹/₂ teaspoon baking soda
  ¹/₄ teaspoon salt
  1 cup raisins

Place oats in a food processor; process until coarsely ground. Add sugar, flours, buttermilk powder, baking powder, orange peel, baking soda, and salt; pulse process just until well blended. Stir in raisins. Store in an airtight container. Give with serving instructions.

Yield: 2¹/₂ cups muffin mix

To serve: Preheat oven to 400 degrees. Combine muffin mix, ¹/₂ cup water, ¹/₃ cup vegetable oil, and 2 eggs; stir just until moistened. Fill lightly greased muffin cups about three-fourths full. Bake 15 to 18 minutes or until a toothpick inserted in center of muffin comes out clean.

Yield: about 1 dozen muffins

CAPPUCCINO WAFFLE MIX WITH COFFEE SYRUP

CAPPUCCINO WAFFLES
- ½ cup butter or margarine, softened
- 1 cup sugar
- 1 teaspoon vanilla extract
- 1⅓ cups all-purpose flour
- ⅓ cup nonfat dry milk
- ¼ cup non-dairy powdered creamer
- 2 tablespoons instant coffee granules
- 2 teaspoons baking powder
- ¼ teaspoon salt
- ¼ teaspoon ground cinnamon

COFFEE SYRUP
- 1 cup strongly brewed coffee
- 2 cups sugar

For cappuccino waffles, cream butter, sugar, and vanilla in a medium bowl until fluffy. In a small bowl, combine remaining ingredients. On low speed of an electric mixer, beat dry ingredients into creamed mixture (mixture will be crumbly). Transfer to a resealable plastic bag; store in refrigerator. Give with serving instructions.

For coffee syrup, combine coffee and sugar in a heavy medium saucepan. Stirring constantly over medium-high heat, cook mixture until sugar dissolves. Without stirring, bring mixture to a boil; boil 2 minutes. Remove from heat; cool to room temperature. Store in an airtight container in refrigerator.

Yield: about 4 cups waffle mix and 1¾ cups syrup

To serve: Preheat waffle iron. Transfer bag of waffle mix into a medium bowl. Add ¾ cup water and 2 eggs; stir just until blended. For each waffle, pour about ⅔ cup batter into waffle iron. Bake 3 to 5 minutes or according to manufacturer's instructions. Serve hot waffles with coffee syrup.

Yield: about five 8-inch waffles

CINNAMON OAT PANCAKE MIX

- 4 cups quick-cooking oats
- 4 cups whole wheat blend flour (or 2 cups all-purpose flour combined with 2 cups whole wheat flour)
- 1 cup nonfat dry milk
- 2 tablespoons ground cinnamon
- 5 teaspoons salt
- 3 tablespoons baking powder
- ½ teaspoon cream of tartar

Combine all ingredients in a large bowl; stir well. Store in airtight container in refrigerator. Give with serving instructions.

Yield: about 8 cups of mix, enough for 4 batches of pancakes

To serve: In a mixing bowl, beat 2 eggs. Gradually beat in ⅓ cup vegetable oil. Alternately beat in 2 cups of pancake mix and 1 cup of water. Heat a lightly greased skillet over medium-high heat. Pour a heaping spoonful of batter onto hot skillet. Cook pancakes until bubbles appear on surface and begin to break (about 2 to 3 minutes). Turn and cook 2 to 3 minutes more or until golden brown.

Yield: about twelve 5-inch pancakes

LEMON-OATMEAL PANCAKE MIX

Make several batches of mix to give with Blueberry Syrup.

PANCAKE MIX

- 2 cups all-purpose baking mix
- 1/2 cup nonfat milk powder
- 1/2 cup quick-cooking oats
- 2 tablespoons sugar
- 2 teaspoons grated lemon zest

In a large bowl, combine baking mix, milk powder, oats, sugar, and lemon zest. Store in an airtight container in refrigerator. Give with serving instructions.

Yield: about 3 cups mix

To serve: In a medium bowl, combine 3 cups pancake mix, 1 3/4 cups water, and 2 slightly beaten eggs. Stir just until moistened. Heat a greased griddle over medium heat. For each pancake, pour about 1/4 cup batter onto griddle and cook until top of pancake is full of bubbles and underside is golden brown. Turn with a spatula and cook until remaining side is golden brown. Grease griddle as necessary. Serve warm with Blueberry Syrup.

Yield: about 14 pancakes

BLUEBERRY SYRUP

- 1 package (12 ounces) frozen blueberries
- 2 cups water
- 1 cup light corn syrup
- 1 package (1 3/4 ounces) powdered fruit pectin
- 4 cups sugar

In a Dutch oven, combine blueberries, water, corn syrup, and pectin over medium-high heat. Stirring constantly, bring to a rolling boil. Add sugar. Stirring constantly, bring to a rolling boil again and boil 1 minute. Remove from heat. Pour into heat-resistant jars; cover and cool to room temperature. Store in refrigerator.

Yield: about 5 1/2 cups syrup

APPLE-NUT PANCAKE MIX

- 3 cups nonfat dry milk
- 2 1/2 cups all-purpose flour
- 1 cup whole-wheat flour
- 1 cup coarsely ground pecans
- 1/3 cup sugar
- 1/4 cup baking powder
- 1 1/2 teaspoons salt
- 1/2 teaspoon ground cinnamon
- 1 package (6 ounces) dried apples, cut into small pieces

Combine dry milk, flours, pecans, sugar, baking powder, salt, and cinnamon in a large bowl. Stir in dried apples. Store in an airtight container in a cool place. Give with serving instructions.

Yield: about 8 1/2 cups pancake mix

To serve: Combine 2 3/4 cups pancake mix, 1 1/4 cups water, 1 egg, and 2 tablespoons vegetable oil in a medium bowl. Stir just until moistened. Grease and preheat griddle. For each pancake, pour about 1/4 cup batter onto griddle. Cook until top of pancake is full of bubbles and underside is golden brown. Turn with a spatula and cook until remaining side is golden brown. Serve warm.

Yield: about 14 pancakes

These lightly sweet biscuits feature chocolate chips and pecans.

CHOCOLATE BISCUIT MIX

1³/₄ cups all-purpose flour
¹/₄ cup cocoa
¹/₄ cup sugar
1 tablespoon baking powder
¹/₂ teaspoon salt
¹/₄ teaspoon ground cinnamon
¹/₂ cup butter or margarine
²/₃ cup finely chopped pecans
¹/₂ cup semisweet chocolate mini
      chips

In a large bowl, combine flour, cocoa, sugar, baking powder, salt, and cinnamon. Using a pastry blender or 2 knives, cut in butter until mixture resembles coarse meal. Stir in pecans and chocolate chips. Place about 2 cups mix in each of 2 resealable plastic bags. Store in refrigerator. Give with serving instructions.

Yield: about 4 cups mix

To serve: Store mix in refrigerator until ready to serve. Preheat oven to 425 degrees. Place 2 cups mix in a medium bowl. Add ¹/₃ cup milk; stir just until a soft dough forms. On a lightly floured surface, use a floured rolling pin to roll out dough to ¹/₂-inch thickness. Use a 2-inch-diameter biscuit cutter to cut out biscuits. Transfer to a greased baking sheet. Bake 10 to 15 minutes or until bottoms are lightly browned. Serve warm.

Yield: about 1 dozen biscuits

Need a last-minute gift in a hurry? This mix whips up fast.

CHEDDAR-GARLIC BISCUIT MIX

- 4 cups all-purpose baking mix
- 2 cups (8 ounces) shredded sharp Cheddar cheese
- 2 teaspoons garlic powder
- 2 teaspoons dried Italian herb seasoning

In a large bowl, combine baking mix, cheese, garlic powder, and Italian seasoning. Divide mix in half. Place each half in a resealable plastic bag. Store in refrigerator. Give with serving instructions.

Yield: about 5 cups biscuit mix, about 2¹/₂ cups each bag

To serve: Store biscuit mix in refrigerator until ready to prepare. Preheat oven to 425 degrees. Place mix (about 2¹/₂ cups) in a medium bowl. Add ³/₄ cup milk; stir until well blended. On a lightly floured surface, use a floured rolling pin to roll out dough to ¹/₂-inch thickness. Use a 2-inch-diameter biscuit cutter to cut out biscuits. Transfer to a greased baking sheet. Bake 11 to 13 minutes or until golden brown. Brush with melted butter. Serve warm.

Yield: about 1¹/₂ dozen biscuits

RANCH-STYLE DRESSING AND DIP MIX

    2 teaspoons salt
    2 teaspoons dried minced garlic
    8 teaspoons dried minced onion
    2 teaspoons freshly ground
         pepper
    2 teaspoons granulated sugar
 2½ teaspoons paprika
 2½ teaspoons parsley flakes

Combine all ingredients. Store in airtight container. Use mix in the recipes for Dressing and Dip. Give with serving instructions.

Yield: ½ cup of mix

To make Dressing: Combine 1 tablespoon mix with 1 cup mayonnaise and 1 cup buttermilk. Blend well.

To make Dip: Combine 1 tablespoon mix with 1 cup sour cream. Blend well. Refrigerate 1 hour before serving with vegetables.

BUTTERMILK DRESSING MIX

    2 tablespoons dried thyme leaves
 1½ tablespoons dried parsley flakes
    1 tablespoon lemon pepper
    2 teaspoons salt
    1 teaspoon dried sage leaves
    1 teaspoon garlic powder
    1 teaspoon ground black pepper

Process all ingredients in a small food processor until well blended. Store in an airtight container. Give with serving instructions.

Yield: about ¼ cup dressing mix

To make: For salad dressing, combine 1½ teaspoons dressing mix, ½ cup buttermilk, and ½ cup mayonnaise; stir until blended. Cover and chill 1 hour to allow flavors to blend.

To make Dip: Combine 1½ teaspoons dressing mix, ½ cup sour cream, and ½ cup mayonnaise; stir until blended. Cover and chill 1 hour to allow flavors to blend.

BARBECUE SPICE MIX

1 cup paprika
³/₄ cup firmly packed brown sugar
1 tablespoon ground black pepper
1 tablespoon garlic powder
2 teaspoons chili powder
2 teaspoons ground ginger
1 teaspoon ground nutmeg
1 teaspoon salt
¹/₂ teaspoon ground thyme
¹/₂ teaspoon onion powder
¹/₂ teaspoon celery seed
¹/₄ teaspoon ground coriander
¹/₄ teaspoon ground red pepper
¹/₄ teaspoon ground cloves

Combine all ingredients in a small bowl; stir until well blended. Store in an airtight container. Give with recipe for Barbecue Snack Mix.

Yield: about 2 cups spice mix

BARBECUE SNACK MIX

3 cups square corn cereal
3 cups small pretzel twists
3 cups corn chips
3 cups cheese snack crackers
2 cups lightly salted peanuts
¹/₂ cup butter or margarine
1 tablespoon Worcestershire sauce
¹/₄ cup Barbecue Spice Mix

Preheat oven to 250 degrees. Combine corn cereal, pretzels, corn chips, cheese crackers, and peanuts in a large roasting pan. In a small saucepan, melt butter over medium-low heat. Remove from heat and stir in Worcestershire sauce and ¹/₄ cup spice mix. Pour butter mixture over cereal mixture; stir until well coated. Bake 1 hour, stirring every 15 minutes. Spread on aluminum foil to cool. Store in an airtight container.

Yield: about 14 cups snack mix

BOURSIN CHEESE SPREAD MIX

1 container (1⁵/₈ ounces) caraway seed
1 container (¹/₂ ounce) dried basil leaves
1 container (0.56 ounce) dried dill weed
1 container (0.12 ounce) dried chives
¹/₄ cup lemon pepper
2 tablespoons garlic salt
1¹/₂ tablespoons freshly ground black pepper

In a small bowl, combine caraway seed, basil leaves, dill weed, chives, lemon pepper, garlic salt, and black pepper. Store in an airtight container. Give with serving instructions.

Yield: about 2 cups dry mix (8 gifts)

To serve: For 2 cups cheese spread, combine 2 tablespoons mix with two 8-ounce packages softened cream cheese; beat until well blended. Serve with crackers.

A bagel lover will have something to smile about when you give this mix, which they simply add to softened cream cheese.

SAVORY HERB BAGEL MIX

- 1 cup dried parsley flakes
- 1/3 cup dried dill weed
- 2 1/2 tablespoons dried oregano leaves
- 2 1/2 tablespoons dried thyme leaves
- 2 tablespoons salt
- 4 teaspoons dried rosemary leaves
- 4 teaspoons dried marjoram leaves
- 2 teaspoons paprika

Combine all ingredients in an airtight container. Give with serving instructions.

Yield: about 2 cups mix

To serve: Process 2 teaspoons mix with one 8-ounce package softened cream cheese in a food processor until smooth. Transfer to an airtight container. Chill 2 hours to let flavors blend. Serve spread on bagel slices.

Yield: about 1 cup spread

Give friends a taste of the tropics with these mixes made with gelatin and dried fruit.

FRUITY BAGEL SPREAD MIXES

Try variations of these mixes using your favorite gelatin and dried fruit.

VERY BERRY MIX

    1 package (3 ounces) raspberry
          gelatin
    ½ cup dried sweetened cranberries

In a small bowl, combine gelatin and dried fruit. Store in a resealable plastic bag in refrigerator. Give with serving instructions.

Yield: about ¾ cup mix

TROPICAL FRUIT MIX

    1 package (3 ounces) pineapple
          gelatin
    ½ cup chopped dried pineapple
    ¼ cup flaked coconut

In a small bowl, combine gelatin, dried fruit, and coconut. Store in a resealable plastic bag in refrigerator. Give with serving instructions.

Yield: about 1 cup mix

To serve: In a small bowl, beat 3 tablespoons mix into one 8-ounce package softened cream cheese until well blended. Cover and chill 2 hours to let flavors blend. Serve spread on bagels.

Yield: about 1 cup spread

HOLIDAY BEAN SOUP MIX

- 1 pound dried black beans
- 1 pound dried red beans
- 1 pound dried kidney beans
- 1 pound dried navy beans
- 1 pound dried great Northern beans
- 1 pound dried baby lima beans
- 1 pound dried large lima beans
- 1 pound dried pinto beans
- 1 pound dried green split peas
- 1 pound dried yellow split peas
- 1 pound dried black-eyed peas
- 1 pound dried red lentils
- 1 pound dried green lentils
- 1 pound dried brown lentils

Combine dried beans in a very large bowl. Store in an airtight container. Give with recipe to make Holiday Bean Soup.

Yield: about 34 cups beans

HOLIDAY BEAN SOUP

- 2 cups Holiday Bean Soup Mix
- 1 smoked ham hock
- 2 cans (14.5 ounces each) stewed tomatoes
- 1 medium onion, chopped
- 2 ribs celery, chopped
- 1 clove garlic, minced
- 1 bay leaf
- 6 cups water
- 1/4 cup chopped fresh parsley
- 1 tablespoon red wine vinegar
- 2 teaspoons salt
- 1 teaspoon ground black pepper
- 1 teaspoon chili powder
- 1 teaspoon ground cumin seed

Cover bean mix with water and soak overnight. Drain beans and place in a stockpot. Add ham hock, tomatoes, onion, celery, garlic, bay leaf, and 6 cups water. Bring to a boil over medium-high heat; reduce to medium-low, cover, and simmer 1 hour. Add remaining ingredients; continue to simmer 1 hour or until beans are tender. Remove bay leaf. Serve warm.

Yield: about 11 cups soup

INSTANT RANCH POTATO SOUP

- 4 cups potato flakes
- 2 cups nonfat milk powder
- 1/4 cup chicken bouillon granules
- 1 package (0.4 ounce) ranch-style salad dressing mix
- 1 teaspoon garlic powder
- 1/2 teaspoon ground black pepper

Combine all ingredients in a large bowl; stir until well blended. Store in an airtight container.

Yield: about 6 1/4 cups of mix

To serve: Place 1/2 cup soup mix in a soup bowl or mug. Add 1 cup boiling water and stir until smooth. Let soup stand 1 to 2 minutes to thicken slightly.

CURRY SOUP MIX

- 2 cups uncooked instant rice
- 1/2 cup raisins
- 1/3 cup chopped walnuts
- 1/4 cup dried minced onions
- 2 tablespoons salt
- 1 tablespoon curry powder
- 1 tablespoon granulated sugar
- 2 teaspoons paprika
- 1 1/2 teaspoons dried dill weed
- 1 teaspoon dry mustard
- 1 teaspoon ground coriander
- 1 teaspoon garlic powder
- 1/2 teaspoon ground cardamom

In a large bowl, combine all ingredients, stirring until well blended. Store in an airtight container. Give with instructions for making soup.

To make soup: Bring 10 cups water to a boil in a large stockpot over high heat. Add soup mix; reduce heat to medium. Simmer, stirring occasionally, until rice is tender and soup thickens (about 20 minutes). Stir in about 2 cups shredded cooked chicken or cooked peeled shrimp; cook until heated through. Serve immediately. Store in an airtight container in refrigerator.

Yield: 6 to 8 servings

CHILI SEASONING MIX

- 1/2 cup chili powder
- 1/4 cup dried minced onions
- 2 tablespoons dried minced garlic
- 2 tablespoons ground cumin
- 2 tablespoons cornstarch
- 2 tablespoons salt
- 1 tablespoon sweet pepper flakes
- 1 tablespoon ground coriander
- 1 tablespoon ground black pepper
- 1 tablespoon dried cilantro
- 1 teaspoon dried oregano leaves
- 1/2 teaspoon ground red pepper
- 1/8 teaspoon ground cloves

In a small bowl, combine all ingredients; stir until well blended. Store in an airtight container. Give with recipe to make Chili.

Yield: about 1 1/4 cups seasoning mix

CHILI

- 2 pounds ground beef
- 2 cans (8 ounces each) tomato sauce
- 1 can (16 ounces) pinto beans, undrained
- 1 can (14 1/2 ounces) diced tomatoes, undrained
- 1/4 cup Chili Seasoning Mix

In a large skillet, cook beef over medium heat until brown; drain meat. Stir in tomato sauce, beans, tomatoes, and chili seasoning mix. Reduce heat to low. Stirring occasionally, cover and simmer 30 minutes. Serve warm.

Yield: about 7 cups chili

This "souper" gift of colorful Dried Bean Soup Mix is made with six types of beans to symbolize the blessings of health and prosperity. Layered inside a glass jar, the beans will make an appealing countertop display—and a hearty soup when they're prepared with the spicy seasoning mix and soup recipe that you provide.

DRIED BEAN SOUP MIX AND SEASONING

DRIED BEAN MIX
1/2 cup of *each* of the following:
kidney beans, split yellow peas, black beans, red lentils, small red beans, and split green peas

SEASONING MIX
- 1 tablespoon dried sweet pepper flakes
- 2 teaspoons chicken bouillon granules
- 2 teaspoons dried minced onion
- 1 1/2 teaspoons salt
- 1 teaspoon dried parsley flakes
- 1/2 teaspoon ground black pepper
- 1/2 teaspoon garlic powder
- 1/2 teaspoon celery seed

For dried bean mix, layer each type of bean in a clear gift container.

For seasoning mix, combine all ingredients. Store in a resealable plastic bag. Give with recipe to make Seasoned Bean Soup.

Yield: about 3 cups dried bean mix and about 1/4 cup seasoning mix

SEASONED BEAN SOUP

Dried Bean Mix (3 cups)
2 cans (14 1/2 ounces each) stewed tomatoes
Seasoning Mix (1/4 cup)

Rinse beans and place in a large Dutch oven. Pour 4 cups boiling water over beans; cover and let soak overnight.

Drain beans and return to Dutch oven. Add 6 cups water, cover, and bring to a boil over high heat. Reduce heat to low and simmer 1 to 1 1/2 hours or until beans are almost tender. Add tomatoes and seasoning mix. Stirring occasionally, cover and simmer 30 minutes. Uncover beans and continue to simmer about 1 hour longer or until beans are tender and soup thickens. Serve warm.

Yield: about 10 cups soup

BUSY DAY POTATO SOUP MIX

- 1 package (6.6 ounces) dried potato flakes
- 2 tablespoons dried minced onions
- 2 tablespoons chicken bouillon granules
- 2 teaspoons celery salt
- 2 teaspoons dried parsley flakes
- 2 teaspoons dried chopped chives
- 1/2 teaspoon garlic powder
- 1/2 teaspoon salt
- 1/4 teaspoon ground black pepper
- 1/8 teaspoon ground red pepper

In a medium bowl, combine potato flakes, minced onions, bouillon, celery salt, parsley flakes, chopped chives, garlic powder, salt, black pepper, and red pepper. Store in an airtight container. Give with serving instructions.

Yield: about 4 cups soup mix

To serve: In a 2-cup microwave-safe container, combine 1/3 cup soup mix with 1 cup milk. Microwave on high power (100%) 3 minutes or until soup is thick and smooth and onions are tender, stirring after each minute.

Yield: about 1 cup soup

CHERRY-NUT CHEESE BALL MIX

1¼ cups dried cherries (available at gourmet food stores)
1¼ cups finely chopped walnuts
2 teaspoons ground ginger, divided
Vanilla wafers to serve

In a medium bowl, combine cherries and walnuts. Place about 1¼ cups cherry mixture into each of 2 small resealable plastic bags. Spoon 1 teaspoon ginger into each container and seal. Give with serving instructions.

Yield: about 2½ cups mix, enough to make 2 cheese balls

To make cheese ball: Combine 1¼ cups mix with one 8-ounce package softened cream cheese and 1 teaspoon ginger. Shape into a ball; wrap in plastic wrap and refrigerate until firm. To serve, let stand at room temperature 20 to 30 minutes or until softened. Serve with vanilla wafers.

Yield: 1 cheese ball

CHOCOLATE-MINT CHEESE BALL MIX

1 package (12 ounces) semisweet chocolate chips
2 cups chopped pecans
1 cup 1-inch diameter peppermint candies (about thirty-six candies or 7 ounces)

In a blender or food processor, finely grind all ingredients. Store in an airtight container. Give with serving instructions.

Yield: about 6 cups mix, enough to make 4 cheese balls

To make cheese ball: Stir 1½ cups mix into one 8-ounce package softened cream cheese. Shape into a ball; wrap in plastic wrap and refrigerate until firm. To serve, let stand at room temperature 20 to 30 minutes or until softened. Serve with cookies.

Yield: 1 cheese ball

A blend of chocolate chips, pecans, and peppermint candies, this cheese ball is a creamy delight. To make your gift doubly delicious, pack a prepared cheese ball with chocolate wafers; for later, include a bag of mix and instructions for making another cheese ball.

FAVORITE FISH-FRY SEASONING

2 cups yellow cornmeal
1 cup all-purpose flour
2 teaspoons paprika
1 teaspoon dried parsley flakes, crushed
1 teaspoon salt
1 teaspoon celery salt
1 teaspoon onion salt
1 teaspoon lemon pepper
1/2 teaspoon ground red pepper

In a large bowl, combine cornmeal, flour, paprika, parsley, salt, celery salt, onion salt, lemon pepper, and red pepper. Store in a resealable plastic bag. Give with serving instructions.

Yield: about 3 cups mix (will coat about 4 pounds of fish)

To serve: Heat about 1 1/2 inches vegetable oil to 375 degrees in a deep skillet. In a small bowl, combine 1 egg and 1 cup buttermilk. Dip fish into buttermilk mixture. Place in bag of mix; shake until fish is well coated. Fry until fish is golden brown and flakes easily with a fork. Drain on paper towels. Serve warm.

HUSH PUPPY MIX

1 1/2 cups yellow cornmeal
3/4 cup all-purpose flour
3 tablespoons dried minced onion
1 teaspoon baking powder
1 teaspoon sugar
1 teaspoon salt
1/2 teaspoon baking soda
1/4 teaspoon ground red pepper

In a large bowl, combine cornmeal, flour, onion, baking powder, sugar, salt, baking soda, and red pepper. Store in a resealable plastic bag. Give with serving instructions.

Yield: about 2 1/4 cups mix

To serve: Heat about 1 1/2 inches vegetable oil to 350 degrees in a deep skillet. In a medium bowl, combine 1 1/4 cups buttermilk, 1 beaten egg, and mix; stir until well blended. Drop mixture by tablespoonfuls into hot oil. Fry until golden brown and thoroughly cooked. Drain on paper towels. Serve warm.

Yield: about 3 dozen hush puppies

SPECIAL SEASONING SALT
Use seasoning salt in place of table salt.

1 cup salt
2 teaspoons paprika
1 teaspoon dry mustard
1 teaspoon garlic powder
1 teaspoon onion powder
1/2 teaspoon ground oregano leaves
1/2 teaspoon ground thyme leaves
1/2 teaspoon curry powder
1/2 teaspoon dried dill weed
1/2 teaspoon celery seed

In a small bowl, combine salt, paprika, dry mustard, garlic powder, onion powder, oregano, thyme, curry powder, dill weed, and celery seed. Store in an airtight container.

Yield: about 1 1/4 cups seasoning salt

STIR-FRY SAUCE

Include chow mein noodles, fortune cookies, green tea, and chopsticks with sauce.

- 1/4 cup soy sauce
- 1/4 cup oyster sauce (in Oriental section of supermarket)
- 2 tablespoons freshly squeezed lime juice
- 1 tablespoon freshly grated gingerroot
- 1 tablespoon sugar
- 1/2 teaspoon crushed red pepper flakes

In a small bowl, combine soy sauce, oyster sauce, lime juice, gingerroot, sugar, and red pepper flakes. Store in an airtight container in refrigerator. Give sauce with purchased items and recipe for Stir-Fry Chicken.

Yield: about 2/3 cup sauce

STIR-FRY CHICKEN

- 1 container of Stir-Fry Sauce
- 1 pound skinless, boneless chicken breasts, cut into bite-size pieces
- 3 tablespoons dark sesame oil, divided
- 3 carrots, peeled and cut into thin diagonal slices
- 1 large green pepper, thinly sliced
- 1 large sweet red pepper, thinly sliced
- 1 large onion, thinly sliced
- 1 package (8 ounces) fresh mushrooms, sliced
- 4 cups cooked rice to serve

Pour Stir-Fry Sauce over chicken in a shallow dish. Cover and refrigerate 30 minutes, stirring after 15 minutes.

Drain chicken, reserving sauce. In a large skillet or wok, heat 2 tablespoons sesame oil over medium-high heat. Stirring constantly, cook chicken 5 minutes or until chicken is tender. Remove chicken and set aside. Add remaining tablespoon sesame oil to skillet. Add carrots, peppers, and onion. Stir fry on medium high 5 minutes or until vegetables are crisp tender. Stir in chicken, mushrooms, and reserved sauce. Bring sauce to a boil; cook about 2 minutes or until mushrooms are tender. Serve warm over rice with chow mein noodles on top.

Yield: 6 to 8 servings

FRUITED RICE MIX

Yield: about 5 cups of rice mix

3 cups uncooked long-grain white rice
3 tablespoons dried minced onion
1½ tablespoons instant chicken bouillon
1 tablespoon salt
1 cup chopped dried apples
⅓ cup golden raisins
⅓ cup toasted slivered almonds

Combine all ingredients, mixing well. Store in an airtight container. Give with serving instructions.

To make Fruited Rice: In heavy 2-quart saucepan, combine 1 cup Fruited Rice Mix with 2 cups water and 2 tablespoons butter or margarine. Cover tightly. Bring to a boil. Reduce heat to medium-low. Without lifting lid, simmer 30 minutes or until water is absorbed.

Yield: about 3½ cups of cooked rice

This Fruited Rice Mix is twice as nice when it's packaged in a pretty bottle and presented in a hand-painted basket.

Our Favorite
SIMPLE SUPPERS

You don't need a special occasion to serve your family the very best. This mouth-watering collection of everyday recipes is chock-full of taste and substance without a lot of extra fuss. Whether you're looking for a hearty soup, a zesty casserole, or a new variation on salad, you'll find plenty of practical ideas here.

Stroganoff Stew, p. 164

CHICKEN-BLACK BEAN CASSEROLE

²/₃ cup freshly squeezed lime juice
¹/₃ cup olive oil
¹/₂ teaspoon ground black pepper
2 teaspoons garlic powder, divided
2 teaspoons salt, divided
1¹/₂ pounds boneless, skinless chicken breasts, cut into bite-size pieces
4 cups cooked white rice
2 cans (15 ounces each) black beans
1 cup finely chopped fresh cilantro
1 teaspoon onion powder
1 teaspoon chili powder
1 teaspoon ground cumin

In a medium bowl, whisk lime juice, oil, pepper, 1 teaspoon garlic powder, and 1 teaspoon salt. Add chicken; stir until evenly coated. Cover and refrigerate 2 hours.

In a 2-quart casserole, combine rice, undrained beans, cilantro, onion powder, chili powder, cumin, remaining 1 teaspoon garlic powder, and remaining 1 teaspoon salt; set aside.

Preheat oven to 350 degrees. Using a slotted spoon, place chicken in a large skillet. Cook over medium heat until juices run clear when chicken is pierced with a fork. Stir chicken into rice mixture. Cover and bake 40 to 45 minutes or until heated through.

Yield: about nine 1-cup servings

ITALIAN CHICKEN AND DUMPLINGS

2 cans (24 ounces each) chicken and dumplings
1 package (10 ounces) frozen green peas
1 jar (2 ounces) diced pimientos
1 package (0.7 ounces) Italian salad dressing mix
¹/₂ cup sliced almonds
¹/₂ cup Italian-style bread crumbs
4 tablespoons grated Parmesan cheese

Combine chicken and dumplings, peas, pimientos, and salad dressing mix in a medium bowl. Spread mixture evenly in two 7 x 11-inch baking dishes. Evenly sprinkle almonds, bread crumbs, and cheese over each casserole. Cover and store in refrigerator. Give with serving instructions.

Yield: 2 casseroles, about 6 servings each

To serve: Bake covered casserole in a 350-degree oven 25 to 30 minutes. Remove cover and broil about 3 minutes or until topping is lightly browned. Serve warm.

GARDEN CHICKEN CASSEROLE

2 cups chicken broth
²/₃ cup sherry, divided
1 package (6 ounces) long grain and wild rice mix
1 small onion, chopped
2 small carrots, grated
1 small green pepper, chopped
¹/₄ cup butter or margarine
3 cups diced cooked chicken

1 can (4 ounces) sliced
   mushrooms
1 package (8 ounces) cream
   cheese
2 cups (8 ounces) shredded
   American cheese
1 cup evaporated milk
⅓ cup grated Parmesan cheese
½ cup sliced almonds
   Carrots and green onions for
   garnish, optional

In a medium saucepan, bring broth and ⅓ cup sherry to a boil. Add contents of rice package, cover, and simmer over low heat 25 to 30 minutes or until all liquid is absorbed.

Preheat oven to 350 degrees. In a Dutch oven, sauté onion, carrots, and green pepper in butter until soft, about 5 minutes. Add rice, chicken, and mushrooms, mixing well. Place cream cheese, American cheese, and milk in saucepan and melt over medium heat, stirring until smooth. Add to Dutch oven with remaining sherry, mixing thoroughly. Pour into a buttered 13 x 9 x 2-inch casserole dish. Top with Parmesan cheese and almonds. Cover and bake 35 minutes; uncover and bake 15 minutes longer or until bubbly. If desired, garnish with carrots and green onions.

Yield: about 8 servings

Note: Casserole may be refrigerated overnight before baking. If refrigerated, increase baking time to 45 minutes covered and 15 minutes uncovered.

Garden Chicken Casserole is a wholesome meal filled with vegetables, rice, and chicken in a creamy cheese sauce.

CHICKEN PAPRIKA

½ cup butter or margarine
1 medium onion, chopped
½ cup chopped celery
1 teaspoon dried minced garlic
2 teaspoons paprika
1 teaspoon salt
½ teaspoon ground black pepper
2 cans (5 ounces each) chicken, drained
½ cup all-purpose flour
1 can (10½ ounces) chicken broth
1 cup half and half
2 cups cooked rice

In a large stockpot, melt butter over medium heat. Add next 3 ingredients and sauté until onion and celery are tender. Stir in next 4 ingredients. Sprinkle flour evenly over chicken mixture; stir until well blended. Cook until heated through. Stirring constantly, gradually add chicken broth and cook until mixture begins to thicken. Stir in half and half and rice. Cook 5 to 10 minutes or until heated through. Remove from heat.

To serve, preheat oven to 350 degrees. Bake covered 25 to 30 minutes or until heated through.

Yield: 6 to 8 servings

SOUTHWESTERN CHICKEN CASSEROLE

1 teaspoon salt
½ teaspoon ground black pepper
¼ teaspoon garlic powder
1½ pounds boneless, skinless chicken breasts, cut into bite-size pieces
¼ cup butter or margarine
1 cup finely chopped fresh cilantro leaves
3½ cups fresh broccoli flowerets
1 pound process cheese, cut into pieces
1 can (10 ounces) diced tomatoes and green chilies
4 cups cooked rice
Sour cream to serve

Sprinkle salt, pepper, and garlic powder evenly over chicken. In a large skillet, heat butter over medium heat. Add cilantro and chicken; cook 10 minutes, stirring occasionally. Add broccoli to skillet and cook, stirring occasionally, until broccoli is tender and juices run clear when chicken is pierced. Remove from heat.

Preheat oven to 350 degrees. In a small saucepan, combine cheese with tomatoes and green chilies. Stirring occasionally, cook over medium-low heat until cheese melts. Remove from heat. Spoon rice into a greased 2½-quart casserole. Spoon chicken mixture over rice. Pour cheese mixture over chicken. Cover and bake 25 to 30 minutes or until cheese is bubbly. Serve with sour cream.

Yield: 6 to 8 servings

BAKED CHICKEN STEW

1 can (14½ ounces) chicken broth
1 can (10 ounces) diced tomatoes
  and green chiles
2 tablespoons cornstarch
2 teaspoons sugar
1½ teaspoons salt
1 teaspoon lemon pepper
1¼ pounds boneless skinless
  chicken breasts, cut into
  1-inch pieces
1½ cups thickly sliced carrots
4 cups cubed potatoes
1½ cups 1-inch celery pieces
1 large onion, coarsely chopped

Preheat oven to 375 degrees. In a large bowl, combine chicken broth, tomatoes and green chiles, cornstarch, sugar, salt, and lemon pepper. Stir in chicken, carrots, potatoes, celery, and onion. Place mixture in a greased 9 x 13-inch baking dish. Cover and bake 1½ to 2 hours or until meat and vegetables are tender. Serve warm.

Yield: about 6 servings

LAYERED MEXICAN CASSEROLE

1 pound ground beef
1 jar (8 ounces) chunky salsa
1 package (1.5 ounces) taco
  seasoning
1 container (12 ounces) cottage
  cheese
1 package (8 ounces) shredded
  Cheddar cheese, divided
2 eggs, beaten
10 flour tortillas (about 7-inch
  diameter)
1 can (4.5 ounces) chopped green
  chiles, drained
1 can (4¼ ounces) chopped ripe
  olives, drained

Stirring occasionally, brown ground beef in a medium skillet over medium-high heat. Remove from heat; drain grease. Stir in salsa and taco seasoning.

In a medium bowl, combine cottage cheese, 1 cup Cheddar cheese, and eggs. Grease two 8-inch square baking pans. Place 4 tortillas over bottom and up sides of each pan. Spoon one-fourth of meat mixture and one-fourth of cottage cheese mixture over tortillas in each pan. Place 1 tortilla in center of each pan. Spoon remaining one-fourth of meat mixture and remaining one-fourth of cottage cheese mixture over tortilla in each pan. Sprinkle with green chiles, olives, and remaining 1 cup Cheddar cheese. Cover and store in refrigerator.

Yield: two 8-inch casseroles, about 6 servings each

To serve: Bake covered casserole in a 350-degree oven 45 to 50 minutes or until heated through. Uncover and bake 5 minutes longer or until cheese is bubbly. Serve warm.

Named for a popular quilt pattern, Cheesy "Butter and Eggs" Casserole layers sliced bread with a peppery mushroom, onion, and egg mixture. Before baking, shredded cheese and buttery cracker crumbs are sprinkled over the top in the shape of the quilt pattern.

154

CHEESY "BUTTER AND EGGS" CASSEROLE

Assemble casserole one night ahead.

2 tablespoons butter or margarine softened
6 slices white bread, crusts removed
1/3 cup finely chopped green onions
1 tablespoon vegetable oil
9 eggs
2 1/2 cups half and half
2 cans (7 ounces each) mushroom pieces, drained
1 can (4.5 ounces) chopped green chiles, drained
1 1/4 teaspoon salt
1/8 teaspoon ground black pepper
2 cups (8 ounces) shredded Monterey Jack cheese, divided
1 1/2 cups butter-flavored cracker crumbs
Sweet red pepper ring and chopped green onions to garnish

Spread butter over bread slices. Place in bottom of a greased 9 x 13-inch baking dish. In a small skillet, sauté 1/3 cup green onions in oil over medium heat until onions are tender. Beat eggs in a medium bowl. Stir onions, half and half, mushrooms, green chilies, salt, and black pepper into eggs. Stir in 1 1/2 cups cheese. Pour egg mixture over bread slices. Cover and chill overnight.

Preheat oven to 350 degrees. Sprinkle cracker crumbs over casserole in the shape of inside section of "Butter and Eggs" quilt pattern. Sprinkle remaining 1/2 cup cheese over casserole in the shape of outer sections of "Butter and Eggs" quilt pattern. Bake 45 minutes or until egg mixture is set and cracker crumbs are golden brown. Garnish with pepper ring and green onions. Serve warm.

Yield: about 12 servings

POTATOES AU GRATIN CASSEROLE

2 cups (8 ounces) shredded Cheddar cheese, divided
1 package (20 ounces) fresh shredded potatoes
1 cup sour cream
1/2 cup milk
1 jar (2 ounces) real bacon pieces
2 tablespoons butter or margarine, melted
1 teaspoon onion powder
1/2 teaspoon ground black pepper

In a 2-quart casserole, combine 1 cup cheese and remaining ingredients. Sprinkle remaining 1 cup cheese over top. Cover and store in refrigerator.

Yield: about 8 servings

To serve: Bake uncovered in a preheated 350-degree oven about 45 minutes; cover and continue to bake 30 minutes or until heated through and cheese is bubbly.

CHEESY VEGETABLE PIE

This pie is made with previously cooked vegetables, or you may substitute canned or frozen.

- 1 cup green beans, drained
- 1 cup green peas, drained
- 1 cup sliced carrots, drained
- 1 cup broccoli flowerets
- 1/2 cup whole kernel corn, drained
- 1 cup chopped uncooked onion
- 1/4 cup chopped uncooked green pepper
- 1 clove garlic, minced
- 3/4 teaspoon salt
- 1/4 teaspoon ground black pepper
- 1 cup sour cream
- 1 cup (4 ounces) shredded mozzarella cheese
- 1 tablespoon chopped fresh parsley
- 1 package (15 ounces) refrigerated pie crusts, at room temperature

Preheat oven to 350 degrees. In a large bowl, combine green beans, green peas, carrots, broccoli, corn, onion, green pepper, garlic, salt, and black pepper; toss until well blended. Stir in sour cream, cheese, and parsley. Press 1 crust into bottom of a 9-inch deep-dish pie plate. Cut decorative shapes from top crust. Spoon vegetable mixture into crust. Place top crust over vegetables. Arrange cutout pieces of dough on top crust. Crimp edges of crust with a fork. Bake 60 to 65 minutes or until cheese is bubbly and crust is golden brown. If edges of crust brown too quickly, cover with strips of aluminum foil. Allow pie to stand 10 minutes before serving.

Yield: 8 to 10 servings

EASY TAMALE PIE

- 1 1/4 pounds ground beef
- 1/2 cup chopped onion
- 1 clove garlic, minced
- 1 can (11 ounces) Mexican-style whole kernel corn, drained
- 1 can (8 ounces) tomato sauce
- 1 can (4 ounces) chopped green chiles
- 1 teaspoon chili powder
- 1/2 teaspoon salt
- 1/2 cup sour cream
- 1 egg
- 2 cups (8 ounces) shredded Cheddar cheese, divided
- 1 package (6 ounces) Mexican-style corn bread mix and ingredients to prepare corn bread

Preheat oven to 375 degrees. In a large skillet, cook ground beef, onion, and garlic over medium-high heat until meat is brown and onion is tender; drain. Reduce heat to medium-low. Stir in corn, tomato sauce, green chiles, chili powder, and salt. Remove from heat.

In a small bowl, beat sour cream and egg until well blended. Stir in 1 cup cheese. Combine sour cream mixture with ground beef mixture. Spoon into a lightly greased 8 3/8 x 12 3/8 x 1 1/8-inch baking pan. In a medium bowl, prepare corn bread mix according to package directions. Spread corn bread batter over casserole. Sprinkle with remaining 1 cup cheese. Bake uncovered 25 to 30 minutes or until mixture is heated through and corn bread topping is golden brown. Serve warm.

Yield: 6 to 8 servings

Bacon bits and cheese cracker crumbs top Spinach-Squash Casserole.

SPINACH-SQUASH CASSEROLE

6   medium yellow squash, sliced
2   packages (10 ounces each) frozen chopped spinach, thawed and drained
1   package (8 ounces) cream cheese, softened
2   eggs, lightly beaten
6   tablespoons butter or margarine, melted
1   tablespoon sugar
1/2   teaspoon salt
1/2   teaspoon garlic salt
1   teaspoon ground black pepper
1   cup cheese cracker crumbs
6   slices bacon, cooked and crumbled
    Paprika

Preheat oven to 350 degrees. Cook squash in salted boiling water until tender (about 10 minutes); drain. Place squash in a large bowl and mash. Add spinach, cream cheese, eggs, melted butter, sugar, salt, garlic salt, and pepper to squash; stir until well blended. Pour into a lightly greased 2-quart baking dish; top with cracker crumbs, bacon, and paprika. Cover and bake 45 minutes. Remove cover and bake 15 minutes longer or until center is set. Serve warm.

Yield: 8 to 10 servings

QUESADILLAS CASSEROLE

1   can (16 ounces) refried beans
1   can (8 ounces) tomato sauce
1   can (4 ounces) chopped green chilies
1   teaspoon ground cumin seed
1   teaspoon chili powder
1   teaspoon onion powder
1   teaspoon garlic powder
4   8-inch flour tortillas
    vegetable cooking spray
2   cups (8 ounces) shredded Cheddar cheese, divided

In a small bowl, combine first 7 ingredients. Place 1 tortilla in an 8-inch round cake pan sprayed with vegetable cooking spray. Spread about 1/4 of bean mixture over tortilla. Repeat with second tortilla and bean mixture. Sprinkle 1 cup cheese over bean mixture. Repeat with remaining tortillas and bean mixture. Sprinkle remaining 1 cup cheese over top. Cover and refrigerate.

Yield: about 8 servings

To serve: Bake uncovered in a preheated 350-degree oven 35 to 40 minutes or until heated through and cheese is bubbly.

CHICKEN-MUSHROOM LASAGNA

2   cans (10³/₄ ounces each) cream of
     mushroom soup
2   cups milk
¹/₈ teaspoon ground white pepper
1   container (15 ounces) ricotta
     cheese
1   package (10 ounces) frozen
     chopped spinach, thawed and
     squeezed dry
1   egg
1   package (8 ounces) uncooked
     lasagna noodles
1   jar (6 ounces) marinated artichoke
     hearts, drained and coarsely
     chopped
1   jar (4¹/₂ ounces) sliced
     mushrooms, drained
2   cups chopped cooked chicken
2   cups (8 ounces) shredded
     Monterey Jack cheese
¹/₂ cup freshly grated Parmesan
     cheese

In a medium bowl, combine soup, milk, and white pepper; stir until well blended. In another medium bowl, combine ricotta cheese, spinach, and egg; stir until well blended. Spoon ¹/₂ cup of soup mixture over bottom of a greased 9 x 13-inch baking dish. Layer half of uncooked lasagna noodles over soup mixture. Layer half of artichoke pieces, half of mushrooms, 1 cup chicken, ³/₄ cup Monterey Jack cheese, and half of spinach mixture over noodles. Spoon 2 cups soup mixture over layers. Repeat layers with remaining lasagna noodles, artichoke pieces, mushrooms, chicken, ³/₄ cup Monterey Jack cheese, and spinach mixture. Spoon remaining soup mixture over layers. Sprinkle top with Parmesan cheese and remaining ¹/₂ cup Monterey Jack cheese. Cover and refrigerate overnight to allow lasagna noodles to absorb liquids.

Yield: about 12 servings

To serve: Bake uncovered in a 350-degree oven 55 to 60 minutes or until golden brown. Let stand about 15 minutes before serving. Serve warm.

MAKE-AHEAD VEGETABLE LASAGNA

1   package (10 ounces) frozen
     chopped spinach, thawed and
     squeezed dry
1   container (15 ounces) ricotta
     cheese
¹/₂ cup shredded Parmesan cheese
1   egg
1¹/₂ teaspoons dried Italian herb
     seasoning
1   jar (27¹/₂ ounces) spaghetti
     sauce
1   can (14.5 ounces) stewed
     tomatoes
1   can (4.5 ounces) sliced
     mushrooms, drained
1   package (8 ounces) lasagna
     noodles, uncooked
1   large green pepper, cut into rings
1   package (8 ounces) shredded
     mozzarella cheese

In a medium bowl, combine spinach, ricotta cheese, Parmesan cheese, egg, and Italian seasoning. In a second medium bowl, combine spaghetti sauce, tomatoes, and mushrooms. Place 1 cup spaghetti sauce mixture in bottom of a greased 9 x 13 x 2-inch baking dish. Layer half of uncooked lasagna noodles over sauce. Spoon half of cheese mixture over noodles. Layer again with half of remaining sauce and remaining noodles. Place remaining cheese mixture over noodles. Pour remaining spaghetti sauce mixture over cheese mixture. Arrange green pepper rings on top. Sprinkle mozzarella cheese over pepper rings. Cover and refrigerate overnight to allow lasagna noodles to absorb liquids.

Yield: about 12 servings

To serve: Bake uncovered lasagna in a 350-degree oven 50 to 60 minutes or until noodles are tender and cheese is bubbly. Allow to stand about 15 minutes before serving.

SPAGHETTI PIE

    6 cups water
    4 tablespoons olive oil, divided
    1 tablespoon salt
    1 pound uncooked thin spaghetti
    2 medium onions, chopped
    1 green pepper, seeded and
          chopped
    3 eggs, beaten
    1 container (15 ounces) ricotta
          cheese
  3/4 cup grated Parmesan cheese
    1 teaspoon dried oregano
    1 teaspoon dried basil
  1/2 teaspoon crushed red pepper
          flakes
    1 cup (4 ounces) grated Cheddar
          cheese
    1 pound mild pork sausage,
          cooked, crumbled, and
          drained well

In a large stockpot, bring water, 2 tablespoons oil, and salt to a boil over high heat. Stir in spaghetti and cook 10 to 12 minutes or until tender. Drain and rinse with cold water; set aside.

Preheat oven to 350 degrees. In a large skillet, heat remaining oil over medium heat. Sauté onions and pepper until soft; transfer to a large bowl. Add next 6 ingredients; beat until well blended using medium speed of an electric mixer. Add spaghetti; toss until well coated. Spoon 1/2 of spaghetti mixture into bottoms of 2 greased 7-inch springform pans. Spread cheese and sausage evenly over spaghetti. Top with remaining 1/2 of spaghetti mixture. Bake 30 to 35 minutes or until center of pie is set. Cool in pans 15 minutes; remove sides of pans. Store in an airtight container in refrigerator.

To reheat, preheat oven to 350 degrees. Transfer pie to an ungreased baking sheet. Cover loosely with aluminum foil. Bake 10 to 12 minutes or until heated through.

Yield: 2 pies

Overnight Ham-and-Egg Casserole can be prepared ahead and simply popped in the oven the next morning for a convenient breakfast.

OVERNIGHT HAM-AND-EGG CASSEROLE

      8   slices Texas-style (thick-slice)
          bread, cut into 1-inch cubes
   2¼   cups cubed smoked ham
          (about 1 pound)
      2   cups (8 ounces) shredded
          Cheddar cheese, divided
    12   eggs, beaten
      3   cups half and half
    ¼   cup chopped fresh parsley
      1   teaspoon salt
      1   teaspoon dry mustard
    ½   teaspoon garlic powder
    ½   teaspoon ground black pepper
    ¼   teaspoon paprika to garnish

Layer half of bread cubes in a greased 9 x 13-inch baking dish. Sprinkle half of ham and 1 cup cheese over bread. Layer remaining bread and ham. In a large bowl, combine eggs, half and half, parsley, salt, dry mustard, garlic powder, and pepper. Beat until well blended. Pour egg mixture over ham and bread. Sprinkle with remaining 1 cup cheese and paprika. Cover and chill overnight.

Yield: 8 to 10 servings

To bake: Remove casserole from refrigerator and let stand 30 minutes before baking. Bake uncovered in a 350-degree oven 50 to 60 minutes or until a knife inserted in center comes out clean. Serve warm.

SPINACH-FETA STRATA

6 croissants, cut in half
    horizontally
6 eggs, beaten
1½ cups milk
1 package (10 ounces) frozen
    chopped spinach, thawed and
    well drained
½ teaspoon salt
¼ teaspoon ground black pepper
¼ teaspoon ground nutmeg
1½ cups (6 ounces) shredded
    Monterey Jack cheese
7 ounces crumbled feta cheese

Arrange croissant halves with sides overlapping in a greased 9 x 13-inch baking dish. In a medium bowl, combine eggs, milk, spinach, salt, pepper, and nutmeg. Pour over croissants. Sprinkle cheeses over spinach mixture. Cover and refrigerate 8 hours or overnight.

Preheat oven to 350 degrees. Uncover and bake 40 to 45 minutes or until lightly browned. Cut into squares. Serve warm.

Yield: about 15 servings

Spinach-Feta Strata is a pleasing combination of spinach, eggs, and cheeses baked atop croissant halves.

SAUSAGE-GRITS PIE

CRUST

1½ cups water
½ teaspoon garlic powder
½ cup quick-cooking grits
½ cup (2 ounces) shredded
     Cheddar cheese
¼ cup all-purpose flour
1 egg, beaten

FILLING

6 eggs
½ teaspoon dry mustard
½ teaspoon salt
¼ teaspoon ground black pepper
½ pound ground mild pork
     sausage, cooked, drained,
     and crumbled
1 cup (4 ounces) shredded
     Cheddar cheese
4 green onions, chopped

For crust, combine water and garlic powder in a medium saucepan. Bring to a boil. Stir in grits and bring to a boil again. Reduce heat to medium-low, cover, and cook 5 to 7 minutes or until thick, stirring occasionally. Remove from heat. In a small bowl, combine cheese, flour, and egg. Stir cheese mixture into grits. Press grits mixture into bottom and 2 inches up sides of a greased 9-inch springform pan.

Preheat oven to 350 degrees. For filling, whisk eggs, mustard, salt, and pepper in a large bowl. Stir in sausage, cheese, and onions. Pour into crust. Bake 45 to 50 minutes or until a knife inserted in center comes out clean. Serve hot or cool completely on a wire rack, cover, and refrigerate.

To reheat, cover and bake in a preheated 350-degree oven 30 to 35 minutes or until heated through. Remove sides of pan. Serve warm.

Yield: 8 to 10 servings

CHEESY PEPPERONI-MACARONI BAKE

1 package (3.5 ounces) sliced
     pepperoni, divided
1 can (14.5 ounces) diced tomatoes
1 can (10¾ ounces) cream of
     mushroom soup
1 package (8 ounces) elbow
     macaroni, uncooked
1 package (8 ounces) shredded
     pasteurized process cheese,
     divided
1 cup water

Reserving several pepperoni slices for garnish, combine remaining pepperoni, tomatoes, soup, uncooked macaroni, 1 cup cheese, and water in a large bowl. Pour into a 2-quart baking dish. Sprinkle remaining 1 cup cheese on top. Garnish with reserved pepperoni. Cover and refrigerate overnight to allow macaroni to absorb liquids.

Yield: about 8 to 10 servings

To serve: Bake covered casserole in a 350-degree oven 45 minutes. Uncover and bake 15 minutes longer or until heated through and cheese is bubbly. Serve warm.

HOT REUBEN CASSEROLE

- 2 cans (10 ounces each) chopped sauerkraut, drained
- 1 pound thinly sliced corned beef, coarsely chopped
- 3/4 cup Thousand Island dressing
- 8 ounces thinly sliced Swiss cheese
- 5 1/2 cups (about 8 ounces) coarsely crumbled rye bread
- 1/4 cup butter, melted

In a greased 8 x 11 1/2-inch baking dish, layer first 5 ingredients and drizzle with butter. Cover and store in refrigerator.

Yield: about 6 to 8 servings

To serve: Bake uncovered in a preheated 375-degree oven 30 to 40 minutes or until casserole is heated through and bread crumbs are lightly browned.

MEXICAN CORN CASSEROLES

- 2 cans (11 ounces each) Mexican-style corn, drained
- 1 can (16 1/2 ounces) yellow cream-style corn
- 1 package (8.5 ounces) corn muffin mix
- 1 cup (4 ounces) shredded sharp Cheddar cheese
- 1/2 cup sour cream
- 1 can (4 ounces) chopped green chilies, drained
- 1/4 cup butter or margarine, melted

Preheat oven to 350 degrees. Stir all ingredients in a large bowl until just combined. Pour batter into 2 greased 9-inch iron skillets or two 8-inch square baking pans. Bake 45 to 55 minutes or until lightly browned. Cover and store in refrigerator.

Yield: 2 casseroles, about 8 servings each

To serve: Cover and bake in a preheated 350-degree oven to 20 to 25 minutes or until heated through.

HOPPIN' JOHN

- 4 cans (15.8 ounces each) black-eyed peas, undrained
- 1 pound smoked sausage, sliced into bite-size pieces
- 1 can (10 ounces) diced tomatoes and green chiles
- 1 can (4 ounces) mild chopped green chiles
- 1 envelope from a package (2.20 ounces) of beefy onion dried soup mix
- 4 cups uncooked rice to serve

Combine all ingredients except rice in a Dutch oven. Stirring occasionally, cook over medium heat 20 minutes or until heated through. Store in an airtight container in refrigerator.

Yield: 2 suppers, about 5½ cups each

To serve: Bring 2 cups rice and 4 cups water to a boil in a medium saucepan over high heat; cover and reduce heat to low. Cook 20 minutes or until rice is tender. Heat Hoppin' John until hot. Serve over cooked rice.

Yield: about 8 servings per supper

STROGANOFF STEW

- ¼ cup all-purpose flour
- 1 teaspoon salt
- ½ teaspoon ground black pepper
- 1⅓ pounds stew meat
- 1 tablespoon vegetable oil
- 2 cans (10½ ounces each) beef broth
- 1½ cups water
- 2 large potatoes, peeled and chopped
- 6 carrots, peeled and chopped
- 1 pound fresh mushrooms, sliced
- 2 teaspoons dried minced garlic
- 1 cup sour cream

Sprinkle flour, salt, and pepper evenly over meat. In a large stockpot, heat oil over medium heat. Add meat; cook until brown, stirring occasionally.

Stirring constantly, gradually add beef broth and water. Add next 4 ingredients. Bring to a boil, reduce heat to medium-low, and simmer 50 to 55 minutes or until potatoes are tender.

Remove from heat; stir in sour cream. Serve hot.

Yield: 8 to 10 servings

Nourishing Stroganoff Stew is filled with chunks of beef, potatoes, carrots, and mushrooms in rich sour cream gravy.

THREE-BEAN CHILI

 2 pounds ground round
 1 tablespoon vegetable oil
 1 large red onion, cut into chunks
 1 large green pepper, cut into chunks
 1 jalepeño pepper, seeded and diced
 2 cloves garlic, minced
 1 cup red wine
 1/2 cup worcestershire sauce
 2 tablespoons chili powder
 1 teaspoon dry mustard
 1 teaspoon celery seeds
 1 teaspoon salt
 1/2 teaspoon ground black pepper
 3 cans (14.5 ounces each) Italian-style tomatoes, chopped with liquid
 1 can (15 ounces) black beans
 1 can (15 ounces) garbanzo beans
 1 can (15 ounces) kidney beans

Brown meat in a large Dutch oven; drain and remove from pan. Add oil to Dutch oven and sauté onion, green pepper, jalepeño, and garlic until soft, about 6 minutes. Add wine and Worcestershire; simmer 10 minutes. Stir in next 5 ingredients and simmer 10 minutes longer. Add tomatoes, beans (undrained), and meat to Dutch oven. Heat chili to boiling; reduce heat, cover, and simmer 30 minutes, stirring occasionally. Remove cover and simmer 30 minutes longer.

Yield: about 4 1/2 quarts of chili

VEGETARIAN CHILI

 1 package (16 ounces) frozen vegetable gumbo mix (okra, corn, celery, onion, and sweet red pepper)
 2 cans (16 ounces each) pinto beans, undrained
 2 cans (15 ounces each) black beans, undrained
 2 cans (14 1/2 ounces each) stewed tomatoes
 1 can (4 ounces) chopped green chilies, undrained
 2 tablespoons chili powder
 1 tablespoon sugar
 3/4 teaspoon salt
 1/4 teaspoon ground red pepper

In a Dutch oven over medium-high heat, combine all ingredients. Stirring occasionally, bring to a boil. Reduce heat to medium-low; simmer 20 to 30 minutes.

Yield: about 12 cups chili

WHITE CHILI

2 tablespoons vegetable oil
1 medium white onion, finely chopped
1 can (4½ ounces) chopped green chiles
2 teaspoons garlic powder
2 teaspoons salt
2 teaspoons ground cumin
2 teaspoons ground oregano
2 teaspoons ground coriander
½ teaspoon cayenne pepper
2 cans (15.8 ounces each) great Northern beans
2 cans (10½ ounces each) chicken broth
2 cans (5 ounces each) chicken, drained

In a large stockpot, heat oil over medium heat. Add onion; sauté until tender. Add green chiles, garlic powder, salt, cumin, oregano, coriander, and cayenne pepper; stir until well blended. Stir in undrained beans, chicken broth, and chicken. Bring to a boil; reduce heat to low and simmer 15 to 20 minutes or until heated through. Serve warm. Store in an airtight container in refrigerator.

Yield: 8 to 10 servings

TOMATO AND LEEK BISQUE

¼ cup olive oil
8 cups chopped leeks, white and pale green parts only (about 3 to 4 leeks)
2 ribs celery, coarsely chopped
1 clove garlic, chopped
2 cans (14½ ounces each) whole peeled tomatoes
1 can (14½ ounces) chicken broth
¾ cup dry white wine
1 tablespoon fresh lemon juice
1½ tablespoons chopped fresh basil leaves or 2 teaspoons dried basil leaves
½ teaspoon salt
¼ teaspoon ground white pepper
¾ cup whipping cream
Fresh or dried basil leaves to garnish

In a heavy Dutch oven, heat oil, leeks, celery, and garlic over medium-high heat; cook 8 to 10 minutes or until leeks are soft. Add tomatoes, chicken broth, wine, and lemon juice. Bring mixture to a boil; reduce heat to medium-low, cover, and simmer 30 minutes. Remove from heat; add 1½ tablespoons fresh basil, salt, and white pepper. Purée soup mixture in a food processor until smooth. Return soup to Dutch oven over low heat. Stirring occasionally, add whipping cream and simmer about 10 minutes or until thickened. Garnish with basil. Serve warm.

Yield: about 9 cups soup

Peanut butter, soy sauce, and chicken broth give Creamy Peanut Soup its unusual and robust taste.

CREAMY PEANUT SOUP

¼ cup butter or margarine
¾ cup finely chopped onion
¾ cup finely chopped celery
3 cloves garlic, minced
¼ teaspoon crushed red pepper flakes
3 tablespoons all-purpose flour
6 cups chicken broth
1½ cups smooth peanut butter
1 tablespoon soy sauce
Coarsely chopped peanuts to garnish

In a large saucepan, melt butter over medium-high heat. Add onion, celery, garlic, and red pepper flakes. Cook 5 minutes or until vegetables are tender. Sprinkle flour over vegetable mixture. Stirring constantly, cook 1 minute or until well blended. Whisking constantly, add chicken broth, peanut butter, and soy sauce. Reduce heat to medium low; whisking frequently, simmer about 15 minutes. Garnish with peanuts and serve hot.

Yield: about 8 cups soup

CHEESY CORN CHOWDER

2 cans (17 ounces each) yellow cream-style corn
1 can (10¾ ounces) cream of potato soup, undiluted
1 can (10¾ ounces) Cheddar cheese soup, undiluted
½ cup real bacon pieces (½ of a 2-ounce jar)
2 cups milk
2 teaspoons dried chopped onion
1 teaspoons dried parsley flakes
¼ teaspoon ground red pepper

In a large saucepan, combine all ingredients. Stirring occasionally, cook soup on medium-high heat until heated through. Store in an airtight container in refrigerator.

Yield: about 8 cups soup

A hearty blend of canned potato and Cheddar cheese soups with cream-style corn, Cheesy Corn Chowder is super easy to stir together.

"CRAZY QUILT" SOUP

4 cups vegetable cocktail juice
3 medium tomatoes, peeled, seeded, and finely chopped
1 medium cucumber, peeled, seeded, and finely chopped
1 medium green pepper, finely chopped
1 medium sweet yellow pepper, finely chopped
1/2 cup finely chopped celery
1/3 cup finely chopped green onions
2 tablespoons olive oil
2 tablespoons red wine vinegar
1 teaspoon Worcestershire sauce
1 clove garlic, minced
1/2 teaspoon salt
1/2 teaspoon ground black pepper
1/2 teaspoon hot pepper sauce
Cucumber slices and fresh dill weed to garnish

Combine all ingredients in a 3-quart nonmetal container. Cover and chill overnight.

To serve, stir soup; garnish each serving with cucumber slices and dill weed.

Yield: about 8 cups soup

BLACK-EYED PEA SOUP

6 slices bacon
1 large onion, finely chopped
1 clove garlic, minced
1 teaspoon salt
1/2 teaspoon ground black pepper
1 can (4 ounces) chopped jalapeño peppers
4 cans (15.8 ounces each) black-eyed peas
2 cans (14 1/2 ounces each) beef stock
1 can (10 ounces) diced tomatoes and green chilies

In a large stockpot, cook bacon over medium heat until crisp. Transfer to paper towels to drain; crumble bacon. Add next 5 ingredients to bacon drippings in pot; sauté until onion is brown. Add bacon and remaining ingredients. Increase heat to medium-high and bring to a boil. Remove from heat. Store in an airtight container in refrigerator.

To serve, transfer soup to a stockpot. Cook over medium-high heat 10 to 15 minutes or until heated through, stirring occasionally.

Yield: 12 to 14 servings

COCK-A-NOODLE SOUP

STOCK

1	(3½ to 4-pound) chicken
6	sprigs fresh parsley, stems included
2	onions, quartered
2	celery stalks, leaves included
2	bay leaves
1	turnip, quartered
1	teaspoon salt
1	teaspoon black peppercorns, crushed
½	teaspoon dried thyme

SOUP

3	quarts stock
⅔	cup finely chopped celery
½	cup finely chopped carrots
½	cup finely copped onion
2	teaspoons salt
½	teaspoons ground black pepper
2	cups uncooked thin egg noodles
3 to 4 cups shredded cooked chicken

For stock, place chicken in a Dutch oven with 5 quarts water. Add remaining stock ingredients and bring to a boil. Reduce heat to medium and simmer 30 minutes, skimming foam from the top. Partially cover pan; simmer 30 minutes longer or until juices run clear when chicken is pierced with a fork. Remove chicken and set aside to cool. Add 1 quart water to Dutch oven, partially cover, and simmer 1 hour longer. When chicken has cooled, remove skin and shred meat. Cover and refrigerate until ready to use.

Strain stock through a cheesecloth-lined sieve into a large bowl. Cover and refrigerate at least 8 hours. After refrigerating, skim fat from surface of stock.

For soup, combine 3 quarts stock in large Dutch oven with next 5 ingredients. Bring soup to a boil; cover and reduce heat to low. Cook 30 minutes or until vegetables are tender.

Prepare noodles following package instructions. Add noodles and shredded chicken to soup and simmer 5 minutes.

Yield: about 4 quarts of soup

Chopped green chiles and cumin give our Chicken and Rice Soup a hot, peppery flavor.

CHICKEN AND RICE SOUP

3 pound broiler-fryer chicken
  (discard giblets)
6½ cups water
1 medium onion, cut into large
  pieces
2 ribs celery with leaves, cut into
  pieces
1 clove garlic
1 bay leaf
1 cup thinly sliced carrots
⅔ cup uncooked long-grain rice
½ cup finely chopped onion
1 can (4½ ounces) chopped
  green chiles
2 chicken bouillon cubes
¼ teaspoon salt
¼ teaspoon ground white pepper
¼ teaspoon ground cumin
  Chopped green onions to
  garnish

Place chicken, water, onion pieces, celery, garlic, and bay leaf in a stockpot over high heat; bring to a boil. Cover and reduce heat to medium-low; simmer 1 hour or until chicken is tender. Strain chicken stock and chill; discard vegetables. Skin and bone chicken. Cut meat into bite-size pieces; chill.

Skim fat from chicken stock. Combine chicken stock, carrots, rice, chopped onion, green chiles, bouillon, salt, white pepper, and cumin in a Dutch oven over medium-high heat; bring mixture to a boil. Reduce heat to low; cover and simmer 30 minutes, adding chicken pieces during last 10 minutes. Garnish with green onions and serve warm.

Yield: about 9 cups soup

CHEESY BROCCOLI SOUP

  1 quart water
  2 packages (10 ounces each) frozen chopped broccoli
  1 cup frozen chopped onion
  1 can ($10^3/_4$ ounces) cream of celery soup
  1 can ($10^3/_4$ ounces) Cheddar cheese soup
  2 packages (8 ounces each) shredded pasteurized process cheese
  1 teaspoon paprika
 $^1/_8$ teaspoon ground red pepper

Combine water, broccoli, and onion in a Dutch oven over medium-high heat. Bring to a boil and cook about 2 minutes or until broccoli is tender (do not drain). Reduce heat to medium-low and stir in soups, cheese, paprika, and red pepper. Stirring frequently, cook about 5 minutes or until cheese melts. Serve warm. Store in an airtight container in refrigerator.

Yield: about $10^1/_2$ cups soup

EASY FOUR-BEAN SOUP

  4 slices bacon
 $1^1/_2$ cups chopped onions
  1 can ($4^1/_2$ ounces) chopped green chiles
  1 clove garlic, minced
  2 cans ($14^1/_2$ ounces each) beef broth
  1 can (16 ounces) pinto beans
  1 can (16 ounces) navy beans
  1 can (15.8 ounces) great Northern beans
  1 can (15 ounces) black beans
  1 can (10 ounces) diced tomatoes and green chiles
  1 teaspoon ground cumin
  1 teaspoon ground black pepper
 $^1/_2$ teaspoon salt

In a Dutch oven, cook bacon over medium-low heat until crisp. Reserving drippings in skillet, drain bacon on paper towels and crumble. Increase heat to medium. Sauté onions, green chiles, and garlic in bacon drippings until onions are tender and begin to brown. Add beef broth, undrained beans, tomatoes and green chiles, cumin, pepper, salt, and bacon. Increase heat to medium high; bring mixture to a boil. Reduce heat to low; cover and simmer 30 minutes to let flavors blend. Serve warm.

Yield: about 12 cups soup

BUSY DAY POTATO SOUP MIX

- 1 package (6.6 ounces) dried potato flakes
- 2 tablespoons dried minced onions
- 2 tablespoons chicken bouillon granules
- 2 teaspoons celery salt
- 2 teaspoons dried parsley flakes
- 2 teaspoons dried chopped chives
- 1/2 teaspoon garlic powder
- 1/2 teaspoon salt
- 1/4 teaspoon ground black pepper
- 1/8 teaspoon ground red pepper

In a medium bowl, combine potato flakes, minced onions, bouillon, celery salt, parsley flakes, chopped chives, garlic powder, salt, black pepper, and red pepper. Store in an airtight container.

Yield: about 4 cups soup mix

To serve: In a 2-cup microwave-safe container, combine 1/3 cup soup mix with 1 cup milk. Microwave on high power (100%) 3 minutes or until soup is thick and smooth and onions are tender, stirring after each minute.

Yield: about 1 cup soup

BLACK BEAN SOUP

- 1 package (16 ounces) dried black beans
- 10 cups water
- 8 slices bacon
- 1 can (10 1/2 ounces) chicken broth
- 3 large carrots, finely chopped
- 1 large onion, finely chopped
- 2 tablespoons garlic powder
- 1 tablespoon salt
- 1 teaspoon ground cumin
- 1 teaspoon ground black pepper
- 1 cup cooked rice

In a large stock pot, soak beans in water 8 hours or overnight. In a small skillet, cook bacon until crisp, drain on paper towels, and crumble. Add bacon and next 7 ingredients to beans; mix well. Bring to a boil over medium-high heat. Reduce heat to medium, cover, and simmer 3 hours or until beans are soft. Remove from heat; stir in rice. Store in an airtight container in refrigerator.

To reheat, transfer soup to a large stockpot. Cook over medium heat 10 to 15 minutes or until heated through.

Yield: about 8 cups soup

TURKEY AND SAUSAGE GUMBO

- ½ cup vegetable oil
- ¾ cup all-purpose flour
- 1 package (1 pound, 2 ounces) frozen sliced okra, thawed
- 1 cup chopped onion
- ¾ cup chopped celery
- ¾ cup chopped green onions
- ½ cup chopped green pepper
- 2 cloves garlic, minced
- 6 cups turkey stock or canned chicken broth
- 4 cups chopped cooked turkey
- 1 pound smoked sausage, sliced
- 1 can (14½ ounces) diced tomatoes
- 2 teaspoons hot pepper sauce
- 1 teaspoon dried thyme leaves
- 1 teaspoon dried marjoram leaves
- 1 teaspoon salt
- ½ teaspoon ground black pepper
- ¼ teaspoon ground red pepper
- 2 bay leaves
- 1 package (16 ounces) frozen cooked and peeled cocktail shrimp, thawed
- 1 teaspoon filé powder
  Cooked rice to serve

Combine oil and flour in a heavy large Dutch oven over medium heat. Stirring constantly, cook 13 to 15 minutes or until mixture forms a brown roux. Reduce heat to medium-low and stir in okra, onion, celery, green onions, green pepper, and garlic. Cook 15 minutes or until vegetables are tender. Stir in turkey stock, turkey, sausage, tomatoes, pepper sauce, thyme, marjoram, salt, black pepper, red pepper, and bay leaves. Increase heat to medium-high and bring to a boil. Reduce heat to low; cover and simmer 1 hour, stirring occasionally. Remove lid and simmer 30 minutes or until desired thickness. Remove from heat; stir in shrimp and filé powder. Remove bay leaves. Serve gumbo over rice.

Yield: about 4 quarts gumbo

SPICY GAZPACHO

- 3 tomatoes, chopped
- 1 cucumber, chopped
- 1 green pepper, chopped
- 1 onion, chopped
- ¾ cup chopped fresh parsley
- 2 cloves garlic, minced
- 3½ cups liquid Bloody Mary mix
- ¼ cup white wine vinegar
- ¼ cup olive oil
- ½ teaspoon salt
- ¼ teaspoon ground black pepper

In a large bowl, combine first 6 ingredients. In a separate bowl, use a wire whisk to blend remaining ingredients. Add liquid to vegetable mixture, stirring to combine. Cover and refrigerate at least 2 hours before serving. Serve cold. Store in airtight container in refrigerator.

Yield: about 8 cups of soup

A glass trifle bowl provides a taste-tempting view of Seventh Heaven Layered Salad.

SEVENTH HEAVEN LAYERED SALAD

DRESSING
    1 package (8 ounces) cream cheese,
         softened
    1 cup mayonnaise
    1 cup sour cream
    1 teaspoon dried ground basil
         leaves
  ½ teaspoon garlic powder
  ½ teaspoon onion powder

SALAD
  ½ head iceberg lettuce, chopped
    2 large tomatoes, chopped
    1 large cucumber, sliced
    4 large carrots, peeled and sliced
  10 green onions, finely chopped
    2 cups (8 ounces) grated sharp
         Cheddar cheese
    1 pound bacon, cooked and
         crumbled

For dressing, combine all ingredients in a medium bowl; blend well using medium speed of an electric mixer. Cover and set aside.

For salad, layer vegetables and cheese in desired order in a trifle bowl or large glass container. Spread dressing evenly over vegetables. Garnish with crumbled bacon. Cover and store in refrigerator.

Yield: about 10 servings

Filled with juicy pineapple, tender chicken, and crunchy celery, tropical Chicken Chutney Salad is enhanced with curry powder and sweet chutney. Toasted almonds lend delicious texture to the dish.

CHICKEN CHUTNEY SALAD

- 3 cups diced cooked chicken
- 1 cup canned pineapple chunks, drained with juice reserved
- ³/₄ cup sliced celery
- ¹/₂ cup mayonnaise
- ¹/₄ cup sour cream
- 3 tablespoons prepared chutney
- 1 teaspoon curry powder
- ¹/₂ cup slivered almonds, toasted

In a large bowl, combine chicken, pineapple, and celery. In a separate bowl, use a wire whisk to blend 3 tablespoons reserved juice with remaining ingredients, except almonds. Stir into chicken mixture. Cover and refrigerate at least 1 hour. Stir in almonds before serving. If desired, serve on lettuce leaves.

Yield: about 4 to 6 servings

"BOWL OF FRUIT" SALAD

DRESSING

- 1 package (3 ounces) cream cheese, softened
- 1/3 cup apple cider
- 1/4 cup honey
- 3 egg yolks
- 3 tablespoons apple cider vinegar
- 1/2 teaspoon ground cinnamon
- 1/8 teaspoon salt

SALAD

- 1 pear, cored and chopped
- 1 red apple, cored and chopped
- 1 green apple, cored and chopped
- 2 teaspoons freshly squeezed lemon juice
- 1 1/2 cups miniature marshmallows
- 1 cup seedless red grapes
- 1 cup seedless green grapes
- 1 cup chopped walnuts, toasted
- 1/2 cup finely sliced celery

For dressing, beat cream cheese until smooth in a medium bowl; beat in apple cider, honey, egg yolks, vinegar, cinnamon, and salt. Pour mixture into the top of a double boiler over simmering water. Whisking constantly, cook 12 to 15 minutes or until thickened. Remove from heat; cool.

For salad, combine pear and apple pieces in a large bowl. Sprinkle lemon juice over fruit and toss. Stir in marshmallows, grapes, walnuts, and celery. Pour dressing over fruit mixture; stir until well blended. Cover and chill until ready to serve.

Yield: 14 to 16 servings

ROSEMARY CHICKEN-POTATO SALAD

- 1/4 cup chicken broth
- 4 tablespoons freshly squeezed lemon juice, divided
- 3 tablespoons honey
- 2 tablespoons coarsely chopped fresh rosemary
- 1 clove garlic, minced
- 1 1/2 teaspoons salt, divided
- 1/4 plus 1/8 teaspoon ground black pepper, divided
- 1 1/4 pounds boneless, skinless chicken breasts
- 2 pounds red potatoes, peeled and cubed
- 1 cup mayonnaise
- 1/2 cup finely chopped celery
- 1/4 cup finely chopped green onions
- 1/4 cup chopped sweet red pepper
- 1 tablespoon finely chopped fresh parsley
- 1/2 teaspoon grated lemon zest

In a medium bowl, combine chicken broth, 3 tablespoons lemon juice, honey, rosemary, garlic, 1/4 teaspoon salt, and 1/8 teaspoon black pepper. Place chicken in marinade, turning to coat well. Cover and chill 30 minutes.

Place potatoes in a heavy medium saucepan. Add water to cover potatoes. Add 3/4 teaspoon salt. Cover and cook over medium-high heat about 15 minutes or just until tender. Drain and cool.

Place chicken and marinade in a medium skillet. Cover and cook over medium-low heat 25 to 30 minutes, turning once halfway through cooking time. Discard liquid and cool chicken slightly; cut into about 1/2-inch pieces. In a large bowl, combine chicken and potatoes.

In a medium bowl, combine mayonnaise, celery, green onions, red pepper, parsley, remaining 1 tablespoon lemon juice, lemon zest, remaining 1/2 teaspoon salt, and remaining 1/4 teaspoon black pepper. Add dressing to chicken mixture; gently toss until coated. Cover and store in refrigerator.

Yield: about 8 cups salad

NUTTY CHICKEN-BROCCOLI SALAD

- 1 cup mayonnaise
- 1/4 cup sugar
- 5 tablespoons raspberry vinegar
- 2 cups cubed cooked chicken breast
- 8 ounces bacon, cooked and crumbled
- 4 cups small fresh broccoli flowerets (about 2 pounds)
- 1/2 cup dry-roasted cashews
- 1/2 cup sunflower kernels
- 1/2 cup chopped red onion
- 1/2 cup golden raisins

In a small bowl, combine mayonnaise, sugar, and vinegar; whisk dressing until well blended. In a large bowl, combine chicken, bacon, broccoli, cashews, sunflower kernels, onion, and raisins. Add dressing to chicken mixture; stir until well coated. Cover and chill 2 hours to let flavors blend. Store in an airtight container in refrigerator.

Yield: about 8 cups salad

SALMON PASTA SALAD

- 1 1/3 cups mayonnaise
- 1 cup finely chopped green onions
- 2/3 cup finely chopped celery
- 1/4 cup chopped fresh dill weed
- 2 tablespoons freshly squeezed lemon juice
- 2 teaspoons prepared mustard
- 1/2 teaspoon ground black pepper
- 1 package (12 ounces) seashell pasta, cooked
- 4 packages (3 ounces each) smoked salmon, cut into pieces
  Fresh dill weed sprigs to garnish

In a large bowl, combine mayonnaise, green onions, celery, dill weed, lemon juice, mustard, and pepper; stir until well blended. Add pasta; stir until well coated. Stir in salmon. Cover and chill 2 hours to let flavors blend. Garnish with dill weed.

Yield: about 9 1/2 cups salad

CHICKEN-CUCUMBER SALAD

1½ pounds boneless, skinless chicken breasts
1 package (8 ounces) cream cheese, softened
½ cup sour cream
2 tablespoons dry white wine
1½ teaspoons garlic powder
1 teaspoon salt
½ teaspoon ground black pepper
½ teaspoon dried dill weed
½ teaspoon hot pepper sauce
1 cup peeled, diced cucumber
½ cup chopped green onions
4 acorn squash, halved lengthwise and seeded
Fresh carrot and green pepper slices to garnish

In a medium saucepan, cover chicken with water. Bring to a boil, reduce heat to medium-low, and simmer 30 to 35 minutes or until chicken is cooked; drain. Cool 10 minutes and cut into bite-size pieces.

In a medium bowl, beat cream cheese and sour cream until fluffy. Beat in wine, garlic powder, salt, pepper, dill weed, and pepper sauce. Stir in chicken, cucumber, and green onions. Cut a thin slice off bottom of each squash half so squash will sit level. Spoon chicken salad into each squash half. Refer to photo and garnish with carrot and green pepper slices. Cover and refrigerate until ready to serve.

Yield: 8 servings

Cool, creamy Chicken-Cucumber Salad is attractively presented in acorn squash halves.

For a Waldorf salad with a twist, try Apple-Pecan Salad.

APPLE-PECAN SALAD

 6 cups unpeeled, coarsely
    chopped apples
 2 tablespoons lemon juice
 1/2 cup finely chopped celery
 1/2 cup raisins
 1/2 cup chopped pecans, toasted
 1/2 cup sour cream
 1/2 cup mayonnaise
 6 tablespoons sugar
    Red leaf lettuce to serve

In a large bowl, toss apples and lemon juice. Stir in celery, raisins, and pecans. In a small bowl, combine sour cream, mayonnaise, and sugar. Stir sour cream mixture into apple mixture. Cover and chill until ready to serve. Serve in a lettuce-lined bowl.

Yield: about 7 cups salad

SUMMER VEGETABLE SALAD

 3 cups fresh broccoli flowerets
 3 cups shredded cabbage
 2 cups thinly sliced zucchini
 1 1/2 cups sliced red onion
 1 1/2 cups thinly sliced carrots
 1 1/2 cups (about 6 ounces)
        shredded sharp Cheddar cheese
 1/3 cup olive oil
 1/3 cup buttermilk
 1/4 cup red wine vinegar
 1 teaspoon grainy mustard
 2 teaspoons salt
 1/2 teaspoon ground black pepper
 1/4 teaspoon garlic powder

In a large bowl, combine vegetables and cheese. In a medium bowl, whisk together remaining ingredients. Pour oil mixture over vegetables; toss until well coated. Cover and store in refrigerator.

Yield: about 10 cups salad

BACON BATTER BREAD

1 pound bacon
3 cups all-purpose flour
¼ cup granulated sugar
2 tablespoons baking powder
2 teaspoons salt
3 eggs
½ teaspoon liquid smoke flavoring
1½ cups milk

In a large skillet, cook bacon over medium heat until crisp. Transfer to paper towels to drain; reserve ⅓ cup bacon drippings. Cool bacon to room temperature, crumble, and set aside.

Preheat oven to 350 degrees. In a large bowl, combine next 4 ingredients. In a medium bowl, whisk together reserved bacon drippings and next 3 ingredients. Add egg mixture to dry ingredients; stir just until moistened. Fold in bacon. Pour batter into a greased 5 x 9-inch loaf pan. Bake 45 to 50 minutes or until a toothpick inserted in center comes out clean. Cool in pan 10 minutes; turn onto a wire rack to cool completely. Store in an airtight container.

Yield: 1 loaf bread

MEXICAN CORN BREAD

MIX

2 cups yellow cornmeal
½ cup all-purpose flour
1 tablespoon sugar
2 teaspoons baking powder
1 teaspoon salt
1 teaspoon ground red pepper
½ teaspoon baking soda

In a large bowl, combine cornmeal, flour, sugar, baking powder, salt, red pepper, and baking soda. Store in a resealable plastic bag.

Yield: about 2½ cups mix

BREAD

2 tablespoons butter or margarine
1 bag (about 2½ cups) Mexican Corn Bread Mix
1 can (12 ounces) beer
2 eggs, lightly beaten

Preheat oven to 425 degrees. Place butter in an 8-inch round baking pan or skillet. Place pan in oven to melt butter and to heat pan. In a medium bowl, combine corn bread mix, beer, and eggs. Stir just until blended. Pour into hot pan. Bake 25 to 30 minutes or until lightly browned. Serve warm.

Yield: 6 to 8 servings

HONEY-CHEESE ROLLS

8 cups all-purpose flour, divided
2 teaspoons salt
2 packages active dry yeast
3/4 cup butter or margarine, divided
2 cups (8 ounces) grated Cheddar
  cheese
1 1/2 cups milk
1/3 cup honey
3 eggs

In a large bowl, combine 6 cups flour, salt, and yeast; stir until well blended. In a medium saucepan, combine 1/2 cup butter and next 3 ingredients. Cook over medium heat until a thermometer registers 130 degrees (butter may not be completely melted). Add eggs and cheese mixture alternately to dry ingredients, mixing until a soft dough forms. Gradually stir in remaining flour. Turn dough onto a lightly floured surface; knead about 10 minutes or until dough becomes soft and elastic. Transfer to a large greased bowl. Melt remaining butter in a small saucepan over low heat. Brush top of dough with 1/2 of melted butter and cover. Let rise in a warm place (80 to 85 degrees) 1 hour or until doubled in size.

Turn dough onto a lightly floured surface and punch down. Shape dough into 3-inch balls and place with sides touching in greased round 9-inch cake pans. If necessary, remelt remaining butter. Brush tops of rolls with melted butter and cover. Let rise about 1 hour or until doubled in size.

Preheat oven to 375 degrees. Bake 30 to 35 minutes or until golden brown. Cool completely in pan. Store in an airtight container.

To reheat, preheat oven to 350 degrees. Bake rolls uncovered 3 to 5 minutes or until heated through.

Yield: about 2 dozen rolls

CUMIN BREAD

3 cups all-purpose flour
1/4 cup granulated sugar
2 tablespoons baking powder
4 teaspoons ground cumin
2 teaspoons salt
1 teaspoon cumin seed, crushed
1/2 teaspoon dry mustard
3 eggs
1 1/2 cups milk
1/3 cup vegetable oil
3 tablespoons picante sauce

Preheat oven to 350 degrees. In a large bowl, combine first 7 ingredients. In a medium bowl, whisk together remaining ingredients. Add egg mixture to dry ingredients; stir just until batter is moist. Pour batter evenly into 3 greased 3 x 5 1/2-inch loaf pans. Bake 25 to 30 minutes or until a toothpick inserted in center comes out clean. Cool in pans 10 minutes; turn onto a wire rack to cool completely. Store in an airtight container. Bread may be served at room temperature or warm.

To reheat, preheat oven to 350 degrees. Bake uncovered on an ungreased baking sheet 3 to 5 minutes or until heated through.

Yield: 3 loaves bread

Hot Garlic-Cheese Loaves are easily prepared with buttermilk baking mix and shredded sharp Cheddar cheese.

HOT GARLIC-CHEESE LOAVES

3½ cups buttermilk baking mix
2½ cups (10 ounces) shredded
    sharp Cheddar cheese
  1 teaspoon garlic powder
 ¼ teaspoon ground red pepper
1¼ cups milk
  2 eggs, beaten

Preheat oven to 350 degrees. In a large bowl, combine baking mix, cheese, garlic powder, and red pepper. Add milk and eggs to dry ingredients; mix only until ingredients are moistened. Spoon batter into 4 greased and floured 3¼ x 6-inch baking pans. Bake 30 to 35 minutes or until lightly browned. Cool in pans 5 minutes. Remove from pans and cool completely on a wire rack. Store in an airtight container.

Yield: 4 mini loaves bread

BUCKWHEAT ROLLS

2 packages dry yeast
$1/2$ cup warm water
$1^1/4$ cups buckwheat groats
$1/2$ cup old-fashioned rolled oats
$1/4$ cup firmly packed brown sugar
$1/4$ cup butter or margarine, melted
1 tablespoon salt
$1^3/4$ cups boiling water
4 cups bread flour, divided
Vegetable cooking spray
$1/8$ cup blue cornmeal

In a small bowl, dissolve yeast in $1/2$ cup warm water. In a large bowl, combine buckwheat, oats, sugar, butter, salt, and $1^3/4$ cups boiling water; let stand 10 minutes. Stir in yeast mixture and 1 cup flour. Gradually add remaining flour; stir until a soft dough forms. Turn onto a lightly floured surface and knead until dough becomes smooth and elastic. Place in a large bowl sprayed with cooking spray, turning once to coat top of dough. Cover and let rise in a warm place (80 to 85 degrees) $1^1/2$ to 2 hours or until doubled in size. Turn dough onto a lightly floured surface and punch down. Shape dough into 2-inch balls and place 2 inches apart on a greased baking sheet. Using a serrated knife, make decorative cuts $1/4$-inch-deep in tops of rolls. Spray tops of rolls with cooking spray, sprinkle with cornmeal, cover, and let rise in a warm place 1 hour or until doubled in size. Preheat oven to 400 degrees. Bake 18 to 20 minutes or until golden brown. Serve warm.

Yield: about $2^1/2$ dozen rolls

Lightly sprinkled with blue cornmeal, old-fashioned Buckwheat Rolls are great warm or cold.

SPAGHETTI BREAD

3½ ounces (½ of 7-ounce package)
    thin spaghetti, cooked, drained,
    and rinsed with cold water
2 cups all-purpose flour
1 cup whole wheat flour
⅓ cup grated Parmesan cheese
1 package active dry yeast
1 tablespoon granulated sugar
1 teaspoon garlic salt
½ teaspoon dried basil leaves
½ teaspoon dried oregano leaves
1½ cups warm water
1 tablespoon olive oil

In a large bowl, combine first 9 ingredients. In a medium bowl, whisk together water and oil. Gradually add oil mixture to dry ingredients; knead until a soft dough forms. Turn dough onto a lightly floured surface and knead about 5 minutes or until dough becomes elastic and pliable. Place dough in a greased bowl; grease top of dough. Cover and let rise in a warm place (80 to 85 degrees) 1 hour or until doubled in size. Turn dough onto a lightly floured surface and punch down. Shape into a loaf and place in a greased 5 x 9-inch loaf pan. Grease top of dough. Cover and let rise in a warm place 1 hour or until doubled in size.

Preheat oven to 350 degrees. Bake 30 to 35 minutes or until brown and bread sounds hollow when tapped. Transfer to a wire rack to cool completely. Store in an airtight container.

Yield: 1 loaf bread

CHICKEN TURNOVERS

1 tablespoon sesame oil
6 green onions, chopped
½ pound fresh mushrooms, chopped
3 cloves garlic, minced
½ teaspoon salt
¼ teaspoon ground black pepper
1 can (5 ounces) chicken, drained
1 package (17¼ ounces) frozen
    puff pastry dough, thawed
    according to package directions
4 ounces Havarti cheese, grated

Preheat oven to 350 degrees. In a large skillet, heat oil over medium heat. Add next 5 ingredients; sauté until onions are brown. Stir in chicken. Remove from heat.

On a lightly floured surface, use a floured rolling pin to roll out each sheet of pastry to an 8 x 12-inch rectangle. Using a sharp knife, cut pastry into 4-inch squares. Spoon about 1 tablespoon chicken mixture into center of each square. Sprinkle about 2 teaspoons cheese over chicken mixture. Fold pastry over chicken and cheese, forming a triangle. Crimp edges together with a fork. Transfer to a greased baking sheet. Bake 20 to 25 minutes or until brown. Transfer to a wire rack to cool completely. Serve at room temperature. Store leftovers in an airtight container in refrigerator.

To reheat, preheat oven to 350 degrees. Bake uncovered on an ungreased baking sheet 8 to 10 minutes or until heated through.

Yield: 1 dozen turnovers

CORN BREAD LOAF

Slices of sage-flavored Corn Bread Loaf are a tasty variation of traditional dressing.

    6   tablespoons butter or margarine
    1   cup chopped green onions
  3/4   cup chopped celery
    4   cups corn bread crumbs
    4   cups finely crumbled white bread
   10   slices bacon, cooked and
          crumbled
 1 1/2 teaspoons ground sage
  3/4   teaspoon salt
  1/2   teaspoon ground black pepper
    6   eggs, beaten
    1   cup chicken broth

Preheat oven to 350 degrees. In a large skillet, melt butter over medium-high heat. Stir in onions and celery; sauté 8 minutes or until soft. In a large bowl, combine bread crumbs. Stir in onion mixture and next 4 ingredients. Stir in eggs and chicken broth. Spoon evenly into a greased and floured 4 x 12-inch loaf pan. Bake 30 to 40 minutes or until top is brown. Unmold onto serving plate and slice. Serve immediately.

Yield: about 10 servings

HUSH PUPPY MIX

 1 1/2 cups yellow cornmeal
  3/4   cup all-purpose flour
    3   tablespoons dried minced onion
    1   teaspoon baking powder
    1   teaspoon sugar
    1   teaspoon salt
  1/2   teaspoon baking soda
  1/4   teaspoon ground red pepper

In a large bowl, combine cornmeal, flour, onion, baking powder, sugar, salt, baking soda, and red pepper. Store in a resealable plastic bag.

Yield: about 2 1/4 cups mix

To serve: Heat about 1 1/2 inches vegetable oil to 350 degrees in a deep skillet. In a medium bowl, combine 1 1/4 cups buttermilk, 1 beaten egg, and mix; stir until well blended. Drop mixture by tablespoonfuls into hot oil. Fry until golden brown and thoroughly cooked. Drain on paper towels. Serve warm.

Yield: about 3 dozen hush puppies

SOUTHWEST OLIVE BREAD

3 cups self-rising yellow cornmeal mix
1 teaspoon ground cumin
1/4 teaspoon ground red pepper
1 1/2 cups milk
2 eggs
1/4 cup vegetable oil
1 cup (4 ounces) shredded sharp Cheddar cheese
2 jars (5 3/4 ounces each) whole stuffed green olives, drained

Preheat oven to 375 degrees. In a medium bowl, combine cornmeal mix, cumin, and red pepper. Add milk, eggs, and oil; stir until well blended. Add remaining ingredients, stirring well. Spoon batter into 4 greased and floured 3 x 5 1/2-inch loaf pans. Bake 35 to 40 minutes or until bread is golden brown and a toothpick inserted in center of bread comes out clean. Cool in pans on a wire rack 5 minutes. Run a knife around edges of pans to loosen bread; remove from pans. Serve warm.

Yield: 4 mini loaves bread

SWISS CHEESE BREAD

4 cups all-purpose flour
2 tablespoons sugar
1 tablespoon baking powder
1 1/2 teaspoons salt
1/2 cup chilled butter or margarine, cut into pieces
4 cups (16 ounces) shredded Swiss cheese
1 tablespoon dried dill weed
2 cups milk
2 eggs

Preheat oven to 400 degrees. In a large bowl, combine flour, sugar, baking powder, and salt. Using a pastry blender or 2 knives, cut in butter until mixture resembles coarse meal. Stir in cheese and dill weed. In a medium bowl, whisk together milk and eggs. Add milk mixture to flour mixture; stir just until moistened. Pour batter evenly into 7 greased 3 x 5 1/2-inch loaf pans. Bake 20 to 25 minutes or until a toothpick inserted in center of bread comes out clean. Cool 10 minutes in pans. Remove from pans and serve warm or cool completely on a wire rack.

Yield: 7 mini loaves bread

EASY PUMPERNICKEL BREAD

- 1 package (16 ounces) hot roll mix
- 3/4 cup warm (105 to 115 degrees) strongly brewed coffee
- 2 eggs
- 1/4 cup molasses
- 3/4 cup rye flour
- 3 teaspoons caraway seed, divided
- 2 teaspoons cocoa
  Vegetable cooking spray
- 1 egg white, lightly beaten

In a small bowl, sprinkle yeast from roll mix over coffee; allow yeast to soften. Stir in eggs and molasses. In a medium bowl, combine roll mix, rye flour, 2 teaspoons caraway seed, and cocoa. Add yeast mixture; stir until a soft dough forms. Place in a large bowl sprayed with cooking spray, turning once to coat top of dough. Cover and let rise in a warm place (80 to 85 degrees) about 1 hour or until doubled in size.

Turn dough onto a lightly floured surface and knead 3 minutes or until dough becomes smooth and elastic. Shape dough into 2 round loaves and place on a greased baking sheet. Spray tops of dough with cooking spray, cover, and let rise in a warm place 1 hour or until doubled in size.

Preheat oven to 350 degrees. Brush dough with egg white and sprinkle with remaining 1 teaspoon caraway seed. Bake 25 to 30 minutes or until bread is golden brown and sounds hollow when tapped. Transfer to a wire rack to cool completely. Store in an airtight container.

Yield: 2 loaves bread

STUFFED FRENCH LOAF

- 1 loaf (16 ounces) French bread
- 8 ounces spicy bulk pork sausage
- 1/3 cup chopped onion
- 1 clove garlic, minced
- 1 egg
- 2 tablespoons chopped fresh parsley
- 1 tablespoon Dijon-style mustard, divided
- 3/4 cup shredded extra-sharp Cheddar cheese
- 1/2 cup grated Parmesan cheese
- 1/4 cup olive oil
- 1 teaspoon ground black pepper

Preheat oven to 350 degrees. Slice bread in half lengthwise and slightly hollow out each half, leaving a 1/2-inch-thick layer of bread. Place bread crumbs in container of a blender or food processor and process 15 to 20 seconds or until finely chopped.

Cook sausage, onion, and garlic in a heavy skillet over medium heat until meat is brown; drain. In a large bowl, combine bread crumbs, meat mixture, egg, parsley, and 1 teaspoon mustard; set aside.

Using a blender or food processor, process cheeses, olive oil, remaining 2 teaspoons mustard, and pepper until mixture forms a paste, about 1 minute. Spread cheese mixture evenly over inside of each bread half. Spoon meat mixture into cavity of each bread half. Place bread halves together. Wrap loaf in foil. Bake 30 to 35 minutes or until heated through. Cut into 1-inch-thick slices.

Yield: about 16 servings

"SOUP-ER" BREADS

- 4 cups all-purpose flour
- 2 teaspoons backing powder
- 2 teaspoons baking soda
- ¼ cup dry tomato soup mix
- ¼ teaspoon basil
- ⅓ cup dry herb soup mix
- 2 tablespoons dry golden onion soup mix
- 2 eggs
- ½ cup butter or margarine
- ½ cup granulated sugar
- 2 cups sour cream
- ⅔ cup milk

Preheat over to 350 degrees. In a large bowl, combine flour, baking powder, and baking soda. Using 3 smaller bowls, place 1⅓ cups dry mixture into each bowl. Add tomato soup mix and basil to first bowl for Tomato-Basil Bread, herb soup mix to second for Herb Bread, and onion soup mix to third for Onion Bread. Blend each thoroughly.

In a separate bowl, beat eggs, butter, and sugar until smooth. Stir in sour cream and milk. Pour 1⅓ cups batter into each dry mixture. Stir just until combined.

For a total of 6 loaves, spoon each batter into 2 greased and floured 5¾ x 3 x 2-inch loaf pans. Bake 30 to 35 minutes, testing for doneness with a toothpick. Cool in pans 10 minutes; remove and serve warm.

To reheat bread, wrap in aluminum foil heat 10 to 15 minutes at 350 degrees or lightly toast in toaster oven.

Yield: 6 small loaves

Note: If desired, 1 or 2 varieties of soup may be used to flavor the entire batter mix. Adjust amount of dry soup mixture accordingly.

COOKING TIPS

MEASURING INGREDIENTS

Liquid measuring cups have a rim above the measuring line to keep liquid ingredients from spilling. Nested measuring cups are used to measure dry ingredients, butter, shortening, and peanut butter. Measuring spoons are used for measuring both dry and liquid ingredients.

To measure flour or granulated sugar: Spoon ingredient into nested measuring cup and level off with a knife. Do not pack down with spoon.

To measure dry ingredients equaling less than ¼ cup: Dip measuring spoon into ingredient and level off with a knife.

To measure butter, shortening, or peanut butter: Pack ingredient firmly into nested measuring cup and level off with a knife.

You can create a trio of hearty breads from a single recipe! Three equal portions are each flavored with a dry soup mix to make Tomato-Basil Bread, Herb Bread, or Onion Bread.

SWEET POTATO QUICK BREAD

BREAD

- 2 cups all-purpose baking mix
- ¾ cup firmly packed brown sugar
- ½ cup quick-cooking oats
- 1½ teaspoons ground cinnamon
- ⅛ teaspoon ground cloves
- ⅛ teaspoon ground nutmeg
- 1 cup cooked, mashed sweet potatoes
- ½ cup milk
- 2 eggs
- ¼ cup butter or margarine, melted
- ½ cup chopped walnuts

TOPPING

- 2 tablespoons chopped walnuts
- 2 tablespoons firmly packed brown sugar
- 2 tablespoons quick-cooking oats
- 2 tablespoons butter, melted

Preheat oven to 350 degrees. For bread, combine baking mix, brown sugar, oats, cinnamon, cloves, and nutmeg in a large bowl. In a medium bowl, combine sweet potatoes, milk, eggs, and melted butter; beat until well blended. Stir into dry ingredients; beat until blended. Stir in walnuts. Spoon into a greased 5 x 9-inch loaf pan.

For topping, combine walnuts, brown sugar, oats, and melted butter in a small bowl; stir until blended. Sprinkle topping over batter. Bake 45 to 55 minutes or until a toothpick inserted in center of bread comes out with a few crumbs attached. Cool in pan 5 minutes. Remove from pan and cool completely on a wire rack. Store in an airtight container.

Yield: 1 loaf bread

HOMESTYLE SWEET POTATO BISCUITS

- 2 cups all-purpose flour
- 2½ teaspoons baking powder
- ½ teaspoon salt
- ¼ cup chilled butter or margarine
- ¼ cup vegetable shortening
- 1 cup cooked, mashed sweet potatoes
- 5 to 7 tablespoons buttermilk

Preheat oven to 450 degrees. In a large bowl, combine flour, baking powder, and salt. Using a pastry blender or 2 knives, cut in butter and shortening until well blended. Add sweet potatoes and enough buttermilk to make a soft dough. Lightly knead dough about 20 times. On a lightly floured surface, roll out dough to ½-inch thickness. Use a 2-inch biscuit cutter to cut out biscuits. Bake on an ungreased baking sheet 12 to 15 minutes or until biscuits are light golden brown. Serve warm.

Yield: about 2 dozen biscuits

ZUCCHINI-BRAN BREAD

3 eggs
1 cup vegetable oil
2 cups grated zucchini
2 cups granulated sugar
3 teaspoons vanilla extract
2 cups all-purpose flour
1 cup whole bran cereal
3 teaspoons ground cinnamon
$1/2$ teaspoons salt
1 teaspoon baking soda
$1/4$ teaspoon baking powder
1 cup chopped walnuts

Preheat oven to 325 degrees. Grease and flour 5 pint-size wide mouth canning jars. In a large bowl, beat eggs and oil until foamy. Add zucchini, sugar, and vanilla, mixing well. In a separate bowl, combine remaining ingredients. Add flour mixture to zucchini mixture, stirring just until combined. Fill jars with batter just over half full. Place jars on baking sheet and bake 40 to 45 minutes, testing for doneness with a toothpick. Place jars on a rack to cool.

Bread may also be baked in two $8\frac{1}{2}$ x $4\frac{1}{2}$ x $2\frac{3}{4}$-inch loaf pans 50 to 60 minutes at 350 degrees.

Yield: 5 jars or 2 loaves of bread

Note: This is not a canning technique; bread should be eaten fresh or stored in the refrigerator or freezer.

CARROT-RAISIN BREAD

3 cups all-purpose flour
3 teaspoons caraway seeds
$1/4$ teaspoon salt
1 teaspoon baking soda
$1\frac{1}{2}$ teaspoons ground cinnamon
$1/4$ teaspoon ground allspice
$1/4$ teaspoon ground cloves
$1\frac{1}{2}$ cups finely grated carrots
$1\frac{1}{2}$ cups raisins
$1/3$ cup butter or margarine, softened
2 cups brown sugar, firmly packed
2 eggs
1 cup buttermilk

Preheat oven to 325 degrees. Grease and flour 5 pint-size wide mouth canning jars. In a medium bowl, combine first 9 ingredients, mixing well. In a large bowl, cream butter, sugar, and eggs. Stir in buttermilk. Add flour mixture, stirring just until combined. Fill jars with batter just over half full. Place jars on baking sheet and bake 45 to 50 minutes, testing for doneness with a toothpick. Place jars on a rack to cool.

Bread may also be baked in two $8\frac{1}{2}$ x $4\frac{1}{2}$ x $2\frac{3}{4}$ –inch loaf pans 1 hour to 1 hour and 10 minutes at 350 degrees.

Yield: 5 jars or 2 loaves of bread

Note: This is not a canning technique; bread should be eaten fresh or stored in the refrigerator or freezer.

Enriched with pecans, Pumpkin Bread is especially good topped with microwave Orange Sauce.

PUMPKIN BREAD

3½ cups all-purpose flour
2 teaspoons baking soda
1 teaspoon salt
1 teaspoon ground cinnamon
1 teaspoon ground nutmeg
1 teaspoon ground cloves
1 teaspoon ground allspice
3 cups granulated sugar
1 cup vegetable oil
4 eggs, lightly beaten
2 cups pumpkin
⅔ cup water
1½ cups chopped pecans

Preheat the oven to 350 degrees. In large mixing bowl, combine flour, baking soda, salt, spices, and sugar. Add oil, eggs, pumpkin, and water, beating until well blended. Stir in pecans. Pour batter into two lightly greased 9 x 5 x 3-inch loaf pans. Bake 1 hour or until toothpick inserted in the center of a loaf comes out clean. Remove from pans and cool on wire racks. Serve with Orange Sauce.

Yield: 2 loaves of bread

ORANGE SAUCE

Juice of one orange
1 tablespoon lemon juice
1 cup water
½ cup granulated sugar
3 tablespoons cornstarch
Grated rind of one orange
1 egg, lightly beaten
1 teaspoon butter or margarine

In medium micro-proof bowl, combine juices and water. Add sugar and cornstarch, stirring to dissolve. Stir in rind, egg, and butter. Microwave on high 5 minutes, or until mixture boils and thickens. Allow to cool and store in airtight container in refrigerator. Serve warm or cold.

Yield: about 1⅓ cups of sauce

Our Favorite
PARTY FARE

Planning a get-together? Treat your guests to satisfying snacks guaranteed to please. Choose light and luscious hors d'oeuvres for a girls-only night, hearty appetizers for the big game, or energizing snacks for the office party. Our delicious drinks, from kid-friendly punches to coffees and cocktails, will earn raves, too!

Layered Crab Taco Dip, p. 196

(Shown on page 195) *Layered Crab Taco Dip is a marinated mixture of crabmeat and vegetables nestled on a bed of cream cheese and avocado.*

Coated with toasted pecans, Cream Cheese Grapes are arranged in a cluster, then garnished with grapevine twigs and silk leaves.

CREAM CHEESE GRAPES

1 package (8 ounces) cream
   cheese, softened
2 tablespoons mayonnaise
1 pound seedless grapes
1½ cups finely chopped toasted
   pecans
   Artificial grapevine twigs and silk
   leaves to decorate

In a medium bowl, combine cream cheese and mayonnaise, beating until smooth. Add grapes to cream cheese and stir gently just until coated. Spread pecans on a large sheet of waxed paper. Roll the cheese-coated grapes in the pecans until well coated. Place grapes on a baking sheet and chill at least 1 hour. If desired, arrange on a serving platter in the shape of a grape cluster and decorate with grapevine twigs and silk leaves.

Yield: about 6 dozen grapes

LAYERED CRAB TACO DIP
(Shown on page 195)

2 cans (6 ounces each) lump
   crabmeat, drained
2 green onions, minced
½ cup diced cucumber
½ cup diced red onion
1 medium tomato, finely chopped
2 tablespoons minced fresh parsley
¼ cup lime juice
¼ cup lemon juice
¼ cup orange juice
   Salt and ground black pepper
2 packages (8 ounces each)
   cream cheese, softened
¼ cup mayonnaise
1 avocado, peeled, pitted, and diced
   Tortilla chips to serve

In a glass bowl, combine crabmeat, green onions, cucumber, red onion, tomato, and parsley. In a small bowl, combine juices. Stir into crab mixture. Salt and pepper to taste. Cover and refrigerate at least 6 hours or overnight.

Combine cream cheese and mayonnaise, blending well. Spread mixture over the bottom of a serving platter. Place avocado pieces over cream cheese mixture. Drain crab mixture, pressing out as much moisture as possible. Spread mixture over avocado. Serve with tortilla chips.

Yield: about 5¾ cups of dip

FRUIT WREATH WITH SWEET CHEESE DIP

The wreath may be prepared ahead of time, but keep the cut fruit fresh by sprinkling with lemon juice.

- 2 packages (8 ounces each) cream cheese, softened
- 1 jar (7 ounces) marshmallow creme
- 1/4 cup milk
- 1 1/2 teaspoons vanilla extract
- 1/2 teaspoon ground nutmeg
  Assorted fruits to serve

In a medium mixing bowl, combine cream cheese, marshmallow creme, milk, vanilla, and nutmeg, beating until smooth.

Place dip in a serving bowl. Arrange fruit around bowl.

Yield: about 3 1/2 cups of dip

A pretty tray of fruit and dip is really quick and easy party fare.

STRAWBERRY SPREAD

- 1 package (8 ounces) cream cheese, softened
- 1 jar (10 ounces) strawberry jam or preserves
- 1 teaspoon dried grated orange peel
- 1 cup finely chopped pecans

In a medium bowl, combine cream cheese, jam, and orange peel. Stir in pecans. Cover and chill until firm. Store in an airtight container in refrigerator. Serve with toast or muffins.

Yield: about 3 cups spread

SPICY PECANS

- 1/2 cup butter
- 3 tablespoons steak sauce
- 6 drops hot pepper sauce
- 4 cups pecan halves
  Cajun seasoning

Melt butter in a 15 1/2 x 10 1/2-inch jellyroll pan in a preheated 200-degree oven. Add steak sauce and pepper sauce; stir in pecans. Spread pecans on pan and bake 1 hour. Stir often while baking. Drain on paper towels and sprinkle with Cajun seasoning. Store in airtight containers.

Yield: 4 cups pecans

CRUNCHY CHEESE BALL

1 package (3 ounces) chicken-flavored ramen noodle soup
2 packages (8 ounces each) cream cheese, softened
1 cup sour cream
1/2 cup dry-roasted shelled sunflower seeds
4 green onions, chopped
1/3 cup dried parsley flakes

In a food processor fitted with a steel blade, process noodles, contents of seasoning packet, and next 4 ingredients until well blended. Divide mixture in half. Shape each half into a ball. Roll in parsley. Wrap in plastic wrap and refrigerate.

To serve, let stand at room temperature 20 to 30 minutes or until softened. Serve with crackers or bread.

Yield: 2 cheese balls

ZESTY RIPE OLIVE DIP

1 can (10 ounces) diced tomatoes and green chilies, well drained
2 cans (4 1/2 ounces each) chopped green chilies, well drained
2 cans (4 1/4 ounces each) chopped ripe olives, well drained
1 tablespoon red wine vinegar
2 teaspoons olive oil
1/2 teaspoon ground black pepper
1/4 teaspoon salt
1/4 teaspoon garlic powder
Tortilla chips to serve

In a medium bowl, combine tomatoes and green chilies, chopped green chilies, ripe olives, vinegar, oil, pepper, salt, and garlic powder. Cover and allow mixture to stand 1 hour for flavors to blend. Serve at room temperature with tortilla chips.

Yield: about 2 2/3 cups dip

MARINATED OLIVES

These stuffed olives fortified with vinegar and herbs give an everyday treat party flavor. The recipe can easily be doubled for larger crowds.

1 jar (8 ounces) pimiento-stuffed green olives, drained
1/4 cup tarragon wine vinegar
1/4 cup olive oil
1 tablespoon dried chives
1 clove garlic, minced
1/4 teaspoon whole black peppercorns

Place olives in a glass container with a lid. Combine remaining ingredients and pour over olives. Secure lid on jar and shake to coat olives well. Marinate at room temperature for 2 days, shaking jar daily. Drain before serving.

Yield: about 1 cup of olives

BLACK BEAN DIP

2 jalapeño peppers, seeded and coarsely chopped
2 cloves garlic, chopped
2 cans (15.5 ounces each) black beans, drained
1/2 teaspoon salt
1/2 cup sour cream
2 tablespoons freshly squeezed lime juice
Lime slice to garnish

Process peppers and garlic in a food processor until finely chopped. Add beans and salt; pulse process until beans are coarsely chopped. Transfer bean mixture to a small bowl. Stir in sour cream and lime juice. Cover and store in refrigerator.

To serve, bring bean dip to room temperature. Garnish with lime slice.

Yield: about 1½ cups dip

MONTEREY CHEESE CRISPS

You won't believe how easy these are to make. A sprinkling of cayenne pepper gives them an added bite.

1 pound Monterey Jack cheese, softened (use only Monterey Jack cheese)
Cayenne pepper or chili powder

Cut cheese into ¼-inch-thick slices, then cut slices into circles using a 1½-inch round cookie cutter. Place cheese rounds 3 inches apart on an ungreased non-stick baking sheet (cheese will spread while baking). Sprinkle with cayenne or chili powder.

Bake in a preheated 400-degree oven 10 minutes or until golden brown. (Do not overbake.)

Remove crisps with a spatula and cool on paper towels. Store in airtight containers.

Yield: 36 to 42 crisps

SALSA SUPREME

1/2 small onion, coarsely chopped
3 tablespoons fresh cilantro leaves
2 cloves garlic
1 tablespoon pickled jalapeño pepper slices
1 tablespoon ground cumin
1 can (14.5 ounces) diced tomatoes
1 can (10 ounces) diced tomatoes and green chiles
Jalepeno pepper slices to garnish
Tortilla chips to serve

Process onion, cilantro, garlic, 1 tablespoon pepper slices, and cumin in a small food processor until onion is finely chopped. Combine onion mixture, tomatoes, and tomatoes and green chiles in a heavy medium saucepan. Cook over medium-high heat until mixture comes to a boil. Reduce heat to medium-low and simmer 5 minutes. Allow mixture to cool to room temperature. Garnish with pepper slices. Serve at room temperature with tortilla chips.

Yield: about 3 cups salsa

MARMALADE CHEESE TARTS

The tangy flavors of marmalade and Cheddar cheese are a winning combination. Definitely give these a try.

- 1 cup butter, softened
- 2 cups all-purpose flour
- 1 cup grated sharp Cheddar cheese
- 3/4 cup orange marmalade
- 1 egg, lightly beaten

In a medium mixing bowl, combine butter, flour, and cheese. Knead until well blended. Wrap dough in plastic wrap and refrigerate 1 hour.

Preheat oven to 350 degrees. On a lightly floured surface, use a floured rolling pin to roll out dough to 1/8-inch thickness. Cut out dough using a 2-inch round cookie cutter. Place about 1/2 teaspoon marmalade in center of each circle of dough. Fold dough in half and seal edges by pressing with a fork. Transfer tarts to ungreased baking sheets and brush tops with egg. Bake 10 to 15 minutes or until tarts are set and lightly browned. Remove from pans and cool on wire racks.

Yield: about 5 dozen tarts

BROCCOLI DIP

The special combination of flavors makes this a light and refreshing dip.

- 1 package (10 ounces) frozen chopped broccoli, thawed and drained
- 1/2 cup minced fresh parsley
- 1/2 cup chopped green onions
- 1 cup chopped celery
- 1 tablespoon Worcestershire sauce
- 1 teaspoon Greek seasoning
- 1 cup sour cream
- 1 cup mayonnaise
- 1 tablespoon lemon juice
- 1 loaf (1 pound) round Hawaiian bread (found in freezer or deli section)
  Chopped fresh parsley to garnish
  Crackers to serve

In a large bowl, combine broccoli, minced parsley, green onions, celery, Worcestershire sauce, Greek seasoning, sour cream, mayonnaise, and lemon juice. Cover and refrigerate overnight.

Before serving, cut the top from the loaf of bread. Hollow out the inside of the bread, leaving about a 1-inch shell. Fill bread round with dip. Serve dip with crackers.

Yield: about 3 1/2 cups dip

Sweet orange marmalade paired with tangy Cheddar cheese makes our Marmalade Cheese Tarts an unusual (and delicious) treat.

Guacamole tops off our irresistible Tortilla Roll-Ups.

TORTILLA ROLL-UPS

These are so easy to make ahead. Have them waiting in the refrigerator ready to top with our creamy guacamole just before serving.

    1   package (8 ounces) cream
          cheese, softened
    1/3 cup chunky salsa
    1/4 cup chopped green onion
    1/2 teaspoon garlic salt
    1/2 teaspoon chili powder
    12 (6-inch) flour tortillas
          Guacamole (recipe follows)
          Small red chili peppers to garnish

Beat cream cheese until smooth. Add salsa, green onion, garlic salt, and chili powder, mixing well. Spread a heaping tablespoon of the cream cheese mixture on each tortilla. Roll up each tortilla tightly, jellyroll fashion, and place seam side down on a baking sheet. Cover and chill at least 2 hours. Slice each roll into 4 pieces. Top each appetizer with a small amount of Guacamole and garnish with a small red chili pepper. Serve with additional Guacamole.

Yield: 4 dozen roll-ups

GUACAMOLE

    2   ripe avocados, mashed (about
          1 cup)
    1/3 cup mayonnaise
    1/4 cup chopped ripe olives
    2   tablespoons lemon juice
    2   tablespoons grated onion
    1   clove garlic, minced
    1   teaspoon salt
    1/4 teaspoon chili powder
          Dash cayenne pepper

Using a food processor or blender, process all ingredients until creamy. Chill. Use as topping for Tortilla Roll-Ups.

201

NUTTY GARLIC CHEESE SPREAD

- 3 heads (about 30 cloves) garlic, peeled
- 2 tablespoons vegetable oil
- 2 teaspoons white wine vinegar
- 1½ teaspoons Worcestershire sauce
- 1 package (8 ounces) cream cheese, softened
- 1¼ cups slivered almonds, toasted and finely chopped
- 1 cup sour cream
- ¼ cup chopped fresh parsley
- ½ teaspoon dry mustard
- ½ teaspoon dried oregano leaves
- ½ teaspoon salt
- ¼ teaspoon ground white pepper
  Crackers or bread to serve

Preheat oven to 300 degrees. Place garlic and oil in a shallow baking dish, stirring until well coated. Bake 30 minutes or until garlic is light brown. Drain garlic on paper towels and cool completely.

In a blender or food processor fitted with a steel blade, process garlic, vinegar, and Worcestershire sauce until garlic is finely chopped. In a medium bowl, beat cream cheese until smooth. Stir in garlic mixture and remaining ingredients until thoroughly blended. Cover and refrigerate 8 hours or overnight.

To serve, bring to room temperature and serve with crackers or bread.

Yield: about 3 cups of spread

BASIL-GARLIC SNACK WAFERS

- 1 cup butter or margarine, softened
- ½ cup shredded sharp Cheddar cheese
- 3 ounces (½ of 6-ounce package) Kraft® pasteurized process cheese food with garlic, softened
- 2 cups all-purpose flour
- 1 teaspoon dried basil leaves
- 1 teaspoon garlic powder
- ½ teaspoon salt

Preheat oven to 350 degrees. In a large bowl; beat first 3 ingredients together until well blended. Add remaining ingredients; mix until a soft dough forms. Divide dough in half. Shape each half into a 1¼-inch diameter roll. Cover with plastic wrap and refrigerate until firm. Cut each roll into ¼-inch slices and place on greased baking sheets. Bake 10 to 12 minutes or until light brown on bottom. Transfer to a wire rack to cool completely. Store in an airtight container.

Yield: about 8 dozen snack wafers

TURKEY NACHOS

- 1 can (16 ounces) regular or vegetarian refried beans
- 1 teaspoon chili powder
- 1 teaspoon ground cumin
- 2 tablespoons vegetable oil
- 1 pound cooked turkey breast, diced (about 3½ cups)
- ½ cup chopped onion (about 1 medium onion)
- 1 can (4 ounces) chopped mild green chilies
- 2 tablespoons chopped fresh cilantro leaves
- 1 teaspoon salt
- ½ teaspoon ground black pepper
- 1 cup finely chopped tomato (about 1 large tomato)
- 1 bag (10½ ounces) round tortilla chips
- 2 cups (about 8 ounces) shredded Monterey Jack cheese

Bite-size Turkey Nachos make spicy little appetizers.

In a small saucepan, combine beans, chili powder, and cumin. Cook, stirring occasionally, over medium-low heat until heated through. Remove from heat and cover.

In a large skillet, heat oil over medium heat. Add turkey, onion, chilies, cilantro, salt, and pepper. Cook, stirring occasionally, until onion is tender. Remove from heat and stir in tomato.

Preheat oven to 425 degrees. Spread about 1 teaspoon bean mixture evenly over each tortilla chip; place in a single layer on a greased baking sheet. Spoon about 1 tablespoon turkey mixture over bean mixture. Sprinkle cheese evenly over turkey mixture. Bake 5 to 7 minutes or until cheese melts. Serve warm.

Yield: about 4½ dozen nachos

MADEIRA CHEESE SPREAD

1/2 cup Madeira wine
1/3 cup butter, melted
14 ounces Gouda cheese
1 cup sour cream
1 teaspoon salt
1/8 teaspoon cayenne pepper

In a small bowl, combine wine and butter. In a food processor or blender, combine cheese, sour cream, salt, and cayenne. Process until smooth. With motor running, gradually add wine mixture, blending until smooth. Refrigerate 24 hours before serving to allow flavors to blend.

Yield: about 2 1/2 cups of spread

SEASONED PRETZELS

6 cups pretzels (mix shapes if desired)
1/2 cup butter or margarine, melted
1 package (1 ounce) ranch-style party dip mix
1 tablespoon Worcestershire sauce
1/2 teaspoon seasoned salt

Preheat oven to 250 degrees. Place pretzels in a large shallow baking pan. In a small bowl, combine butter, dip mix, Worcestershire sauce, and salt. Pour butter mixture over pretzels; stir well. Bake 1 hour, stirring every 15 minutes. Pour onto waxed paper to cool. Store in an airtight container.

Yield: about 6 cups of snack mix

MARINATED CHICKEN BITES

These moist chunks of chicken are perfect to make ahead. Just place the marinated meat and vegetables on the skewers, cover, and refrigerate until ready to broil. Inexpensive bamboo skewers are available in the party supplies section of most grocery stores.

1 1/2 pounds boneless, skinless chicken breasts, cut into 1-inch pieces
1/2 cup mango chutney
1/3 cup white wine
1/4 cup olive oil
1 tablespoon raspberry vinegar
1 green pepper, cut into 1-inch pieces
1 sweet red pepper, cut into 1-inch pieces
1/2 cup red plum jam

In a large glass bowl, combine chicken, chutney, wine, olive oil, and vinegar. Cover and marinate in refrigerator overnight.

Drain chicken. On each 6-inch skewer, place 2 chicken pieces and 2 pepper pieces.

In a small saucepan, melt jam over low heat. Generously brush chicken and peppers with jam. Place on wire rack in baking pan. Brushing often with jam, broil 12 to 15 minutes or until chicken is thoroughly cooked.

Yield: about 24 skewers

CHILI CON QUESO DIP

2 slices bacon, chopped
2 tablespoons chopped onion
1 clove garlic, minced
1 can (14.5 ounces) whole
    tomatoes undrained
1 can (4 ounces) chopped green
    chilies
1 teaspoon ground cumin
$1/2$ teaspoon salt
$1/2$ teaspoon dried whole oregano
$1/4$ teaspoon ground black pepper
4 cups (16 ounces) grated American
    cheese

In a large saucepan, cook bacon until crisp. Add onion and garlic and cook until onion is soft, about 5 minutes. Stir in next 6 ingredients, blending well. Reduce heat to low and gradually add cheese, stirring until melted. Serve hot with tortilla or corn chips.

Yield: about 4 cups of dip

HOT BACON-CHEESE DIP

3 rolls (6 ounces each) pasteurized
    process cheese food with
    garlic, quartered
2 cups sour cream
1 can ($11^1/2$ ounces) bean and
    bacon soup
2 tablespoons dried chopped onion
2 teaspoons hot pepper sauce
2 teaspoons liquid smoke
2 teaspoons garlic powder
1 jar (2 ounces) real bacon pieces
    Chips to serve

In a blender or food processor, process first 7 ingredients until smooth. Transfer cheese mixture to a medium bowl; stir in bacon. Cover and refrigerate 8 hours or overnight to allow flavors to blend. Spoon dip into a large saucepan. Stirring occasionally, cook over medium heat until heated through. Serve warm with chips.

Yield: about 5 cups dip

CRUNCHY SNACK MIX

Here is our version of the traditional cereal snack mix. This mixture freezes well, so it may be made in advance.

$1/2$ cup butter or margarine,
    melted
1 package Caesar garlic cheese
    salad dressing mix
1 tablespoon Worcestershire
    sauce
1 teaspoon seasoned salt
4 cups bite-size shredded wheat
    cereal
3 cups chow mein noodles
2 cups unblanched whole
    almonds
2 cups walnut halves

Preheat oven to 250 degrees. In a small bowl, combine butter, salad dressing mix, Worcestershire sauce, and seasoned salt; stir to blend. In a large bowl, combine the remaining ingredients. Pour butter mixture over cereal mixture, stirring until thoroughly coated. Pour onto a baking sheet and bake 1 hour, stirring every 15 minutes; cool in pan. Store in a tightly sealed container.

Yield: about 11 cups of snack mix

Cucumber Bites present two delicious sour cream toppings: one with salmon and dill, the other with Gruyère cheese and herbs.

CUCUMBER BITES

SALMON TOPPING

  1 package (3 ounces) smoked salmon, broken into small pieces

  1/2 cup sour cream

  1 teaspoon chopped fresh dill weed

  1 teaspoon freshly squeezed lemon juice

  1 teaspoon capers, finely chopped

CHEESE TOPPING

  1/2 cup sour cream

  1/4 cup shredded Gruyère cheese

  2 teaspoons chopped fresh parsley

  1/4 teaspoon dried oregano leaves

  1/4 teaspoon dried thyme leaves

  1/8 teaspoon garlic salt

  3 to 4 cucumbers
     Salt and ground white pepper
     Fresh dill weed and parsley to garnish

For salmon topping, combine salmon, sour cream, dill weed, lemon juice, and capers in a small bowl: stir until well blended. Cover and chill 2 hours to allow flavors to blend.

For cheese topping, combine sour cream, cheese, parsley, oregano, thyme and garlic salt in a small bowl. Stir with fork until well blended. Cover and cool 2 hours to allow flavors to blend.

Score peel of cucumbers with fork tines. Cut cucumbers into 1/2-inch slices. Use a melon ball scoop to remove a small amount of cucumber from center of each slice, leaving bottom of slice intact. Lightly sprinkle slices with salt and pepper. Place 1 tablespoon desired topping on each cucumber slice. Garnish salmon appetizers with dill weed and cheese appetizers with parsley. Serve immediately.

Yield: about 4 dozen appetizers

Pineapple preserves lend a lightly sweet taste to Sausage "Pinwheel" Pastries. The spicy filling is baked in refrigerated pie crust cutouts.

SAUSAGE "PINWHEEL" PASTRIES

Sausage mixture may be prepared a day ahead.

  1   pound mild pork sauage
 ¹/₂ cup chopped onion
 ²/₃ cup pineapple preserves
  1   tablespoon dry mustard
 ¹/₂ teaspoon salt
 ¹/₄ teaspoon ground black
      pepper
 ¹/₈ teaspoon rubbed sage
  1   package (15 ounces) refrigerated
      pie crusts, at room temperature

In a large skillet, cook sausage over medium heat until it begins to brown; drain well. Add onion; cook until onion is tender and sausage is thoroughly cooked. Remove from heat. Stir in preserves, dry mustard, salt, pepper, and sage. Cover and chill 1 hour.

Preheat oven to 400 degrees. On a lightly floured surface, use a floured rolling pin to roll 1 crust into a 12-inch square. Use a pastry wheel to cut dough into sixteen 3-inch squares; place 1 inch apart on a greased baking sheet. Repeat with remaining crust. For each pinwheel, use pastry wheel to make a 1-inch-long diagonal cut from each corner. Place about 2 teaspoons sausage mixture in center of each square. Bring every other dough tip to center of square over filling, sealing tips together with water. (Pastries can be covered with plastic wrap and refrigerated until ready to bake.) Bake 9 to 11 minutes or until filling is hot and edges are lightly browned. Serve warm.

Yield: 32 pastries

HERB CHIPS

1 can (10 ounces) refrigerated
　　pizza crust dough
2 tablespoons butter or
　　margarine, melted
　 Salt
　 Paprika, dried chives, and dried
　　parsley flakes

Preheat oven to 350 degrees. On a lightly floured surface, use a floured rolling pin to roll out dough into a 12 x 18-inch rectangle. Use a large-tooth pastry cutter or pastry wheel to cut dough into 3 x 4-inch rectangles; cut each rectangle diagonally into 2 triangles. Brush with melted butter and sprinkle with salt. Transfer triangles to a greased baking sheet. Sprinkle 12 triangles with paprika, 12 with chives, and 12 with parsley. Bake 8 to 10 minutes or until edges begin to brown. Serve warm.

Yield: 3 dozen chips

HOT SPINACH DIP

1 package (10 ounces) frozen
　　chopped spinach, thawed
　　and well drained
$1/2$ pound cooked lean ham, diced
1 cup (4 ounces) shredded fat-
　　free mozzarella cheese
$1/2$ cup fat-free sour cream
3 ounces fat-free cream cheese,
　　softened
$1/4$ cup chopped green onions
1 tablespoon prepared
　　horseradish
1 fresh jalapeño pepper, seeded
　　and minced
1 teaspoon salt
$1/2$ teaspoon ground black pepper
　 Vegetable cooking spray
　 Fat-free sour cream and green
　　onion to garnish
　 Pita bread, cut in wedges, to serve

Preheat oven to 375 degrees. In a large bowl, combine spinach, ham, mozzarella cheese, sour cream, cream cheese, green onions, horseradish, jalapeño pepper, salt, and black pepper. Spread mixture into a 9-inch pie plate sprayed with cooking spray. Bake 15 to 18 minutes or until heated through. Garnish with sour cream and green onion. Serve warm with pita bread.

Yield: about 3 cups dip or 9 servings

SAUSAGE-CREAM CHEESE SQUARES

2 cans (8 ounces each) refrigerated crescent rolls
2 packages (8 ounces each) cream cheese, softened
1/2 teaspoon dried basil leaves, crushed
1/4 teaspoon garlic powder
1 1/2 pounds mild pork sausage, cooked, drained, and crumbled
12 ounces provolone cheese, shredded (about 3 cups)
3/4 cup finely chopped sweet red pepper

Preheat oven to 350 degrees. Unroll 1 can of crescent roll dough onto a greased baking sheet, being careful not to separate dough into pieces. Press dough into an 8 x 13-inch rectangle. Using a second greased baking sheet, repeat for remaining can of rolls. Bake 12 to 15 minutes or until golden brown. Remove from oven.

In a medium bowl, combine next 3 ingredients. Spread cream cheese mixture evenly over baked dough. Sprinkle remaining ingredients evenly over cream cheese mixture. Bake 5 to 7 minutes or until cheese melts. Cut into 2-inch squares and serve warm.

Yield: about 4 dozen appetizers

SHRIMP SPREAD

Shrimp Spread should be made 1 day in advance.

1 1/2 pounds cooked and peeled shrimp
1 package (8 ounces) cream cheese, softened
1/4 cup finely chopped onion
2 tablespoons sour cream
2 teaspoons sweet pickle relish
1 1/2 teaspoons Dijon-style mustard
1 1/2 teaspoons hot pepper sauce
Crackers or bread to serve

Reserve several shrimp for garnish. Finely chop remaining shrimp. In a large bowl, combine chopped shrimp, cream cheese, onion, sour cream, pickle relish, mustard, and hot pepper sauce; stir until well blended. Cover and refrigerate 8 hours or overnight to allow flavors to blend. Garnish with reserved shrimp. Serve with crackers or bread.

Yield: about 4 cups spread

The crisp, wholesome taste of Caraway Wafers makes them an excellent snack. When served with soups and salads, they're a flavorful complement to the meal.

CARAWAY WAFERS

1 cup all-purpose flour
1 teaspoon dry mustard
1/4 teaspoon salt
1/2 cup shredded Swiss cheese
2 teaspoons caraway seed
1/2 teaspoon paprika
1/4 teaspoon cayenne pepper
1/3 cup butter or margarine, softened
3 tablespoons cold water
1 teaspoon Worcestershire sauce
Paprika

Preheat oven to 425 degrees. Sift flour, dry mustard, and salt into bowl. Stir in cheese, caraway seed, 1/2 teaspoon paprika, and cayenne. Cut in butter until mixture resembles coarse meal. Add water and Worcestershire sauce; blend with a fork until dough sticks together, adding more water if necessary. Shape into a ball.

On a lightly floured surface, roll out dough to 1/8-inch thickness and cut out using a 11/2-inch biscuit cutter. Place on an ungreased baking sheet. Sprinkle with paprika. Bake 5 to 7 minutes or until lightly browned.

Yield: about 4 dozen wafers

SUGARED CRANBERRY TRAIL MIX

1 cup whole almonds
2 cups small pretzels
1 cup (about 4 ounces) dried cranberries
1 egg white
1/2 cup granulated sugar
1/2 teaspoon ground cinnamon
1/2 teaspoon salt

Preheat oven to 350 degrees. Spread almonds evenly on an ungreased baking sheet. Bake 7 to 8 minutes or until nuts are slightly darker in color. Cool completely on pan.

Reduce oven temperature to 225 degrees. In a large bowl, combine almonds, pretzels, and cranberries. In a small bowl, beat egg white until foamy. Pour over pretzel mixture; toss until well coated. In another small bowl, combine remaining ingredients. Sprinkle over pretzel mixture; toss until well coated. Spread evenly on a greased baking sheet. Bake 1 hour, stirring every 15 minutes. Cool completely on pan. Store in an airtight container.

Yield: about 5 cups trail mix

CHEESY CRAB TOASTS

Cheese mixture can be made 1 day in advance and chilled.

2 small (2¼ x 14-inches each)
   French bread loaves
   (1 pound total)
2 cups (8 ounces) shredded sharp
   Cheddar cheese
1 can (6 ounces) crabmeat,
   drained
⅓ cup mayonnaise
2 teaspoons prepared
   horseradish
1 teaspoon dried chopped chives

Preheat oven to 375 degrees. Cut each French bread loaf in half lengthwise. Combine cheese, crabmeat, mayonnaise, horseradish, and chives in a food processor until smooth. Spread cheese mixture over each loaf half. Bake on an ungreased baking sheet 20 to 25 minutes or until cheese mixture is hot and edges of bread are lightly browned. Cut into 1-inch slices. Serve warm.

Yield: about 52 toasts

SAVORY BREADSTICKS

¾ cup butter or margarine
½ tablespoon instant beef
   bouillon granules
1 tablespoon dried parsley flakes
⅛ teaspoon dried marjoram
   leaves
2 packages (4½ ounces each)
   prepared breadsticks
2 tablespoons grated Parmesan
   cheese

Melt butter in a jellyroll pan. Stir in bouillon, parsley, and marjoram. Roll breadsticks in butter mixture and sprinkle with cheese. Bake in a preheated 300-degree oven 10 minutes. Store in an airtight container.

Yield: 30 breadsticks

ITALIAN CRACKER SNACKS

1 package (9 ounces) small
   butter-flavored crackers
¼ cup butter or margarine,
   melted
1 package zesty Italian salad
   dressing mix
1 tablespoon Worcestershire
   sauce
¼ teaspoon seasoned salt

Preheat oven to 250 degrees. Place crackers in a large shallow baking pan. In a small bowl, combine butter, salad dressing mix, Worcestershire sauce, and salt. Pour butter mixture over crackers; stir well. Bake 1 hour, stirring every 15 minutes. Pour onto waxed paper to cool. Store in an airtight container.

Yield: about 4 cups of snack mix

SPICY SNACK MIX

- 1 package (10.5 ounces) corn chips
- 1 package (10 ounces) small pretzels
- 1 package (7 ounces) cheese stick crackers
- 2 cups oyster crackers
- 2 packages (3 ounces each) sweet and salty peanuts
- 3/4 cup butter or margarine, melted
- 1 container (6 ounces) frozen limeade concentrate, thawed
- 1 package (1 3/4 ounces) chili seasoning mix

Preheat oven to 250 degrees. In a large roasting pan, combine corn chips, pretzels, cheese crackers, oyster crackers, and peanuts. In a small bowl, combine melted butter, limeade concentrate, and chili seasoning mix; stir until well blended. Pour over snack mixture; stir until well coated. Bake 1 hour, stirring every 15 minutes. Spread mixture on foil to cool. Store in an airtight container.

Yield: about 20 cups snack mix

TROPICAL GRANOLA SNACK MIX

- 4 cups graham cereal squares
- 4 cups round toasted oat cereal
- 1 package (6 ounces) dried pineapple chunks (about 1 1/4 cups)
- 1 package (5 ounces) dried banana chips (about 1 1/2 cups)
- 1 cup dried coconut chips
- 1 cup sunflower kernels
- 1 cup golden raisins
- 3/4 cup slivered almonds
- 3/4 cup firmly packed brown sugar
- 1/3 cup vegetable oil
- 6 tablespoons frozen orange juice concentrate, thawed
- 3 tablespoons honey

Preheat oven to 300 degrees. In a large roasting pan, combine cereals, pineapple chunks, banana chips, coconut chips, sunflower kernels, raisins, and almonds. In a small bowl, combine brown sugar, oil, juice concentrate, and honey; stir until well blended. Pour over cereal mixture; stir until well coated. Stirring every 10 minutes, bake 40 to 45 or until lightly browned (mixture will be slightly moist). Spread on waxed paper and allow to cool. Store in an airtight container in a cool place.

Yield: about 14 cups snack mix.

SPICE CHEESE MOLD

This cheese ball is a blend of cheeses with the bite of jalapeño peppers and hot-flavored pecans.

2 packages (8 ounces each)
   cream cheese, softened
8 ounces sharp Cheddar cheese,
   softened
8 ounces Monterey Jack cheese
   with jalapeño peppers,
   softened
3 drops hot pepper sauce
1¼ cups Spicy Pecans, chopped
   and divided (recipe on page 197)
   Fresh grapes and assorted crackers
   to serve

In a food processor or blender, combine cheeses and pepper sauce. Process until well blended. Place mixture in a bowl and add ¾ cup chopped Spicy Pecans. Form into a large ball or mold in a 1-quart round bowl. Cover tightly and refrigerate overnight.

To serve, remove from refrigerator and garnish with remaining Spicy Pecans. Serve with fresh grapes and assorted crackers.

Yield: 1 cheese ball

CHINESE CHICKEN WINGS

1½ pounds chicken wings, disjointed
    and wing tips discarded
½ cup red plum jam
3 tablespoons soy sauce
2 tablespoons prepared horseradish
1 tablespoon prepared mustard
3 to 4 drops hot pepper sauce
    Chinese hot mustard to serve

Preheat oven to 425 degrees. Place wings in a single layer on a baking sheet. Combine jam, soy sauce, horseradish, prepared mustard, and pepper sauce; brush generously over wings. Bake 15 to 20 minutes, basting frequently. Serve with Chinese hot mustard, if desired.

Yield: about 20 chicken wings

CHEESE POCKETS

1 package (10 ounces)
    refrigerated pizza dough
¼ cup strawberry jam
¾ cup shredded sharp Cheddar
    cheese
¼ cup chopped green onion
5 slices bacon, cooked and crumbled
¼ cup chopped pecans

Preheat oven to 400 degrees. Unroll pizza dough and cut into 12 equal pieces. Place 1 teaspoon jam on each piece of dough. Top with cheese, green onion, bacon, and pecans. Brush edges of dough with water. Fold dough over filling and seal edges with fork. Place pockets on a lightly greased baking sheet. Bake 12 to 15 minutes or until golden brown. Serve warm.

Yield: 12 pockets

Succulent Chinese Chicken Wings (right) are basted with a mixture of soy sauce, horseradish, and plum jam. Cheese Pockets get their sensational taste from strawberry jam, bacon, and pecans.

CREAMY CHICKEN-MUSHROOM DIP

1 can (10 3/4 ounces) golden mushroom soup, undiluted
1 package (8 ounces) cream cheese, softened
1 can (5 ounces) chunk white chicken, drained
1/2 cup sliced fresh mushrooms
1/2 cup slivered almonds, toasted
2 tablespoons white wine
1 small clove garlic, minced
1/8 teaspoon ground white pepper
Chips or crackers to serve

In a heavy medium saucepan, combine soup and cream cheese. Stir over medium heat until smooth. Add chicken, mushrooms, almonds, wine, garlic, and white pepper; stir until well blended and heated through. Serve warm with chips or crackers.

Yield: about 2 1/2 cups dip

BACON-CHEDDAR CHEESE BALL

A miniature cookie cutter is all you need to cut out simple garnishes. We cut the tiny stars from a sweet red pepper.

2 packages (8 ounces each) cream cheese, softened
1/2 pound sharp Cheddar cheese, shredded
1/2 cup chopped green onions
6 slices bacon, cooked and crumbled
1 clove garlic, minced
3 tablespoons diced pimiento
3 tablespoons minced fresh parsley
Crackers to serve

Combine all ingredients, blending well. Form into a ball. Cover with plastic wrap.

Refrigerate overnight to allow flavors to blend. Serve with crackers.

Yield: 1 cheese ball

CHEDDAR SPREAD

2 cups (8 ounces) shredded sharp Cheddar cheese
1 package (8 ounces) cream cheese, softened
1/3 cup sherry
1/2 teaspoon garlic powder
1/2 teaspoon salt
1/4 teaspoon ground white pepper
1/4 teaspoon dry mustard

In a large bowl, combine all ingredients until well blended using an electric mixer. Refrigerate overnight to allow flavors to blend.

Yield: about 2 cups spread

To serve: Let stand at room temperature 20 to 30 minutes or until softened. Serve with crackers or bread.

DILLY OYSTER CRACKERS

1 package (1.6 ounces) ranch-style salad dressing mix
1 tablespoon dried dill weed
1/2 teaspoon garlic powder
1 box (16 ounces) unseasoned oyster crackers
1 cup vegetable oil

In a large bowl, combine dressing mix, dill weed, and garlic powder. Add crackers and blend thoroughly. Pour oil over mixture and stir thoroughly; allow crackers to absorb oil and seasonings. Store in an airtight container.

Yield: about 8 cups

SPICY ROASTED PEANUTS

- 2 tablespoons vegetable oil
- 4 cloves garlic, minced
- 1 tablespoon red pepper flakes
- 2 cans (16 ounces each) salted peanuts
- 2 teaspoons paprika
- 1 teaspoon chili powder

Preheat oven to 350 degrees. In a heavy large skillet, cook oil, garlic, and red pepper flakes over medium heat about 1 minute. Remove from heat. Add peanuts and stir until well coated. Pour peanut mixture onto a baking sheet. Stirring occasionally, bake about 20 minutes or until lightly browned. Sprinkle paprika and chili powder over peanuts and stir. Allow peanuts to cool completely.

Yield: about 6 cups peanuts

HUMMUS DIP

- 2 cans (15 ounces each) chick-peas, drained
- 1/2 cup olive oil
- 3 tablespoons freshly squeezed lemon juice
- 2 cloves garlic, coarsely chopped
- 1 tablespoon tahini (ground sesame seed)
- 1 tablespoon chopped onion
- 1 tablespoon minced parsley
- 1/4 teaspoon salt
- 1/4 teaspoon ground black pepper
- 1/8 teaspoon curry powder
  Sliced black olives, fresh parsley, and red onion wedges to garnish
  Pita bread triangles to serve

In a food processor, combine first 10 ingredients; process until smooth. Spoon hummus into a serving dish. Garnish with black olives, parsley, and red onion wedges. Serve at room temperature with pita bread triangles.

Yield: about 3 cups dip

CURRIED SNACK STICKS

- 1 can (16 ounces) salted peanuts
- 1 package (10 ounces) pretzel sticks
- 1 can (7 ounces) potato sticks
- 1/2 cup vegetable oil
- 2 packages (1.2 ounces each) curry sauce mix
- 1/2 teaspoon ground red pepper
- 1/2 teaspoon ground cumin seed

Preheat oven to 300 degrees. In a large bowl, combine peanuts, pretzel sticks, and potato sticks. In a small bowl, combine remaining ingredients until well blended. Pour sauce mixture over peanut mixture; stir until well coated. Spread evenly in a large jellyroll pan. Bake 20 minutes, stirring after 10 minutes. Spread on aluminum foil to cool. Store in an airtight container.

Yield: about 14 cups snack mix

DOUBLE DILL DIP

- 1 cup coarsely chopped refrigerated kosher dill pickles
- 1 package (8 ounces) cream cheese, softened
- 1/4 cup sour cream
- 1 tablespoon fresh dill weed
- 1/8 teaspoon ground red pepper
  Fresh dill weed to garnish
  Corn chips to serve

Process pickles in a food processor until finely chopped. Add remaining ingredients and process until well blended. Cover and chill 2 hours. Garnish with dill weed. Serve with chips.

Yield: about 2 cups dip

217

ZESTY CHEESECAKE SPREAD

2 packages (8 ounces each) cream cheese, softened
1 cup finely chopped celery
1 medium green pepper, finely chopped
1 small onion, finely chopped
3 hard-cooked eggs, chopped
2 tablespoons freshly squeezed lime juice
1 teaspoon salt
1 teaspoon Worcestershire sauce
1 teaspoon paprika
$1/4$ teaspoon hot pepper sauce
$1^1/2$ cups crushed cheese crackers
$1^1/4$ cups thick and chunky picante sauce
Crackers to serve

In a large bowl, combine cream cheese, celery, green pepper, onion, eggs, lime juice, salt, Worcestershire sauce, paprika and pepper sauce. Spread mixture into lightly greased 9-inch springform pan. Cover and chill 24 hours to allow flavor to blend.

To serve, remove sides of pan. Sprinkle top with cracker pieces. Spoon picante sauce in center of cheesecake. Serve with crackers.

Yield: about $6^1/2$ cups spread

ITALIAN KABOBS
Allow enough time for kabobs to marinate.

1 package (9 ounces) uncooked refrigerated cheese-filled tortellini
1 can (14 ounces) artichoke hearts, drained and quartered
1 can (6 ounces) pitted ripe olives, drained
1 package (3.5 ounces) pepperoni slices (about $1^1/2$-inch diameter)
6-inch long wooden skewers
1 bottle (8 ounces) Italian salad dressing
8 ounces farmer cheese, cut into $1/2$-inch cubes
1 pint cherry tomatoes, halved

Prepare tortellini according to package directions; drain and cool. Place tortellini, artichoke hearts, olives, and pepperoni on skewers. Place skewers in a 9 x 13-inch baking dish; drizzle with salad dressing, turning skewers to coat. Cover and chill 8 hours, turning occasionally.

To serve, remove skewers from dressing; add cheese cubes and tomato halves.

Yield: about $4^1/2$ dozen kabobs

Start pregame activities with these spicy nibbles! Zesty Cheesecake Spread (top) drafts green pepper, picante sauce, and hot pepper sauce for a taste that is sure to score. Our Italian Kabobs team tortellini, pepperoni, vegetables, and cheese.

CINNAMON-APPLE POPCORN

   2   cups chopped dried apples
   10 cups popped popcorn
   2   cups pecan halves
   4   tablespoons butter, melted
   2   tablespoons firmly packed
          brown sugar
   1   teaspoon ground cinnamon
   1/4 teaspoon ground nutmeg
   1/4 teaspoon vanilla extract

Preheat oven to 250 degrees. Place apples in a large shallow baking pan. Bake 20 minutes. Remove pan from oven and stir in popcorn and pecans. In a small bowl, combine remaining ingredients. Drizzle butter mixture over popcorn mixture, stirring well. Bake 30 minutes, stirring every 10 minutes. Pour onto waxed paper to cool. Store in an airtight container.

Yield: about 14 cups of snack mix

NUTTY BUTTERSCOTCH POPCORN

   1   package (12 ounces)
          butterscotch chips
   16 cups unsalted popped popcorn
   1   can (16 ounces) salted peanuts

Place butterscotch chips in a small microwave-safe bowl. Microwave on high power (100%) 3 minutes, stirring every minute until chips are melted. Place popcorn and peanuts in a very large bowl.

Pour melted chips over popcorn mixture; stir until well coated. Pour onto greased aluminum foil; allow to cool. Store in an airtight container.

Yield: about 20 cups flavored popcorn

CINNAMON CANDY CORN

   6   quarts popped white popcorn
   1 3/4 cups sugar
   1   cup butter or margarine
   1/2 cup light corn syrup
   1/2 teaspoon salt
   3   cups miniature marshmallows
   1/4 teaspoon cinnamon-flavored oil
   1/4 teaspoon red liquid food coloring

Preheat oven to 250 degrees. Place popcorn in a greased large roasting pan. In a large saucepan, combine sugar, butter, corn syrup, and salt. Stirring constantly, cook over medium heat 8 to 10 minutes or until mixture boils. Boil 2 minutes without stirring. Remove from heat; add marshmallows. Stir until marshmallows melt. Stir in cinnamon oil and food coloring. Pour syrup over popcorn, stirring until well coated. Bake 1 hour, stirring every 15 minutes. Spread on lightly greased aluminum foil to cool. Store in an airtight container.

Yield: about 25 cups candy corn

BROWN SUGAR SNACK MIX

24 cups popped popcorn
2 packages (12.3 ounces each) bite-size crispy corn-rice cereal
2 cans (12 ounces each) mixed nuts
2 cups butter or margarine
2 cups firmly packed brown sugar
3/4 cup light corn syrup
2 teaspoons vanilla extract
1/2 teaspoon baking soda

Preheat oven to 275 degrees. Evenly divide popcorn, cereal, and nuts into 2 large roasting pans; set aside. In a large saucepan over medium heat, combine butter, brown sugar, and corn syrup. Stirring occasionally, bring mixture to a boil; boil 5 minutes. Remove from heat. Stir in vanilla and baking soda (mixture will foam). Pour syrup over cereal mixture, tossing to coat. Bake 1 hour, stirring every 15 minutes. Pour mixture onto ungreased aluminum foil to cool. Store in airtight containers.

Yield: about 46 cups snack mix.

CARAMEL CRACKERS

2 packages (9 ounces each) small butter-flavored crackers
1 cup dry-roasted peanuts
1 cup granulated sugar
1/2 cup butter or margarine
1/2 cup light corn syrup
1 teaspoon vanilla extract
1 teaspoon baking soda

Preheat oven to 250 degrees. Combine crackers and peanuts in a greased large shallow baking pan. In a saucepan, bring sugar, butter, and corn syrup to a boil and cook 5 minutes. Remove from heat; add vanilla and baking soda. Pour caramel mixture over crackers and peanuts; stir well. Bake 1 hour, stirring every 15 minutes. Pour onto waxed paper and break apart; allow to cool. Store in an airtight container.

Yield: about 9 cups of snack mix

PEANUT BUTTER SNACK MIX

2 bags (11 ounces each) small pretzels
1 package (12 ounces) peanut butter-flavored chips
1 jar (7 ounces) marshmallow creme
1/2 cup butter or margarine
4 tablespoons honey
4 tablespoons milk
6 cups confectioners sugar, sifted

Place pretzels in a very large bowl. Stirring constantly, melt peanut butter chips in a medium saucepan over low heat. Add next 4 ingredients; stir until smooth. Pour peanut butter mixture over pretzels; stir until evenly coated. Coat pretzel mixture with sugar in batches. For each batch, place 2 cups sugar into a large brown paper bag. Add one third of pretzel mixture, close bag, and shake briefly. Spread mix on waxed paper. Cool completely. Store in an airtight container.

Yield: about 23 cups snack mix

Apple slices and cinnamon sticks garnish glasses of frosty Spiced Apple Punch.

SPICED APPLE PUNCH

    2 teaspoons ground cinnamon
    1 teaspoon dried grated lemon peel
    1/4 teaspoon ground cloves
    1/4 teaspoon ground allspice
    1/4 teaspoon ground nutmeg
    1 gallon apple cider
    1 liter ginger ale, chilled
    2 Red Delicious apples, cut
         crosswise into 1/4-inch slices,
         and cinnamon sticks to garnish

Place spices in a 6-inch square of cheesecloth or a coffee filter and tie with string. Pour cider into a stockpot. Add bundle of spices. Stirring occasionally, cook over medium-low heat 1½ hours. Remove from heat; cool to room temperature. Remove spice bundle and discard. Place punch in a covered container and freeze.

Remove punch from freezer 4 hours before serving to partially thaw. To serve, break into chunks, add ginger ale, and stir until slushy. Ladle into glasses and garnish with apple slices and cinnamon sticks.

Yield: about twenty-two 6-ounce servings

CITRUS CIDER PUNCH

We made apple cider ice cubes to serve in our punch.

    1 gallon apple cider, chilled
    1 can (12 ounces) frozen limeade
         concentrate
    1 can (12 ounces) frozen lemonade
         concentrate
    1 bottle (2 liters) lemon-lime soft
         drink, chilled
       Lemon and lime slices and
         maraschino cherries with stems
         to garnish

In a 2-gallon container, combine cider and concentrates. Stir until concentrates thaw. Stir in soft drink. Garnish servings with lemon and lime slices and maraschino cherries. Serve immediately.

Yield: about 27 cups punch

Pink lemonade and raspberry sherbet give this punch its "punch."

RASPBERRY-LEMON PUNCH

Prepare ice ring a day ahead of time.

2 cans (12 ounces each) pink lemonade concentrate, thawed and divided
6 cups water, divided
1 lemon, thinly sliced
6 whole fresh or frozen raspberries
1 half-gallon raspberry sherbet
4 cans (12 ounces each) lemon-lime soda, chilled

For ice ring, combine 1 can pink lemonade concentrate and 3 cups water in a half-gallon container. Pour 3½ cups lemonade in an 8-cup ring mold; reserve remaining lemonade. Freeze ice ring 4 hours.

Place lemon slices about 1 inch apart over frozen lemonade. Place raspberries between slices. Pour remaining 1 cup lemonade over fruit. Cover and freeze until firm.

To serve, combine remaining can lemonade concentrate and remaining 3 cups water in a half-gallon container. Pour lemonade into a punch bowl; add spoonfuls of sherbet. Dip ice mold into warm water 15 seconds. Place ice ring in punch bowl. Add lemon-lime soda; stir until blended. Serve immediately.

Yield: about 5¼ quarts punch

223

CHRISTMAS PUNCH

- 2 quarts cranberry juice
- 4 cups orange juice
- 2 cups water
- 2 cups granulated sugar
- 1 can (12 ounces) frozen cranberry-orange juice concentrate, thawed
- 1 package (0.14 ounces) unsweetened strawberry-flavored soft drink mix
- 2 liters club soda, chilled
- 1 package (12 ounces) frozen unsweetened strawberries

In a 6-quart container, stir together first 6 ingredients. Cover and refrigerate until well chilled. To serve, stir together chilled mixture, club soda, and strawberries in a large punch bowl. If desired, add crushed ice.

Yield: about thirty-two 6-ounce servings

HOT CRANBERRY PUNCH

- 6 cups cranberry juice
- 4 cups orange juice
- 1 cup water
- 1 can (6 ounces) frozen lemonade concentrate, thawed
- 1/2 cup firmly packed brown sugar
- 3 teaspoons whole cloves
- 3 teaspoons ground allspice
- 1 whole nutmeg, crushed
- 4 3-inch-long cinnamon sticks, broken into pieces

In a large saucepan or Dutch oven, combine first 5 ingredients. Place spices in a piece of cheesecloth and tie with string; add to punch. Bring to a boil, stirring occasionally.

Reduce to low heat, cover, and simmer 30 minutes. Serve hot.

Yield: about 3 quarts of punch

FIRESIDE PUNCH

- 6 cups apple cider
- 1 can (12 ounces) frozen lemonade concentrate
- 1 cup granulated sugar
- 1 cup peach schnapps
- 1 cup rum
  Fresh lemon peel to garnish

In a Dutch oven, combine first 3 ingredients; bring to a boil. Remove from heat; stir in schnapps and rum. Serve hot in mugs and garnish with lemon peel.

Yield: about twelve 6-ounce servings

CHERRY-APPLE PUNCH
Make punch the day of party.

- 1 cup boiling water
- 1 package (3 ounces) cherry gelatin
- 1 can (6 ounces) frozen pink lemonade concentrate, thawed
- 3 cups apple juice
- 2 cans (12 ounces each) cherry-lemon-lime soda, chilled

In a medium bowl, stir boiling water into gelatin until gelatin dissolves. In a large container, combine gelatin, lemonade concentrate, and apple juice. Cover and chill 2 hours. To serve, stir in cherry-lime soda; serve immediately.

Yield: about 7 1/2 cups punch

HOT CRANBERRY-BANANA PUNCH

1 bottle (48 ounces) cranberry juice cocktail
1 can (6 ounces) frozen lemonade concentrate
1/2 cup firmly packed brown sugar
2 1/2 cups mashed bananas (about 6 medium bananas)
1 tablespoon ground allspice
1 teaspoon ground nutmeg
1/2 teaspoon ground cinnamon

In a large saucepan or Dutch oven, combine cranberry juice, lemonade, brown sugar, and bananas. Cook over medium-high heat, stirring until well blended. Layer four 4-inch squares of cheesecloth. Place allspice, nutmeg, and cinnamon in center of cheesecloth square and tie with string; add to punch. Stirring occasionally, bring to a boil. Reduce heat to low. Cover and simmer 30 minutes. Remove spice bag. Serve hot.

Yield: about 9 cups punch

SPARKLING FRUIT PUNCH

1 can (12 ounces) frozen apple-grape-raspberry juice concentrate, thawed
1 can (6 ounces) frozen lemonade concentrate, thawed
1 bottle (25 ounces) sparkling red grape juice *or* 1 fifth (750 ml) sparkling wine, chilled

Combine frozen juice concentrates in a 1-quart container. Cover and store in refrigerator. To serve, combine blended concentrates and sparkling grape juice or wine. Serve chilled.

Yield: about seven 6-ounce servings

ORANGE-PINEAPPLE PUNCH

Punch must be made 1 day in advance.

2 quarts water
2 cans (20 ounces each) unsweetened crushed pineapple, undrained
3 cups granulated sugar
3 ripe bananas, mashed
1 can (12 ounces) frozen orange juice concentrate, thawed
1 can (6 ounces) frozen lemonade concentrate, thawed
1 package (0.14 ounces) unsweetened orange-flavored soft drink mix
1 liter ginger ale, chilled
1 jar (10 ounces) maraschino cherries, drained

In a 6-quart container, combine first 7 ingredients. Place punch in a covered container and freeze.

Remove punch from freezer 4 hours before serving to partially thaw. To serve, break into chunks. Add ginger ale and cherries; stir until slushy.

Yield: about twenty-seven 6-ounce servings

Freezer Margaritas are an invigorating complement to party food.

FREEZER MARGARITAS

2 cups water
1 cup sugar
1½ cups freshly squeezed lime
    juice (about 8 limes)
1½ cups tequila
¾ cup Triple Sec liqueur
    Lime zest to garnish

In a small saucepan, combine water and sugar over high heat. Stirring frequently, bring mixture to a boil. Remove syrup from heat and cool 1 hour.

In a 2-quart freezer container, combine syrup, lime juice, tequila, and liqueur. Cover and freeze overnight.

To serve, spoon into glasses and garnish with lime zest.

Yield: about 6½ cups margaritas

ORANGE CREAM

- 4 cups orange juice
- 3 cinnamon sticks
- 1 tablespoon vanilla extract
- 1 pint vanilla ice cream
  Miniature marshmallows to serve

In a large saucepan, combine orange juice, cinnamon sticks, and vanilla over medium-high heat. Bring mixture to a boil and reduce to low heat. Simmer 10 minutes. Remove cinnamon sticks. Stir in ice cream. Cook over low heat, stirring constantly, until heated through. Do not allow mixture to boil. Serve with miniature marshmallows.

Yield: 4 to 6 servings

FRUITY YOGURT SHAKE

- 1 cup orange juice
- 1 container (8 ounces) lemon yogurt
- 1/2 banana
- 1/2 cup orange pieces
- 1/2 cup chopped apple
- 1/2 cup grapefruit pieces
- 2 cups frozen vanilla yogurt

Combine orange juice, lemon yogurt, banana, orange, apple, grapefruit, and frozen yogurt in a blender. Blend just until combined. Chill in freezer about 30 minutes or until mixture is desired consistency, stirring after 15 minutes.

Yield: about 4 cups

Flavored with a hint of cinnamon, Orange Cream is made from orange juice and vanilla ice cream and is luscious served warm.

STRAWBERRY FIZZ

- 3 packages (10 ounces each) frozen sweetened sliced strawberries
- 3 cartons (8 ounces each) strawberry yogurt
- 2 tablespoons sugar
- 4 cans (12 ounces each) strawberry-flavored soft drink, chilled

Process frozen strawberries, yogurt, and sugar in a food processor until smooth. Spoon strawberry mixture into a punch bowl; stir in soft drink. Serve immediately.

Yield: about 16 cups punch

SUNSHINE PUNCH

- 3 bananas, peeled and cut into pieces
- 1 can (6 ounces) frozen lemonade concentrate, thawed
- 4 cups water
- 2 cups red grape juice
- 1 can (6 ounces) frozen pineapple juice concentrate, thawed

In a blender or food processor fitted with a steel blade, process bananas and lemonade concentrate until well blended. Transfer to a 3-quart container. Add remaining ingredients; stir until well blended. Cover and refrigerate. Serve chilled.

Yield: about 2½ quarts punch

WINE PUNCH

- 2 bottles (720 ml each) dry white wine
- 2 cans (12 ounces each) frozen pineapple juice concentrate, thawed
- 1 can (6 ounces) frozen lemonade concentrate, thawed
- 1 can (6 ounces) frozen orange juice concentrate, thawed
- 1 jar (10 ounces) maraschino cherries

In a 1 gallon container, combine first 4 ingredients, stirring until well blended. Stir in cherries. Cover and chill 8 hours or overnight to allow flavors to blend. Serve chilled.

Yield: about 3 quarts punch

CRANBERRY-CHAMPAGNE COCKTAILS

- 1 quart cranberry juice cocktail, chilled
- 1 bottle (750 ml) champagne, chilled

Combine cranberry juice and champagne in a 2-quart pitcher; stir until well blended. Serve chilled.

Yield: about nine 6-ounce servings

FRESH MINT LEMONADE

- 6 cups sugar
- 2 cups water
- 2 cups coarsely chopped fresh mint leaves
- 3 cups freshly squeezed lemon juice (about 16 lemons)
- 2 tablespoons grated lemon zest

In a Dutch oven, combine sugar and water over medium heat; stir until sugar dissolves. Increase heat to medium-high. Add mint leaves and bring to a boil. Stirring constantly, boil 1 minute. Strain syrup into a heat-resistant container; allow to cool. Stir in lemon juice and lemon zest. Cover and chill. To serve, combine 2 parts club soda with 1 part lemonade concentrate. Serve over ice; garnish with lemon slices and mint leaves.

Yield: about 8 cups lemonade concentrate

ZESTY TOMATO JUICE

- 1 can (48 ounces) tomato juice
- 1/2 cup lemon juice
- 1/4 cup Worcestershire sauce
- 2 tablespoons juice from canned or bottled jalapeño peppers
- 1 1/2 teaspoons hot pepper sauce
- 1/2 teaspoon onion juice

Combine tomato juice, lemon juice, Worcestershire sauce, pepper juice, pepper sauce, and onion juice; stir well. Store in refrigerator.

Yield: about 6 servings

CHERRY-BERRY CIDER

- 1 package (12 ounces) frozen whole blackberries
- 1 package (12 ounces) frozen whole dark sweet cherries
- 3 cinnamon sticks
- 2 teaspoons whole allspice
- 1 gallon apple cider
  Cinnamon sticks to serve

In a Dutch oven, combine blackberries, cherries, 3 cinnamon sticks, and allspice. Add apple cider. Bring to a simmer over medium-high heat. Use a potato masher to mash fruit. Reduce heat to medium; cover and simmer 30 minutes. Strain mixture and serve warm with cinnamon sticks.

Yield: about 16 1/2 cups cider

SPICY TOMATO PUNCH
May be made one day in advance.

- 4 cups tomato juice
- 1 cup pineapple juice
- 1 cup orange juice
- 2 tablespoons prepared horseradish
- 1 teaspoon ground black pepper
- 1 teaspoon Worcestershire sauce
- 1 teaspoon hot pepper sauce
  Celery stalks to garnish

In a 2-quart container, combine tomato juice, pineapple juice, orange juice, horseradish, black pepper, Worcestershire sauce, and pepper sauce; stir until well blended. Cover and refrigerate 8 hours or overnight to allow flavors to blend. Serve chilled with celery stalks.

Yield: about 6 cups punch

Pretty in pink and brimming with raspberries, Silver Bells Punch makes a lovely drink for a tea party or shower.

SILVER BELLS PUNCH

1 can (46 ounces) unsweetened pineapple juice, chilled
2 cups piña colada drink mixer, chilled
1 can (12 ounces) frozen orange juice concentrate, thawed
1 liter club soda, chilled
1 liter lemon-lime soft drink, chilled
1 package (10 ounces) frozen raspberries in syrup, slightly thawed

In a punch bowl, stir together first 5 ingredients. To serve, stir in raspberries. Serve chilled.

Yield: about twenty-four 6-ounce servings

CRANBERRY-BRANDY PUNCH

Cranberry-Brandy Punch may be served warm or chilled.

5 cups cranberry juice cocktail
3 cups orange juice
2 cups brandy

To serve warm, combine all ingredients in a large saucepan or Dutch oven. Cook over medium heat until heated through. Serve immediately.

To serve chilled, combine all ingredients in a 3-quart container. Serve over ice.

Yield: about 10 cups punch

MERRY CHERRY COCKTAILS

- ²/₃ cup half and half
- ½ cup cream of coconut
- ⅓ cup dark rum
- ⅓ cup cherry brandy
- 3 tablespoons maraschino cherry juice
- 3 teaspoons grenadine syrup
- 1½ to 2 cups ice cubes
  Whipped cream and maraschino cherries to garnish

Place half and half, cream of coconut, rum, brandy, cherry juice, grenadine, and ice in a blender; process until well blended. Pour into glasses; garnish each serving with whipped cream and a cherry.

Yield: 5 to 6 servings

Merry Cherry Cocktails are a frothy combination of cherry and coconut flavors.

CHAMPAGNE PUNCH

- 1 bottle (64 ounces) cranberry juice cocktail, chilled
- 1 can (12 ounces) frozen pineapple juice concentrate, thawed
- 2 cups brandy
- 2 bottles (750 ml each) champagne, chilled

Combine cranberry juice, pineapple juice, and brandy in a large punch bowl. Stir in champagne. Serve immediately.

Yield: about 18 cups punch

Champagne Punch is a refreshing mix of fruit juices, brandy, and chilled bubbly.

STRAWBERRY PUNCH

Strawberry Punch must be made 1 day in advance.

- 2 quarts water
- 3 cups granulated sugar
- 1 package (16 ounces) frozen unsweetened strawberries, thawed and puréed
- 3 ripe bananas, peeled and mashed
- 1 can (6 ounces) frozen orange juice concentrate, thawed
- 1 can (6 ounces) frozen lemonade concentrate, thawed
- 3 packages (0.14 ounces each) unsweetened cherry-flavored soft drink mix
- 1 liter ginger ale, chilled

In a 6-quart container, mix together first 7 ingredients. Loosely cover and freeze until firm.

Remove punch from freezer 4 hours before serving; partially thaw. To serve, break into chunks. Add ginger ale and stir until slushy.

Yield: about twenty-eight 6-ounce servings

FUZZY NAVEL PUNCH

- 9 cups orange juice with pulp
- 3 cups peach schnapps
- 1 bottle (750 ml) brut champagne, chilled
  Crushed ice or ice ring

Combine orange juice, peach schnapps, and champagne. Pour into a punch bowl and add crushed ice or ice ring.

Yield: about 1 gallon of punch

HONEY-OF-A-PUNCH

- 5 cups unsweetened pineapple juice
- 5 cups cranberry juice cocktail
- 2 cups water
- 1 cup honey
- 2 tablespoons whole allspice
- 4 two-inch cinnamon sticks

Place first 4 ingredients in a large Dutch oven. Place allspice and cinnamon sticks in center of a 6-inch square of cheesecloth and tie with string. Add spices to punch mixture and simmer over medium-low heat 1 hour. Serve hot. (Punch may also be prepared by placing first 4 ingredients in a large electric percolator. Stir until well blended. Place allspice and cinnamon sticks in percolator basket. Perk through complete cycle.)

Yield: about seventeen 6-ounce servings

CARIBBEAN COOLER PUNCH

- 2½ cups peach nectar
- 2 cups orange juice
- 1 cup pineapple juice
- 1½ cups light rum
- 1 cup club soda
- ½ cup granulated sugar
- 2 teaspoons grenadine

Combine all ingredients in a 2-quart pitcher. Serve chilled or over ice. Store in refrigerator.

Yield: about 2 quarts of punch

STRAWBERRY WINE PUNCH

- 1/2 cup sugar
- 1/4 cup water
- 2 packages (10 ounces each) frozen sweetened sliced strawberries, partially thawed
- 2 bottles (750 ml each) red wine, chilled
- 1 bottle (2 liters) lemon-lime soda, chilled

In a small saucepan, combine sugar and water over medium-high heat. Stirring frequently, bring to a boil. Remove from heat and cool. Cover and chill syrup until ready to serve.

To serve, place strawberries in a 1 1/2-gallon container. Pour wine and lemon-lime soda over strawberries; carefully stir to break up strawberries. Sweeten punch to taste by adding 1 tablespoon syrup at a time; stir well after each addition. Serve immediately.

Yield: about 16 cups punch

PEACH EGGNOG

- 1 quart prepared eggnog
- 3 cups half and half
- 1 can (12 ounces) apricot nectar
- 1 cup rum
- 1 cup peach-flavored brandy

In a 3-quart container, combine all ingredients; stir until well blended. Store in an airtight container in refrigerator. Serve chilled.

Yield: about fourteen 6-ounce servings

FRUIT SIP

- 1 bottle (48 ounces) apple-cherry juice
- 3 3-inch cinnamon sticks
- 1/2 cup dried apples
- 1/2 cup dried chopped dates
- 1/2 cup raisins
- 2 teaspoons vanilla extract

In a large saucepan, combine all ingredients. Bring to a simmer and remove from heat. Allow to cool. Steep in refrigerator overnight. Drain the liquid through a strainer or doubled layer of cheesecloth into a bowl. Pour the liquid into a glass bottle. Cap bottle tightly. Store in refrigerator. Serve hot or cold.

Yield: six 8-ounce servings

CHOCOLATE EGGNOG

- 1 quart prepared eggnog
- 1/2 cup chocolate syrup
- 1/4 teaspoon ground nutmeg
- 1 tablespoon vanilla extract
  Ground nutmeg for garnish

In a large saucepan, combine eggnog, chocolate syrup, and 1/4 teaspoon nutmeg. Stirring occasionally, cook over medium-low heat 20 to 25 minutes or until heated through (do not boil). Remove from heat; stir in vanilla. To serve, pour into cups; sprinkle tops lightly with nutmeg. Serve warm.

Yield: six 6-ounce servings

Raspberry Cider is simple to heat up in just minutes by combining apple cider, raspberry jelly, and powdered soft drink mixes.

RASPBERRY CIDER

1 quart apple cider
1 jar (12 ounces) raspberry jelly
1 teaspoon presweetened lemonade-flavored soft drink mix
1/8 teaspoon unsweetened raspberry-flavored soft drink mix
Fresh lemon slices to serve

In a large saucepan, bring cider to a simmer. Add jelly and drink mixes, stirring until jelly is dissolved. Serve hot with lemon slices.

Yield: about seven 6-ounce servings

PEANUT BUTTER HOT COCOA

9 cups milk, divided
1/2 cup smooth peanut butter
1 1/2 cups chocolate mix for milk
Whipped cream to garnish

In a Dutch oven, combine 1 cup milk and peanut butter. Stirring frequently, cook over low heat until smooth. Increase heat to medium. Slowly stir in remaining 8 cups milk and chocolate mix. Stirring occasionally, cook just until mixture simmers. Garnish each serving with whipped cream; serve immediately.

Yield: about 9 1/2 cups cocoa

CHERRY-MOCHA WARMER

2 cups very hot strongly brewed
   coffee *or* 2 cups boiling water
   and 2 tablespoons instant
   coffee granules
4 ounces semisweet baking
   chocolate, chopped
2/3 cup granulated sugar
1/8 teaspoon salt
4 cups half and half
2 cups milk
3/4 cup crème de cacao
3/4 cup cherry brandy
1 cup whipping cream
1/4 cup sifted confectioners sugar
   Maraschino cherries with stems
   to garnish

Chill a small bowl and beaters from an electric mixer in freezer. In a double boiler over hot water, combine coffee, chocolate, granulated sugar, and salt. Whisk until chocolate is melted and smooth. In a medium saucepan, scald half and half and milk; whisk into chocolate mixture. Whisk in crème de cacao and brandy. Keep chocolate mixture warm.

In chilled bowl, beat whipping cream until soft peaks form. Gradually add confectioners sugar and beat until stiff peaks form. Serve each warm beverage with a dollop of whipped cream and a maraschino cherry.

Yield: about fourteen 6-ounce servings

PRALINE COFFEE

2 quarts brewed coffee
3 cans (12-ounce each)
   evaporated skimmed milk
1/2 cup firmly packed brown sugar
3 cups fat-free vanilla ice cream,
   softened
1 cup vodka
1 tablespoon vanilla extract
2 teaspoons maple flavoring

In a Dutch oven, combine coffee, milk, and sugar. Stirring occasionally, cook over medium-high heat until mixture begins to boil; remove from heat. Stir in ice cream, vodka, vanilla, and maple flavoring. Serve hot.

Yield: about twenty 6-ounce servings

MOCHA-CARDAMOM CAPPUCCINO

3 cups brewed coffee
3 cups half and half
1 cup rum
1 cup coffee-flavored liqueur
2 teaspoons ground cardamom

In a large saucepan or Dutch oven, combine coffee, half and half, rum, liqueur, and cardamom. Cook over medium heat until mixture begins to boil. Remove from heat. Serve immediately.

Yield: about 7 1/2 cups cappuccino

SPICED IRISH COFFEE

⅓ cup plus 2 tablespoons sugar, divided
¼ teaspoon ground cinnamon
2 cups skim milk
2 cinnamon sticks
1 whole nutmeg, crushed
2½ quarts hot, strongly brewed coffee
3 tablespoons fat-free non-dairy powdered creamer
⅔ cup Irish whiskey
Fat-free frozen whipped topping, thawed to garnish

In a small bowl, combine 2 tablespoons sugar and ground cinnamon; set aside. Combine remaining ⅓ cup sugar, milk, cinnamon sticks, and nutmeg in a Dutch oven. Cook over medium-low heat, stirring until sugar dissolves. Stir in coffee and creamer. Cover and heat 5 minutes to allow flavors to blend. Remove from heat; strain and discard cinnamon sticks and nutmeg. Stir in Irish whiskey. Pour into 8-ounce Irish coffee glasses. Garnish each serving with 1 tablespoon whipped topping and sprinkle with sugar-cinnamon mixture. Serve immediately.

Yield: about 12 cups coffee

HONEY-CINNAMON COFFEE

1½ tablespoons ground coffee
½ teaspoon ground cinnamon
3 cups water
6 tablespoons honey
¼ cup warm half and half

Combine coffee and cinnamon in a coffee filter. Pour water into a drip coffee maker and brew coffee. Stir honey and half and half into brewed coffee; serve immediately.

Yield: about 3 cups coffee

HOLIDAY COFFEE

⅓ cup ground coffee
2 cinnamon sticks, broken into pieces
6 whole cloves
1 vanilla bean (about 3 inches long)
1½ quarts water

Combine coffee, cinnamon pieces, and cloves in an airtight container. Split vanilla bean and scrape seeds into mixture. Cut vanilla bean into 3 pieces and add to mixture. Cover and store overnight to allow flavors to blend.

To serve, brew coffee mixture and water in a 10-cup coffee maker. Serve hot.

Yield: about eight 6-ounce servings

Blend together four simple ingredients and add freshly brewed coffee for aromatic Cinnamon Mocha, a tasty sensation!

CINNAMON MOCHA

6 ounces semisweet baking chocolate, chopped
1/2 cup half and half
1/4 cup sugar
1/2 teaspoon ground cinnamon
1 1/2 quarts hot brewed coffee

Combine chocolate, half and half, sugar, and cinnamon in top of a double boiler over hot water; stir until chocolate melts. Transfer chocolate mixture to a large heat-resistant container. Pour brewed coffee over chocolate mixture; whisk until frothy. Pour into cups and serve hot.

Yield: about ten 6-ounce servings

CARAMEL MOCHA

- 1 can (14 ounces) sweetened condensed milk
- 1 container (12 ounces) caramel ice cream topping
- 1/2 cup chocolate-flavored syrup
- 2 1/2 quarts hot, strongly brewed coffee (we used espresso roast coffee)

In a small Dutch oven, combine sweetened condensed milk, caramel topping, and chocolate syrup. Stirring constantly, cook over medium-low heat about 8 minutes or until mixture is well blended and hot. Add coffee; stir until blended. Serve hot.

Yield: about 12 cups coffee

RASPBERRY COFFEE

- 1 cup half and half
- 2/3 cup sugar
- 1 quart hot, strongly brewed raspberry-flavored coffee

For hot coffee, place half and half and sugar in a small saucepan over medium-low heat. Stirring frequently, heat about 10 minutes or until hot. Combine coffee and half and half mixture in a 1 1/2-quart heatproof container; serve hot.

For iced coffee, combine coffee and sugar in a 1 1/2-quart heatproof container. Stir until sugar dissolves; cover and chill. To serve, stir half and half into coffee mixture; serve over ice.

Yield: about 5 cups coffee

ALMOND CAPPUCCINO

- 8 cups brewed coffee
- 4 cups evaporated skimmed milk
- 1/2 cup firmly packed brown sugar
- 1 tablespoon vanilla extract
- 1 teaspoon almond extract

In a large saucepan or Dutch oven, combine coffee, evaporated milk, and brown sugar. Stirring occasionally, cook over medium-high heat until mixture begins to boil; remove from heat. Stir in vanilla and almond extracts. Serve hot.

Yield: about 12 cups cappuccino

CREAMY COFFEE PUNCH

- 2 quarts hot, strongly brewed coffee
- 3 tablespoons sugar
- 2 teaspoons vanilla extract
- 2 cups coffee-flavored liqueur
- 1 quart vanilla ice cream, softened
- 2 cups whipping cream, whipped

Place coffee in a 3-quart heatproof container. Add sugar and vanilla; stir until sugar dissolves. Allow mixture to cool. Stir in liqueur; cover and chill.

To serve, pour chilled coffee mixture into a punch bowl. Stir in ice cream. Fold in whipped cream. Serve immediately.

Yield: about 16 cups punch

CHRISTMAS TEA

    Maraschino cherries with stems,
        drained and frozen in ice
        cubes
2 quarts water, divided
3 large tea bags
1 can (6 ounces) frozen orange
      juice concentrate, thawed
2 teaspoons orange extract
12 packets sugar substitute

In a large saucepan or Dutch oven, bring 1 quart water to a boil. Remove from heat. Add tea bags; let stand 15 minutes. Remove tea bags. Stir in remaining 1 quart cold water. Add remaining ingredients; stir until well blended. Cover and refrigerate until well chilled. To serve, pour tea over prepared ice cubes.

Yield: about ten 6-ounce servings

SPARKLING FRUIT TEA

4 cups water
15 orange and spice-flavored tea bags
1 cup sugar
1 can (12 ounces) frozen apple juice
      concentrate, thawed
4 1/2 cups cold water
1 bottle (750 ml) sparkling white
      grape juice, chilled

In a large saucepan, bring 4 cups water to a boil. Remove from heat; add tea bags. Cover and steep 10 minutes; remove tea bags. Add sugar; stir until dissolved. In a 1-gallon container, combine apple juice concentrate and cold water. Stir in tea mixture. Cover and chill.

To serve, add grape juice to tea mixture. Serve immediately.

Yield: about 13 cups fruit tea

HOT FRUITED TEA

This hot beverage will fill your home with a wonderful spicy aroma. After it is brewed, the tea may be refrigerated and reheated later. For larger crowds, we suggest serving the tea from an electric coffee server.

1 1/2 cups water
1/3 cup unsweetened powdered
      instant tea
1 can (46 ounces) pineapple juice
6 cups orange juice
6 cups lemonade
1 1/2 cups sugar
3 whole nutmegs
3 tablespoons whole cloves
4 2-inch cinnamon sticks
      Sliced oranges or lemons to
      serve

In a large Dutch oven, bring water to a boil; stir in instant tea until dissolved. Stir in pineapple juice, orange juice, lemonade, and sugar, mixing well. Place nutmegs and cloves in center of a small square of cheesecloth and tie corners together to form a bag. Add spice bag and cinnamon sticks to tea. Stirring occasionally, simmer 2 to 3 hours over medium-low heat (do not allow mixture to boil). Remove spice bag and serve hot tea with slices of orange or lemon.

Yield: about 16 cups tea

ROSEMARY TEA

½ cup tea leaves
1 tablespoon dried rosemary leaves

In a blender or food processor, finely grind tea and rosemary. Store in an airtight container.

To brew tea, place 1 teaspoon tea for each 8 ounces of water in a warm teapot. Bring water to a rolling boil and pour over tea. Steep tea 5 minutes, stir, and strain through cheesecloth. Serve hot or over ice.

Yield: about ⅓ cup tea leaves

HOT CRANBERRY-LEMON TEA

8 cups boiling water
4 regular-size tea bags
1 stick cinnamon
1¼ cups sugar
4 cups cranberry juice cocktail
¼ cup freshly squeezed lemon juice
Cinnamon sticks to serve

In a heavy large Dutch oven, pour boiling water over tea bags and cinnamon stick; steep 5 minutes. Remove tea bags and cinnamon stick. Add sugar; stir until dissolved. Stir in cranberry juice cocktail and lemon juice. Place over medium heat until mixture is heated through. Serve hot with cinnamon sticks.

Yield: about 12 cups tea

Rosemary Tea has a distinctive flavor that enhances sweet treats.

Our Favorite FAMILY FEASTS

Nothing compares to the warmth and welcome of a family gathering. Whether it's an intimate gathering around the kitchen table or a four-course holiday celebration, food can comfort, nourish, and delight. That's why we've compiled some of our favorite recipes in this collection. Whatever the occasion, your family will enjoy feasting on our mouthwatering fare.

Ginger-Glazed Turkey, p. 242

FAMILY FEAST

Sweet Red Pepper-Crab Bisque

Cherry Salad

Ginger-Glazed Turkey

Apple Rings with Sweet Potato Topping

Honey-Glazed New Potatoes

Asparagus en Croûte with Tarragon Sauce

Cheddar-Pumpkin Soufflé

Lemon Mousse with Raspberry Sauce

GINGER-GLAZED TURKEY

GLAZE

     6 tablespoons finely chopped
         crystallized ginger
    1/4 cup vegetable oil
     1 cup soy sauce
     6 tablespoons firmly packed
         brown sugar
     6 tablespoons rum

TURKEY

    13 to 15 pound turkey
     2 tablespoons vegetable oil
        Salt and ground black pepper
     1 cup water

GRAVY

     1 tablespoon cornstarch
     2 tablespoons water

For glaze, combine ginger and oil in a medium saucepan. Cook over medium heat until ginger begins to brown. Stir in soy sauce, brown sugar, and rum. Bring to a boil; remove from heat.

For turkey, remove giblets and neck from turkey. Place giblets and neck in a medium saucepan and add enough water to cover; bring to a boil. Continue to boil 20 minutes; remove from heat. Cover saucepan, cool 10 minutes, and refrigerate.

Preheat oven to 350 degrees. Rinse turkey and pat dry with paper towels. Rub turkey with oil. Liberally salt and pepper turkey inside and out. Tie ends of legs to tail with kitchen twine; lift wing tips up and over back so they are tucked under bird. Place in a large roasting pan with breast side up. Insert a meat thermometer into thickest part of thigh without touching bone. Pour 1 cup water into pan. Brush glaze on turkey. Loosely cover with aluminum foil and roast 3 to 3 1/2 hours, basting with glaze every 30 minutes. To test for doneness, meat thermometer should register 180 degrees and juices run clear when thickest part of thigh is pierced with a fork. Transfer turkey to a serving platter and let stand 20 minutes before carving. Reserve remaining glaze and 1 cup drippings from roasting pan for gravy.

For gravy, dissolve cornstarch in water in a small bowl. Pour remaining glaze and reserved drippings into saucepan containing giblet mixture. Bring to a boil over medium heat. Remove neck and giblets. Stirring constantly, add cornstarch mixture and continue to cook 5 to 8 minutes or until gravy thickens. Serve with turkey.

Yield: 18 to 20 servings

Baked to a golden brown, Ginger-Glazed Turkey looks picture-perfect. A bed of Apple Rings with Sweet Potato Topping (recipe on page 244) is an attractive way to combine two traditional flavors.

APPLE RINGS WITH SWEET POTATO TOPPING

(Shown on page 243)

SWEET POTATO TOPPING

- 1 can (29 ounces) sweet potatoes, drained
- 1 tablespoon butter or margarine, melted
- 1 tablespoon firmly packed brown sugar
- 1/4 teaspoon salt
- 1/8 teaspoon ground cloves
- 1/8 teaspoon ground cinnamon

APPLE RINGS

- 6 tablespoons butter or margarine
- 1/4 cup firmly packed brown sugar
- 2 tablespoons water
- 2 tablespoons freshly squeezed lemon juice
- 1 teaspoon dried lemon peel
- 1/2 teaspoon ground ginger
- 3 unpeeled Red Delicious apples (about 1 1/4 pounds), cored and cut into 1/2-inch rings (about 20 rings)

For sweet potato topping, process sweet potatoes, melted butter, brown sugar, salt, cloves, and cinnamon in a food processor until smooth. Transfer to a medium saucepan. Stirring occasionally, cook over medium heat 10 to 12 minutes or until heated through. Remove from heat, cover, and set aside.

For apple rings, melt butter in a large skillet over medium heat. Add brown sugar, water, lemon juice, lemon peel, and ginger; stir until sugar dissolves. Cook 1 layer of apple rings at a time 5 to 6 minutes in sugar mixture; turn and cook 5 to 6 minutes longer or until tender. Arrange on serving platter. If necessary, reheat sweet potato topping over low heat, stirring occasionally. Spoon sweet potato topping into a pastry bag fitted with a large star tip and pipe in center of each apple ring. Serve warm.

Yield: about 10 servings

SWEET RED PEPPER-CRAB BISQUE

Bisque may be made one day in advance.

- 2 tablespoons olive oil
- 3 cups coarsely chopped sweet red peppers (about 3 large sweet red peppers)
- 3 green onions, chopped
- 1 cup coarsely chopped celery (about 3 ribs celery)
- 2/3 cup coarsely chopped carrots (about 2 medium carrots)
- 1/2 cup coarsely chopped red onion
- 2 teaspoons salt
- 1/2 teaspoon dried tarragon leaves
- 1/8 teaspoon ground red pepper
- 4 cups coarsely chopped tomatoes (about 4 large tomatoes)
- 1 1/2 cups whipping cream
- 1 cup dry sherry
- 2 tablespoons rum
- 1/2 pound lump crabmeat
- 1/2 teaspoon freshly squeezed lemon juice or to taste

In a 6-quart saucepan, heat oil over medium heat. Add sweet red peppers, green onions, celery, carrots, red onion, salt, tarragon, and ground red pepper; cook, stirring occasionally, until vegetables are tender. Add tomatoes; stir until well blended. Stir in whipping cream, sherry, and rum. Reduce heat to low and simmer 1 hour, stirring occasionally. Stir in crabmeat and lemon juice; cook 5 to 10 minutes longer or until crabmeat is heated through. Serve warm. (If making bisque in advance, cover and refrigerate. Reheat over low heat until warm.)

Yield: 8 to 10 servings

CHERRY SALAD

    2 cups boiling water
    2 packages (3 ounces each)
         cherry gelatin
    1 can (16 ounces) pitted cherries
         packed in water, drained
    1 pint vanilla ice cream, softened
    1 cup sour cream
         Whipped cream to garnish

In a large bowl, combine boiling water and gelatin; stir until gelatin dissolves. Cool to room temperature.

Purée cherries in a food processor. Add to gelatin mixture; stir until well blended. In a medium bowl, beat ice cream and sour cream using medium speed of an electric mixer. Stir ice cream mixture into gelatin mixture. Pour into a 9 x 13-inch baking pan. Cover and refrigerate until set. Cut into 3-inch squares and garnish with whipped cream.

Yield: about 12 servings

HONEY-GLAZED NEW POTATOES

    2½ pounds new potatoes, cut into
           quarters
    ½   cup butter or margarine
    ¼   cup water
    2   tablespoons honey
    1   teaspoon salt
    ¼   teaspoon ground black pepper

In a large saucepan or Dutch oven, cover potatoes with salted water. Bring water to a boil and cook until potatoes are tender; drain.

In a large skillet, melt butter over medium heat. Stir in water, honey, salt, and pepper. Stirring occasionally, cook 1 layer of potatoes at a time 10 to 12 minutes or until brown. Transfer to serving dish and cover with aluminum foil to keep warm. Serve warm.

Yield: 6 to 8 servings

ASPARAGUS EN CROÛTE WITH TARRAGON SAUCE
Sauce may be made one day in advance.

ASPARAGUS EN CROÛTE
    1 cup water
    3 packages (8 ounces each)
         frozen asparagus spears, cut
         into 4-inch spears
    1 can (8 ounces) refrigerated
         crescent rolls
    2 tablespoons butter or margarine,
         melted

TARRAGON SAUCE
    ½ cup butter or margarine
    2 tablespoons all-purpose flour
    1 tablespoon Dijon-style mustard
    ½ teaspoon dried tarragon leaves,
         crushed
    ½ teaspoon salt
    ¼ teaspoon ground black pepper
    1 cup whipping cream
         (Continued on page 246)

(Continued on page 246)

245

For asparagus en croûte, bring water to a rolling boil in a large skillet. Add asparagus; cook 5 to 8 minutes or until tender. Drain well and pat dry with paper towels.

Preheat oven to 375 degrees. Separate crescent rolls into triangles. Stack about 5 spears of asparagus on wide end of each triangle. Beginning with wide end, roll up each triangle and place on an ungreased baking sheet with point side down. Brush asparagus and crescent roll with melted butter. Bake 10 to 13 minutes or until rolls are golden brown.

For tarragon sauce, melt butter in a medium saucepan over medium heat while asparagus-crescent rolls are baking. Add flour, mustard, tarragon, salt, and pepper to melted butter; stir to form a thin paste. Slowly stir in whipping cream. Cook, stirring constantly, 5 to 8 minutes or until sauce thickens. (If making sauce in advance, cover and refrigerate. To reheat, transfer to a saucepan and cook over medium-low heat until warm.)

To serve, spoon about 2 tablespoons sauce onto each plate. Place asparagus-crescent roll on top of sauce. Serve immediately.

Yield: 8 servings

LEMON MOUSSE WITH RASPBERRY SAUCE

Lemon Mousse and Raspberry Sauce may be made one day in advance and stored in separate containers in refrigerator.

LEMON MOUSSE
1 1/2 teaspoons unflavored gelatin
  2 tablespoons cold water

3/4 cup freshly squeezed lemon juice
3/4 cup sugar
  4 eggs
  3 tablespoons butter or margarine
  2 tablespoons grated lemon zest
  1 cup whipping cream

RASPBERRY SAUCE
  2 packages (12 ounces each) frozen red raspberries, thawed
  1 bottle (1 1/2 liters) Beaujolais wine
  1 cup sugar

For lemon mousse, place a large bowl and beaters from an electric mixer in refrigerator until well chilled. In a small bowl, sprinkle gelatin over water; allow to stand 1 minute to soften. In top of a double boiler over simmering water, whisk lemon juice, sugar, eggs, butter, and lemon zest. Stir in gelatin mixture. Stirring constantly, cook over simmering water 12 to 15 minutes or until lemon mixture thickens and coats the back of a spoon. Remove from heat and cool to room temperature.

In chilled bowl, beat whipping cream until stiff. Gently fold into lemon mixture. Spoon evenly into 12 paper-lined muffin cups. Cover and refrigerate until set.

For raspberry sauce, purée raspberries in a food processor. Strain purée; discard seeds. Combine purée, wine, and sugar in a heavy large saucepan. Cook over medium-high heat, stirring until sugar dissolves and mixture begins to boil. Reduce heat to medium-low and simmer about 3 hours or until mixture reduces to about 2 cups. Remove from heat, cover, and refrigerate until well chilled.

To serve, invert onto a serving plate and remove paper from each mousse. Spoon about 2½ tablespoons sauce over each mousse. Serve chilled.

Yield: 12 servings

CHEDDAR-PUMPKIN SOUFFLÉ

- ⅓ cup grated Parmesan cheese
- ¼ cup butter or margarine
- ¼ cup all-purpose flour
- 1½ cups water
- 1 can (16 ounces) pumpkin
- 6 eggs, separated
- ½ teaspoon salt
- ¼ teaspoon ground black pepper
- ¼ teaspoon cream of tartar
- 1¾ cups (about 7 ounces) shredded sharp Cheddar cheese

Prepare a 1½-quart soufflé dish by fitting an aluminum foil collar around outside of dish with top extending 3 to 4 inches above rim. Use transparent tape to secure. Grease dish and collar. Dust dish and collar with Parmesan cheese; discard excess.

Preheat oven to 400 degrees. In a large saucepan, melt butter over medium heat. Add flour, stirring to make a paste. Cook 3 to 4 minutes or until flour begins to brown. Whisk in water. Stirring constantly, bring to a boil and cook 5 minutes. Add pumpkin and stir until well blended. Remove from heat.

Place egg yolks in a large bowl. Whisk about ½ cup pumpkin mixture into yolks. Whisk salt, pepper, and remaining pumpkin mixture into yolk mixture.

In another large bowl, beat egg whites and cream of tartar until stiff. Fold ½ of egg white mixture into pumpkin mixture. Fold Cheddar cheese and remaining egg white mixture into pumpkin mixture. Pour into soufflé dish. Bake 1 hour 10 minutes to 1 hour 15 minutes or until brown and set in center. Remove collar and serve immediately.

Yield: 10 to 12 servings

Complete a memorable meal with this creamy and colorful dessert. Individual portions of tangy Lemon Mousse with Raspberry Sauce are shaped in muffin cups.

HOME FOR THE HOLIDAYS

Orange-Carrot Soup • Dill Crackers
Stuffed Holiday Ham
Cheesy Spinach Soufflé
Pickled Yellow Squash
Overnight Fruit Salad
Creamy Garlic Mashed Potatoes
Cornmeal Yeast Muffins
Eggnog Custard Pie
Banana-Nut Cream Tart
Coconut-Orange Cake

ORANGE-CARROT SOUP

- ¼ cup finely chopped onion
- 1 tablespoon butter or margarine
- 4 cups chicken or vegetable stock
- 1 pound carrots, shredded
- 1 can (11 ounces) mandarin oranges in syrup,
- ½ cup orange juice
- 2 teaspoons grated orange zest
- 2 teaspoons honey
- ¼ teaspoon ground ginger
- ¼ cup cold water
- 1 tablespoon cornstarch
- ½ cup half and half

In a Dutch oven over medium heat, cook onion and butter about 5 minutes or until onion is clear. Add chicken stock and carrots. Increase heat to medium-high and bring to a boil. Reduce heat to medium; cook about 15 minutes or until carrots are almost tender. Remove from heat.

Remove 1 cup carrots from liquid using a slotted spoon; set aside. Add oranges and syrup, orange juice, orange zest, honey, and ginger to soup. Batch process soup in a food processor until puréed.

Return soup to Dutch oven over medium heat. Add reserved carrots to soup; bring to a simmer. Combine cold water and cornstarch in a small bowl. Add cornstarch mixture and half and half to soup; stir until thickened. Serve warm with Dill Crackers.

Yield: about 8 cups soup

STUFFED HOLIDAY HAM

- 1 small head green cabbage, coarsely chopped
- ½ pound mustard greens, spinach, or other fresh greens
- 1 medium onion, quartered
- 1 rib celery, coarsely chopped
- 1 small sweet red pepper, quartered
- 2 cloves garlic
- 2 teaspoons crushed red pepper flakes
- 8 to 9 pound fully cooked butt portion bone-in ham

Combine first 7 ingredients in small batches in a food processor; pulse process until finely chopped. Place ham in center of 2 layers of cheesecloth large enough to cover ham. Make random cuts in ham down to the bone. Open cuts with fingers and stuff as much vegetable mixture as possible into each cut. Press remaining vegetable mixture onto surface of ham. Gather cheesecloth around ham; tie with kitchen string. Place stuffed ham in a large stockpot or roasting pan; add water to cover at least half of ham. Cover and bring water to a boil over high heat. Reduce heat to medium-low and simmer 1½ to 2 hours or until vegetables are tender and ham is heated through, adding hot water as needed. Remove from heat and cool 1 hour. Remove ham from stockpot. Carefully unwrap cheesecloth, leaving vegetables on ham. Cover ham and refrigerate overnight. Serve chilled.

Yield: about 22 servings

Dressed in a colorful medley of chopped greens, cabbage, sweet red pepper, and savory spices, Stuffed Holiday Ham is cooked to succulent perfection.

DILL CRACKERS

1 package (10 ounces) oyster
   crackers
1/4 cup vegetable oil
2 teaspoons dried dill weed

Preheat oven to 300 degrees. Place crackers in a large bowl. Combine oil and dill weed in a small bowl. Pour oil mixture over crackers; stir until well coated. Transfer to an ungreased jellyroll pan. Bake 15 minutes, stirring every 5 minutes. Place pan on a wire rack to cool. Store in an airtight container.

Yield: about 6 cups crackers

CHEESY SPINACH SOUFFLÉ

1 container (16 ounces) cottage
   cheese
1 1/2 cups (about 6 ounces)
   shredded Parmesan cheese
2 packages (10 ounces each)
   frozen chopped spinach,
   cooked and well drained
2 eggs, separated
1/4 cup butter or margarine, melted
2 tablespoons minced onion
1 clove garlic, minced
2 tablespoons all-purpose flour
1/2 teaspoon baking powder
1/2 teaspoon lemon pepper

Preheat oven to 350 degrees. In a medium bowl, combine cottage cheese, Parmesan cheese, spinach, egg yolks, melted butter, onion, and garlic. In a small bowl, combine flour, baking powder, and lemon pepper. Add dry ingredients to spinach mixture; stir until well blended. In a small bowl, beat egg whites until stiff; fold into spinach mixture. Pour into a greased 2-quart soufflé dish. Bake uncovered 50 to 60 minutes or until center is set. Serve warm.

Yield: about 10 servings

PICKLED YELLOW SQUASH

2 quarts cold water
1 cup canning and pickling salt
8 cups sliced yellow squash
4 green peppers, chopped
2 cups chopped white onions
3 cups sugar
2 cups white vinegar (5% acidity)
1 teaspoon celery seed
1 teaspoon mustard seed

In a large nonmetal bowl, combine water and salt; stir until well blended. Place squash in salt mixture. Cover and allow to stand 2 hours. Using a colander, drain and thoroughly rinse squash with cold water. In a large bowl, combine squash, peppers, and onions. Combine sugar, vinegar, celery seed, and mustard seed in a large Dutch oven (preferably enamelware). Bring vinegar mixture to a boil over high heat. Add vegetables; bring to a boil again. Spoon mixture into heat-resistant jars with lids; cool. Store in refrigerator.

Yield: about 5 pints pickled squash

OVERNIGHT FRUIT SALAD

1 can (20 ounces) pineapple
   chunks in heavy syrup
3 egg yolks, beaten
2 tablespoons sugar
2 tablespoons white vinegar
1 tablespoon butter or margarine

250

1/8 teaspoon salt
2 cans (17 ounces each) pitted white Royal Anne cherries, drained
2 cans (11 ounces each) mandarin oranges, drained
1 1/2 cups miniature marshmallows
1 cup whipping cream, whipped

Drain pineapple, reserving 2 tablespoons syrup. In the top of a double boiler over hot water, combine egg yolks, sugar, vinegar, reserved pineapple syrup, butter, and salt. Stirring constantly, cook mixture about 4 minutes or until thickened. Transfer to a large bowl and let cool. Cover and chill 30 minutes.

Stir in pineapple, cherries, mandarin oranges, and marshmallows. Fold whipped cream into fruit mixture. Cover and chill overnight.

Yield: about 16 servings

CREAMY GARLIC MASHED POTATOES

4 pounds russet potatoes, peeled and cut into pieces
6 cloves garlic
2 teaspoons salt, divided
2 packages (3 ounces each) cream cheese, softened
1/2 cup butter or margarine
1 cup warm milk

Place potatoes in a Dutch oven. Cover with water; add garlic and 1 teaspoon salt. Cover and bring to a boil over medium-high heat. Reduce heat to medium and continue cooking 10 minutes or until potatoes are just tender; drain. Return potatoes and garlic to low heat. Add cream cheese, butter, and remaining 1 teaspoon salt; mash until cream cheese and butter are melted. Add milk and continue mashing until potatoes are coarsely mashed. Serve warm.

Yield: about 14 servings

CORNMEAL YEAST MUFFINS

1 package dry yeast
1/4 cup plus 1 teaspoon sugar, divided
1/3 cup warm water (105 to 115 degrees)
1 cup milk
1/2 cup butter or margarine
1 1/2 teaspoons salt
1 can (15 1/4 ounces) whole kernel corn, drained
1 cup cream-style corn
2 eggs, beaten
1 1/2 cups yellow cornmeal
3 cups all-purpose flour

In a small bowl, dissolve yeast and 1 teaspoon sugar in warm water. In a small saucepan, combine milk, butter, remaining 1/4 cup sugar, and salt over medium heat; whisk until butter melts and sugar is dissolved. Remove from heat and pour into a large bowl. Add whole kernel corn, cream-style corn, eggs, and yeast mixture; stir until well blended. Add cornmeal and flour, 1 cup at a time; stir until a thick batter forms. Cover and let rise in a warm place (80 to 85 degrees) 1 to 1 1/2 hours or until almost doubled in size. Stir batter down.

(Continued on page 252)

CORNMEAL YEAST MUFFINS
(Continued from page 251)

Spoon batter into greased muffin cups, filling each two-thirds full. Let rise uncovered in a warm place about 45 minutes.

Preheat oven to 375 degrees. Bake 20 to 25 minutes or until golden brown. Allow muffins to cool in pan 5 minutes. Serve warm or transfer to a wire rack to cool completely.

Yield: about 2 dozen muffins

COCONUT-ORANGE CAKE
(Continued from page 255)

For icing, combine sugar, orange juice, egg whites, corn syrup, and cream of tartar in top of a double boiler. Beat with a mixer until sugar is well blended. Place over boiling water and continue beating about 7 minutes or until soft peaks form. Remove from heat and add vanilla. Continue beating 2 minutes or until icing is desired consistency. Ice cake. Sprinkle coconut on top and sides of cake. Decorate with orange segments. Store in an airtight container in refrigerator.

Yield: about 16 servings

A new twist on a traditional treat, Eggnog Custard Pie is laced with bourbon and ground nutmeg. Coconut-Orange Cake (right) is a dreamy dessert featuring an orange-flavored filling between two layers of moist goodness. Iced with fluffy frosting sweetened with orange juice, the cake is covered with coconut and mandarin orange segments. (Recipes are on pages 254 and 255.)

For our Banana-Nut Cream Tart (recipe on page 254), a light pudding fillling covers a layer of banana slices on a crust of vanilla wafer crumbs and chopped pecans. Alternating rows of banana slices and caramelized nuts top the yummy delight.

253

EGGNOG CUSTARD PIE
(Shown on page 252)

CRUST

- 1½ cups all-purpose flour
- ¼ teaspoon salt
- ½ cup vegetable shortening
- ¼ cup water

FILLING

- 4 eggs
- ½ cup sugar
- 2 cups half and half
- 2 tablespoons bourbon
- 1 teaspoon vanilla extract
- ¼ teaspoon ground nutmeg
- ⅛ teaspoon salt

TOPPING

- ½ cup whipping cream
- 1½ tablespoons sugar
- 1 teaspoon bourbon

For crust, combine flour and salt in a medium bowl. Using a pastry blender or 2 knives, cut in shortening until mixture resembles coarse meal. Sprinkle with water; mix until a soft dough forms. On a lightly floured surface, use a floured rolling pin to roll out dough to ⅛-inch thickness. Transfer to a 9-inch pie plate. Crimp edges of crust; use a sharp knife to trim excess crust.

Preheat oven to 450 degrees. For filling, beat eggs and sugar in a medium bowl until well blended. Add half and half; beat until smooth. Stir in bourbon, vanilla, nutmeg, and salt. Pour filling into crust. Bake 10 minutes. Reduce heat to 325 degrees and bake an additional 35 to 40 minutes or until a knife inserted in center of pie comes out clean. Cool pie on a wire rack.

For topping, beat whipping cream and sugar in a small bowl until stiff peaks form. Beat in bourbon. To serve, spoon topping onto each piece of pie.

Yield: about 8 servings

BANANA-NUT CREAM TART *(Shown on page 253)*

FILLING

- ½ cup sugar
- 3 tablespoons all-purpose flour
- 3 cups half and half
- 3 eggs, beaten
- 3 tablespoons butter or margarine
- ¾ teaspoon vanilla extract
- ¼ teaspoon butter flavoring

CRUST

- 1 cup vanilla wafer crumbs (about 20 cookies)
- 1 cup chopped pecans, toasted and coarsely ground
- ¼ cup butter or margarine, softened
- ¼ cup sugar

TOPPING

- 1 egg white
- 2 teaspoons water
- 1 cup chopped pecans
- ¼ cup firmly packed brown sugar
- 2 tablespoons apple jelly
- 6 medium bananas

For filling, combine sugar and flour in the top of a double boiler. Add half and half, eggs, and butter; place over simmering water. Stirring frequently, cook about 20 minutes or until thick enough to coat back of a spoon. Stir in vanilla and butter flavoring. Remove from heat and pour into a medium bowl. Place plastic wrap directly on surface of filling; chill.

Preheat oven to 350 degrees. For crust, combine all ingredients in a medium bowl. Press mixture into bottom and up sides of a lightly greased 8 x 11-inch tart pan with a removable bottom. Bake 10 to 12 minutes or until crust is firm; chill.

Reduce oven temperature to 225 degrees. For topping, combine egg white and water in a small bowl; beat until foamy. Stir in pecans and brown sugar. Spread coated pecans on an ungreased baking sheet. Bake 45 minutes, stirring every 15 minutes, or until golden brown. Cool pan on a wire rack.

To serve, melt apple jelly in a small saucepan over medium heat. Slice 2 bananas and place a single layer in pie crust. Spoon half of chilled filling over bananas. Place another single layer of 2 sliced bananas on filling. Top with remainder of filling. Alternate rows of caramelized nuts and slices of remaining bananas on top of filling. Brush melted apple jelly over bananas.

Yield: about 12 servings

COCONUT-ORANGE CAKE
(Shown on page 252)

CAKE
    1 package (18¼ ounces) yellow
         cake mix
    3 eggs
 ⅓ cup vegetable oil
    1 can (8½ ounces) cream of
         coconut
    1 cup sour cream

ORANGE FILLING
 ½ cup sugar
 1½ tablespoons all-purpose flour
    1 can (11 ounces) mandarin
         oranges, drained
    2 egg yolks (reserve egg whites
         for icing)
 ½ teaspoon butter or margarine
 ½ teaspoon vanilla extract

ICING
 1½ cups sugar
 ¼ cup orange juice
    2 egg whites
    1 tablespoon light corn syrup
 ¼ teaspoon cream of tartar
    1 teaspoon vanilla extract
    1 cup fllaked coconut
         Mandarin orange segments to
         decorate

Preheat oven to 350 degrees. For cake, line bottoms of two 9-inch round cake pans with waxed paper. Grease paper and sides of pans. In a large bowl, combine cake mix, eggs, and oil; beat until well blended. Add cream of coconut and sour cream; beat until smooth. Pour batter into prepared pans. Bake 32 to 36 minutes or until a toothpick inserted in center of cake comes out clean. Cool in pans 10 minutes on a wire rack. Run knife around edge of pans to loosen cake; remove from pans and place on wire rack to cool completely.

For orange filling, combine sugar and flour in a heavy small saucepan. Add oranges, egg yolks, and butter. Stirring constantly, bring mixture to a boil over medium heat; cook 4 minutes or until mixture thickens. Stir in vanilla. Cool to room temperature. Spread filling between cake layers.

(Continued on page 252)

YULETIDE REUNION

Parmesan Cheese Crisps
Roasted Red Pepper Soup
Christmas Sangria
Brie-Stuffed Chicken Breasts with Green Peppercorn Sauce
Elegant Cranberry Salad
Oven-Roasted Vegetables
Corn Soufflés
Eggnog Trifle

PARMESAN CHEESE CRISPS

These crackers freeze well.

- 1 cup butter, softened
- 1 clove garlic, minced
- 2 cups all-purpose flour
- 1 cup freshly grated Parmesan cheese
- 2 tablespoons dried parsley flakes

Process butter and garlic in a large food processor until smooth. Add flour, Parmesan cheese, and parsley flakes; process until well blended. Shape cheese mixture into two 10-inch-long rolls. Wrap in plastic wrap and chill 2 hours or until firm enough to slice.

Preheat oven to 350 degrees. Cut rolls into ¼-inch slices. Place slices on an ungreased baking sheet. Bake 13 to 15 minutes or until crackers are golden brown. Transfer to a wire rack to cool. Store in an airtight container.

Yield: about 6½ dozen crackers

ROASTED RED PEPPER SOUP

- 4 sweet red peppers
- 3 tablespoons butter or margarine
- 1¾ cups chopped onions
- ½ cup sliced carrot
- 3 cloves garlic, minced
- 2 tablespoons all-purpose flour
- 2 cans (14½ ounces each) chicken broth
- 1 can (14½ ounces) whole tomatoes
- 1 cup whipping cream
- ¼ cup white wine
- 2 tablespoons freshly squeezed lemon juice
- 1 teaspoon honey
- 1 teaspoon salt
- ¼ teaspoon ground white pepper
  Parsley to garnish

To roast peppers, cut in half lengthwise and remove seeds and membranes. Place, skin side up, on a greased baking sheet; flatten with hand. Broil about 3 inches from heat about 15 to 20 minutes or until skin of peppers blackens. Immediately seal peppers in a plastic bag and allow to steam 10 to 15 minutes. Remove and discard charred skin.

In a large Dutch oven, melt butter over medium heat. Sauté onions, carrot, and garlic about 5 minutes or until onion is tender. Stirring constantly, add flour and cook about 2 minutes. Stir in chicken broth, tomatoes, and peppers; bring to a simmer. Reduce heat to medium low. Stirring occasionally, cover and simmer about 25 minutes or until vegetables are tender. Process mixture in batches in a food processor until vegetables are puréed. Return mixture to Dutch oven. Stir in whipping cream, wine, lemon juice, honey, salt, and white pepper. Cook until heated through (do not boil). Garnish individual servings with parsley, if desired.

Yield: about 7 cups soup

CHRISTMAS SANGRIA

- 4 navel oranges, sliced
- 2 lemons, sliced
- 1¹/₂ cups sugar
- 2 bottles (750 ml each) dry white wine, chilled
- 1 can (12 ounces) frozen cranberry juice cocktail concentrate, thawed
- 2 tablespoons orange-flavored liqueur
- 2 tablespoons brandy
- 1 bottle (1 liter) club soda, chilled

Place fruit slices in a large bowl. Pour sugar over fruit; stir with a wooden spoon until fruit is coated with sugar. Cover and let stand at room temperature 1 hour.

In a large container combine fruit mixture, wine, cranberry juice concentrate, liqueur, and brandy. Cover and chill 2 hours.

To serve, transfer wine mixture to a 5-quart serving container; stir in club soda. Serve immediately.

Yield: about 14 cups wine

Guests can warm up to a bowl of creamy Roasted Red Pepper Soup. Complete the course with homemade Parmesan Cheese Crisps and finish with a glass of spirited Christmas Sangria.

BRIE-STUFFED CHICKEN BREASTS WITH GREEN PEPPERCORN SAUCE

(Shown on page 260)

CHICKEN BREASTS

- 6 boneless, skinless chicken breasts
- 1/4 cup mayonnaise
- 2 tablespoons Dijon-style mustard
- 1/2 teaspoon ground white pepper
- 8 ounces Brie cheese, rind removed and shredded
- 1/2 cup purchased plain bread crumbs
- 1/2 cup chopped pecans, toasted and ground
- 1 tablespoon finely chopped fresh parsley

GREEN PEPPERCORN SAUCE

- 1/4 cup butter or margarine
- 1/4 cup minced onion
- 2 tablespoons green peppercorns, crushed
- 1 can (14 1/2 ounces) chicken broth
- 1/4 cup finely chopped fresh parsley
- 2 tablespoons Dijon-style mustard
- 3/4 teaspoon salt
- 2 cups half and half
- 2 tablespoons cornstarch
- 1/4 cup water

Preheat oven to 350 degrees. Place chicken between sheets of waxed paper. Using a mallet, gently pound chicken pieces until 1/4-inch thick. In a small bowl, combine mayonnaise and mustard. Spread 1 tablespoon mixture over each chicken breast. Sprinkle chicken breasts with white pepper. Place 1/4 cup cheese in center of each chicken piece. Beginning at 1 short edge, roll up chicken jellyroll style; secure with a toothpick. (Chicken may be covered and chilled until ready to bake.) In a shallow bowl, combine bread crumbs, pecans, and parsley. Coat chicken with crumb mixture. Place chicken in a lightly greased jellyroll pan. Bake 35 minutes (40 minutes if chilled) or until juices run clear when pierced with a fork.

For green peppercorn sauce, melt butter in a medium saucepan over medium heat. Sauté onion and peppercorns in butter about 5 minutes or until onion is tender; stir in chicken broth. Stirring occasionally, cook mixture 25 minutes or until volume is reduced by half. Add parsley, mustard, and salt; stir until well blended. Stirring frequently, add half and half and bring mixture to a simmer over medium-high heat. In a small bowl, combine cornstarch and water. Stirring constantly, add cornstarch mixture and cook about 1 minute or until sauce is bubbly and thickened. Serve warm or store in an airtight container in refrigerator until ready to serve.

To reheat sauce, place in a medium microwave-safe bowl. Microwave on medium-high power (80%) about 6 minutes or until heated through, stirring every 2 minutes. Remove toothpicks from chicken. Serve 1/2 cup sauce with each chicken piece.

Yield: 6 servings

ELEGANT CRANBERRY SALAD

(Shown on page 260)

- 1 can (8 ounces) crushed pineapple in juice
- 1 cup boiling water
- 2 packages (3 ounces each) cranberry gelatin
- 1 cup cold water
- 1 can (16 ounces) whole berry cranberry sauce

1 cup chopped walnuts
1 cup chopped unpeeled red apple
    (we used Red Delicious)
½ cup finely chopped celery
    Lettuce leaves to serve

Drain pineapple, reserving juice in a measuring cup. Add enough water to juice to make 1 cup. In a medium bowl, stir boiling water into gelatin; stir until gelatin dissolves. Add pineapple juice mixture, cold water, and cranberry sauce; stir until well blended. Chill gelatin mixture about 45 minutes or until partially set, stirring occasionally, Fold pineapple, walnuts, apple, and celery into gelatin mixture. Pour into a lightly oiled 9 x 13-inch baking dish. Cover and chill about 2 hours or until firm. Cut gelatin into 3-inch squares. Serve on lettuce leaves.

Yield: about 12 servings

OVEN-ROASTED VEGETABLES

1 package (16 ounces) frozen
    bean and carrot blend, thawed
1 package (16 ounces) frozen
    peas with baby corn and snow
    peas, thawed
¾ cup butter or margarine
2 tablespoons freshly grated ginger
1½ tablespoons finely chopped fresh
    thyme leaves
1 teaspoon salt
½ teaspoon ground black pepper
1 jar (15 ounces) whole small
    onions, drained

Preheat oven to 400 degrees. In a large roasting pan, combine first 2 ingredients. In a small saucepan, combine butter, ginger, thyme, salt, and pepper. Stirring constantly, cook over medium-low heat until butter melts. Pour over vegetables. Bake 30 minutes, stirring after 15 minutes. Stir in onions and bake 15 minutes or until vegetables are tender and lightly browned.

Yield: about 6 cups vegetables

CORN SOUFFLÉS
(Shown on page 260)

Soufflés can be made ahead and chilled until ready to bake.

1½ cups water
¾ cup yellow cornmeal
2 cups (8 ounces) shredded sharp
    Cheddar cheese
1 can (11 ounces) whole kernel
    corn, drained
1 small clove garlic, minced
½ teaspoon salt
⅛ teaspoon ground white pepper
¾ cup milk
4 eggs, separated

Preheat oven to 325 degrees. In a large saucepan, combine water and cornmeal. Stirring constantly, cook over medium heat 3 to 4 minutes or until mixture thickens. Reduce heat to low. Add cheese, corn, garlic, salt, and white pepper; stir until cheese melts. Remove from heat. In a small bowl, combine milk and egg yolks; beat until blended. Stir into cornmeal mixture. In a medium bowl, beat egg whites until stiff. Fold egg whites into cornmeal mixture. Spoon into 7 greased 1 cup ramekins. (Mixture may be covered and chilled until ready to bake.) Bake 30 to 35 minutes (40 to 45 minutes if chilled) or until puffed and lightly browned. Serve immediately.

Yield: 7 servings

A scrumptious spread of holiday fare begins with Elegant Cranberry Salad featuring crunchy celery, walnuts, and chopped apples. A light side dish, Corn Soufflés can be made ahead and baked just before serving. Our Brie-Stuffed Chicken Breasts with Green Peppercorn Sauce are bursting with the robust flavor of Dijon mustard. (Recipes are on pages 258 and 259.)

Eye-catching Eggnog Trifle contrasts rich pudding with colorful oranges and cherries, all layered with slices of moist pound cake.

EGGNOG TRIFLE

- 2 packages (3 ounces each) vanilla pudding mix
- 1 carton (1 quart) eggnog
- 1/4 teaspoon freshly grated nutmeg (optional)
- 2 loaves (10 3/4 ounces each) pound cake
- 1/3 cup cream sherry
- 2 1/4 cups whipping cream, divided
- 3 cans (11 ounces each) mandarin oranges, drained
- 1 jar (10 ounces) maraschino cherry halves, drained
- 2 tablespoons confectioners sugar
- 1 teaspoon vanilla extract

Combine pudding mix and eggnog in a medium saucepan. Stirring constantly, cook over medium heat until mixture comes to a full boil. Pour mixture into a large heatproof bowl. Stir in nutmeg, if desired. Place plastic wrap directly on surface of pudding; chill 1 hour.

Cut top of pound cake flat and trim edges from cake. Cut cake into 1/2-inch slices. Place slices on waxed paper.

Brush slices with sherry. Beat 1 1/4 cups whipping cream in a medium bowl until stiff peaks form. Fold whipped cream into pudding. Place one-third of cake slices in bottom of a 16-cup trifle bowl. Spoon 2 cups pudding over cake. Using 1 1/2 cups oranges, line outside edge of bowl and place remaining oranges over pudding. Using 1/2 cup cherries, line outside edge of bowl and place remaining cherries over oranges. Continue layering using half of remaining cake, 2 cups pudding, 1 1/2 cups oranges, 1/2 cup cherries, remaining cake, and remaining pudding. Cover and chill until ready to serve.

To serve, beat remaining 1 cup whipping cream, confectioners sugar, and vanilla in a small bowl until stiff peaks form. Spoon whipped cream into a pastry bag fitted with a large star tip. Pipe dollops of whipped cream onto top of trifle.

Yield: about 24 servings

DASHING THROUGH THE SNOW

These recipes are perfect for an old-fashioned progressive dinner with friends and neighbors.

Sparkling Wine Punch
Hot Fruited Tea
Curried Blue Cheesecake
Beef Saté with Hot Peanut Dipping Sauce
Seafood Crêpes with Creamy Lemon-Dill
and Basil Red Sauces
Mushroom Soup
Herbed Breadsticks • Roasted Garlic
Pear and Blue Cheese Salad with
Toasted Walnut Dressing
Smoked Cornish Hens with
Red Currant Sauce
Whole Green Beans with Dilled Butter Curls
Stuffed Deviled Onions
Spicy Christmas Trees
Bavarian Creams with Raspberry Sauce
Steamed Cranberry Pudding with
Orange Hard Sauce

SPARKLING WINE PUNCH

Make ice ring at least 24 hours in advance.

- Seedless red grapes
- 1 bottle (48 ounces) red grape juice, chilled and divided
- 1 bottle (32 ounces) club soda, chilled
- 1 bottle (750 ml) sparkling white wine, chilled
- ¼ cup orange-flavored liqueur

Make ice ring by placing grapes in a 4-cup ring mold. Add 3 cups grape juice; cover and freeze.

To serve, combine remaining grape juice, club soda, wine, and liqueur in punch bowl. Float ice ring on top and serve.

Yield: about eighteen 6-ounce servings

HOT FRUITED TEA

- 1 whole orange
- 10 cups water
- 4 regular-size tea bags
- 2 cinnamon sticks
- 1 teaspoon whole cloves
- 2 cans (12 ounces each) frozen cranberry-raspberry-strawberry juice beverage concentrate
- 1 cup firmly packed brown sugar
- Orange slices to serve

Peel whole orange in one continuous strip; set peel aside and reserve orange meat for another use. Place water, tea bags, cinnamon sticks, cloves, and orange peel in a heavy large saucepan. Bring to a simmer over medium-high heat. Cover and continue to simmer 15 minutes. Strain tea into a Dutch oven; discard tea bags, orange peel, and spices. Add concentrate and brown sugar; stir over medium-low heat until sugar dissolves and tea is hot. Serve hot with orange slices.

Yield: about seventeen 6-ounce servings

CURRIED BLUE CHEESECAKE

- 1¼ cups butter-flavored cracker crumbs
- ¼ cup freshly grated Parmesan cheese

1/4 cup butter or margarine, melted
3 packages (8 ounces each) cream cheese, softened
4 eggs
1/2 cup mayonnaise
1/2 cup finely minced onion
1 tablespoon lemon juice
3/4 teaspoon curry powder
1/2 teaspoon Worcestershire sauce
8 ounces blue cheese, crumbled
Purchased chutney to garnish
Crackers to serve

Preheat oven to 300 degrees. In a medium bowl, combine cracker crumbs, Parmesan cheese, and melted butter. Press into bottom of a greased 9-inch springform pan. In a large bowl, beat cream cheese until fluffy. Add eggs, 1 at a time, beating 2 minutes after each addition. Continue beating while adding mayonnaise, onion, lemon juice, curry powder, and Worcestershire sauce; beat until well blended. Stir in blue cheese. Pour filling over crust. Bake 1 1/2 hours. Turn oven off. With oven door partially open, leave cheesecake in oven 1 hour. Transfer to a wire rack to cool. Remove sides of pan. Spoon chutney over top of cheesecake. Serve chilled or at room temperature with crackers.

Yield: about 50 servings

BEEF SATÉ WITH HOT PEANUT DIPPING SAUCE

HOT PEANUT DIPPING SAUCE
1/4 cup smooth peanut butter
1/4 cup beef broth
2 tablespoons peanut oil
1 tablespoon soy sauce
1 tablespoon seasoned rice wine vinegar
1 teaspoon dark sesame oil
1 teaspoon freshly grated ginger
1/2 teaspoon crushed red pepper flakes

BEEF SATÉ
3/4 cup seasoned rice wine vinegar
1/3 cup peanut oil
1/3 cup soy sauce
3 cloves garlic, minced
1 tablespoon firmly packed brown sugar
1 tablespoon grated fresh ginger
1 teaspoon crushed red pepper flakes
2 pounds flank steak, trimmed of fat and partially frozen
Six-inch-long bamboo skewers

For hot peanut dipping sauce, combine all ingredients in a food processor; process until well blended. Transfer to a small bowl; cover and let stand at room temperature 2 hours to allow flavors to blend. Store in refrigerator.

For beef sate´, combine vinegar, oil, soy sauce, garlic, brown sugar, ginger, and red pepper flakes in a large bowl; stir until well blended. Slice chilled meat diagonally across the grain into thin slices. Place beef strips in marinade and refrigerate overnight. Soak bamboo skewers in water overnight.

Bring sauce to room temperature. Thread marinated beef strips onto skewers. Broil or grill about 4 inches from heat 5 to 6 minutes; turning once after 3 minutes. Serve warm with sauce.

Yield: about 1/2 cup sauce and about 4 dozen appetizers

SEAFOOD CRÊPES WITH CREAMY LEMON-DILL AND BASIL RED SAUCES

FILLING
    3   tablespoons butter
    1/4 cup finely minced green onion
    1   clove garlic, minced
    1/2 pound boiled shrimp, shelled, deveined, and cut into bite-size pieces
    2   cans (6 ounces each) lump crabmeat, drained
    1/2 cup ricotta cheese
    2   tablespoons grated Parmesan cheese
    1/8 teaspoon ground white pepper

CRÊPES
    1 1/2 cups sifted all-purpose flour
    1/4   teaspoon salt
    4   eggs
    1 1/4 cups milk
    1   cup cold water
    2   tablespoons vegetable oil

For filling, melt butter in a medium saucepan over medium-low heat. Add onion and garlic; sauté until onion is tender. Transfer onion mixture to a medium bowl. Stir in shrimp, crabmeat, cheeses, and white pepper until well blended. Place in an airtight container in refrigerator until ready to use.

For crêpes, combine flour and salt in a medium bowl. Add eggs, milk, water, and oil; beat until well blended.

Preheat and lightly grease a griddle or large skillet over medium heat. For each crêpe, spoon about 1 tablespoon batter onto griddle, using back of spoon to smooth into a 4-inch circle. Cook until edges are lightly browned; remove from griddle. Place crêpes in a single layer between sheets of waxed paper.

Fill each crêpe with about 1 tablespoon of filling; roll up crêpe. Serve with Creamy Lemon-Dill Sauce and Basil Red Sauce.

Yield: about 50 appetizers

CREAMY LEMON-DILL SAUCE
    1/2 cup whipping cream
    4   cloves garlic, minced
    1/4 cup fresh lemon juice
    3/4 cup olive oil
    1/4 cup minced fresh dill weed
    1/4 teaspoon salt
    1/8 teaspoon ground white pepper

In a heavy small saucepan, heat whipping cream over medium heat until it comes to a boil. Reduce heat to low and add garlic. Simmer mixture about 15 minutes or until garlic is tender and cream has reduced in volume almost by half. Place warm cream mixture in a food processor. With processor running, add lemon juice and process until well blended. Continue processing and gradually add oil; process until an emulsion is formed. Stir in dill weed, salt, and white pepper. Serve with Seafood Crêpes.

Yield: about 1 cup sauce

BASIL RED SAUCE
    2   cans (14 1/2 ounces each) undrained plum tomatoes, coarsely chopped
    1   package (3 ounces) sun-dried tomatoes
    1/3 cup chopped fresh basil leaves
    1/4 cup minced onion
    4   cloves garlic, minced
    1/4 teaspoon salt
    1/4 teaspoon ground black pepper

¼ teaspoon sugar
1 tablespoon seasoned rice wine vinegar
1 tablespoon olive oil

Place canned tomatoes and sun-dried tomatoes in a medium saucepan over medium heat. Bring to a boil and cook 2 minutes. Remove from heat and allow to cool 5 minutes.

Place tomato mixture, basil, onion, garlic, salt, pepper, and sugar in a food processor; pulse process briefly to blend ingredients. With processor running, gradually add vinegar and oil; process until well blended. Serve with Seafood Crêpes.

Yield: about 3⅔ cups sauce

Filled with shrimp, crabmeat, and mild cheeses, Seafood Crêpes are a scrumptious appetizer. Guests can choose from two delicious toppings—Creamy Lemon-Dill Sauce or hearty Basil Red Sauce.

MUSHROOM SOUP

- 1 pound fresh mushrooms
- ¼ cup butter or margarine
- 1 onion, coarsely chopped
- 2 ribs celery, coarsely chopped
- 2 cloves garlic, minced
- 6 cups beef broth
- 1 teaspoon dried thyme leaves
- ½ teaspoon dried parsley flakes
- 1 bay leaf
  Chopped fresh parsley to garnish

Separate mushroom caps from stems; set aside. Coarsely chop mushroom stems. In a Dutch oven over medium heat, combine mushroom stems, butter, onion, celery, and garlic; sauté about 8 minutes or until tender. Add beef broth, thyme, dried parsley, and bay leaf. Cover and reduce heat to medium-low; simmer about 45 minutes. Strain and return liquid to Dutch oven. Discard cooked vegetables. Slice mushroom caps and add to soup. Cover and simmer over medium-low heat about 15 minutes or until mushrooms are just tender. Garnish with fresh parsley and serve warm.

Yield: about 8 servings

HERBED BREADSTICKS

- 2 packages dry yeast
- 4 tablespoons sugar, divided
- ¼ cup warm water
- 2 cups milk
- ¼ cup butter or margarine
- 2 teaspoons salt
- 6 cups all-purpose flour, divided
- 1 egg white, beaten
- 3 tablespoons dried Italian herb seasoning

In a small bowl, dissolve yeast and 1 tablespoon sugar in warm water; set aside. In a small saucepan, cook milk, butter, remaining 3 tablespoons sugar, and salt over medium heat until butter melts. In a large bowl, combine 5 cups flour, yeast mixture, and milk mixture; stir until a soft dough forms. Turn onto a lightly floured surface. Adding remaining flour as needed, knead 10 to 15 minutes or until dough becomes smooth and elastic. Place in a large greased bowl, turning once to coat top of dough. Cover and let rise in a warm place (80 to 85 degrees) 1 hour or until doubled in size.

Turn dough onto a lightly floured surface and punch down. Divide dough in half. Shape half of dough into 12 equal pieces. Roll each piece into a 15-inch-long rope. Twist each rope of dough several times. Place breadsticks on a well-greased baking sheet. Repeat with remaining dough. Cover and let rise in a warm place 20 to 30 minutes or until dough rises slightly.

Preheat oven to 400 degrees. Lightly brush breadsticks with beaten egg white and sprinkle with herb seasoning. Bake about 15 minutes or until golden brown. Serve warm or transfer to a wire rack to cool.

Yield: 2 dozen breadsticks

ROASTED GARLIC

- 6 large heads garlic
- 1 loaf (8 ounces) 2½-inch-diameter French bread, cut into ¼-inch slices

Preheat oven to 375 degrees. Remove the outermost papery skin from each head of garlic, leaving cloves of garlic intact. Slice across stem end of each garlic head. Place garlic heads in a baking dish; cover with heavy aluminum foil. Bake about 1 hour. Allow garlic to cool 10 to 15 minutes before serving. Place French bread slices on a baking sheet. Toast in a 375-degree oven 5 minutes, turning slices over after 3 minutes. To serve, press garlic pulp out of each clove and spread on toast.

Yield: about 50 servings

PEAR AND BLUE CHEESE SALAD WITH TOASTED WALNUT DRESSING

Salad may be prepared ahead of time and refrigerated; prepare dressing immediately before serving.

SALAD
    8 to 10 cups mixed salad greens
    1 small red onion, thinly sliced
    2 red pears, quartered, cored, and
         thinly sliced (dip pears in a
         mixture of 3 tablespoons
         each water and lemon juice)

DRESSING
    1 cup coarsely chopped walnuts
  1/2 cup vegetable oil
    6 tablespoons red wine vinegar
    1 teaspoon sugar
  1/2 teaspoon salt
  1/8 teaspoon ground white pepper
    4 ounces Gorgonzola cheese,
         crumbled

For salad, arrange salad greens and onion and pear slices on 8 salad plates. Cover and refrigerate until ready to serve.

For dressing, toast walnuts in oil over medium heat in a heavy medium skillet about 5 minutes or until lightly browned. Reserving oil in skillet, place walnuts on a paper towel to drain. Add vinegar, sugar, salt, and white pepper to oil in skillet; stir over medium heat until well blended. Spoon dressing over salads and sprinkle with toasted walnuts and crumbled cheese.

Yield: 8 servings

SMOKED CORNISH HENS WITH RED CURRANT SAUCE
(Shown on page 269)

    1 jar (10 ounces) red currant jelly
  1/4 cup dry white wine
    2 tablespoons orange juice
  1/2 teaspoon ground allspice
  1/8 teaspoon salt
  1/8 teaspoon ground black pepper
    4 Cornish hens, smoked, halved,
         and chilled

Combine jelly, wine, orange juice, allspice, salt, and pepper in a food processor. Process until well blended. Place hens in a single layer in a deep roasting pan. Baste with jelly mixture. Cover and heat hens in a 350-degree oven 45 minutes or until heated through or until temperature registers 165 degrees on a meat thermometer. Baste hens with jelly mixture while baking. Serve warm.

Yield: 8 servings

WHOLE GREEN BEANS WITH DILLED BUTTER CURLS

Make butter curls several hours ahead.

½ cup butter, softened
2 tablespoons chopped fresh dill weed **or** 1 teaspoon dried dill weed
1 teaspoon lemon juice
1 teaspoon minced onion
3 cans (14½ ounces each) vertical pack whole green beans

In a small bowl, combine butter, dill weed, lemon juice, and onion. Shape mixture into a stick of butter slightly wider than a butter curler. Wrap in plastic wrap and chill until firm.

To prepare butter curls, dip butter curler in warm water. Pull curler across surface of seasoned butter to make each curl. Place curls in ice water. Store in refrigerator until ready to serve.

Pour ¾ cup green bean liquid into a large saucepan over medium-high heat. Place vegetable steamer in saucepan. Drain remaining liquid from green beans. Place green beans in steamer; cover and steam until heated through. Serve warm with chilled butter curls.

Yield: about 8 servings

STUFFED DEVILED ONIONS

8 whole white onions (about 3 inches in diameter)
2 tablespoons olive oil
2 cloves garlic, minced
8 medium fresh mushrooms, finely chopped
⅓ cup Dijon-style mustard
¼ cup white wine
¾ cup chicken broth, divided
½ teaspoon hot pepper sauce
¾ cup (3 ounces) shredded Cheddar cheese
1 package (8 ounces) seasoned corn bread stuffing

Cut a small slice off bottom of each onion to flatten. Cut an "X" in bottom of each onion about ¼-inch deep. In a Dutch oven, cook onions in boiling water 15 minutes. Drain onions; allow to cool enough to handle. Make a thin slice across top to level and scoop out center of each onion, leaving a ½-inch shell; reserve onion centers. Finely chop reserved onion centers to yield ½ cup.

Preheat oven to 350 degrees. Stirring frequently, cook oil, garlic, and chopped onion in a large saucepan over medium heat until onion is almost soft but not brown. Add mushrooms and continue to cook 2 to 3 minutes or until mushrooms are soft. Add mustard, wine, ¼ cup chicken broth, and hot pepper sauce; stir until well blended. Remove from heat. Stir in cheese and corn bread stuffing. Fill each onion with stuffing mixture. Place onions in a 9 x 13-inch baking dish. In a microwave-safe cup, microwave remaining ½ cup chicken broth on high power (100%) 1 minute. Pour broth into baking dish. Cover and bake onions 45 minutes or until heated through. Serve warm.

Yield: 8 servings

Succulent Smoked Cornish Hens (recipe on page 267) are slow-roasted and basted with flavorful Red Currant Sauce. Whole Green Beans with Dilled Butter Curls and Stuffed Deviled Onions are the perfect side dishes to complete this delightful entrée.

SPICY CHRISTMAS TREES

COOKIES
- 1/3 cup butter or margarine, softened
- 1/3 cup vegetable shortening
- 1 1/4 cups sugar
- 1 cup sour cream
- 1/2 cup molasses
- 2 eggs
- 1 teaspoon vanilla extract
- 5 1/4 cups all-purpose flour
- 1/4 cup cocoa
- 1 tablespoon ground cinnamon
- 2 teaspoons baking powder
- 2 teaspoons ground ginger
- 1 teaspoon ground allspice
- 1 teaspoon baking soda
- 1 teaspoon salt

ICING
- 1 cup sifted confectioners sugar
- 1 tablespoon plus 1 teaspoon milk

For cookies, cream butter, shortening, and sugar in a large bowl until fluffy. Add sour cream, molasses, eggs, and vanilla; beat until smooth. In another large bowl, combine flour, cocoa, cinnamon, baking powder, ginger, allspice, baking soda, and salt. Add half of dry ingredients to creamed mixture; stir until a soft dough forms. Stir remaining dry ingredients, 1 cup at a time, into dough; use hands if necessary to mix well. Divide dough into fourths. Wrap in plastic wrap and chill 2 hours or until dough is firm.

Preheat oven to 350 degrees. On a lightly floured surface, use a floured rolling pin to roll out one fourth of dough to slightly less than 1/4-inch thickness. Use 3 1/4 x 4-inch and 2 1/4 x 3 1/4-inch Christmas tree-shaped cookie cutters to cut out cookies. Transfer to a greased baking sheet. Bake 7 to 9 minutes or until firm to the touch. Transfer cookies to a wire rack to cool. Repeat with remaining dough.

For icing, combine confectioners sugar and milk in a small bowl; stir until smooth. Spoon icing into a pastry bag fitted with a small round tip. Pipe outline onto each cookie. Allow icing to harden. Store in an airtight container.

Yield: about 7 dozen cookies

BAVARIAN CREAMS WITH RASPBERRY SAUCE

CUSTARD
- 1 envelope unflavored gelatin
- 1/3 cup cold orange juice
- 3/4 cup sugar
- 4 egg yolks
- 1/8 teaspoon salt
- 1 3/4 cups milk, scalded
- 1 cup whipping cream

RASPBERRY SAUCE
- 1 tablespoon cornstarch
- 2 tablespoons cold water
- 1 package (12 ounces) frozen red raspberries, partially thawed
- 1/4 cup raspberry jelly
- 1 tablespoon orange-flavored liqueur
  Shaved bittersweet chocolate to garnish

For custard, soften gelatin in orange juice in a small bowl. Combine sugar, egg yolks, and salt in a small bowl; beat until well blended. Whisking constantly, add egg mixture to scalded milk in a heavy medium saucepan. Stirring constantly, cook over medium-low heat about 20 minutes or until custard thickens enough to coat the back of a spoon. Stir gelatin mixture into hot custard, stirring until well blended. Pour custard into a medium bowl; cover and chill 1½ hours.

Beat whipping cream until soft peaks form; fold into chilled custard. Spoon into individual serving dishes; cover and chill 30 minutes.

For raspberry sauce, combine cornstarch and cold water in a small bowl. In a heavy medium saucepan, combine raspberries and jelly. Bring to a boil over medium-high heat. Stirring constantly, add cornstarch mixture; stir until thickened. Press raspberry mixture through a sieve into a medium bowl; discard seeds and pulp. Stir liqueur into raspberry sauce; spoon over custard. Garnish with shaved chocolate.

Yield: about 8 servings

STEAMED CRANBERRY PUDDING WITH ORANGE HARD SAUCE

ORANGE HARD SAUCE
- ½ cup butter, softened
- 1½ cups sifted confectioners sugar
- 1½ tablespoons brandy
- 2 teaspoons grated orange zest
- 1 teaspoon orange extract
- ½ teaspoon vanilla extract

CRANBERRY PUDDING
- 1 cup raisins
- ½ cup brandy
- ½ cup butter or margarine, softened
- ½ cup granulated sugar
- ½ cup firmly packed brown sugar
- 1 cup whole berry cranberry sauce
- 2 eggs
- ¾ teaspoon butter flavoring
- 2 cups all-purpose flour
- 1½ teaspoons baking powder
- 1 teaspoon ground cinnamon
- ½ teaspoon ground allspice
- ½ teaspoon baking soda
- ½ teaspoon salt
- 1 cup coarsely chopped fresh cranberries
- ¾ cup finely chopped toasted pecans

For orange hard sauce, cream butter in a medium bowl. Gradually add remaining ingredients while continuing to beat; beat until fluffy. Spoon into serving dish and chill.

For cranberry pudding, combine raisins and brandy in a small saucepan over medium-low heat. Heat 5 minutes; remove from heat and set aside. In a large bowl, cream butter and sugars. Add cranberry sauce, eggs, and butter flavoring; beat until smooth. In a small bowl, combine flour, baking powder, cinnamon, allspice, baking soda, and salt. Add dry ingredients to creamed mixture; stir until well blended. Stir in cranberries, pecans, and brandied raisin mixture. Spoon batter into a greased and floured 8-cup pudding mold. Cover with mold lid or aluminum foil. Set mold on a rack inside a large stockpot. Add boiling water to stockpot to come halfway up sides of mold. Cover stockpot and keep water at a gentle boil, adding boiling water as necessary. Steam 2 to 2¼ hours or until a toothpick inserted in center comes out clean. Unmold steamed pudding onto serving plate and serve warm with orange hard sauce.

Yield: about 14 servings

271

SKI LODGE SUPPER

Citrus Cider Punch

*Turkey Enchiladas with
Sweet Red Pepper Sauce*

Christmas Pasta Snacks

Mango Buttermilk Dressing

Pear and Spinach Salad

Black Bean Salsa

Hearty Corn Chowder

Orange-Walnut Pie

Honey Spice Cake

TURKEY ENCHILADAS WITH SWEET RED PEPPER SAUCE

- 3 sweet red peppers
- $\frac{1}{2}$ cup plus 3 tablespoons finely chopped onion, divided
- 2 cloves garlic, minced
- 2 tablespoons vegetable oil
- 1 can (28 ounces) crushed tomatoes
- 1 can (14$\frac{1}{2}$ ounces) chicken broth
- $\frac{1}{2}$ teaspoon salt
- $\frac{1}{2}$ teaspoon ground cumin
- $\frac{1}{4}$ teaspoon dried oregano leaves, crushed
- 4 cups finely chopped cooked turkey
- 1 container (8 ounces) sour cream
- 20 corn tortillas (6 inches in diameter)
- 4 cups combined shredded Monterey Jack and Cheddar cheeses, divided
  Chopped fresh cilantro to garnish

To roast red peppers, cut in half lengthwise; remove seeds and membranes. Place, skin side up, on an ungreased baking sheet; flatten with hand. Broil about 3 inches from heat 12 to 15 minutes or until skin is evenly blackened. Immediately seal peppers in a plastic bag and allow to steam 10 to 15 minutes. Remove charred skin. Cut peppers into $\frac{1}{2}$-inch x 1-inch strips.

In a heavy large saucepan, sauté $\frac{1}{2}$ cup onion and garlic in oil over medium-high heat until vegetables are tender. Stir in pepper strips, tomatoes, chicken broth, salt, cumin, and oregano. Bring mixture to a boil. Stirring frequently, reduce heat to medium-low and simmer about 20 minutes or until sauce thickens.

Preheat oven to 375 degrees. Spread $\frac{2}{3}$ cup sauce in each of 2 greased 7 x 11-inch baking dishes. In a medium bowl, combine turkey, remaining 3 tablespoons chopped onion, and sour cream. Soften tortillas in a microwave according to package directions. Place 2 rounded tablespoons turkey mixture and 2 tablespoons cheese on each tortilla. Tightly roll up tortillas and place, seam side down, in baking dishes. Spoon remaining sauce down each side of baking dishes, covering ends of tortillas. Sprinkle remaining cheese over middle of enchiladas. Bake 12 to 15 minutes or until heated through and cheese melts. Garnish with cilantro. Serve warm.

Yield: 20 enchiladas

Turkey Enchiladas with Sweet Red Pepper are flavored with Monterey Jack and Cheddar cheeses. Golden Citrus Cider Punch is a sweet, slightly tangy blend of lemon-lime and apple.

CITRUS CIDER PUNCH

We made apple cider ice cubes to serve in our punch.

- 1 gallon apple cider, chilled
- 1 can (12 ounces) frozen limeade concentrate
- 1 can (12 ounces) frozen lemonade concentrate
- 1 bottle (2 liters) lemon-lime soft drink, chilled
  Lemon and lime slices and maraschino cherries with stems to garnish

In a 2-gallon container, combine cider and concentrates. Stir until concentrates thaw. Stir in soft drink. Garnish servings with lemon and lime slices and maraschino cherries. Serve immediately.

Yield: about 27 cups punch

CHRISTMAS PASTA SNACKS

- 2 tablespoons grated Parmesan cheese
- 1 teaspoon ground cumin
- 3/4 teaspoon ground oregano
- 3/4 teaspoon salt
- 1/2 teaspoon garlic powder
  Vegetable oil
- 8 ounces tree-shaped pasta, cooked, drained, and patted dry

In a small bowl, combine cheese, cumin, oregano, salt, and garlic powder. In a heavy medium saucepan, heat oil to 375 degrees. Stirring occasionally, deep fry 1 cup pasta 4 to 5 minutes or until pasta is golden brown and oil stops bubbling. Drain on paper towels. Transfer warm pasta to lightly greased aluminum foil. Sprinkle about 2 teaspoons cheese mixture over warm pasta. Repeat with remaining pasta and cheese mixture. Cool completely and store in an airtight container.

Yield: about 4$\frac{1}{2}$ cups snack mix

PEAR AND SPINACH SALAD

- 12 cups washed and torn fresh spinach
- 3 avocados
- 3 cans (15$\frac{1}{4}$ ounces each) pear slices in heavy syrup, drained
- 2 cups fresh grapefruit segments (about 3 grapefruit)
- 1 cup (4 ounces) shredded Cheddar cheese
- 1/3 cup sliced almonds, toasted and coarsely chopped

Place 1 cup spinach on each serving plate. Peel each avocado and cut into 12 slices. Arrange about 3 slices each of pear, grapefruit, and avocado on each plate. Garnish each serving with about 1 tablespoon cheese and 1 teaspoon almonds. Serve with Mango Buttermilk Dressing.

Yield: 12 servings

MANGO BUTTERMILK DRESSING

Chilled jars of mango slices can be found in the produce department.

- 1 cup mayonnaise
- ¼ cup buttermilk
- ½ teaspoon curry powder
- 1 cup finely chopped mango
- 1 tablespoon chopped fresh parsley
- 2 teaspoons finely chopped onion

In a small bowl, combine mayonnaise, buttermilk, and curry powder; whisk until well blended. Stir in mango, parsley, and onion. Serve with Pear and Spinach Salad.

Yield: about 2 cups dressing

BLACK BEAN SALSA

- 1 can (15 ounces) black beans, rinsed and drained
- 1 cup seeded and chopped fresh plum tomatoes
- 1 cup chopped sweet yellow pepper
- ½ cup chopped fresh cilantro
- ½ cup sliced green onions
- 1 jalapeño pepper, seeded and chopped
- 3 tablespoons freshly squeezed lime juice
- 1 tablespoon olive oil
- 1 tablespoon red wine vinegar
- 1 clove garlic, minced
- 1 teaspoon salt
- ½ teaspoon ground cumin
  Tortilla chips to serve

In a medium bowl, combine beans, tomatoes, yellow pepper, cilantro, green onions, and jalapeño pepper. In a small bowl, combine lime juice, olive oil, vinegar, garlic, salt, and cumin; stir until blended. Pour lime juice mixture over bean mixture and gently toss. Cover and chill 2 hours to let flavors blend. Serve with tortilla chips.

Yield: about 3½ cups salsa

HEARTY CORN CHOWDER

- ¼ cup butter or margarine
- 1¼ cups chopped sweet red pepper
- ½ cup finely chopped celery
- ½ cup chopped onion
- 3 cups peeled and diced potatoes
- 1 can (14½ ounces) chicken broth
- 2¼ cups half and half, divided
- 3 tablespoons all-purpose flour
- 2 packages (10 ounces each) frozen whole kernel corn, thawed
- 1 teaspoon salt
- ½ teaspoon ground white pepper

In a large Dutch oven, melt butter over medium-high heat. Add red pepper, celery, and onion; sauté until tender. Add potatoes and chicken broth; bring to a boil. Reduce heat to medium-low. Cover and cook 15 minutes or until potatoes are tender.

In a medium bowl, combine ¼ cup half and half and flour; whisk until smooth. Whisk in remaining 2 cups half and half. Stir corn, half and half mixture, salt, and white pepper into soup. Increase heat to medium. Stirring frequently, cook 15 minutes longer or until heated through and thickened. Serve warm.

Yield: about 8½ cups soup

ORANGE-WALNUT PIE

CRUST
- 1¼ cups all-purpose flour
- ½ teaspoon salt
- ½ teaspoon grated orange zest
- ⅓ cup vegetable shortening
- 3 to 4 tablespoons cold orange juice

FILLING
- 3 eggs
- 1 cup light corn syrup
- ½ cup sugar
- ¼ teaspoon salt
- ¼ cup butter or margarine, melted
- ½ teaspoon orange extract
- 1 cup chopped walnuts

For crust, combine flour, salt, and orange zest in a medium bowl. Using a pastry blender or 2 knives, cut in shortening until mixture resembles coarse meal. Sprinkle with orange juice; mix until a soft dough forms. On a lightly floured surface, use a floured rolling pin to roll out dough. Transfer to a 9-inch pie plate and use a sharp knife to trim edge of dough. Flute edge of dough.

Preheat oven to 400 degrees. For filling, beat eggs, corn syrup, sugar, and salt in a medium bowl until blended. Add melted butter and orange extract; beat until well blended. Stir in walnuts. Pour mixture into prepared crust. Bake 10 minutes. Reduce temperature to 350 degrees. Bake 35 to 40 minutes longer or until center is almost set. Cool completely. Store in an airtight container in refrigerator.

Yield: about 8 servings

HONEY SPICE CAKE

CAKE
- ½ cup butter or margarine, softened
- ½ cup granulated sugar
- ½ cup firmly packed brown sugar
- 1 container (8 ounces) sour cream
- 3 eggs
- ¼ cup honey
- 1¾ cups plus 2 tablespoons all-purpose flour
- 2 teaspoons ground cinnamon
- 1 teaspoon baking soda
- ½ teaspoon ground allspice
- ½ teaspoon salt
- ¾ cup chopped pecans, toasted

SYRUP
- ¼ cup honey
- 2 tablespoons butter or margarine

ICING
- 1 cup firmly packed brown sugar
- ¾ cup butter or margarine
- 1 tablespoon light corn syrup
- ⅓ cup milk
- 1 teaspoon vanilla extract
- 2¼ cups sifted confectioners sugar
- 1 cup finely chopped pecans, toasted

Preheat oven to 325 degrees. For cake, grease three 8-inch round cake pans and line bottoms with waxed paper; set aside. In a large bowl, cream butter and sugars until well blended. Add sour cream, eggs, and honey; beat until smooth. In a medium bowl, combine flour, cinnamon, baking soda, allspice, and salt. Add dry ingredients to creamed mixture; beat until well blended. Stir in pecans. Pour batter into prepared pans. Bake 20 to 25 minutes or until a toothpick inserted in center of cake comes out clean. Cool in pans 10 minutes. Remove from pans and cool completely on a wire rack.

For syrup, combine honey and butter in a small saucepan over medium heat. Stir constantly until butter melts. Brush syrup between cake layers.

For icing, combine brown sugar, butter, and corn syrup in a heavy medium saucepan. Whisking constantly, cook over medium heat until mixture comes to a full boil (about 8 minutes); boil 5 minutes. Turn off heat, leaving pan on burner. Slowly whisk in milk and vanilla until smooth. Transfer to a heatproof bowl and let cool 20 minutes. Place bowl of icing in a larger bowl filled with ice. Beat in confectioners sugar, beating until mixture is smooth and begins to hold its shape (about 3 minutes). Spread icing on top and sides of cake. Press pecans into sides of cake. Let icing harden. Store in an airtight container.

Yield: 12 to 14 servings

Buttery honey syrup is brushed between layers of sour cream-moistened Honey Spice Cake. Toasted pecan pieces are pressed into the brown sugar icing.

COZY LITTLE BUFFET

Tomato and Leek Bisque

Homestyle Sweet Potato Biscuits

Wild Rice Dressing

Butternut Squash and Apple Purée

Herb-Pecan Stuffed Turkey Breasts

Cranberry-Port Sauce

Caramelized Onions

Herbed Zucchini Bundles

Parmesan Spinach and Artichokes

*Pumpkin Cheesecake with
Ginger Cream Topping*

Deep-Dish Berry Pie

TOMATO AND LEEK BISQUE

    ¼ cup olive oil
    8 cups chopped leeks, white and
       pale green parts only (about 3
       to 4 leeks)
    2 ribs celery, coarsely chopped
    1 clove garlic, chopped
    2 cans (14½ ounces each) whole
       peeled tomatoes
    1 can (14½ ounces) chicken
       broth
    ¾ cup dry white wine
    1 tablespoon fresh lemon juice
 1½ tablespoons chopped fresh basil
       leaves or 2 teaspoons dried
       basil leaves
    ½ teaspoon salt
    ¼ teaspoon ground white pepper
    ¾ cup whipping cream
       Fresh or dried basil leaves to
       garnish

In a heavy Dutch oven, heat oil, leeks, celery, and garlic over medium-high heat; cook 8 to 10 minutes or until leeks are soft. Add tomatoes, chicken broth, wine, and lemon juice. Bring mixture to a boil; reduce heat to medium-low, cover, and simmer 30 minutes. Remove from heat; add 1½ tablespoons fresh basil, salt, and white pepper. Purée soup mixture in a food processor until smooth. Return soup to Dutch oven over low heat. Stirring occasionally, add whipping cream and simmer about 10 minutes or until thickened. Garnish with basil. Serve warm.

Yield: about 9 cups soup

HOMESTYLE SWEET POTATO BISCUITS

    2 cups all-purpose flour
 2½ teaspoons baking powder
    ½ teaspoon salt
    ¼ cup chilled butter or margarine
    ¼ cup vegetable shortening
    1 cup cooked, mashed sweet
       potatoes
    5 to 7 tablespoons buttermilk

Preheat oven to 450 degrees. In a large bowl, combine flour, baking powder, and salt. Using a pastry blender or 2 knives, cut in butter and shortening until well blended. Add sweet potatoes and enough buttermilk to make a soft dough. Lightly knead dough about 20 times. On a lightly floured surface, roll out dough to ½-inch thickness. Use a 2-inch biscuit cutter to cut out biscuits. Bake on an ungreased baking sheet 12 to 15 minutes or until biscuits are light golden brown. Serve warm.

Yield: about 2 dozen biscuits

WILD RICE DRESSING

- 1 cup minced onions
- 1 cup finely chopped celery
- 1/2 cup olive oil
- 1/2 cup chopped green pepper
- 2 green onions, finely chopped
- 1 tablespoon chopped fresh parsley
- 1 clove garlic, minced
- 1 teaspoon dried basil leaves
- 1 teaspoon ground black pepper
- 1/2 teaspoon ground sage
- 1/2 teaspoon dried rosemary leaves
- 1/2 teaspoon dried thyme leaves
- 1 package (6 1/4 ounces) long grain and wild rice, cooked according to package directions
- 2 cups corn bread crumbs
- 1 can (14 1/2 ounces) chicken broth
- 1 cup sliced fresh mushrooms

Preheat oven to 350 degrees. In a heavy large skillet over medium heat, cook minced onions and celery in olive oil until vegetables are almost tender. Add green pepper, green onions, parsley, and garlic to skillet; continue cooking 2 minutes, stirring frequently. Remove from heat; stir in basil, black pepper, sage, rosemary, and thyme until well blended. In a large bowl, combine onion mixture and remaining ingredients; spoon into a greased 8 x 11 1/2-inch baking dish. Bake 35 to 40 minutes or until lightly browned. Serve warm.

Yield: about 8 to 10 servings

BUTTERNUT SQUASH AND APPLE PURÉE

- 1 butternut squash (about 2 1/2 pounds), peeled, seeded, and cut into 1/2-inch cubes
- 1 tart baking apple, peeled, cored, and coarsely chopped
- 2 tablespoons butter or margarine
- 1 tablespoon honey
- 1 teaspoon grated orange zest
- 1 teaspoon finely chopped crystallized ginger
- 1/8 teaspoon ground nutmeg

In a heavy large saucepan, cover squash and apple with water. Cover and cook over medium-high heat 15 to 20 minutes or until tender; drain. Reduce heat to medium-low; add remaining ingredients to squash mixture. Stirring constantly, cook squash mixture about 10 minutes or until smooth. Serve warm.

Yield: about 8 servings

A spicy stuffing makes moist Herb-Pecan Stuffed Turkey Breasts a succulent alternative to traditional holiday turkey. Tart and tangy Cranberry-Port Sauce is kissed with a hint of orange.

HERB-PECAN STUFFED TURKEY BREASTS

1 turkey breast (about 6 pounds), halved and boned
1⅓ cups coarsely chopped pecans, toasted
2 ribs celery, coarsely chopped
2 medium onions, coarsely chopped
2 tablespoons chopped fresh parsley
1 teaspoon ground sage
1 teaspoon salt
½ teaspoon dried rosemary leaves
½ teaspoon dried thyme leaves
½ teaspoon ground black pepper

Make a lengthwise cut along center of each breast half, cutting halfway through meat. In each side of first cut, make lengthwise cuts perpendicular to the first cut. Spread each breast half flat between two pieces of plastic wrap. Pound meat to ½-inch thickness. Cover and place in refrigerator.

Preheat oven to 350 degrees. Combine remaining ingredients in a food processor. Process 15 to 20 seconds. Spread herb mixture over each breast half. Beginning at 1 long edge, roll up each breast half jellyroll style; tie with twine. Place on a rack in a roasting pan. Pour ½ inch of water into pan (to add moisture and to help prevent burning of meat drippings). Insert meat thermometer into center of 1 breast half. Loosely cover meat with foil. Bake 1½ hours. Remove foil and twine. Continue baking 30 to 45 minutes or until thermometer registers 170 degrees. Allow meat to stand 15 minutes before slicing. Serve warm with Cranberry-Port Sauce.

Yield: about 10 to 12 servings

CRANBERRY-PORT SAUCE

1 cup sugar
½ cup ruby port wine
1 package (12 ounces) fresh cranberries
1 tablespoon grated orange zest
4 tablespoons butter or margarine
¼ cup chicken broth

In a medium saucepan over low heat, stir sugar and wine until sugar dissolves; add cranberries and orange zest. Increase heat to medium-high and bring to a boil. Cook about 10 minutes or until berries pop. Reduce heat to medium-low. Adding one tablespoon butter at a time, stir until well blended. Stir in chicken broth. Serve warm with Herb-Pecan Stuffed Turkey Breasts.

Yield: about 3 cups sauce

CARAMELIZED ONIONS

2 pounds pearl onions, peeled
¼ cup butter or margarine
2 tablespoons firmly packed brown sugar
1 tablespoon grated orange zest
⅛ teaspoon salt
⅛ teaspoon paprika

In a large saucepan, cover onions with water. Cover and cook 10 to 12 minutes or until onions are almost tender; drain. In a large skillet, combine onions and butter. Stirring frequently, cook about 30 minutes or until golden brown. In a small bowl, combine remaining ingredients. Add brown sugar mixture to onions. Stirring constantly, cook until onions are evenly coated and browned. Serve warm.

Yield: about 6 servings

HERBED ZUCCHINI BUNDLES

1 pound unpeeled zucchini, cut into 3-inch-long by 1/8-inch-thick julienne strips
2 medium sweet red peppers, sliced into ten 1/4-inch rings
2 tablespoons butter or margarine
1 teaspoon dried marjoram leaves
1/4 teaspoon dried oregano leaves

Divide zucchini strips into 10 equal bundles and place a pepper ring around each bundle. Place in a microwave-safe baking dish and cover with plastic wrap. Make 2 slits in top of plastic wrap. Microwave on medium-high power (90%) 3 1/2 to 4 minutes, turning dish halfway through cooking time. Remove dish from microwave. Place butter, marjoram, and oregano in a small microwave-safe bowl. Microwave on high power (100%) 20 to 30 seconds or until butter is melted; pour over zucchini. Serve warm.

Yield: 10 servings

PARMESAN SPINACH AND ARTICHOKES

1/2 cup chopped green onions
1/2 cup chopped celery
1/2 cup butter or margarine
2 packages (10 ounces each) frozen chopped spinach, cooked and drained
2 cups sour cream
1 can (14 ounces) artichoke hearts, drained and chopped
1/2 teaspoon hot pepper sauce
1/2 teaspoon salt
1/4 teaspoon ground black pepper
8 ounces bacon, cooked, crumbled, and divided
1/2 cup shredded Parmesan cheese

Preheat oven to 350 degrees. In a small saucepan over medium heat, cook onions and celery in butter until vegetables are tender. In a greased 2-quart baking dish, combine onion mixture, spinach, sour cream, artichoke hearts, hot pepper sauce, salt, and black pepper. Reserving 2 tablespoons bacon for garnish, stir remaining bacon into spinach mixture. Sprinkle cheese over top of casserole. Bake 30 to 40 minutes or until edges are lightly browned. Garnish with reserved bacon. Serve warm.

Yield: about 8 to 10 servings

Topped with crisp bacon pieces and shredded cheese, creamy Parmesan Spinach and Artichokes will be a family favorite.

PUMPKIN CHEESECAKE WITH GINGER CREAM TOPPING

(Shown on page 286)

CRUST
- ¾ cup graham cracker crumbs
- ½ cup finely chopped pecans
- ¼ cup firmly packed brown sugar
- ¼ cup granulated sugar
- 4 tablespoons butter or margarine, melted

FILLING
- 1 can (15 ounces) pumpkin
- 3 eggs
- ½ cup firmly packed brown sugar
- 1 teaspoon vanilla extract
- 1½ teaspoons ground cinnamon
- ½ teaspoon ground ginger
- ½ teaspoon ground nutmeg
- ¼ teaspoon salt
- 3 packages (8 ounces each) cream cheese, softened
- ½ cup granulated sugar
- 1 tablespoon all-purpose flour

TOPPING
- 1 cup whipping cream
- 1 cup sour cream
- 2 tablespoons sugar
- 3 tablespoons dark rum
- ½ teaspoon vanilla extract
- ¼ cup minced crystallized ginger
- 16 pecan halves to garnish

For crust, combine cracker crumbs, pecans, and sugars in a medium bowl until well blended; stir in melted butter. Press mixture into bottom and halfway up sides of a greased 9-inch springform pan; chill 1 hour.

Preheat oven to 350 degrees. For filling, beat pumpkin, eggs, brown sugar, vanilla, spices, and salt in a medium bowl. In a large bowl, beat cream cheese and granulated sugar until well blended. Beat flour and pumpkin mixture into cream cheese mixture until smooth. Pour filling into crust; bake 50 to 55 minutes or until center is set. Cool completely in pan.

For topping, chill a medium bowl and beaters from an electric mixer in freezer. In chilled bowl, beat whipping cream, sour cream, and sugar until stiff peaks form. Fold in rum, vanilla, and ginger. Spread topping over cheesecake. Cover and refrigerate overnight.

To serve, remove sides of pan and garnish top with pecan halves.

Yield: 16 servings

DEEP-DISH BERRY PIE

(Shown on page 286)

CRUST
2¼ cups all-purpose flour
½ teaspoon salt
½ cup chilled vegetable shortening
¼ cup chilled butter or margarine
¼ cup ice water

FILLING
2 cans (16 ounces each) tart red
    pitted cherries, drained
1 package (12 ounces) frozen
    whole blueberries
1 package (12 ounces) frozen
    whole red raspberries
1½ cups plus 2 tablespoons sugar,
    divided
2 tablespoons fresh lemon juice
¼ teaspoon ground cinnamon
⅓ cup cornstarch
⅓ cup cold water
2 tablespoons chilled butter or
    margarine
1 egg white, beaten

For crust, combine flour and salt in a medium bowl. Using a pastry blender or 2 knives, cut in shortening and butter until mixture resembles coarse meal. Sprinkle with water; mix until a soft dough forms. Shape dough into 2 balls. Wrap each ball with plastic wrap and chill while preparing filling.

For filling, combine cherries, blueberries, raspberries, 1½ cups sugar, lemon juice, and cinnamon in a large saucepan over medium-high heat; stir until well blended. In a small bowl, combine cornstarch and water. Stirring constantly as fruit mixture begins to boil, add cornstarch mixture. Stir until mixture thickens. Remove from heat; place pan in cool water in sink. Allow filling to cool while rolling out dough.

Use a rolling pin to roll out half of dough between pieces of plastic wrap to ⅛-inch thickness. Transfer to a 9-inch deep-dish pie plate. Leaving ½ inch of dough over edge, use a sharp knife to trim dough. Cover crust and chill in refrigerator while filling cools to room temperature.

Preheat oven to 375 degrees. Roll out remaining dough for top crust. Spoon filling into bottom pie crust. Cut butter into small pieces and place over filling. Place top crust over filling; crimp edges of crust and make several slits in top. Brush with egg white and sprinkle remaining 2 tablespoons sugar over crust. Bake on a baking sheet 50 to 60 minutes or until crust is golden brown. (If edge of crust browns too quickly, cover edge with aluminum foil.) Serve warm.

Yield: about 10 servings

Pumpkin Cheesecake with Ginger Cream Topping is irresistible. (Recipe is on page 284.)

Deep-Dish Berry Pie has a treasure of cherries, blueberries, and raspberries hidden beneath a flaky sugar-coated crust. (Recipe is on page 285.)

Hooray For
QUICK MEALS

With these timesaving recipes, you'll get dinner ready and be out of the kitchen faster than ever! Each dish features easy-to-gather ingredients and short cooking times or convenient make-ahead plans. You'll turn to these family favorites even when you're not in a hurry!

Kielbasa-Vegetable Dinner, p. 296

STIR UP A STIR-FRY

PEPPER STEAK STIR-FRY

1¼ pounds sirloin steak (1 inch thick)
1 tablespoon cornstarch
¼ cup water
½ cup canned diluted beef broth
¼ cup soy sauce
¼ cup vegetable oil
1 clove garlic, minced
1 teaspoon ground ginger
½ teaspoon salt
½ teaspoon pepper
1 large green pepper, cut
   into strips
1 large sweet red pepper, cut
   into strips
1 large onion, thinly sliced
1 (6-ounce) can sliced water
   chestnuts, drained
4 green onions, cut into 1-inch
   pieces
   Hot cooked rice

Partially freeze steak; slice diagonally across the grain into 1½ x ⅛-inch strips. Set aside.

Combine cornstarch and water in a small bowl, stirring until smooth; add beef broth and soy sauce. Set aside.

Heat oil in a skillet over medium-high heat; add garlic, ginger, salt, and pepper, and cook 1 minute, stirring constantly. Add steak, and cook 2 minutes or until browned; remove from skillet. Add pepper strips and onion, and cook 3 minutes or until crisp-tender. Add beef, water chestnuts, green onions, and broth mixture; cook 2 minutes or until thickened. Serve over rice.

Yield: 4 servings.

TANGY SAUCE

⅓ cup frozen lemonade
   concentrate, thawed
⅓ cup vegetable oil
⅓ cup honey
1 teaspoon celery seeds

Combine all ingredients in container of an electric blender or mixer; blend 1 minute. Serve with fresh fruit.

Yield: 1 cup.

TIMESAVER
• Peppers are easier to slice if you cut from the flesh (not the skin) side.

Pepper Steak Stir-Fry

SUPPER OLÉ

SOFT BEEF TACOS

- 1 pound ground beef
- 1 small onion, minced
- 2 cloves garlic, minced
- 1/2 green pepper, chopped
- 1 jalapeño pepper, seeded and minced
- 1 cup water
- 1 teaspoon ground cumin
- 1 teaspoon chili powder
- 1/2 teaspoon dried oregano
- 1/4 teaspoon salt
- 1/8 teaspoon pepper
- 8 (7-inch) flour tortillas
- 2 cups shredded lettuce
- 2 tomatoes, chopped
- 1 cup (4 ounces) shredded Cheddar cheese
- 1 (8-ounce) carton guacamole
  Commercial taco or picante sauce

Cook first 5 ingredients in a large skillet until meat is browned, stirring to crumble; drain well. Stir in water and next 5 ingredients; bring to a boil. Cover, reduce heat, and simmer over low heat 20 minutes, stirring occasionally. Uncover and cook 5 minutes.

Wrap tortillas securely in aluminum foil; bake at 350° for 10 minutes or until thoroughly heated.

Spoon equal amounts of meat mixture lengthwise down center of each tortilla. Top with lettuce, tomato, cheese, guacamole, and desired amount of taco sauce. Fold bottom third of tortillas over filling. Fold sides of tortillas in toward center, leaving top open. Secure with wooden picks, if necessary. Serve with additional taco sauce, if desired.

Yield: 4 servings.

CANTALOUPE SALAD

- 1/2 cup mayonnaise
- 3 tablespoons frozen orange juice concentrate, thawed and undiluted
- 1 small cantaloupe, chilled
  Leaf lettuce
- 1 1/3 cups seedless green grapes, divided

Combine mayonnaise and orange juice concentrate, mixing well; set aside.

Cut cantaloupe into 4 sections; remove seeds, and peel. Place cantaloupe sections on lettuce leaves; spoon 1/3 cup grapes over and around each section. Drizzle with mayonnaise mixture.

Yield: 4 servings.

FESTIVE FAMILY SUPPER

GRILLED MARINATED PORK TENDERLOIN

2 (³/₄-pound) pork tenderloins
1 (8-ounce) bottle Italian salad
    dressing
    Garnishes: cherry tomato halves,
    fresh parsley sprigs

Place pork tenderloins in a heavy-duty, zip-top plastic bag. Pour dressing over tenderloins; seal and chill 8 hours.

Remove tenderloins from marinade. Insert meat thermometer into tenderloins, being careful not to touch fat. Grill tenderloins, covered with grill lid, over medium-hot coals (350° to 400°) 12 to 15 minutes or until thermometer registers 160°, turning them once. Garnish, if desired.

Yield: 6 servings.

JULIENNE SQUASH

1½ tablespoons vegetable oil
1½ tablespoons lemon juice
1½ tablespoons white vinegar
1 teaspoon salt-free herb-and-spice
    blend
⅛ teaspoon garlic salt
2 yellow squash
2 large zucchini

Combine first 5 ingredients. Stir well; set aside.

Cut yellow squash and zucchini into very thin strips. Arrange on a steaming rack, and place over boiling water; cover and steam 4 minutes.

Place vegetables in a bowl. Pour sauce over vegetables; toss gently to coat.

Yield: 6 servings.

FUDGE PIE

1 cup sugar
¼ cup all-purpose flour
¼ cup cocoa
½ cup butter or margarine, melted
2 large eggs, beaten
¼ teaspoon vanilla extract
½ cup chopped pecans
1 unbaked 9-inch pastry shell
    Ice cream (optional)

Combine first 6 ingredients; stir well. Stir in pecans. Pour mixture into pastry shell. Bake at 350° for 25 minutes or until a wooden pick inserted in center comes out clean. Serve with ice cream, if desired.

Yield: one 9-inch pie.

TIMESAVER
• Marinate pork tenderloins in a heavy-duty, zip-top plastic bag for easy clean-up.

SKILLET DINNER

CHICKEN AND VEGETABLES

- 2 carrots, scraped and sliced
- 1/4 cup chopped onion
- 1 to 2 tablespoons vegetable oil
- 2 skinned and boned chicken breast halves, cut into 1/4-inch strips
- 1/4 teaspoon dried basil
- 1/4 teaspoon garlic powder
- 1/8 teaspoon salt
- 1/8 teaspoon pepper
- 1/4 cup chicken broth
- 2 tablespoons white wine
- 1 (6-ounce) package frozen snow pea pods, thawed and drained
- 1 medium tomato, cut into 8 pieces
- 1/3 cup minced fresh parsley

Cook carrot and onion in 1 tablespoon hot oil in a large skillet over medium heat, stirring constantly, until crisp-tender. Remove vegetables from skillet, reserving pan drippings.

Add chicken to skillet; sprinkle with basil, garlic powder, salt, and pepper. Cook chicken 3 minutes on each side or until browned, adding 1 tablespoon oil if needed. Add reserved vegetables, chicken broth, and wine.

Cover, reduce heat, and simmer 10 minutes. Stir in snow peas, tomato, and parsley; cook until thoroughly heated.

Yield: 2 servings.

CHEESY PITA TRIANGLES

- 1 (8-inch) white or whole wheat pita bread round
- 1/4 cup (1 ounce) shredded Swiss cheese

Cut pita bread round into 6 triangles; sprinkle Swiss cheese inside each triangle, and place on a baking sheet. Bake at 350° for 10 minutes. Serve immediately.

Yield: 2 servings.

INDIVIDUAL POTS DE CRÈME

- 1/2 (4-ounce) package sweet baking chocolate
- 2 tablespoons egg substitute
- 2 teaspoons sugar
- 1/4 cup whipping cream
- 1/4 teaspoon vanilla extract
  Garnish: whipped cream

Melt chocolate in a heavy saucepan over low heat. Combine egg substitute, sugar, and whipping cream; gradually stir into melted chocolate.

Cook over low heat, stirring constantly, 5 minutes or until thickened. Remove from heat; stir in vanilla.

Spoon mixture into individual serving containers. Cover and chill at least 3 hours. Garnish, if desired.

Yield: 2 servings.

Chicken and Vegetables

TIMESAVERS
• Save time and nutrients by leaving peel on tomato. Substitute cherry tomatoes, if desired.

• Press thawed snow peas between paper towels to speed draining.
• Use kitchen shears to cut pita bread into triangles.

A FAMILY AFFAIR

GOLDEN CHOPS WITH VEGETABLES

- 6 ($^1/_2$-inch-thick) pork chops (about 2$^1/_4$ pounds)
- 1 (10$^3/_4$-ounce) can golden mushroom soup, undiluted
- $^1/_4$ cup water
- $^1/_2$ teaspoon rubbed sage
- 1 cup sliced carrot
- $^1/_2$ cup chopped onion
- 1 medium-size green pepper, cut into strips

Brown pork chops in a large nonstick skillet; remove pork chops and drain. Combine soup, water, and sage in skillet; add carrot and onion.

Arrange pork chops over soup mixture; cover and simmer over medium heat 15 minutes, stirring and rearranging pork chops once. Add green pepper; cover and cook 10 additional minutes.

Yield: 6 servings.

SOUFFLÉ POTATOES

- 2$^2/_3$ cups mashed potato mix
- 1 large egg, beaten
- 1 (2.8-ounce) can French-fried onions
- $^1/_4$ teaspoon salt
- $^1/_2$ cup (2 ounces) shredded Cheddar cheese

Prepare mashed potato mix according to package directions. Add egg, onions, and salt, stirring until blended.

Spoon mixture into a greased 2-quart baking dish; sprinkle with cheese. Bake, uncovered, at 350° for 5 minutes.

Yield: 6 to 8 servings.

QUICK FRUIT COBBLER

- 1 (21-ounce) can cherry or blueberry pie filling
- 1 (8-ounce) can unsweetened crushed pineapple, drained
- 1 (9-ounce) package yellow cake mix
- $^1/_3$ cup butter or margarine, melted

Spoon pie filling into a lightly greased 8-inch square baking dish. Spoon pineapple over pie filling.

Sprinkle cake mix evenly over pineapple. Drizzle butter over cake mix. Bake at 425° for 20 to 22 minutes.

Yield: 6 to 8 servings.

SHORTCUT SUPPER

BROCCOLI-SHRIMP STUFFED POTATOES

- 2 large baking potatoes (about 1¼ pounds)
- ⅓ cup loaf process cheese spread
- 2 tablespoons milk
- 1 cup fresh broccoli flowerets
- 1 (6-ounce) can shrimp, drained and rinsed
- 1 green onion, chopped

Scrub potatoes; prick several times with a fork. Place potatoes 1 inch apart on a microwave-safe rack or paper towel.

Microwave potatoes at HIGH 10 to 13 minutes, turning and rearranging once; let stand 2 minutes. Cut an X to within ½ inch of bottom of each potato. Squeeze potatoes from opposite sides and opposite ends to open; fluff with a fork.

Combine cheese spread and milk in a heavy saucepan; cook over low heat until cheese melts, stirring often. Remove from heat, and set aside.

Place broccoli in a 9-inch pieplate; cover and microwave at HIGH 2 to 3 minutes or until tender. Arrange broccoli and shrimp in potatoes. Spoon cheese sauce over potatoes, and sprinkle with green onions.

Yield: 2 servings.

LAYERED FRUIT SALAD

- ½ cup sliced strawberries
- ¼ cup sliced banana
- ¼ cup sour cream
- ½ cup pineapple chunks

Layer half each of strawberries and banana in a small serving dish; lightly spread fruit with one-fourth of sour cream. Top with half of pineapple and one-fourth of sour cream. Repeat procedure with remaining ingredients.

Yield: 2 servings.

PITA CRISPS

- 1 (6-inch) whole wheat pita bread round
- 1 tablespoon butter or margarine, melted

Split pita round to yield 2 flat discs. Cut each disc into 4 triangles; brush each triangle with melted butter.

Place triangles on paper towels in microwave. Microwave at HIGH 20 seconds or until edges curl.

Let stand to cool.

Yield: 2 servings.

BUSY DAY DINNER

KIELBASA-VEGETABLE DINNER
(Shown on page 287)

3 slices bacon
1½ pounds small red potatoes, thinly sliced
1 cup chopped onion
1½ cups thinly sliced carrot
½ teaspoon dried marjoram
1½ pounds kielbasa sausage, cut into ½-inch slices
1½ pounds fresh broccoli flowerets
1 cup water

Cook bacon in a large Dutch oven until crisp; remove bacon, reserving drippings in Dutch oven. Crumble bacon, and set aside.

Cook potato, onion, carrot, and marjoram in reserved drippings in Dutch oven over medium heat 7 minutes, stirring often.

Add kielbasa, broccoli, and water to vegetables in Dutch oven; bring mixture to a boil. Cover, reduce heat, and simmer 15 minutes or until vegetables are crisp-tender, stirring occasionally. Spoon into soup bowls; sprinkle with bacon.

Yield: 6 servings.

SPOON ROLLS

1 package active dry yeast
2 tablespoons warm water (105° to 115°)
½ cup vegetable oil
¼ cup sugar
1 large egg, beaten
4 cups self-rising flour
2 cups warm water (105° to 115°)

Dissolve yeast in 2 tablespoons warm water in a large bowl; let stand 5 minutes. Add oil and remaining ingredients to yeast mixture, and stir until mixture is smooth.

Cover; chill 4 hours or up to 3 days.

Stir batter, and spoon into greased muffin pans, filling three-fourths full. Bake at 400° for 20 minutes or until golden.

Yield: 1½ dozen.

TART LEMON PIE

3 large eggs
1 medium lemon, unpeeled, quartered, and seeded
1¼ cups sugar
2 tablespoons lemon juice
¼ cup butter or margarine, melted
1 unbaked 9-inch pastry shell
Frozen whipped topping, thawed

Combine first 4 ingredients in an electric blender; process 3 minutes or until smooth. Add butter; process 30 seconds. Pour into pastry shell. Bake at 350° for 30 to 35 minutes. Serve pie at room temperature or chilled with whipped topping.

Yield: one 9-inch pie.

ONE-DISH DINNER FOR TWO

SAUSAGE RATATOUILLE

- ½ pound Italian sausage
- 1 small onion, chopped
- ¼ cup olive oil
- 1 small eggplant (¾ pound), cut into ½-inch cubes
- 1 zucchini, sliced
- 1 clove garlic, minced
- 1 large tomato, peeled and chopped
- ½ teaspoon dried oregano
- ¼ teaspoon salt
- ¼ teaspoon pepper
  Garnish: fresh parsley sprigs

Remove casings from sausage. Cook sausage in a large skillet over medium heat until browned, stirring to crumble. Drain well; set aside.

Cook onion in hot oil in a large skillet over medium heat, stirring constantly, until tender. Add eggplant, and cook 3 minutes, stirring constantly. Add zucchini and garlic; reduce heat, and simmer 10 minutes. Add tomato, sausage, and seasonings; cover and simmer 5 minutes, stirring once. Garnish, if desired.

Yield: 2 servings.

TIMESAVER
• Cut all the vegetables for entrée and arrange on cutting board in order of use.

TIMESAVERS FOR BUSY DAY DINNER
(opposite page)

• To save time, use frozen chopped onion, and buy broccoli flowerets and scraped baby carrots from the produce section.
• Wash the potatoes well, but leave the skins on to save time and preserve nutrients.
• Make batter for rolls ahead of time.

SUNDAY NIGHT SUPPER

HONEY-MUSTARD TURKEY SALAD

- 2 cups chopped cooked turkey
- 6 slices bacon, cooked and crumbled
- 1 (4.5-ounce) jar whole mushrooms, drained
- 1/4 cup sweet red pepper strips
- 1/4 cup sliced green onions
- 1/2 cup mayonnaise or salad dressing
- 2 tablespoons honey
- 1 1/2 tablespoons Dijon mustard
- 3/4 teaspoon soy sauce
- 3/4 teaspoon lemon juice
- 1 (2-ounce) package roasted cashews
  Lettuce leaves
  Sweet red pepper rings
  Chow mein noodles

Combine first 5 ingredients in a medium bowl; set aside. Combine mayonnaise and next 4 ingredients; fold into turkey mixture. Cover and chill. Just before serving, stir in cashews. Serve on lettuce leaves and red pepper rings; sprinkle with chow mein noodles.

Yield: 4 servings.

TIMESAVERS

- Use leftover cooked turkey or sliced turkey from the deli.
- Chop canned tomatoes right in the can with kitchen shears.

CREAMY TOMATO SOUP

- 1 (10 3/4-ounce) can tomato soup, undiluted
- 1 (12-ounce) can evaporated milk
- 1 (14 1/2-ounce) can stewed tomatoes, undrained and chopped
- 1/2 cup (2 ounces) shredded Cheddar cheese

Combine soup and milk in a medium saucepan, stirring with a wire whisk. Add tomatoes and cheese.

Cook over low heat until cheese melts and soup is hot.

Yield: 4 2/3 cups.

SESAME KNOTS

- 1 (11-ounce) package refrigerated soft breadsticks
- 2 tablespoons butter or margarine, melted
- 1/2 teaspoon sesame seeds or poppy seeds

Separate dough, and loosely tie each piece of dough into a knot. Arrange rolls 1 inch apart on an ungreased baking sheet. Brush with butter; sprinkle with sesame seeds.

Bake at 350° for 15 minutes or until golden brown.

Yield: 10 servings.

Honey-Mustard Turkey Salad

FIRESIDE SUPPER

EASY RED BEANS AND RICE

1 pound smoked link sausage, cut into 1/2-inch slices
1 medium onion, chopped
1 green pepper, chopped
1 clove garlic, minced
2 (15-ounce) cans kidney beans, drained
1 (16-ounce) can whole tomatoes, undrained and chopped
1/2 teaspoon dried oregano
1/2 teaspoon pepper
Hot cooked rice

Cook sausage over low heat 5 to 8 minutes. Add onion, green pepper, and garlic; cook until tender. Drain, if necessary. Add beans, tomatoes, and seasonings; simmer, uncovered, 20 minutes. Serve over rice.

Yield: 4 to 6 servings.

OVERNIGHT SLAW

5 cups shredded cabbage
1/4 cup chopped purple onion
3/4 cup sugar
3/4 cup white vinegar
3/4 cup water
2 teaspoons salt

Combine cabbage and purple onion in a large bowl. Combine sugar and remaining ingredients, stirring until sugar dissolves. Pour over cabbage mixture; toss gently.

Cover and chill 8 hours. Serve with a slotted spoon.

Yield: 4 to 6 servings.

QUICK CORN MUFFINS

1 (8 1/2-ounce) package corn muffin mix
2 tablespoons chopped onion
1 large egg, beaten
1/3 cup milk

Combine muffin mix and onion; add egg and milk, stirring just until dry ingredients are moistened. Pour batter into well-greased muffin pans, filling two-thirds full. Bake at 400° for 15 minutes or until lightly browned.

Yield: 6 to 8 muffins.

TIMESAVERS
• Use kitchen shears to chop canned tomatoes in the can.
• Purchase shredded cabbage or coleslaw mix and make slaw the night before. Chop and bag onion and green pepper for the entrée and muffins for a headstart.
• Use a corn muffin mix for a really quick bread. The yield depends on the size of the muffin pan.

A TASTE OF TEX-MEX

MEXICAN CHEF SALAD
(Shown on page 7)

  1   pound ground beef
 3/4 cup water
  1   (1¼-ounce) package taco
        seasoning mix
  8   cups torn iceberg lettuce
  1   (16-ounce) can kidney beans,
        drained and rinsed
  2   tomatoes, chopped
  1   (2¼-ounce) can sliced ripe olives,
        drained
 ½   cup (2 ounces) shredded
        Cheddar cheese
      Commercial guacamole
      Tortilla chips

Cook ground beef in a skillet until meat is browned, stirring to crumble; drain. Return meat to skillet; add water and taco seasoning mix. Bring to a boil; reduce heat, and simmer 10 minutes, stirring occasionally.

Layer lettuce, beans, beef mixture, tomato, olives, and cheese. Serve with guacamole and tortilla chips.

Yield: 4 servings.

TIMESAVER
• To save time with dessert, substitute frozen strawberries for fresh, and 2 cups frozen whipped topping, thawed, for whipped cream; omit sugar.

STRAWBERRY FOOL

  2   cups fresh strawberries, hulled
 ¼   cup sugar
  1   cup whipping cream, whipped
      Garnish: 4 fresh strawberries

Place 2 cups strawberries and sugar in container of a food processor or electric blender, and process until smooth. Pour mixture into a large bowl.

Fold whipped cream into strawberry mixture. Spoon into individual serving bowls. Garnish, if desired. Serve immediately, or chill 1 hour.

Yield: 4 servings.

SOUTHERN SANGRÍA

 ⅓   cup sugar
 ⅓   cup lemon juice
 ⅓   cup orange juice
  1   (25.4-ounce) bottle sparkling red
        grape juice, chilled

Combine first 3 ingredients in a large pitcher, stirring until sugar dissolves. Add grape juice, and gently stir to mix well. Serve over crushed ice.

Yield: 5 cups.

FETTUCCINE WITH HAM AND PEAS

2 cloves garlic, crushed
1 tablespoon butter or
   margarine, melted
1/2 pound thinly sliced cooked ham
1 cup frozen English peas, thawed
12 ounces fettuccine, uncooked
1/2 cup butter or
   margarine, softened
1 cup grated Parmesan cheese
1 (8-ounce) carton sour cream
1/2 teaspoon pepper

Cook garlic in 1 tablespoon melted butter in a large skillet over medium heat. Stir in ham and peas; cook, stirring constantly, 3 to 5 minutes. Remove from heat; cover and keep warm.

Cook fettuccine according to package directions, omitting salt. Drain well; place in a large serving bowl. Add 1/2 cup softened butter, stirring until completely melted; add Parmesan cheese and sour cream, stirring gently to coat well.

Fold ham mixture into fettuccine mixture. Add pepper; toss gently. Serve immediately.

Yield: 6 servings.

Fettuccine with Ham and Peas Techniques

Stack several slices of ham on cutting board; cut ham into 1/4-inch slices. Repeat procedure with remaining ham slices.

Thaw peas in microwave oven at HIGH 1 to 2 minutes, stirring to melt ice crystals.

HAM AND SWISS ON NOODLES

16 ounces egg noodles, uncooked
1/4 cup sliced green onions
1/2 cup butter or margarine, divided
1 (4-ounce) can sliced
    mushrooms, drained
1 (10-ounce) package frozen English
    peas, thawed and drained
1/4 cup all-purpose flour
3 cups milk
1/2 teaspoon salt
1/2 teaspoon ground white pepper
2 cups (8 ounces) shredded
    Swiss cheese
2 cups cubed cooked ham
1 cup chopped canned
    tomatoes, drained

Cook noodles according to package directions. Drain and keep noodles warm.

Cook green onions in 2 tablespoons melted butter in a large heavy saucepan 3 minutes; add mushrooms and peas, and cook until heated. Remove from saucepan, and set aside.

Melt remaining 6 tablespoons butter in saucepan; add flour, stirring until smooth. Cook, stirring constantly, 1 minute. Gradually add milk, and cook over medium heat, stirring constantly, until mixture is thickened and bubbly. Add salt and pepper, stirring well. Add cheese, and stir until mixture is smooth.

Add vegetables, ham, and tomatoes; mix well. Cook until thoroughly heated. Serve over noodles.

Yield: 8 servings.

Pasta Cooking Technique

Add pasta to boiling water in small batches. A few drops of oil added to the water prevents pasta from sticking together.

FIERY CAJUN SHRIMP

1 cup butter, melted
1 cup margarine, melted
1/2 cup Worcestershire sauce
1/4 cup lemon juice
1/4 cup ground pepper
2 teaspoons hot sauce
2 teaspoons salt
4 cloves garlic, minced
5 pounds unpeeled, medium-size
  fresh shrimp
2 lemons, thinly sliced
  French bread

Combine first 8 ingredients; pour half of mixture into a large ceramic heat-proof dish. Layer shrimp and lemon slices in sauce; pour remaining sauce over shrimp and lemon.

Bake, uncovered, at 400° for 20 minutes or until shrimp turn pink, stirring twice. Drain sauce, and serve with shrimp and French bread.

Yield: 6 to 8 servings.

QUICK CHICKEN AND PASTA

2 quarts water
1/2 teaspoon salt
4 ounces vermicelli, uncooked
3/4 cup frozen English peas
1/3 cup Italian salad dressing
1 cup chopped cooked chicken
1/4 teaspoon sweet red pepper flakes
2 tablespoons grated Parmesan
  cheese

Combine water and salt in a large saucepan; bring to a boil. Add vermicelli and peas. Return water to a boil; reduce heat, and cook 10 minutes. Drain and set aside.

Heat salad dressing in saucepan. Add chicken and red pepper flakes; cook, stirring constantly, 2 minutes.

Add pasta mixture, and cook until thoroughly heated. Sprinkle with Parmesan cheese, tossing mixture well.

Yield: 2 servings.

BEEF HASH

1 cup cubed cooked lean beef
1 cup peeled, cubed potato
1/2 cup chopped onion
1 tablespoon chopped fresh parsley
1/4 teaspoon salt
1/4 teaspoon pepper
2 teaspoons vegetable oil
1/3 cup fat-free milk

Combine first 6 ingredients; cook in hot oil in a large nonstick skillet over medium-high heat, stirring occasionally, 10 minutes or until mixture is browned and tender. Stir in milk; cover, reduce heat, and simmer 5 minutes.

Yield: 2 servings.

QUICK SPAGHETTI

1 large onion, chopped
1 green pepper, chopped
1 pound ground beef
1 (3 1/2-ounce) package sliced
   pepperoni, chopped
1 (32-ounce) jar spaghetti sauce
   with mushrooms
1 (12-ounce) package spaghetti,
   uncooked
1 cup (4 ounces) shredded
   mozzarella cheese
1 tablespoon grated Parmesan
   cheese

Cook first 4 ingredients in a large skillet over medium heat, stirring until beef browns and crumbles. Remove from heat; drain. Return mixture to skillet.

Add spaghetti sauce to beef mixture, and bring to a boil. Cover, reduce heat, and simmer 20 minutes, stirring occasionally.

Cook spaghetti according to package directions, omitting salt. Drain. Arrange on an ovenproof platter; spoon meat sauce on top. Sprinkle mozzarella cheese over sauce.

Bake at 400° for 3 to 5 minutes. Remove from oven; top with Parmesan cheese. Serve immediately.

Yield: 6 servings.

SPAGHETTI-HAM PIE

6 ounces spaghetti, uncooked
4 cloves garlic, minced
2 1/2 tablespoons olive oil
1/4 cup all-purpose flour
1/4 teaspoon salt
1/8 teaspoon freshly ground pepper
3/4 cup half-and-half
1 1/2 cups milk
1/4 to 1/2 cup chopped cooked ham
1/4 cup grated Parmesan cheese,
   divided

Cook spaghetti according to package directions; drain and set aside.

Cook garlic in olive oil in a Dutch oven over medium heat, stirring constantly, 5 minutes. Stir in flour, salt, and pepper. Cook, stirring constantly, 1 minute.

Add half-and-half and milk; cook over medium heat, stirring constantly, until thickened and bubbly. Stir in spaghetti.

Spoon half of spaghetti mixture into a lightly greased 9-inch pieplate; sprinkle with ham and 2 tablespoons Parmesan cheese. Top with remaining spaghetti mixture; sprinkle with remaining 2 tablespoons Parmesan cheese.

Bake at 425° for 15 to 20 minutes or until lightly browned.

Yield: 6 servings.

WINTER WARM-UP

CHILI-CHICKEN STEW

6 skinned, boned chicken breast
   halves
1 medium onion, chopped
1 medium-size green pepper,
   chopped
2 cloves garlic, minced
1 tablespoon vegetable oil
2 (14$\frac{1}{2}$-ounce) cans stewed
   tomatoes, undrained
   and chopped
1 (15-ounce) can pinto beans,
   drained
$\frac{2}{3}$ cup picante sauce
1 teaspoon chili powder
1 teaspoon ground cumin
$\frac{1}{2}$ teaspoon salt
   Shredded Cheddar cheese,
   diced avocado, sliced green
   onions, and sour cream

Cut chicken into 1-inch pieces. Cook chicken, onion, green pepper, and garlic in hot oil in a Dutch oven until lightly browned. Add tomatoes and next 5 ingredients; cover, reduce heat, and simmer 20 minutes.

Top individual servings with remaining ingredients.

Yield: 6 servings.

SEASONED CORNBREAD

1 (8$\frac{1}{2}$-ounce) package corn muffin
   mix
$\frac{1}{2}$ teaspoon poultry seasoning
1 large egg, beaten
$\frac{2}{3}$ cup milk

Combine muffin mix and poultry seasoning; add egg and milk, stirring just until dry ingredients are moistened. Pour batter into a well-greased 8-inch square baking dish; bake at 400° for 18 to 20 minutes.

Yield: 9 servings.

BROWNIE CHIP COOKIES

1 (23.7-ounce) pkg. brownie mix
2 large eggs
$\frac{1}{3}$ cup vegetable oil
1 (6-ounce) package semisweet
   chocolate morsels
$\frac{1}{2}$ cup chopped pecans

Combine brownie mix, eggs, and oil; beat about 50 strokes with a spoon. Stir in chocolate morsels and pecans. Drop dough by rounded teaspoonfuls onto greased cookie sheets.

Bake at 350° for 10 to 12 minutes. Cool slightly on cookie sheets; then remove to wire racks, and cool completely.

Yield: about 6 dozen.

Chili-Chicken Stew, Seasoned Cornbread, and Brownie Chip Cookies

PIZZA CASSEROLE

1 pound lean ground beef
1 large onion, chopped
1 green pepper, chopped
$1/2$ teaspoon garlic salt
$1/4$ teaspoon pepper
$1/4$ teaspoon dried oregano
$1/4$ teaspoon dried basil
1 (14-ounce) jar pizza sauce
1 (8-ounce) package macaroni, uncooked
1 ($3^1/2$-ounce) package sliced pepperoni
1 (4-ounce) package shredded mozzarella cheese

Cook ground beef, onion, and green pepper in a large Dutch oven, stirring until meat browns and crumbles. Drain well.

Add garlic salt and next 4 ingredients. Stir well; cover, reduce heat, and simmer 15 minutes.

Cook macaroni according to package directions, omitting salt; drain. Add to meat mixture; stir well. Spoon into a lightly greased 13 x 9 x 2-inch baking dish; top evenly with pepperoni.

Cover and bake at 350° for 20 minutes; top with cheese, and bake, uncovered, 5 additional minutes.

Yield: 6 to 8 servings.

SHORTCUT STRATEGIES

• To streamline your time, read all the recipes in the menu and assemble all the ingredients and equipment.
• Make a game plan. First start with make-aheads; then plan the portion of the meal that involves more total time than active time — such as cooking rice.
• Plan for leftovers by fixing a large quantity or simply doubling a recipe; freeze or refrigerate the remainder so you will have a heat-and-eat meal to serve another day.
• Measure dry ingredients before moist ones to minimize cleanup. Before measuring honey or other sticky ingredients, rinse the measure with hot water; then the honey will slide right out.
• Chop and freeze half-cup portions of green pepper, onion, and parsley in zip-top freezer bags, or purchase prepackaged frozen chopped onion and green pepper.
• When slicing vegetables like carrots, green onions, or celery, slice 3 or 4 pieces at a time.
• Cut vegetables into small pieces or thin slices to cook faster.

CREAMY SHRIMP AND NOODLES

1 pound unpeeled medium-size fresh shrimp
6 ounces fettuccine, uncooked
1 small sweet red pepper, cut into strips
2 tablespoons butter or margarine, melted
1¼ cups milk
2 (0.6-ounce) envelopes cream of chicken-flavored instant soup mix
½ cup frozen English peas
3 tablespoons grated Parmesan cheese
¼ teaspoon garlic powder

Peel shrimp, and devein, if desired; set aside.

Cook fettuccine according to package directions; drain and set aside.

Cook shrimp and red pepper in butter in a large skillet over medium-high heat, stirring constantly, 3 minutes or until shrimp turn pink.

Combine milk and soup mix; add to shrimp mixture. Stir in peas, cheese, and garlic powder.

Bring to a boil; reduce heat and simmer, stirring often, 5 minutes or until thickened. Toss shrimp mixture with fettuccine. Serve immediately.

Yield: 3 to 4 servings.

PASTA TIPS

• When cooking long pasta shapes (spaghetti, fettuccine, linguine, and angel hair), it's not necessary to break the pasta into shorter pieces. Hold one end of the pasta by the handful, and set the other end in boiling water, pushing pasta gently until it softens enough to submerge.

• Pasta is best served piping hot, but it cools quickly when placed on serving dishes that are at room temperature. To avoid the cool down, preheat the serving platter or bowls. Warm heat-proof dishes in a 250-degree oven about 10 minutes, or drain some of the hot pasta cooking liquid into the serving bowl and let stand about 2 minutes. Pour off the water, and transfer the pasta to the dish.

• To save time, use refrigerated or fresh pasta. It cooks faster than dried.

PATIO SUPPER

STROMBOLI

1 (16-ounce) loaf frozen bread
    dough, thawed
1/4 pound thinly sliced ham
1/4 pound sliced hard salami
1/2 teaspoon dried basil, divided
1/2 teaspoon dried oregano, divided
3 ounces sliced provolone cheese
1 cup (4 ounces) shredded
    mozzarella cheese
2 tablespoons butter or margarine,
    melted
1 teaspoon cornmeal

Place bread dough on a lightly greased baking sheet; pat to a 15 x 10-inch rectangle. Arrange ham slices lengthwise down center; place salami on top. Sprinkle with 1/4 teaspoon basil and 1/4 teaspoon oregano. Arrange provolone cheese over herbs, and top with mozzarella cheese; sprinkle with remaining herbs.

Moisten all edges of dough with water. Bring each long edge of dough to center; press edges together securely to seal. Seal ends.

Brush dough with 1 tablespoon butter. Sprinkle with cornmeal, and carefully invert. Brush top with remaining butter. Bake at 375° for 20 to 22 minutes.

Yield: 4 servings.

GRAPE JUICE-FRUIT REFRESHER

1 quart pineapple or lime sherbet
1 1/3 cups sliced fresh strawberries
1/4 to 1/2 cup white grape juice

Spoon sherbet equally into 4 compotes. Top each with 1/3 cup sliced strawberries. Just before serving, pour 1 to 2 tablespoons grape juice over top.

Yield: 4 servings.

TIMESAVERS

• Buy sliced meat and cheese at deli.
• Thaw frozen bread dough at room temperature, or follow quick thawing instructions on package.

Stromboli

HEALTHY HEROES

 ³/₄ cup thinly sliced fresh mushrooms
 ¹/₂ cup seeded and chopped
     cucumber
 1 tablespoon sliced green onions
 1 clove garlic, minced
 2 tablespoons balsamic vinegar
 ¹/₈ teaspoon freshly ground pepper
 1 (2-ounce) hoagie bun
 2 lettuce leaves
 2 ounces thinly sliced lean ham
 2 ounces thinly sliced turkey breast
 4 slices tomato
 ¹/₄ cup (1 ounce) shredded part-skim
     mozzarella cheese

Combine first 6 ingredients in a small bowl; let mixture stand 30 minutes.

Slice bun in half lengthwise; pull out soft inside of top and bottom, leaving a shell (reserve crumbs for another use).

Spoon mushroom mixture into each half of bun; cover with a lettuce leaf. Top with ham, turkey, tomato, and cheese. Cut in half to serve.

Yield: 2 servings.

SNACK SMART

Instead of high-fat snacks, try one of these low-fat alternatives; each has less than 5 grams of total fat:

 1 apple
 1 bagel
 1 banana
 8 carrot sticks
 ¹/₂ cup dried fruit
 1 English muffin
 2 fig bars
 3 gingersnaps
 1 orange
 20 pretzel sticks
 2 rice cakes
 5 vanilla wafers

RELAX WITH SOUP AND SANDWICHES

DOUBLE-DECKER BLT

1 (13-ounce) loaf unsliced French bread
  Olive oil-flavored cooking spray
  Garlic-Basil Mayonnaise
  Salad greens
4 tomatoes, thinly sliced
16 slices bacon, cooked

Cut bread into 12 slices. Coat one side of each with cooking spray. Grill or toast until golden.

Spread Garlic-Basil Mayonnaise on other side of each bread slice; layer 4 slices with half each of salad greens, tomato slices, and bacon. Top each with a second bread slice and remaining salad greens, tomato, and bacon. Top with remaining bread slices.

Yield: 4 sandwiches.

GARLIC-BASIL MAYONNAISE

$1/2$ cup mayonnaise or salad dressing
1 tablespoon chopped fresh basil or 1 teaspoon dried basil
$1/4$ teaspoon garlic salt
$1/4$ teaspoon freshly ground pepper

Combine all ingredients; cover and chill.

Yield: $1/2$ cup.

BROCCOLI-CHEESE SOUP

$3/4$ cup water
1 (10-ounce) package frozen chopped broccoli
1 ($10^3/4$-ounce) can cream of chicken soup
$1/2$ cup milk
$1/8$ teaspoon ground red pepper
$1/2$ cup (2 ounces) shredded Cheddar cheese

Bring water to a boil in a large saucepan; add broccoli. Cover, reduce heat, and simmer 5 minutes or until tender. Stir in soup and milk.

Cook over medium heat, stirring constantly, until thoroughly heated. Stir in pepper. Pour into serving bowls. Top each serving with cheese.

Yield: 1 quart.

TIMESAVER

• Microwave bacon in advance on a microwave-safe rack or paper plate with a double layer of paper towels between each layer of slices. Cook 8 slices at HIGH 6 to 7 minutes.

SOUTH OF THE BORDER

OVEN-FRIED CHICKEN CHIMICHANGAS

    3 (5-ounce) cans white chicken,
        drained and flaked
    1 (4.5-ounce) can chopped green
        chiles, drained
    1 cup (4 ounces) shredded
        Monterey Jack cheese
   1/2 cup sliced green onions
    8 (9-inch) flour tortillas
        Vegetable oil
        Shredded lettuce, salsa or picante
        sauce, sour cream

Combine first 4 ingredients; set aside. Wrap tortillas in damp paper towels; microwave at HIGH 15 seconds or until hot. Brush both sides of tortillas, one at a time, with vegetable oil (keep remaining tortillas warm).

Place a scant 1/2 cup chicken mixture just below center of each tortilla. Fold in left and right sides of tortilla to partially enclose filling. Fold up bottom edge of tortilla; fold into a rectangle, and secure with a wooden pick. Repeat with remaining tortillas and chicken mixture.

Place filled tortillas on a lightly greased baking sheet. Bake at 425° for 10 minutes or until crisp and lightly browned. Serve with shredded lettuce, salsa, and sour cream.

Yield: 4 servings.

SUNNY FRUIT SALAD

   1/2 cup plain yogurt
    2 tablespoons honey
    1 teaspoon lemon juice
        Pinch of grated nutmeg
    1 cup orange sections
    2 large bananas, peeled and cut into
        1/2-inch slices
    3 kiwifruit, peeled and cut into
        1/2-inch slices
        Lettuce leaves

Combine first 4 ingredients in a medium bowl. Add fruit, and toss gently. Serve on lettuce leaves.

Yield: 4 servings.

QUICK-FIX LUNCH

MEXICAN EGG SALAD TACOS

- 4 large hard-cooked eggs, chopped
- 1/4 cup (1 ounce) shredded sharp Cheddar cheese
- 1 tablespoon chopped green onions
- 2 tablespoons mayonnaise or salad dressing
- 2 tablespoons salsa
- 1 tablespoon sour cream
- 1/8 teaspoon salt
- 1/8 teaspoon pepper
- 6 taco shells
  Lettuce leaves
- 3/4 cup (3 ounces) shredded sharp Cheddar cheese
  Avocado slices
  Additional salsa

Combine first 3 ingredients in a medium bowl; set aside.

Combine mayonnaise and next 4 ingredients; fold into egg mixture.

Line taco shells with lettuce. Spoon egg salad evenly into taco shells. Sprinkle 2 tablespoons cheese on each taco. Serve with avocado slices and salsa.

Yield: 6 servings.

PEACH CRINKLE

- 1 (29-ounce) can sliced peaches, drained
- 1 teaspoon grated lemon rind
- 1 (11-ounce) package piecrust mix
- 1 cup firmly packed brown sugar
- 1/4 cup cold butter or margarine, cut into small pieces

Place peaches in a lightly greased 11 x 7 x 1 1/2-inch baking dish. Sprinkle with lemon rind, and set aside.

Combine piecrust mix and sugar; sprinkle over top. Dot with butter.

Bake at 375° for 30 minutes. Serve with vanilla ice cream or frozen yogurt.

Yield: 6 servings.

TIMESAVER
• To seed avocado, cut lengthwise all the way around and twist halves in opposite directions to separate. Remove seed; brush cut surface with lemon juice to keep from turning brown.

SOUP & SALAD, ANYTIME MEAL

CREAMY ONION-AND-POTATO SOUP

2 tablespoons butter or margarine
2 tablespoons all-purpose flour
1 cup chopped onion
1 large clove garlic, minced
2 (14$^1/_2$-ounce) cans ready-to-serve chicken broth
4 cups peeled, cubed potato (about 3 large)
$^1/_2$ cup sliced green onions
$^1/_8$ teaspoon salt
$^1/_4$ teaspoon ground white pepper
1 cup milk
Garnish: green onion strips

Melt butter in a Dutch oven over low heat; add flour, stirring until smooth. Cook, stirring constantly, 1 minute. Add onion and garlic; cook 1 minute or until onion is tender. Gradually add broth, stirring constantly. Add potato and next 3 ingredients.

Bring to a boil; cover, reduce heat, and simmer 15 minutes, stirring occasionally, or until potato is tender. Stir in milk, and heat thoroughly. Garnish, if desired.

Yield: 7 cups.

TIMESAVERS
• Cut potatoes into small cubes to help them cook faster.
• Use leftover cooked ham for biscuits.

HAM-CHEESE BISCUITS

2 cups biscuit mix
$^1/_2$ cup minced cooked ham
$^1/_2$ cup (2 ounces) shredded Cheddar cheese
$^2/_3$ cup milk

Combine first 3 ingredients in a medium bowl, stirring well. Sprinkle milk over dry mixture, stirring just until moistened.

Pat dough out onto a floured surface to $^1/_2$-inch thickness; cut with a 2-inch biscuit cutter.

Place biscuits on a greased baking sheet. Bake at 450° for 8 minutes or until lightly browned.

Yield: 14 biscuits.

SPINACH SALAD

1 (10-ounce) package fresh trimmed spinach
1 cup strawberries, halved
1 cup pecan halves, toasted
Commercial poppy seed dressing

Tear spinach leaves into bite-size pieces. Combine spinach, strawberries, and pecans; drizzle with poppy seed dressing. Serve immediately.

Yield: 6 servings.

COOL SUMMER LUNCH

RANCH-STYLE TURKEY 'N' PASTA SALAD

 2 cups penne pasta, uncooked
 2 cups chopped cooked turkey
 1 small zucchini, sliced
 2 small yellow squash, sliced
 1 small green pepper, chopped
 1 small sweet red pepper, chopped
 1/4 cup grated Parmesan cheese
 3/4 cup commercial Ranch-style dressing

Cook pasta according to package directions; drain. Rinse with cold water; drain.

Combine pasta and remaining ingredients in a large bowl. Cover and chill at least 2 hours. Toss before serving.

Yield: 6 to 8 servings.

TIMESAVER
• Save time by cooking extra pasta for another meal. Toss it with a small amount of olive oil, and store in a covered container in the refrigerator up to 3 days. To reheat, place pasta in a colander and pour hot water over it.

GREEN GRAPES SURPRISE

 1/4 cup firmly packed light brown sugar
 1/2 cup sour cream
 5 cups seedless green grapes, washed and stemmed
 Garnish: mint sprigs

Combine brown sugar and sour cream in a large bowl. Stir in grapes. Chill several hours.

Spoon into individual serving dishes. Garnish, if desired.

Yield: 6 to 8 servings.

LIGHT IDEAS
• Fresh fruit, loaded with vitamins, minerals, and fiber, is always a good dessert choice.
• Angel food cake contains no fat and is a smart selection for healthy eating.
• Frozen fruit sorbet or nonfat frozen yogurt is a delicious substitution for ice cream.

LATE-MORNING MEAL

CURRIED CHICKEN-RICE SALAD

    3 cups chopped cooked chicken
 1½ cups cooked rice
    1 cup chopped celery
    1 cup seedless green grapes, halved
 ½ cup chopped pecans, toasted
 ⅓ cup sweet pickle relish
 ¾ cup mayonnaise
    1 teaspoon curry powder
 ½ teaspoon salt
 ½ teaspoon pepper
       Lettuce leaves
    1 pint fresh strawberries
    1 fresh pineapple, peeled and cut
          into spears

Combine first 6 ingredients in a medium bowl.

Combine mayonnaise and next 3 ingredients; add to chicken mixture, stirring well.

Serve on lettuce leaves with strawberries and pineapple.

Yield: 6 servings.

SOUR CREAM MUFFINS

 ½ cup butter, softened
    1 (8-ounce) carton sour cream
    2 cups biscuit mix

Cream butter; stir in sour cream. Gradually add biscuit mix, stirring just until moistened.

Spoon into lightly greased miniature muffin pans, filling two-thirds full. Bake at 350° for 15 minutes or until lightly browned.

Yield: 3 dozen.

Note: Muffins can be made in regular muffin pans. Bake at 350° for 20 minutes.

Yield: 1 dozen.

TIMESAVERS
• Purchase chicken from the deli and use quick-cooking rice.
• Buy cored and peeled fresh pineapple.

Curried Chicken-Rice Salad

TURKEY-IN-THE-SLAW SANDWICH

- 1 cup shredded green cabbage
- 1 cup shredded red cabbage
- 1/2 cup shredded carrot
- 1/4 cup reduced-calorie mayonnaise
- 1/4 cup plain nonfat yogurt
- 1 1/2 teaspoons sugar
- 1/4 teaspoon ground white pepper
- 8 slices whole wheat bread
- 1 tablespoon commercial reduced-calorie Thousand Island salad dressing
- 3/4 pound thinly sliced cooked turkey

Combine first 7 ingredients in a large bowl; cover and chill.

Spread 4 slices of bread equally with dressing. Place 3 ounces sliced turkey and one-fourth of slaw on each slice of bread; top with remaining bread slices. Cut each sandwich in half, and secure with wooden picks.

Yield: 4 servings.

TURKEY-RICE SOUP

- 3/4 pound turkey tenderloin, cut into bite-size pieces
- 1 1/2 quarts water
- 2 stalks celery, sliced
- 1 medium onion, chopped
- 2 chicken-flavored bouillon cubes
- 1 teaspoon salt
- 1/4 teaspoon poultry seasoning
- 1 bay leaf
- 1/2 cup long-grain rice, uncooked
- 2 carrots, scraped and sliced

Combine first 8 ingredients in a Dutch oven. Bring to a boil; cover, reduce heat, and simmer 40 minutes. Add rice and carrot; cover and simmer 20 additional minutes or until rice is tender. Remove bay leaf.

Yield: 1 1/2 quarts.

SALMON BURGERS

 1 (15-ounce) can pink salmon,
    undrained
 1 large egg, lightly beaten
 1/2 cup unsalted saltine cracker
    crumbs
 1/4 cup finely chopped onion
 1/4 cup finely chopped celery
 1/2 teaspoon baking powder
    Vegetable cooking spray
 1/2 cup nonfat mayonnaise
 2 tablespoons lemon juice
 1/2 teaspoon dried dillweed
 1/4 teaspoon pepper
 1/4 teaspoon hot sauce
 6 onion sandwich rolls, split
 6 tomato slices
 1 cup shredded lettuce

Drain salmon, reserving liquid; remove
and discard skin and bones. Flake salmon
with a fork.

Combine salmon and next 5 ingredients.
Add 1 to 2 tablespoons reserved liquid,
stirring until mixture sticks together.
Shape into 6 patties; set aside.

Coat a large nonstick skillet with cooking
spray; add salmon patties, and cook over
medium heat about 4 minutes on each
side or until lightly browned. Keep warm.

Combine mayonnaise and next 4
ingredients; spread on cut sides of rolls.
Place a salmon patty on bottom half of
each roll; top each with a tomato slice,
lettuce, and top half of bun.

Yield: 6 servings.

COLD DILL SOUP

 2 cups half-and-half
 2 (8-ounce) cartons plain yogurt
 2 cucumbers, peeled, seeded, and
    diced
 3 tablespoons minced fresh dill or
    1 tablespoon dried dillweed
 2 tablespoons lemon juice
 1 tablespoon chopped green onions
 1/2 teaspoon salt
 1/8 to 1/4 teaspoon ground white
    pepper
    Garnishes: cucumber slices, fresh
    dill sprigs

Combine first 8 ingredients, stirring well;
cover and chill thoroughly. Stir well;
garnish, if desired.

Yield: 1 quart.

LEMON-DILL CHICKEN SAUTÉ

1/2 cup dry breadcrumbs
1 1/2 teaspoons lemon-pepper
    seasoning
1/2 teaspoon dried dillweed
6 skinned and boned chicken breast
    halves
1 large egg, beaten
2 tablespoons vegetable oil

Combine first 3 ingredients in a dish. Dip chicken in egg; dredge in breadcrumb mixture.

Heat oil in a large skillet over medium heat. Add chicken, and cook 5 minutes on each side or until golden. Cover and cook 5 minutes.

Yield: 6 servings.

TIMESAVER
• For easy cleanup, use a plastic bag to dredge chicken.

HAM-PECAN-BLUE CHEESE PASTA SALAD

(Shown on page 7)

3 cups farfalle (bow tie pasta),
    uncooked
4 ounces cooked ham, cut into
    strips
1 cup coarsely chopped pecans
1 (4-ounce) package crumbled blue
    cheese
2 tablespoons chopped fresh
    parsley
1 tablespoon minced fresh
    rosemary or 1 teaspoon dried
    rosemary
1 clove garlic, minced
1/2 teaspoon coarsely ground pepper
1/4 cup olive oil
1/3 cup grated Parmesan cheese

Cook pasta according to package directions; drain. Rinse with cold water and drain.

Combine pasta and remaining ingredients except Parmesan cheese, tossing well. Sprinkle with Parmesan cheese. Serve immediately or chill, if desired.

Yield: 6 servings.

FIESTA QUICHE

Vegetable cooking spray
4 (8¹/₂-inch) flour tortillas
¹/₂ cup (2 ounces) shredded reduced-
   fat Cheddar cheese
1 (4.5-ounce) can chopped green
   chiles, drained
¹/₄ cup sliced green onions
¹/₂ cup picante sauce
1 cup egg substitute
¹/₃ cup fat-free milk
¹/₂ teaspoon chili powder
¹/₄ teaspoon cracked black pepper
6 tomato slices
2 tablespoons plain nonfat yogurt
   Fresh cilantro

Coat a 12-inch quiche dish with cooking spray; layer tortillas in dish. Sprinkle cheese, chiles, and green onions over tortillas; dollop with picante sauce.

Combine egg substitute and next 3 ingredients; pour into quiche dish.

Bake at 350° for 30 to 35 minutes. Remove from oven, and arrange tomato slices around edge of quiche; top each tomato slice with 1 teaspoon yogurt and a sprig of cilantro. Cut into wedges.

Yield: 6 servings.

ZIPPY OMELET BRUNCH

EASY MEXICAN OMELET

    3 large eggs
 1/2 teaspoon salt
 1/4 teaspoon pepper
    1 tablespoon water
    1 tablespoon butter or margarine
 3/4 cup (3 ounces) shredded
         Monterey Jack cheese
    2 tablespoons sliced jalapeño
         peppers
    2 tablespoons salsa

Combine first 4 ingredients; stir with a wire whisk just until blended.

Heat a heavy 8-inch skillet over medium heat until hot enough to sizzle a drop of water. Add butter, and rotate skillet to coat bottom.

Pour egg mixture into skillet; sprinkle with cheese and jalapeño peppers. As mixture starts to cook, gently lift edges of omelet with a spatula, and tilt skillet so that uncooked portion flows underneath. Fold omelet in half, and transfer to plate. Top with salsa.

Yield: 2 servings.

HASH BROWN POTATOES

    1 tablespoon bacon drippings
    1 tablespoon butter or margarine
    2 cups diced cooked potato
 1/3 cup minced onion
    1 tablespoon minced fresh parsley
    1 clove garlic, minced
       Salt and pepper to taste

Melt bacon drippings and butter in a heavy 9-inch skillet. Add remaining ingredients, stirring gently until coated. Cook mixture, uncovered, 15 to 20 minutes or until browned on all sides, turning occasionally.

Yield: 2 servings.

TIMESAVERS
• Begin omelet with a heated nonstick skillet or omelet pan.
• Use leftover cooked potatoes, or cut potatoes into small pieces to cook faster.

OUT-OF-THE-ORDINARY BREAKFAST

APPLE BREAKFAST SANDWICHES

- 1/3 cup firmly packed brown sugar
- 2 tablespoons all-purpose flour
- 1/2 teaspoon ground cinnamon
- 1 (10-ounce) can refrigerated buttermilk biscuits
- 1 cup (4 ounces) shredded sharp Cheddar cheese
- 2 large apples, peeled, cored, and cut into rings
- 1 tablespoon butter or margarine, melted

Combine first 3 ingredients in a small bowl; set aside.

Separate biscuits, and press each into a 3-inch circle. Place on lightly greased baking sheets; sprinkle with cheese, and top each with an apple ring. Sprinkle with reserved sugar mixture, and drizzle with butter.

Bake at 350° for 15 minutes or until crust is golden. Serve immediately.

Yield: 10 servings.

PERKY CRANBERRY PUNCH

- 2 (32-ounce) bottles cranberry juice
- 1 (46-ounce) can unsweetened pineapple juice
- 2 cups water
- 1 cup firmly packed brown sugar
- 2 tablespoons whole allspice
- 2 tablespoons whole cloves
- 6 (3-inch) sticks cinnamon

Pour first 3 ingredients into a large percolator. Place brown sugar and remaining ingredients in percolator basket.

Perk through complete cycle of electric percolator.

Yield: 1 gallon.

FAVORITE FAMILY BREAKFAST

EASY PANCAKES

2½ cups biscuit mix
2 large eggs, beaten
1⅓ cups milk
2 tablespoons vegetable oil

Place biscuit mix in a medium bowl; make a well in center. Combine eggs, milk, and oil; add to biscuit mix, stirring just until dry ingredients are moistened.

Pour about ¼ cup batter for each pancake onto a moderately hot, lightly greased griddle. Turn pancakes when tops are covered with bubbles and edges of pancakes look cooked.

Yield: 16 pancakes.

TIMESAVERS
• Stir pancake batter only until dry ingredients are moistened — batter will still be lumpy. Beating batter until smooth produces tough pancakes.
• Save time by using a wide-mouth pitcher to mix and pour pancake batter.
• Make sausage patties and sauce for pancakes ahead of time.

CRANBERRY-APPLE SAUCE

1 (16-ounce) can whole-berry cranberry sauce
2 small cooking apples, cored and chopped
⅓ cup apple juice

Combine all ingredients in a small saucepan; bring to a boil, stirring constantly. Reduce heat and simmer, stirring occasionally, 6 minutes or until apples are tender.

Serve warm over pancakes. Store sauce in refrigerator.

Yield: 2½ cups.

BAKED SAUSAGE PATTIES

1 pound ground pork sausage

Shape sausage into 8 patties about ¾-inch thick; place on a rack in a broiler pan. Bake at 375° for 15 to 20 minutes or until done. Drain on paper towels.

Yield: 8 servings

To make ahead: Prepare as directed; let cool. Wrap in aluminum foil; chill. Bake at 350° in foil 10 minutes or until thoroughly heated.

BACKYARD PICNIC

SPEEDY CHILI DOGS

1 pound ground beef
1 large onion, chopped
1 clove garlic, crushed
1 (16-ounce) can tomato sauce
$1/4$ teaspoon salt
$1/8$ teaspoon pepper
1 to 2 tablespoons chili powder
1 cup water
8 frankfurters, cooked
8 hot dog buns, split and toasted
  Shredded Cheddar cheese
  Chopped green onions

Combine first 3 ingredients in a skillet; cook until beef is browned, stirring until it crumbles. Drain. Add tomato sauce and next 4 ingredients; cover, reduce heat, and simmer 25 minutes, stirring occasionally.

Place frankfurters in hot dog buns. Spoon chili mixture over frankfurters; top with cheese and green onions.

Yield: 8 servings.

OLD-FASHIONED SWEET COLESLAW

5 cups finely chopped cabbage
   (about 1 small head)
2 carrots, scraped and shredded
1 to 2 tablespoons sugar
$1/2$ teaspoon salt
$1/4$ teaspoon pepper
$1/3$ cup mayonnaise or salad dressing

Combine cabbage and carrot in a large bowl. Sprinkle with sugar, salt, and pepper; toss gently. Stir in mayonnaise. Cover and chill thoroughly.

Yield: 8 servings.

LEMON ICE CREAM TARTS

1 quart vanilla ice cream, slightly
   softened
1 (6-ounce) can frozen lemonade
   concentrate, undiluted
12 (3-inch) commercial graham
   cracker tart shells

Place softened ice cream and lemonade concentrate in container of an electric blender; process until smooth. Pour mixture into tart shells.

Place tart shells on a baking sheet, and freeze until firm. Place frozen tarts in heavy-duty, zip-top plastic bags. Carefully remove filled crusts about 5 minutes before serving.

Yield: 12 (3-inch) tarts.

TIMESAVERS
• Select a packaged slaw mix that has shredded carrot in it.
• Make tarts in advance and freeze.

KIDS' SUMMER CELEBRATION

SLOPPY JOES

1½ pounds ground beef
1   small onion, chopped
1   small green pepper, chopped
1   (10¾-ounce) can tomato soup
1   (8-ounce) can tomato sauce
2   tablespoons brown sugar
    (optional)
1   tablespoon Worcestershire sauce
1   teaspoon prepared mustard
    Pinch of garlic powder
6   hamburger buns, split and toasted

Cook ground beef, onion, and green pepper in a large skillet until beef is browned, stirring to crumble; drain.

Stir in tomato soup and next 5 ingredients; simmer 10 to 15 minutes, stirring mixture often. Serve on toasted buns.

Yield: 6 servings.

TIMESAVERS

• Microwave Jiffy Beans and Franks while Sloppy Joe mixture is simmering.
• Allow ice cream time to soften before scooping, or peel away the carton and cut into slices with an electric knife.

JIFFY BEANS AND FRANKS

2   (16-ounce) cans pork and beans
½   cup chopped onion
½   cup ketchup
¼   cup firmly packed brown sugar
½   teaspoon dry mustard
4   frankfurters, cut into ⅜-inch slices

Combine first 5 ingredients; spoon into a lightly greased, shallow 2-quart casserole. Cover with heavy-duty plastic wrap; fold back a small edge of wrap to allow steam to escape.

Microwave at HIGH 8 to 9 minutes, stirring once. Add frankfurters. Microwave at HIGH 8 to 9 minutes, stirring once.

Yield: 6 servings.

ROOT BEER FLOATS

1   (1-liter) bottle root beer or other
    cola, divided
1   quart vanilla ice cream

Pour ½ cup root beer into each of 6 (12-ounce) soda glasses; spoon ice cream equally into glasses. Top each with remaining root beer.

Yield: 6 servings.

Jiffy Beans and Franks, Sloppy Joes

AFTER THE GAME

ALL-AMERICAN PIZZA BURGERS

1½ pounds lean ground beef
1½ pounds ground turkey sausage
   Vegetable cooking spray
1 (14-ounce) jar pizza sauce, divided
¾ cup grated Parmesan cheese
1 medium onion, chopped
   (optional)
12 hamburger buns
12 slices mozzarella cheese

Combine ground beef and sausage; shape into 12 patties. Coat grill rack with cooking spray; place on grill over medium-hot coals (350° to 400°).

Place patties on rack, and cook, uncovered, 5 minutes on each side or until done, brushing patties occasionally with ¾ cup pizza sauce. (Discard any remaining pizza sauce used for brushing patties.)

Sprinkle with Parmesan cheese and, if desired, onion. Serve on buns with mozzarella cheese and remaining pizza sauce.

Yield: 12 servings.

RANCH-STYLE DIP

¾ cup low-fat cottage cheese
1 (8-ounce) carton sour cream
1 cup mayonnaise or salad dressing
1 (1-ounce) envelope Ranch-style
   dressing mix

Place cottage cheese in container of an electric blender or food processor; process until smooth. Add sour cream and remaining ingredients; process until blended, stopping once to scrape down sides. Serve dip with fresh vegetables.

Yield: 2½ cups.

TIMESAVERS
• Shape ground meat into ½-inch-thick patties (¼ pound each), and stack between sheets of wax paper. If making patties ahead to freeze, place 2 pieces of wax paper between each patty, and place in a freezer bag.
• Preheat gas grill 20 minutes, or light charcoal 30 minutes before grilling burgers.

KIDS' COMPANY SUPPER

MEXICAN FRANKS

10 (6-inch) corn tortillas
   Vegetable oil
1 (15-ounce) can chili without beans
1 (8-ounce) can tomato sauce,
   divided
1 tablespoon minced onion
1/4 teaspoon hot sauce
10 frankfurters
1 (4.5-ounce) can chopped green
   chiles, drained
1 cup (4 ounces) shredded Cheddar
   cheese

Fry tortillas, one at a time, in 1/4-inch hot oil 3 to 5 seconds on each side or just until softened. Drain on paper towels. Set aside.

Combine chili, 1/4 cup tomato sauce, onion, and hot sauce in a small bowl. Place a frankfurter in center of each tortilla; top each with 2 tablespoons chili mixture. Roll up, and place seam side down in a lightly greased 11 x 7 x 1 1/2-inch baking dish. Combine remaining tomato sauce and remaining chili mixture; pour over tortillas.

Sprinkle with chiles. Cover and bake at 350° for 20 to 25 minutes. Uncover and sprinkle evenly with cheese; bake 5 additional minutes.

Yield: 10 servings.

FIESTA DIP

1 (8-ounce) package cream cheese,
   softened
1 (8-ounce) jar mild picante sauce
   Garnish: sliced green onions

Combine cream cheese and picante sauce; beat mixture at low speed of an electric mixer until smooth. Spoon into a small bowl, and garnish, if desired. Serve with corn chips or tortillas.

Yield: 2 cups.

FROZEN COOKIE CRUNCH

1 (20-ounce) package cream-filled
   chocolate sandwich cookies,
   crushed
1/2 cup butter or margarine, melted
1 cup chopped pecans
1/2 gallon vanilla ice cream, softened

Combine first 3 ingredients. Pat one-third of cookie mixture in bottom of a lightly greased 13 x 9 x 2-inch pan; spread half of ice cream on top. Repeat procedure; sprinkle remaining crumbs on top. Freeze 8 hours.

Yield: 15 servings.

KIDS' EASY BREAKFAST TREAT

ORANGE JUICY

1 (6-ounce) can frozen orange juice
   concentrate, undiluted
1 cup water
1 cup milk
1/4 cup sugar
1 teaspoon vanilla extract
2 cups ice cubes

Combine all ingredients in container of an electric blender; process until smooth. Serve immediately.

Yield: 5 cups.

TIMESAVER

• Microwave bacon on a microwave-safe rack or paper plate. Cover bacon with paper towels; cook 6 slices at HIGH 5 minutes.

STRAWBERRY-FRENCH TOAST SANDWICHES

1/4 cup plus 2 tablespoons whipped
   cream cheese
12 slices sandwich bread
3 tablespoons strawberry jam
3 large eggs
3 tablespoons milk
1/8 teaspoon salt
2 to 3 tablespoons butter or
   margarine, divided
   Powdered sugar
   Garnish: strawberry fans

Spread 1 tablespoon cream cheese on each of six bread slices; spread 1 1/2 teaspoons jam over cream cheese. Top with remaining slices of bread.

Combine eggs, milk, and salt in a shallow dish, beating well. Dip each sandwich into egg mixture, turning to coat both sides.

Melt 2 tablespoons butter in a large skillet; cook 3 sandwiches in butter until browned, turning to brown both sides. Repeat procedure with remaining sandwiches, adding more butter if necessary.

Sprinkle sandwiches with powdered sugar; serve immediately with fresh-cooked bacon. Garnish, if desired.

Yield: 6 servings.

Hooray For
CHICKEN

Whether roasted, fried, sautéed, or simmered, chicken goes great with a huge variety of seasonings and ingredients. These kitchen-tested recipes are simply delicious, as well as simple to make. So gather your family and invite your friends for a feast of flavorful chicken that you'll be proud to serve.

Chicken-in-a-Garden, p. 361

LAYERED CHICKEN SALAD

    3 cups chopped cooked chicken,
          divided
    2 cups torn lettuce
    1 cup cooked long-grain rice
    1 (10-ounce) package frozen English
          peas, thawed
  1/4 cup chopped fresh parsley
    2 large tomatoes, seeded and
          chopped
    1 cup thinly sliced cucumber
    1 small sweet red pepper, chopped
    1 small green pepper, chopped
       Creamy Dressing
       Red pepper rings

Layer 1 1/2 cups chicken and lettuce in a 3-quart bowl. Combine rice, peas, and parsley; spoon evenly over lettuce.

Layer tomato, cucumber, chopped red pepper, green pepper, and remaining 1 1/2 cups chicken.

Spoon Creamy Dressing evenly over top of salad, sealing to edge of bowl. Top with red pepper rings; cover and chill 8 hours. Toss before serving.

Yield: 8 servings.

CREAMY DRESSING

    1 cup mayonnaise
  1/2 cup sour cream
  1/2 cup raisins
  1/2 cup finely chopped onion
  1/4 cup sweet pickle relish
    2 tablespoons milk
  1/2 teaspoon celery seeds
  1/2 teaspoon dillseeds
  1/2 teaspoon dry mustard
  1/2 teaspoon garlic salt

Combine all ingredients; stir well.

Yield: about 2 3/4 cups.

BLT CHICKEN SALAD
(Shown on page 7)

  1/2 cup mayonnaise
  1/4 cup commercial barbecue sauce
    2 tablespoons grated onion
    1 tablespoon lemon juice
  1/2 teaspoon pepper
    2 large tomatoes, chopped
    8 cups torn leaf lettuce or iceberg
          lettuce
    3 cups chopped cooked chicken
   10 slices bacon, cooked and
          crumbled
    2 hard-cooked eggs, sliced

Combine first 5 ingredients in a small bowl; stir well. Cover and chill dressing mixture thoroughly.

Press chopped tomato between several layers of paper towels to remove excess moisture.

Arrange lettuce on individual salad plates; top each serving with tomato and chopped cooked chicken.

Spoon dressing mixture over salads; sprinkle with crumbled bacon, and garnish with egg slices. Serve immediately.

Yield: 4 servings.

HOT MEXICAN CHICKEN SALADS

5 cups chopped cooked chicken
2 cups (8 ounces) shredded sharp
    Cheddar cheese, divided
1 (15-ounce) can red kidney beans,
    drained
1 large sweet red pepper, chopped
$^3/_4$ cup finely chopped onion
$^1/_2$ cup sliced ripe olives
$^1/_2$ cup sour cream
$^1/_2$ cup mayonnaise
1 (4.5-ounce) can chopped green
    chiles
1 ($1^1/_4$-ounce) package taco
    seasoning
    Vegetable oil
6 (8-inch) flour tortillas
    Garnishes: avocado slices,
        cilantro sprigs

Hot Mexican Chicken Salads

Combine chicken, 1 cup cheese, and next 8 ingredients, stirring well. Cover and chill.

Pour oil to depth of $^1/_4$ inch into a large deep skillet; heat to 375°. Fry tortillas, one at a time, until crisp and golden. Drain on paper towels.

Spoon chicken mixture evenly onto fried tortillas. Sprinkle with remaining 1 cup cheese. Place on baking sheets.

Broil 4 inches from heat (with door partially opened if using an electric oven) 30 seconds or just until cheese melts. Garnish, if desired. Serve immediately.

Yield: 6 servings.

SOUTHWESTERN CHICKEN SALAD

- 4 skinned chicken breast halves
- 1/2 teaspoon salt
- 1/4 cup mayonnaise
- 1/4 cup sour cream
- 1 (4.5-ounce) can chopped green chiles, undrained
- 1 teaspoon ground cumin
- 1/4 teaspoon salt
- 1/8 teaspoon pepper
- 1/4 cup chopped onion
- 4 (8-inch) flour tortillas
- 1 cup (4 ounces) shredded Longhorn cheese
- 3 cups shredded lettuce
  Garnishes: sour cream, diced tomato, picante sauce

Place chicken in a large saucepan; add 1/2 teaspoon salt and water to cover. Bring to a boil; cover, reduce heat, and simmer 30 minutes or until chicken is tender. Drain chicken, reserving broth for another use. Bone chicken, and shred into small pieces. Set aside. Combine mayonnaise and 1/4 cup sour cream, stirring well. Add chiles and next 3 ingredients; stir well. Combine chicken and onion; add sour cream mixture, stirring to coat well. Cover and refrigerate 2 hours. Place tortillas on a baking sheet; sprinkle cheese evenly over each tortilla. Bake at 300° for 10 minutes or until cheese melts; transfer to individual serving plates. Arrange lettuce on tortillas; top each with one-fourth of chicken mixture. Garnish, if desired. Serve with picante sauce.

Yield: 4 servings.

GRILLED CHICKEN SALAD

- 4 skinned and boned chicken breast halves
- 3 tablespoons soy sauce
- 3 tablespoons butter or margarine, softened
- 3 (3/4-inch-thick) slices French bread
- 1/3 cup olive oil
- 2 cloves garlic, crushed
- 1 1/2 tablespoons lemon juice
- 2 teaspoons Dijon mustard
- 2 dashes of hot sauce
- 1 large head romaine lettuce, torn
- 1/4 cup freshly grated Parmesan cheese
  Freshly ground pepper

Place chicken and soy sauce in a heavy-duty, zip-top plastic bag; marinate 30 minutes in refrigerator. Spread butter over both sides of bread slices; cut slices into 3/4-inch cubes. Place on a baking sheet, and bake at 350° for 15 minutes or until croutons are crisp and dry. Set aside.

Remove chicken from soy sauce; discard soy sauce. Grill chicken, covered, over medium coals (300° to 350°) 5 minutes on each side or until done. Cool 5 minutes; slice crosswise into 1/2-inch-wide strips. Set aside.

Combine olive oil and next 4 ingredients in a large bowl; stir with a wire whisk until blended. Add chicken strips, tossing to coat. Add romaine, cheese, croutons, and pepper, tossing gently to combine. Serve immediately.

Yield: 4 servings.

BROCCOLI-CHICKEN SALAD

4 cups chopped cooked chicken
1/4 cup sliced pimiento-stuffed olives
1 pound fresh broccoli, broken into flowerets
2/3 cup mayonnaise or salad dressing
1/4 teaspoon curry powder
Lettuce leaves (optional)

Combine chicken, olives, and broccoli. Combine mayonnaise and curry powder, stirring well; add to chicken mixture, and toss well.

Cover and chill. Serve in a lettuce-lined bowl, if desired.

Yield: 6 to 8 servings.

HOT CHICKEN SALAD CASSEROLE

4 cups chopped cooked chicken
1 1/2 cups chopped celery
4 hard-cooked eggs, chopped
1 (2-ounce) jar diced pimiento, drained
1 tablespoon finely chopped onion
3/4 cup mayonnaise
2 tablespoons lemon juice
3/4 teaspoon salt
1 cup (4 ounces) shredded Cheddar cheese
2/3 cup sliced almonds, toasted

Combine first 8 ingredients in a bowl; mix well. Spoon into a lightly greased 12 x 8 x 2-inch baking dish; cover and bake at 350° for 20 minutes.

Sprinkle with cheese; top with almonds. Bake, uncovered, 3 additional minutes or until cheese melts.

Yield: 6 to 8 servings.

CHICKEN-FRUIT SALAD

1 small head Bibb lettuce
1 avocado
2 chicken breast halves, cooked and cubed
1 small apple, diced
1 small banana, sliced
1 (8-ounce) can pineapple chunks, drained
1/2 cup chopped pecans
1/3 to 1/2 cup mayonnaise or salad dressing

Remove 6 outer leaves of lettuce; tear remaining lettuce. Peel and seed avocado. Slice half of avocado and set aside; chop remaining avocado.

Combine torn lettuce, chopped avocado, chicken, and next 5 ingredients; toss gently. Serve on reserved lettuce leaves, and garnish with avocado slices.

Yield: 2 servings.

ASPARAGUS-CHICKEN SALAD

1 pound fresh asparagus
1 1/2 cups chopped cooked chicken
3 cups iceberg lettuce, torn into bite-size pieces
1/4 cup slivered almonds, toasted
1/4 cup chopped parsley
1 1/2 tablespoons raisins
1 red apple, unpeeled
Lettuce leaves (optional)
Italian Cream Dressing

Snap off tough ends of asparagus. Remove scales with a knife or vegetable peeler, if desired.

Cook asparagus, covered, in a small amount of boiling water 3 minutes. Plunge in ice water. Drain well.

Cut asparagus into 1 1/2-inch pieces; reserve 8 pieces for garnish. Combine remaining asparagus, chicken, lettuce, almonds, parsley, and raisins in a large bowl. Cut half of apple into 1/2-inch cubes; stir into chicken mixture. (Reserve remaining apple for garnish.)

Arrange salad in a lettuce-lined bowl, if desired. Garnish with reserved asparagus and apple slices. Pour Italian Cream Dressing over salad.

Yield: 4 servings.

ITALIAN CREAM DRESSING

3/4 cup sour cream
1/4 cup crumbled Gorgonzola cheese or blue cheese
1 tablespoon lemon juice
1/4 teaspoon garlic powder
Freshly ground pepper

Combine all ingredients in a small bowl; stir well.

Yield: 1 cup.

ARTICHOKE-CHICKEN-RICE SALAD

2 (6-ounce) jars marinated artichoke hearts, undrained
1 (6.9-ounce) package chicken-flavored rice and vermicelli mix
2 1/2 cups chopped cooked chicken
1 (6-ounce) can sliced water chestnuts, drained and chopped
1 (3-ounce) jar pimiento-stuffed olives, drained and sliced
1 cup chopped green onions
1 cup reduced-fat mayonnaise
1 1/2 tablespoons curry powder
1 teaspoon pepper
Lettuce leaves

Drain artichoke hearts, reserving marinade; coarsely chop artichokes. Cook rice mix according to package directions; stir in reserved marinade. Cool.

Combine artichoke hearts, rice mixture, chopped chicken, and next 3 ingredients. Combine mayonnaise, curry powder, and pepper; stir into chicken mixture.

Cover and chill 1 to 2 hours. Serve on lettuce leaves.

Yield: 8 servings.

CHICKEN SALAD ORIENTAL

  $^1/_2$ cup uncooked macaroni
  2 cups chopped cooked chicken
  $^1/_2$ cup sliced green onions
  1 (8-ounce) can sliced water
      chestnuts, drained
  $^1/_2$ cup mayonnaise or salad dressing
  2 teaspoons soy sauce
  $^1/_4$ teaspoon ground ginger
  $^1/_8$ teaspoon pepper

  2 cups ($^3/_4$-pound) fresh snow pea
      pods, blanched
  $^1/_2$ cup slivered almonds, toasted

Cook macaroni according to package directions; drain. Combine macaroni and next 3 ingredients; toss well.

Combine mayonnaise and next 3 ingredients, stirring well; fold into chicken mixture. Cover and chill 2 hours.

Divide snow peas among 4 plates. Top with chicken salad, and sprinkle with toasted almonds.

Yield: 4 servings.

Chicken Salad Oriental

CHUTNEY-CHICKEN SALAD

4 1/2 cups chopped cooked chicken
3/4 cup mayonnaise
1/2 cup chutney
1 1/2 teaspoons curry powder
1/4 teaspoon salt
1 tablespoon lime juice
1 1/2 cups sliced almonds, toasted
  Lettuce leaves
  Garnish: apple slices

Combine first 6 ingredients in a large bowl; toss to mix. Cover and let chill thoroughly. Stir in toasted almonds before serving. Serve salad on lettuce leaves. Garnish, if desired.

Yield: 6 servings.

BAKED LEMON CHICKEN

4 skinned chicken breast halves
1/3 cup lemon juice
1/2 cup butter or margarine, melted
1 teaspoon garlic powder
1 teaspoon poultry seasoning
1/2 teaspoon salt
1/4 teaspoon pepper
  Hot cooked rice (optional)

Place chicken in a lightly greased 11 x 7 x 1 1/2-inch baking dish. Combine remaining ingredients except rice; pour over chicken. Bake, uncovered, at 350° for 1 hour or until juices run clear, basting frequently. Serve with rice, if desired.

Yield: 4 servings.

DILLED CHICKEN SALAD

8 skinned chicken breast halves
1 teaspoon salt
1 cup chopped celery
3 hard-cooked eggs, chopped
1 (3-ounce) package cream cheese, softened
1/2 cup mayonnaise or salad dressing
1/4 cup sour cream
1 1/2 tablespoons chopped fresh dillweed
1 teaspoon dry mustard
1/4 teaspoon salt
1/8 teaspoon pepper
  Lettuce leaves
  Slices of raw carrot and yellow squash

Combine chicken and 1 teaspoon salt in a Dutch oven; add water to cover. Bring to a boil; cover, reduce heat, and simmer 30 minutes or until tender.

Drain chicken, reserving broth for another use. Bone chicken, and cut into bite-size pieces. Combine chicken, celery, and eggs in a large bowl, and set aside.

Combine cream cheese and next 6 ingredients in a medium bowl. Add to chicken mixture, and toss well. Cover and chill thoroughly.

Serve salad on lettuce leaves with sliced carrot and squash.

Yield: 8 servings.

CHICKEN TORTELLINI SALAD

- 1 pound boneless chicken breasts, cut into strips
- 2 cloves garlic, minced
- 2 tablespoons olive oil
- 1 (8-ounce) package tortellini with Parmesan cheese
- 2 tablespoons olive oil
- 3 stalks celery, chopped
- 1 medium-size red pepper, cut into strips
- $1/3$ cup chopped purple onion
- 5 ounces smoked Gouda cheese, cut into strips
- $3/4$ cup olive oil
- $3/4$ cup cider vinegar
- 2 tablespoons honey
- 2 tablespoons Dijon mustard
- 1 teaspoon dry mustard
  Bibb lettuce leaves
- 5 slices Canadian bacon, cut into strips
  Garnish: celery leaves

Cook chicken and garlic in 2 tablespoons hot oil, stirring constantly, until chicken is done; drain and set aside.

Cook tortellini according to package directions; drain well. Combine tortellini and 2 tablespoons oil in a large bowl, tossing gently. Add chicken, celery, red pepper, onion, and cheese.

Combine $3/4$ cup olive oil and next 4 ingredients in a jar; cover tightly, and shake vigorously. Pour mixture over salad, and toss gently.

Serve salad immediately or chill. Arrange on lettuce leaves, and top with Canadian bacon. Garnish, if desired.

Yield: 6 servings.

OLD-FASHIONED CHICKEN SALAD

- 4 cups chopped cooked chicken
- 2 hard-cooked eggs, chopped
- 1 cup chopped celery
- $1/4$ cup chopped onion
- $3/4$ teaspoon salt
- $1/2$ teaspoon celery salt
- $1/8$ to $1/4$ teaspoon white pepper
  Dash of red pepper
- 2 tablespoons lemon juice
- $1/2$ to $3/4$ cup mayonnaise
  Paprika
  Garnishes: fresh parsley sprigs, cherry tomatoes

Combine first 9 ingredients; toss gently. Fold in mayonnaise; cover and chill 2 hours.

Spoon salad into a serving dish; sprinkle with paprika. Garnish, if desired.

Yield: 6 servings.

HERB-ROASTED CHICKEN

2 tablespoons butter or margarine, melted
1/3 cup white vinegar
3 tablespoons lemon juice
3 tablespoons chopped fresh tarragon
2 tablespoons olive oil
1 clove garlic, minced
1 teaspoon salt
1 teaspoon freshly ground pepper
1 pound round red potatoes, unpeeled
1 cup diagonally sliced celery
1 (2-ounce) jar sliced pimiento, drained
1/4 cup chopped fresh parsley
1 (5- to 6-pound) stewing chicken
Garnishes: fresh parsley, fresh tarragon

Combine first 8 ingredients in a small bowl, mixing well. Set aside.

Cover potatoes with water in saucepan; cook, covered, over medium heat 15 minutes or until tender. Drain potatoes; cool.

Cut potatoes into bite-size pieces. Add celery, pimiento, and 1/4 cup parsley, tossing gently. Add 2 tablespoons tarragon-oil mixture, tossing to coat. Set aside.

Remove giblets from cavity of chicken, and reserve for another use. Rinse chicken with cold water; pat dry with paper towels. Fold neck skin over back; secure with a wooden pick. Lift wingtips up and over back, and tuck under chicken.

Stuff chicken with potato mixture. Close cavity with wooden picks or skewers; tie ends of legs together with string or cord. Place chicken, breast side up, on a roasting rack. Brush entire chicken with remaining tarragon-oil mixture.

Insert meat thermometer in meaty part of thigh, making sure it does not touch bone. Bake at 375° until meat thermometer inserted in meaty part of thigh registers 180° (about 2 hours), basting frequently with tarragon-oil mixture. Let cool 10 to 15 minutes before slicing. Place on a serving platter; garnish, if desired.

Yield: 4 servings.

TIP

• If cooked chicken is stuffed, remove stuffing and refrigerate chicken and stuffing in separate containers.

RICE-STUFFED ROASTED CHICKEN

2 1/2 cups cooked brown rice
1 cup chopped apple
1/2 cup chopped dried prunes
1/2 cup chopped dried apricots
1/4 cup chopped celery
1/4 teaspoon garlic powder
1/2 teaspoon grated lemon rind
1 teaspoon ground ginger
1/4 teaspoon salt
1/4 cup butter or margarine, melted
1 (2 1/2- to 3-pound) broiler-fryer
2 tablespoons butter or margarine, melted
1/4 teaspoon paprika

Combine first 10 ingredients in a large bowl; mix well. Place chicken, breast side up, on a rack in a shallow roasting pan. Stuff cavity lightly with brown rice mixture. Close cavity with wooden picks or skewers.

Combine 2 tablespoons melted butter and paprika; brush over chicken. Bake at 375° for 1 1/2 hours or until meat thermometer inserted in meaty part of thigh registers 180° and in rice mixture registers 165°.

Spoon remaining rice mixture into a lightly greased 1-quart casserole; bake in oven with chicken the last 15 to 20 minutes of baking time.

Place chicken on a serving platter, and spoon rice around it.

Yield: 4 servings.

SPICY ALMOND CHICKEN

3 tablespoons butter or margarine
1 (3- to 3 1/2-pound) broiler-fryer, cut up and skinned
1 (14-ounce) jar red currant jelly
1/2 cup prepared mustard
1/2 cup slivered almonds
3 tablespoons brown sugar
2 tablespoons lemon juice
1/2 teaspoon ground cinnamon

Melt butter in a large skillet over medium heat. Add chicken, and cook about 10 minutes or until lightly browned on all sides.

Place chicken in a lightly greased 13 x 9 x 2-inch baking dish.

Add jelly and remaining ingredients to skillet; cook over medium heat until jelly melts, stirring occasionally. Pour over chicken.

Cover and bake at 350° for 30 minutes. Uncover and bake 10 additional minutes or until juices run clear.

Yield: 4 servings.

CREOLE CHICKEN

1 medium onion, sliced
8 cloves garlic, minced
1/4 cup olive oil
1/2 cup orange juice
1/3 cup fresh lime juice
3 tablespoons Chablis or chicken broth
1 teaspoon sugar
1 teaspoon salt
1/4 teaspoon pepper
1 teaspoon white vinegar
1 (3- to 3 1/2-pound) broiler-fryer
Garnishes: lime slices, orange slices, fresh cilantro

Cook onion and garlic in olive oil in a medium saucepan over medium-high heat 2 minutes. Add orange juice and next 6 ingredients.

Bring to a boil. Remove from heat; cool. Reserve 1/4 cup marinade, and refrigerate it.

Place chicken in a shallow dish or heavy-duty, zip-top plastic bag. Pour remaining marinade over chicken. Cover or seal, and refrigerate 8 hours, turning chicken occasionally.

Remove chicken from marinade; discard marinade. Dry chicken with a paper towel. Place on a lightly greased rack, and place rack in a broiler pan.

Bake at 400° for 15 minutes; reduce heat to 350°, and bake 1 hour or until meat thermometer in thigh registers 180°, basting with reserved 1/4 cup marinade. Cover chicken with aluminum foil after 1 hour to prevent excessive browning. Place on a serving platter, and garnish, if desired.

Yield: 4 servings.

EXTRA CHICKEN BROTH?
• Fresh broth can be refrigerated 3 to 4 days.
• Freeze broth in a variety of containers or try ice-cube trays. Transfer the cubes to a plastic bag once frozen. Each cube yields about 2 tablespoons of broth.

DIJON CHICKEN WITH PASTA

6 chicken breast halves
$^3/_4$ cup butter or margarine, softened
$^1/_3$ cup sliced green onions
$^1/_4$ cup chopped fresh parsley
3$^1/_2$ tablespoons Dijon mustard
12 ounces uncooked fettuccine
Garnish: fresh parsley sprigs

Loosen skin from chicken, forming a pocket without detaching skin. Set aside.

Combine butter and next 3 ingredients, mixing well. Place 1$^1/_2$ tablespoons butter mixture under skin of each piece of chicken; reserve remaining mixture.

Place chicken, skin side up, in a lightly greased 13 x 9 x 2-inch baking dish. Bake at 350° for 1 hour, basting occasionally with pan drippings.

Cook fettuccine in a Dutch oven according to package directions; drain and return to pan. Add remaining butter mixture, tossing well. Serve with chicken. Garnish, if desired.

Yield: 6 servings.

Dijon Chicken with Pasta

CHICKEN IN FOIL

1 (2½-pound) broiler-fryer,
     skinned and quartered
¼ teaspoon garlic salt
⅛ teaspoon paprika
1 large onion, cut into 4 slices
1 large potato, cut into 8 slices
2 carrots, scraped and cut into
     ¾-inch pieces
2 stalks celery, cut into
     ¾-inch pieces
1 (4-ounce) can sliced mushrooms,
     drained
1 (10¾-ounce) can cream of
     chicken soup, undiluted

Cut 4 (24 x 18-inch) pieces of heavy-duty aluminum foil.

Place a chicken quarter in center of each; sprinkle with garlic salt and paprika. Top evenly with onion and next 4 ingredients.

Spoon soup evenly over each portion. Seal each packet, and place on 15 x 10 x 1-inch jellyroll pan.

Bake at 400° for 1 hour and 15 minutes or until juices run clear.

Yield: 4 servings.

CRISPY WALNUT CHICKEN

3 cups crispy rice cereal
½ cup walnuts
½ cup butter or margarine, melted
1 teaspoon garlic powder
½ teaspoon salt
½ teaspoon pepper
3 pounds chicken pieces, skinned

Position knife blade in food processor bowl. Add cereal and walnuts; top with cover, and process until finely ground. Set aside.

Combine butter and next 3 ingredients; stir well. Dredge chicken in butter mixture and then in cereal mixture.

Arrange chicken in a 15 x 10 x 1-inch jellyroll pan; pour any remaining butter mixture over chicken. Bake at 350° for 1 hour or until chicken is tender.

Yield: 6 servings.

ORANGE-PECAN CHICKEN DRUMMETTES

- 1 (6-ounce) can frozen orange juice concentrate, thawed and undiluted
- 3 large eggs, lightly beaten
- 2 tablespoons water
- 1 cup all-purpose flour
- 1/3 cup finely chopped pecans
- 3 pounds chicken drummettes, skinned
- 1/3 cup butter or margarine, melted
  Red Hot Sauce
  Hot cooked rice

Combine first 3 ingredients, and set aside. Combine flour and pecans, and set aside.

Dip drummettes in orange juice mixture; dredge in flour mixture. Pour butter into a 15 x 10 x 1-inch jellyroll pan; arrange drummettes in a single layer. Bake at 375° for 25 minutes.

Spoon Red Hot Sauce over drummettes, and bake 30 additional minutes. Serve over rice.

Yield: 8 to 10 servings.

RED HOT SAUCE

- 2 cups ketchup
- 3/4 cup firmly packed brown sugar
- 1 to 2 teaspoons hot sauce

Combine all ingredients, stirring until smooth.

Yield: 2½ cups.

OVEN-BARBECUED CHICKEN

- 1/2 cup all-purpose flour
- 1 teaspoon paprika
- 1/2 teaspoon salt
- 1/8 teaspoon pepper
- 1 (2½- to 3-pound) broiler-fryer, cut up
- 1/4 cup butter or margarine, melted
- 1/2 cup ketchup
- 1/2 medium onion, chopped
- 2 tablespoons water
- 1 tablespoon white vinegar
- 1 tablespoon Worcestershire sauce
- 1/2 teaspoon salt
- 1/2 teaspoon chili powder
- 1/4 teaspoon pepper

Combine first 4 ingredients; stir well. Dredge chicken in flour mixture.

Pour butter into a 13 x 9 x 2-inch pan. Arrange chicken in pan, skin side down. Bake at 350° for 30 minutes.

Combine ketchup and remaining ingredients, stirring well.

Remove chicken from oven, and turn; spoon sauce over chicken. Bake 30 additional minutes.

Yield: 4 servings.

GRILLED CUMIN CHICKEN

2 (2½- to 3-pound) broiler-fryers,
    quartered
  Juice of 3 lemons
2 tablespoons vegetable oil
2 tablespoons ground cumin
1 teaspoon salt
1 tablespoon coarsely ground
    pepper
2½ teaspoons celery salt
¼ teaspoon red pepper

Place chicken in a large shallow dish; pour lemon juice over chicken. Cover and marinate in refrigerator 2 to 3 hours, turning once. Remove chicken from lemon juice; rub with oil.

Combine cumin and remaining ingredients; stir well. Sprinkle seasoning over chicken.

Grill chicken, skin side up, over medium-hot coals (350° to 400°) 30 to 35 minutes or until juices run clear, turning once.

Yield: 8 servings.

BARBECUED CHICKEN LEGS AND THIGHS

4 chicken legs, skinned
4 chicken thighs, skinned
¾ cup ketchup
⅓ cup firmly packed brown sugar
3 tablespoons Worcestershire sauce
2 tablespoons orange juice
1 tablespoon dried onion flakes
1 tablespoon prepared mustard
½ teaspoon garlic powder

Place chicken in a greased 13 x 9 x 2-inch baking dish; set aside.

Combine ketchup and remaining ingredients, and pour over chicken. Bake at 350° for 1 hour, turning chicken once.

Yield: 4 to 6 servings.

MAPLE SYRUP BARBECUE SAUCE

1 cup maple syrup
1 cup ketchup
1 cup finely chopped onion
¼ cup firmly packed brown sugar
¼ cup cider vinegar
¼ cup lemon juice
¼ cup water
2 tablespoons olive oil
2 tablespoons Worcestershire sauce
2 teaspoons finely chopped garlic
2 teaspoons grated lemon rind
1 teaspoon salt
¼ teaspoon hot sauce

Combine all ingredients in a saucepan. Bring to a boil; reduce heat, and simmer 20 minutes. Cool.

Pour mixture into container of an electric blender; process until smooth.

Remove 1 cup sauce, and brush over chicken the last 30 minutes of cooking time. Serve chicken with remaining sauce. Refrigerate sauce up to 1 month.

Yield: 3½ cups.

ROAST CHICKEN WITH PINEAPPLE-MUSTARD GLAZE

2 (2½- to 3-pound) broiler-fryers, quartered
4 large cloves garlic, sliced
¼ cup butter or margarine, melted
¼ cup minced fresh parsley
1 teaspoon dried thyme
1 (20-ounce) can sweetened pineapple chunks
⅓ cup honey
¼ cup Dijon mustard
1 tablespoon cornstarch
 Hot cooked rice
 Garnish: fresh parsley sprigs

Place chicken, skin side up, on a rack in a roasting pan. Place garlic slices under skin of chicken.

Combine butter, parsley, and thyme; brush over chicken. Bake at 350° for 45 minutes.

Drain pineapple, reserving juice. Combine ¼ cup pineapple juice, honey, and mustard. Brush mixture over chicken, and bake 15 to 20 additional minutes or until juices run clear.

Combine cornstarch, remaining honey mixture, pineapple, and remaining juice in a sauce-pan; cook over medium heat, stirring constantly, until thickened and bubbly. Boil 1 minute, stirring constantly. Serve chicken and sauce over cooked rice. Garnish, if desired.

Yield: 8 servings.

Roast Chicken with Pineapple-Mustard Glaze

PESTO-STUFFED CHICKEN ROLLS

- 6 large skinned and boned chicken breast halves
- $1/4$ teaspoon salt
- $1/4$ teaspoon pepper
- 1 (3-ounce) package cream cheese, softened
- $1/4$ cup commercial pesto
- $1/2$ cup finely chopped sweet red pepper
- $3/4$ cup corn flake crumbs
- $1/2$ teaspoon paprika
  Vegetable cooking spray
  Garnish: fresh basil sprigs

Place chicken between 2 sheets of heavy-duty plastic wrap; flatten to $1/4$-inch thickness, using a meat mallet or rolling pin. Sprinkle with salt and pepper; set aside.

Combine cream cheese, pesto, and sweet red pepper in a small bowl, stirring with a fork until smooth. Spread 2 tablespoons over each chicken breast; roll up lengthwise, securing with wooden picks.

Combine corn flake crumbs and paprika; dredge chicken rolls in crumb mixture. Place in an 11 x 7 x 1$1/2$-inch baking dish coated with cooking spray.

Bake, uncovered, at 350° for 35 minutes; let stand 10 minutes. Remove wooden picks, and slice into 1-inch rounds.

(An electric knife works best.) Garnish, if desired.

Yield: 6 servings.

Note: Chicken Rolls may be prepared ahead. Prepare as directed above; do not bake. Cover and refrigerate overnight. Remove from refrigerator; let stand, covered, 30 minutes. Uncover and bake as directed above.

PECAN CHICKEN

- 4 skinned and boned chicken breast halves
- $1/4$ cup honey
- $1/4$ cup Dijon mustard
- 1 cup finely chopped pecans

Place chicken between 2 sheets of heavy-duty plastic wrap; flatten to $1/4$-inch thickness, using a meat mallet or rolling pin. Set aside.

Combine honey and mustard; spread on both sides of chicken, and dredge chicken in pecans.

Arrange chicken in a lightly greased shallow baking dish. Bake at 350° for 30 minutes or until juices run clear.

Yield: 4 servings.

CRUNCHY SEASONED CHICKEN

- $1/2$ cup sour cream
- 2 tablespoons lemon juice
- $1^1/2$ tablespoons Worcestershire sauce
- $1^1/2$ teaspoons celery salt
- $1/4$ teaspoon garlic powder
- $1/4$ teaspoon onion powder
- $1/8$ teaspoon pepper
- 6 skinned chicken breast halves
- $1^3/4$ cups saltine cracker crumbs (about 40 crackers)
- $1^1/2$ teaspoons paprika
- 2 tablespoons butter or margarine, melted
  Garnish: lemon slices

Combine first 7 ingredients in a small bowl; mix well. Brush mixture on chicken, coating well.

Place chicken in a 13 x 9 x 2-inch dish; cover and refrigerate 8 hours.

Combine cracker crumbs and paprika; roll chicken in cracker crumb mixture, coating well.

Place chicken in a lightly greased 3-quart casserole. Drizzle with melted butter.

Bake, uncovered, at 350° for 1 hour or until juices run clear. Garnish, if desired.

Yield: 6 servings.

PARMESAN CHICKEN

- 1 large egg, lightly beaten
- 1 tablespoon milk
- $1/2$ cup grated Parmesan cheese
- $1/4$ cup all-purpose flour
- 1 teaspoon paprika
- $1/2$ teaspoon salt
- $1/4$ teaspoon pepper
- 4 skinned chicken breast halves
- 3 tablespoons butter or margarine, melted

Combine egg and milk in a small bowl; stir well. Combine cheese and next 4 ingredients; stir well.

Dip chicken in egg mixture; dredge in flour mixture. Arrange chicken in an 11 x 7 x $1^1/2$-inch baking dish. Drizzle melted butter over top.

Bake at 350° for 40 to 45 minutes or until juices run clear.

Yield: 4 servings.

Note: Six large chicken thighs may be substituted for chicken breasts. Bake as directed for 35 to 40 minutes.

BISCUIT-TOPPED CHICKEN PIE

    1 (3-pound) broiler-fryer, cut up
1 1/2 teaspoons salt, divided
    1 cup chopped carrot
    1 cup frozen English peas, thawed
2 1/2 cups diced potato
  1/4 cup chopped celery
  1/2 teaspoon white pepper
    1 teaspoon onion powder
  3/4 teaspoon poultry seasoning
    3 tablespoons all-purpose flour
    1 (5-ounce) can evaporated milk
    1 cup chopped fresh mushrooms
       Biscuit Topping
       Butter or margarine, melted
         (optional)

Place chicken in a Dutch oven; add 1 teaspoon salt and water to cover. Bring to a boil; cover, reduce heat, and simmer 45 minutes or until chicken is tender.

Drain chicken, reserving 2 3/4 cups broth. Set chicken aside. Add remaining 1/2 teaspoon salt, carrot, and next 6 ingredients to broth; cook 20 minutes or until vegetables are tender.

Combine flour and milk; add to vegetable mixture, stirring constantly until mixture is thickened.

Bone chicken, and cut into bite-size pieces. Stir chicken and mushrooms into vegetable mixture. Spoon into a lightly greased 13 x 9 x 2-inch baking dish. Arrange Biscuit Topping rounds over chicken mixture.

Bake at 400° for 25 minutes or until biscuits are golden. Brush tops of biscuits with butter, if desired.

Yield: 6 to 8 servings.

BISCUIT TOPPING
  1/2 cup shortening
    2 cups self-rising flour
  2/3 cup milk

Cut shortening into flour with a pastry blender until mixture is crumbly. Add milk, and mix well.

Turn dough out onto a lightly floured surface. Roll dough to 1/3-inch thickness; cut rounds with a 2 3/4-inch biscuit cutter.

Yield: 15 biscuit rounds.

COUNTRY CHICKEN AND DUMPLINGS

    1 (3- to 3 1/2-pound) broiler-fryer
    2 quarts water
    2 stalks celery, cut into pieces
    1 teaspoon salt
    2 cups all-purpose flour
    2 teaspoons baking powder
  1/2 teaspoon salt
  1/4 cup butter or margarine, softened

Place chicken in a Dutch oven; add water, celery, and 1 teaspoon salt. Bring to a boil; cover, reduce heat, and simmer 1 hour or until chicken is tender.

Remove chicken from broth, and cool. Discard celery. Bone chicken, and cut into bite-size pieces; set aside chicken and $3/4$ cup broth. Leave remaining broth in pan.

Combine flour, baking powder, and $1/2$ teaspoon salt; cut in butter until mixture is crumbly. Add $3/4$ cup reserved broth, stirring with a fork until dry ingredients are moistened. Turn dough out onto a well-floured surface, and knead. Pat dough to $1/2$-inch thickness. Cut dough in 4 x $1/2$-inch pieces, and sprinkle with additional flour.

Bring broth to a boil. Drop dough, one piece at a time, into boiling broth, gently stirring after each addition. Reduce heat to low; cover and cook 8 to 10 minutes. Stir in chicken, and serve immediately.

Yield: 4 servings.

OLD-FASHIONED CHICKEN AND DUMPLINGS

  1 (3$1/2$-pound) broiler-fryer, cut up
     and skinned
  1 stalk celery, cut into thirds
  1 medium onion, quartered
  2 quarts water
  1 teaspoon salt
$1/2$ teaspoon pepper
  2 cups all-purpose flour
$1/2$ teaspoon baking soda
$1/2$ teaspoon salt
  3 tablespoons margarine
  2 tablespoons chopped fresh
     parsley
$3/4$ cup nonfat buttermilk

Combine first 5 ingredients in a Dutch oven; bring to a boil. Cover, reduce heat, and simmer 1 hour or until chicken is tender. Remove chicken, reserving broth in Dutch oven; discard vegetables. Let chicken and broth cool.

Bone and cut chicken into bite-size pieces. Place chicken and broth in separate containers; cover and chill 8 hours. Remove fat from broth; bring to a boil, and add pepper.

Combine flour, soda, and $1/2$ teaspoon salt; cut in margarine with a pastry blender until mixture is crumbly. Add parsley and buttermilk, stirring with a fork until dry ingredients are moistened.

Turn dough out onto a heavily floured surface, and knead lightly 4 or 5 times. Pat dough to $1/4$-inch thickness. Pinch off $11/2$-inch pieces, and drop into boiling broth. Add chicken. Reduce heat to medium-low, and cook 8 to 10 minutes, stirring occasionally.

Yield: 8 servings.

KENTUCKY BURGOO

1 (4-pound) broiler-fryer
1 pound beef for stewing, cut into
    2-inch pieces
1 pound veal for stewing, cut into
    2-inch pieces
1 stalk celery with leaves
1 carrot, scraped
1 onion, quartered
6 fresh parsley sprigs
4 quarts water
1 ($10^3/_4$-ounce) can tomato puree
$1^1/_2$ tablespoons salt
1 tablespoon sugar
3 tablespoons Worcestershire sauce
$1^1/_2$ teaspoons pepper
$^1/_2$ teaspoon ground red pepper
4 large tomatoes, peeled and
    chopped
2 large onions, chopped
2 large green peppers, chopped
2 cups sliced celery
2 cups chopped cabbage
1 (16-ounce) package frozen lima
    beans
1 (16-ounce) package frozen sliced
    okra
2 ($8^3/_4$-ounce) cans whole kernel
    corn

Combine first 14 ingredients in a large stockpot. Bring to a boil; cover, reduce heat, and simmer 3 hours. Remove from heat, and let cool.

Strain soup, discarding vegetables; return meat and stock to stockpot. Let chicken cool; remove skin, bone, and chop chicken. Return chopped chicken to soup; cover and refrigerate 8 hours.

Skim and discard fat from surface of soup; add tomato and remaining ingredients. Bring to a boil; cover, reduce heat, and simmer 1 hour.

Uncover; simmer 1 hour and 45 minutes to 2 hours, stirring frequently.

Yield: 5 quarts.

CREAMY CHICKEN-AND-BROCCOLI SOUP

$^1/_2$ cup sliced fresh mushrooms
$^1/_2$ cup chopped onion
$^1/_4$ cup butter or margarine, melted
$^1/_4$ cup all-purpose flour
2 cups half-and-half
$1^1/_2$ cups chicken broth
1 cup chopped cooked chicken
1 cup frozen chopped broccoli,
    thawed
$^1/_2$ teaspoon dried rosemary
$^1/_2$ teaspoon salt
$^1/_4$ teaspoon dried thyme
$^1/_4$ teaspoon pepper

Cook mushrooms and onion in butter in a medium saucepan over low heat until tender; add flour, stirring until smooth. Cook, stirring constantly, 1 minute.

Add half-and-half and chicken broth; cook over medium heat, stirring constantly, until mixture is thickened and bubbly.

Stir in chicken and remaining ingredients. Cover and simmer 10 minutes, stirring occasionally.

Yield: 1 quart.

CHICKEN-AND-RICE SOUP

1 (3½- to 4-pound) broiler-fryer, cut
    up and skinned
2 quarts water
1 medium onion, chopped
2 stalks celery, thinly sliced
1½ teaspoons salt
1 to 1½ teaspoons pepper
1 bay leaf
1 cup uncooked long-grain rice
2 carrots, diced

Combine first 7 ingredients in a Dutch oven. Bring to a boil; cover, reduce heat, and simmer 45 minutes.

Remove chicken, reserving broth. Discard bay leaf. Set chicken aside.

Add rice and carrot to broth; bring to a boil. Cover, reduce heat, and simmer 20 minutes or until rice is tender.

Bone chicken, and cut into bite-size pieces. Add chicken to broth; heat thoroughly.

Yield: 2 quarts.

CHICKEN-AND-SAUSAGE GUMBO

1 pound hot smoked sausage, cut
    into ¼-inch slices
4 skinned chicken breast halves
¼ to ⅓ cup vegetable oil
¾ cup all-purpose flour
1 cup chopped onion
½ cup chopped green pepper
½ cup sliced celery
2 quarts hot water
3 cloves garlic, minced
2 bay leaves
2 teaspoons Creole seasoning
½ teaspoon dried thyme
1 tablespoon Worcestershire sauce
½ to 1 teaspoon hot sauce
½ cup sliced green onions
¼ teaspoon salt (optional)
    Hot cooked rice
    Gumbo filé (optional)

Brown sausage in a Dutch oven over medium heat. Remove to paper towels, reserving drippings.

Brown chicken in drippings; remove to paper towels, reserving drippings. Measure drippings, adding enough oil to measure ½ cup. Heat in Dutch oven over medium heat until hot.

Add flour to hot oil; cook, stirring constantly, until roux is the color of chocolate (about 30 minutes). Add onion, green pepper, and celery; cook until vegetables are tender, stirring often.

Stir in water; bring to a boil. Return chicken to pan; add garlic and next 5 ingredients. Reduce heat; simmer, uncovered, 1 hour. Remove chicken; return sausage to pan, and cook, uncovered, 30 minutes. Stir in green onions; cook, uncovered, 30 minutes. Add salt, if desired.

Bone chicken, and cut into strips. Add to gumbo, and thoroughly heat. Remove bay leaves; serve gumbo over rice. Sprinkle with gumbo filé, if desired.

Yield: 8 servings.

INDIVIDUAL CHICKEN POT PIES

- 1 cup chopped onion
- 1 cup chopped celery
- 1 cup chopped carrot
- 1/3 cup butter or margarine, melted
- 1/2 cup all-purpose flour
- 2 cups chicken broth
- 1 cup half-and-half
- 4 cups chopped cooked chicken
- 1 cup frozen English peas, thawed
- 1 teaspoon salt
- 1/4 teaspoon pepper
  Basic Pastry

Cook first 3 ingredients in butter in a skillet over medium heat until tender. Add flour; stir until smooth. Cook, stirring constantly, 1 minute.

Add chicken broth and half-and-half; cook, stirring constantly, until thickened and bubbly.

Stir in chicken, peas, salt, and pepper.

Divide Basic Pastry into 8 equal portions. Roll 4 portions of pastry into 10-inch circles on a floured surface. Place in 4 (6-inch) pie pans.

Spoon chicken mixture evenly into each of the prepared pie pans.

Roll remaining 4 portions of pastry to 7-inch circles on a floured surface. Place pastry circles over filling; fold edges under and flute. Cut slits in tops to allow steam to escape.

Bake, uncovered, at 400° for 35 minutes or until crust is golden brown.

Yield: 4 servings.

BASIC PASTRY

- 4 cups all-purpose flour
- 2 teaspoons salt
- 1 1/2 cups plus 1 tablespoon shortening
- 1/3 to 1/2 cup cold water

Combine flour and salt; cut in shortening with a pastry blender until mixture is crumbly. Sprinkle cold water, 1 tablespoon at a time, over surface; stir with a fork until dry ingredients are moistened. Shape into a ball; chill.

Yield: pastry for 4 (6-inch) pies.

CHICKEN RAGOÛT WITH CHEDDAR DUMPLINGS

- 2 cups diagonally sliced carrot
- 1 cup sweet red pepper strips
- 3 tablespoons butter or margarine
- 1/4 cup all-purpose flour
- 2 cups chicken broth
- 1 cup milk
- 1 tablespoon lemon juice
- 1/2 teaspoon salt
- 1/2 teaspoon pepper
- 3 cups chopped cooked chicken
- 1 cup frozen English peas, thawed
- 2 cups biscuit mix
- 2/3 cup milk
- 3/4 cup (3 ounces) shredded Cheddar cheese
- 1 (2-ounce) jar diced pimiento, drained

Chicken Ragoût with Cheddar Dumplings

Arrange carrot and pepper strips in a steamer basket; place over boiling water. Cover and steam 8 minutes or until crisp-tender; set aside.

Melt butter in a large heavy saucepan over low heat; add flour, stirring until smooth. Cook, stirring constantly, 1 minute.

Add chicken broth and 1 cup milk; cook over medium heat, stirring constantly, until mixture is thickened and bubbly. Remove from heat. Stir in lemon juice, salt, and pepper. Add chicken, steamed vegetables, and peas, stirring gently. Spoon into a greased 11 x 7 x 1¹/₂-inch baking dish.

Combine biscuit mix and ²/₃ cup milk, stirring until dry ingredients are moistened. Stir vigorously 30 seconds. Turn out onto a lightly floured surface, and knead 4 or 5 times.

Roll dough into a 12 x 9-inch rectangle. Sprinkle with cheese and pimiento, leaving a ¹/₂-inch border; roll up jellyroll fashion, starting with a long side, and turn seam side down. Cut into 1-inch-thick slices, and place over chicken mixture.

Bake at 400° for 30 minutes or until golden brown.

Yield: 6 servings.

CHILI-CHICKEN STEW

6 skinned and boned chicken breast
  halves
1 medium onion, chopped
1 medium-size green pepper,
  chopped
2 cloves garlic, minced
1 tablespoon vegetable oil
2 (14 1/2-ounce) cans stewed
  tomatoes, undrained and
  chopped
1 (15-ounce) can pinto beans,
  drained
2/3 cup picante sauce
1 teaspoon chili powder
1 teaspoon ground cumin
1/2 teaspoon salt
  Condiments: shredded Cheddar
  cheese, sour cream, diced
  avocado, sliced green onions

Cut chicken into 1-inch pieces. Cook
chicken and next 3 ingredients in hot oil
in a Dutch oven until lightly browned.

Add tomatoes and next 5 ingredients;
cover, reduce heat, and simmer
20 minutes. Top individual servings
with desired condiments.

Yield: 6 servings.

WHITE LIGHTNING
TEXAS CHILI

1 pound dried navy beans
4 (14 1/2-ounce) cans ready-to-serve
  chicken broth, divided
1 large onion, chopped
2 cloves garlic, minced
1 tablespoon ground white pepper
1 tablespoon dried oregano
1 tablespoon ground cumin
1 teaspoon salt
1/2 teaspoon ground cloves
5 cups chopped cooked chicken
1 (4.5-ounce) can chopped green
  chiles, undrained
1 cup water
1 jalapeño pepper, seeded and
  chopped (optional)
  Shredded Monterey Jack cheese
  Commercial salsa
  Sour cream
  Sliced green onions

Sort and wash beans; place in a large
Dutch oven. Cover with water 2 inches
above beans; let soak 8 hours.

Drain beans, and return to pan.
Add 3 cans chicken broth and next
7 ingredients; bring to a boil. Cover,
reduce heat, and simmer 2 hours or until
beans are tender, stirring occasionally.

Add remaining can of chicken broth,
chicken, and next 3 ingredients. Cover
and simmer 1 hour, stirring occasionally.

Serve with cheese, salsa, sour cream, and
green onions.

Yield: 2 1/2 quarts.

BRUNSWICK STEW

(Shown on page 365)

       8 skinned and boned chicken breast
          halves
    1 1/2 cups chopped onion
       1 cup chopped green pepper
       1 tablespoon vegetable oil
       3 (16-ounce) cans tomatoes,
          undrained and chopped
       1 (8-ounce) can tomato sauce
     1/4 cup sugar
       3 tablespoons white vinegar
       2 tablespoons Worcestershire sauce
       2 tablespoons all-purpose flour
       1 cup water
       1 pound red potatoes, peeled and
          cubed
       1 (16-ounce) can pork and beans
       1 tablespoon hot sauce
    1 1/2 teaspoons salt
     1/2 teaspoon ground turmeric
     1/2 teaspoon pepper
       1 (16-ounce) can whole kernel corn,
          drained
       1 (16-ounce) can lima beans,
          drained

Place chicken in a large Dutch oven; add water to cover. Bring to a boil; cover, reduce heat, and simmer 20 minutes or until chicken is tender.

Remove chicken from broth, reserving broth for another use. Let chicken cool. Chop chicken, and set aside.

Cook onion and green pepper in hot oil in Dutch oven, stirring constantly. Add chicken, tomatoes, and next 4 ingredients.

Combine flour and 1 cup water, stirring until smooth. Stir flour mixture into chicken mixture.

Add potato and next 5 ingredients; stir well. Cover and cook over medium heat 20 to 30 minutes or until potato is tender, stirring occasionally. Add corn and lima beans, and cook 10 minutes or until thoroughly heated.

Yield: 4 quarts.

DIJON-HERB CHICKEN

       8 skinned and boned chicken breast
          halves
     1/4 cup butter or margarine, melted
     1/4 cup lemon juice
       2 tablespoons Worcestershire sauce
       1 tablespoon Dijon mustard
     1/2 teaspoon salt
       2 tablespoons chopped fresh chives
       2 tablespoons chopped fresh
          parsley

Cook chicken in butter in a skillet over medium heat 10 minutes on each side. Remove chicken to a serving platter, reserving pan drippings in skillet; keep chicken warm.

Add lemon juice and next 3 ingredients to pan drippings. Bring to a boil, stirring occasionally.

Stir in chives and parsley. Pour over chicken.

Yield: 8 servings.

CHICKEN ROLLUPS

- 1 (6-ounce) package wild rice-and-mushroom stuffing mix
- 6 large skinned and boned chicken breast halves
- 1/4 teaspoon pepper
- 2 tablespoons butter or margarine, melted
- 2 tablespoons Dijon mustard
- 1 1/4 cups ground pecans
- 3 tablespoons vegetable oil
- 3/4 cup chicken broth
- 3/4 cup sour cream

Prepare wild rice-and-mushroom stuffing mix according to package directions. Set aside. Place each chicken breast between 2 sheets of heavy-duty plastic wrap. Flatten to 1/4-inch thickness, using a meat mallet or rolling pin.

Divide stuffing mixture evenly, and place on top of each chicken breast; fold sides of chicken breast over stuffing, roll up, and secure with wooden picks. Sprinkle with pepper.

Combine butter and mustard in a small bowl; stir well. Brush mustard mixture over chicken, completely coating all sides; roll in pecans. Brown chicken on all sides in hot oil in skillet; drain and discard pan drippings, retaining chicken in skillet. Add chicken broth to skillet; cover, reduce heat, and simmer 20 minutes. Place chicken on a serving dish; keep warm. Stir sour cream into broth in skillet; cook over low heat, stirring constantly, until heated. Spoon over chicken.

Yield: 6 servings.

CHICKEN KIEV

- 1/4 cup plus 2 tablespoons butter, softened
- 1 tablespoon chopped fresh parsley
- 1 small clove garlic, minced
- 1/4 teaspoon dried tarragon
- 1/4 teaspoon salt
- 1/8 teaspoon ground white pepper
- 6 skinned and boned chicken breast halves
- 1 large egg, beaten
- 1 tablespoon water
- 1/2 cup all-purpose flour
- 1 1/2 to 2 cups soft breadcrumbs
  Vegetable oil

Combine first 6 ingredients in a small bowl; stir until blended. Shape butter mixture into a 3-inch stick; cover and freeze about 45 minutes or until firm.

Place chicken between 2 sheets of heavy-duty plastic wrap; flatten to 1/4-inch thickness, using a meat mallet or rolling pin. Cut butter into 6 pats; place one pat in center of each chicken breast. Fold long sides of chicken over butter; fold ends over, and secure with wooden picks.

Combine egg and water, beating well. Dredge chicken in flour; dip in egg mixture, and dredge in breadcrumbs.

Pour oil to depth of 2 to 3 inches into a Dutch oven; heat to 350°. Fry chicken 3 to 4 minutes on each side or until browned. Drain well on paper towels.

Yield: 6 servings.

CHICKEN-IN-A-GARDEN

(Shown on page 333)

    3 tablespoons peanut or vegetable
        oil, divided
    2 tablespoons soy sauce, divided
1 1/2 teaspoons cornstarch
  1/2 teaspoon garlic powder
  1/4 teaspoon pepper
    6 skinned and boned chicken breast
        halves, cut into 1-inch pieces
    3 green peppers, cut into 1-inch
        pieces
    1 cup diagonally sliced celery
        (1-inch pieces)
    8 scallions, cut into 1/2-inch slices
    1 (6-ounce) package frozen snow
        pea pods, thawed and drained
2 1/2 tablespoons cornstarch
  3/4 cup water
  3/4 teaspoon chicken-flavored
        bouillon granules
  1/8 teaspoon ground ginger
    3 medium tomatoes, peeled and cut
        into eighths
      Hot cooked rice

Combine 1 tablespoon oil, 1 tablespoon soy sauce, 1 1/2 teaspoons cornstarch, garlic powder, and pepper in a medium bowl; stir well. Add chicken; cover and refrigerate 20 minutes.

Pour remaining 2 tablespoons oil around top of preheated wok, coating sides; heat at medium-high (350°) for 2 minutes. Add green pepper, and stir-fry 4 minutes. Add celery, scallions, and snow peas; stir-fry 2 minutes. Remove vegetables from wok, and set aside.

Combine remaining 1 tablespoon soy sauce and 2 1/2 tablespoons cornstarch; stir in water, bouillon granules, and ginger. Set mixture aside.

Add chicken to wok, and stir-fry 3 minutes; add stir-fried vegetables, tomato, and bouillon mixture. Stir-fry over low heat (225°) for 3 minutes or until thickened and bubbly. Serve over rice.

Yield: 6 servings.

CREAMY CHICKEN TETRAZZINI

1	(3 to 4-pound) broiler-fryer
1	teaspoon salt
1	teaspoon pepper
1	(8-ounce) package spaghetti
1	large green pepper, chopped
1	cup sliced fresh mushrooms
1	small onion, chopped
$1/4$	cup butter or margarine, melted
$1/4$	cup all-purpose flour
$1/2$	teaspoon salt
$1/2$	teaspoon garlic powder
$1/2$	teaspoon poultry seasoning
$1/2$	teaspoon pepper
1	cup half-and-half
2	cups (8 ounces) shredded sharp Cheddar cheese, divided
1	($10^3/4$-ounce) can cream of mushroom soup, undiluted
$3/4$	cup grated Parmesan cheese, divided
$1/4$	cup dry sherry
1	(4-ounce) jar sliced pimiento, drained
1	teaspoon paprika
$3/4$	cup sliced almonds, toasted

Combine first 3 ingredients in a Dutch oven; add water to cover. Bring to a boil. Cover, reduce heat, and simmer 45 minutes or until chicken is tender. Remove chicken from broth, reserving broth.

Let chicken cool slightly. Bone and coarsely shred chicken; set aside.

Add enough water to reserved broth to measure 3 quarts; bring to a boil. Cook spaghetti in broth according to package directions. Drain and set aside.

Cook green pepper, mushrooms, and onion in butter in a Dutch oven over medium heat, stirring constantly, until tender. Add flour and next 4 ingredients; stir until smooth. Cook, stirring constantly 1 minute. Gradually stir in half-and-half, and cook until thickened, stirring gently.

Add $3/4$ cup Cheddar cheese, stirring until cheese melts. Add chicken, mushroom soup, $1/2$ cup Parmesan cheese, sherry, and pimiento; stir well.

Combine chicken mixture and cooked spaghetti, tossing gently until thoroughly combined. Spoon into a greased 13 x 9 x 2-inch baking dish.

Bake, uncovered, at 350° for 20 to 25 minutes or until thoroughly heated.

Combine remaining $1/4$ cup Parmesan cheese and paprika; stir well. Sprinkle remaining $1^1/4$ cups Cheddar cheese in diagonal rows across top of casserole. Repeat procedure with almonds and Parmesan-paprika mixture. Bake 5 additional minutes or until Cheddar cheese melts.

Yield: 6 to 8 servings.

ITALIAN CHICKEN CUTLETS

    6 skinned and boned chicken breast
         halves
    1 cup Italian-seasoned breadcrumbs
 1/2 cup freshly grated Romano or
         Parmesan cheese
 1/4 cup all-purpose flour
    1 (0.8-ounce) envelope light Italian
         salad dressing mix
    2 teaspoons dried oregano
 1/4 teaspoon garlic powder
    2 large eggs, beaten
 1/3 cup vegetable oil
         Garnish: green onion strips

Place chicken between 2 sheets of heavy-duty plastic wrap; flatten to 1/4-inch thickness, using a meat mallet or rolling pin.

Combine breadcrumbs and next 5 ingredients; dip chicken in eggs, and dredge in breadcrumbs.

Heat oil in a large skillet over medium heat. Add chicken, and cook 3 to 4 minutes on each side or until golden brown, adding extra oil, if necessary. Drain on paper towels. Garnish, if desired.

Yield: 6 servings.

CRISPY FRIED CHICKEN

    1 (3- to 3 1/2-pound) broiler-fryer,
         cut up
 1/2 teaspoon salt
 1/8 teaspoon black pepper
 1 1/2 cups all-purpose flour
    1 teaspoon salt
 3/4 teaspoon black pepper
 1/2 teaspoon ground red pepper
 1/4 teaspoon paprika
    1 large egg, beaten
 1/2 cup buttermilk
         Vegetable oil

Season chicken with 1/2 teaspoon salt and 1/8 teaspoon black pepper; set aside.

Combine flour and next 4 ingredients; stir well, and set aside. Combine egg and buttermilk; stir well.

Dip chicken in egg mixture; dredge in flour mixture, coating each piece well. Repeat procedure, heavily coating chicken pieces.

Pour oil to depth of 1 inch into a large heavy skillet; heat to 350°. Fry chicken 20 to 25 minutes or until golden, turning to brown both sides. Drain well on paper towels.

Yield: 4 servings.

SPICY FRIED CHICKEN

6 skinned and boned chicken breast
   halves
2 cups water
2 tablespoons hot sauce
1 cup self-rising flour
1 teaspoon garlic salt
$^1/_2$ teaspoon pepper
1 teaspoon paprika
1 teaspoon red pepper
   Vegetable oil

Place chicken in a shallow dish or heavy-duty, zip-top plastic bag. Combine water and hot sauce; pour over chicken. Cover or seal, and marinate 1 hour in refrigerator, turning once.

Combine flour and next 4 ingredients. Remove chicken from marinade, and dredge in flour mixture, coating well. Discard marinade.

Pour oil to depth of 1 inch into a heavy skillet; heat to 350°. Fry chicken 5 to 6 minutes on each side or until golden brown. Drain well on paper towels.

Yield: 6 servings.

FRIED CHEESE-STUFFED CHICKEN THIGHS

8 skinned and boned chicken thighs
$^1/_2$ (8-ounce) package Swiss cheese
8 slices bacon, partially cooked
2 egg whites, slightly beaten
$1^1/_2$ tablespoons lemon juice
$^3/_4$ cup all-purpose flour
$1^1/_2$ teaspoons lemon-pepper
   seasoning
   Vegetable oil

Place chicken between 2 sheets of heavy-duty plastic wrap; flatten to $^1/_4$-inch thickness, using a meat mallet or rolling pin.

Slice cheese lengthwise to make 8 even strips. Place 1 strip of cheese in center of each chicken thigh. Fold long sides of chicken over cheese; fold ends of chicken over, and wrap each with a slice of bacon. Secure with wooden picks.

Combine egg white and lemon juice; combine flour and lemon-pepper seasoning. Dip chicken in egg mixture; dredge in flour mixture.

Pour oil to depth of 1 inch into a heavy skillet; heat to 350°. Fry chicken 15 minutes or until golden, turning once. Drain on paper towels.

Yield: 8 servings.

ITALIAN-SEASONED FRIED CHICKEN

3/4 cup Italian-seasoned breadcrumbs
1/2 cup grated Parmesan cheese
1/4 cup minced fresh parsley
3/4 teaspoon dried oregano
1 large egg, beaten
1/2 cup milk
1 tablespoon all-purpose flour
1 (3 to 3 1/2-pound) broiler-fryer, cut up
  Vegetable oil

Combine first 4 ingredients; stir well, and set aside. Combine egg, milk, and flour; stir well. Dip chicken in egg mixture; dredge in breadcrumb mixture, coating well.

Pour oil to depth of 1 inch into a large, heavy skillet; heat to 350°. Fry chicken 20 to 25 minutes or until golden, turning to brown both sides. Drain well on paper towels.

Yield: 4 servings.

Brunswick Stew (recipe on page 359)

LEMON CHICKEN AND VEGETABLES

- 3 tablespoons vegetable oil, divided
- 4 skinned and boned chicken breast halves, cut into $1/2$-inch strips
- 1 lemon, sliced
- $1/2$ cup sliced celery
- $1/2$ medium onion, sliced
- 1 cup sliced yellow squash or zucchini
- $1/2$ cup sliced fresh mushrooms
- $1/2$ cup sweet red pepper strips
- $1/2$ cup frozen English peas, thawed
- $1/2$ cup fresh snow pea pods
- 1 teaspoon pepper
- 1 tablespoon lemon juice

Heat $1^1/2$ tablespoons oil to medium-high (350°) in a large skillet. Add chicken and lemon slices, and stir-fry 2 minutes or until lightly browned. Remove from skillet. Set aside.

Heat remaining $1^1/2$ tablespoons oil to medium-high in skillet. Add celery and next 4 ingredients; stir-fry 2 minutes or until vegetables are crisp-tender.

Add chicken, peas, and remaining ingredients to skillet. Stir-fry on medium-high until thoroughly heated. Serve immediately.

Yield: 4 servings.

CHICKEN-VEGETABLE STIR-FRY

- $1/2$ cup soy sauce
- $1/4$ cup vegetable oil or sesame seed oil
- 2 teaspoons sesame seeds
- 6 skinned and boned chicken breast halves
- 2 cups broccoli flowerets
- 1 onion, thinly sliced and separated into rings
- $1/2$ pound fresh snow pea pods
- $1/2$ cup thinly sliced celery
- $1/2$ cup sliced fresh mushrooms
- 1 tablespoon cornstarch
- $1/2$ cup water
  Hot cooked brown rice

Combine first 3 ingredients in a medium bowl, stirring well; set aside. Cut chicken into 2-inch strips, and add to marinade, mixing well. Cover and refrigerate at least 30 minutes.

Preheat wok to medium-high (350°). Add chicken mixture, and stir-fry 2 to 3 minutes. Remove chicken from wok, and set aside.

Add broccoli and onion to wok; stir-fry 2 minutes. Add snow peas, celery, and mushrooms; stir-fry 2 minutes or until vegetables are crisp-tender. Add chicken to wok.

Combine cornstarch and water; add to wok. Cook, stirring constantly, until thickened. Serve over brown rice.

Yield: 6 servings.

CHEESY CHICKEN SPAGHETTI

1 (6-pound) hen
1 (10-ounce) package spaghetti
1 1/2 cups chopped onion
1 cup chopped green pepper
1 cup chopped celery
1 (4-ounce) jar diced pimiento, drained
1 (6-ounce) jar sliced mushrooms, drained
1 (16-ounce) loaf process American cheese, cubed
1/2 teaspoon salt
1/2 teaspoon pepper

Place hen in a Dutch oven; add water to cover. Bring to a boil; cover, reduce heat, and simmer 1 1/2 hours or until tender.

Remove hen, reserving 6 cups broth; let hen cool slightly. Bone, and cut into bite-size pieces; set aside.

Bring 1 quart reserved broth to a boil in Dutch oven; gradually add spaghetti. Cook, uncovered, over medium heat 10 to 13 minutes. Do not drain.

Combine onion, green pepper, celery, and remaining 2 cups reserved broth in a medium saucepan. Bring to a boil; reduce heat and simmer 10 minutes or until vegetables are tender. Drain.

Add chicken, cooked vegetables, pimiento, and mushrooms to spaghetti, stirring well. Add cheese cubes, salt, and pepper, stirring until cheese melts.

Yield: 8 servings.

CHICKEN MANICOTTI

8 manicotti shells
1 (10 3/4-ounce) can creamy chicken mushroom soup, undiluted
1/2 cup sour cream
2 cups chopped cooked chicken
1/4 cup chopped onion
2 tablespoons butter or margarine, melted
1 (4-ounce) can sliced mushrooms, undrained
1 cup (4 ounces) shredded Cheddar or Monterey Jack cheese

Cook manicotti shells according to package directions, omitting salt; drain and set aside.

Combine soup and sour cream; stir well. Combine half of soup mixture and chicken; stir well. Set aside remaining soup mixture. Stuff manicotti shells with chicken mixture; place in a greased 11 x 7 x 1 1/2-inch baking dish.

Cook onion in butter over medium heat in a large skillet, stirring constantly, until tender; add mushrooms and reserved soup mixture. Spoon over manicotti.

Bake, uncovered, at 350° for 15 minutes. Sprinkle with cheese, and bake 5 additional minutes.

Yield: 4 servings.

CHICKEN LASAGNA

1 (2½- to 3-pound) broiler-fryer
6 cups water
1 teaspoon salt
1 clove garlic, minced
2 tablespoons butter, melted
1 (10¾-ounce) can cream of celery soup, undiluted
½ teaspoon dried oregano
¼ teaspoon pepper
8 lasagna noodles, uncooked
1 (8-ounce) loaf process American cheese, cut in ¼-inch slices, divided
2 cups (8 ounces) shredded mozzarella cheese, divided
2 tablespoons grated Parmesan cheese

Combine first 3 ingredients in a Dutch oven; bring to a boil. Cover, reduce heat, and simmer 45 minutes or until chicken is tender. Drain, reserving broth, and let cool slightly. Bone chicken and cut into bite-size pieces; set aside.

Cook garlic in butter in a skillet over medium-high heat, stirring constantly, 2 minutes. Add celery soup, ¾ cup reserved chicken broth, oregano, and pepper.

Cook lasagna noodles according to package directions in remaining reserved chicken broth, adding more water, if necessary; drain. Spoon a small amount of sauce into a lightly greased 11 x 7 x 1½-inch baking dish. Layer with half each of lasagna noodles, sauce, chicken, and American and mozzarella cheeses. Repeat procedure with noodles, sauce, and chicken, reserving remaining cheeses to add later. Bake at 350° for 25 minutes; top with remaining cheeses, and bake 5 additional minutes. Let stand 10 minutes.

Yield: 6 servings.

Note: To save time, cook chicken in a pressure cooker; follow manufacturer's instructions.

CHICKEN PICCATA

6 skinned and boned chicken breast halves
⅓ cup all-purpose flour
1 teaspoon salt
¼ teaspoon pepper
¼ cup butter or margarine
¼ cup lemon juice
1 lemon, thinly sliced
2 tablespoons chopped fresh parsley

Place chicken between 2 sheets of heavy-duty plastic wrap; flatten to ¼-inch thickness, using a meat mallet or rolling pin. Combine flour, salt, and pepper; dredge chicken in flour mixture.

Melt butter in a large skillet over medium heat. Add chicken, and cook 3 to 4 minutes on each side or until golden brown. Remove chicken, and drain on paper towels; keep warm. Add lemon juice and lemon slices to pan drippings in skillet; cook until thoroughly heated. Pour lemon mixture over chicken; sprinkle with parsley.

Yield: 6 servings.

CHICKEN FETTUCCINE SUPREME

1/4 cup butter or margarine
1 1/4 pounds skinned and boned chicken breast halves, cut into 3/4-inch pieces
3 cups sliced fresh mushrooms
1 cup chopped green onions
1 small sweet red pepper, cut into thin strips
1 clove garlic, crushed
1/2 teaspoon salt
1/2 teaspoon pepper
10 ounces uncooked fettuccine
3/4 cup half-and-half
1/2 cup butter or margarine, melted
1/4 cup chopped fresh parsley
1/4 teaspoon salt
1/4 teaspoon pepper
1/2 cup grated Parmesan cheese
1 cup chopped pecans, toasted

Melt 1/4 cup butter in a large skillet over medium heat; add chicken, and cook, stirring constantly, until browned.

Remove chicken from skillet, reserving pan drippings in skillet; set chicken aside.

Add mushrooms and next 5 ingredients to pan drippings in skillet, and cook, stirring constantly, until vegetables are tender. Add chicken; reduce heat, and cook 15 minutes or until chicken is tender and mixture is thoroughly heated. Set aside, and keep warm.

Cook fettuccine according to package directions, omitting salt; drain. Place fettuccine in a large bowl.

Combine half-and-half and next 4 ingredients in a small bowl; stir well. Add to fettuccine; toss gently to combine.

Add chicken mixture and Parmesan cheese to fettuccine; toss gently to combine. Sprinkle with pecans, and serve immediately.

Yield: 6 servings.

Chicken Fettuccine Supreme

COUNTRY CAPTAIN CHICKEN

$^1/_2$ cup all-purpose flour
1 teaspoon salt
$^1/_2$ teaspoon pepper
1 ($2^1/_2$- to 3-pound) broiler-fryer, cut up
  Vegetable oil
2 medium onions, chopped
2 medium-size green peppers, chopped
$^1/_4$ cup chopped celery
1 clove garlic, minced
2 (16-ounce) cans whole tomatoes, undrained and chopped
$^1/_4$ cup currants
2 teaspoons curry powder
$^3/_4$ teaspoon salt
$^1/_2$ teaspoon ground white pepper
$^1/_2$ teaspoon ground thyme
3 cups hot cooked rice
$1^1/_2$ tablespoons minced fresh parsley
3 tablespoons cornstarch
$^1/_4$ cup cold water
$^1/_4$ cup sliced natural almonds, toasted

Combine first 3 ingredients; stir well. Dredge chicken in flour mixture. Pour oil to a depth of $^1/_2$ inch into a large heavy skillet. Fry chicken in hot oil (350°) until browned.

Arrange chicken in a 13 x 9 x 2-inch baking dish; set aside. Drain pan drippings, reserving 2 tablespoons drippings in skillet.

Cook onion, green pepper, celery, and garlic in pan drippings until vegetables are tender. Add tomatoes and next 5 ingredients; stir well. Spoon sauce over chicken in baking dish.

Cover and bake at 350° for 40 to 50 minutes or until chicken is tender.

Transfer chicken to a large serving platter with a slotted spoon, reserving sauce in baking dish. Combine rice and parsley, tossing gently to combine; spoon around chicken. Set aside, and keep warm.

Transfer sauce to a medium saucepan. Combine cornstarch and water, stirring until smooth; stir into sauce. Bring sauce to a boil; cook, stirring constantly, 1 minute or until slightly thickened. Spoon sauce over chicken. Sprinkle almonds over chicken. Serve immediately.

Yield: 4 servings.

SPICY TORTILLA SOUP

1 large onion, coarsely chopped
  Vegetable oil
4 corn tortillas, coarsely chopped
6 cloves garlic, minced
1 tablespoon chopped fresh cilantro or parsley
2 ($10^3/_4$-ounce) cans tomato purée
2 quarts chicken broth
1 tablespoon ground cumin
2 teaspoons chili powder
2 bay leaves
$^1/_8$ teaspoon ground red pepper
3 corn tortillas

2 skinned and boned chicken breast halves, cut into strips
1 avocado, peeled, seeded, and cubed
1 cup (4 ounces) shredded Cheddar cheese

Position knife blade in food processor bowl; add chopped onion, and process until smooth. Measure 1 cup onion purée, and set aside; reserve any remaining puree for another use.

Heat 3 tablespoons vegetable oil in a Dutch oven over medium heat; cook 4 chopped tortillas, garlic, and cilantro in hot oil until tortillas are soft.

Add 1 cup onion purée, tomato purée, and next 5 ingredients. Bring to a boil; cover, reduce heat, and simmer 30 minutes. Remove and discard bay leaves.

Cut 3 tortillas into thin strips. Pour oil to depth of $1/2$ inch into a large, heavy skillet. Fry strips in hot oil over medium heat until browned. Remove tortillas, reserving $1/2$ tablespoon oil in skillet; drain tortillas on paper towels, and set aside.

Add chicken strips to skillet; cook over medium heat, stirring constantly, about 8 minutes or until chicken is done.

Spoon soup into bowls; add chicken strips, avocado, and cheese. Top with tortilla strips. Serve immediately.

Yield: 2½ quarts.

CHICKEN TOSTADAS

4 skinned and boned chicken breast halves, cut into $1/4$-inch-wide strips
$1/4$ cup chopped onion
2 tablespoons butter or margarine, melted
1 (16-ounce) jar salsa
1 (1$1/4$-ounce) package taco seasoning mix
1 (16-ounce) can refried beans
1 (4$1/2$-ounce) package tostada shells
2 small tomatoes, chopped
2 cups shredded lettuce
1 cup (4 ounces) shredded Cheddar cheese

Cook half each of chicken strips and onion in 1 tablespoon butter in a large skillet over medium-high heat 2 to 3 minutes, stirring often. Remove mixture, and set aside. Repeat procedure with remaining chicken, onion, and butter.

Return chicken mixture to skillet; add salsa and taco seasoning mix. Cook over low heat 10 minutes, stirring occasionally. Heat refried beans in a small saucepan; set aside.

Place tostada shells on a baking sheet, slightly overlapping. Bake at 350° for 5 minutes. Spread about 2 tablespoons refried beans on each tostada; top evenly with chicken mixture, tomato, lettuce, and cheese.

Yield: 6 servings.

NO-FUSS FAJITAS

3 tablespoons lemon juice
3/4 teaspoon salt
1/4 teaspoon coarsely ground pepper
1/4 teaspoon garlic powder
1/2 teaspoon liquid smoke
3 skinned and boned chicken breast halves, cut into strips
6 (6-inch) flour tortillas
2 tablespoons vegetable oil
1 green or sweet red pepper, cut into strips
1 medium onion, sliced and separated into rings
Condiments: chopped tomato, green onions, lettuce, guacamole, sour cream, shredded cheese, and picante sauce

Combine first 5 ingredients in a medium bowl; reserve 1 1/2 tablespoons marinade. Add chicken to remaining marinade in bowl; stir to coat. Cover and refrigerate at least 30 minutes. Drain chicken, discarding marinade.

Wrap tortillas in aluminum foil; bake at 350° for 15 minutes.

Heat oil in a heavy skillet. Add chicken; cook, stirring constantly, 2 to 3 minutes. Add 1 1/2 tablespoons reserved marinade, pepper, and onion; cook, stirring constantly, until vegetables are crisp-tender. Remove from heat. Divide mixture evenly, and spoon a portion onto each tortilla. If desired, top with several condiments; then wrap.

Yield: 6 fajitas.

EASY CHICKEN ENCHILADAS

2 cups chopped cooked chicken
2 cups sour cream
1 (10 3/4-ounce) can cream of chicken soup
1 1/2 cups (6 ounces) shredded Monterey Jack cheese
1 1/2 cups (6 ounces) shredded longhorn cheese
1 (4.5-ounce) can chopped green chiles, drained
2 tablespoons chopped onion
1/8 teaspoon salt
1/4 teaspoon pepper
10 (10-inch) flour tortillas
Vegetable oil
1 cup (4 ounces) shredded longhorn cheese

Combine first 9 ingredients; mix well. Fry tortillas, one at a time, in 2 tablespoons oil in a skillet 5 seconds on each side or until softened; add additional oil, if necessary. Drain.

Place a heaping 1/2 cup chicken mixture on each tortilla; roll up each tortilla, and place seam side down in a 13 x 9 x 2-inch baking dish.

Cover and bake at 350° for 20 minutes. Sprinkle with 1 cup longhorn cheese, and bake, uncovered, 5 additional minutes.

Yield: 5 servings.

BREAST-OF-CHICKEN FIESTA

1 cup Cheddar cheese cracker
    crumbs
2 tablespoons taco seasoning mix
8 skinned and boned chicken breast
    halves
4 green onions, chopped
2 tablespoons butter or margarine,
    melted
2 cups whipping cream
1 cup (4 ounces) shredded
    Monterey Jack cheese
1 cup (4 ounces) shredded Cheddar
    cheese
1 (4.5-ounce) can chopped green
    chiles, drained
$1/2$ teaspoon chicken-flavored
    bouillon granules

Combine cracker crumbs and seasoning mix in a small bowl, stirring well. Dredge chicken in crumb mixture; place in a greased 13 x 9 x 2-inch baking dish.

Cook green onions in butter in a large skillet over medium heat until tender. Stir in whipping cream and remaining ingredients; pour over chicken. Bake, uncovered, at 350° for 45 minutes.

Yield: 8 servings.

MEXICAN CHICKEN ROLLS

$1/2$ cup fine, dry breadcrumbs
$1/4$ cup grated Parmesan cheese
1 teaspoon chili powder
$1/4$ teaspoon ground cumin
$1/4$ teaspoon pepper
8 skinned and boned chicken breast
    halves
1 (8-ounce) package Monterey Jack
    cheese with jalapeño peppers
$1/3$ cup butter or margarine, melted

Combine first 5 ingredients in a shallow dish; set aside.

Place chicken between 2 sheets of heavy-duty plastic wrap; flatten to $1/4$-inch thickness, using a meat mallet or rolling pin. Cut cheese crosswise into 8 equal slices; place a slice of cheese on each chicken breast. Roll up from short side, and secure with wooden picks.

Dip chicken rolls in butter, and dredge in breadcrumb mixture. Place rolls, seam side down, in a lightly greased 11 x 7 x $1^{1}/_{2}$-inch baking dish; bake at 350° for 25 to 30 minutes.

Yield: 8 servings.

PEPPERY CHICKEN IN PITA

  6 skinned and boned chicken breast halves (about 1 1/2 pounds)
1/4 cup teriyaki sauce
  1 teaspoon dried thyme
  1 teaspoon ground white pepper
  1 teaspoon black pepper
1/2 teaspoon garlic powder
1/2 teaspoon ground red pepper
  2 tablespoons olive oil, divided
1/3 cup mayonnaise or salad dressing
  1 tablespoon prepared horseradish
  6 (8-inch) pita bread rounds
  2 cups shredded lettuce

Cut chicken lengthwise into 1/2-inch-wide strips, and place in a shallow dish. Pour teriyaki sauce over chicken; cover and marinate in refrigerator 2 hours.

Remove chicken from marinade, discarding marinade. Combine thyme and next 4 ingredients; sprinkle evenly over chicken.

Heat 1 tablespoon olive oil in a large skillet over medium-high heat. Cook half of chicken 5 to 7 minutes, turning once. Drain on paper towels. Repeat procedure with remaining olive oil and chicken.

Combine mayonnaise and horseradish. Spread each pita round with about 1 tablespoon mayonnaise mixture; sprinkle evenly with lettuce, and top with chicken. Fold two sides of pita over chicken, and secure with a wooden pick.

Yield: 6 servings.

Note: Before spreading pita rounds with mayonnaise mixture, wrap in heavy-duty plastic wrap, and microwave at HIGH 45 seconds or until thoroughly heated. This will prevent bread from cracking when folding.

OPEN-FACED CHICKEN SANDWICHES

  2 tablespoons butter or margarine
  2 tablespoons all-purpose flour
  1 cup milk
1/2 teaspoon salt
1/8 teaspoon white pepper
1/2 cup (2 ounces) shredded Cheddar cheese
  1 pound sliced cooked chicken
  4 slices sandwich bread, toasted
  8 slices bacon, cooked, drained, and crumbled
1/4 cup grated Parmesan cheese

Melt butter in a heavy saucepan over low heat; add flour, stirring until smooth. Cook, stirring constantly, 1 minute. Gradually add milk; cook over medium heat, stirring constantly, until thickened and bubbly. Add salt, pepper, and Cheddar cheese, stirring until cheese melts.

Place chicken on toast, and cover with sauce. Sprinkle with bacon and Parmesan cheese. Bake at 400° for 10 minutes.

Yield: 4 servings.

SOUTHWESTERN CHICKEN DRUMMETTES

- ²/₃ cup fine, dry breadcrumbs
- ²/₃ cup finely crushed corn chips
- 1 (1¼-ounce) package taco seasoning mix
- 2 pounds chicken drummettes, skinned
- 1 (16-ounce) jar taco sauce, divided
  Garnish: fresh cilantro sprigs

Combine first 3 ingredients in a small bowl. Dip drummettes, one at a time, into ¹/₂ cup taco sauce, and dredge in crumb mixture; place on a lightly greased baking sheet.

Bake at 375° for 30 to 35 minutes. Serve with remaining taco sauce. Garnish, if desired.

Yield: 8 to 10 appetizer servings.

Southwestern Chicken Drummettes

FESTIVE CHICKEN SPREAD

1 (8-ounce) package cream cheese, softened
3 tablespoons mayonnaise
1 tablespoon lemon juice
$^1/_2$ teaspoon salt
$^1/_4$ teaspoon ground ginger
$^1/_8$ teaspoon pepper
4 drops of hot sauce
2 cups diced cooked chicken
2 hard-cooked eggs, diced
$^1/_4$ cup diced green onions
3 tablespoons chopped green pepper
Green pepper strips
2 tablespoons sesame seeds, toasted
3 tablespoons chopped black olives
3 tablespoons chopped sweet red pepper
5 slices cucumber, halved (optional)
Parsley sprigs (optional)

Combine first 7 ingredients in a large bowl; beat at medium speed of an electric mixer until smooth. Add chicken, eggs, green onions, and chopped green pepper; stir well.

Line a 1-quart bowl or mold with plastic wrap. Spoon mixture into bowl; press firmly with the back of a spoon. Cover and chill at least 4 hours.

Invert bowl onto serving platter. Remove bowl, and peel off plastic wrap. Garnish mound with green pepper strips, sesame seeds, black olives, and sweet red pepper. Arrange cucumber slices and parsley sprigs around bottom of mound, if desired; serve with assorted crackers.

Yield: 3 cups.

CHICKEN SALAD SPREAD

1$^1/_2$ cups coarsely ground cooked chicken
$^1/_4$ cup sweet pickle relish
3 to 4 tablespoons mayonnaise
2 tablespoons finely chopped onion
$^3/_4$ teaspoon salt
$^1/_2$ teaspoon celery seeds
$^1/_4$ teaspoon pepper

Combine all ingredients, stirring well. Store in refrigerator; serve with crackers.

Yield: 1$^1/_2$ cups.

SPICY CHICKEN STRIPS

   8 skinned and boned chicken breast
      halves
 3/4 cup all-purpose flour
   1 to 1 1/2 teaspoons chili powder
 3/4 teaspoon salt
 1/2 teaspoon garlic powder
 1/4 teaspoon ground cumin
 1/4 teaspoon pepper
   1 large egg, beaten
 1/2 cup water
      Vegetable oil
      Tomato-Garlic Dip

Cut chicken into long, thin strips (about
3/4-inch wide). Combine flour and next
5 ingredients; stir well. Stir in egg and
water. Dip chicken strips in batter.

Fry strips, a few at a time, in hot oil
(375°) for 2 to 3 minutes or until
golden. Drain on paper towels. Serve
immediately with Tomato-Garlic Dip.

Yield: 16 appetizer servings.

TOMATO-GARLIC DIP

   1 (6-ounce) can tomato paste
 1/3 cup mayonnaise
 1/4 cup sour cream
 1/4 cup tomato sauce
   2 cloves garlic, crushed
 1/4 teaspoon ground cumin
 1/4 teaspoon chili powder
 1/4 teaspoon hot sauce

Combine all ingredients in a small bowl;
stir well. Serve dip in a hollowed-out
cabbage bowl, if desired.

Yield: 1 1/2 cups.

GREAT GRILLING

The key to perfectly grilled chicken is low temperature and nonrushed cooking time. When preparing the grill, consider whether you'll cook using direct or indirect heat.

GRILLING WITH DIRECT HEAT:
• Arrange the coals in a single layer; allow 1 pound charcoal to 2 pounds chicken. Light charcoal 30 minutes before grilling. If using a gas grill, preheat grill for 20 minutes. Coals are ready when covered with light gray ash.
• Coat food rack with cooking spray or vegetable oil; place rack 6 to 8 inches above coals.
• Place chicken on rack, skin side up, with smaller pieces near the edges.
• Turn chicken often during cooking for even doneness.

GRILLING WITH INDIRECT HEAT:
• Place 2 cups hickory or mesquite chips in center of a large square of aluminum foil; fold into a rectangle, and seal. Punch several holes in top of packet.
• Arrange charcoal or lava rocks on each side of grill, leaving center empty. Place packet on one side of coals or rocks, and ignite. Let charcoal burn 30 minutes until coals turn white. If using a gas grill, preheat grill for 20 minutes. Place a drip pan in center.
• Coat food rack with cooking spray or vegetable oil; place rack 6 to 8 inches above coals.
• Place chicken, skin side up, on rack directly over medium-hot coals (350° to 400°); cook, covered with grill lid, about 15 minutes.
• Turn chicken, and cook, covered with grill lid, 10 to 15 minutes or until golden. Move chicken over drip pan; cook, covered with grill lid, indirectly 25 to 35 minutes, brushing often with sauce and turning skin side up after 5 minutes.

QUICK CHICKEN FOR SALAD

When time is short and your recipe calls for tender chunks of chicken, remember that chicken and the microwave are ideal partners. For 2 cups chopped cooked chicken:
• Arrange 4 skinned and boned chicken breast halves around sides of an 8-inch square dish. Pour $1/2$ cup water over chicken and sprinkle with pepper.
• Cover with heavy-duty plastic wrap; vent corner. Microwave at HIGH 6 minutes or until juice is no longer pink.
• Let stand, covered, 5 minutes; drain. When cool enough to handle, chop chicken.

Hooray For
SIDE DISHES

Once you've chosen the entrée for a meal, your thoughts turn to what you should serve with it. Our quick dishes will stand up to any main course and take the ho-hum out of mealtime in the blink of an eye.

Macaroni and Cheese, p. 392

GREEN BEANS WITH MUSHROOMS

1 tablespoon minced onion
1 tablespoon vegetable oil
1 (8-ounce) can cut green beans, drained
1 tablespoon diced pimiento
1 teaspoon chopped fresh parsley
1 (4-ounce) can sliced mushrooms, drained
$1/8$ teaspoon salt
$1/8$ teaspoon pepper

Cook onion in hot oil in a medium skillet until transparent. Stir in beans and remaining ingredients; cover and cook over medium heat 10 minutes or until thoroughly heated.

Yield: 2 servings.

QUICK POTATOES

1 tablespoon olive oil
1 large onion, chopped
2 cloves garlic, minced
$1/2$ cup chopped sweet red pepper
$1/2$ teaspoon salt
$1/4$ teaspoon pepper
$1/4$ teaspoon hot sauce
3 cups unpeeled cubed potato
2 tablespoons butter or margarine

Heat olive oil in a 10-inch cast-iron skillet. Add onion and garlic; cook over medium heat, stirring constantly, until tender.

Stir in red pepper and next 3 ingredients; cook 2 minutes, stirring constantly. Add potato and butter, stirring well.

Bake in skillet at 400° for 20 to 30 minutes.

Yield: 4 servings.

BAKED RANCH TOMATOES

2 tomatoes, cut in half
Vegetable cooking spray
$1/4$ teaspoon dried Italian seasoning
$1 1/2$ tablespoons commercial Ranch-style dressing
Garnish: fresh parsley sprigs

Place tomato halves in an 8-inch square pan. Coat top of halves with cooking spray.

Bake tomato halves at 350° for 15 minutes.

Sprinkle with Italian seasoning, and top evenly with dressing.

Broil 3 inches from heat (with door partially opened, if using an electric oven) 2 to 3 minutes or until tomato halves begin to brown. Garnish, if desired.

Yield: 4 servings.

GRILLED ZUCCHINI FANS

 3 tablespoons olive oil
 1/4 teaspoon garlic powder
 4 small zucchini, cut into fans

Combine olive oil and garlic powder. Cut each zucchini into lengthwise slices, leaving slices attached on stem end. Fan slices out, and place on grill; brush zucchini with olive oil mixture.

Grill zucchini, covered with grill lid, over medium coals (300° to 350°) 5 minutes on each side, basting once with olive oil mixture.

Yield: 4 servings.

LEMONY CORN ON THE COB

 1/4 cup butter or margarine, softened
 1/2 to 1 teaspoon lemon-pepper
        seasoning
 4 ears fresh corn

Combine butter and lemon-pepper seasoning; spread on corn, and place each ear on a piece of heavy-duty aluminum foil. Roll foil lengthwise around each ear, and twist at each end.

Grill corn, covered with grill lid, over medium coals (300° to 350°) 20 minutes, turning after 10 minutes.

Yield: 4 servings.

Grilled Zucchini Fans and Lemony Corn on the Cob go great with grilled chicken!

HERBED POTATOES

Vegetable cooking spray
4 medium baking potatoes,
    cut into 1/4-inch slices
    (1 1/2 pounds)
2 medium-size white onions, cut
    into 1/4-inch slices (12 ounces)
5 plum tomatoes, sliced (1 pound)
1/2 teaspoon salt
1 teaspoon dried thyme
3/4 teaspoon dried rosemary, crushed
1 tablespoon olive oil
2 tablespoons chopped fresh
    parsley

Coat a 13 x 9 x 2-inch baking dish with cooking spray. Layer half each of potato, onion, and tomato in dish; sprinkle with half each of salt, thyme, and rosemary. Repeat layers, and drizzle evenly with olive oil.

Cover and bake at 425° for 35 to 40 minutes or until tender. Sprinkle with parsley.

Yield: 8 (3/4-cup) servings.

SHREDDING CHEESE
To shred cheese easily, place wrapped cheese in freezer for 10 to 20 minutes before shredding.

GRILLED SWEET POTATOES

2 pounds sweet potatoes, peeled
    and cut into wedges
3 tablespoons reduced-sodium soy
    sauce
2 tablespoons dry sherry
2 tablespoons honey
2 tablespoons water
1 clove garlic, minced
    Vegetable cooking spray
1 tablespoon sesame oil

Arrange sweet potato in a steamer basket; place over boiling water. Cover and steam 5 to 7 minutes.

Combine soy sauce and next 4 ingredients in a shallow dish; add sweet potato, and toss gently.

Drain sweet potato, reserving soy sauce mixture. Arrange sweet potato in a single layer in a grill basket coated with cooking spray; brush wedges with sesame oil.

Cook, covered with grill lid, over medium coals (300° to 350°) 15 minutes, basting with reserved soy sauce mixture and turning several times.

Yield: 6 servings.

MEXICAN-STUFFED POTATOES

    4   medium baking potatoes
            (1½ pounds)
    1   (8-ounce) carton plain low-fat
            yogurt
    ¼   cup fat-free milk
    ⅛   teaspoon pepper
    1   (4.5-ounce) can chopped green
            chiles, drained
    1   (2-ounce) jar diced pimiento,
            drained
    4   large, pitted ripe olives, chopped
    ½   cup (2 ounces) shredded reduced
            fat sharp Cheddar cheese,
            divided

Wash potatoes; prick several times with a fork. Bake at 400° for 1 hour or until done. Let cool to touch. Cut potatoes in half lengthwise; carefully scoop out pulp, leaving shells intact. Set aside.

Combine potato pulp, yogurt, milk, and pepper; mash until light and fluffy.

Stir chiles, pimiento, olives, and half of Cheddar cheese into potato mixture. Stuff shells with potato mixture; place on an ungreased baking sheet.

Bake at 375° for 10 minutes. Sprinkle evenly with remaining cheese, and bake 2 additional minutes.

Yield: 8 servings.

GREEN BEANS AND POTATOES

    4   medium-size red potatoes, cut
            into eighths
    2   (16-ounce) cans no-salt-added
            green beans, drained
    1   medium onion, sliced and
            separated into rings
    1   teaspoon beef-flavored bouillon
            granules
    ½   teaspoon garlic powder
    ¼   teaspoon pepper
    1   cup water

Layer all ingredients in a large saucepan in the order given; bring to a boil.

Cover, reduce heat, and simmer 20 minutes or until potato is fork tender.

Yield: 6 (1-cup) servings.

NEW POTATO MEDLEY

    1   tablespoon reduced-calorie
            margarine
    3   cups cubed new potato
    1½ cups diagonally sliced carrot
    1   cup chopped onion
    ¼   teaspoon salt
    ¼   teaspoon pepper

Melt margarine in a saucepan over medium heat. Add potato and remaining ingredients; toss.

Cover, reduce heat, and cook 20 minutes, stirring once.

Yield: 6 (¾-cup) servings.

ROASTED RED PEPPER CORN

4 medium ears fresh corn
Butter-flavored cooking spray
$^1/_4$ cup diced sweet red pepper

Remove husks and silks from corn. Place each ear on a piece of heavy-duty aluminum foil, and coat with cooking spray. Sprinkle 1 tablespoon sweet red pepper on each ear of corn.

Roll foil lengthwise around corn, and twist foil at each end. Bake at 500° for 20 minutes.

Yield: 4 servings.

BUTTERBEANS

2 cups water
1 ounce chopped lean ham
2 cups shelled fresh butterbeans or lima beans (about 1$^3/_4$ pounds)
$^1/_4$ teaspoon salt
$^1/_8$ teaspoon pepper

Combine water and ham in a saucepan; bring to a boil, and cook 5 to 10 minutes. Add beans, salt, and pepper; bring to a boil.

Cover, reduce heat, and simmer 45 minutes or until beans are tender.

Yield: 4 ($^1/_2$-cup) servings.

STUFFED SCALLOPED TOMATOES

2 medium tomatoes ($^3/_4$ pound)
Vegetable cooking spray
2 tablespoons diced onion
$^1/_2$ teaspoon brown sugar
$^1/_4$ teaspoon salt
$^1/_4$ teaspoon pepper
$^2/_3$ cup soft breadcrumbs, toasted
1 tablespoon grated Parmesan cheese

Cut tops from tomatoes; chop tops, and set aside. Scoop out pulp, leaving shells intact. Reserve pulp.

Coat a nonstick skillet with cooking spray; place over medium-high heat until hot. Add onion, and sauté until tender.

Add chopped tomato tops, reserved tomato pulp, brown sugar, and next 3 ingredients; stir well, and remove from heat.

Spoon stuffing mixture into tomato shells, and place in an 8-inch square baking dish coated with cooking spray. Sprinkle with Parmesan cheese, and bake at 350° for 10 minutes or until thoroughly heated.

Yield: 2 servings.

PARMESAN-STUFFED TOMATOES

- 4 medium tomatoes (2$\frac{1}{2}$ pounds)
- 3 tablespoons chopped green onions
- 2 tablespoons chopped green pepper
- 1 teaspoon reduced-calorie margarine, melted
- $\frac{1}{4}$ cup Italian-seasoned breadcrumbs
- 2 tablespoons chopped fresh parsley
- $\frac{1}{8}$ teaspoon dried oregano
- $\frac{1}{8}$ teaspoon ground red pepper
- $\frac{1}{8}$ teaspoon black pepper
  Vegetable cooking spray
- 2 tablespoons grated Parmesan cheese

Slice off top of each tomato, and carefully scoop out pulp. Set tomato shells and pulp aside.

Cook green onions and green pepper in margarine in a large skillet over medium-high heat, stirring constantly, until tender. Remove from heat.

Stir in tomato pulp, breadcrumbs, and next 4 ingredients. Spoon into shells, and place in an 8-inch square baking dish coated with cooking spray.

Cover and bake at 350° for 25 minutes. Sprinkle with cheese, and broil 5 inches from heat (with door partially opened, if using an electric oven) 3 minutes or until golden.

Yield: 4 servings.

Parmesan-Stuffed Tomatoes

CORN ON THE COB WITH HERB BUTTER

1/4 cup butter or margarine, softened
1 tablespoon chopped fresh parsley
1 tablespoon chopped fresh chives
1/4 teaspoon dried salad herbs
   About 2 quarts water
6 ears fresh corn

Combine first 4 ingredients; set aside.

Bring water to a boil, and add corn. Return to a boil, and cook 8 to 10 minutes. Drain well. Spread butter mixture over hot corn.

Yield: 6 servings.

TIME SAVERS
• Purchase frozen corn on the cob if fresh corn is unavailable.
• Substitute any type of 16-ounce package slaw mix for slaw.

ZESTY BROCCOLI SLAW

1/2 cup cider vinegar
1/2 cup vegetable oil
1 clove garlic, pressed
1 1/2 teaspoons dried dillweed
1/2 teaspoon salt
1 (16-ounce) package fresh broccoli, carrot, and red cabbage slaw mix

Combine first 5 ingredients; pour over slaw mix, stirring gently to coat.

Cover and chill at least 2 hours. Drain slaw mix before serving, or serve with a slotted spoon.

Yield: 6 servings.

VEGETABLE SAUTÉ

2 tablespoons olive oil
1 large zucchini, sliced
1 large yellow squash, sliced
1 carrot, scraped and sliced
1 clove garlic, crushed
1/2 teaspoon pepper
1/4 teaspoon hot sauce

Heat olive oil in a large skillet until hot; add remaining ingredients, and toss gently. Cover, reduce heat, and cook 10 minutes or until crisp-tender.

Yield: 4 servings.

VEGETABLE-CHEESE ENCHILADAS

8 (6-inch) corn tortillas
1 medium zucchini, cut into $1/2$-inch cubes
1 cup (4 ounces) shredded reduced-fat Monterey Jack cheese, divided
1 cup cooked brown rice (cooked without salt or fat)
$1/4$ cup chopped green onions
$1/3$ cup low-fat sour cream
$1/4$ teaspoon salt
$1/4$ teaspoon pepper
Vegetable cooking spray
2 (10-ounce) cans chopped tomatoes and green chiles, undrained

Wrap tortillas in aluminum foil, and bake at 350° for 7 minutes.

Cook zucchini in boiling water to cover 2 minutes; drain and pat dry with paper towels.

Combine zucchini, half of cheese, and next 5 ingredients. Spoon mixture evenly down center of each tortilla; fold opposite sides over filling, and roll up tortillas. Place, seam side down, in an 11 x 7 x $1/2$-inch baking dish coated with cooking spray.

Pour chopped tomatoes and green chiles over tortillas.

Bake at 350° for 15 minutes; sprinkle with remaining cheese, and bake 5 additional minutes.

Yield: 4 servings.

CORN CHOWDER

1 ($10\frac{3}{4}$-ounce) can cream of potato soup
1 (17-ounce) can reduced-sodium whole kernel corn, drained
$1\frac{1}{3}$ cups milk
1 tablespoon butter or margarine
$1/2$ teaspoon pepper
4 slices bacon, cooked and crumbled
2 small green onions, sliced

Combine first 5 ingredients in a saucepan. Cook over medium heat, stirring occasionally, until thoroughly heated. Sprinkle each serving with crumbled bacon and green onions.

Yield: 1 quart.

TIME SAVER

• Substitute bacon bits for crumbled bacon if you don't have a supply of cooked bacon in the freezer.

VEGETABLE KABOBS

- 3 medium onions, quartered
- 1 medium zucchini, cut into 1-inch slices
- 3 medium-size yellow squash, cut into 1-inch slices
- 12 medium fresh mushrooms
- 12 cherry tomatoes
- 1/4 cup butter or margarine, melted
- 1/4 teaspoon ground cumin

Arrange vegetables on 6 skewers. Combine butter and cumin; brush vegetables with butter mixture.

Grill kabobs, covered with grill lid, over medium-hot coals (350° to 400°) 10 to 15 minutes or until zucchini and yellow squash are crisp-tender, turning occasionally and brushing with butter mixture.

Yield: 6 servings.

GREEN BEANS WITH BUTTERED PECANS

- 2 cups water
- 1/4 teaspoon salt
- 1/2 pound trimmed green beans
- 1 tablespoon butter or margarine
- 2 tablespoons chopped pecans
- 1/8 teaspoon pepper

Bring water and salt to a boil in a medium saucepan. Add green beans; cook, uncovered, 10 minutes or just until crisp-tender. Drain beans, and set aside.

Melt butter in a nonstick skillet; add pecans, and cook until golden, stirring often. Add beans; toss gently, and cook until thoroughly heated. Sprinkle with pepper.

Yield: 2 servings.

KRAUT RELISH

- 1 (16-ounce) jar sauerkraut, drained
- 1/2 cup finely chopped celery
- 1/2 cup finely chopped green pepper
- 1/2 cup finely chopped carrot
- 1/2 cup finely chopped onion
- 1/4 cup sugar

Combine all ingredients; cover and chill 8 hours. Serve relish with hot dogs, vegetables, or meats.

Yield: 1 quart.

OVEN-FRIED OKRA

1 pound fresh okra
1/4 cup egg substitute
1/4 cup nonfat buttermilk
2/3 cup cornmeal
1/3 cup all-purpose flour
1 teaspoon baking powder
1/2 teaspoon salt
1 tablespoon vegetable oil
  Vegetable cooking spray

Wash okra and drain. Remove tips and stem ends; cut okra crosswise into 1/2-inch slices.

Combine egg substitute and buttermilk; add okra, stirring to coat well. Let stand 10 minutes.

Combine cornmeal and next 3 ingredients in a zip-top plastic bag. Drain okra, small portions at a time, using a slotted spoon; place okra in bag with cornmeal mixture, shaking gently to coat.

Brush oil on a 15 x 10 x 1-inch jellyroll pan; add okra in a single layer.

Coat okra with cooking spray, and bake at 450° for 8 minutes. Stir well, and spray with cooking spray again; bake 7 to 8 additional minutes. After last baking, broil 4 inches from heat (with door partially opened, if using an electric oven) 4 to 5 minutes or until browned, stirring occasionally.

Yield: 7 (1/2-cup) servings.

DEVILED PURPLE HULL PEAS

3 cups shelled fresh purple hull peas
    or black-eyed peas (1 pound)
2 cups water
1/2 teaspoon salt
2 tablespoons cider vinegar
1 teaspoon dry mustard
1/4 teaspoon sugar
1/4 teaspoon pepper
1 clove garlic, minced
1 tablespoon chopped fresh parsley

Combine first 3 ingredients in a large saucepan; bring to a boil. Cover, reduce heat, and simmer 30 minutes or until tender; drain, reserving 1/2 cup liquid.

Combine reserved liquid, vinegar, and next 4 ingredients in saucepan. Add peas, and cook, stirring occasionally, over medium heat 5 minutes or until thoroughly heated. Spoon into a serving bowl; top with parsley.

Yield: 6 (1/2-cup) servings.

SOUTHERN-STYLE CREAMED CORN

6 medium ears fresh corn
1 cup 1% low-fat milk, divided
2 teaspoons cornstarch
2 ($\frac{1}{2}$-inch thick) onion slices
$\frac{1}{4}$ teaspoon salt
$\frac{1}{4}$ teaspoon ground white or black pepper

Cut off tips of kernels into a large bowl; scrape milk and remaining pulp from cob, using a small paring knife. Set aside.

Combine $\frac{1}{4}$ cup milk and cornstarch; set mixture aside.

Combine remaining $\frac{3}{4}$ cup milk and onion in a heavy saucepan; bring to a boil over medium heat. Cover, reduce heat, and simmer 5 minutes; remove and discard onion.

Add corn; cook over medium heat, stirring frequently, 5 minutes. Gradually stir in cornstarch mixture, salt, and pepper. Cook, stirring constantly, until thickened and bubbly (about 3 minutes).

Yield: 6 ($\frac{1}{2}$-cup) servings.

PASTA PRIMAVERA

1 pound fresh asparagus
2 cups fresh broccoli flowerets
1 medium onion, chopped
1 large clove garlic, chopped
1 tablespoon olive oil
1 large carrot, scraped and diagonally sliced
1 sweet red pepper, coarsely chopped
1 sweet yellow pepper, coarsely chopped
1 cup whipping cream
$\frac{1}{2}$ cup chicken broth
3 green onions, chopped
2 tablespoons chopped fresh basil or 2 teaspoons dried basil
$\frac{1}{2}$ teaspoon salt
8 ounces linguine, uncooked
$\frac{1}{2}$ pound fresh mushrooms, sliced
1 cup freshly grated Parmesan cheese
$\frac{1}{4}$ teaspoon freshly ground pepper

Snap off tough ends of asparagus. Remove scales with a vegetable peeler or knife, if desired. Cut asparagus diagonally into $1\frac{1}{2}$-inch pieces.

Place asparagus pieces and broccoli flowerets in a vegetable steamer over boiling water. Cover; steam 6 to 8 minutes. Set aside.

Cook onion and garlic in oil in a large skillet, stirring constantly, until tender. Add carrot and chopped peppers; cook, stirring constantly, until crisp-tender. Remove from heat; drain.

Combine whipping cream and next 4 ingredients in a medium skillet; cook over medium-high heat 5 minutes, stirring occasionally.

Break linguine noodles in half; cook according to package directions. Drain well; place in a large serving bowl.

Add reserved vegetables, whipping cream mixture, and mushrooms; toss gently. Sprinkle with Parmesan cheese and pepper; toss gently. Serve immediately.

Yield: 8 servings.

Pasta Primavera

MACARONI AND CHEESE
(Shown on page 379)

- 1 (8-ounce) package elbow
  macaroni, uncooked
- 1/4 cup butter or margarine
- 1/4 cup plus 2 tablespoons all-
  purpose flour
- 1/4 teaspoon salt
- 2 cups milk
- 2 cups (8 ounces) shredded
  Cheddar cheese
- 1 (2-ounce) jar diced pimiento,
  drained
- 1 tablespoon butter or margarine
- 1/3 cup fine, dry breadcrumbs
- 1/2 teaspoon dried parsley flakes

Cook macaroni according to package directions; drain and set aside.

Place 1/4 cup butter in a 4-cup glass measure; microwave, uncovered, at HIGH 55 seconds or until melted.

Blend in flour and salt, stirring until smooth. Gradually stir in milk; microwave, uncovered, at HIGH 5 to 6 minutes or until thickened, stirring after every minute. Add cheese, stirring until melted; stir in pimiento.

Add cheese sauce to macaroni, stirring well. Place macaroni mixture in a 1 1/2-quart baking dish. Cover with heavy-duty plastic wrap; fold back a small edge of wrap to allow steam to escape.

Microwave at MEDIUM HIGH (70% power) 7 to 8 minutes or until thoroughly heated, stirring after 4 minutes.

Place 1 tablespoon butter in a 1-cup glass measure; microwave, uncovered, at HIGH 35 seconds or until melted. Stir in breadcrumbs and parsley flakes; sprinkle over macaroni mixture. Let stand, uncovered, 1 minute. Serve immediately.

Yield: 6 servings.

HANDY SUBSTITUTIONS FOR DAIRY PRODUCTS

1 cup milk	1/2 cup evaporated milk plus 1/2 cup water
1 cup whipping cream	3/4 cup milk plus 1/3 cup melted butter (for baking only; will not whip)
1 cup plain yogurt	1 cup buttermilk
1 cup sour cream	1 cup yogurt plus 3 tablespoons melted butter or 1 cup yogurt plus 1 tablespoon cornstarch

JACK-IN-THE-MACARONI BAKE

1 (8-ounce) package elbow
    macaroni, uncooked
2 tablespoons butter or margarine
$1/4$ cup chopped onion
$1/4$ cup chopped sweet red pepper
2 cups (8 ounces) shredded
    Monterey Jack cheese with
    jalapeño peppers
1 ($10^3/4$-ounce) can cream of celery
    soup, undiluted
$1/2$ cup sour cream
    Chili powder
    Garnish: celery leaves

Cook macaroni according to package directions; drain. Rinse with cold water; drain.

Melt butter in a Dutch oven; add onion and sweet red pepper. Cook over medium heat, stirring constantly, until vegetables are crisp-tender. Remove from heat.

Stir cheese, soup, and sour cream into Dutch oven. Stir in macaroni; spoon into a lightly greased 2-quart shallow baking dish. Sprinkle with chili powder.

Bake at 350° for 30 minutes. Garnish, if desired.

Yield: 6 servings.

GLORIOUS MACARONI

1 (8-ounce) package shell macaroni,
    uncooked
$1/4$ cup chopped onion
1 (2-ounce) jar diced pimiento,
    drained
1 tablespoon butter or margarine,
    melted
2 cups (8 ounces) shredded
    Cheddar cheese
1 ($10^3/4$-ounce) can cream of
    mushroom soup, undiluted
$1/2$ cup mayonnaise
1 ($2^1/2$-ounce) jar sliced mushrooms,
    drained

Cook macaroni in a Dutch oven according to package directions; drain.

Cook onion and pimiento in butter until onion is crisp-tender.

Combine macaroni, onion mixture, cheese, and remaining ingredients; mix well. Spoon into a lightly greased 2-quart shallow baking dish.

Bake at 350° for 30 minutes.

Yield: 6 servings.

OLD-FASHIONED MACARONI AND CHEESE

- 1 (8-ounce) package elbow macaroni, uncooked
- 2¹/₂ cups (10 ounces) shredded Cheddar cheese, divided
- 2 large eggs, lightly beaten
- 1¹/₂ cups milk
- 1 teaspoon salt
- ¹/₈ teaspoon ground white pepper
  Paprika

Cook macaroni according to package directions; drain.

Layer one-third each of macaroni and cheese in a lightly greased 2-quart baking dish. Repeat procedure, and top with remaining macaroni. (Reserve remaining cheese.)

Combine eggs, milk, salt, and pepper; pour over macaroni and cheese.

Cover and bake at 350° for 45 minutes. Uncover and sprinkle with remaining cheese and paprika.

Cover and let stand 10 minutes before serving.

Yield: 6 to 8 servings.

DELUXE MACARONI AND CHEESE

- 1 (8-ounce) package elbow macaroni, uncooked
- 2 cups (8 ounces) shredded Cheddar cheese
- 2 cups cottage cheese
- 1 (8-ounce) carton sour cream
- 1 cup diced cooked ham
- 3 tablespoons finely chopped onion
- 1 large egg, lightly beaten
- ¹/₄ teaspoon salt
- ¹/₄ teaspoon pepper
- 1 cup soft breadcrumbs
- 2 tablespoons butter or margarine, melted
- ¹/₄ teaspoon paprika
  Garnishes: sliced cherry tomatoes, fresh parsley sprigs.

Cook macaroni according to package directions; drain well.

Place macaroni and next 8 ingredients in a large bowl; stir gently to combine. Spoon mixture into a lightly greased 2-quart baking dish.

Combine breadcrumbs, melted butter, and paprika in a small bowl, stirring well. Sprinkle breadcrumb mixture diagonally across top of casserole, forming stripes.

Bake at 350° for 30 to 40 minutes or until golden. Garnish, if desired.

Yield: 6 servings.

Deluxe Macaroni and Cheese

MUSHROOM-MACARONI CASSEROLE

1 (8-ounce) package elbow
    macaroni, uncooked
1 (10¾-ounce) can cream of
    mushroom soup, undiluted
1 cup mayonnaise
2 cups (8 ounces) shredded sharp
    Cheddar cheese
1 (4-ounce) can sliced mushrooms,
    drained
1 (2-ounce) jar diced pimiento,
    drained (optional)
¾ cup crushed round buttery
    crackers (about 15 crackers)
1 tablespoon butter or margarine,
    melted

Cook macaroni according to package directions; drain. Rinse with cold water; drain.

Combine macaroni, soup, and next 3 ingredients; add pimiento, if desired. Spoon into a lightly greased 2-quart baking dish.

Combine cracker crumbs and melted butter; sprinkle evenly over macaroni mixture.

Bake at 300° for 30 minutes or until thoroughly heated.

Yield: 6 to 8 servings.

ST. LOUIS TOASTED RAVIOLI

1 large egg, lightly beaten
2 tablespoons milk
¾ cup dry Italian-seasoned
    breadcrumbs
½ teaspoon salt (optional)
½ (27.5-ounce) package frozen
    cheese-filled ravioli, thawed
    Vegetable oil
    Grated Parmesan cheese
    Commercial spaghetti sauce or
    pizza sauce

Combine egg and milk in a small bowl. Place breadcrumbs and, if desired, salt, in a shallow bowl. Dip ravioli in milk mixture, and coat with breadcrumbs.

Pour oil to a depth of 2 inches into a Dutch oven; heat to 350°.

Fry ravioli, a few at a time, 1 minute on each side or until golden. Drain on paper towels.

Sprinkle with Parmesan cheese, and serve immediately with warm spaghetti sauce or pizza sauce.

Yield: about 2 dozen appetizers or 4 to 6 side-dish servings.

Note: Refrigerated fresh ravioli may be substituted for the frozen. Vary the flavor by using sausage, chicken, Italian, or other meat-filled varieties.

FETTUCCINE ALFREDO

8 ounces fettuccine, uncooked
$1/2$ cup butter
$1/2$ cup whipping cream
$3/4$ cup grated Parmesan cheese
$1/4$ teaspoon ground white pepper
2 tablespoons chopped fresh
  parsley
  Garnish: fresh parsley

Cook fettuccine according to package directions, omitting salt. Drain well, and place in a large bowl.

Combine butter and whipping cream in a small saucepan; cook over low heat until butter melts. Stir in cheese, pepper, and parsley.

Pour mixture over hot fettuccine; toss until fettuccine is coated. Garnish, if desired.

Yield: 4 servings.

TOSS A PASTA SALAD
Turn leftover plain pasta into an impromptu pasta salad — simply add chopped raw or cooked vegetables, and toss with your favorite salad dressing. Add diced or shredded cheese and cooked ham, poultry, or seafood for other variations.

GREEN PEAS AND PASTA

4 ounces spinach linguine,
  uncooked
1 cup whipping cream
1 cup chicken broth
$1/2$ cup freshly grated Parmesan
  cheese
$1/2$ cup frozen English peas
3 slices bacon, cooked and
  crumbled

Cook linguine according to package directions; drain and keep warm.

Combine whipping cream and chicken broth in a saucepan; bring to a boil. Reduce heat, and simmer 25 minutes or until thickened and reduced to 1 cup. Remove mixture from heat.

Add cheese, peas, and bacon, stirring until cheese melts. Toss with linguine, and serve immediately.

Yield: 2 servings.

Note: Whipping cream and chicken broth may be simmered longer for a thicker sauce. Peeled, cooked shrimp or chopped, cooked chicken may be added with the cheese, peas, and bacon for a heartier dish.

ITALIAN ZUCCHINI SPAGHETTI

1 1/2   pounds hot Italian sausage links, cut into bite-size pieces
2   medium-size green peppers, seeded and chopped
1   cup chopped onion
2   cloves garlic, minced
3   medium zucchini, coarsely shredded
2   cups chopped peeled tomato
1   (7 1/2-ounce) can tomatoes and jalapeño peppers, undrained
1   teaspoon dried Italian seasoning
1   teaspoon chili powder
1/2   teaspoon salt
1   teaspoon lemon juice
1/2   teaspoon hot sauce
1/2   cup grated Parmesan cheese
   Hot cooked spaghetti

Cook first 4 ingredients in a Dutch oven, stirring until meat browns; drain well.

Add zucchini and next 7 ingredients; cook over medium heat 10 to 15 minutes or until zucchini is tender, stirring occasionally. Remove from heat; stir in cheese. Serve sauce over spaghetti.

Yield: 8 servings.

NOODLES ROMANOFF

1   (8-ounce) package medium-size curly egg noodles, uncooked
1   cup small-curd cottage cheese
1   (8-ounce) carton sour cream
1/2   cup sliced ripe olives
1/2   cup sliced green onions
1   teaspoon Worcestershire sauce
1/2   teaspoon salt
1/8   teaspoon ground red pepper
1/2   cup (2 ounces) shredded Cheddar cheese

Cook noodles according to package directions, omitting salt. Drain well.

Combine noodles, cottage cheese, and next 6 ingredients, stirring well. Spoon mixture into a lightly greased 11 x 7 x 1 1/2-inch baking dish.

Bake, uncovered, at 350° for 30 minutes. Sprinkle with shredded Cheddar cheese, and bake 5 additional minutes or until cheese melts.

Yield: 6 to 8 servings.

Noodles Romanoff

PASTA WITH GREENS

- 1 (8-ounce) package fettuccine, uncooked
- 1 (16-ounce) package frozen collards or other greens
- 2 to 3 cloves garlic, minced
- 3 tablespoons olive oil
- 1/2 teaspoon salt
- 1/4 teaspoon freshly ground pepper
- 1/2 cup freshly grated Parmesan cheese
- 1 (1 3/4-ounce) jar pine nuts, toasted
- Garnishes: grated Parmesan cheese, toasted pine nuts

Cook pasta according to package directions; drain and set aside.

Cook greens according to package directions; drain and set aside.

Cook garlic in olive oil in a large skillet over medium-high heat until tender but not brown. Add greens, salt, and pepper; cook until heated.

Combine pasta, greens, Parmesan cheese, and pine nuts in a large serving bowl. Garnish, if desired.

Yield: 2 servings.

LEMON-GARLIC PASTA

- 8 ounces thin spaghetti, uncooked
- 2 tablespoons butter or margarine
- 2 tablespoons olive oil
- 4 to 5 cloves garlic, minced
- 1/4 cup lemon juice
- 1/4 teaspoon salt
- 1/2 to 1 teaspoon pepper
- 1/3 cup chopped fresh parsley

Cook pasta according to package directions; drain and set aside.

Melt butter in a large skillet over medium-high heat; add olive oil and minced garlic. Cook, stirring constantly, 1 minute. Add lemon juice, salt, and pepper.

Bring mixture to a boil; pour over pasta. Add parsley; toss gently. Serve immediately.

Yield: 4 servings.

MATCH PASTA WITH A SAUCE

• Thin sauces, such as marinara sauce or pesto sauce, should be served with thin pasta.
• Thicker, chunkier meat and vegetable sauces go well with tubular and shell pastas that are designed to "trap" the toppings.
• Chunky vegetable or meat sauces should be served with thick pasta: ziti, mostaccioli, rigatoni, or fettuccine.
• Rich, thick smooth sauces need a flat pasta that won't trap too much of the sauce.

PASTA POTPOURRI

      4 ounces penne or rigatoni (short
        tubular pasta), uncooked
      1 teaspoon sesame oil
  1 1/2 tablespoons olive oil
  1 1/2 tablespoons sesame oil
      1 small purple onion, chopped
      2 medium carrots, scraped and
        diagonally sliced
      2 medium zucchini, halved
        lengthwise and sliced
      2 cloves garlic, crushed
  1 1/2 teaspoons peeled, grated
        gingerroot
    1/2 teaspoon dried crushed red
        pepper
      2 tablespoons soy sauce
      2 teaspoons rice wine vinegar
      1 tablespoon freshly grated
        Parmesan cheese
      2 teaspoons chopped fresh cilantro

Cook pasta according to package directions; drain and toss with 1 teaspoon sesame oil. Set pasta aside.

Pour olive oil and 1 1/2 tablespoons sesame oil around top of a preheated wok, coating sides; heat at high 1 minute. Add onion and carrot; cook, stirring constantly, 2 minutes or until onion is tender.

Add zucchini and next 3 ingredients; cook, stirring constantly, 1 minute.

Stir in cooked pasta, soy sauce, and vinegar; cook 1 minute or until thoroughly heated.

Transfer to a serving dish; sprinkle with cheese and cilantro.

Yield: 4 to 6 servings.

Note: For a quick main dish, add leftover chopped cooked chicken or beef.

PARMESAN NOODLES

      1 (8-ounce) package medium egg
        noodles
      3 tablespoons butter or margarine,
        melted
    1/8 teaspoon garlic powder
      2 tablespoons chopped fresh
        parsley
      2 tablespoons grated Parmesan
        cheese

Cook noodles according to package directions; drain well. Toss noodles with butter, garlic powder, and parsley. Spoon into a serving bowl, and sprinkle with Parmesan cheese. Serve immediately.

Yield: 4 servings.

TOASTED RICE AND PASTA

1 1/2 cups long-grain rice, uncooked
4 ounces angel hair pasta or vermicelli, uncooked and broken into 1 1/2-inch pieces
2 tablespoons vegetable oil
1 large onion, chopped
2 (14 1/2-ounce) cans ready-to-serve chicken broth
1/4 cup chopped fresh parsley

Cook rice and pasta in oil in a Dutch oven over medium heat, stirring constantly, 3 to 5 minutes or until golden. Add onion, and cook mixture 3 minutes.

Stir in broth; bring to a boil. Cover, reduce heat to low, and simmer 15 to 17 minutes.

Stir in parsley, and serve immediately.

Yield: 4 to 6 servings.

HOPPING JOHN WITH GRILLED PORK MEDAILLONS

3/4 cup chopped onion
1/2 cup chopped celery
1 teaspoon olive oil
2 (15.75-ounce) cans ready-to-serve, reduced-sodium, fat-free chicken broth
1 teaspoon dried thyme
1/2 cup wild rice, uncooked
1 cup frozen black-eyed peas
1/2 cup long-grain rice, uncooked
3/4 cup chopped tomato
2 teaspoons lemon juice
2 tablespoons chopped fresh parsley
1/2 teaspoon salt
1/4 teaspoon ground red pepper
1/4 teaspoon freshly ground black pepper
Grilled Pork Medaillons
1 Red Delicious apple, cut into 12 wedges
Garnish: fresh thyme sprig

Cook onion and celery in olive oil in a large saucepan over medium heat, stirring constantly, until tender. Add chicken broth and dried thyme; bring mixture to a boil. Add wild rice. Cover, reduce heat, and cook 30 minutes.

Add black-eyed peas and next 7 ingredients; cover and cook 20 minutes or until rice is tender.

Serve with medaillons and apple wedges. Garnish, if desired.

Yield: 4 (1 1/4-cup) servings.

GRILLED PORK MEDAILLONS

1/4 cup lemon juice
2 tablespoons reduced-sodium soy
   sauce
2 cloves garlic, pressed
1 (3/4-pound) pork tenderloin,
   trimmed
   Vegetable cooking spray

Combine first 3 ingredients in a shallow container or a large heavy-duty, zip-top plastic bag. Add tenderloin; cover or seal and chill 8 hours.

Remove tenderloin from marinade, discarding marinade. Coat food rack with cooking spray; place rack on grill, and place tenderloin on rack.

Cook, covered with grill lid, over medium-hot coals (350° to 400°), 12 minutes on each side or until a meat thermometer registers 160°. Cut into 12 slices.

Yield: 4 servings.

Hopping John with Grilled Pork Medaillons

BLACK-EYED PEA JAMBALAYA

1½ cups dried black-eyed peas
3 (15.75-ounce) cans ready-to-serve, reduced-sodium, fat-free chicken broth
2 cups chopped tomato
1½ cups cubed lean cooked ham
1 cup chopped onion
¾ cup chopped green pepper
¼ cup chopped celery
2 cloves garlic, minced
1 bay leaf
½ teaspoon salt
¼ teaspoon dried thyme
⅛ teaspoon ground cloves
1½ cups long-grain rice, uncooked
1½ teaspoons hot sauce
½ cup sliced green onions

Sort and wash peas; place in a 5- or 6-quart pressure cooker. Add next 11 ingredients; stir well.

Close lid securely; according to manufacturer's directions, bring to high pressure over high heat (about 10 to 12 minutes). Reduce heat to medium-low or level needed to maintain high pressure; cook 15 minutes.

Remove from heat; run cold water over pressure cooker to reduce pressure instantly. Remove lid so that steam escapes away from you. Drain, reserving 3 cups liquid. Remove pea mixture from cooker, and keep warm. Discard bay leaf.

Add rice and reserved liquid to cooker. Close lid; bring to high pressure over high heat (about 5 minutes). Reduce heat to medium-low or level needed to maintain high pressure; cook 5 minutes.

Remove from heat; let stand 10 minutes or until pressure drops. Remove lid. Add pea mixture, hot sauce, and green onions; toss.

Yield: 8 servings.

ALMOND RICE

1 (10½-ounce) can chicken broth, undiluted
1¼ cups water
1 cup long-grain rice, uncooked
½ cup slivered almonds
2 tablespoons butter or margarine, melted

Combine broth and water in a heavy saucepan; bring to a boil, and add rice. Cover, reduce heat, and simmer 20 minutes or until liquid is absorbed.

Cook almonds in butter in a skillet until lightly browned; stir into rice.

Yield: 4 to 6 servings.

RICE-VEGETABLE PILAF

1 1/3 cups water
1 teaspoon chicken-flavored
     bouillon granules
1/2 cup long-grain rice, uncooked
1 1/2 cups sliced fresh mushrooms
1 1/2 cups coarsely shredded carrot
1/2 cup chopped fresh parsley
1/3 cup thinly sliced green onions
1/4 cup chopped sweet red pepper
1/4 teaspoon pepper
1/4 cup chopped pecans, toasted

Combine water and bouillon granules in a saucepan; bring to a boil. Add rice; cover, reduce heat, and simmer 20 minutes. Remove from heat; uncover and stir in mushrooms and next 5 ingredients. Cover and let stand 5 minutes.

Cook over low heat 5 minutes or until excess moisture has evaporated. Sprinkle with pecans.

Yield: 8 (1/2 cup) servings.

SOUTHWESTERN RICE

3 (10 1/2-ounce) cans low-sodium
     chicken broth
2 teaspoons ground cumin
1 1/2 cups long-grain rice, uncooked
1/4 teaspoon salt
1/2 cup thinly sliced green onions

Bring chicken broth to a boil in a Dutch oven. Add cumin, rice, and salt; cover, reduce heat, and simmer 20 minutes or until rice is tender and liquid is absorbed. Add green onions; toss gently.

Yield: 8 (1/2-cup) servings.

KEEP PARSLEY FRESH
Extend the life of fresh parsley by placing it in a glass jar with a small amount of water. Cover the jar tightly, and refrigerate, changing the water at least every 5 days.

HANDY SUBSTITUTIONS FOR VEGETABLE PRODUCTS

1 pound fresh mushrooms, sliced	1 (8-ounce) can sliced mushrooms, drained, or 3 ounces dried
1 medium onion, chopped	1 tablespoon instant minced onion or 1 tablespoon onion powder
3 tablespoons chopped sweet red or green pepper	1 tablespoon dried pepper flakes or 2 tablespoons chopped pimiento

BROWNED RICE PILAF

Vegetable cooking spray
- 1/4 cup long-grain rice, uncooked
- 1 small clove garlic, minced
- 1/8 teaspoon dried oregano
- 1/8 teaspoon dried thyme
- 1/8 teaspoon salt
- 3/4 cup water
- 2 tablespoons diced carrot
- 2 tablespoons diced sweet red pepper

Coat a medium saucepan with cooking spray; place over medium-high heat until hot. Add rice and garlic; sauté 3 minutes or until rice is lightly browned, stirring often.

Add oregano, thyme, salt, and water, stirring well. Cover, reduce heat, and simmer 15 minutes. Add carrot and red pepper; toss gently. Cover and cook 5 additional minutes or until liquid is absorbed and rice is tender.

Yield: 2 servings.

VEGETABLE-RICE TOSS
(Shown on page 8)

- 1 teaspoon sesame oil
- 3/4 cup diced onion
- 1/2 cup diced carrot
- 2 cloves garlic, minced
- 2 (10½-ounce) cans low-sodium chicken broth
- 1/4 teaspoon Chinese five-spice powder
- 1/4 teaspoon pepper
- 1/4 teaspoon salt
- 1¼ cups long-grain rice, uncooked
- 1/2 cup frozen English peas, thawed
- 1/2 cup diagonally sliced green onions

Heat oil in a wok or large nonstick skillet until hot. Add onion, carrot, and garlic; sauté until tender.

Add chicken broth and next 3 ingredients; bring to a boil. Stir in rice; return to a boil. Cover, reduce heat, and cook 20 minutes. Add peas and green onions; toss gently.

Yield: 8 (2/3-cup) servings.

HANDY SUBSTITUTIONS FOR SEASONING PRODUCTS

1 tablespoon chopped fresh herbs	1 teaspoon dried herbs or 1/4 teaspoon powdered herbs
1 clove garlic	1/8 teaspoon garlic powder or 1/8 teaspoon minced dried garlic
1 tablespoon chopped chives	1 tablespoon chopped green onion tops
1 tablespoon grated fresh gingerroot or candied ginger	1/8 teaspoon ground ginger

RED CABBAGE AND APPLE SLAW

(Shown on page 8)

- 7 cups finely shredded red cabbage
- 1 1/2 cups diced Golden Delicious apple
- 1/3 cup cider vinegar
- 2 teaspoons olive oil
- 1 teaspoon sugar
- 1 teaspoon Dijon mustard
- 1/4 teaspoon salt
- 1/4 teaspoon pepper
- 1/2 teaspoon caraway seeds (optional)
- 8 red cabbage leaves (optional)

Combine cabbage and apple, and set mixture aside.

Combine vinegar and next 5 ingredients in a jar; add caraway seeds, if desired. Cover tightly, and shake vigorously.

Drizzle over shredded cabbage; toss gently. Cover and chill thoroughly. Serve slaw on red cabbage leaves, if desired.

Yield: 8 (3/4-cup) servings.

HEALTHY SLAW

- 4 cups finely shredded cabbage
- 2 cups finely shredded red cabbage
- 3/4 cup shredded carrot
- 3 tablespoons sliced green onions
- 1/4 cup low-fat mayonnaise
- 1/4 cup plain low-fat yogurt
- 2 tablespoons white vinegar
- 1 teaspoon sugar
- 1/2 teaspoon pepper

Combine first 4 ingredients in a bowl; set aside.

Combine mayonnaise and next 4 ingredients; add to cabbage mixture, tossing well. Cover and chill.

Yield: 6 (1-cup) servings.

ORIENTAL FLAVOR ACCENTS

• Chinese five-spice powder is a blend of equal parts of cinnamon, cloves, fennel seed, star anise, and Szechwan peppercorns. It has a pungent, slightly sweet licorice flavor.

• Sesame oil, a golden-brown seasoning oil pressed from toasted sesame seeds, adds an aromatic, nutty flavor. Two types are available — the darker version has a much stronger flavor.

FRESH CORN PUDDING

(Shown on page 8)

- 2 cups corn cut from cob (about 4 medium ears)
- 1 tablespoon minced green pepper
- 1¹/₂ tablespoons all-purpose flour
- 2 teaspoons sugar
- ¹/₄ teaspoon salt
- ¹/₄ teaspoon ground mace
  Dash of ground red pepper
- ¹/₂ cup egg substitute
- 1 cup evaporated fat-free milk
  Vegetable cooking spray

Combine first 7 ingredients, stirring well. Combine egg substitute and evaporated milk; add to corn mixture.

Spoon mixture into a 1-quart baking dish coated with cooking spray. Place dish in a large shallow pan; add water to pan to a depth of 1 inch.

Bake at 350° for 1 hour or until a knife inserted in center comes out clean.

Yield: 6 (¹/₂-cup) servings.

GREEN BEAN SLAW

- ¹/₂ pound fresh green beans
- ¹/₄ small onion, cut into thin strips (about ¹/₄ cup)
- ¹/₂ cup thin sweet red pepper strips
- 1 medium cucumber, peeled, seeded, and cut into thin strips
- 2¹/₂ tablespoons tarragon vinegar or other herb vinegar
- 2 tablespoons nonfat process cream cheese
- 1 tablespoon skim milk
- 1 teaspoon sugar
- ¹/₄ teaspoon salt
- ¹/₄ teaspoon pepper

Wash beans; remove ends. Cook in boiling water 8 minutes or until crisp-tender; drain. Plunge into ice water to stop cooking process; drain.

Combine beans, onion, sweet red pepper, and cucumber; toss gently, and set aside.

Combine vinegar and next 5 ingredients, stirring until smooth. Pour dressing over bean mixture; toss gently. Cover and chill thoroughly before serving.

Yield: 4 (1-cup) servings.

STUFFED VIDALIA ONIONS

4   medium Vidalia onions (about 1 1/2 pounds)
2   tablespoons oil-free Italian dressing
1/2 cup diced sweet red pepper
1   cup diced zucchini
1/2 cup soft breadcrumbs
1/2 cup (2 ounces) shredded part-skim mozzarella cheese
2   tablespoons minced fresh parsley
1/4 teaspoon dried oregano
    Dash of hot sauce
    Vegetable cooking spray
    Garnishes: paprika, fresh parsley sprigs

Peel onions, and cut a slice from top and bottom; chop slices, and set aside.

Cook onions in boiling water 15 to 20 minutes or until tender but not mushy. Cool. Remove center of onions, leaving shells intact; reserve onion centers for another use. Set onion shells aside.

Heat Italian dressing in a medium skillet until hot; add chopped onion, red pepper, and zucchini, and cook until tender, stirring constantly. Remove from heat; stir in breadcrumbs and next 4 ingredients.

Fill each onion shell with 1/2 cup vegetable mixture; place filled shells in an 8-inch square baking dish coated with cooking spray.

Cover and bake at 350° for 20 minutes. Uncover and bake 5 additional minutes. Garnish, if desired.

Yield: 4 servings.

FREEZING TIME

These vegetables can be frozen two months to one year if kept at zero degrees or colder:

Asparagus
Green beans
Lima beans
Broccoli
Carrots
Whole kernel corn
Chopped onion
English peas
Snow pea pods
Chopped pepper
Spinach

APPLE-CARROT SLAW

4 cups shredded cabbage
2 cups shredded carrot
1³/₄ cups unpeeled, chopped Red
    Delicious apple
²/₃ cup fat-free mayonnaise
2 tablespoons sugar
¹/₃ cup white vinegar
1 teaspoon celery seeds
8 cabbage leaves (optional)

Combine first 3 ingredients in a large bowl. Combine mayonnaise and next 3 ingredients; pour over cabbage mixture, tossing gently to coat. Cover and chill. Serve on cabbage leaves, if desired.

Yield: 8 (1-cup) servings.

BEAN AND CORNBREAD CASSEROLE

Vegetable cooking spray
1 cup chopped onion
¹/₂ cup chopped green pepper
2 cloves garlic, minced
1 (16-ounce) can kidney beans,
    drained
1 (16-ounce) can pinto beans,
    drained
1 (16-ounce) can no-salt-added
    tomatoes, undrained and
    chopped
1 (8-ounce) can no-salt-added
    tomato sauce
1 teaspoon chili powder
¹/₂ teaspoon pepper
¹/₂ teaspoon prepared mustard
¹/₈ teaspoon hot sauce
1 cup yellow cornmeal
1 cup all-purpose flour
2¹/₂ teaspoons baking powder
¹/₂ teaspoon salt
1 tablespoon sugar
1¹/₄ cups skim milk
¹/₂ cup frozen egg substitute,
    thawed
3 tablespoons vegetable oil
1 (8¹/₂-ounce) can no-salt-added,
    cream-style corn
Garnish: green pepper strips

Coat a large nonstick skillet with cooking spray; place over medium-high heat until hot. Add onion, chopped green pepper, and garlic; cook, stirring constantly, until vegetables are tender.

Stir in kidney beans and next 7 ingredients. Cover and cook 5 minutes; spoon into a 13 x 9 x 2-inch baking dish coated with cooking spray. Set aside.

Combine cornmeal and next 4 ingredients in a medium bowl.

Combine milk and next 3 ingredients; add to dry mixture, stirring until dry ingredients are moistened. Spoon evenly over bean mixture to within 1 inch of edges of dish.

Bake at 375° for 30 to 35 minutes or until cornbread is done. Cut into 8 squares. Garnish, if desired.

Yield: 8 servings.

Bean and Cornbread Casserole with Apple-Carrot Slaw

PRETTY PEPPER KABOBS

- 12 (6-inch) wooden skewers
- 1 large onion, cut into wedges
- 1 large sweet yellow pepper, cubed
- 1 large sweet red pepper, cubed
- 1 large green pepper, cubed
  Olive oil-flavored cooking spray

Soak wooden skewers in water at least 30 minutes.

Alternate vegetables on skewers; spray each kabob with cooking spray.

Cook, covered with grill lid, over medium-hot coals (350° to 400°) 8 to 10 minutes or until done, turning frequently.

Yield: 8 servings.

FREEZING ROASTED PEPPERS

Whenever you are roasting sweet red or yellow peppers, make extra to freeze and use later to add flavor to soups, pastas, pizzas, and salads. To freeze, cut roasted peppers into strips, and place in a single layer on a baking sheet sprayed with cooking spray. Freeze; remove from baking sheet, and place in a heavy-duty, zip-top plastic bag. Return to the freezer, and use as needed.

SUMMER VEGETABLES

- Vegetable cooking spray
- 4 cloves garlic, minced
- 2 cups sliced zucchini
- 2 cups sliced yellow squash
- 1 cup chopped tomato
- 1/2 cup julienne-sliced green pepper
- 1/2 cup ready-to-serve, no-salt-added chicken broth
- 1 tablespoon chopped fresh basil or 1 teaspoon dried basil

Coat a large nonstick skillet with cooking spray; place over medium-high heat until hot. Add garlic, and cook 1 minute.

Add zucchini and next 4 ingredients. Cook 3 minutes or until vegetables are crisp-tender, stirring constantly. Stir in basil.

Yield: 4 (3/4- cup) servings.

BROTH OPTIONS

• Give canned broth a flavor boost by simmering it with aromatic vegetables for 30 minutes.

• To defat commercial beef or chicken broth, place the unopened can in the refrigerator at least 1 hour before using. Open the can, and skim off the layer of solidified fat.

LIGHT SCALLOPED POTATOES

Vegetable cooking spray
2 cloves garlic, minced
1/3 cup diced onion
1 1/2 tablespoons all-purpose flour
1 (12-ounce) can evaporated skimmed milk
1 1/2 cups skim milk
1 teaspoon salt
1/2 teaspoon dried crushed red pepper
1/4 teaspoon freshly ground black pepper
9 cups thinly sliced unpeeled red potato (about 4 pounds)
3/4 cup (3 ounces) shredded Gruyére cheese
1/3 cup freshly grated Parmesan cheese

Coat a Dutch oven with cooking spray; place over medium-high heat until hot. Add garlic and onion; sauté until tender.

Add flour; cook 1 minute, stirring constantly. Add evaporated milk and next 4 ingredients; cook over medium heat, stirring constantly, until mixture boils. Add potato, and return to a boil, stirring occasionally.

Layer half each of potato, Gruyére cheese, and Parmesan cheese in a 13 x 9 x 2-inch baking dish coated with cooking spray. Repeat layers.

Bake at 350° for 45 minutes or until bubbly and golden. Let stand 30 minutes before serving.

Yield: 16 (1/2-cup) servings.

ROASTED NEW POTATOES

24 small new potatoes (about 2 2/3 pounds)
Olive oil-flavored vegetable cooking spray
1/4 cup Italian-seasoned breadcrumbs
1/4 cup freshly grated Parmesan cheese
3/4 teaspoon paprika

Cook unpeeled potatoes in boiling water 15 minutes; drain and cool slightly. Quarter potatoes; coat cut sides with cooking spray.

Combine breadcrumbs, cheese, and paprika; dredge cut sides of potatoes in breadcrumb mixture.

Arrange in a single layer on a baking sheet coated with cooking spray. Bake at 450° for 15 minutes.

Yield: 8 servings.

SIMMERING SUCCESS
An enameled cast-iron Dutch oven allows steady simmering with little risk of scorching. Heavy stainless steel and aluminum pots are also good choices.

ASPARAGUS SALAD

1 pound fresh asparagus spears
1/4 cup lemon juice
2 tablespoons honey
2 teaspoons vegetable oil
8 lettuce leaves

Snap off tough ends of asparagus. Remove scales from stalks, if desired. Arrange asparagus in a steamer basket; place over boiling water. Cover and steam 6 minutes or until crisp-tender.

Plunge asparagus into ice water to stop the cooking process; drain and chill.

Combine lemon juice, honey, and oil in a jar; cover tightly, and shake vigorously. Chill.

Arrange lettuce leaves on individual plates; top with asparagus, and drizzle with dressing.

Yield: 4 servings.

BEFORE YOU SQUEEZE

• One medium lemon yields 2 to 3 tablespoons juice and 2 to 3 teaspoons grated rind. Four tablespoons juice is the equivalent of 1/4 cup liquid.
• To remove the most lemon juice from an unpeeled fruit, use one of these methods: roll lemon firmly on a countertop; microwave at HIGH 20 seconds; or submerge in hot water 15 minutes.

ROSEMARY ROASTED POTATOES

3 large baking potatoes, unpeeled
  Olive oil-flavored cooking spray
1/4 teaspoon salt
1 1/2 teaspoons fresh or dried rosemary
1/2 teaspoon freshly ground pepper
  Garnish: fresh rosemary sprigs

Wash potatoes, and pat dry; cut into 1/4-inch slices. Arrange slices into 4 rows on a baking sheet coated with cooking spray, overlapping half of each slice with the next. Sprinkle with salt.

Combine rosemary and pepper; sprinkle potato slices with half of mixture. Set remaining mixture aside.

Bake at 375° for 20 minutes; turn potato slices over. Coat potato slices with cooking spray, and sprinkle with remaining rosemary mixture. Bake 20 additional minutes. Garnish, if desired.

Yield: 4 servings.

OVEN FRENCH FRIES

$1/2$ cup grated Parmesan cheese
2 teaspoons dried oregano
2 (8-ounce) baking potatoes, unpeeled
1 egg white, beaten
Vegetable cooking spray

Combine Parmesan cheese and oregano, and set aside.

Cut each potato lengthwise into 8 wedges; dip wedges into egg white, and dredge in Parmesan cheese mixture.

Place fries on a baking sheet coated with cooking spray. Bake at 425° for 25 minutes.

Yield: 4 (4-wedge) servings.

SOFTENING CREAM CHEESE

To soften cream cheese, remove wrapper and place cream cheese on a microwave-safe plate. Microwave 1 to $1^1/2$ minutes at MEDIUM (50% power) for one 8-ounce package or 30 to 45 seconds for one 3-ounce package.

TWICE-BAKED POTATO

1 (12-ounce) baking potato
3 tablespoons light process cream cheese
3 tablespoons plain nonfat yogurt
2 teaspoons chopped fresh chives or $3/4$ teaspoon freeze-dried chives
$1/4$ teaspoon pepper
$1/8$ teaspoon salt
$1/8$ teaspoon paprika

Wash potato; prick several times with a fork. Place potato on a paper towel in microwave oven. Microwave at HIGH 4 to 6 minutes. Let potato stand 5 minutes.

Cut potato in half lengthwise; carefully scoop out pulp, leaving shells intact. Combine potato pulp, cream cheese, and next 4 ingredients.

Stuff shells with potato mixture; sprinkle evenly with paprika. Place on a microwave-safe plate; microwave at HIGH 1 minute or until hot.

Yield: 2 servings.

HONEY-GLAZED CARROTS

4½ cups sliced carrot (about
   2 pounds)
1 tablespoon reduced-calorie
   margarine
1½ tablespoons honey
1 tablespoon lemon juice

Arrange carrot in a steamer basket over boiling water. Cover and steam 4 to 8 minutes.

Melt margarine in a skillet over medium heat; add honey and lemon juice, stirring well. Add warm carrot; toss.

Yield: 4 (1-cup) servings.

MEASURING HONEY
For an accurate measurement, lightly spray measuring cup or spoon with cooking spray before measuring so the liquid will release easily from cup or spoon.

CHOWDER DEFINED
Chowder is a thick, chunky soup rich with seafood, meat, or vegetables. The name chowder comes from the French chaudière, a large kettle fishermen used when making their soups or stews.

POTATO-CORN CHOWDER

¾ cup chopped green pepper
⅓ cup chopped onion
   Vegetable cooking spray
2¾ cups no-salt-added chicken
   broth
1½ cups finely chopped potato
½ teaspoon salt
¼ teaspoon pepper
¼ cup cornstarch
2¼ cups skim milk
2¼ cups frozen whole kernel corn
1 (2-ounce) jar chopped pimiento

Cook green pepper and onion in a saucepan coated with cooking spray over medium heat, stirring constantly, 5 minutes or until tender.

Stir in chicken broth and next 3 ingredients. Bring to a boil; reduce heat, and simmer 5 to 7 minutes or until potato is tender.

Combine cornstarch and milk, stirring until smooth. Gradually add to potato mixture, stirring constantly.

Stir in corn and pimiento. Bring to a boil over medium heat, stirring constantly; cook, stirring constantly, 1 minute or until thickened.

Yield: 4 (1½-cup) servings.

HONEY RUTABAGA

- 1/2 cup dry white wine
- 1 tablespoon brown sugar
- 2 tablespoons honey
- 2 teaspoons reduced-calorie margarine
- 4 cups cubed, uncooked rutabaga

Combine all ingredients in a large saucepan. Bring to a boil; cover, reduce heat, and simmer 40 to 45 minutes.

Yield: 5 (3/4-cup) servings.

ORANGY CARROT STRIPS

- 8 cups thin carrot strips
- 2 teaspoons grated orange rind
- 3/4 cup orange juice
- 2 tablespoons honey
- 1 tablespoon cornstarch
- 1/4 cup water

Combine first 4 ingredients in a Dutch oven. Bring to a boil; cover, reduce heat, and simmer 8 to 10 minutes or until carrot strips are tender.

Combine cornstarch and water; stir into carrot strips, and bring to a boil, stirring constantly. Cook 1 minute, stirring constantly.

Yield: 16 (1/2-cup) servings.

HANDY SUBSTITUTIONS FOR COOKING PRODUCTS

1 cup honey	1 1/4 cups sugar plus 1/4 cup water
1 cup light corn syrup	1 cup sugar plus 1/4 cup water
1 teaspoon baking powder	1/4 teaspoon baking soda plus 1/2 teaspoon cream of tartar
1 tablespoon cornstarch (for thickening)	2 tablespoons all-purpose flour

LEMON BROCCOLI

2 tablespoons grated lemon rind
1/4 teaspoon salt
1/4 teaspoon freshly ground pepper
1 1/2 pounds fresh broccoli
2 tablespoons lemon juice

Combine first 3 ingredients; set aside.

Remove broccoli leaves, and discard tough ends of stalks; cut into spears.

Arrange broccoli in a steamer basket over boiling water. Cover and steam 5 minutes or until crisp-tender.

Arrange broccoli on a serving platter. Sprinkle with lemon rind mixture and lemon juice.

Yield: 6 servings.

PREPARING CITRUS FRUIT ZEST
To remove outer portion of peel (colored part) from lemons, oranges, or other citrus fruits, use a fine grater or fruit zester while fruit is still whole. Be careful not to grate the white portion of inner peel, which is bitter. Zest is also referred to as grated rind in some recipes.

ROSEMARY CARROTS

2 1/4 cups thinly sliced carrots
1/2 cup water
1 tablespoon brown sugar
1 tablespoon chopped chives
1 teaspoon chicken-flavored bouillon granules
1/2 teaspoon fresh rosemary
1/8 teaspoon pepper

Combine carrots and water in a saucepan; bring to a boil. Cover, reduce heat, and simmer 7 minutes or until carrots are crisp-tender. Drain, reserving 2 tablespoons liquid.

Combine reserved liquid, brown sugar, and remaining ingredients in a saucepan.

Bring mixture to a boil over medium heat, stirring constantly; pour over carrots and toss.

Yield: 4 (1/2-cup) servings.

ITALIAN GREEN BEANS

- 1 pound fresh green beans
- 1 medium onion, sliced and separated into rings
- 3 cloves garlic
- 1 teaspoon vegetable oil
- 2 tablespoons water
- 1 teaspoon sugar
- 1 teaspoon dried basil
- 1/4 teaspoon salt
- 2 tablespoons grated Parmesan cheese

Wash green beans; trim ends, and remove strings.

Add water to depth of 1 inch in a large skillet; bring to a boil, and add beans. Cover, reduce heat, and cook 6 to 8 minutes. Drain and immediately place in ice water. Let stand 5 minutes; drain well.

Cook onion and garlic in oil in a large skillet over medium-high heat, stirring constantly, until tender. Add green beans; cook 1 minute, stirring constantly.

Add 2 tablespoons water, sugar, basil, and salt; cook 1 to 2 minutes, stirring constantly. Remove and discard garlic; sprinkle with Parmesan cheese.

Yield: 3 (1-cup) servings.

BLACK-EYED PEAS

- 6 cups fresh black-eyed peas
- 3 (14.25-ounce) cans ready-to-serve, reduced-sodium, fat-free chicken broth
- 2 teaspoons Creole seasoning
- 1 teaspoon olive oil
- 1/4 teaspoon hot sauce

Combine all ingredients in a Dutch oven; bring to a boil. Cover, reduce heat, and simmer 45 minutes or until tender, stirring occasionally. Serve with a slotted spoon.

Yield: 6 (1-cup) servings.

Note: 2 (16-ounce) packages frozen black-eyed peas may be substituted for 6 cups fresh black-eyed peas.

CUT THE FAT: PUMP UP THE FLAVOR

- Cook with bold-flavored ingredients. Some good choices are chiles, citrus, garlic, mustard, onion, spices, and vinegar.
- Romano, Parmesan, and feta cheeses add a lot of flavor with only a little fat.
- Salsas can make a routine meal special. And most salsas are fat-free.

GREEN BEANS WITH CREAMY TARRAGON DRESSING

1½ pounds fresh green beans
1 cup nonfat mayonnaise
⅓ cup chopped fresh parsley
¼ cup chopped onion
¼ cup 1% low-fat cottage cheese
3 tablespoons tarragon vinegar
2 tablespoons fat-free milk
1½ teaspoons lemon juice
½ teaspoon anchovy paste
   Belgian endive, sliced

Wash beans; trim ends, if desired, and remove strings. Arrange beans in a steamer basket, and place over boiling water. Cover and steam 12 minutes or until crisp-tender. Remove beans, and plunge into ice water. Drain; cover and chill.

Position knife blade in food processor bowl; add mayonnaise and next 7 ingredients. Process 1 minute or until smooth, stopping once to scrape down sides. Cover and chill at least 1 hour.

Arrange endive on individual plates; place beans in center of plates, and top each serving with ½ tablespoon dressing.

Yield: 6 servings.

Note: When preparing young, tender green beans, trim the stem end only, leaving the pointed end of beans on to enhance the appearance and fiber content of the salad.

COOKING VEGETABLES
The most nutritious vegetables are those that aren't overcooked. Steaming, stir-frying, sautéing, and grilling are great ways to cook vegetables to bring out their natural flavors. Try adding herbs or spices to further enhance the taste.

GLAZED CARROTS

5 cups thinly sliced carrot
2 tablespoons brown sugar
1 teaspoon dry mustard
¼ teaspoon salt
¼ teaspoon hot sauce
1½ tablespoons reduced-calorie margarine

Cook carrot in a small amount of boiling water 5 to 8 minutes or until crisp-tender; drain.

Combine brown sugar and next 4 ingredients in a small saucepan; cook over medium heat, stirring constantly, until margarine melts. Add to carrot; toss gently.

Yield: 10 (½-cup) servings.

SEASONED GREEN BEANS

2 pounds fresh green beans
¼ cup chopped lean cooked ham
1 beef-flavored bouillon cube
¼ teaspoon freshly ground pepper
1½ cups water

Wash beans, and remove strings; cut beans into 1½-inch pieces. Place in a 5-quart Dutch oven; add ham and remaining ingredients.

Bring to a boil; cover, reduce heat, and simmer 20 minutes, stirring occasionally.

Yield: 10 (½-cup) servings.

Glazed Carrots and Seasoned Green Beans

COLD DILL SOUP

2   cups half-and-half
2   (8-ounce) cartons plain yogurt
2   cucumbers, peeled, seeded, and
      diced
3   tablespoons minced fresh dill or
      1 tablespoon dried dillweed
2   tablespoons lemon juice
1   tablespoon chopped green onions
$1/2$ teaspoon salt
$1/8$ to $1/4$ teaspoon ground white
      pepper
      Garnishes: cucumber slices,
        fresh dill sprigs

Combine first 8 ingredients, stirring well; cover and chill thoroughly. Stir well; garnish, if desired.

Yield: 1 quart.

CREAMY MUSHROOM SOUP

4   ($10^3/4$-ounce) cans cream of
      mushroom soup, undiluted
2   cups half-and-half
2   cups milk
1   (8-ounce) carton sour cream
1   (8-ounce) loaf process cheese
      spread, cubed
$1/8$ teaspoon ground red pepper
1   pound fresh mushrooms, sliced
$1/4$ cup dry white wine
      Garnish: fresh chives

Combine first 6 ingredients in a large Dutch oven; stir well. Cook over low to medium heat, stirring frequently, until cheese melts.

Stir mushrooms into soup; cook over low heat 20 minutes, stirring frequently. Stir wine into soup just before serving. Garnish, if desired.

Yield: about $3^1/2$ quarts.

PASTA MEASURES UP

Uncooked pasta of similar sizes and shapes may be interchanged in recipes if it is measured by weight, not volume. Cooked pasta, however, should be substituted cup for cup. In general, allow 1 to 2 ounces of uncooked pasta or $1/2$ to 1 cup cooked pasta per person.

Fine or Medium Egg Noodles:
4 ounces dry = 2 to 3 cups cooked
8 ounces dry = 4 to 5 cups cooked

Macaroni, Penne, Rotini, or Shells:
4 ounces dry = 2½ cups cooked
8 ounces dry = 4½ cups cooked

Linguine, Spaghetti, or Vermicelli:
4 ounces dry = 2 to 3 cups cooked
8 ounces dry = 4 to 5 cups cooked
16 ounces dry = 8 to 9 cups cooked

PERFECT PASTA EVERY TIME

• Cook pasta in a pasta pot with a removable perforated inner basket, or create one using a large Dutch oven or stockpot with a colander or large wire basket placed inside. The pasta needs plenty of room to bubble in boiling water. To drain, lift the basket, and shake off excess water.

• Use 4 to 6 quarts of water to cook 1 pound of dried pasta. Add pasta gradually to rapidly boiling water so that the water never stops boiling. (A rapid boil means the water is bubbling and moving around swiftly.) After all pasta has been added, stir once, and begin timing.

• Add salt and 1 teaspoon oil to boiling water, if desired. The oil helps keep the pasta from sticking; however, too much oil will cause the sauce to slide off the pasta. If you do not add oil, stir pasta frequently to prevent sticking.

• Cooking times vary with the size, shape, and moisture content of the pasta. Dried pasta cooks in 4 to 15 minutes, while refrigerated pasta requires only 2 to 3 minutes. Follow package directions. Begin checking pasta for doneness 1 minute before its minimum cooking time. Remove a piece of pasta from the water, and cut a bite from it. It is ready when it is al dente ("to the tooth" in Italian) —firm but tender, chewy not soggy.

• If the pasta is to be used in a dish that requires further cooking, slightly undercook the pasta.

• Drain pasta immediately. If pasta is to be reheated or chilled, rinse under cold water to stop the cooking process and to remove excess starch.

• Rinse pasta under running water if it sticks together. For warm pasta dishes, use hot water, and for cold pasta dishes use cold water.

• Save a small amount of the hot cooking liquid to toss with the pasta if it seems too dry.

• Get a head start on a future meal by cooking a little extra. To store cooked pasta, toss lightly with 1 to 2 teaspoons vegetable oil to prevent sticking. Cover and chill up to 4 days, or freeze up to 6 months.

• To reheat cooked pasta, place it in a colander, and run hot water over it. Or drop the pasta in boiling water, let stand for 1 to 2 minutes, and then drain.

LOW-FAT INGREDIENT SUBSTITUTIONS

ITEM	SUBSTITUTION
DAIRY PRODUCTS:	
Cheeses	Cheeses with 5 grams of fat or less per ounce (American, Cheddar, colby, edam, Monterey Jack, mozzarella, Swiss)
Cottage cheese	Nonfat or 1% low-fat cottage cheese
Cream cheese	Nonfat or light cream cheese, Neufchâtel cheese
Ricotta cheese	Nonfat, light, or part-skim ricotta cheese
Ice cream	Nonfat or low-fat frozen yogurt, low-fat frozen dairy dessert, low-fat ice cream, sherbet, sorbet
Milk, whole or 2%	Fat-free milk, 1% low-fat milk, evaporated fat-free milk diluted equally with water
Sour cream	Nonfat sour cream, light sour cream, low-fat or nonfat yogurt
Whipping cream	Chilled evaporated fat-free milk, whipped
FATS AND OILS:	
Butter or Margarine	Reduced-calorie margarine or margarine with liquid polyunsaturated or monounsaturated oil listed as the first ingredient; also, polyunsaturated or monounsaturated oil
Chocolate, unsweetened	3 tablespoons unsweetened cocoa plus 1 tablespoon polyunsaturated oil or margarine
Mayonnaise	Nonfat or reduced-calorie mayonnaise
Oil	Polyunsaturated or monounsaturated oil in reduced amount
Salad dressing	Nonfat or oil-free salad dressing
Shortening	Polyunsaturated or monounsaturated oil in amount reduced by one-third

Hooray For
SALADS

In an age fascinated by both fitness and good food, salad has naturally come into its own. It appears as the main course at lunch or dinner, or as a substantial side dish. Whatever the occasion, salads have never before offered such versatile, fresh choices.

Bow Tie Shrimp Salad, p. 452

CAESAR SALAD WITH TORTELLINI AND ASPARAGUS

(Shown on page 8)

- 4 cups hot water
- 1 (9-ounce) package refrigerated cheese-filled tortellini, uncooked
- 1/2 pound fresh asparagus, cut into 2-inch pieces
- 1/4 cup lemon juice
- 3 tablespoons olive oil
- 2 tablespoons water
- 1 tablespoon Worcestershire sauce
- 1/4 teaspoon freshly ground pepper
- 1 clove garlic, pressed
- 1 head romaine lettuce, torn
- 1/4 cup grated Parmesan cheese

Bring water to a boil in a 4-quart Dutch oven. Add tortellini and asparagus, and cook 4 minutes. Drain; rinse in cold water and drain. Set mixture aside.

Combine lemon juice and next 5 ingredients, stirring with a wire whisk; set aside.

Place lettuce, tortellini, and asparagus in a large bowl; add dressing, tossing gently. Sprinkle with cheese.

Yield: 4 servings.

QUICK SUMMER ITALIAN SALAD

- 15 small fresh mushrooms
- 1 large cucumber, unpeeled and sliced
- 1 large green pepper, cut into strips
- 2 medium tomatoes, cut into wedges
- 1/2 cup chopped green onions
- 1 cup commercial Italian salad dressing
  Lettuce leaves

Clean mushrooms with damp paper towels. Remove stems, and reserve for another use. Combine mushroom caps and next 5 ingredients in a large bowl; toss gently. Cover and chill. Serve on lettuce leaves.

Yield: 6 servings.

MIXED GREEN SALAD

- 3 cups torn romaine lettuce
- 3 cups torn Bibb lettuce
- 3 cups torn red leaf lettuce
- 3 cups torn endive
- 18 cherry tomatoes, halved
- 1 (8-ounce) bottle fat-free Italian dressing

Combine all ingredients, and toss gently.

Yield: 8 (1 1/2-cup) servings.

Warm Chinese Chicken Salad (recipe on page 428)

WARM CHINESE CHICKEN SALAD

(Shown on page 427)

1/4 cup cider vinegar
2 tablespoons walnut oil
2 tablespoons vegetable oil
2 tablespoons chicken broth
1 teaspoon dried tarragon
1/2 teaspoon Dijon mustard
1/2 teaspoon Worcestershire sauce
1/4 teaspoon salt
1/8 teaspoon ground nutmeg
2 cups torn Chinese cabbage
2 cups torn romaine lettuce
2/3 cup chopped walnuts, toasted
3 cups coarsely chopped cooked chicken
1 1/2 cups halved seedless red grapes

Combine first 9 ingredients in a small bowl, stirring well. Toss cabbage and lettuce with half of dressing mixture in a large shallow bowl. Sprinkle walnuts over cabbage mixture.

Combine chicken and 3 tablespoons remaining dressing mixture in a skillet over medium heat. Cook, stirring occasionally, until chicken is thoroughly heated.

Toss hot chicken mixture and grape halves with cabbage mixture. Serve salad warm with remaining dressing.

Yield: 4 servings.

MANDARIN ORANGE-LETTUCE SALAD

1 (16-ounce) package mixed lettuces
1 (11-ounce) can mandarin oranges, chilled and drained
1/3 cup golden raisins
1 (2-ounce) package cashew nuts, toasted (1/3 cup)
1/2 cup commercial Italian or sweet-and-sour salad dressing

Combine first 4 ingredients in a large bowl. Just before serving, pour dressing over salad and toss.

Yield: 4 servings.

QUICK CHEESE AND MUSHROOM SALAD

2 cups torn Bibb lettuce
2 cups torn iceberg lettuce
6 slices bacon, cooked and crumbled
1/4 pound sliced fresh mushrooms
1/3 cup grated Parmesan cheese
3/4 cup (3 ounces) shredded Swiss cheese
Commercial creamy Italian salad dressing

Combine all ingredients, except dressing; toss gently. Serve with dressing.

Yield: 4 servings.

SALAD MANDARIN

1 medium head Bibb or Boston lettuce, torn
1 (11-ounce) can mandarin oranges, chilled and drained
1/2 medium avocado, peeled and thinly sliced
1/2 cup coarsely chopped pecans, toasted
2 green onions, thinly sliced
Freshly ground pepper to taste
1/3 cup commercial Italian dressing

Combine first 6 ingredients in a medium bowl. Add Italian dressing, tossing gently.

Yield: 6 servings.

SPINACH-PECAN SALAD

1 cup sliced fresh mushrooms
1/2 cup commercial Italian salad dressing
1 (10-ounce) package fresh, trimmed spinach, torn into bite-size pieces
1/3 cup golden raisins
1/3 cup coarsely chopped pecans
2 hard-cooked eggs

Toss mushrooms with salad dressing; set aside.

Combine spinach, mushrooms, raisins, and pecans in a bowl; toss gently. Add additional dressing, if necessary. Grate egg over salad before serving.

Yield: 6 servings.

CITRUS SPINACH SALAD

2 tablespoons orange juice
2 tablespoons rice vinegar
2 1/2 teaspoons vegetable oil
1 tablespoon honey
1/4 teaspoon grated orange rind
6 cups torn spinach
2 oranges, peeled, seeded, and sectioned
3/4 medium-size purple onion, sliced and separated into rings

Combine first 5 ingredients in a jar; cover tightly, and shake vigorously. Chill thoroughly. Combine spinach, orange sections, and onion rings in a salad bowl.

Drizzle dressing over spinach mixture; toss gently.

Yield: 6 (1-cup) servings.

TOMATO-ASPARAGUS SALAD

 1 pound fresh asparagus
 8 romaine lettuce leaves
12 cherry tomatoes, halved
1/3 cup commercial Italian salad
    dressing
1/4 cup grated Parmesan cheese

Snap off tough ends of asparagus. Place asparagus in steaming rack over boiling water; cover and steam 4 minutes. Drain and plunge into ice water to cool. Drain asparagus well.

Arrange lettuce leaves on individual plates. Arrange asparagus spears and tomato on top; drizzle with salad dressing, and sprinkle with Parmesan cheese.

Yield: 4 servings.

Note: 1 (16-ounce) can asparagus spears may be substituted for fresh asparagus.

SUNBURST CHICKEN-AND-WALNUT SALAD

1 1/2 cups water
 1 medium onion, halved
 1 stalk celery, halved
 4 black peppercorns
 4 (4-ounce) skinned and boned
    chicken breast halves
 2 tablespoons cider vinegar
2 1/2 teaspoons vegetable oil
 2 teaspoons honey
1/2 teaspoon dry mustard
1/2 teaspoon dried tarragon
1/2 teaspoon grated orange rind
 2 oranges, peeled and sectioned
 8 lettuce leaves
1 1/2 tablespoons chopped walnuts,
    toasted

Combine first 4 ingredients in a large skillet, and bring to a boil. Cover, reduce heat, and simmer 10 minutes. Place chicken in skillet; cover and simmer 10 minutes or until tender.

Remove chicken, and let cool (discard vegetables, and reserve broth for another use). Cut chicken into strips; set aside.

Combine vinegar and next 5 ingredients in a medium bowl, stirring with a wire whisk. Add orange sections; set aside.

Line each salad plate with 2 lettuce leaves. Remove orange sections from dressing, and divide evenly among plates. Place chicken strips in dressing, and toss gently; divide strips evenly among plates. Drizzle remaining dressing evenly over salads; sprinkle evenly with walnuts.

Yield: 4 servings.

Sunburst Chicken-and-Walnut Salad

ITALIAN SALAD

1 (12-ounce) package rotini (corkscrew pasta), uncooked
2 (6-ounce) jars marinated artichoke hearts, undrained
1 1/4 cups pitted ripe olives, sliced
1 cup chopped green pepper
1/4 pound hard salami, cut into 1/4-inch strips
1/2 cup grated Parmesan cheese
1/4 cup chopped onion
1/4 cup chopped fresh parsley
1 (0.7-ounce) package Italian salad dressing mix

Cook pasta according to package directions; drain. Rinse with cold water; drain.

Drain artichokes, reserving 1/4 cup liquid; set aside. Cut artichoke hearts into quarters; set aside.

Combine pasta, artichokes, reserved artichoke liquid, olives, and remaining ingredients in a large bowl; toss gently. Cover and chill.

Yield: 6 servings.

MARINATED CHICKEN-GRAPE SALAD

2/3 cup dry white wine
3 tablespoons lemon juice
4 chicken breast halves, cooked and cut into strips
1 cup mayonnaise
1/4 teaspoon salt
1/8 teaspoon white pepper
Red-leaf lettuce
1 cup halved seedless green grapes
1 cup halved seedless red grapes
1 1/2 cups diagonally-sliced celery
1/2 cup cashews

Combine wine and lemon juice; pour over chicken. Cover and chill 2 hours. Drain, reserving marinade. Strain marinade, reserving 1/3 cup. Combine reserved marinade, mayonnaise, salt, and pepper.

Line 4 plates with lettuce. Arrange chicken, grapes, celery, and cashews over lettuce. Serve with mayonnaise mixture.

Yield: 4 servings.

DILLED CHICKEN SALAD

  8 skinned chicken breast halves
  1 teaspoon salt
  1 cup chopped celery
  3 hard-cooked eggs, chopped
  1 (3-ounce) package cream cheese,
     softened
$1/2$ cup mayonnaise or salad dressing
$1/4$ cup sour cream
$1^{1}/_{2}$ tablespoons chopped fresh
     dillweed
  1 teaspoon dry mustard
$1/4$ teaspoon salt
$1/8$ teaspoon pepper
     Lettuce leaves
     Slices of raw carrot and
     yellow squash

Combine chicken and 1 teaspoon salt in a Dutch oven; add water to cover. Bring to a boil; cover, reduce heat, and simmer 30 minutes or until tender.

Drain chicken, reserving broth for another use. Bone chicken, and cut into bite-size pieces. Combine chicken, celery, and eggs in a large bowl, and set aside.

Combine cream cheese and next 6 ingredients in a medium bowl. Add to chicken mixture, and toss well. Cover and chill thoroughly.

Serve salad on lettuce leaves with sliced carrot and squash.

Yield: 8 servings.

MARINATED SQUASH MEDLEY

$3/4$ cup olive oil
$1/3$ cup tarragon-flavored wine
     vinegar
  2 tablespoons finely chopped
     shallots
  1 clove garlic, minced
$1/2$ teaspoon salt
$1/4$ teaspoon pepper
$1/4$ teaspoon dried thyme
  3 medium-size yellow squash, sliced
  3 medium zucchini, sliced

Combine first 7 ingredients in a jar. Cover tightly, and shake vigorously. Pour dressing over squash; toss gently. Cover and chill 4 hours.

Yield: 8 servings.

ASPIC-TOPPED CHICKEN SALAD

- 1 envelope unflavored gelatin
- 1/2 cup cold water
- 3 cups tomato juice
- 3 cups finely chopped celery, divided
- 2 tablespoons chopped onion
- 1 tablespoon Worcestershire sauce
  Dash of salt
- 1/4 teaspoon white pepper
- 1 envelope unflavored gelatin
- 1/4 cup cold water
- 1 cup mayonnaise
- 1 cup whipping cream, whipped
- 3 cups chopped cooked chicken
  (about 6 breast halves)
  Lettuce leaves

Sprinkle 1 envelope gelatin over 1/2 cup cold water; let stand 1 minute. Combine tomato juice, 1 cup celery, and onion in a saucepan; bring to a boil, and cook 1 minute. Remove from heat; strain, discarding vegetables.

Combine vegetable liquid and gelatin mixture, stirring until gelatin dissolves. Stir in Worcestershire sauce, salt, and pepper. Pour mixture into a lightly oiled 11-cup mold; chill until the consistency of unbeaten egg white.

Sprinkle 1 envelope gelatin over 1/4 cup cold water in a small saucepan; let stand 1 minute. Cook over medium heat until gelatin dissolves. Remove from heat; cool.

Fold mayonnaise and gelatin mixture into whipped cream. Fold in chicken and remaining 2 cups celery; gently spoon over aspic in mold. Chill until firm. Unmold aspic onto a lettuce-lined serving dish.

Yield: 8 servings.

CHUTNEY-CHICKEN SALAD

- 4 1/2 cups chopped cooked chicken
- 3/4 cup mayonnaise
- 1/2 cup chutney
- 1 1/2 teaspoons curry powder
- 1/4 teaspoon salt
- 1 tablespoon lime juice
- 1 1/2 cups sliced almonds, toasted
  Lettuce leaves
  Garnish: apple slices

Combine first 6 ingredients in a large bowl; toss to mix. Cover and let chill thoroughly.

Stir in toasted almonds before serving. Serve salad on lettuce leaves. Garnish, if desired.

Yield: 6 servings.

FRUITED CHICKEN SALAD

- 4 cups chopped cooked chicken
- 2 cups diced celery
- 2 cups halved seedless red or green grapes
- 1 (15$\frac{1}{4}$-ounce) can pineapple tidbits, drained
- 1 (11-ounce) can mandarin oranges, drained
- 1 cup slivered almonds, toasted
- $\frac{1}{2}$ cup mayonnaise
- $\frac{1}{2}$ cup sour cream
- 2 tablespoons lemon juice
- $\frac{1}{4}$ teaspoon salt
- $\frac{1}{4}$ teaspoon white pepper
  Fresh escarole
  Cheese Tart Shells

Combine first 6 ingredients, and toss well. Combine mayonnaise and next 4 ingredients; add to chicken mixture, stirring well. Chill. Arrange escarole around inside edges of 8 Cheese Tart Shells; spoon chicken mixture on top.

Yield: 8 servings.

CHEESE TART SHELLS

- 2 cups all-purpose flour
- $\frac{1}{2}$ teaspoon salt
- $\frac{3}{4}$ cup shortening
- 1 cup (4 ounces) shredded Cheddar cheese
- 4 to 5 tablespoons cold water

Combine flour and salt in a bowl; cut in shortening with a pastry blender until mixture is crumbly. Stir in cheese.

Sprinkle cold water, 1 tablespoon at a time, evenly over surface; stir with a fork until dry ingredients are moistened. Shape into 8 balls; cover and chill.

Roll dough into 8 (6$\frac{1}{2}$-inch) circles on a lightly floured surface. Line 8 (4$\frac{1}{2}$-inch) tart pans with pastry; trim excess pastry.

Bake at 450° for 8 to 10 minutes or until lightly browned.

Yield: 8 tart shells.

CHICKEN SALAD IN PUFF PASTRY

3¹/₂ cups chopped cooked chicken
1¹/₂ cups chopped celery
 ¹/₂ cup mayonnaise
 ¹/₃ cup honey mustard
  3 tablespoons finely chopped onion
  1 teaspoon salt
 ³/₄ teaspoon cracked pepper
 ¹/₂ teaspoon dry mustard
 ³/₄ cup slivered almonds, toasted
    Puff Pastry Ring
    Curly leaf lettuce

Combine chicken and celery in a bowl. Combine mayonnaise and next 5 ingredients; stir well. Add to chicken; toss gently. Stir in almonds.

Split Puff Pastry Ring in half horizontally; remove and discard soft dough inside. Line bottom half of pastry ring with lettuce; top with chicken salad. Replace pastry ring top.

Yield: 12 servings.

PUFF PASTRY RING

1¹/₃ cups water
 ²/₃ cup butter
1¹/₃ cups all-purpose flour
 ¹/₄ teaspoon salt
 ¹/₄ to ¹/₂ teaspoon celery seeds
  6 large eggs

Trace a 9-inch circle on parchment paper. Turn paper over, and place on a greased baking sheet.

Combine water and butter in a medium saucepan; bring to a boil. Combine flour, salt, and celery seeds; stir well. Add to butter mixture, all at once, stirring vigorously over medium-high heat until mixture leaves sides of pan and forms a smooth ball. Remove from heat, and let cool 2 minutes.

Add eggs, one at a time, beating thoroughly with a wooden spoon after each addition; beat until dough is smooth.

Spoon dough into a large pastry bag fitted with a large fluted tip. Working quickly, pipe into 12 rosettes on 9-inch circle on baking sheet. Bake at 400° for 40 to 50 minutes or until puffed and golden. Cool on a wire rack.

Yield: 12 servings.

Chicken Salad in Puff Pastry

TARRAGON PASTA-CHICKEN SALAD

  1 (8-ounce) bottle Italian salad
    dressing
¼ cup white wine vinegar
  2 tablespoons chopped fresh
    tarragon
  1 clove garlic, minced
  4 skinned and boned chicken breast
    halves
  4 ounces shell macaroni, uncooked
  2 cups sliced celery
½ cup chopped sweet red pepper or
    green pepper
¼ cup chopped green onions
  1 tablespoon chopped fresh parsley
½ cup mayonnaise

Combine first 4 ingredients in a jar, and cover tightly. Shake vigorously until well mixed.

Place chicken in a heavy-duty, zip-top plastic bag; pour ¾ cup dressing mixture over chicken, reserving remaining mixture. Seal bag, and chill at least 8 hours.

Transfer chicken and marinade from bag to an 11 x 7 x 1½-inch baking dish. Bake at 350° for 25 to 30 minutes or until done. Drain chicken, and cool slightly; coarsely chop.

Cook pasta according to package directions; drain and cool slightly.

Combine chicken, reserved dressing mixture, pasta, celery, and remaining ingredients in a large bowl; toss gently. Cover and chill thoroughly.

Yield: 4 to 6 servings.

FRUITED PASTA SALAD

1⅓ cups rotini (corkscrew pasta),
    uncooked
  2 cups chopped cooked chicken
1½ cups sliced celery
  1 cup seedless green grapes, halved
¼ cup chopped green pepper
¼ cup chopped purple onion
  1 (11-ounce) can mandarin oranges,
    drained
  1 (8-ounce) can sliced water
    chestnuts, drained
¼ cup commercial buttermilk
    dressing
¼ cup mayonnaise
  1 teaspoon Beau Monde seasoning
¼ teaspoon salt
⅛ teaspoon pepper

Cook pasta according to package directions; drain. Rinse with cold water; drain.

Combine pasta and next 7 ingredients in a large bowl, tossing gently.

Combine buttermilk dressing and next 4 ingredients. Pour over pasta mixture, tossing gently. Cover and chill.

Yield: 4 to 6 servings.

GRILLED CHICKEN-PASTA SALAD

- 4 ounces bow tie pasta, uncooked
- 1/2 cup Italian salad dressing, divided
- 2 skinned and boned chicken breast halves
- 1/2 small cucumber
- 1 cup Marinara Sauce, chilled

Cook pasta according to package directions, omitting salt; drain.

Combine pasta and 2 tablespoons salad dressing in a bowl, and toss gently. Cover pasta mixture, and chill at least 8 hours.

Place chicken in a shallow dish; drizzle with remaining salad dressing, turning to coat. Cover and chill 2 hours.

Cut cucumber half crosswise into 2 equal portions. Peel and chop 1 portion of cucumber; cut remaining portion into thin strips, and set aside. Stir chopped cucumber into Marinara Sauce, and set aside.

Drain chicken breasts; cook, without grill lid, over hot coals (450° to 500°) for 5 to 7 minutes on each side or until chicken is tender.

Arrange pasta on individual salad plates; spoon sauce over pasta, and top with chicken breasts and cucumber strips.

Yield: 2 servings.

MARINARA SAUCE

- 1/2 cup chopped onion
- 2 cloves garlic, crushed
- 1 tablespoon olive oil
- 4 (14 1/2-ounce) cans tomatoes, drained and chopped
- 2 tablespoons lemon juice
- 1 tablespoon dried Italian seasoning
- 2 bay leaves

Cook onion and garlic in olive oil in a Dutch oven over medium-high heat, stirring constantly, until tender. Stir in tomatoes and remaining ingredients.

Bring mixture to a boil; reduce heat to medium, and cook 20 minutes or until most of liquid evaporates, stirring occasionally. Remove and discard bay leaves.

Yield: 5 cups.

COLD PASTA PLATTER

1   (3-pound) broiler-fryer
1/4   cup white wine vinegar
2   teaspoons Dijon mustard
2   teaspoons chopped garlic
1/2   teaspoon salt
1/2   teaspoon freshly ground pepper
2   tablespoons olive oil
2   tablespoons vegetable oil
8   ounces vermicelli, uncooked
1/2   cup mayonnaise
    Leaf lettuce
2   tablespoons chopped fresh
      parsley (optional)
    Pickled beets
    Marinated mushrooms
    Marinated artichoke hearts
    Cherry tomatoes
    Garnish: parsley sprigs

Place chicken in a Dutch oven; add water to cover. Bring to a boil; cover, reduce heat, and simmer 45 minutes or until chicken is tender.

Remove chicken from broth, and cool. Bone chicken, and cut into 1/2-inch pieces; set aside. Reserve broth for other uses, if desired.

Combine vinegar and next 4 ingredients, mixing well. Gradually add olive oil and vegetable oil; whisk until blended. Set dressing aside.

Cook vermicelli according to package directions, omitting salt; drain. Rinse with cold water; drain well.

Combine pasta and dressing, tossing well. Add chicken and mayonnaise, mixing well; cover and chill at least 1 hour.

Spoon mixture into center of a lettuce-lined platter. Sprinkle with chopped parsley, if desired. Arrange beets, mushrooms, artichoke hearts, and tomatoes around pasta. Garnish, if desired.

Yield: about 6 servings.

TOMATO-FETA SALAD

3/4   cup crumbled feta cheese
1/4   cup chopped green onions
3/4   teaspoon vegetable oil
1/2   teaspoon dried oregano
3   medium tomatoes, cut into
      wedges
    Boston lettuce leaves

Combine first 5 ingredients; toss gently. Cover and chill at least 2 hours. Spoon onto Boston lettuce leaves to serve.

Yield: 4 servings.

TOMATO-CUCUMBER SALAD WITH YOGURT-HERB DRESSING

 1 head Boston lettuce
 4 small tomatoes, cut into wedges
 1 medium cucumber, scored and sliced
 1/2 small purple onion, sliced and separated into rings
   Yogurt-Herb Dressing

Line individual plates with lettuce leaves; arrange tomato, cucumber, and onion in pinwheel fashion on plates. Top with 2 tablespoons Yogurt-Herb Dressing.

Yield: 8 servings

YOGURT-HERB DRESSING

 3/4 cup plain nonfat yogurt
 3/4 cup nonfat mayonnaise
 1 teaspoon chopped fresh dillweed
 1 teaspoon chopped fresh chives
 1/8 teaspoon white pepper

Combine all ingredients; cover and chill.

Yield: 1 cup.

GAZPACHO MOLDED SALAD

 2 envelopes unflavored gelatin
 1/4 cup cold water
 1 1/2 cups no-salt-added vegetable juice
 1/4 cup red wine vinegar
 1/4 teaspoon hot sauce
 1 clove garlic, minced
 1/4 cup fat-free mayonnaise
 1 cup finely chopped cucumber
 1/2 cup finely chopped green pepper
 1/2 cup finely chopped onion
   Vegetable cooking spray
 6 lettuce leaves
   Garnish: cucumber slices

Sprinkle gelatin over cold water in a medium saucepan; let stand 1 minute. Add vegetable juice and next 3 ingredients. Cook over medium heat, stirring until gelatin dissolves (about 2 minutes).

Add mayonnaise; whisk until blended. Chill until the consistency of unbeaten egg white.

Fold in cucumber, green pepper, and onion; spoon into six 1/2-cup molds lightly coated with cooking spray.

Cover and chill 8 hours. Unmold onto lettuce leaves; garnish, if desired.

Yield: 6 servings.

THREE-LAYER ASPIC

YOGURT LAYER

 1 envelope unflavored gelatin
 $1/4$ cup water
 1 tablespoon lemon juice
 1 (8-ounce) carton plain low-fat
   yogurt
   Vegetable cooking spray

GREEN PEPPER LAYER

 1 envelope unflavored gelatin
 1 cup water
 1 tablespoon lemon juice
 1 teaspoon reduced-sodium
   Worcestershire sauce
 1 cup diced green pepper

TOMATO LAYER

 1 ($14^{1/2}$-ounce) can stewed
   tomatoes, undrained
 1 (12-ounce) can vegetable
   cocktail juice
 1 tablespoon sugar
 1 teaspoon celery salt
 1 teaspoon reduced-sodium
   Worcestershire sauce
 $1/4$ teaspoon hot sauce
 2 tablespoons lemon juice
 1 bay leaf
 2 envelopes unflavored gelatin
 1 cup thinly sliced celery

   Lettuce leaves
   Garnish: lemon slices

Sprinkle 1 envelope gelatin over $1/4$ cup water in a small saucepan; let stand 1 minute. Cook over medium heat, stirring constantly, until gelatin dissolves; remove from heat.

Stir in 1 tablespoon lemon juice and yogurt. Pour into a 6-cup mold that has been coated with cooking spray; cover and chill until firm.

Sprinkle 1 envelope gelatin over 1 cup water in a small saucepan; let stand 1 minute. Cook over medium heat, stirring constantly, until gelatin dissolves; remove from heat.

Stir in 1 tablespoon lemon juice and 1 teaspoon Worcestershire sauce; chill until the consistency of unbeaten egg white. Stir in green pepper. Spoon over yogurt layer. Cover; chill.

Drain tomatoes, reserving liquid; chop tomatoes. Combine liquid, tomatoes, vegetable juice, and next 6 ingredients in a saucepan. Cook over low heat 30 minutes; remove from heat.

Remove bay leaf. Sprinkle 2 envelopes gelatin over hot mixture; stir until gelatin dissolves.

Chill until the consistency of unbeaten egg white. Stir in celery; spoon over green pepper layer. Cover; chill. Unmold onto lettuce leaves. Garnish, if desired.

Yield: 12 ($1/2$-cup) servings.

FROZEN STRAWBERRY SALAD

1 (8-ounce) package nonfat cream cheese, softened
1/2 cup sugar
1 (8-ounce) container reduced-fat frozen whipped topping, thawed
2 cups frozen no-sugar-added whole strawberries, thawed and halved
1 (15 1/4-ounce) can unsweetened crushed pineapple, undrained
1 1/2 cups sliced banana (2 medium)

Beat cream cheese at medium speed of an electric mixer until creamy; gradually add sugar, beating until smooth.

Fold in whipped topping and remaining ingredients; spoon into a 13 x 9 x 2-inch dish. Cover and freeze until firm.

Yield: 12 servings.

HERBED TOMATOES

1/3 cup vegetable oil
2 tablespoons white wine vinegar
1/4 cup chopped fresh parsley
1/4 cup chopped fresh chives
1/8 teaspoon pepper
   Pinch of dried thyme
3 tomatoes, unpeeled and quartered
   Lettuce

Combine first 6 ingredients in a 2-cup glass measure; mix well. Place tomato in a shallow container; pour dressing over tomato. Cover and chill 8 hours or overnight.

Drain tomato, reserving dressing. Arrange tomato on lettuce leaves; spoon dressing over tomato.

Yield: 6 servings.

MARINATED ARTICHOKE SALAD

1 (6-ounce) jar marinated artichoke hearts, undrained
1 (4-ounce) can sliced mushrooms, drained
1 (4-ounce) can sliced ripe olives, drained
1/2 cup chopped onion
2 stalks celery, sliced
1 medium tomato, cut into wedges
   Lettuce leaves

Combine first 6 ingredients in a large bowl, stirring well. Cover and chill thoroughly. Transfer salad with a slotted spoon into a lettuce-lined bowl.

Yield: 4 servings.

PASTA SALAD

- 4 cups uncooked rotini
- 1 medium zucchini, sliced
- 2 carrots, peeled and sliced
- $1/2$ sweet red pepper, cut into thin strips
- 1 cup broccoli flowerets
- 1 (6-ounce) can sliced ripe olives
- 1 (8-ounce) bottle Italian salad dressing

Cook rotini according to package directions; drain. Rinse pasta with cold water and drain.

Combine pasta and remaining ingredients, tossing well. Serve immediately or, if desired, chill.

Yield: 6 to 8 servings.

BOW TIE PASTA PRIMAVERA

- 8 ounces bow tie pasta, uncooked
- 2 tablespoons olive oil, divided
- 3 green onions, cut into 1-inch pieces
- 2 cloves garlic, minced
- $1/2$ pound fresh asparagus
- 2 cups broccoli flowerets
- 1 (10-ounce) package frozen English peas, thawed and drained
- $1/2$ pound fresh mushrooms, sliced
- 1 small tomato, finely chopped
- 1 small sweet red pepper, seeded and chopped
- 1 cup freshly grated Parmesan cheese
- $1/4$ cup minced fresh parsley
- $1/4$ cup white wine vinegar
- $1/4$ cup olive oil
- $1/2$ teaspoon salt
- $1/2$ teaspoon dried oregano
- $1/2$ teaspoon dried basil
- $1/2$ teaspoon dried thyme
- $1/4$ teaspoon black pepper
- $1/8$ teaspoon ground red pepper

Cook pasta according to package directions; drain. Rinse with cold water; drain. Place pasta in a large serving bowl; toss with 1 tablespoon olive oil.

Cook green onions and garlic in 1 tablespoon hot olive oil in a large skillet over medium-high heat, stirring constantly, until crisp-tender; add to pasta, tossing gently.

Snap off tough ends of asparagus. Remove scales with a vegetable peeler or knife, if desired. Cut asparagus into 1-inch pieces.

Arrange asparagus and broccoli in a vegetable steamer over boiling water; cover and steam 4 minutes or until crisp-tender.

Add asparagus mixture, peas, and remaining ingredients to pasta mixture; toss gently. Cover and chill 3 to 4 hours, tossing occasionally.

Yield: 8 servings.

Bow Tie Pasta Primavera

ASPARAGUS-CARROT-SQUASH TOSS

1/2 pound asparagus, cut into
   1-inch pieces
1/2 pound carrots, cut into very thin
   strips
1 yellow squash, sliced
3 tablespoons butter or margarine,
   melted
3 tablespoons lemon juice
1 tablespoon chopped fresh dill
   or 1 teaspoon dried dillweed
1/4 teaspoon salt

Combine vegetables, and place in a steamer rack over boiling water in a Dutch oven. Steam 8 to 10 minutes or until vegetables are crisp-tender.

Combine butter and remaining ingredients, and toss gently with vegetables. Serve immediately.

Yield: 4 to 6 servings.

MARINATED ASPARAGUS AND HEARTS OF PALM

1 1/2 pounds fresh asparagus
1 (14-ounce) can hearts of palm,
   drained and cut into 1/2-inch
   slices
1/2 cup vegetable oil
1/4 cup cider vinegar
1 clove garlic, crushed
3/4 teaspoon salt
1/2 teaspoon pepper
   Cherry tomatoes

Snap off tough ends of asparagus. Place asparagus in steaming rack over boiling water; cover and steam 4 minutes. Drain and submerge in ice water to cool. Drain asparagus well.

Combine asparagus and hearts of palm in a heavy-duty, zip-top plastic bag. Combine oil and next 4 ingredients in a jar; cover and shake vigorously. Pour over vegetables. Seal bag, and marinate in refrigerator 8 hours; turn bag occasionally. Add tomatoes.

Yield: 6 servings.

CRAB-AND-ASPARAGUS SALAD

18 fresh asparagus spears ($^3/_4$ pound)
$^1/_4$ cup nonfat mayonnaise
1 tablespoon lemon juice
1 teaspoon chopped capers
$^1/_2$ teaspoon prepared mustard
$^1/_2$ teaspoon white wine
    Worcestershire sauce
12 large lettuce leaves
$^3/_4$ pound fresh lump crabmeat,
    drained
$^1/_8$ teaspoon paprika

Snap off tough ends of asparagus. Remove scales from stalks with a vegetable peeler or knife, if desired. Arrange asparagus in a steamer basket over boiling water. Cover and steam 6 minutes or until crisp-tender.

Plunge asparagus into ice water to stop the cooking process; drain and chill.

Combine mayonnaise and next 4 ingredients. Arrange lettuce leaves on individual serving plates; top with equal amounts of asparagus and crabmeat. Serve each salad with 1 tablespoon mayonnaise mixture, and sprinkle with paprika.

Yield: 6 servings.

MARINATED SALAD

1 (15-ounce) can white asparagus
    spears, drained
1 (14-ounce) can artichoke hearts,
    drained and cut in half
1 (14-ounce) can hearts of palm,
    drained and cut into $^1/_2$-inch
    slices
1 (4-ounce) can sliced mushrooms,
    drained
$^1/_4$ cup sliced ripe olives
$^1/_4$ cup sliced pimiento-stuffed olives
12 cherry tomatoes, halved
$^1/_2$ purple onion, sliced and separated
    into rings
1 (8-ounce) bottle Italian salad
    dressing
    Romaine lettuce

Combine all ingredients except romaine lettuce in a bowl, stirring gently. Chill at least 30 minutes. Drain salad, and serve on lettuce.

Yield: 6 servings.

CRABMEAT SALAD

- 1 dozen fresh asparagus spears
- 1/3 cup sour cream
- 1/3 cup mayonnaise or salad dressing
- 2 teaspoons Dijon mustard
- 2 teaspoons white wine vinegar
- 1/2 teaspoon dried tarragon
- 1/4 teaspoon dried basil
- 1 tablespoon chopped green onions
- 1/2 teaspoon prepared horseradish
- 4 cups shredded lettuce
- 1 pound fresh lump crabmeat, drained
- 4 marinated artichoke hearts, halved
- 2 hard-cooked eggs, quartered
  Garnish: pimiento strips

Snap off tough ends of asparagus. Arrange asparagus in a steaming rack, and place over boiling water. Cover and steam 5 minutes or until crisp-tender. Drain. Chill 1 hour.

Combine sour cream and next 7 ingredients in a small bowl. Line each of 4 individual salad plates with 1 cup lettuce.

Divide crabmeat among plates. Divide artichokes, asparagus, and hard-cooked eggs among plates, and arrange around crabmeat. Serve with dressing. Garnish, if desired.

Yield: 4 servings.

CRABMEAT-SHRIMP PASTA SALAD

- 3 cups water
- 1 pound unpeeled medium-size fresh shrimp
- 6 ounces shell macaroni, uncooked
- 1 cup thinly sliced celery
- 1/2 medium-size green pepper, finely chopped
- 1/2 medium-size sweet red pepper, finely chopped
- 1/2 small purple onion, chopped
- 2 green onions, chopped
- 1 tablespoon chopped fresh parsley
- 1/4 cup mayonnaise
- 1/4 cup commercial Italian salad dressing
- 1 tablespoon lemon juice
- 1/2 teaspoon dried oregano, crushed
- 1/4 teaspoon salt
  Dash of pepper
- 8 ounces lump crabmeat, drained

Bring water to a boil; add shrimp, and cook 3 to 5 minutes or just until shrimp turn pink. Drain well; rinse shrimp with cold water. Chill. Peel shrimp, and devein, if desired; set aside.

Cook pasta according to package directions, omitting salt; drain. Rinse with cold water; drain. Stir in celery and next 5 ingredients.

Combine mayonnaise and next 5 ingredients; add to pasta mixture. Stir in crabmeat and shrimp. Cover and chill.

Yield: 7 servings.

RICE-SHRIMP SALAD

- 2 unpeeled, medium tomatoes ($^3/_4$ pound)
- 3 cups water
- 1 pound unpeeled medium-size fresh shrimp
- 2 cups cooked rice (cooked without salt or fat)
- 1 cup unpeeled, chopped apple
- $^3/_4$ cup chopped green pepper
- $^1/_2$ cup sliced celery
- $^1/_4$ cup chopped green onions
- 1 tablespoon chopped fresh parsley
- 3 tablespoons white wine vinegar
- 1 tablespoon olive oil
- $^1/_2$ teaspoon salt
- $^1/_4$ teaspoon pepper
- 2 cloves garlic, minced
- 6 red cabbage leaves (optional)
- 6 lemon wedges (optional)

Cut tomatoes in half. Carefully squeeze each half over a small bowl to remove seeds; pour juice through a wire-mesh strainer into a small bowl, discarding seeds. Reserve 2 tablespoons juice. Chop tomatoes.

Bring water to a boil; add shrimp, and cook 3 to 5 minutes. Drain well, and rinse with cold water. Peel and devein shrimp.

Combine chopped tomato, shrimp, rice, and next 5 ingredients in a large bowl; set aside.

Combine reserved tomato juice, vinegar, and next 4 ingredients; stir with a wire whisk until blended. Pour over shrimp mixture, and toss gently; chill.

Spoon salad over cabbage leaves, and serve with a lemon wedge, if desired.

Yield: 6 ($1^1/_4$-cup) servings.

SPINACH SALAD

- 1 (10-ounce) package fresh, trimmed spinach
- 1 cup strawberries, halved
- 1 cup pecan halves, toasted
  Commercial poppy seed dressing

Tear spinach leaves into bite-size pieces. Combine spinach, strawberries, and pecans; drizzle with poppy seed dressing. Serve immediately.

Yield: 6 servings.

SHRIMP VERMICELLI SALAD

    5 cups water
 1½ pounds unpeeled medium-size
        fresh shrimp
    1 (12-ounce) package vermicelli,
        uncooked
    3 hard-cooked eggs, chopped
 1½ cups chopped green onions
    1 cup chopped dill pickle
  ¼ cup minced fresh parsley
    1 small green pepper, seeded and
        chopped
    1 (2-ounce) jar diced pimiento,
        drained
    1 (10-ounce) package frozen tiny
        English peas, thawed and
        drained
    1 cup mayonnaise
    1 (8-ounce) carton sour cream
  ¼ cup lemon juice
    2 tablespoons prepared mustard
    1 teaspoon celery seeds
    1 teaspoon salt
  ¼ teaspoon pepper
        Leaf lettuce
  ¼ to ½ teaspoon paprika

Bring water to a boil; add shrimp, and cook 3 to 5 minutes or just until shrimp turn pink. Drain well; rinse with cold water. Chill. Peel shrimp, and devein, if desired.

Break vermicelli into 3-inch pieces. Cook according to package directions; drain. Rinse with cold water; drain.

Add shrimp, eggs, and next 6 ingredients to pasta; set aside.

Combine mayonnaise and next 6 ingredients; stir well. Pour over shrimp mixture; toss gently. Cover and chill 2 hours.

Serve on a lettuce-lined platter; sprinkle with paprika.

Yield: 8 servings.

SHRIMP-AND-RICE SALAD

    3 cups water
    1 pound unpeeled medium-size
        fresh shrimp
    2 cups cooked rice (cooked without
        salt or fat)
  ½ cup chopped celery
  ½ cup chopped green pepper
  ¼ cup sliced pimiento-stuffed olives
  ¼ cup chopped onion
    2 tablespoons diced pimiento
    3 tablespoons commercial oil-free
        Italian dressing
    2 tablespoons reduced-calorie
        mayonnaise
    2 tablespoons prepared mustard
    1 tablespoon lemon juice
    1 teaspoon salt-free lemon-pepper
        seasoning
  ⅛ teaspoon pepper
        Lettuce leaves
        Garnishes: fresh parsley sprig,
        cooked shrimp, pimiento-
        stuffed olive

Bring water to a boil; add shrimp, and cook 3 to 5 minutes or until shrimp turn pink. Drain well; rinse with cold water. Chill. Peel and devein shrimp.

Combine shrimp, rice, and next 5 ingredients in a medium bowl. Combine Italian dressing and next 5 ingredients, stirring until well blended. Pour over shrimp mixture, and toss gently to coat.

Cover; chill 3 to 4 hours. Line a serving plate with lettuce leaves. Spoon salad onto plate and garnish, if desired.

Yield: 5 (1-cup) servings.

SHRIMP-PASTA MEDLEY

    5 cups water
 1¹/₂ pounds unpeeled medium-size
         fresh shrimp
    1 cup rotini (corkscrew pasta),
         uncooked
    1 (6-ounce) package frozen snow
         pea pods, thawed
    1 (4-ounce) can button mushrooms,
         drained
 ¹/₃ to ¹/₂ cup grated Parmesan
         cheese

 ¹/₄ cup sliced celery
 ¹/₄ cup sliced pimiento-stuffed olives
 ¹/₄ cup sliced ripe olives
    1 teaspoon chopped parsley
    1 teaspoon white wine
 ¹/₄ teaspoon anise flavoring
    1 (8-ounce) bottle Italian salad
         dressing
         Lettuce leaves
         Parmesan cheese
         Garnish: cherry tomato halves

Bring water to a boil; add shrimp, and cook 3 to 5 minutes or just until shrimp turn pink. Drain well, and rinse with cold water. Chill. Peel shrimp, and devein, if desired.

Cook pasta according to package directions, omitting salt; drain. Rinse with cold water; drain.

Combine pasta, shrimp, snow peas, and next 9 ingredients, tossing well; chill at least 1 hour.

Spoon mixture onto a lettuce-lined platter. Sprinkle with Parmesan cheese. Garnish, if desired.

Yield: 6 servings.

BOW TIE SHRIMP SALAD
(Shown on page 425)

      10 ounces bow tie pasta, uncooked
       2 cups water
     3/4 pound unpeeled medium-size
           fresh shrimp
   1 1/2 cups frozen tiny English peas,
           thawed
       1 (7-ounce) jar dried tomatoes in oil,
           drained and coarsely chopped
       1 small purple onion, finely
           chopped
     1/2 cup finely chopped green pepper
     1/2 cup finely chopped sweet yellow
           pepper
       5 radishes, chopped
       2 tablespoons minced fresh parsley
       1 tablespoon minced fresh basil
       3 tablespoons olive oil
       2 tablespoons lemon juice
       2 tablespoons white wine vinegar
       1 teaspoon Dijon mustard
     1/4 teaspoon salt
           Freshly ground pepper to taste

Cook pasta according to package directions; drain. Rinse with cold water; drain. Set aside.

Bring 2 cups water to a boil; add shrimp, and cook 3 to 5 minutes or just until shrimp turn pink. Drain; rinse with cold water. Chill. Peel shrimp, and devein, if desired.

Combine pasta, shrimp, peas, and next 7 ingredients in a large salad bowl. Toss gently, and set aside.

Combine olive oil and next 5 ingredients in a jar. Cover tightly; shake vigorously. Pour dressing over pasta mixture; toss gently.

Yield: 8 to 10 servings.

MINTED MARINATED FRUIT

       1 (20-ounce) can unsweetened
           pineapple chunks, undrained
   1 1/2 cups unpeeled, chopped red
           apple
   1 1/2 cups unpeeled, chopped green
           apple
       1 cup unpeeled, chopped pear
       1 cup sliced banana
     1/2 cup orange juice
       2 tablespoons chopped fresh mint
       1 tablespoon honey

Drain pineapple chunks, reserving juice. Combine fruit in an 11 x 7 x 1 1/2-inch dish.

Combine reserved pineapple juice, orange juice, and remaining ingredients; pour over fruit. Cover and chill 3 hours, stirring occasionally.

Yield: 7 (1-cup) servings.

TUNA-PASTA SALAD

6 ounces spinach or tricolored corkscrew noodles, uncooked
$1/2$ cup sliced green onions
$1/2$ cup sweet yellow or green pepper strips
$1/2$ cup sliced ripe olives
1 cup halved cherry tomatoes
1 carrot, scraped and shredded
2 ($6^1/2$-ounce) cans chunk light tuna, drained and flaked
$1/2$ cup vegetable oil
3 tablespoons white wine vinegar
2 tablespoons lemon juice
3 tablespoons minced fresh parsley
$1/2$ teaspoon salt
$1/4$ teaspoon pepper
1 green onion, cut into 1-inch pieces
1 large clove garlic, halved
Lettuce leaves

Cook pasta according to package directions; drain. Rinse with cold water; drain. Combine pasta and next 6 ingredients; set aside.

Combine oil and remaining ingredients except lettuce leaves in an electric blender, and process until mixture is smooth.

Pour dressing over salad, and toss gently. Cover and chill at least 8 hours, stirring occasionally. Spoon salad over lettuce leaves, using a slotted spoon.

Yield: 6 to 8 servings.

Tuna-Pasta Salad

453

SMOKED TURKEY PASTA PRIMAVERA

1 (12-ounce) package fettuccine, uncooked
1½ pounds fresh broccoli, cut into flowerets
2 medium zucchini, thinly sliced
6 green onions, thinly sliced
1 sweet red pepper, sliced into thin strips
1 (6-ounce) can pitted ripe olives, drained and sliced
4 cups chopped cooked smoked turkey
⅔ cup grated Parmesan cheese
½ teaspoon salt
½ teaspoon freshly ground pepper
  Basil Sauce
2 cups cherry tomatoes, halved
  Lettuce leaves

Cook fettuccine according to package directions; drain. Rinse with cold water; drain.

Combine fettuccine and next 9 ingredients. Add Basil Sauce and cherry tomatoes; toss gently.

Cover and chill. Serve on lettuce leaves.

Yield: 12 servings.

BASIL SAUCE

⅓ cup chopped fresh basil
1 clove garlic
¼ teaspoon dry mustard
¼ teaspoon salt
¼ teaspoon lemon juice
2 teaspoons white wine vinegar
⅓ cup mayonnaise
⅓ cup sour cream

Combine basil and garlic in container of an electric blender or food processor; process 30 seconds or until basil is finely chopped.

Add mustard and next 3 ingredients; process 20 seconds, stopping once to scrape down sides.

Add mayonnaise and sour cream. Stir well.

Yield: ⅔ cup.

PRIMAVERA SALAD

1 pound broccoli
1 (12-ounce) package bow tie pasta, uncooked
  Versatile Vinaigrette
1 (10-ounce) package fresh spinach
1 pound smoked turkey breast, cut into thin strips
1 pint cherry tomatoes, halved
½ cup chopped fresh basil
¼ cup chopped fresh parsley
⅓ cup pine nuts, toasted

Remove broccoli leaves, and cut off tough

ends of stalks; discard. Wash broccoli thoroughly, and cut into 1-inch pieces.

Cook broccoli in boiling water to cover 1 minute; drain immediately, and plunge into ice water. Drain and pat dry with paper towels; chill.

Cook pasta according to package directions; drain. Rinse with cold water; drain.

Combine pasta and Versatile Vinaigrette, tossing to coat. Place in a large heavy-duty, zip-top plastic bag. Chill at least 2 hours or overnight.

Remove stems from spinach; wash leaves thoroughly, and pat dry.

Combine spinach, broccoli, pasta, turkey, and remaining ingredients, tossing gently.

Yield: 8 to 10 servings.

VERSATILE VINAIGRETTE
- $2/3$ cup vegetable oil
- $1/4$ cup white wine vinegar
- $1/4$ cup water
- $1^1/2$ teaspoons salt
- 1 tablespoon freshly ground pepper
- 1 clove garlic, crushed

Combine all ingredients in a jar. Cover tightly, and shake vigorously.

Yield: 1 cup.

RANCH-STYLE TURKEY 'N' PASTA SALAD

- 2 cups penne (short tubular pasta), uncooked
- 2 cups chopped cooked turkey
- 1 small zucchini, sliced
- 2 small yellow squash, sliced
- 1 small green pepper, seeded and chopped
- 1 small sweet red pepper, seeded and chopped
- $1/4$ cup grated Parmesan cheese
- $3/4$ cup commercial Ranch-style dressing

Cook pasta according to package directions; drain. Rinse with cold water; drain.

Combine pasta and remaining ingredients in a large bowl. Cover and chill at least 2 hours. Toss before serving.

Yield: 6 to 8 servings.

VEGETABLE PASTA SALAD

8 ounces rotini (corkscrew pasta),
    uncooked
1 teaspoon salt
1 medium onion, chopped
1 cup sliced fresh mushrooms
1 clove garlic, minced
2 tablespoons olive oil
1 medium carrot, thinly sliced
1 cup broccoli flowerets
1 medium zucchini, thinly sliced
1 cup frozen English peas
2 tablespoons chopped fresh basil
    or 2 teaspoons dried basil
2 tablespoons chopped fresh
    parsley
1 pint cherry tomatoes, cut in half
    Vinaigrette Dressing
    Lettuce leaves
    Garnish: grated Parmesan cheese

Cook pasta according to package directions, using 1 teaspoon salt; drain. Rinse with cold water; drain. Set aside.

Cook onion, mushrooms, and garlic in 2 tablespoons olive oil in a Dutch oven, stirring constantly, until onion is tender. Add carrot, broccoli, zucchini, and peas; cook 2 minutes.

Add pasta, basil, and parsley to Dutch oven, mixing well. Stir in tomatoes.

Toss pasta mixture with Vinaigrette Dressing, and serve on lettuce leaves. Garnish, if desired.

Yield: 10 to 12 servings.

VINAIGRETTE DRESSING

$1/3$ cup olive oil
$1/4$ cup red wine vinegar
1 tablespoon water
1 teaspoon minced onion
1 clove garlic, minced
$1/4$ teaspoon salt
$1/4$ teaspoon sugar
$1/4$ teaspoon paprika
$1/4$ teaspoon pepper
$1/8$ teaspoon dry mustard

Combine all ingredients in a jar. Cover tightly, and shake vigorously.

Yield: $2/3$ cup.

HAM AND CHEESE SALAD

8 ounces rotini (corkscrew pasta), uncooked
$^{1}/_{2}$ pound cooked ham, cut into 2-inch strips
1 cup broccoli flowerets
1 cup frozen English peas, thawed
1 small yellow squash, thinly sliced
1 small sweet red pepper, cut into thin strips
4 ounces Swiss cheese, cubed
$^{1}/_{2}$ cup mayonnaise
$^{1}/_{4}$ cup Dijon mustard
$^{1}/_{4}$ cup milk
$^{1}/_{4}$ cup grated Parmesan cheese

Cook pasta according to package directions; drain. Rinse with cold water; drain.

Combine pasta and next 6 ingredients in a large bowl.

Combine mayonnaise, mustard, and milk; stir well. Add to vegetable mixture, tossing gently. Sprinkle with Parmesan cheese. Cover and chill at least 2 hours.

Yield: 6 servings.

Ham and Cheese Salad

GARDEN TORTELLINI SALAD

1 (9-ounce) package refrigerated cheese-filled tortellini, uncooked
1 (7-ounce) package refrigerated cheese-filled spinach tortellini, uncooked
3 cups broccoli flowerets
1/2 pound carrots, scraped and sliced
2 small green onions, sliced
1 small sweet red pepper, cut into strips
1/4 cup finely chopped fresh basil
2 tablespoons egg substitute
1 tablespoon lemon juice
1 1/2 teaspoons Dijon mustard
1 1/2 teaspoons balsamic vinegar
1/2 cup vegetable oil
1/4 cup olive oil
1 1/2 teaspoons grated orange rind
1/2 teaspoon dried thyme
1/2 teaspoon salt
1/8 teaspoon ground white pepper

Cook tortellini according to package directions; drain. Rinse with cold water; drain.

Cook broccoli and carrot in a small amount of boiling water 5 minutes or just until crisp-tender; drain well.

Combine tortellini, broccoli, carrot, and next 3 ingredients in a large bowl.

Position knife blade in food processor bowl; add egg substitute and next 3 ingredients. Process 30 seconds. Remove food pusher.

Pour oils slowly through food chute with processor running, blending just until smooth. Add orange rind and next 3 ingredients to dressing; process 30 seconds.

Pour dressing over pasta mixture; toss well. Cover and chill salad at least 2 hours before serving.

Yield: 10 to 12 servings.

CANTALOUPE COOLER SALAD

3 cups cubed cantaloupe
  Lettuce leaves
1/2 small onion, thinly sliced and separated into rings
6 slices bacon, cooked and crumbled
  Commercial poppy seed dressing

Arrange cantaloupe on lettuce leaves. Top with onion and crumbled bacon. Drizzle dressing over salad.

Yield: 4 servings.

CONFETTI ORZO SALAD

1½ cups orzo (rice-shaped pasta), uncooked
1 carrot, scraped and chopped
1¼ cups chopped sweet red, green, or yellow pepper
½ cup peeled, seeded, and chopped cucumber
¼ cup thinly sliced green onions
¼ cup chopped purple onion
¼ cup chopped fresh parsley
2 tablespoons white wine vinegar
½ teaspoon grated lemon rind
3 tablespoons lemon juice
¾ teaspoon salt
⅛ teaspoon coarsely ground pepper
2 cloves garlic, minced
⅓ cup olive oil

Cook orzo according to package directions; drain. Rinse with cold water; drain.

Combine orzo, carrot, and next 5 ingredients; set aside.

Combine vinegar and next 5 ingredients. Gradually add oil, beating with a wire whisk until blended. Pour over orzo mixture, tossing gently. Cover and chill.

Yield: 8 to 10 servings.

TORTELLINI-PESTO SALAD

1 (9-ounce) package refrigerated cheese-filled tortellini, uncooked
1 small sweet red pepper, cut into thin strips
¾ cup broccoli flowerets
⅓ cup carrot slices
⅓ cup sliced pimiento-stuffed olives
½ cup mayonnaise
¼ cup commercial pesto sauce
¼ cup milk
2 tablespoons grated Parmesan cheese
1 tablespoon olive oil
1 teaspoon white wine vinegar
1 clove garlic, minced
Fresh spinach leaves (optional)

Cook tortellini according to package directions; drain. Rinse with cold water; drain.

Combine tortellini and next 4 ingredients in a medium bowl; set aside.

Combine mayonnaise and next 6 ingredients; spoon over tortellini mixture, and toss gently.

Cover and chill until ready to serve. Serve on fresh spinach leaves, if desired.

Yield: 4 to 6 servings.

CRANBERRY ORIENTAL

- 1 (16-ounce) can whole-berry cranberry sauce
- 1 (8-ounce) can crushed pineapple, drained
- 1 teaspoon lemon juice
- 1 (8-ounce) carton sour cream
   Lettuce leaves

Combine first 4 ingredients; stir until blended. Pour mixture into an $8^1/_2$ x $4^1/_2$ x 3-inch loafpan, and freeze until firm. Cut into 1-inch slices. Serve on lettuce leaves.

Yield: 8 servings.

ASIAN PORK SALAD

- $^3/_4$ cup orange juice, divided
- $^1/_4$ cup low-sodium teriyaki sauce, divided
- 1 tablespoon rice vinegar
- 1 tablespoon mirin (sweet rice wine)
- 2 teaspoons hoisin sauce
- 1 teaspoon sesame oil
- 1 garlic clove, minced
- 3 tablespoons brown sugar
- 2 tablespoons bourbon
- $^1/_4$ teaspoon dried crushed red pepper
- 1 (1-pound) pork tenderloin
   Vegetable cooking spray
- 8 cups gourmet salad greens
- $^1/_2$ cup sliced purple onion, separated into rings
- 1 (11-ounce) can mandarin oranges in light syrup, drained
- 1 (8-ounce) can sliced water chestnuts, drained
- 1 large sweet red pepper, sliced into rings
- 2 tablespoons sesame seeds, toasted

Combine $^1/_2$ cup plus 2 tablespoons orange juice, 2 tablespoons teriyaki sauce, vinegar, and next 4 ingredients; stir well. Cover and chill.

Combine 2 tablespoons orange juice, 2 tablespoons teriyaki sauce, brown sugar, bourbon, and dried crushed red pepper in a large zip-top plastic bag. Trim fat from pork; slice pork into 3 x $^1/_2$-inch strips. Add pork to bag. Seal; toss to coat. Marinate in refrigerator 15 minutes.

Heat a large nonstick skillet coated with cooking spray over medium-high heat. Add pork and marinade; cook 8 minutes or until pork is done and liquid almost evaporates. Remove from heat.

Divide greens, onion, oranges, water chestnuts, and red pepper rings evenly among 4 plates. Top each with 1 cup pork mixture; drizzle $^1/_4$ cup orange juice mixture over each salad. Sprinkle evenly with sesame seeds.

Yield: 4 servings.

CHEDDAR-PASTA TOSS

1½ cups tri-colored rotini (corkscrew pasta), uncooked
½ (10-ounce) package frozen English peas
1 cup julienne-sliced cooked ham
1 (8-ounce) package Cheddar cheese, cut into ¾-inch cubes
½ cup chopped celery
½ cup sliced ripe olives
3 green onions, chopped
⅓ cup mayonnaise
2 tablespoons red wine vinegar
1 tablespoon olive oil
¼ teaspoon garlic powder
¼ teaspoon pepper
⅛ teaspoon dried oregano
1 (4-ounce) jar diced pimiento, drained
Lettuce leaves

Cook rotini according to package directions; drain. Rinse with cold water; drain.

Cook peas according to package directions; drain well. Combine pasta, peas, ham, and next 4 ingredients in a large bowl; toss gently.

Combine mayonnaise and next 5 ingredients in a small bowl; stir well. Add to pasta mixture; toss gently to coat.

Cover and chill thoroughly. Stir in pimiento just before serving. Serve on lettuce leaves.

Yield: 6 servings.

Cheddar-Pasta Toss

GARLIC-TARRAGON GREEN SALAD

1 clove garlic, minced
¼ teaspoon salt
⅛ teaspoon freshly ground pepper
  Pinch of dry mustard
1 tablespoon tarragon vinegar
¼ cup vegetable oil
8 cups mixed salad greens

Combine first 4 ingredients in a large bowl; blend with a fork. Add vinegar and oil, mixing well. Add lettuce; toss gently.

Yield: 4 to 6 servings.

VERSATILE PASTA SALAD

4 ounces rotini (corkscrew pasta), uncooked
1 cup sliced fresh mushrooms
1 cup broccoli flowerets
1 cup diced Cheddar cheese
½ cup shredded carrot
½ cup chopped sweet red pepper
¼ teaspoon seasoned salt
¼ teaspoon pepper
⅓ cup vegetable oil
¼ cup white wine vinegar
1 tablespoon Dijon mustard
¼ cup finely chopped green onions
1 tablespoon minced fresh parsley
2 cloves garlic, crushed
½ teaspoon sugar
½ teaspoon dried basil
¼ teaspoon salt
¼ teaspoon dried oregano
¼ teaspoon dried crushed red pepper flakes

Cook rotini according to package directions; drain. Rinse with cold water; drain.

Combine pasta and next 7 ingredients in a large bowl. Set aside.

Combine vegetable oil and next 10 ingredients in a jar. Cover tightly, and shake vigorously. Pour dressing over pasta mixture; toss well.

Chill in a tightly covered container at least 2 hours and up to 3 days.

Yield: 4½ cups.

VARIATIONS:
SUMMER PASTA SALAD
Substitute 1 small zucchini, thinly sliced, 1 small yellow squash, thinly sliced, and 6 to 8 cherry tomatoes, halved, for mushrooms and broccoli.

Yield: about 4½ cups.

PASTA SALAD ROMA
Substitute 1 (14-ounce) can artichoke hearts, drained and quartered, 1 cup cubed salami, 1 cup diced mozzarella cheese, and ½ cup sliced ripe olives for broccoli, carrot, and Cheddar cheese.

Yield: 4 cups.

FRUIT CUP WITH RUM

- 1 (17-ounce) can apricot halves, drained
- 1 (16-ounce) can sliced peaches, drained
- 1 (16-ounce) can sliced pears, drained
- 1 (15$\frac{1}{4}$-ounce) can pineapple chunks, drained
- 1 (11-ounce) can mandarin oranges, drained
- $\frac{1}{2}$ cup rum

Combine fruit in a large bowl; add rum, and toss gently. Cover and chill 8 hours.

Yield: 12 servings.

RAMEN NOODLE SALAD

- 2 cups water
- 1 (3-ounce) package chicken-flavored Ramen noodles
- 1 teaspoon butter
- $\frac{1}{4}$ cup finely chopped celery
- $\frac{1}{4}$ cup shredded carrot
- $\frac{1}{4}$ cup thinly sliced green onions
- 1 tablespoon finely chopped green pepper
- 1 teaspoon lemon juice
- 1 teaspoon soy sauce
- 2 tablespoons mayonnaise

Bring water to a boil. Crumble noodles, and add to water; stir in seasoning packet. Return to a boil, and cook 2 minutes, stirring often. Drain.

Combine noodles and butter, stirring until butter melts. Add celery and remaining ingredients, stirring gently to coat. Cover and chill 3 to 4 hours.

Yield: 2 servings.

COLORFUL PASTA SALAD

- 1 pound tri-colored rotini (corkscrew pasta), uncooked
- 1 green pepper, seeded and chopped
- 1 sweet red pepper, seeded and chopped
- 1 (8-ounce) can sliced water chestnuts, drained
- 1 bunch green onions, chopped
  Cherry tomatoes (optional)
- $\frac{3}{4}$ cup vegetable oil
- $\frac{1}{4}$ cup cider vinegar
- 1$\frac{1}{2}$ teaspoons salt
- 1$\frac{1}{2}$ teaspoons pepper
- 1 clove garlic, crushed

Cook pasta according to package directions, omitting salt; drain. Rinse with cold water; drain.

Combine pasta, peppers, water chestnuts, green onions and, if desired, cherry tomatoes in a bowl.

Combine oil and next 4 ingredients; mix well. Pour over pasta; toss well. Cover and chill 8 hours, stirring occasionally.

Yield: 12 servings.

TOMATO-HERB SALAD

3 small tomatoes, sliced
2 tablespoons vegetable oil
2 tablespoons white wine vinegar
1/2 teaspoon salt
1/4 teaspoon pepper
2 tablespoons chopped fresh chives
  Lettuce leaves

Arrange tomato in a 13 x 9 x 2-inch dish. Combine oil and next 3 ingredients in a jar; cover tightly, and shake vigorously. Pour dressing over tomato. Sprinkle with chives. Cover and chill at least 2 hours. Serve on lettuce leaves.

Yield: 4 servings.

BLACK BEAN-AND-BARLEY SALAD

3/4 cup barley, uncooked
1/4 cup lime juice
2 tablespoons water
1 tablespoon vegetable oil
1 teaspoon sugar
1/2 teaspoon garlic powder
1/4 teaspoon salt
1/4 teaspoon ground black pepper
1/4 teaspoon ground cumin
1/4 teaspoon ground red pepper
1 (15-ounce) can black beans, drained and rinsed
  Leaf lettuce
1 cup chopped tomato
1/4 cup (2 ounces) shredded reduced-fat Cheddar cheese
1/4 cup sliced green onions

Cook barley according to package directions; drain and set aside.

Combine lime juice and next 8 ingredients in a jar. Cover tightly, and shake vigorously.

Pour half of dressing over barley; cover and chill 8 hours, stirring mixture occasionally.

Combine beans and remaining dressing; cover and chill 8 hours, stirring occasionally.

Spoon barley mixture evenly onto lettuce-lined plates. Top evenly with black beans, tomato, cheese, and green onions.

Yield: 4 servings.

CREAMY POTATO SALAD

2 pounds unpeeled red potatoes (about 6 medium)
1/4 cup chopped green onions
1 (2-ounce) jar diced pimiento, drained
1/3 cup nonfat mayonnaise
1/4 cup plain low-fat yogurt
1 1/2 tablespoons prepared mustard
1 tablespoon sugar
1 tablespoon white wine vinegar
1/2 teaspoon salt
1/2 teaspoon celery seeds
1/4 teaspoon pepper
1/8 teaspoon garlic powder

Place potatoes in a medium saucepan; cover with water, and bring to a boil. Cover, reduce heat, and simmer 25 minutes or until tender; drain and let cool.

Peel potatoes, and cut into 1/2-inch cubes. Combine potato, green onions, and pimiento in a large bowl.

Combine mayonnaise and remaining ingredients; stir into potato mixture, and toss gently. Cover and chill.

Yield: 10 (1/2-cup) servings.

MIXED GREENS WITH BLUE CHEESE VINAIGRETTE

1/4 cup vegetable oil
1 1/2 tablespoons white wine vinegar
1 ounce crumbled blue cheese
1/2 teaspoon dried oregano
1/8 teaspoon salt
1/8 teaspoon freshly ground pepper
1 cup torn radicchio
1 cup torn Bibb lettuce

Combine first 6 ingredients in a jar; cover tightly and shake. Chill at least 1 hour.

Place salad greens in a bowl. Toss with dressing just before serving.

Yield: 2 servings.

MARINATED BLACK-EYED PEA SALAD

1 1/2 cups water
1 medium onion, halved
1/2 teaspoon salt
1/2 teaspoon dried crushed red pepper
1/8 teaspoon hickory-flavored liquid smoke
1 (16-ounce) package frozen black-eyed peas
1/2 cup raspberry wine vinegar
1/4 cup water
3 tablespoons chopped fresh parsley
1 clove garlic, minced
1 teaspoon olive oil
1/4 teaspoon salt
1/4 teaspoon freshly ground pepper
1/2 cup chopped sweet red pepper
1/3 cup small purple onion rings
Leaf lettuce
3/4 cup croutons

Combine first 5 ingredients in a saucepan; bring to a boil. Add peas; return to a boil. Cover, reduce heat, and simmer 40 to 45 minutes or until peas are tender. Remove and discard onion; drain. Rinse with cold water; drain. Place in a bowl; set aside.

Combine vinegar and next 7 ingredients. Pour over peas; toss to coat. Cover; chill 8 hours, stirring occasionally. Stir in purple onion. Serve on lettuce-lined plates. Sprinkle with croutons.

Yield: 5 (3/4-cup) servings.

BLACK-EYED PEA SALAD

1 (16-ounce) package dried black-eyed peas
6 cups water
1 (6-ounce) jar marinated artichoke hearts, undrained
2 cups cooked wagon wheel pasta
1 medium-size sweet red pepper, seeded and chopped
1 medium-size green pepper, seeded and chopped
3/4 cup canned garbanzo beans
1/2 cup chopped purple onion
1 (6-ounce) package sliced provolone cheese, cut into strips
1 (3 1/2-ounce) package sliced pepperoni, cut into strips
3 tablespoons chopped fresh parsley
1 (0.7-ounce) envelope Italian salad dressing mix
1/4 cup sugar
1/2 teaspoon pepper
1/2 cup white wine vinegar
1/4 cup vegetable oil

Sort and wash peas; place in a large Dutch oven. Cover with water 2 inches above peas; let soak 8 hours. Drain. Add 6 cups water, and bring to a boil. Cover, reduce heat, and simmer 45 minutes or until peas are tender. Drain and let cool.

Drain artichoke hearts, reserving liquid. Chop artichokes, and set aside.

Combine peas, chopped artichoke, pasta, and next 7 ingredients in a large bowl. Toss gently.

Combine reserved artichoke liquid, salad dressing mix, and next 4 ingredients in a jar; cover tightly, and shake vigorously.

Pour dressing over pea mixture, stirring gently. Cover and chill salad at least 2 hours before serving.

Yield: 12 servings.

Black-Eyed Pea Salad

RED CABBAGE-CITRUS SALAD

2 cups shredded red cabbage
4 large oranges, peeled and sectioned
½ cup coarsely chopped pecans, toasted
¼ cup chopped green onions
Commercial poppy seed dressing or sweet-and-sour salad dressing

Arrange cabbage evenly on individual salad plates; place orange sections in center. Sprinkle with pecans and green onions. Serve with dressing.

Yield: 4 to 6 servings.

APPLE CARROT SLAW

4 cups shredded cabbage
2 cups shredded carrot
1¾ cups unpeeled, chopped Red Delicious apple
⅔ cup fat-free mayonnaise
2 tablespoons sugar
⅓ cup white vinegar
1 teaspoon celery seeds
8 cabbage leaves (optional)

Combine first 3 ingredients in a large bowl. Combine mayonnaise and next 3 ingredients; pour over cabbage mixture, tossing gently to coat. Cover and chill. Serve on cabbage leaves, if desired.

Yield: 8 (1-cup) servings.

CHINESE CABBAGE SLAW

1 tablespoon sugar
⅓ cup cider vinegar
1 tablespoon sesame oil
10 cups shredded Chinese cabbage (about 2 pounds)
1 tablespoon sesame seeds, toasted

Combine first 3 ingredients in a small bowl; pour over cabbage, and toss gently. Cover and chill 8 hours.

Toss gently before serving, and sprinkle with sesame seeds.

Yield: 16 (½-cup) servings.

APPLE-APRICOT SALAD
(Shown on page 8)

 1 envelope unflavored gelatin
 2 cups unsweetened apple juice, divided
 2 teaspoons lemon juice
1 1/2 cups chopped apple
 8 canned apricot halves in extra-light syrup, drained and chopped
   Vegetable cooking spray
   Lettuce leaves
   Garnish: apple wedges

Sprinkle gelatin over 1 cup apple juice in a small saucepan; let stand 1 minute. Cook over medium heat, stirring constantly, until gelatin dissolves; remove from heat.

Add remaining apple juice and lemon juice. Chill until the consistency of unbeaten egg white.

Fold in apple and apricot; spoon into 7 (1/2-cup) molds coated with cooking spray. Cover and chill until firm. Unmold onto lettuce-lined plates. Garnish, if desired.

Yield: 7 (1/2-cup) servings.

RED AND GREEN APPLE SALAD

1/3 cup unsweetened apple juice
 2 tablespoons lemon juice
 2 tablespoons cider vinegar
 1 tablespoon vegetable oil
 1 teaspoon Dijon mustard
1/4 teaspoon pepper
1/8 teaspoon salt
1/8 teaspoon ground cinnamon
 2 small unpeeled red apples, cored and sliced
 1 small unpeeled Granny Smith apple, cored and sliced
 4 cups loosely packed torn leaf lettuce
 4 cups loosely packed torn romaine lettuce
 2 tablespoons sliced almonds, toasted

Combine first 8 ingredients in a jar. Cover tightly, and shake vigorously. Pour into a large serving bowl. Add apples, tossing to coat. Cover and chill up to 4 hours.

Combine apples and lettuce; toss gently, and sprinkle with almonds.

Yield: 8 servings.

CABBAGE-PINEAPPLE SLAW

1 (8-ounce) can unsweetened
    pineapple tidbits, undrained
3 cups finely shredded cabbage
1 1/2 cups unpeeled, chopped Red
    Delicious apple
1/2 cup chopped celery
1/4 cup golden raisins
1/4 cup reduced-calorie mayonnaise
    Lettuce leaves
    Garnishes: apple wedges,
      celery leaves

Drain pineapple, reserving 3 tablespoons juice. Combine pineapple, cabbage, and next 3 ingredients in a large bowl.

Combine reserved pineapple juice and mayonnaise; add to cabbage mixture, tossing gently. Cover and chill. Spoon into a lettuce-lined bowl and garnish, if desired.

Yield: 5 (1-cup) servings.

Cabbage-Pineapple Slaw

Hooray For
DESSERTS

Sweet endings have been dinnertime essentials for generations. From cakes and pies to puddings and frosty favorites, you'll find lots of easy, delicious choices here to delight your family and friends every day.

Pineapple Upside-Down Cake, p. 480

APPLE CAKE WITH BROWN SUGAR GLAZE

- 2 cups sugar
- 1 cup vegetable oil
- 3 large eggs
- 3 cups all-purpose flour
- 1 teaspoon baking soda
- 1/2 teaspoon salt
- 1 teaspoon ground cinnamon
- 3 cups peeled, finely chopped cooking apple
- 1/2 cup chopped pecans
  Brown Sugar Glaze

Beat first 3 ingredients at medium speed of an electric mixer until creamy. Combine flour and next 3 ingredients; add to sugar mixture, beating well. Stir in apple and pecans. Spoon batter into a greased and floured 12-cup Bundt pan. Bake at 350° for 1 hour and 20 minutes or until a wooden pick inserted in center comes out clean. Cool in pan on a wire rack 10 to 15 minutes; remove from pan, and cool completely on wire rack. Drizzle Brown Sugar Glaze over cake.

Yield: one 10-inch cake.

BROWN SUGAR GLAZE

- 1/2 cup firmly packed brown sugar
- 1/4 cup butter or margarine
- 2 tablespoons evaporated milk

Combine all ingredients in a small saucepan; cook over high heat, stirring constantly, 2 minutes or until butter melts. Cool to lukewarm.

Yield: 1/2 cup.

OLD-FASHIONED GINGERBREAD

- 1/2 cup butter or margarine, softened
- 1/2 cup sugar
- 1 large egg
- 1 cup molasses
- 2 1/2 cups all-purpose flour
- 1 1/2 teaspoons baking soda
- 1/2 teaspoon salt
- 1 teaspoon ground cinnamon
- 1 teaspoon ground cloves
- 1 teaspoon ground ginger
- 1 cup hot water
  Sweetened whipped cream

Beat butter at medium speed of an electric mixer until creamy; gradually add sugar, beating well. Add egg and molasses, mixing well.

Combine flour and next 5 ingredients; add to butter mixture alternately with water, beginning and ending with flour mixture. Beat at low speed until blended after each addition.

Pour batter into a lightly greased and floured 9-inch square pan.

Bake at 350° for 35 to 40 minutes or until a wooden pick inserted in center comes out clean. Serve with a dollop of whipped cream.

Yield: 9 servings.

WHIPPING CREAM POUND CAKE

1 cup butter or margarine, softened
3 cups sugar
6 large eggs
3 cups sifted cake flour
1 cup whipping cream
2 teaspoons vanilla extract
  Powdered sugar
  Garnish: fresh strawberries,
    mint sprigs

Beat butter at medium speed of an electric mixer 2 minutes or until creamy. Gradually add 3 cups sugar, beating 5 to 7 minutes. Add eggs, one at a time, beating just until yellow disappears.

Add flour to butter mixture alternately with whipping cream, beginning and ending with flour. Beat at low speed just until blended after each addition. Stir in vanilla. Spoon batter into a greased and floured 10-inch Bundt pan.

Bake at 325° for 1 hour or until a wooden pick inserted in center comes out clean. Cool in pan on a wire rack 10 minutes; remove from pan, and cool completely on wire rack.

Sift powdered sugar over cake. Garnish, if desired.

Yield: one 10-inch cake.

Whipping Cream Pound Cake

LEMON-COCONUT CAKE

    1 cup butter, softened
    2 cups sugar
    3¼ cups sifted cake flour
    2½ teaspoons baking powder
    ½ teaspoon salt
    1 cup milk
    ¾ teaspoon coconut extract
    ½ teaspoon lemon extract
    6 egg whites
    ¾ teaspoon cream of tartar
       Lemon-Coconut Filling
       Fluffy Lemon Frosting
    1½ to 2 cups flaked coconut
       Garnish: lemon rind curls

Beat softened butter at medium speed of an electric mixer until creamy; gradually add sugar, beating well.

Combine flour, baking powder, and salt; add to butter mixture alternately with milk, beginning and ending with flour mixture. Beat mixture at low speed until blended after each addition. Stir in flavorings.

Beat egg whites in a large mixing bowl at high speed until foamy. Add cream of tartar; beat until stiff peaks form. Gently fold one-third of egg whites into batter; fold in remaining egg whites. Pour batter into 3 greased and floured 9-inch round cakepans.

Bake at 350° for 20 to 25 minutes or until a wooden pick inserted in center comes out clean. Cool in pans on wire racks 10 minutes; remove from pans, and cool completely on wire racks.

Spread Lemon-Coconut Filling between layers; spread Fluffy Lemon Frosting on sides and top of cake. Gently press coconut into frosting. Garnish.

Yield: one 3-layer cake.

LEMON-COCONUT FILLING
    1 cup sugar
    3 tablespoons cornstarch
    ⅛ teaspoon salt
    1 tablespoon grated lemon rind
    ⅔ cup lemon juice
    ⅓ cup water
    5 egg yolks, beaten
    ½ cup butter or margarine
    ½ cup flaked coconut

Combine first 3 ingredients in a heavy saucepan; stir well.

Stir in lemon rind, juice, and water. Cook over medium heat, stirring constantly, until mixture thickens and comes to a boil. Boil 1 minute, stirring constantly.

Stir half of hot mixture gradually into egg yolks; add to remaining hot mixture, stirring constantly. Cook 1 minute, stirring constantly.

Remove from heat; add butter and coconut, stirring until butter melts. Cool completely.

Yield: 2½ cups.

FLUFFY LEMON FROSTING
    1 cup sugar
    ⅓ cup water
    2 tablespoons light corn syrup

2 egg whites
1/4 cup sifted powdered sugar
1 teaspoon grated lemon rind
1/2 teaspoon lemon extract

Combine first 3 ingredients in a heavy saucepan. Cook over medium heat, stirring constantly, until clear. Cook, without stirring, until candy thermometer registers 232°. Beat egg whites at high speed of an electric mixer until soft peaks form; continue to beat, adding hot syrup mixture. Add powdered sugar, lemon rind, and lemon extract; continue beating until stiff peaks form and frosting is spreading consistency.

Yield: about 3 cups.

ITALIAN CREAM CAKE

1 cup butter or margarine, softened
2 cups sugar
5 large eggs, separated
2 1/2 cups all-purpose flour
1 teaspoon baking soda
1 cup milk
2/3 cup finely chopped pecans
1 (3 1/2-ounce) can flaked coconut
1 teaspoon vanilla extract
1/2 teaspoon cream of tartar
3 tablespoons light rum
Cream Cheese Frosting

Grease three 9-inch round cakepans, and line with wax paper; grease and flour paper. Set aside.

Beat butter at medium speed of an electric mixer until creamy; add sugar, beating well. Add egg yolks, one at a time, beating until blended after each addition.

Combine flour and baking soda; add to butter mixture alternately with milk, beginning and ending with flour mixture. Beat at low speed after each addition. Stir in chopped pecans, coconut, and vanilla.

Beat egg whites in a large mixing bowl at high speed until foamy. Add cream of tartar; beat until stiff peaks form. Gently fold one-third of egg whites into batter; fold in remaining egg whites. Pour batter into pans.

Bake at 350° for 25 to 30 minutes or until a wooden pick inserted in center comes out clean. Cool in pans on wire racks 10 minutes. Remove from pans; peel off wax paper, and cool completely on wire racks.

Sprinkle each layer with 1 tablespoon light rum. Let stand 10 minutes. Spread frosting between layers and on sides and top of cake.

Yield: one 3-layer cake.

CREAM CHEESE FROSTING

1 (8-ounce) package cream cheese, softened
1/2 cup butter, softened
1 (16-ounce) package powdered sugar, sifted
1 cup chopped pecans
2 teaspoons vanilla extract

Combine cream cheese and butter, beating until smooth. Gradually add powdered sugar, and beat until light and fluffy. Stir in pecans and vanilla.

Yield: 4 cups.

CHOCOLATE-SOUR CREAM POUND CAKE

1 cup butter or margarine, softened
2 cups sugar
1 cup firmly packed brown sugar
6 large eggs
2 1/2 cups all-purpose flour
1/4 teaspoon baking soda
1/2 cup cocoa
1 (8-ounce) carton sour cream
2 teaspoons vanilla extract
Powdered sugar (optional)

Beat butter at medium speed of an electric mixer 2 minutes or until creamy. Gradually add sugars, beating 5 to 7 minutes.

Add eggs, one at a time, beating just until yellow disappears.

Combine flour, baking soda, and cocoa; add to butter mixture alternately with sour cream, beginning and ending with flour mixture. Beat at low speed just until blended after each addition. Stir in vanilla. Spoon batter into a greased, floured 10-inch tube pan.

Bake at 325° for 1 hour and 20 minutes or until a wooden pick inserted in center comes out clean. Cool in pan on a wire rack 10 to 15 minutes; remove from pan, and cool completely on wire rack. Sprinkle with powdered sugar, if desired.

Yield: one 10-inch cake.

PEANUT BUTTER SURPRISE CAKE

10 (6-ounce) peanut butter cup candies
1 cup creamy peanut butter
3/4 cup butter or margarine, softened
1 cup sugar
3/4 cup firmly packed brown sugar
3 large eggs
2 cups all-purpose flour
2 teaspoons baking powder
1/2 teaspoon salt
1 cup milk
Chocolate-Peanut Butter Frosting
1/4 cup chopped roasted peanuts

Freeze peanut butter cup candies. Beat peanut butter and butter at medium speed of an electric mixer until creamy. Add sugars, beating until light and fluffy. Add eggs, one at a time, beating until blended after each addition.

Combine flour, baking powder, and salt; add to butter mixture alternately with milk, beginning and ending with flour mixture. Beat at low speed until blended after each addition. Coarsely chop frozen candies, and fold into batter.

Pour batter into a greased and floured 13 x 9 x 2-inch pan. Bake at 350° for 55 minutes to 1 hour or until a wooden pick inserted in center comes out clean. Cool in pan on a wire rack. (Cake may sink slightly in center.)

Spread Chocolate-Peanut Butter Frosting over top of cake. Sprinkle with peanuts.

Yield: 15 servings.

CHOCOLATE-PEANUT BUTTER FROSTING

    1 (6-ounce) package semisweet
         chocolate morsels
 1¹/₃ cups creamy peanut butter
    ¹/₂ cup butter or margarine, softened
    ¹/₂ cup sifted powdered sugar

Melt chocolate morsels in a small saucepan over low heat; set aside.

Combine peanut butter, butter, and powdered sugar in a mixing bowl; beat at medium speed of an electric mixer until smooth. Add melted chocolate; beat until smooth. Chill 30 minutes or until spreading consistency.

Yield: 2¹/₂ cups.

Peanut Butter Surprise Cake

SPECIAL SPICE CAKE

- 1 cup butter or margarine, softened
- 2 cups firmly packed light brown sugar
- 3 large eggs
- 1 teaspoon baking soda
- 1 cup buttermilk
- 2 cups all-purpose flour
- 2 teaspoons ground cinnamon
- 1 teaspoon vanilla extract
- 1/2 cup golden raisins
- 1/2 cup raisins
- 1 cup chopped pecans
  Chocolate-Coffee Frosting

Beat butter at medium speed of an electric mixer until creamy; gradually add sugar, beating well. Add eggs, one at a time, beating until blended after each addition.

Dissolve soda in buttermilk. Combine flour and cinnamon; add to butter mixture alternately with buttermilk mixture, beginning and ending with flour mixture. Beat at low speed until blended after each addition. Stir in vanilla, raisins, and pecans. Pour batter into 3 greased and floured 9-inch round cakepans.

Bake at 325° for 25 to 27 minutes or until a wooden pick inserted in center comes out clean. Cool in pans on wire racks 10 minutes; remove from pans, and cool completely on wire racks. Spread Chocolate-Coffee Frosting between layers and on sides and top of cake.

Yield: one 3-layer cake.

CHOCOLATE-COFFEE FROSTING

- 1 teaspoon instant coffee granules
- 1/2 cup boiling water
- 7 cups sifted powdered sugar
- 2/3 cup cocoa
- 1/2 cup butter or margarine, softened
- 1 teaspoon vanilla extract

Dissolve coffee granules in boiling water, and set aside. Combine powdered sugar and cocoa; mix well. Set aside.

Beat butter at medium speed of an electric mixer until creamy; add sugar mixture and vanilla. Gradually add coffee mixture, beating at high speed to desired spreading consistency.

Yield: frosting for one 3-layer cake.

ANGEL FOOD CAKE

- 12 egg whites
- 1 1/2 teaspoons cream of tartar
- 1/4 teaspoon salt
- 1 1/2 cups sugar
- 1 cup sifted cake flour
- 1 1/2 teaspoons vanilla extract

Beat egg whites in a large mixing bowl at high speed of an electric mixer until foamy. Add cream of tartar and salt; beat until soft peaks form. Add sugar, 2 tablespoons at a time, beating until stiff peaks form.

Sprinkle flour over egg white mixture, 1/4 cup at a time; fold in carefully. Fold in vanilla. Spoon batter into an ungreased 10-inch tube pan, spreading evenly.

Bake at 375° for 30 to 35 minutes or until cake springs back when lightly touched. Invert pan, and cool 40 minutes. Loosen cake from sides of pan using a narrow metal spatula; remove from pan.

Yield: one 10-inch cake.

OLD-FASHIONED CARROT CAKE

    3 cups shredded carrot
    2 cups all-purpose flour
    1 teaspoon baking soda
    1 teaspoon baking powder
  1/2 teaspoon salt
    2 cups sugar
    1 teaspoon ground cinnamon
    4 large eggs, beaten
  3/4 cup vegetable oil
    1 teaspoon vanilla extract
       Cream Cheese Frosting
       Garnish: chopped pecans

Grease three 9-inch round cakepans; line with wax paper. Grease and flour paper. Set aside.

Combine first 7 ingredients in a large bowl; add eggs, oil, and vanilla, stirring until blended. Pour into prepared pans.

Bake at 350° for 25 minutes or until a wooden pick inserted in center comes out clean. Cool in pans on wire racks 10 minutes; remove from pans, and cool completely on wire racks.

Spread Cream Cheese Frosting between layers and on sides and top of cake. Garnish, if desired, and chill. Freeze up to 3 months, if desired.

Yield: one 3-layer cake.

CREAM CHEESE FROSTING

    1 (8-ounce) package cream cheese, softened
  1/2 cup butter or margarine, softened
    1 (16-ounce) package powdered sugar, sifted
    1 teaspoon vanilla extract

Beat cream cheese and butter at medium speed of an electric mixer until creamy. Gradually add powdered sugar, beating until light and fluffy. Stir in vanilla.

Yield: about 3 cups.

PINEAPPLE UPSIDE-DOWN CAKE

(Shown on page 471)

- 1/2 cup butter or margarine
- 1 cup firmly packed brown sugar
- 3 (8 1/4-ounce) cans pineapple slices, undrained
- 10 pecan halves
- 11 maraschino cherries, halved
- 2 large eggs, separated
- 1 egg yolk
- 1 cup sugar
- 1 cup all-purpose flour
- 1 teaspoon baking powder
- 1/2 teaspoon ground cinnamon
- 1/4 teaspoon salt
- 1 teaspoon vanilla extract
- 1/4 teaspoon cream of tartar

Melt butter in a 10-inch cast-iron skillet over low heat. Sprinkle brown sugar in skillet. Remove from heat.

Drain pineapple, reserving 1/4 cup juice. Cut pineapple slices in half, reserving 1 whole slice.

Place whole pineapple slice in center of skillet. Arrange 10 pineapple pieces in a spoke fashion around whole slice in center of skillet.

Place a pecan half and a cherry half between each piece of pineapple. Place a cherry half in center of whole pineapple slice. Arrange remaining pineapple pieces, cut side up, around sides of skillet. Place a cherry half in center of each piece of pineapple around sides of skillet.

Beat 3 egg yolks at medium speed of an electric mixer until thick and pale; gradually add 1 cup sugar, beating well.

Combine flour and next 3 ingredients; stir well. Add to yolk mixture alternately with reserved pineapple juice. Stir in vanilla.

Beat egg whites and cream of tartar at high speed until stiff peaks form; fold into batter. Spoon batter evenly over pineapple in skillet.

Bake at 350° for 45 to 50 minutes or until set. Invert onto a serving plate immediately. Cut into wedges to serve.

Yield: one 10-inch cake.

HUMMINGBIRD CAKE

- 3 cups all-purpose flour
- 1 teaspoon baking soda
- 1/2 teaspoon salt
- 2 cups sugar
- 1 teaspoon ground cinnamon
- 3 large eggs, lightly beaten
- 3/4 cup vegetable oil
- 1 1/2 teaspoons vanilla extract
- 1 (8-ounce) can crushed pineapple, undrained
- 1 cup chopped pecans
- 1 3/4 cups mashed banana
  Cream Cheese Frosting
    (recipe on page 479)
  Garnish: fresh rose petals

Combine first 5 ingredients in a large bowl; add eggs and oil, stirring until dry ingredients are moistened. (Do not beat.)

Stir in vanilla and next 3 ingredients. Pour batter into 3 greased and floured 9-inch round cakepans.

Bake at 350° for 23 to 28 minutes or until a wooden pick inserted in center comes out clean. Cool in pans on wire racks 10 minutes; remove from pans, and cool completely on wire racks.

Spread Cream Cheese Frosting between layers and on sides and top of cake. Store in refrigerator up to 3 days, or freeze up to 3 months. Garnish, if desired.

Yield: one 3-layer cake.

QUICK CHOCOLATE-COLA CAKE

- 1 (18.25-ounce) package devil's food cake mix without pudding
- 1 (3.9-ounce) package chocolate instant pudding mix
- 4 large eggs
- $1/2$ cup vegetable oil
- 1 (10-ounce) bottle cola-flavored carbonated beverage ($1^1/4$ cups)
  Chocolate-Cola Frosting

Combine first 4 ingredients in a large mixing bowl; beat at low speed of an electric mixer until blended, and set aside.

Bring cola to a boil in a small saucepan over medium heat. With mixer on low speed, gradually pour hot cola into cake batter. Increase speed to medium; beat 2 minutes.

Pour batter into a greased and floured 13 x 9 x 2-inch pan. Bake at 350° for 30 minutes or until a wooden pick inserted in center comes out clean. Cool in pan on a wire rack 10 minutes.

Spread Chocolate-Cola Frosting over top of warm cake; cool cake completely on wire rack.

Yield: 15 servings.

CHOCOLATE-COLA FROSTING

- $1/2$ cup butter or margarine
- $1/4$ cup plus 2 tablespoons cola-flavored carbonated beverage
- 3 tablespoons cocoa
- 1 (16-ounce) package powdered sugar, sifted
- 1 teaspoon vanilla extract
- 1 cup chopped pecans

Combine first 3 ingredients in a large saucepan; cook over medium heat, stirring constantly, until butter melts. (Do not boil.)

Remove from heat; add powdered sugar and vanilla, stirring until smooth. Stir in pecans.

Yield: about $2^1/4$ cups.

CREAMY CHOCOLATE CAKE

- 1 (4-ounce) package sweet baking chocolate
- 1/2 cup boiling water
- 1 cup butter or margarine, softened
- 2 cups sugar
- 4 large eggs
- 1 teaspoon baking soda
- 1 cup buttermilk
- 3 3/4 cups sifted cake flour
- 1/2 teaspoon salt
- 2 teaspoons vanilla extract
  Buttercream Filling
  Creamy Frosting
- 1 cup finely chopped pecans
  Garnish: pecan halves

Grease three 9-inch round cakepans, and line with wax paper; grease and flour paper. Set aside.

Combine chocolate and boiling water; stir until chocolate melts. Set aside.

Beat butter at medium speed of an electric mixer until creamy. Add sugar; beat 5 minutes. Add eggs, one at a time, beating after each addition.

Dissolve soda in buttermilk. Combine flour and salt; add to butter mixture alternately with buttermilk mixture, beginning and ending with flour mixture. Beat at low speed until blended after each addition. Stir in chocolate and vanilla. Pour batter into prepared pans.

Bake at 350° for 30 minutes or until a wooden pick inserted in center comes out clean. Remove from pans. Remove wax paper; cool on wire racks.

Spread filling between layers; spread frosting on sides and top of cake. Decorate top of cake, using a cake comb, if desired. Press chopped pecans into frosting on sides of cake. Garnish, if desired.

Yield: one 3-layer cake.

BUTTERCREAM FILLING

- 1/3 cup unsalted butter, softened
- 2 1/4 cups sifted powdered sugar
- 2 to 3 tablespoons half-and-half

Beat butter at medium speed of an electric mixer until creamy; gradually add sugar, beating well. Add half-and-half, 1 tablespoon at a time, beating until spreading consistency.

Yield: 1 1/3 cups.

CREAMY FROSTING

- 3/4 cup sugar
- 1/3 cup water
- 3 egg yolks
- 1 cup unsalted butter, softened
- 2 (1-ounce) squares unsweetened chocolate, melted and cooled
- 2 (1-ounce) squares semisweet chocolate, melted and cooled
- 1 teaspoon chocolate extract

Combine sugar and water in a medium saucepan. Bring to a boil; cook over medium heat, without stirring, until mixture reaches soft ball stage (240°).

Beat egg yolks at high speed of an electric mixer until thick and pale; continue beating, adding 240° syrup in a heavy stream. Beat until mixture thickens and cools.

Add butter, 3 tablespoons at a time, beating until smooth. Stir in melted chocolate and extract. Chill to spreadable consistency.

Yield: 2 cups.

Mint-Chocolate Chip Ice Cream Squares

MINT-CHOCOLATE CHIP ICE CREAM SQUARES

  3 cups cream-filled chocolate sandwich cookie crumbs (about 30 cookies, crushed)
  ¹/₄ cup butter or margarine, melted
  ¹/₂ gallon mint-chocolate chip ice cream, slightly softened
  1 (5-ounce) can evaporated milk
  ¹/₂ cup sugar
1¹/₂ (1-ounce) squares unsweetened chocolate
  1 tablespoon butter or margarine
  1 (12-ounce) carton frozen whipped topping, thawed
  1 cup chopped pecans, toasted
    Garnish: fresh mint sprigs

Combine cookie crumbs and ¹/₄ cup butter. Press mixture into a lightly greased 13 x 9 x 2-inch pan; freeze until firm.

Spread ice cream evenly over crust; freeze until firm.

Combine evaporated milk and next 3 ingredients in a small heavy saucepan. Bring to a boil over low heat, stirring constantly with a wire whisk. Cook, stirring constantly, 3 to 4 minutes or until mixture thickens. Cool mixture to room temperature.

Spread chocolate mixture over ice cream; top with whipped topping, and sprinkle with pecans. Freeze until firm.

Let stand 10 minutes at room temperature before serving. Cut into squares, and garnish, if desired.

Yield: 15 servings.

LAYERED SHERBET DESSERT

2²/₃ cups chocolate wafer crumbs, divided
½ cup butter or margarine, melted
1 quart orange sherbet, slightly softened
1 quart rainbow sherbet, slightly softened
1 quart lime sherbet, slightly softened
   Raspberry-Orange Sauce
   Garnishes: chocolate curls, orange rind curls, fresh mint sprigs

Combine 1²/₃ cups chocolate crumbs and butter; press onto bottom of a 10-inch springform pan. Freeze until firm. Spread orange sherbet evenly over frozen crust. Sprinkle with ½ cup chocolate crumbs; freeze until firm. Repeat procedure with rainbow sherbet and remaining crumbs; freeze until firm.

Spread lime sherbet over frozen crumb layer. Cover and freeze at least 8 hours. Remove sides of springform pan. Spoon 2 to 3 tablespoons Raspberry-Orange Sauce onto each serving plate. Place wedge of sherbet dessert over sauce. Garnish, if desired.

Yield: 12 to 14 servings

RASPBERRY-ORANGE SAUCE

2 (10-ounce) packages frozen raspberries in light syrup, thawed
2 tablespoons frozen orange juice concentrate, thawed and undiluted
1 tablespoon plus 1 teaspoon cornstarch

Place raspberries in container of a food processor or electric blender. Process 1 minute or until smooth. Press raspberry purée through a wire-mesh strainer; discard seeds. Set purée aside.

Combine orange juice concentrate and cornstarch in a saucepan; add purée, and stir well. Cook over medium heat, stirring constantly, until mixture comes to a boil. Cook 1 minute, stirring constantly. Pour sauce into a bowl. Cover and chill.

Yield: 2¹/₃ cups.

MICROWAVE CHOCOLATE PIE

2 cups miniature marshmallows
1 cup milk chocolate morsels
1 cup milk
1 (1-ounce) square unsweetened chocolate
1 cup whipping cream, whipped
1 (6-ounce) chocolate-flavored crumb crust

Combine first 4 ingredients in a 2-quart glass mixing bowl. Microwave at HIGH 4 to 5 minutes, stirring once. Cool. Fold in whipped cream, and pour mixture into chocolate crust. Freeze until firm.

Yield: one (9-inch) pie.

CHOCOLATE ICE CREAM BROWNIES

1 (23.6-ounce) package fudge brownie mix
1/2 gallon vanilla ice cream, slightly softened
2 cups sifted powdered sugar
2/3 cup semisweet chocolate morsels
1 1/2 cups evaporated milk
1/2 cup butter or margarine
1 teaspoon vanilla extract
1 1/2 cups chopped pecans or walnuts

Prepare brownie mix according to package directions in a lightly greased 13 x 9 x 2-inch pan. Cool in pan on a wire rack.

Spread ice cream over brownies; freeze until ice cream is firm.

Combine sugar and next 3 ingredients in a saucepan. Bring to a boil; reduce heat to medium, and cook 8 minutes. Remove from heat, and stir in vanilla and pecans. Cool. Spread frosting over ice cream. Freeze.

Remove from freezer 5 to 10 minutes before serving. Cut into squares.

Yield: 15 servings.

STRAWBERRY-BANANA TOPPING

2 tablespoons butter or margarine
2 tablespoons brown sugar
2 tablespoons lemon juice
1/4 cup light rum
3 medium bananas, sliced
6 fresh strawberries, cut in half

Melt butter in a skillet on grill. Add sugar, lemon juice, and rum; stir well. Cook, stirring constantly, until sugar dissolves (2 to 3 minutes). Add bananas and strawberries, and cook until bananas are soft but not mushy (about 2 minutes). Serve over ice cream or pound cake.

Yield: 4 servings.

CHOCOLATE-MINT SUNDAES

6 chocolate-covered mint patties
1 tablespoon milk
   Vanilla ice cream

Combine mint patties and milk in a 1-cup glass measure. Cover with heavy-duty plastic wrap, and microwave at MEDIUM (50% power) 45 seconds or until patties melt. Serve warm over ice cream.

Yield: 2 servings.

PINEAPPLE ANGEL FOOD TRIFLE

1 (16-ounce) can pineapple tidbits, undrained
2 (3.4-ounce) packages vanilla instant pudding mix
3 cups milk
1 (8-ounce) carton sour cream
1 (10-inch) angel food cake, cut into 1-inch cubes
1 (8-ounce) carton frozen whipped topping, thawed
Garnishes: mint leaves, pineapple slices

Drain pineapple tidbits, reserving 1 cup juice; set aside.

Combine pudding mix, $1/2$ cup reserved juice, and milk in a mixing bowl; beat at low speed of an electric mixer 2 minutes or until thickened. Fold in sour cream and pineapple tidbits.

Place one-third of cake cubes in bottom of a 16-cup trifle bowl; drizzle with 2 to 3 tablespoons remaining reserved pineapple juice. Spoon one-third of pudding mixture over cake. Repeat procedure twice, ending with pudding mixture. Cover and chill at least 3 hours.

Spread top with whipped topping just before serving. Garnish, if desired.

Yield: 12 servings.

TENNESSEE BREAD PUDDING

2 cups hot water
$1^1/2$ cups sugar
1 (12-ounce) can evaporated milk
4 large eggs
1 cup flaked coconut
$1/2$ cup crushed pineapple, drained
$1/2$ cup raisins
$1/3$ cup butter or margarine, melted
1 teaspoon vanilla extract
$1/2$ teaspoon ground nutmeg
9 slices white bread with crust, cut into $1/2$-inch cubes

Combine water and sugar in a bowl, stirring until sugar dissolves. Add milk and eggs, stirring with a wire whisk until blended.

Stir in coconut and next 5 ingredients. Add bread cubes; let mixture stand 30 minutes, stirring occasionally. Pour into a greased 13 x 9 x 2-inch pan.

Bake at 350° for 45 minutes or until a knife inserted in center comes out clean. Serve warm.

Yield: 12 servings.

From left: Creamy Vanilla Cheesecake and variations – Chocolate Marble, Black Forest, Crème de Menthe, and Praline

CREAMY VANILLA CHEESECAKE

    5 (8-ounce) packages cream cheese,
         softened
 1¹/₂ cups sugar
    3 large eggs
 2¹/₂ teaspoons vanilla extract
         Graham Cracker Crust (recipe on
             page 488)
         Garnish: strawberry fans

Beat cream cheese at high speed of an electric mixer until fluffy; gradually add sugar, beating well. Add eggs, one at a time, beating after each addition. Stir in vanilla. Pour into Graham Cracker Crust.

Bake at 350° for 40 minutes; turn oven off, and partially open oven door. Leave cheesecake in oven 30 minutes. Remove from oven, and cool on a wire rack in a draft-free place.

Cover and chill at least 8 hours. Garnish, if desired.

Yield: 10 to 12 servings.

VARIATIONS
BLACK FOREST CHEESECAKE

Use Graham Cracker Crust or Chocolate Wafer Crust. Prepare basic cheesecake mixture; stir in 6 ounces melted semisweet chocolate. Pour half of chocolate mixture into crust; top with 1 cup canned dark, sweet, pitted cherries, drained and patted dry. Spoon remaining chocolate mixture evenly over cherries. Bake at 350° for 45 minutes. Garnish with whipped cream and additional cherries, if desired.

Continued on page 488

BROWN SUGAR AND SPICE CHEESECAKE

Use Gingersnap Crust. For cheesecake mixture, substitute brown sugar for white sugar, and add 1 teaspoon ground cinnamon, 1/2 teaspoon ground cloves, and 1/2 teaspoon ground nutmeg when sugar is added. Bake at 350° for 45 minutes. Garnish with whipped cream, and sprinkle with nutmeg, if desired.

CHOCOLATE MARBLE CHEESECAKE

Use Chocolate Wafer Crust. Prepare basic cheesecake mixture, and divide in half. Stir 6 ounces melted semisweet chocolate into half of cheesecake mixture. Pour half of plain cheesecake mixture into prepared crust; top with half of chocolate mixture. Repeat layers to use all of mixture. Gently swirl batter with a knife to create a marbled effect. Bake at 350° for 40 minutes. Garnish with mint sprigs, if desired.

CRÈME DE MENTHE CHEESECAKE

Use Chocolate Wafer Crust. Stir 1/4 cup green crème de menthe into cheesecake mixture when vanilla is added. Bake at 350° for 45 minutes. Garnish with chocolate leaves, if desired.

PRALINE CHEESECAKE

Use Graham Cracker Crust. Substitute dark brown sugar for white sugar in cheesecake mixture. Sauté 1 cup chopped pecans in 3 tablespoons melted butter or margarine; drain pecans on paper towel. Fold into cheesecake mixture when vanilla is added. Bake at 350° for 45 minutes. Garnish with toasted pecan halves, if desired.

GRAHAM CRACKER CRUST

1 2/3 cups graham cracker crumbs
1/3 cup butter or margarine, melted

Combine crumbs and butter; press onto bottom and 1 inch up sides of a 10-inch springform pan. Bake at 350° for 5 minutes.

Yield: one 10-inch crust.

VARIATIONS
CHOCOLATE WAFER CRUST

Substitute 1 2/3 cups chocolate wafer crumbs for graham cracker crumbs.

GINGERSNAP CRUST

Substitute 1 2/3 cups gingersnap crumbs for graham cracker crumbs.

SMOOTHEST SOUTHERN POUND CAKE

1 cup butter or margarine, softened
3 cups sugar
3 cups sifted cake flour
1/4 teaspoon baking soda
6 large eggs, separated
1 (8-ounce) carton sour cream
1 teaspoon vanilla extract

Beat butter at medium speed of an electric mixer (not a handheld one) 2 minutes or until butter is creamy. Gradually add sugar, beating 5 to 7 minutes.

Combine flour and soda; add to butter mixture 1 cup at a time. (Batter will be extremely thick.)

Add egg yolks to batter, and mix well. Stir in sour cream and vanilla. Beat egg whites in a large mixing bowl at high speed until stiff; fold into batter. Spoon batter into a greased and floured 10-inch Bundt or tube pan.

Bake at 300° for 2 hours or until a wooden pick inserted in center comes out clean. (You may also spoon batter into two 9 x 5 x 3-inch loafpans, and bake at 300° for 1 1/2 hours or until a wooden pick inserted in center comes out clean.)

Cool in pan on a wire rack 10 to 15 minutes; remove from pan, and cool completely on wire rack.

Yield: one 10-inch cake or two loaves.

LEMON CHEESECAKE

3/4 cup graham cracker crumbs
2 tablespoons sugar
1 tablespoon ground cinnamon
1 tablespoon butter or margarine, softened
5 (8-ounce) packages cream cheese, softened
1 2/3 cups sugar
5 large eggs
1/8 teaspoon salt
1 1/2 teaspoons vanilla extract
1/4 cup lemon juice

Combine first 3 ingredients; stir well, and set aside. Grease bottom and sides of a 10-inch springform pan with butter. Add crumb mixture; tilt pan to coat sides and bottom. Chill.

Beat cream cheese at medium speed of an electric mixer until fluffy; gradually add 1 2/3 cups sugar, beating well. Add eggs, one at a time, beating after each addition. Stir in salt, vanilla, and lemon juice; pour into prepared crust.

Bake at 300° for 1 hour and 20 minutes. (Center may be soft but will set when chilled.) Cool on a wire rack; cover and chill 8 hours.

Yield: 10 to 12 servings.

BOSTON CREAM PIE

1/2 cup butter or margarine, softened
1 cup sugar
3 large eggs
2 cups sifted cake flour
2 teaspoons baking powder
1/4 teaspoon salt
1/2 cup milk
2 teaspoons vanilla extract
   Cream Filling
   Chocolate Glaze

Beat butter at medium speed of an electric mixer until creamy; gradually add sugar, beating well. Add eggs, one at a time, beating after each addition.

Combine flour, baking powder, and salt; add to butter mixture alternately with milk, beginning and ending with flour mixture. Mix after each addition. Stir in vanilla.

Pour batter into 2 greased and floured 9-inch round cakepans.

Bake at 350° for 20 to 25 minutes or until a wooden pick inserted in center comes out clean. Cool in pans on wire racks 10 minutes; remove from pans, and cool completely on wire racks.

Spread Cream Filling between cake layers. Spread Chocolate Glaze over top of cake, letting excess drip down sides of cake. Chill until ready to serve.

Yield: 8 to 10 servings.

CREAM FILLING

1/2 cup sugar
1/4 cup cornstarch
1/4 teaspoon salt
2 cups milk
4 egg yolks, lightly beaten
1 teaspoon vanilla extract

Combine first 3 ingredients in a heavy saucepan. Add milk and egg yolks, stirring with a wire whisk until blended.

Cook over medium heat, stirring constantly, until mixture comes to a boil. Boil 1 minute or until thickened, stirring constantly; remove from heat. Stir in vanilla; cool.

Yield: 2 1/2 cups.

CHOCOLATE GLAZE

2 tablespoons butter or margarine
1 (1-ounce) square unsweetened chocolate
1 cup sifted powdered sugar
2 tablespoons boiling water

Melt butter and chocolate in a saucepan, stirring constantly. Cool slightly. Add powdered sugar and water; beat until smooth.

Yield: 1/2 cup.

Boston Cream Pie

NEW-FASHIONED APPLE COBBLER

    1   tablespoon cornstarch
 $1/2$ cup apple juice, divided
    5   cups peeled and sliced cooking
        apple
 $1/3$ cup firmly packed brown sugar
 $1/2$ teaspoon ground cinnamon
 $1/4$ teaspoon ground nutmeg
 $1/4$ teaspoon ground cloves
        Vegetable cooking spray
 $1/2$ cup all-purpose flour
    2   tablespoons corn oil margarine
    1   to 2 tablespoons cold water

Combine cornstarch and $1/4$ cup apple juice; set aside.

Combine remaining $1/2$ cup apple juice, apple, and next 4 ingredients in a heavy saucepan; bring to a boil. Reduce heat, and simmer 10 minutes, stirring occasionally.

Stir in cornstarch mixture; cook over medium heat, stirring constantly, until mixture begins to boil. Boil 1 minute, stirring constantly, until mixture is thickened and bubbly.

Remove from heat; pour into an 8-inch square baking dish coated with cooking spray. Set aside.

Place flour in a small bowl; cut in margarine with a pastry blender until mixture is crumbly. Sprinkle cold water evenly over surface of mixture; stir with a fork until dry ingredients are moistened.

Shape dough into a ball; gently press between 2 sheets of heavy-duty plastic wrap into a 4-inch circle. Chill 15 minutes.

Roll dough to an 8-inch square; freeze 5 minutes. Remove top sheet of plastic wrap; cut dough into strips to fit baking dish. Arrange strips over apples in a lattice design.

Bake at 425° for 30 to 35 minutes or until cobbler is bubbly and crust is golden.

Yield: 6 ($1/2$-cup) servings.

PEACH-BLUEBERRY DESSERT

 $3^{1}/2$ cups peeled, sliced fresh peaches,
            divided
 $1^{1}/2$ cups fresh blueberries, divided
   $1/4$ cup unsweetened apple juice
   $1/8$ to $1/4$ teaspoon ground nutmeg
     3   cups vanilla lowfat ice cream

Combine 1 cup peaches, 1 cup blueberries, apple juice, and nutmeg in a saucepan. Bring to a boil, and cook 2 minutes, stirring occasionally. Remove from heat.

Stir in remaining $2^{1}/2$ cups peaches and $1/2$ cup blueberries. Cover and chill. Spoon into individual dishes; top with ice cream.

Yield: 6 servings.

PUMPKIN CAKE

2³/₄ cups all-purpose flour
1 teaspoon baking soda
¹/₂ teaspoon baking powder
¹/₄ teaspoon salt
1 teaspoon ground nutmeg
1 teaspoon ground cloves
1 teaspoon ground cinnamon
3 large eggs, lightly beaten
2 cups sugar
1 cup unsweetened applesauce
1 (16-ounce) can pumpkin
1 cup raisins, chopped
¹/₂ cup chopped pecans
    Vegetable cooking spray
1 teaspoon powdered sugar
1 cup reduced-calorie frozen
    whipped topping, thawed

Combine first 7 ingredients in a large bowl; make a well in center of mixture.

Combine eggs and next 3 ingredients; add to dry ingredients, stirring just until moistened. Fold in raisins and pecans. Spoon into a 12-cup Bundt pan coated with cooking spray.

Bake at 350° for 1 hour and 10 minutes or until a wooden pick inserted in center comes out clean. Cool in pan on a wire rack 10 minutes; remove from pan, and cool completely on wire rack.

Sprinkle with powdered sugar. Dollop 1 tablespoon whipped topping on each slice.

Yield: 16 servings.

SUMMER STRAWBERRY DESSERT

1 (1.3 ounce) envelope whipped
    topping mix
¹/₂ cup skim milk
1 teaspoon vanilla extract
2 (6-ounce) cartons strawberry low-
    fat yogurt
¹/₂ (10-ounce) commercial angel food
    cake, torn into bite-size pieces.
2 cups fresh strawberries, sliced
3 kiwifruit, sliced
2 tablespoons sliced almonds,
    toasted

Prepare whipped topping mix according to package directions, using ¹/₂ cup skim milk and 1 teaspoon vanilla. Fold in yogurt, and set aside.

Layer half each of cake, yogurt mixture, strawberries, and kiwi fruit in an 8-inch square dish. Repeat layers; sprinkle almonds on top. Cover and chill at least 2 hours.

Yield: 8 (³/₄-cup) servings.

CHOCOLATE ANGEL FOOD CAKE

- 1 (14.5-ounce) package angel food cake mix
- 1/4 cup unsweetened cocoa, sifted
- 1/2 teaspoon chocolate flavoring
- 1 tablespoon sifted powdered sugar
  Garnish: strawberry fans

Combine flour packet from cake mix and cocoa. Mix cake according to package directions; fold chocolate flavoring into batter. Spoon batter into a 10-inch tube pan.

Bake at 375° on lowest rack in oven 30 to 40 minutes or until cake springs back when lightly touched. Invert pan; cool 1 hour.

Loosen cake from sides of pan using a metal spatula; remove from pan. Cool on a wire rack.

Sprinkle cooled cake with sifted powdered sugar. Garnish, if desired.

Yield: 32 servings.

GOLD MEDAL CHOCOLATE BROWNIES

- 2/3 cup reduced-calorie margarine, softened
- 2/3 cup sugar
- 1/2 cup frozen egg substitute, thawed
- 3 tablespoons skim milk
- 1 teaspoon vanilla extract
- 2/3 cup all-purpose flour
- 1/2 teaspoon baking powder
- 1/4 teaspoon salt
- 1/3 cup unsweetened cocoa
- 3 tablespoons finely chopped pecans
  Vegetable cooking spray

Beat margarine at medium speed of an electric mixer until fluffy. Gradually add sugar, 1 tablespoon at a time, beating well. Add egg substitute, milk, and vanilla; mix well.

Combine flour and next 3 ingredients. Add to creamed mixture, mixing well. Stir in pecans. Spoon into an 8-inch square pan coated with cooking spray.

Bake at 325° for 30 minutes or until a wooden pick inserted in center comes out clean. Cool on a wire rack; cut into squares.

Yield: 16 brownies.

SPICE CAKE

Vegetable cooking spray
1¾ cups sugar
¼ cup vegetable oil
½ cup frozen egg substitute, thawed
3 cups all-purpose flour
1 teaspoon baking soda
¾ teaspoon baking powder
1 teaspoon ground allspice
1 teaspoon ground cinnamon
½ cup plain nonfat yogurt
¾ cup unsweetened applesauce
3 cups unpeeled, cored, finely chopped Granny Smith apple
1 cup chopped walnuts
1 teaspoon vanilla extract
½ teaspoon rum flavoring
½ teaspoon black walnut flavoring
½ teaspoon butter flavoring

Coat a 10-inch Bundt pan with cooking spray; dust with flour, and set aside. Beat sugar and oil at medium speed of an electric mixer 1 minute. Add egg substitute, ¼ cup at a time, beating after each addition.

Combine flour and next 4 ingredients; add to sugar mixture alternately with yogurt and applesauce, beginning and ending with flour mixture. Mix after each addition.

Stir in apple and remaining ingredients. Pour batter into prepared pan. Bake at 350° for 55 to 60 minutes or until a wooden pick inserted in center of cake comes out clean. Cool in pan on a wire rack 10 minutes; remove from pan, and cool on wire rack.

Yield: 24 servings.

CAKE BAKING SECRETS

IF CAKE FALLS:
- Oven not hot enough
- Undermixing
- Insufficient baking
- Opening oven door during baking
- Too much leavening, liquid, or sugar

IF CAKE PEAKS IN CENTER:
- Oven too hot at start of baking
- Too much flour
- Not enough liquid

IF CAKE STICKS TO PAN:
- Cooled in pan too long
- Pan not greased and floured properly

IF CAKE CRACKS AND FALLS APART:
- Removed from pan too soon
- Too much shortening, leavening, or sugar

IF CRUST IS STICKY:
- Insufficient baking
- Oven not hot enough
- Too much sugar

IF TEXTURE IS DRY:
- Overbaking
- Overbeaten egg whites
- Too much flour or leavening
- Not enough shortening or sugar

FRUIT KABOBS WITH COCONUT DRESSING

- 1 medium-size red apple, unpeeled
- 1 medium pear, unpeeled
- 1 tablespoon lemon juice
- 21 unsweetened pineapple chunks
- 21 seedless red or green grapes
- 21 fresh strawberries, capped
- Coconut Dressing

Cut apple and pear each into 21 bite-size pieces. Add lemon juice; toss ingredients.

Alternate fruit on 21 wooden skewers. Serve with Coconut Dressing.

Yield: 21 appetizer servings.

COCONUT DRESSING

- 1 1/2 cups vanilla low-fat yogurt
- 1 1/2 tablespoons flaked coconut
- 1 1/2 tablespoons reduced-calorie orange marmalade

Combine all ingredients in a bowl; stir well. Serve with kabobs.

Yield: 1 2/3 cups.

LEMON POPPY SEED CAKE

- 1 (18.25-ounce) package reduced-fat yellow cake mix
- 1/2 cup sugar
- 1/3 cup vegetable oil
- 1/4 cup water
- 1 (8-ounce) carton plain nonfat yogurt
- 1 cup frozen egg substitute, thawed
- 3 tablespoons lemon juice
- 1 tablespoon poppy seeds
- Vegetable cooking spray
- Lemon Glaze

Combine cake mix and sugar in a large mixing bowl; add oil and next 4 ingredients. Beat at medium speed of an electric mixer 6 minutes. Stir in poppy seeds.

Pour batter into a 10-cup Bundt pan coated with cooking spray.

Bake at 350° for 40 minutes or until a wooden pick inserted in center of cake comes out clean. Cool in pan on a wire rack 10 minutes. Remove from pan; drizzle with Lemon Glaze, and cool completely on wire rack.

Yield: 24 servings.

LEMON GLAZE

- 1/2 cup sifted powdered sugar
- 2 tablespoons lemon juice

Combine powdered sugar and lemon juice, stirring until smooth.

Yield: 1/2 cup.

LEMON DELIGHT CHEESECAKE

 1 cup graham cracker crumbs
 3 tablespoons sugar
 2 tablespoons margarine, melted
 3 (8-ounce) packages nonfat cream cheese, softened
 3/4 cup sugar
 2 tablespoons all-purpose flour
 3 tablespoons lemon juice
 3/4 cup frozen egg substitute, thawed
 1 (8-ounce) carton lemon nonfat yogurt
   Garnishes: lemon slices, fresh mint sprigs

Combine first 3 ingredients; press into bottom of a 9-inch springform pan.

Combine cream cheese, 3/4 cup sugar, and all-purpose flour; beat at medium speed of an electric mixer until fluffy.

Add lemon juice and egg substitute, beating well. Add yogurt, beating well; pour into prepared pan. Cover loosely with foil. Bake at 350° for 1 hour or until set. Remove from oven; immediately run a knife around sides of cheesecake to loosen. Cool completely in pan on a wire rack.

Cover and chill at least 8 hours. Remove sides of pan from cheesecake. Garnish, if desired.

Yield: 9 servings.

Note: For a crisper crust, bake crust at 350° for 6 to 8 minutes.

CHOCOLATE-CINNAMON SQUARES

 1 1/2 cups all-purpose flour
 1 teaspoon baking powder
 1/2 teaspoon baking soda
 1/4 teaspoon salt
 1 cup sugar
 1/3 cup unsweetened cocoa
 1 teaspoon ground cinnamon
 1 cup nonfat buttermilk
 1/4 cup frozen egg substitute, thawed
 2 tablespoons margarine, melted
 2 teaspoons vanilla extract
   Vegetable cooking spray
 1/4 cup chopped walnuts

Combine first 7 ingredients in a large bowl. Combine buttermilk and next 3 ingredients; add to dry ingredients, stirring until blended.

Spoon batter into an 8-inch square pan coated with cooking spray; sprinkle with walnuts.

Bake at 350° for 30 minutes or until a wooden pick inserted in center comes out clean. Cool in pan on a wire rack.

Yield: 12 servings.

POUND CAKE

Vegetable cooking spray
1/2 cup margarine, softened
1 cup sugar
1/3 cup egg substitute
2 1/2 cups sifted cake flour
1/2 teaspoon baking powder
1/4 teaspoon baking soda
1/4 teaspoon salt
1 (8-ounce) carton low-fat vanilla yogurt
1 tablespoon vanilla extract
3/4 teaspoon almond extract

Coat the bottom of a 9 x 5 x 3-inch loafpan with cooking spray; dust with flour, and set aside.

Beat margarine at medium speed of an electric mixer until fluffy. Gradually add sugar; beat well. Add egg substitute; beat until blended.

Combine flour and next 3 ingredients; add to creamed mixture alternately with yogurt, beginning and ending with flour mixture. Mix just until blended after each addition. Stir in flavorings.

Spoon batter into prepared pan. Bake at 350° for 1 hour and 5 minutes or until a wooden pick inserted in center comes out clean. Cool in pan on a wire rack 10 minutes; remove from pan, and let cool on wire rack. Serve with 1/2 cup chopped or sliced fruit.

Yield: 18 (1/2-inch) servings.

VANILLA CREAM PIE

3/4 cup sugar
1/4 cup plus 2 teaspoons cornstarch
1/8 teaspoon salt
3 egg yolks, beaten
3 cups milk
1 1/2 tablespoons butter or margarine
1 1/2 teaspoons vanilla extract
1 baked 9-inch pastry shell
3/4 cup whipping cream
1/3 cup sifted powdered sugar

Combine first 3 ingredients in a heavy saucepan; stir well. Combine egg yolks and milk; gradually stir into sugar mixture. Cook over medium heat, stirring constantly, until mixture thickens and boils. Boil 1 minute, stirring mixture constantly.

Remove from heat; stir in butter and vanilla. Immediately pour into pastry shell. Cover filling with wax paper. Cool 30 minutes; chill until firm.

Beat whipping cream at medium speed of an electric mixer until foamy; gradually add powdered sugar, beating until soft peaks form. Spread over filling. Chill.

Yield: one 9-inch pie.

VARIATIONS

BANANA CREAM PIE
Slice 2 small bananas into pastry shell before adding filling.

BUTTERSCOTCH CREAM PIE
Substitute $3/4$ cup firmly packed dark brown sugar for $3/4$ cup sugar; reduce vanilla to $3/4$ teaspoon and add $3/4$ teaspoon butter flavoring.

CHOCOLATE CREAM PIE
Add $1/4$ cup cocoa when combining sugar and cornstarch.

COCONUT CREAM PIE
Add $1/2$ cup flaked coconut with vanilla. Sprinkle $1/4$ cup toasted flaked coconut over whipped cream.

Vanilla Cream Pie (Coconut Cream Pie Variation)

ANGEL FOOD TRIFLE

1 (16-ounce) package angel food
cake mix
$^1/_3$ cup sugar
$^1/_4$ cup cornstarch
$^1/_4$ teaspoon salt
2 cups fat-free milk
$^1/_4$ cup egg substitute
1 teaspoon grated lemon rind
$^1/_4$ cup lemon juice
2 (8-ounce) cartons vanilla low-fat
yogurt
2 cups sliced strawberries
3 kiwifruit, sliced
3 strawberry fans

Prepare cake mix according to package directions. Cut into bite-size cubes; set aside.

Combine sugar, cornstarch, and salt in a saucepan; gradually add milk, stirring well. Cook over medium heat until mixture begins to thicken, stirring constantly.

Remove mixture from heat; gradually add egg substitute, stirring constantly with a wire whisk. Cook over medium-low heat 2 minutes, stirring constantly.

Remove from heat; cool slightly. Stir in lemon rind and lemon juice; chill. Fold yogurt into custard mixture; set aside.

Place one-third of cake in bottom of a 16-cup trifle bowl. Spoon one-third of custard over cake; arrange half each of strawberry slices and kiwi slices around lower edge of bowl and over custard. Repeat process with remaining ingredients, ending with strawberry fans on top. Cover and chill 3 to 4 hours.

Yield: 15 ($^2/_3$-cup) servings.

SWEETHEART FUDGE PIE

$^1/_2$ cup butter or margarine, softened
$^3/_4$ cup firmly packed brown sugar
3 large eggs
1 (12-ounce) package semisweet
chocolate morsels, melted
2 teaspoons instant coffee granules
1 teaspoon rum extract
$^1/_2$ cup all-purpose flour
1 cup coarsely chopped walnuts
1 unbaked 9-inch pastry shell
Garnishes: piped whipped cream,
chopped walnuts

Beat butter at medium speed of an electric mixer until creamy; gradually add brown sugar, beating well. Add eggs, one at a time, beating after each addition.

Add melted chocolate, coffee granules, and rum extract; mix well. Stir in flour and walnuts. Spoon mixture into pastry shell.

Bake at 375° for 25 minutes; cool completely. Chill. Garnish, if desired.

Yield: one 9-inch pie.

AMERICAN APPLE PIE

2 cups all-purpose flour
1 cup firmly packed brown sugar
$1/2$ cup regular oats, uncooked
$1/2$ teaspoon salt
$1/3$ cup chopped pecans
$3/4$ cup butter or margarine, melted
4 cups peeled, sliced cooking apples
$3/4$ cup sugar
1 tablespoon cornstarch
$1/4$ teaspoon salt
$1/2$ cup water
$1/2$ teaspoon vanilla extract
   Vanilla ice cream

Combine first 5 ingredients in a large bowl; add butter, and stir until blended. Measure 1 cup firmly packed mixture; set aside for pie topping.

Press remaining oats mixture in bottom and up sides of a 9-inch deep-dish pieplate. Arrange apple slices in pieplate; set aside.

Combine $3/4$ cup sugar, cornstarch, and salt in a saucepan; stir in water. Cook over medium heat until mixture boils. Stir in vanilla.

Pour hot mixture evenly over apples; crumble reserved topping mixture evenly over pie.

Bake at 375° for 40 minutes, covering with foil the last 15 minutes, if necessary. Serve with ice cream.

Yield: one 9-inch pie.

FRIED APRICOT PIES

1 (6-ounce) package dried apricot
   halves, chopped
$1 1/4$ cups water
$1/2$ cup sugar
$1/2$ teaspoon ground cinnamon
$1/2$ teaspoon ground nutmeg
1 tablespoon lemon or orange juice
1 (15-ounce) package refrigerated
   piecrusts
   Vegetable oil
   Powdered sugar

Combine apricots and $1 1/4$ cups water in a saucepan; bring to a boil. Cover, reduce heat, and simmer 20 minutes or until tender. Drain.

Mash apricots. Stir in sugar and next 3 ingredients; set aside.

Unfold 1 piecrust, and press out fold lines. Roll piecrust to $1/8$-inch thickness on a lightly floured surface. Cut into five 5-inch circles; stack circles between wax paper. Repeat procedure.

Spoon 2 tablespoons apricot mixture on half of each circle. Moisten edges with water; fold dough over apricot mixture, pressing edges to seal. Crimp edges with a fork.

Pour oil to depth of 1 inch into a heavy skillet. Fry pies in hot oil (375°) 2 minutes or until golden, turning once. Drain on paper towels. Sprinkle with powdered sugar.

Yield: 10 pies.

LEMONY CHERRY PIE

2 (16-ounce) cans tart, red pitted
   cherries, undrained
1 cup sugar
3 tablespoons cornstarch
2 tablespoons butter or margarine
1 tablespoon lemon juice
$1/8$ teaspoon liquid red food coloring
   (optional)
1 (15-ounce) package refrigerated
   piecrusts
1 teaspoon all-purpose flour

Drain cherries, reserving $1/2$ cup juice. Set both aside. Combine sugar and cornstarch in a large saucepan; stir in reserved cherry juice. Cook over medium heat, stirring constantly, until mixture comes to a boil; boil 1 minute, stirring constantly. Remove sugar mixture from heat, and stir in cherries, butter, lemon juice, and, if desired, food coloring; cool.

Unfold 1 piecrust, and press out fold lines; sprinkle with flour, spreading over surface. Place piecrust, floured side down, in a 9-inch pieplate; trim off excess pastry along edges. Spoon filling into pastry shell.

Roll remaining piecrust to press out fold lines. Cut into $1/2$-inch strips. Arrange in lattice design over filling; trim strips even with edge. Cut remaining pastry into shapes with a 1-inch cutter, if desired. Moisten edge of piecrust with water, and gently press cutouts around edge.

Bake at 375° for 30 to 35 minutes.

Yield: one 9-inch pie.

EASY LEMON CHESS PIE

$1^3/4$ cups sugar
2 tablespoons yellow cornmeal
$1/4$ teaspoon salt
$1/3$ cup butter or margarine, melted
$1/4$ cup evaporated milk
3 tablespoons lemon juice
4 large eggs
1 unbaked 9-inch pastry shell

Combine first 3 ingredients in a medium bowl, stirring well. Add butter, milk, and lemon juice; stir well.

Add eggs, one at a time, beating after each addition. Pour filling into pastry shell.

Bake at 350° for 45 minutes or until pie is set. Cool on a wire rack.

Yield: one 9-inch pie.

DOUBLE PECAN PIE

1 cup light corn syrup
$3/4$ cup sugar
3 large eggs
3 tablespoons butter or margarine,
   melted
1 tablespoon brandy
1 teaspoon vanilla extract
$1/4$ teaspoon salt
1 cup pecan pieces
   Pecan Pastry
1 cup pecan halves

Combine first 7 ingredients in a medium bowl. Beat at medium speed of an electric mixer just until blended. Stir in pecan pieces.

Pour mixture into Pecan Pastry. Top with pecan halves.

Bake at 350° for 50 to 60 minutes or until set. Cover edges of pastry with aluminum foil, if necessary, to prevent excessive browning.

Yield: one 9-inch pie.

PECAN PASTRY
- 1 cup all-purpose flour
- 1/4 cup ground pecans
- 1/4 teaspoon salt
- 1/4 cup plus 2 tablespoons butter or margarine
- 1 tablespoon brandy
- 1 to 2 tablespoons cold water

Combine first 3 ingredients in a medium bowl; cut in butter with a pastry blender until mixture is crumbly.

Sprinkle brandy over mixture, stirring with a fork. Add water, stirring just until dry ingredients are moistened. Shape pastry into a ball; cover and chill 30 minutes.

Roll pastry to 1/8-inch thickness on a lightly floured surface. Place in a 9-inch pieplate; flute edges.

Yield: pastry for one 9-inch pie.

SPIRITED MINCE PIE

- 3/4 cup raisins
- 3 tablespoons brandy or orange juice
- 1 (15-ounce) package refrigerated piecrusts
- 1 teaspoon all-purpose flour
- 1 (27-ounce) jar mincemeat
- 1 large cooking apple, cored and finely chopped
- 1 cup chopped walnuts
- 1/4 cup firmly packed brown sugar
- 1 teaspoon grated lemon or orange rind
- 1 tablespoon lemon juice

Combine raisins and brandy or orange juice in a large bowl; let stand 2 hours. Unfold 1 piecrust, and press out fold lines; sprinkle with flour, spreading over surface. Place, floured side down, in a 9-inch pieplate; fold edges under, and flute. Set aside.

Combine raisin mixture, mincemeat, and next 5 ingredients; spoon into pastry shell.

Roll remaining piecrust on a lightly floured surface to press out fold lines; cut with a 3 1/4-inch leaf-shaped cutter, and mark veins using a pastry wheel or knife. Roll pastry scraps into small balls representing berries. Arrange pastry on top of filling as desired.

Bake at 375° for 10 minutes; shield edges with aluminum foil, and bake 25 additional minutes. Cool on a wire rack.

Yield: one 9-inch pie.

CRUSTY PEACH COBBLER

    7 to 7½ cups sliced fresh peaches
1½ to 2 cups sugar
    2 to 4 tablespoons all-purpose flour
    ½ teaspoon ground nutmeg
    1 teaspoon almond or vanilla
          extract
    ⅓ cup butter or margarine
          Pastry for double-crust pie
          Vanilla ice cream

Combine first 4 ingredients in a Dutch oven; set aside until syrup forms.

Bring peach mixture to a boil; reduce heat to low, and cook 10 minutes or until peaches are tender. Remove from heat; stir in almond extract and butter.

Roll half of pastry to ⅛-inch thickness on a lightly floured surface; cut into a 9-inch square. Spoon half of peach mixture into a lightly buttered 9-inch square dish; top with pastry square.

Bake at 425° for 14 minutes or until lightly browned. Spoon remaining peach mixture over baked pastry square.

Roll remaining pastry to ⅛-inch thickness, and cut into 1-inch strips; arrange in lattice design over peach mixture.

Bake at 425° for 15 to 18 minutes or until browned. Spoon into serving bowls, and top with ice cream.

Yield: 8 servings.

JUICY BLACKBERRY COBBLER

    4 cups fresh blackberries or
          2 (16-ounce) packages frozen
          blackberries, thawed
    1 cup sugar
    ½ cup water
          Pastry
    2 tablespoons butter, melted
          and divided
    2 tablespoons sugar, divided

Combine first 3 ingredients in a saucepan. Cook over medium heat 10 minutes; stir gently. Pour half of berry mixture into a greased 12 x 8 x 2-inch baking dish.

Roll pastry to ⅛-inch thickness on a floured surface. Cut into 1-inch strips; arrange half of strips in a lattice design over berry mixture. Brush with 1 tablespoon melted butter; sprinkle with 1 tablespoon sugar. Bake at 375° for 10 to 12 minutes or until pastry is lightly browned.

Pour remaining berry mixture over baked pastry. Arrange remaining strips in lattice design over berries. Brush with remaining butter; sprinkle with remaining sugar. Bake at 375° for 20 minutes or until pastry is golden.

Yield: 6 servings.

PASTRY

1½ cups all-purpose flour
    ¾ teaspoon salt
    ½ cup shortening
    5 tablespoons cold water

Combine flour and salt; cut in shortening with a pastry blender until mixture is crumbly.

Sprinkle water, 1 tablespoon at a time, evenly over surface; stir with a fork until dry ingredients are moistened. Shape into a ball; cover and chill.

Yield: pastry for one cobbler.

BEST-EVER LEMON MERINGUE PIE

1^1/$_2$ cups sugar
^{1}/$_3$ cup cornstarch
^{1}/$_8$ teaspoon salt
4 egg yolks
1^3/$_4$ cups water
^{1}/$_2$ cup lemon juice
3 tablespoons butter or margarine
1 teaspoon grated lemon rind
1 baked 9-inch pastry shell
Meringue

Combine first 3 ingredients in a heavy saucepan; set aside. Combine egg yolks, water, and lemon juice; stir into sugar mixture.

Cook over medium heat, stirring constantly, until mixture thickens and boils. Boil 1 minute, stirring constantly. Remove from heat.

Stir in butter and grated lemon rind. Spoon hot filling into pastry shell. Spread Meringue over hot filling, sealing to edge of pastry. Bake at 325° for 25 to 28 minutes.

Yield: one 9-inch pie.

MERINGUE
4 egg whites
^{1}/$_2$ teaspoon cream of tartar
^{1}/$_4$ cup plus 2 tablespoons sugar
^{1}/$_2$ teaspoon vanilla extract

Beat egg whites and cream of tartar at high speed of an electric mixer until foamy. Gradually add sugar, 1 tablespoon at a time, beating until stiff peaks form and sugar dissolves (2 to 4 minutes). Beat in vanilla.

Yield: meringue for one 9-inch pie.

PEANUT BUTTER PIE

1 (8-ounce) package cream cheese, softened
1 cup sifted powdered sugar
1 cup chunky peanut butter
^{1}/$_2$ cup milk
1 (8-ounce) carton frozen whipped topping, thawed
1 (9-inch) graham cracker crust
^{1}/$_4$ cup coarsely chopped peanuts

Combine first 4 ingredients in a bowl; beat at medium speed of an electric mixer until blended. Fold in whipped topping. Spoon into crust; sprinkle with peanuts. Chill.

Yield: one 9-inch pie.

CHOCOLATE DREAM PIE

(Shown on page 9)

- ³/₄ cup sugar
- ¹/₄ cup cornstarch
- 1 tablespoon cocoa
- ¹/₄ teaspoon salt
- 2¹/₂ cups milk
- 1 cup half-and-half
- 3 egg yolks
- 1 (6-ounce) package semisweet chocolate morsels, melted
- 1 teaspoon vanilla extract
  Chocolate Pastry Shell
- 1 cup whipping cream
- 2 tablespoons powdered sugar
  Grated semisweet chocolate

Combine first 4 ingredients in a saucepan. Add milk and half-and-half; cook over medium heat, stirring constantly, until thickened and bubbly.

Beat egg yolks at medium speed of an electric mixer until thick and pale. Gradually add ¹/₄ of hot mixture to yolks; add to remaining hot mixture, stirring constantly. Cook over low heat, stirring constantly, until mixture thickens. Remove from heat. Stir in melted chocolate and vanilla. Cool completely. Pour filling into Chocolate Pastry Shell. Cover loosely; chill several hours.

Beat whipping cream at medium speed until foamy. Add powdered sugar, and beat until soft peaks form; spoon over pie. Sprinkle with grated chocolate. Garnish with pastry cutouts, if desired.

Yield: one 9-inch pie.

CHOCOLATE PASTRY SHELL

- 1¹/₂ cups all-purpose flour
- ¹/₄ cup plus 2 tablespoons firmly packed brown sugar
- 3 tablespoons cocoa
- ¹/₄ teaspoon salt
- ¹/₂ cup shortening
- 5 to 6 tablespoons cold water

Combine first 4 ingredients; cut in shortening with a pastry blender until mixture is crumbly.

Sprinkle cold water, 1 tablespoon at a time, over surface; stir with a fork until moistened. Shape into a ball; cover and chill 1 hour.

Pinch off ¹/₄ cup pastry, and set aside to make decorative cutouts, if desired. Roll remaining pastry to ¹/₈-inch thickness on a floured surface. Fit into a greased 9-inch pieplate; fold edges under, and flute. Freeze 10 minutes.

Prick bottom and sides of pastry with a fork; bake at 450° for 6 to 8 minutes or until done.

Roll reserved ¹/₄ cup pastry to ¹/₄-inch thickness. Cut into decorative shapes, using small cookie cutters. Place on a baking sheet. Bake at 450° for 5 to 6 minutes. Cool.

Yield: pastry for one 9-inch pastry shell and pastry cutouts.

BANANA PUDDING

(Shown on page 9)

  ²/₃ cup sugar
3¹/₂ tablespoons all-purpose flour
     Dash of salt
  1 (14-ounce) can sweetened
     condensed milk
2¹/₂ cups milk
  4 large eggs, separated
  2 teaspoons vanilla extract
  1 (12-ounce) package vanilla wafers
  6 large bananas
  ¹/₄ cup plus 2 tablespoons sugar
  ¹/₂ teaspoon banana or vanilla extract

Combine first 3 ingredients in a saucepan. Combine milks and yolks; add to dry ingredients.

Cook over medium heat, stirring constantly, until smooth and thickened. Remove from heat; stir in 2 teaspoons vanilla.

Arrange one-third of wafers in bottom of a 3-quart baking dish. Slice 2 bananas, and layer over wafers. Pour one-third of pudding mixture over bananas. Repeat layers twice, arranging remaining wafers around outside edge of dish.

Beat egg whites at high speed of an electric mixer until soft peaks form. Add ¹/₄ cup plus 2 tablespoons sugar, 1 tablespoon at a time, beating until stiff peaks form and sugar dissolves. Fold in ¹/₂ teaspoon extract. Spread over pudding, sealing to edge of dish. Bake at 325° for 25 minutes or until meringue is golden.

Yield: 8 to 10 servings.

NO-BAKE BANANA PUDDING

  2 (3.4-ounce) packages vanilla
     instant pudding mix
  1 (8-ounce) carton sour cream
3¹/₂ cups milk
     Vanilla wafers
  3 large bananas
  1 (8-ounce) carton frozen whipped
     topping, thawed

Combine first 3 ingredients in a large bowl; beat at low speed of an electric mixer 2 minutes or until thickened.

Line bottom and sides of a 3-quart bowl with vanilla wafers. Slice 1 banana, and layer over wafers. Spoon one-third of pudding mixture over banana. Repeat layers two more times. Cover and chill. Spread whipped topping over pudding just before serving.

Yield: 10 servings.

ICE CREAM PIE SPECTACULAR

   1 cup graham cracker crumbs
 1/2 cup chopped walnuts
 1/4 cup butter or margarine, melted
   1 pint coffee ice cream, slightly
      softened
   1 pint vanilla ice cream, slightly
      softened
      Brown Sugar Sauce

Combine first 3 ingredients; press into a buttered 9-inch pieplate. Bake at 375° for 8 to 10 minutes; cool.

Spoon coffee ice cream evenly into cooled crust; freeze until almost firm. Spread vanilla ice cream over coffee ice cream, and freeze until firm. Spoon warm Brown Sugar Sauce over slices.

Yield: one 9-inch pie.

BROWN SUGAR SAUCE

   3 tablespoons butter or margarine
   1 cup firmly packed brown sugar
 1/2 cup half-and-half
   1 cup chopped walnuts
   1 teaspoon vanilla extract

Melt butter in a heavy saucepan over low heat; add brown sugar. Cook 5 to 6 minutes, stirring constantly. Remove from heat, and gradually stir in half-and-half. Return to heat, and cook 1 minute. Remove from heat, and stir in walnuts and vanilla.

Yield: about 1 1/2 cups.

OLD-FASHIONED STIRRED CUSTARD

   3 large eggs
 1/2 cup sugar
   2 tablespoons all-purpose flour
 1/4 teaspoon salt
   3 cups milk
 3/4 teaspoon vanilla extract

Place eggs in top of a double boiler; beat at medium speed of an electric mixer until frothy. Combine sugar, flour, and salt; gradually add to eggs, beating until thick.

Pour milk into a medium saucepan; cook over low heat until thoroughly heated (do not boil). Gradually stir about one-fourth of hot milk into egg mixture; add remaining hot milk, stirring constantly.

Bring water in bottom of double boiler to a boil. Reduce heat to low; cook, stirring constantly, 20 to 25 minutes or until mixture thickens and coats a metal spoon.

Stir in vanilla. Serve warm, or cover and chill thoroughly.

Yield: 4 cups.

PINEAPPLE SODA

1 (8-ounce) can unsweetened
   crushed pineapple, undrained
2 tablespoons milk
1 pint vanilla ice cream
1 cup club soda

Combine first 3 ingredients in container of an electric blender; blend until smooth. Stir in club soda. Serve immediately.

Yield: 3$^1/_2$ cups.

DECADENT MUD PIE

$^1/_2$ gallon coffee ice cream, softened
1 (9-inch) graham cracker crust
1 (11.75-ounce) jar hot fudge sauce, heated
   Commercial whipped topping
   Slivered almonds, toasted

Spread ice cream evenly over crust; cover and freeze until firm. To serve, place pie slice on serving plate; spoon hot fudge sauce over each slice. Dollop with whipped topping, and sprinkle with toasted almonds. Serve immediately.

Yield: one 9-inch pie.

OLD-FASHIONED STRAWBERRY SODAS

1 (10-ounce) package frozen
   strawberries in syrup, thawed
3 cups strawberry ice cream, divided
2 (12-ounce) cans cream soda,
   divided
   Garnish: whipped cream

Mash thawed strawberries with a fork until strawberries are well blended with syrup. Add 1 cup ice cream and $^1/_2$ cup cream soda; stir well.

Spoon an equal amount of strawberry mixture into 4 (14-ounce) soda glasses; top with remaining ice cream, and fill glasses with remaining soda. Garnish, if desired.

Yield: 4 servings.

SUMMER FRUIT BOWL

1$^1/_2$ cups cubed cantaloupe
1 cup sliced fresh strawberries
1 cup cubed fresh pineapple
$^1/_3$ cup fresh blueberries

Combine all fruit; toss gently.

Yield: 4 servings.

AMBROSIA PANCAKES WITH ORANGE SYRUP

- 1 large egg, beaten
- 1 cup milk
- 1/2 cup flaked coconut
- 1 tablespoon vegetable oil
- 1 teaspoon grated orange rind
- 1 cup pancake-and-waffle mix
  Orange Syrup

Combine first 5 ingredients, stirring well. Add pancake mix; stir just until dry ingredients are moistened.

Pour about 2 tablespoons batter for each pancake onto a hot, lightly greased griddle. Turn pancakes when tops are covered with bubbles and edges look cooked. Serve with Orange Syrup.

Yield: 12 pancakes.

ORANGE SYRUP

- 1 cup orange sections, coarsely chopped
- 1 cup maple-flavored syrup

Combine ingredients in a small saucepan. Cook until thoroughly heated.

Yield: 1 1/2 cups

YOGURT-GRANOLA FRUIT MEDLEY

- 2 bananas, sliced
- 1 (8-ounce) carton vanilla yogurt
- 1 cup granola
- 2 cups seedless grapes

Layer half of banana slices in a 1-quart bowl; lightly spread 1/4 of yogurt on top, and sprinkle with 1/4 of granola.

Arrange half of grapes over granola; spread with 1/4 of yogurt, and sprinkle with 1/4 of granola.

Repeat procedure with remaining ingredients. Cover and chill up to 3 hours.

Yield: 4 servings.

COFFEE CRUNCH PARFAITS

- 1 quart coffee ice cream, softened
- 1 (2-ounce) package slivered almonds, chopped and toasted
- 2 (1 1/8-ounce) English toffee-flavored candy bars, crushed
- 1/2 cup chocolate syrup
- 1 cup frozen whipped topping, thawed

Spoon 1/4 cup ice cream into each of 8 (4-ounce) parfait glasses; freeze 15 minutes or until firm.

Layer half each of chopped almonds, crushed candy bars, and chocolate syrup evenly into glasses. Repeat layers with remaining ice cream, almonds, candy bars, and chocolate syrup. Cover and freeze until firm. Top parfaits with whipped topping.

Yield: 8 parfaits.

ALMOND ICE CREAM BALLS

1 pint vanilla ice cream
1 (2-ounce) package slivered almonds, chopped and toasted
1/2 cup commercial fudge sauce
2 teaspoons amaretto or 1 teaspoon almond extract

Scoop ice cream into 4 balls, and place on a baking sheet; freeze at least 1 hour or until firm.

Coat ice cream balls with almonds; freeze.

Combine fudge sauce and amaretto. Place ice cream balls in dessert dishes; top with sauce. Serve immediately.

Yield: 4 servings.

DOUBLE-DELIGHT ICE CREAM PIE

1 1/2 cups butter pecan ice cream, softened
1 (9-inch) graham cracker crust
2 (1 1/8-ounce) English toffee-flavored candy bars, crushed
1 1/2 cups vanilla ice cream, softened

Spread butter pecan ice cream in graham cracker crust. Sprinkle with half of crushed candy bars; freeze. Spread vanilla ice cream over top, and sprinkle with remaining crushed candy bars; freeze until firm.

Yield: one 9-inch pie.

STRAWBERRIES JAMAICA

1 (3-ounce) package cream cheese, softened
1/2 cup firmly packed brown sugar
1 1/2 cups sour cream
1 to 2 tablespoons Grand Marnier or orange juice
Fresh strawberries

Beat cream cheese at medium speed of an electric mixer until smooth. Add brown sugar, sour cream, and Grand Marnier, stirring until blended. Cover and chill 8 hours. Serve with strawberries.

Yield: 2 cups.

COLORFUL FRUIT BOWL

1 (8-ounce) carton plain yogurt
1 tablespoon sugar
1 teaspoon lemon juice
1 cup orange sections, chilled
1 cup grapefruit sections, chilled
1 medium banana, sliced
1 cup sliced strawberries
1 cup cubed honeydew melon

Combine first 3 ingredients; chill. Combine orange sections and remaining fruit, tossing gently.

Drizzle yogurt dressing over each serving; serve immediately.

Yield: 6 servings.

EASY INDIVIDUAL TRIFLES

- 1 (3-ounce) package ladyfingers
- 1/4 cup seedless raspberry jam
- 2 tablespoons dry sherry
- 2 tablespoons orange juice
- 2 cups milk
- 1 (3.4-ounce) package vanilla instant pudding mix
- 1 (8.5-ounce) can refrigerated instant whipped cream
- 2 tablespoons slivered almonds, toasted

Halve ladyfingers lengthwise. Spread 1 teaspoon jam on bottom half of each ladyfinger; cover each with top, and cut in half crosswise.

Arrange 4 filled halves in each individual serving dish; drizzle each with 1 teaspoon sherry and 1 teaspoon orange juice.

Combine milk and pudding mix in a 1-quart container; cover tightly, and shake 45 seconds. Pour over ladyfingers.

Chill at least 4 hours. Just before serving, top with whipped cream and almonds.

Yield: 6 servings.

LAYERED AMBROSIA

- 1 (6-ounce) can pineapple juice
- 1/2 cup orange juice
- 1/4 cup sifted powdered sugar
- 7 large oranges
- 3 medium-size pink grapefruit
- 5 medium bananas
- 1 small fresh pineapple, peeled and cored
- 1 (3 1/2-ounce) can flaked coconut
  Garnish: maraschino cherries with stems

Combine first 3 ingredients; stir well, and set juice mixture aside.

Peel oranges; cut crosswise into 1/2-inch slices. Peel and section grapefruit, catching juice in a bowl.

Peel bananas, and cut diagonally into 1/2-inch slices. Dip banana slices in pineapple juice mixture to prevent browning, using a slotted spoon.

Cut pineapple into 1-inch chunks. Arrange half of orange slices in a 3-quart serving bowl. Top with sliced bananas, grapefruit, half of coconut, and pineapple chunks. Top with remaining orange slices.

Pour grapefruit juice and pineapple juice mixture over fruit. Cover and chill thoroughly.

Sprinkle with remaining coconut, and garnish, if desired.

Yield: 12 servings.

Layered Ambrosia

FANTASTIC AMBROSIA

4 bananas, sliced
1/4 cup orange juice
2 cups orange sections
1 cup fresh strawberries, halved
1/4 cup salad dressing or mayonnaise
1 tablespoon sugar
1/2 cup whipping cream, whipped
2 tablespoons flaked coconut,
    toasted

Toss bananas in orange juice; drain and reserve juice. Layer orange sections, bananas, and strawberries in a serving bowl; cover and chill.

Combine salad dressing, sugar, and reserved orange juice; fold in whipped cream. Spoon mixture over fruit, and sprinkle with coconut.

Yield: 6 to 8 servings.

FESTIVE FRUIT COMPOTE

2 cups cantaloupe or honeydew
    melon balls
2 cups fresh strawberries, halved
2 cups fresh blueberries
3 medium bananas, sliced
1 1/2 cups sliced fresh peaches
1 (25.4-ounce) bottle sparkling
    white grape juice, chilled

Layer first 3 ingredients in a bowl or compote; cover and chill until serving time.

Top with sliced bananas and peaches; pour white grape juice over top. Serve with a slotted spoon.

Yield: 8 to 10 servings.

APPLE CRISP

6 large cooking apples, peeled,
    cored, and sliced
1/2 cup sugar
1/4 teaspoon ground nutmeg
1/4 teaspoon ground cinnamon
1 cup all-purpose flour
1 cup firmly packed brown sugar
1/2 cup butter or margarine
    Vanilla ice cream (optional)

Place apple slices in a lightly greased 13 x 9 x 2-inch baking dish. Combine 1/2 cup sugar, nutmeg, and cinnamon; sprinkle over apple.

Combine flour and brown sugar; cut in butter with a pastry blender until mixture is crumbly. Sprinkle over apple.

Bake, uncovered, at 300° for 1 hour. Serve warm with ice cream, if desired.

Yield: 8 servings.

SPICED PEACHES WITH NUTTY DUMPLINGS

- 1/2 cup all-purpose flour
- 1 teaspoon baking powder
- 1/4 teaspoon salt
- 1/4 cup sugar, divided
- 2 tablespoons chopped pecans, toasted
- 1/4 cup skim milk
- 1/8 teaspoon butter flavoring
- 2 cups sliced fresh peaches (about 1 1/2 pounds)
- 2/3 cup unsweetened white grape juice
- 1/4 teaspoon apple pie spice

Combine flour, baking powder, salt, 2 tablespoons sugar, and pecans; stir well. Stir in milk and butter flavoring; set aside.

Combine peaches, grape juice, remaining 2 tablespoons sugar, and apple pie spice in a saucepan; stir well. Bring to a boil. Drop one-fourth of batter at a time into boiling peach mixture.

Cover; cook over medium heat 10 minutes or until dumplings are done.

Yield: 4 servings.

LIGHT LAYERED AMBROSIA

- 3 cups orange sections
- 1 cup pink grapefruit sections
- 1/2 cup flaked coconut, divided
- 1 (8-ounce) can unsweetened crushed pineapple, undrained
- 3 tablespoons honey

Arrange half of orange sections in a glass bowl; top with grapefruit sections, 1/4 cup coconut, pineapple, and remaining orange sections.

Drizzle with honey, and sprinkle with remaining 1/4 cup coconut. Cover and chill 8 hours.

Yield: 10 (1/2-cup) servings.

PICK AN APPLE
• Choose apples that have good color and smooth skin without bruises.
• For cooking or baking, select one of the following apple varieties: Granny Smith, McIntosh, Rome Beauty, Stayman, Winesap, or York Imperial

HOT CRANBERRY BAKE

4 cups peeled chopped cooking
  apple
2 cups fresh cranberries
1½ teaspoons lemon juice
1 cup sugar
1⅓ cups quick-cooking oats,
  uncooked
1 cup chopped walnuts
⅓ cup firmly packed brown sugar
½ cup butter or margarine, melted
  Vanilla ice cream

Layer apple and cranberries in a lightly greased 2-quart baking dish. Sprinkle with lemon juice; spoon sugar over fruit. Set aside.

Combine oats and next 3 ingredients; stir just until dry ingredients are moistened and mixture is crumbly. Sprinkle over fruit.

Bake, uncovered, at 325° for 1 hour. Serve warm with ice cream.

Yield: 8 servings.

Hot Cranberry Bake

Hooray For
SWEETS

Whether it's for quick energy or a little reward, sweet snacks are always irresistible. These creamy candies and crunchy cookies will satisfy every sweet tooth. And they're great for eating on the run as well as while just hanging out with family or friends.

Triple Chip Cookies, p. 547

CINNAMON CRUNCH BARS

12 cinnamon graham crackers
   (2^1/$_2$ x 4^3/$_4$-inch each)
 2 cups finely chopped walnuts
 1 cup butter
 1 cup firmly packed brown sugar
^{1}/$_2$ teaspoon ground cinnamon

Preheat oven to 400 degrees. Arrange crackers in a single layer with sides touching in bottom of a greased 10^1/$_2$ x 15^1/$_2$-inch jellyroll pan. Sprinkle walnuts evenly over crackers. Combine butter, brown sugar, and cinnamon in a heavy small saucepan. Stirring constantly, cook over medium heat until sugar dissolves and mixture begins to boil. Continue to boil syrup 3 minutes longer without stirring; pour over crackers. Bake 8 to 10 minutes or until bubbly and slightly darker around the edges. Cool completely in pan. Break into pieces. Store in an airtight container.

Yield: about 1^1/$_2$ pounds candy

APPLE-OATMEAL COOKIES

 1 cup all-purpose flour
 1 teaspoon baking soda
^{1}/$_2$ teaspoon salt
 1 cup quick-cooking oats, uncooked
^{1}/$_2$ cup firmly packed brown sugar
 1 teaspoon ground cinnamon
^{1}/$_4$ teaspoon ground nutmeg
 1 large egg
^{1}/$_2$ cup vegetable oil
 1 teaspoon vanilla extract
 1 cup peeled, shredded apple
   (1 medium)

^{1}/$_2$ cup raisins
^{1}/$_3$ cup chopped pecans

Combine first 7 ingredients in a large bowl, mixing well. Combine egg, oil, and vanilla; stir into dry ingredients. Stir in apple, raisins, and pecans. Drop dough by rounded teaspoonfuls onto greased cookie sheets. Bake at 350° for 10 to 12 minutes or until lightly browned. Carefully transfer to wire racks to cool.

Yield: 4 dozen.

CARROT COOKIES

^{1}/$_2$ cup shortening
^{1}/$_2$ cup butter or margarine, melted
^{3}/$_4$ cup sugar
 2 large eggs
1^1/$_4$ cups cooked, mashed carrot
 2 cups all-purpose flour
 2 teaspoons baking powder
^{1}/$_4$ teaspoon salt
 1 cup flaked coconut
^{1}/$_2$ cup chopped pecans

Combine first 3 ingredients in a large mixing bowl; beat at medium speed of an electric mixer until fluffy. Add eggs and carrot, mixing well. Combine flour, baking powder, and salt; add to creamed mixture, and stir well. Stir in coconut and pecans. Drop dough by teaspoonfuls onto greased cookie sheets. Bake at 400° for 10 minutes or until firm. Cool on wire racks.

Yield: about 7 dozen.

GINGERBREAD BARS

1 package (14.5 ounces)
    gingerbread cake mix
½ cup butter or margarine, melted
1 egg
4½ cups sifted confectioners sugar
1 package (8 ounces) cream cheese,
    softened
2 eggs

Preheat oven to 350 degrees. In a medium bowl, combine gingerbread cake mix, butter, and 1 egg. Spread evenly into 2 greased 8-inch square baking pans. Combine cream cheese, 2 eggs, and confectioners sugar in a medium bowl. Spread evenly over gingerbread layer in each pan.

Bake 30 to 35 minutes or until lightly browned. Cool completely in pans. Cut into 1 x 2-inch bars. Store in an airtight container.

Yield: about 2 dozen bars in each pan.

Gingerbread Bars

ESPECIALLY FOR KIDS

Children will love helping you stir up these whimsical snack mixes. Packed in cute decorated bags or jars, the treats make wonderful gifts to share with friends and classmates!

PEANUT BUTTER AND JELLY MUFFINS

- 1 package (18.25 ounces) white cake mix
- 1 teaspoon baking soda
- 1 cup crunchy peanut butter
- 3/4 cup water
- 2 eggs
- 1/3 cup strawberry jam

Preheat oven to 350 degrees. In a large bowl, combine cake mix and baking soda. Add peanut butter, water, and eggs; beat just until blended. Fill paper-lined muffin cups about two-thirds full. Place a teaspoonful of jam in center of batter in each muffin cup.

Bake 18 to 23 minutes or until a toothpick inserted in muffin comes out clean. Serve warm.

Yield: about 18 muffins.

PLEASE DON'T FEED THE ANIMALS

- 2 cups animal crackers
- 2 cups chocolate- or carob-covered raisins
- 1 cup jelly beans
- 1 cup unsalted peanuts

Combine crackers, raisins, jelly beans, and peanuts in a large bowl; store in airtight container.

Yield: 6 cups snack mix.

SOMETHING FOR THE ELEPHANTS

- 2 cups candy corn
- 2 cups candy-coated chocolate pieces
- 2 cups unsalted peanuts

Combine candy corn, chocolate candies, and peanuts in a large bowl; store in airtight container.

Yield: 6 cups snack mix.

GO FISHIN'

- 2 cups gummi fish
- 2 cups yogurt-covered peanuts
- 2 cups small pretzels

Combine gummi fish, peanuts, and pretzels in large bowl; store in airtight container.

Yield: 6 cups snack mix.

CINNAMON PUFFINS

1 1/2 cups all-purpose flour
1 1/2 teaspoons baking powder
1 teaspoon ground nutmeg, divided
1/2 teaspoon salt
1 cup sugar, divided
1/3 cup shortening
1 egg
1/2 teaspoon vanilla extract
1/2 cup milk
1/2 cup butter or margarine
1 teaspoon ground cinnamon

Preheat oven to 350 degrees. In a medium bowl, combine flour, baking powder, 1/2 teaspoon nutmeg, and salt. In another medium bowl, beat 1/2 cup sugar, shortening, egg, and vanilla until well blended.

Add flour mixture to creamed mixture; beat in milk until smooth. Fill each cup of a lightly greased 12-cup muffin pan two-thirds full with batter.

Bake 20 minutes or until light golden brown. Melt butter in a small saucepan. In a small bowl, combine remaining 1/2 cup sugar, cinnamon, and remaining 1/2 teaspoon nutmeg.

While puffins are warm, dip in butter, then in sugar mixture, coating thoroughly. Store in an airtight container.

Yield: 1 dozen puffins.

QUICKIE CINNAMON ROLLS

3/4 cup firmly packed brown sugar
1/4 cup butter or margarine
1 teaspoon ground cinnamon
1/4 cup chopped pecans
1 can (10 biscuits) refrigerated Texas-style biscuits

Stir brown sugar, butter, and cinnamon in a small saucepan over medium heat until butter melts. Pour butter mixture into a 9-inch round cake pan. Sprinkle pecans over butter mixture.

Dip one side of each biscuit in mixture; place coated side up in pan. Bake uncovered in a preheated 400° oven 12 to 18 minutes or until bread is light brown. Serve immediately.

Yield: 10 cinnamon rolls.

Note: Ready-to-bake rolls can be covered and refrigerated 1 to 2 days ahead.

LIGHTENED-UP OLD-FASHIONED CINNAMON ROLLS

$1/3$ cup fat-free milk
$1/3$ cup reduced-calorie margarine
$1/4$ cup firmly packed brown sugar
1 teaspoon salt
1 package active dry yeast
$1/2$ cup warm water (105° to 115°)
$1/2$ cup egg substitute
$3^{1}/2$ cups bread flour, divided
$3/4$ cup quick-cooking oats, uncooked
Vegetable cooking spray
$1/4$ cup reduced-calorie margarine, softened
$3/4$ cup firmly packed brown sugar
$1/4$ cup raisins
2 teaspoons ground cinnamon
1 cup sifted powdered sugar
2 tablespoons water

Combine first 4 ingredients in a saucepan; heat until margarine melts, stirring occasionally. Cool mixture to 105° to 115°.

Combine yeast and warm water; let stand 5 minutes. Combine yeast mixture, milk mixture, egg substitute, 1 cup flour, and oats in a large mixing bowl, mixing well. Gradually stir in enough remaining flour to make a soft dough.

Turn dough out onto a lightly floured surface; knead until smooth and elastic (about 8 minutes). Place dough in a large bowl coated with cooking spray, turning to grease top.

Cover and let rise in a warm place (85°), free from drafts, 1 hour or until doubled in bulk.

Punch dough down. Cover; let rest 10 minutes. Divide in half; roll each half into a 12-inch square. Spread each with 2 tablespoons margarine.

Combine $3/4$ cup brown sugar, raisins, and cinnamon; sprinkle over each square. Roll up jellyroll fashion; pinch seam to seal. Cut each roll into 1-inch slices; place, cut side down, in two 8-inch square pans coated with cooking spray.

Cover; let rise in a warm place, free from drafts, 30 minutes or until almost doubled in bulk.

Bake at 375° for 15 to 20 minutes or until golden. Combine powdered sugar and 2 tablespoons water; drizzle over warm rolls.

Yield: 2 dozen cinnamon rolls.

Lightened-Up Old-Fashioned Cinnamon Rolls

PEANUT BUTTER FUDGE

1 cup granulated sugar
1 cup firmly packed brown sugar
1 cup evaporated milk
$^1/_4$ cup light corn syrup
$^1/_8$ teaspoon salt
1 cup large marshmallows, cut into pieces
$^1/_2$ cup smooth peanut butter
2 tablespoons butter
1 teaspoon vanilla extract

Butter sides of a medium saucepan. Combine sugars, milk, corn syrup, and salt in pan. Stirring constantly, cook over medium-low heat until sugar dissolves. Using a pastry brush dipped in hot water, wash down any sugar crystals on sides of pan. Attach a candy thermometer to pan, making sure thermometer does not touch bottom of pan. Increase heat to medium and bring to a boil. Cook, without stirring, until mixture reaches soft-ball stage (234 to 240 degrees). Test about $^1/_2$ teaspoon mixture in ice water. Mixture will easily form a ball in ice water but will flatten when removed from water. Add marshmallows, peanut butter, and butter; stir until smooth. Stir in vanilla. Using medium speed of an electric mixer, beat until fudge thickens and begins to lose its gloss. Pour into a buttered 8-inch square pan. Cool completely. Cut fudge into $1^1/_2$-inch squares, then cut in half diagonally to form triangles. Store in an airtight container or see Chocolate-Dipped Variation.

Yield: 1 pound, 10 ounces fudge or about 50 triangles.

CHOCOLATE-DIPPED VARIATION

3 ounces chocolate candy coating, melted
$^1/_2$ cup chopped pecans, finely ground

Using half of fudge pieces, dip edges into melted chocolate, then into pecans. Place on waxed paper to let chocolate harden. Store in an airtight container.

SALTED PEANUT COOKIES

1 cup shortening
2 cups firmly packed brown sugar
2 large eggs
2 cups all-purpose flour
1 teaspoon baking powder
1 teaspoon baking soda
$^1/_2$ teaspoon salt
2 cups quick-cooking oats, uncooked
1 cup crispy rice cereal
1 cup salted peanuts

Beat shortening at medium speed of an electric mixer until fluffy; gradually add sugar, beating well. Add eggs, and beat well. Combine flour, baking powder, soda, and salt; add to creamed mixture, mixing well. Stir in oats, cereal, and peanuts. (Dough will be stiff.) Drop dough by rounded teaspoonfuls onto lightly greased cookie sheets. Bake at 375° for 10 to 12 minutes. Remove cookies to wire racks to cool.

Yield: 7 dozen.

PEANUTTY S'MORE BARS

6 graham crackers (2½ x 5-inch rectangles)
2 jars (7 ounces each) marshmallow crème
⅔ cup plus 1 tablespoon crunchy peanut butter, divided
1 package (6 ounces) semisweet chocolate chips

Coarsely crumble crackers into a lightly greased 9 x 13-inch baking pan. Stirring frequently, melt marshmallow crème and ⅔ cup peanut butter in a medium saucepan over medium-low heat.

Immediately pour marshmallow mixture over cracker pieces, spreading with a spatula if necessary.

Stirring frequently, melt chocolate chips and remaining 1 tablespoon peanut butter in a small saucepan over low heat. Drizzle over marshmallow mixture.

Chill 2 hours or until firm. Cut into 1 x 2-inch bars. Store in an airtight container in a single layer in refrigerator.

Yield: about 4 dozen bars.

Peanutty S'more Bars

EASY PEANUT PATTIES

1 1/2 cups sugar
  1 package (3 ounces) vanilla
      pudding and pie filling mix
 3/4 cup evaporated milk
  1 teaspoon vanilla extract
  2 cups Spanish peanuts

Combine sugar, pudding mix, and evaporated milk in a heavy medium saucepan over medium-high heat.

Stirring frequently, bring mixture to a boil. Reduce heat to medium and boil 5 minutes. Remove from heat. Stir in vanilla. Beat 3 minutes or until candy thickens. Stir in peanuts.

Drop by tablespoonfuls onto waxed paper. Allow candy to harden. Store in an airtight container.

Yield: about 2 dozen candies

BUTTER SOFTENING TIP
Use your microwave oven to soften butter or margarine. Place butter in a microwave-safe bowl, and microwave at LOW (10% power) until softened. For 1 to 2 tablespoons, microwave 15 to 30 seconds; for 1/4 to 1/2 cup, microwave 1 to 1 1/4 minutes; and for 1 cup, microwave 1 3/4 minutes.

EASY PRALINES

1 3/4 cups graham cracker crumbs
  1 cup finely chopped toasted
      pecans
 1/8 teaspoon salt
 1/2 cup butter or margarine
  2 cups sugar
  1 can (5 ounces) evaporated milk
  2 cups miniature marshmallows
  1 teaspoon vanilla extract

Combine graham cracker crumbs, pecans, and salt in a medium bowl; set aside. In a heavy large saucepan, melt butter over medium heat.

Add sugar and evaporated milk. Stirring frequently, bring to a boil. Stirring constantly, boil mixture 3 minutes. Remove from heat.

Add marshmallows and vanilla; stir until marshmallows melt. Add graham cracker crumb mixture; stir until well blended. Working quickly, drop tablespoonfuls of warm mixture onto waxed paper; cool. Store in an airtight container.

Yield: about 4 dozen pralines.

MINCEMEAT DROP COOKIES

- 1/2 cup shortening
- 1/2 cup sugar
- 1 large egg
- 1 cup prepared mincemeat
- 1 1/2 cups all-purpose flour
- 1/2 teaspoon baking soda
- 1/4 teaspoon salt

Beat shortening at medium speed of an electric mixer until fluffy; gradually add sugar, beating well. Add egg, and beat well. Add mincemeat, mixing well. Combine flour, soda, and salt; stir into creamed mixture. Drop dough by teaspoonfuls onto greased cookie sheets. Bake at 350° for 16 to 18 minutes. Cool on wire racks.

Yield: 4 1/2 dozen.

TAKE-ALONG BREAKFAST COOKIES

- 3/4 cup all-purpose flour
- 1/2 teaspoon baking soda
- 1/2 teaspoon salt
- 2/3 cup butter or margarine, softened
- 2/3 cup sugar
- 1 large egg
- 1 teaspoon vanilla extract
- 1 1/2 cups regular oats, uncooked
- 1 cup (4 ounces) shredded Cheddar cheese
- 1/2 cup wheat germ
- 6 slices bacon, cooked and crumbled

Combine flour, soda, and salt; mix well, and set aside. Beat butter and sugar at medium speed of an electric mixer until fluffy; add egg and vanilla, beating well. Add flour mixture, mixing well. Stir in oats, cheese, wheat germ, and bacon. Drop dough by rounded tablespoonfuls onto ungreased cookie sheets. Bake at 350° for 14 to 16 minutes. Cool 1 minute on cookie sheets.

Yield: 2 dozen.

GRANOLA COOKIES

- 1 cup butter or margarine, softened
- 3/4 cup firmly packed brown sugar
- 1/2 cup sugar
- 1 large egg
- 1 teaspoon vanilla extract
- 1 1/2 cups all-purpose flour
- 1 teaspoon baking soda
- 1/2 teaspoon salt
- 1 teaspoon ground cinnamon
- 4 cups commercial granola
- 1/2 cup raisins

Beat butter at medium speed of an electric mixer until creamy; gradually add sugars, beating well. Add egg and vanilla, mixing well. Combine flour and next 3 ingredients; add to creamed mixture, mixing well. Stir in granola and raisins. Drop dough by rounded tablespoonfuls onto lightly greased cookie sheets. Bake at 375° for 10 to 12 minutes or until lightly browned. Cool 1 minute on cookie sheets; remove to wire racks to cool completely.

Yield: 4 1/2 dozen.

MICROWAVE ROCKY ROAD FUDGE

4¹/₂ cups sifted confectioners sugar
¹/₂ cup butter or margarine
¹/₃ cup cocoa
¹/₄ cup milk
¹/₄ teaspoon salt
¹/₂ cup chopped pecans
¹/₂ cup miniature marshmallows
1 teaspoon vanilla extract

Line an 8-inch square baking pan with aluminum foil, extending foil over 2 sides of pan; grease foil. In a large microwave-safe bowl, combine confectioners sugar, butter, cocoa, milk, and salt.

Microwave on high power (100%) 2 to 2¹/₂ minutes or until butter is melted. Add pecans, marshmallows, and vanilla; stir until well blended. Pour into prepared pan.

Chill about 1 hour or until firm. Use ends of foil to lift candy from pan. Cut into 1-inch squares and store in an airtight container.

Yield: about 1¹/₂ pounds fudge.

HOLIDAY PACKAGING IDEAS
• Check stores for tins, bags, baskets, and boxes. Line with colorful napkins, plastic wrap, or tissue.
• Decorate small paper bags with stencils or rubber stamps and ink. Trim top of bags with pinking shears. Fold down top; seal with stickers, or weave ribbon through holes punched in bag to close.

STRAWBERRY FUDGE BALLS

1 (8-ounce) package cream cheese, softened
1 (6-ounce) package semisweet chocolate morsels, melted
³/₄ cup vanilla wafer crumbs
¹/₄ cup strawberry preserves
¹/₂ cup almonds, toasted and finely chopped
Powdered sugar

Beat cream cheese at medium speed of an electric mixer until fluffy. Add melted chocolate, beating until smooth. Stir in wafer crumbs and preserves; cover and chill 1 hour.

Shape mixture into 1-inch balls; roll in almonds or powdered sugar. Store in an airtight container in refrigerator, or freeze up to 2 months.

Yield: 4 dozen.

VARIATION
RASPBERRY FUDGE BALLS
Substitute ¹/₄ cup red raspberry jam for strawberry preserves and ²/₃ cup ground pecans, toasted, for ¹/₂ cup almonds.

CRUNCHY TIGER BUTTER

- 1 pound vanilla-flavored candy coating
- 1/2 cup extra-crunchy peanut butter
- 1 package (6 ounces) semisweet chocolate chips

Place candy coating in a medium microwave-safe bowl. Microwave on high power (100%) 2 minutes or until candy coating melts. Stir in peanut butter. Spread peanut butter mixture in a greased 10½ x 15½-inch jellyroll pan.

Place chocolate chips in a small microwave-safe bowl. Microwave on high power (100%) 1½ minutes or until chocolate melts. Pour chocolate over peanut butter mixture; swirl chocolate with a small spatula or knife. Chill until candy hardens. Break into pieces. Store in an airtight container in a cool place.

Yield: about 1½ pounds candy.

Crunchy Tiger Butter

HAZELNUT COOKIES

- 1 cup butter or margarine, softened
- 1/2 cup sifted powdered sugar
- 2 cups all-purpose flour
- 1 cup finely chopped hazelnuts, toasted
- Sifted powdered sugar

Beat butter at medium speed of an electric mixer until creamy. Add 1/2 cup sugar; beat until light and fluffy. Gradually add flour; beat well. Stir in hazelnuts. Cover and chill 30 minutes. Shape dough into 1-inch balls; place on ungreased cookie sheets. Bake at 400° for 12 to 14 minutes. Remove immediately from cookie sheets; roll in powdered sugar.

Yield: 3 1/2 dozen.

ORANGE SLICE COOKIES

- 1 1/2 cups chopped candy orange slices
- 1/4 cup all-purpose flour
- 1 cup butter or margarine, softened
- 1 cup firmly packed brown sugar
- 3/4 cup sugar
- 2 large eggs
- 2 tablespoons milk
- 2 tablespoons vanilla extract
- 2 cups all-purpose flour
- 1 teaspoon baking soda
- 1/2 teaspoon salt
- 1/2 teaspoon ground cinnamon
- 1/2 teaspoon ground nutmeg
- 2 1/2 cups quick-cooking oats, uncooked
- 1 cup flaked coconut

Combine orange slices and 1/4 cup flour in a medium bowl; toss to coat candy. Set aside. Beat butter at medium speed of an electric mixer until creamy; gradually add sugars, beating well. Add eggs, milk, and vanilla; beat well. Combine 2 cups flour and next 4 ingredients; gradually add to creamed mixture, beating well. Stir in candy mixture, oats, and coconut. Drop dough by rounded teaspoonfuls 2 inches apart onto greased cookie sheets. Bake at 375° for 10 minutes. Cool slightly on cookie sheets; remove to wire racks.

Yield: 9 dozen.

ALMOND COOKIES

- 2/3 cup shortening
- 1 2/3 cups sugar
- 2 large eggs
- 1 teaspoon almond extract
- 2 1/2 cups all-purpose flour
- 2 teaspoons baking powder
- 1/2 teaspoon baking soda
- 1/4 teaspoon salt
- 1 egg white, slightly beaten
- About 1/4 cup sliced almonds

Beat shortening at medium speed of an electric mixer until fluffy; gradually add sugar, beating well. Add eggs and almond extract, beating well. Combine flour, baking powder, soda, and salt; stir into creamed mixture. Shape dough into 1 1/2-inch balls; flatten slightly. Brush with beaten egg white. Place 3 sliced almonds in center of each cookie. Bake at 375° for 15 minutes or until lightly browned. Cool on wire racks.

Yield: about 3 dozen.

TEXAN-SIZE ALMOND CRUNCH COOKIES

(Photo on page 9)

- 1 cup sugar
- 1 cup sifted powdered sugar
- 1 cup butter or margarine, softened
- 1 cup vegetable oil
- 2 large eggs
- 2 teaspoons almond extract
- 3 1/2 cups all-purpose flour
- 1 cup whole wheat flour
- 1 teaspoon baking soda
- 1 teaspoon salt
- 1 teaspoon cream of tartar
- 2 cups chopped almonds
- 1 (6-ounce) package almond brickle chips
  Sugar

Combine first 4 ingredients in a large mixing bowl; beat at medium speed of an electric mixer until blended. Add eggs and almond extract, beating well.

Combine flours, soda, salt, and cream of tartar; gradually add to creamed mixture, beating just until blended after each addition. Stir in almonds and brickle chips. Cover and chill 3 to 4 hours.

Shape dough into 1 1/2-inch balls, and place at least 3 inches apart on ungreased cookie sheets. Flatten cookies with a fork dipped in sugar, making a crisscross pattern.

Bake at 350° for 14 to 15 minutes or until lightly browned. Transfer to wire racks to cool.

Yield: about 4 dozen.

EASY WALNUT COOKIES

- 1/2 cup butter or margarine, softened
- 2 tablespoons sugar
- 1 cup all-purpose flour
- 1 teaspoon walnut extract
- 1 cup walnuts, finely chopped
- 3/4 cup sifted powdered sugar

Beat butter and 2 tablespoons sugar at medium speed of an electric mixer until blended. Stir in flour. Add walnut extract and walnuts, stirring well. Cover and chill 30 minutes.

Shape dough into 1-inch balls; place on ungreased cookie sheet. Bake at 350° for 15 minutes. Roll in powdered sugar.

Yield: 2 1/2 dozen.

CRISSCROSS COOKIE TIP

Use a fork to flatten balls of cookie dough in a crisscross pattern. Dip the tines of the fork in sugar or flour so that the dough will not stick.

BROWN SUGAR-PECAN COOKIES

(Photo on page 9)

- 1 cup butter or margarine, softened
- 1/2 cup firmly packed brown sugar
- 1/2 cup sugar
- 1 large egg
- 1 teaspoon vanilla extract
- 2 cups all-purpose flour
- 1/2 teaspoon baking soda
- 1/4 teaspoon salt
- 1/2 cup finely chopped pecans
  - Brown Sugar Frosting
  - Pecan halves

Beat butter at medium speed of an electric mixer until creamy; gradually add sugars, mixing well. Add egg and vanilla; beat well.

Combine flour, soda, and salt; gradually add to creamed mixture, mixing well after each addition. Stir in chopped pecans. Cover and chill 30 minutes.

Shape dough into 1-inch balls; place on ungreased cookie sheets. Bake at 350° for 10 to 12 minutes. Cool on wire racks, and spread Brown Sugar Frosting over tops. Top each cookie with a pecan half.

Yield: 5 dozen.

BROWN SUGAR FROSTING

- 1 cup firmly packed brown sugar
- 1/2 cup half-and-half
- 1 tablespoon butter or margarine
- 1 1/2 to 1 2/3 cups sifted powdered sugar

Combine brown sugar and half-and-half in a saucepan. Cook over medium heat, stirring constantly, until mixture comes to a boil; boil 4 minutes. Remove from heat. Stir in butter.

Add 1 1/2 cups powdered sugar, and beat at medium speed of an electric mixer until smooth. Gradually add remaining powdered sugar to desired spreading consistency.

Yield: 1 1/3 cups.

PECAN-BUTTER COOKIES

- 1 cup butter or margarine, softened
- 1 cup sugar
- 2 egg yolks
- 3/4 teaspoon vanilla extract
- 3/4 teaspoon almond extract
- 1/2 teaspoon lemon extract
- 2 cups all-purpose flour
- 1 teaspoon baking powder
- 1/4 teaspoon salt
  - About 1 cup pecan halves

Beat butter at medium speed of an electric mixer until creamy; gradually add sugar, beating well. Add egg yolks, one at a time, beating until blended after each addition. Stir in flavorings.

Combine flour, baking powder, and salt. Add to creamed mixture, and beat well. Roll dough into 1-inch balls; place about 2 inches apart on ungreased cookie sheets. Press a pecan half into center of each cookie.

Bake at 300° for 20 minutes or until lightly browned. Cool on wire racks.

Yield: about 3 1/2 dozen.

PRALINE GRAHAMS

1 (5⅓-ounce) package graham
    crackers
¾ cup butter or margarine
½ cup sugar
1 cup chopped pecans

Separate each graham cracker into four sections. Arrange in an ungreased 15 x 10 x 1-inch jellyroll pan with edges touching.

Melt butter in a saucepan; stir in sugar and pecans. Bring to a boil; cook 3 minutes, stirring frequently. Spread mixture evenly over graham crackers.

Bake at 300° for 12 minutes. Remove from pan, and cool on wax paper.

Yield: 3½ dozen.

Praline Grahams

GINGERSNAPS

¾ cup shortening
1 cup sugar
1 large egg
¼ cup molasses
2 cups all-purpose flour
2 teaspoons baking soda
¼ teaspoon salt
½ teaspoon ground cinnamon
1 tablespoon ground ginger
   Sugar

Beat shortening at medium speed of an electric mixer until fluffy; gradually add 1 cup sugar, beating well. Add egg and molasses; mix well. Combine flour and next 4 ingredients; mix well. Add about one-fourth of flour mixture at a time to creamed mixture, beating until smooth after each addition. Cover and chill at least 1 hour. Shape dough into 1-inch balls; roll in sugar. Place on ungreased cookie sheets. Bake at 375° for 10 minutes. Cool on wire racks.

Yield: 4 dozen.

SPICE-MOLASSES COOKIES

¾ cup shortening
1 cup sugar
1 large egg
¼ cup molasses
2 cups all-purpose flour
1 teaspoon baking soda
1 teaspoon baking powder
¼ teaspoon salt
1 teaspoon ground ginger
1 teaspoon ground cinnamon
½ teaspoon ground nutmeg

¼ teaspoon ground cloves
¼ teaspoon ground allspice
   Sugar

Beat shortening at medium speed of an electric mixer until fluffy; gradually add 1 cup sugar, beating well. Add egg and molasses; mix well. Combine flour and next 8 ingredients; mix well. Add about one-fourth of flour mixture at a time to creamed mixture, beating until smooth after each addition. Cover and chill 1 hour. Shape dough into 1-inch balls, and roll in sugar. Place 2 inches apart on ungreased cookie sheets. Bake at 375° for 9 to 11 minutes. (Tops will crack.) Cool on wire racks.

Yield: 4 dozen.

RAISIN COOKIES

2 cups raisins
1 cup water
1 cup shortening
1¾ cups sugar
2 large eggs
1 teaspoon vanilla extract
3½ cups all-purpose flour
1 teaspoon baking powder
1 teaspoon baking soda
½ teaspoon salt
½ teaspoon ground cinnamon
½ teaspoon ground nutmeg
1 cup chopped pecans or walnuts

Combine raisins and water in a medium saucepan; bring to a boil, and boil about 3 minutes. Cool. (Do not drain.)

Beat shortening at medium speed of an electric mixer until fluffy; gradually add sugar, beating well. Add eggs; beat well. Stir in raisins (with liquid) and vanilla.

Combine flour and next 5 ingredients; gradually add to raisin mixture, stirring after each addition. Stir in pecans.

Drop dough by teaspoonfuls 2 inches apart onto well-greased cookie sheets. Bake at 375° for 10 to 12 minutes or until browned. Cool on wire racks. (Cookies will be soft.)

Yield: 5 dozen.

SPECIAL OATMEAL COOKIES

1 1/2 cups all-purpose flour
1 teaspoon baking soda
1 teaspoon salt
2 teaspoons ground cinnamon
1/2 teaspoon ground nutmeg
1 cup shortening
1 cup sugar
1 cup firmly packed brown sugar
2 large eggs
1 teaspoon lemon extract
3 cups quick-cooking oats, uncooked
1 cup chopped pecans

Combine first 5 ingredients; set aside.

Beat shortening at medium speed of an electric mixer until fluffy; add sugars, beating well. Add eggs and lemon extract, and beat well. Add flour mixture, mixing well. Stir in oats and pecans.

Shape dough into 1-inch balls, and place on lightly greased cookie sheets. Bake at 350° for 10 to 12 minutes.

Yield: 5 dozen.

OATMEAL-RAISIN COOKIES

1/4 cup margarine, softened
1/2 cup sugar
1/2 cup firmly packed brown sugar
1/2 cup egg substitute
2 teaspoons vanilla extract
3/4 cup all-purpose flour
1/4 teaspoon baking soda
1/8 teaspoon salt
1 1/2 cups quick-cooking oats, uncooked
1/2 cup raisins
    Vegetable cooking spray

Beat margarine at medium speed of an electric mixer. Gradually add sugars, beating well. Add egg substitute and vanilla; mix well.

Combine flour and next 3 ingredients. Gradually add to margarine mixture, mixing well. Stir in raisins.

Drop dough by 2 teaspoonfuls onto cookie sheets coated with cooking spray.

Bake at 350° for 10 to 12 minutes or until lightly browned. Remove to wire racks to cool.

Yield: 3 dozen.

COCOA KISS COOKIES

1 cup butter or margarine, softened
2/3 cup sugar
1 teaspoon vanilla extract
1 2/3 cups all-purpose flour
1/4 cup cocoa
1 cup coarsely ground walnuts
1 (9-ounce) package milk chocolate kisses, unwrapped

Beat butter at medium speed of an electric mixer until creamy; gradually add sugar, beating well. Add vanilla, mixing well. Add flour and cocoa, mixing well. Stir in walnuts. Cover and chill 2 hours or until firm. Wrap 1 tablespoon of dough around each chocolate kiss, and roll to form a ball. Place on ungreased cookie sheets. Bake at 375° for 12 minutes. Cool slightly on cookie sheets; remove to wire racks.

Yield: about 4 dozen.

COOKIE TIPS

• Bake one batch of cookies on the center rack of a preheated oven. If baking two batches at a time, space racks evenly in oven. Allow 1 to 2 inches of space around baking sheet for good air circulation.
• Immediately remove cookies from pan to a cooling rack unless otherwise stated in recipe. If they fall apart or crumble as you are transferring them with a spatula, wait a minute until they firm up before removing the remaining cookies.
• If cookies stick to pan as they cool, return pan to a warm oven for a few minutes to allow cookies to soften.
• Cool baking sheets between batches so cookies will keep their shape.

CINNAMON-PECAN ICEBOX COOKIES

1 cup butter or margarine, softened
3/4 cup sugar
1/4 cup firmly packed brown sugar
1 large egg
1 teaspoon vanilla extract
2 1/4 cups all-purpose flour
1 1/2 teaspoons baking powder
1/2 teaspoon salt
1 cup finely chopped pecans
1/4 cup sugar
1 1/2 teaspoons ground cinnamon

Beat butter at medium speed of an electric mixer until creamy; gradually add 3/4 cup sugar and 1/4 cup brown sugar, beating well. Add egg and vanilla, beating well.

Combine flour, baking powder, and salt; add to creamed mixture, beating well. Stir in pecans. Cover and chill dough 2 hours. Shape into 2 (6 x 2 1/2-inch) rolls; wrap in wax paper, and freeze until firm.

Combine 1/4 cup sugar and cinnamon; stir well. Unwrap dough, and roll in sugar mixture. Slice frozen dough into 1/4-inch slices; place on ungreased cookie sheets.

Bake at 350° for 12 to 14 minutes or until lightly browned. Cool on wire racks.

Yield: 4 dozen.

Note: Dough may be frozen up to 3 months.

Cinnamon-Pecan Icebox Cookies

GOLDEN SUGAR COOKIES

1 cup butter or margarine, softened
1/2 cup sugar
1 large egg
1 teaspoon lemon extract
2 1/4 cups all-purpose flour
1 1/2 teaspoons baking powder
1/2 teaspoon salt
1 tablespoon whipping cream or half-and-half
   Red and green decorator sugar crystals

Beat butter at medium speed of an electric mixer until creamy; gradually add 1/2 cup sugar, beating well. Add egg, beating well. Stir in lemon extract.

Combine flour, baking powder, and salt; add to creamed mixture, beating well. Shape dough into two 12-inch rolls; wrap in wax paper, and chill at least 6 hours.

Unwrap rolls, and cut into 1/4-inch slices; place on lightly greased cookie sheets. Brush tops of cookies with cream, and sprinkle evenly with sugar crystals.

Bake at 400° for 8 minutes. Cool on wire racks.

Yield: 6 dozen.

Note: Dough may be frozen by wrapping securely and freezing up to 1 month. Remove from freezer; slice dough, and bake as directed.

VANILLA SLICE-AND-BAKE COOKIES

1/2 cup butter or margarine, softened
1 cup sugar
1 large egg
2 teaspoons vanilla extract
1 3/4 cups all-purpose flour
1/2 teaspoon baking soda
1/4 teaspoon salt
1/2 cup chopped pecans

Beat butter at medium speed of an electric mixer until creamy; gradually add sugar, beating well. Add egg and vanilla; beat well. Combine flour, soda, and salt; add to creamed mixture, beating well. Stir in pecans. Shape dough into two 12-inch rolls; wrap in wax paper, and chill at least 2 hours.

Unwrap rolls, and cut into 1/4 -inch slices; place on ungreased cookie sheets. Bake at 350° for 10 to 12 minutes. Cool slightly; remove to wire racks to cool completely.

Yield: about 7 dozen.

VARIATION
SLICE OF SPICE COOKIES
Prepare Vanilla Slice-and-Bake Cookies, substituting firmly packed brown sugar for sugar. Combine 1/4 cup granulated sugar and 2 teaspoons ground cinnamon; dip each slice in mixture before baking.

Note: Dough may be frozen up to 3 months. Slice dough while frozen, and bake as directed.

FILLED LEMON COOKIES

    2 cups butter or margarine,
        softened
    1 cup sifted powdered sugar
    4 cups all-purpose flour
    $1/4$ teaspoon salt
    2 teaspoons lemon extract
        Filling
        Additional powdered sugar

Beat butter at medium speed of an electric mixer until creamy; gradually add 1 cup powdered sugar, beating until light and fluffy.

Combine flour and salt; add to creamed mixture, beating well. Stir in lemon extract. Flour hands, and shape dough into two 16-inch rolls; wrap in wax paper, and chill several hours.

Unwrap rolls, and cut into $1/4$-inch slices; place on ungreased cookie sheets. Bake at 400° for 8 minutes or until browned. Cool on wire racks.

Spoon filling on bottom side of half of cookies, spreading evenly. Place a second cookie on top of filling, top side up, and sprinkle lightly with powdered sugar.

Yield: 5 dozen.

FILLING

    1 large egg, beaten
    $2/3$ cup sugar
    2 tablespoons butter or margarine,
        softened
  $1 1/2$ teaspoons grated lemon rind
    3 tablespoons lemon juice
    1 teaspoon cornstarch

Combine all ingredients in top of a double boiler, stirring until blended. Bring water to a boil. Reduce heat to low; cook, stirring constantly, until thickened and smooth. Chill about 1 hour.

Yield: about $3/4$ cup.

CRISPY SHORTBREAD COOKIES

    $1/2$ cup butter or margarine, softened
    $1/2$ cup shortening
  $1 1/2$ cups sifted powdered sugar
  $1 1/2$ teaspoons vanilla extract
  $1 1/4$ cups all-purpose flour
  $1 1/2$ cups cornflakes
    $1/2$ cup finely chopped pecans

Beat butter and shortening at medium speed of an electric mixer until fluffy; gradually add sugar, beating until smooth. Add vanilla and flour, beating well. Stir in cornflakes.

Shape dough into a long roll, 2 inches in diameter; gently roll in pecans. Wrap in wax paper, and chill 8 hours or until firm.

Let roll stand at room temperature about 10 minutes. Cut dough into $1/4$-inch slices; place 2 inches apart on ungreased cookie sheets.

Bake at 350° for 15 minutes or until lightly browned. Cool on wire racks.

Yield: $3 1/2$ dozen.

DOUBLE PEANUT BUTTER COOKIES

1³/₄ cups all-purpose flour
¹/₂ teaspoon baking soda
¹/₄ teaspoon salt
¹/₂ cup sugar
¹/₂ cup shortening
¹/₂ cup creamy peanut butter
¹/₄ cup light corn syrup
1 tablespoon milk
¹/₄ cup creamy peanut butter

Combine first 4 ingredients; cut in shortening and ¹/₂ cup peanut butter with a pastry blender until mixture is crumbly. Stir in corn syrup and milk.

Shape dough into a 12-inch roll; wrap in wax paper, and chill at least 2 hours.

Unwrap roll, and cut into ¹/₄-inch slices; place half of slices on ungreased cookie sheets. Spread each with ¹/₂ teaspoon peanut butter. Top with remaining cookie slices, and seal edges with a fork.

Bake at 350° for 10 to 12 minutes. Cool on wire racks.

Yield: about 2 dozen.

Note: Dough may be frozen up to 3 months. Slice dough while frozen; let thaw slightly. Assemble and bake as directed.

CHOCOLATE-MINT SWIRLS

1 cup butter or margarine, softened
1 cup sugar
1 large egg
1 teaspoon vanilla extract
2 (1-ounce) squares semisweet chocolate, melted and cooled
2 tablespoons green crème de menthe
1¹/₂ teaspoons peppermint extract
3 cups plus 3 tablespoons all-purpose flour, divided
1¹/₂ teaspoons baking powder
¹/₄ teaspoon salt

Beat butter at medium speed of an electric mixer until creamy; gradually add sugar, beating well. Add egg and vanilla; beat well.

Divide mixture in half, transferring one half to a separate bowl. Add melted chocolate to half of batter, beating well. Add green crème de menthe and peppermint extract to other half, beating well.

Combine 3 cups flour, baking powder, and salt; stir well. Add half of flour mixture to each creamed mixture, beating at low speed of electric mixer. Add remaining 3 tablespoons flour to crème de menthe mixture, mixing well. Cover and chill both portions of dough 1 hour.

Roll each half of dough into a 15 x 8-inch rectangle on floured wax paper. Invert crème de menthe dough onto chocolate dough; peel off wax paper. Tightly roll dough, jellyroll fashion, starting at long side, peeling wax paper from dough while rolling. Cover and chill 1 hour.

Slice dough into ¼-inch slices; place on ungreased cookie sheets.

Bake at 350° for 10 to 12 minutes. Remove to wire racks to cool.

Yield: about 5 dozen.

Chocolate-Mint Swirls

CHOCOLATE-GINGER CRINKLES

2/3 cup shortening
1 cup sugar
1 large egg
1/4 cup molasses
2 1/4 cups all-purpose flour
1 1/2 teaspoons baking soda
1/2 teaspoon salt
1 tablespoon ground ginger
2 (1-ounce) squares unsweetened chocolate, melted and cooled
Sugar

Beat shortening at medium speed of an electric mixer until fluffy; gradually add 1 cup sugar, beating well. Add egg, and beat well. Stir in molasses.

Combine flour and next 3 ingredients; add to creamed mixture, stirring well. Stir in melted chocolate.

Shape dough into 1-inch balls; roll balls in sugar. Place 2 inches apart on lightly greased cookie sheets. Bake at 350° for 10 to 12 minutes. Cool on wire racks.

Yield: 4 dozen.

DOUBLE-CHOCOLATE SUGAR COOKIES

1 (12-ounce) package semisweet chocolate morsels, divided
1 cup butter or margarine, softened
1 cup sugar
1 large egg
2 tablespoons milk
1 teaspoon vanilla extract
3 cups all-purpose flour
1 teaspoon baking powder
1/2 teaspoon baking soda
1/2 teaspoon salt
1/2 cup sugar

Melt 1 cup semisweet chocolate morsels in a heavy saucepan over low heat, reserving remaining morsels. Set aside.

Beat butter at medium speed of an electric mixer until creamy; gradually add 1 cup sugar, beating well. Add egg, milk, and vanilla, mixing well. Add melted morsels, mixing until blended.

Combine flour and next 3 ingredients; gradually add to creamed mixture, mixing well. Stir in remaining chocolate morsels.

Shape dough into balls, 1 tablespoon at a time; roll balls in 1/2 cup sugar. Place on lightly greased cookie sheets.

Bake at 400° for 8 to 10 minutes. (Cookies will be soft and will firm up as they cool.) Remove to wire racks to cool.

Yield: 4 1/2 dozen.

WHITE CHOCOLATE CHUNK COOKIES

1/2 cup butter or margarine, softened
1/2 cup shortening
3/4 cup sugar
1/2 cup firmly packed brown sugar
1 large egg
2 cups all-purpose flour
1 teaspoon baking soda
1/2 teaspoon salt
2 teaspoons vanilla extract
10 ounces white chocolate, coarsely chopped
1/2 cup coarsely chopped macadamia nuts, lightly toasted

Beat butter and shortening at medium speed of an electric mixer until creamy; gradually add sugars, beating well. Add egg; beat well. Combine flour, soda, and salt; add to creamed mixture, mixing well. Stir in vanilla. Stir in white chocolate and macadamia nuts. Cover and chill 1 hour.

Drop dough by 2 tablespoonfuls, 3 inches apart, onto lightly greased cookie sheets. Bake at 350° for 12 to 14 minutes (cookies will be soft). Cool slightly on cookie sheets; remove to wire racks to cool completely.

Yield: 1 1/2 dozen.

CHUNKY MACADAMIA NUT-WHITE CHOCOLATE COOKIES

1/2 cup butter or margarine, softened
3/4 cup firmly packed brown sugar
2 tablespoons sugar
1 large egg
1 1/2 teaspoons vanilla extract
2 cups all-purpose flour
3/4 teaspoon baking soda
1/2 teaspoon baking powder
1/8 teaspoon salt
1 (6-ounce) package white chocolate-flavored baking bars, cut into chunks
1 (7-ounce) jar macadamia nuts, coarsely chopped

Beat butter at medium speed of an electric mixer until creamy; gradually add sugars, beating well. Add egg and vanilla, mixing well.

Combine flour and next 3 ingredients; gradually add to creamed mixture, mixing well. Stir in white chocolate chunks and nuts.

Drop by rounded teaspoonfuls onto lightly greased cookie sheets. Bake at 350° for 8 to 10 minutes or until lightly browned. Remove to wire racks to cool.

Yield: 5 dozen.

DID YOU KNOW?

Despite its name and texture, white chocolate is actually not chocolate at all. It's a mixture of cocoa butter, milk solids, sugar, and vanilla; it lacks the cocoa solids that give dark chocolate its color and some of its flavor.

However, don't confuse white chocolate with vanilla-flavored candy coating. While the texture and look are much the same and the ingredients are similar, the cocoa butter is replaced with vegetable fat in candy coating.

PEANUT BUTTER AND CHOCOLATE CHUNK COOKIES

1/2 cup butter or margarine, softened
3/4 cup sugar
2/3 cup firmly packed brown sugar
2 egg whites
1 1/4 cups chunky peanut butter
1 1/2 teaspoons vanilla extract
1 cup all-purpose flour
1/2 teaspoon baking soda
1/4 teaspoon salt
5 (2.1-ounce) chocolate-covered crispy peanut-buttery candy bars, cut into 1/2-inch pieces

Beat butter at medium speed of an electric mixer until creamy; gradually add sugars, beating well. Add egg whites, beating well. Stir in peanut butter and vanilla.

Combine flour, soda, and salt; gradually add to creamed mixture, mixing well. Stir in candy.

Shape dough into 1 1/2-inch balls, and place 2 inches apart on lightly greased cookie sheets.

Bake at 350° for 11 minutes or until browned. Cool 3 minutes on cookie sheets; transfer to wire racks to cool completely.

Yield: 4 dozen.

Note: For chocolate-covered crispy peanut-buttery candy bars, we used Butterfingers.

ORANGE-CHOCOLATE CHIP COOKIES

1/2 cup shortening
1 (3-ounce) package cream cheese, softened
1/2 cup sugar
1 large egg
1 teaspoon vanilla extract
1 teaspoon grated orange rind
1 cup all-purpose flour
1/2 teaspoon salt
1 (6-ounce) package semisweet chocolate morsels

Combine first 4 ingredients in a large bowl; beat until smooth and creamy. Add vanilla and orange rind; beat well.

Combine flour and salt; add to creamed mixture, beating well. Stir in semisweet chocolate morsels.

Drop dough by heaping teaspoonfuls onto ungreased cookie sheets. Bake at 350° for 15 minutes or until edges just begin to brown. Cool on wire racks.

Yield: 3 dozen.

DROP COOKIE TIPS

• Dough for drop cookies is literally dropped from two spoons (not measuring spoons) onto cookie sheets with no further shaping necessary. Or save time by dropping dough using a small, all-purpose scoop.
• Excessive spreading may be caused if the cookie sheet is too hot, oven temperature is incorrect, or dough is too warm. Chilling the dough helps prevent this.
• Allow at least 2 inches between cookies on the cookie sheet.

LOADED-WITH-CHIPS COOKIES

- 1/2 cup butter or margarine, softened
- 1/2 cup shortening
- 1 cup firmly packed brown sugar
- 1/2 cup sugar
- 2 large eggs
- 1 teaspoon vanilla extract
- 1 1/2 cups regular oats, uncooked
- 1 3/4 cups all-purpose flour
- 1 teaspoon baking soda
- 1/2 teaspoon salt
- 1 (12-ounce) package semisweet chocolate morsels
- 3/4 cup chopped pecans

Beat butter and shortening at medium speed of an electric mixer until fluffy; gradually add sugars, beating well. Add eggs and vanilla, beating well.

Combine oats, flour, soda, and salt; add to creamed mixture, mixing well. Stir in chocolate morsels and pecans.

Drop dough by heaping teaspoonfuls onto ungreased cookie sheets. Bake at 350° for 12 to 14 minutes or until lightly browned. Remove to wire racks to cool.

Yield: 6 dozen.

SUPER CHOCOLATE CHUNK COOKIES

- 1 cup butter or margarine, softened
- 1 cup sugar
- 1/2 cup firmly packed brown sugar
- 2 large eggs
- 2 teaspoons vanilla extract
- 2 cups all-purpose flour
- 1 teaspoon baking powder
- 1/2 teaspoon salt
- 1 (12-ounce) package semisweet chocolate chunks
- 1 cup chopped walnuts

Beat butter at medium speed of an electric mixer until creamy; gradually add sugars, beating well. Add eggs and vanilla, beating well.

Combine flour, baking powder, and salt; add to creamed mixture, mixing well. Stir in chocolate chunks and walnuts. Cover and chill at least 1 hour.

Drop dough by tablespoonfuls onto ungreased cookie sheets. Bake at 350° for 12 to 15 minutes or until lightly browned. Cool slightly on cookie sheets; transfer to wire racks to cool completely.

Yield: 4 dozen.

CHOCOLATE OATMEAL CHIPPERS

- 1 cup butter or margarine, softened
- 1½ cups sugar
- 1 large egg
- ¼ cup water
- 1 teaspoon vanilla extract
- 1½ cups all-purpose flour
- ½ teaspoon baking soda
- ½ teaspoon salt
- ½ teaspoon ground cinnamon
- ½ teaspoon ground nutmeg
- 3 cups quick-cooking oats, uncooked
- 1 (6-ounce) package semisweet chocolate morsels
- 1 cup chopped pecans (optional)

Beat butter at medium speed of an electric mixer until creamy; gradually add sugar, beating well. Add egg, water, and vanilla, mixing well. Combine flour, soda, salt, cinnamon, and nutmeg; add to creamed mixture, mixing well. Stir in oats, morsels, and pecans, if desired. Drop dough by rounded teaspoonfuls onto ungreased cookie sheets.

Bake at 350° for 10 to 12 minutes or until lightly browned. Cool slightly on cookie sheets; remove to wire racks to cool completely.

Yield: about 8 dozen.

VARIATIONS
RAISIN OATMEAL COOKIES
Prepare Chocolate Oatmeal Chippers, deleting semisweet chocolate morsels and adding 1 cup raisins.

PEANUT BUTTER OATMEAL CHIPPERS
Prepare Chocolate Oatmeal Chippers, using 1 cup peanut butter morsels instead of 1 (6-ounce) package semisweet chocolate morsels.

BROWNIE CHIP COOKIES

- 1 (23.7-ounce) package brownie mix
- 2 large eggs
- ⅓ cup vegetable oil
- 1 (6-ounce) package semisweet chocolate morsels
- ½ cup chopped pecans

Combine first 3 ingredients; beat about 50 strokes with a spoon. Stir in chocolate morsels and pecans. Drop dough by rounded teaspoonfuls onto greased cookie sheets.

Bake at 350° for 10 to 12 minutes. Cool slightly (about 2 minutes) on cookie sheets. Remove to wire racks, and let cool completely.

Yield: about 6 dozen.

STORING CHOCOLATE
Chocolate morsels can be stored up to 9 months. When conditions are too humid and warm, chocolate develops "bloom" — the morsels look gray on the surface. This doesn't affect quality and disappears when the chocolate is heated.

MEASURING MORSELS
1 (6-ounce) package = 1 cup
1 (12-ounce) package = 2 cups

TRIPLE CHIP COOKIES

(Shown on page 517)

- 1 cup butter or margarine, softened
- 1 cup sugar
- $1/2$ cup firmly packed brown sugar
- 2 large eggs
- 1 teaspoon vanilla extract
- $2^1/4$ cups all-purpose flour
- 1 teaspoon baking soda
- $1/2$ teaspoon salt
- $3/4$ cup semisweet chocolate morsels
- $3/4$ cup milk chocolate morsels
- $3/4$ cup vanilla milk morsels
- $1/2$ cup chopped blanched almonds

Beat butter at medium speed of an electric mixer until creamy; gradually add sugars, beating well. Add eggs and vanilla; beat well.

Combine flour, soda, and salt; gradually add to creamed mixture, mixing well after each addition. Stir in morsels and almonds.

Drop dough by tablespoonfuls onto ungreased cookie sheets. Bake at 350° for 12 to 15 minutes or until lightly browned. Cool slightly on cookie sheets; transfer to wire racks to cool completely.

Yield: 4 dozen.

OATMEAL-PEANUT BUTTER-CHOCOLATE CHIP COOKIES

- $1/2$ cup butter or margarine, softened
- 1 (18-ounce) jar chunky peanut butter
- $1^1/2$ cups sugar
- $1^1/2$ cups firmly packed brown sugar
- 4 large eggs
- 1 teaspoon vanilla extract
- 6 cups quick-cooking oats, uncooked
- $2^1/2$ teaspoons baking soda
- 1 (6-ounce) package semisweet chocolate morsels

Beat butter and peanut butter at medium speed of an electric mixer until fluffy; gradually add sugars, beating well. Add eggs and vanilla, mixing well.

Combine oats and baking soda; add to creamed mixture, mixing well. Stir in morsels.

Drop dough by tablespoonfuls onto ungreased cookie sheets. Bake at 350° for 9 to 10 minutes. Cool on cookie sheets 5 minutes; remove to wire racks to cool completely.

Yield: 7 dozen.

BEST-EVER CHOCOLATE CHIP COOKIES

3/4 cup butter or margarine, softened
1/4 cup shortening
3/4 cup sugar
3/4 cup firmly packed brown sugar
2 large eggs
1 teaspoon vanilla extract
2 1/4 cups all-purpose flour
1 teaspoon baking soda
1/4 teaspoon salt
1 (12-ounce) package semisweet
   chocolate morsels

Beat butter and shortening at medium speed of an electric mixer until fluffy; gradually add sugars, beating well. Add eggs and vanilla, beating well.

Combine flour, soda, and salt; add to creamed mixture, mixing well. Stir in chocolate morsels.

Drop dough by heaping teaspoonfuls onto ungreased cookie sheets. Bake at 375° for 9 to 11 minutes. Cool slightly on cookie sheets; remove to wire racks to cool completely.

Yield: about 6 1/2 dozen.

VARIATIONS
DOUBLE CHIP COOKIES
Prepare Best-Ever Chocolate Chip Cookies, using 1 cup peanut butter morsels or butterscotch morsels and 1 (6-ounce) package semisweet chocolate morsels instead of 1 (12-ounce) package semisweet chocolate morsels.

JUMBO CHOCOLATE CHIP COOKIES
Prepare Best-Ever Chocolate Chip Cookies, dropping them onto ungreased cookie sheets by 1/4 cupfuls. Lightly press each cookie into a 3-inch circle with fingertips. Bake at 350° for 15 to 17 minutes.

Yield: 1 1/2 dozen.

CRISP PEANUTTIEST COOKIES

1/2 cup butter or margarine, softened
1/2 cup chunky peanut butter
1 1/2 cups firmly packed brown sugar
3/4 cup sugar
2 large eggs
2 1/2 cups all-purpose flour
1 teaspoon baking soda
1/2 cup flaked coconut
3/4 cup Spanish peanuts

Beat butter and peanut butter at medium speed of an electric mixer until creamy; gradually add sugars, beating well. Add eggs, and mix well.

Combine flour and soda; add to creamed mixture, mixing well. Stir in coconut and peanuts.

Shape dough into 1-inch balls. Place on ungreased cookie sheets. Bake at 350° for 12 to 15 minutes or until lightly browned. Cool on wire racks.

Yield: 6 dozen.

Crisp Peanuttiest Cookies

549

OLD-FASHIONED PEANUT BUTTER COOKIES

- 1 cup butter or margarine, softened
- 1 cup creamy peanut butter
- 1 cup sugar
- 1 cup firmly packed brown sugar
- 2 large eggs, beaten
- 1 tablespoon milk
- 2 1/2 cups all-purpose flour
- 2 teaspoons baking soda
- 1/4 teaspoon salt
- 1 teaspoon vanilla extract
  Additional sugar

Beat butter and peanut butter at medium speed of an electric mixer until creamy; gradually add 1 cup sugar and brown sugar, beating well. Add eggs and milk, beating well. Combine flour, soda, and salt; add to creamed mixture, beating well. Stir in vanilla. Cover and chill 2 to 3 hours. Shape dough into 1 1/4-inch balls; place 3 inches apart on ungreased cookie sheets. Dip a fork in sugar, and flatten cookies in a crisscross pattern. Bake at 375° for 10 minutes. Remove cookies to wire racks to cool.

Yield: 6 dozen.

CRISPY COCONUT-OATMEAL COOKIES

- 1 cup shortening
- 1 cup sugar
- 1 cup firmly packed brown sugar
- 2 large eggs
- 1 teaspoon vanilla extract
- 2 cups all-purpose flour
- 1 teaspoon baking soda
- 1/2 teaspoon baking powder
- 1/2 teaspoon salt
- 2 cups regular oats, uncooked
- 2 cups crisp rice cereal
- 1 cup flaked coconut

Beat first 3 ingredients at medium speed of an electric mixer until blended; add eggs and vanilla, beating well. Combine flour and next 3 ingredients; add to creamed mixture, mixing well. Stir in oats and remaining ingredients.

Shape dough into 1-inch balls, and place 2 inches apart on lightly greased cookie sheets; flatten slightly with a fork. Bake at 350° for 12 minutes or until done. Transfer to wire racks to cool.

Yield: 7 dozen.

BAKING SHEET TIPS

- Use heavy-gauge, shiny aluminum sheets with low or no sides for even browning of cookies. Nonstick cookie sheets produce cookies that spread less and have smoother bottoms, but their dark coating will affect browning.
- Insulated cookie sheets will help prevent overbaking of cookies, but bottoms will not brown, making it difficult to determine doneness in some cookies. If bottoms do brown, cookies may be overdone. Also, cookies with a high butter content will spread out before the shape is set, so edges may be thin. Baking time will be slightly longer on insulated sheets. Cookies in this book were not tested using insulated sheets, so times will need to be adjusted.

DOUBLE-CHIP PEANUT BUTTER COOKIES

     1 cup butter or margarine, softened
     1 cup creamy peanut butter
     2 cups firmly packed brown sugar
     2 large eggs
     1 teaspoon vanilla extract
 1¼ cups all-purpose flour
 1¼ cups whole wheat flour
 1½ teaspoons baking soda
 ⅔ cup sesame seeds, toasted
 ½ teaspoon ground nutmeg
 ⅔ cup semisweet chocolate morsels
 ⅔ cup peanut butter morsels

Beat butter and peanut butter at medium speed of an electric mixer until creamy; gradually add brown sugar, beating well. Add eggs and vanilla, mixing well.

Combine all-purpose flour and next 4 ingredients; add to creamed mixture, and beat until smooth. Stir in morsels.

Shape dough into 1-inch balls. Place on lightly greased cookie sheets. Bake at 350° for 11 to 13 minutes. Cool on wire racks.

Yield: 7 dozen.

TOASTED OAT-COCONUT COOKIES

 ¼ cup butter or margarine, softened
 ¼ cup shortening
     1 cup sugar
     1 large egg
 ½ teaspoon coconut extract
 1½ cups all-purpose flour
     1 teaspoon baking powder
 ½ teaspoon baking soda
 ½ teaspoon salt
     1 cup flaked coconut
 ½ cup crispy rice cereal
 ½ cup pan-toasted or regular oats, uncooked

Beat softened butter and shortening at medium speed of an electric mixer until fluffy; gradually add sugar, beating well. Add egg and coconut extract; beat well.

Combine flour, baking powder, soda, and salt; stir well. Gradually add to creamed mixture, mixing well. Stir in coconut, cereal, and oats.

Drop dough by heaping teaspoonfuls onto lightly greased cookie sheets. Bake at 325° for 12 to 14 minutes or until golden. Let cool slightly on cookie sheets; remove to wire racks to cool completely.

Yield: 4 dozen.

CHOCOLATE MACAROON COOKIES

1 (4-ounce) package sweet baking chocolate
2 egg whites
$^1/_2$ cup sugar
$^1/_4$ teaspoon vanilla extract
1 (7-ounce) can flaked coconut

Melt chocolate in a heavy saucepan over low heat, stirring occasionally. Remove from heat and cool.

Beat egg whites at high speed of an electric mixer 1 minute. Gradually add sugar, 1 tablespoon at a time, beating until stiff peaks form and sugar dissolves (2 to 4 minutes). Fold in melted chocolate and vanilla; stir in coconut.

Drop mixture by teaspoonfuls onto cookie sheets lined with aluminum foil. Bake at 350° for 12 to 15 minutes. Transfer cookies, leaving them on foil, to wire racks; cool. Carefully remove cookies from foil.

Yield: $4^1/_2$ dozen.

EASY FROSTED BROWNIES

$^1/_2$ cup sugar
$^1/_3$ cup butter or margarine
2 tablespoons water
1 (6-ounce) package semisweet chocolate morsels
1 teaspoon vanilla extract
2 large eggs
$^3/_4$ cup all-purpose flour
$^1/_4$ teaspoon baking soda
$^1/_4$ teaspoon salt
1 cup chopped pecans or walnuts
1 (6-ounce) package semisweet chocolate morsels (optional)
$^1/_2$ cup chopped pecans or walnuts (optional)

Combine first 3 ingredients in a medium saucepan; cook over high heat, stirring frequently, until mixture comes to a boil. Remove mixture from heat.

Add 1 package chocolate morsels and vanilla, stirring until chocolate melts. Add eggs, one at a time, beating after each addition.

Combine flour, soda, and salt; stir dry ingredients and 1 cup pecans into chocolate mixture.

Pour batter into a greased and floured 9-inch square pan. Bake at 325° for 30 minutes. Cool on a wire rack.

Cut brownies into squares and serve plain, or sprinkle 1 package chocolate morsels over hot brownies, if desired. Let stand until morsels are softened; then spread evenly over brownies with a spatula. Sprinkle $^1/_2$ cup pecans on top, if desired. Cool and cut into squares.

Yield: 3 dozen.

CHOCOLATE CHIP COOKIE PIZZAS

Vegetable cooking spray
1 package (18 ounces) refrigerated chocolate chip cookie dough
1 jar (10 ounces) maraschino cherries, drained and halved
1 cup pecan pieces
1 package (6 ounces) semisweet chocolate chips
8 ounces vanilla candy coating, melted

Use the bottom of an 8-inch round cake pan as a pattern to draw 4 circles on cardboard; cut out and set aside.

Preheat oven to 350 degrees. Spray 8-inch round cake pan with vegetable spray until well coated.

Divide cookie dough into fourths. With floured hands, press one fourth of dough into cake pan. Bake 8 to 10 minutes. Carefully remove from pan and cool on a wire rack. Repeat with remaining cookie dough.

Place cookies on cardboard circles. Place cherries, pecans, and chocolate chips on cookies. Drizzle candy coating over cookies; let harden. Store in an airtight container.

Yield: 4 cookie pizzas, 6 servings each.

MELTING CHOCOLATE

• Save on cleanup by melting 1-ounce, paper-wrapped squares of chocolate in the microwave. Keep chocolate in the paper, and microwave at MEDIUM (50% power); 1 square takes $1^1/_2$ to 2 minutes, 2 squares about 3 minutes, and 3 squares about 4 minutes.

• Semisweet chocolate morsels and squares hold their shape when melted until they are stirred.

HELPFUL TIPS

• If cookie dough seems too soft to shape by hand, chill until it's firm enough to shape. If still too soft, mix in 1 to 2 tablespoons flour.

• Unless otherwise specified in recipe, use a tableware teaspoon or tablespoon for drop cookies. Cookie scoops are available in different sizes and are easy to use. They produce uniformly sized cookies that will bake more evenly.

BROWNIE MIX

    7 cups sugar
    4 cups all-purpose flour
2 1/2 cups cocoa
    1 tablespoon plus 1 teaspoon
       baking powder
    1 tablespoon salt
    2 cups shortening

Combine first 5 ingredients; stir well. Cut in shortening with a pastry blender until mixture is crumbly.

Place in an airtight container; store in a cool, dry place or in refrigerator up to 6 weeks.

Yield: 14 cups.

QUICK AND EASY BROWNIES

    3 cups Brownie Mix (recipe above)
 1/2 cup chopped pecans
    3 large eggs, beaten
1 1/2 teaspoons vanilla extract

Combine all ingredients, stirring until blended. Spoon into a greased and floured 8-inch square pan.

Bake at 350° for 35 to 40 minutes. Cool and cut into squares.

Yield: 16 brownies.

BISCUIT MIX BROWNIES

    1 (12-ounce) package semisweet
       chocolate morsels
 1/4 cup butter or margarine
    1 (14-ounce) can sweetened
       condensed milk
    1 large egg, lightly beaten
    2 cups biscuit mix
1 1/2 cups chopped pecans
    1 (16-ounce) container ready-
       to-spread chocolate fudge
       frosting (optional)

Combine chocolate morsels and butter in a microwave-safe bowl; microwave at HIGH 2 minutes, stirring once.

Stir in condensed milk and next 3 ingredients. Spoon into a greased 13 x 9 x 2-inch pan.

Bake at 350° for 25 to 30 minutes. Cool slightly on a wire rack. Spread chocolate frosting on warm brownies, if desired. Cut into squares.

Yield: 3 dozen.

CUTTING BAR COOKIES

• Bar cookies and brownies may be cut into various sizes and shapes. The yield of each recipe depends on the size of the pan as well as the size of the serving. Usually the thicker or richer the bar, the smaller it should be cut. You can adjust the yield of each recipe by cutting larger or smaller portions.
• Besides cutting into bars and squares, bar cookies may be cut into diamond shapes. To do so, cut diagonally in one direction and straight across in the other direction. The yield will be slightly less.

QUICK BROWNIES

1/2 cup chopped pecans
2 (1-ounce) squares unsweetened
  chocolate
1/2 cup butter or margarine, cut into
  4 pieces
1 teaspoon instant coffee granules
1 cup firmly packed light brown
  sugar
2 large eggs, beaten
1 teaspoon vanilla extract
2/3 cup all-purpose flour
1/2 teaspoon baking powder
  Frosting

Spread chopped pecans in a pie plate. Microwave at HIGH 3 to 3 1/2 minutes. Set aside.

Place chocolate and butter in a microwave-safe bowl. Microwave at MEDIUM (50% power) 2 1/2 minutes or until chocolate melts, stirring at 1-minute intervals.

Stir coffee granules into chocolate mixture. Add sugar, and stir until blended. Add eggs and vanilla, mixing well. Stir in pecans, flour, and baking powder.

Spread mixture into a greased and floured 8-inch square baking dish; shield corners with triangles of aluminum foil, keeping foil smooth and close to dish. Place dish on top of a microwave-safe cereal bowl inverted in oven.

Microwave at MEDIUM 8 minutes, giving dish a quarter turn at 4-minute intervals. Remove foil from corners.

Microwave at HIGH 1 to 2 minutes or until a wooden pick inserted in center comes out clean. Place directly on counter, and let stand 20 minutes. Spread frosting over brownies. Cut into squares, and immediately remove from dish.

Yield: 16 brownies.

FROSTING

1 (1-ounce) square unsweetened
  chocolate
1 tablespoon butter or margarine
1 cup sifted powdered sugar
  Dash of ground cinnamon
  Dash of salt
1 to 2 tablespoons milk
1/2 teaspoon vanilla extract

Place unsweetened chocolate and butter in a small microwave-safe bowl. Microwave at MEDIUM (50% power) 1 1/2 to 2 minutes or until chocolate melts, stirring at 1-minute intervals.

Stir in powdered sugar, cinnamon, and salt. Add milk and vanilla, stirring until mixture is smooth.

Yield: 1/2 cup.

CRISPY-CHEWY MOLASSES COOKIES

    1 cup butter or margarine
 2 1/2 cups sugar
    1 teaspoon ground cinnamon
    1 teaspoon ground nutmeg
  1/4 teaspoon salt
    1 large egg
  1/4 cup plus 1 tablespoon water
    1 teaspoon baking soda
  1/4 cup molasses
 3 1/2 cups all-purpose flour

Melt butter; cool to room temperature. Combine butter and next 5 ingredients in a large mixing bowl; beat well at medium speed of an electric mixer. Combine water and soda in a small bowl, stirring until soda dissolves; add soda mixture to creamed mixture, beating well. Stir in molasses and flour. Drop dough by teaspoonfuls, 3 inches apart, onto greased cookie sheets. Bake at 350° for 7 to 9 minutes. Cool completely on wire racks.

Yield: 8 dozen.

MISSISSIPPI MUD BROWNIES

    4 (1-ounce) squares unsweetened
      chocolate
    1 cup butter or margarine
    2 cups sugar
    1 cup all-purpose flour
  1/8 teaspoon salt
    4 large eggs, beaten
    1 cup chopped pecans

    3 cups miniature marshmallows
      Fudge Frosting

Combine chocolate and butter in a large saucepan; cook over low heat, stirring until chocolate and butter melt. Remove from heat.

Combine sugar, flour, and salt; add to chocolate mixture. Add eggs and pecans; stir until blended. Spoon batter into a lightly greased and floured 13 x 9 x 2-inch pan.

Bake at 350° for 25 to 30 minutes or until a wooden pick inserted in center comes out clean.

Sprinkle marshmallows evenly over hot brownies. Spread with Fudge Frosting. Cool and cut into squares.

Yield: 2 dozen.

FUDGE FROSTING

    2 (1-ounce) squares unsweetened
      chocolate
  1/2 cup evaporated milk
  1/2 cup butter or margarine
 4 1/2 to 5 cups sifted powdered sugar
  1/2 teaspoon vanilla extract

Combine first 3 ingredients in a heavy saucepan. Cook over low heat, stirring until chocolate and butter melt. Remove from heat. Transfer to a medium bowl. Gradually add powdered sugar and vanilla, beating at low speed of an electric mixer until smooth.

Yield: 2 1/3 cups.

CANDY BAR BROWNIES
(Shown on page 9)

- 4 large eggs, lightly beaten
- 2 cups sugar
- 3/4 cup butter or margarine, melted
- 2 teaspoons vanilla extract
- 1 1/2 cups all-purpose flour
- 1/2 teaspoon baking powder
- 1/4 teaspoon salt
- 1/3 cup cocoa
- 4 (2.07-ounce) chocolate-coated caramel-peanut nougat bars, coarsely chopped
- 3 (1.55-ounce) milk chocolate candy bars, finely chopped

Combine first 4 ingredients in a large bowl. Combine flour and next 3 ingredients; stir into sugar mixture. Fold in chopped nougat bars.

Spoon mixture into a greased and floured 13 x 9 x 2-inch pan; sprinkle with chopped milk chocolate bars. Bake at 350° for 30 to 35 minutes. Cool and cut into squares.

Yield: 2 1/2 dozen.

Note: For nougat bars, we used Snickers candy bars; for milk chocolate bars, we used Hershey's candy bars.

BUTTERSCOTCH BROWNIES

- 2/3 cup butter or margarine, softened
- 1 1/2 cups firmly packed brown sugar
- 2 large eggs
- 2 teaspoons vanilla extract
- 2 cups all-purpose flour
- 1 teaspoon baking powder
- 1/4 teaspoon baking soda
- 1/4 teaspoon salt
- 1 (6-ounce) package butterscotch morsels
- 1/2 cup chopped pecans

Beat butter at medium speed of an electric mixer until creamy; add sugar, beating well. Add eggs and vanilla; beat well.

Combine flour, baking powder, baking soda, and salt; add dry ingredients to creamed mixture, stirring well.

Pour batter into a greased 13 x 9 x 2-inch baking pan. Sprinkle with butterscotch morsels and pecans. Bake at 350° for 30 minutes. Cool and cut into bars.

Yield: 2 1/2 dozen.

CANDY BAR TIPS
• To easily chop chocolate candy bars with nuts and caramel, use a sharp, sturdy knife.
• To melt milk chocolate candy bars, place in a small, heavy saucepan, and stir over low heat until candy melts. Or place in a small microwave-safe bowl, and microwave at LOW (30% power), stirring often, until candy melts.

CHOCOLATE CHIP-PEANUT BUTTER BROWNIES

1/3 cup butter or margarine, softened
1/2 cup creamy peanut butter
1/2 cup sugar
1/2 cup firmly packed brown sugar
2 large eggs
1 cup all-purpose flour
1 teaspoon baking powder
1/4 teaspoon salt
1 teaspoon vanilla extract
1 (6-ounce) package semisweet chocolate morsels

Beat butter and peanut butter at medium speed of an electric mixer until creamy; gradually add sugars, beating well. Add eggs, one at a time, beating after each addition.

Combine flour, baking powder, and salt; add to creamed mixture, stirring well. Stir in vanilla and chocolate morsels.

Pour batter into a greased 8-inch square pan. Bake at 350° for 30 to 35 minutes. Cool and cut into squares.

Yield: 25 brownies.

YUMMY BARS

1 (14-ounce) package caramels, unwrapped
1 (5-ounce) can evaporated milk, divided
1 (18.25-ounce) package German chocolate cake mix with pudding
3/4 cup butter or margarine, melted
1 large egg
1 (6-ounce) package semisweet chocolate morsels
1 cup coarsely chopped pecans

Combine caramels and 1/4 cup evaporated milk in a small, heavy sauce pan. Cook over low heat, stirring occasionally, until smooth; set aside. Combine cake mix, butter, egg, and remaining evaporated milk. Spoon half of mixture into a greased 13 x 9 x 2-inch pan, spreading mixture evenly.

Bake at 350° for 6 minutes. Remove from oven; sprinkle with morsels and pecans. Spoon caramel mixture on top; carefully spoon remaining cake mixture over caramel layer. Bake at 350° for 20 to 25 minutes. Cool on a wire rack, and cut into bars.

Yield: about 3 dozen.

QUICK TIP
If you line the pan with aluminum foil when making bar cookies, allow foil to overhang 2 inches on each end. Grease foil if recipe calls for a greased pan. After the cookies have baked and cooled, use the foil overhang to lift the cookie slab from the pan. Cutting the cookies outside the pan keeps the pan from getting scratched and marred.

CHERRY BONBON COOKIES

24 maraschino cherries, undrained
1/2 cup butter or margarine, softened
3/4 cup sifted powdered sugar
1 1/2 cups all-purpose flour
1/8 teaspoon salt
2 tablespoons half-and-half
1 teaspoon vanilla extract
   Powdered sugar
   Cherry Glaze

Drain cherries, reserving 1/4 cup juice for glaze; set aside.

Beat butter at medium speed of an electric mixer until creamy; gradually add 3/4 cup sugar, beating well. Stir in flour and next 3 ingredients.

Shape dough into 24 balls. Press each ball around a cherry, covering completely; place on ungreased cookie sheets. Bake at 350° for 18 to 20 minutes. Remove to wire racks to cool completely. Sprinkle with powdered sugar, and drizzle with Cherry Glaze.

Yield: 2 dozen.

CHERRY GLAZE

2 tablespoons butter or margarine, melted
1 cup sifted powdered sugar
1/4 cup reserved cherry juice
   Red food coloring (optional)

Combine first 3 ingredients; add food coloring, if desired. Place in a heavy-duty, zip-top plastic bag; seal. To drizzle, snip a tiny hole at one corner of bag and squeeze.

Yield: 1/2 cup.

Cherry Bonbon Cookies

OAT 'N' CRUNCH BROWNIES

1 (21.5-ounce) package fudge
    brownie mix
1/2 cup chopped pecans
1/3 cup quick-cooking oats, uncooked
1/4 cup firmly packed brown sugar
1/4 teaspoon ground cinnamon
    (optional)
2 tablespoons butter or margarine,
    melted
3/4 cup candy-coated chocolate
    pieces

Grease bottom of a 13 x 9 x 2-inch pan. Prepare brownie mix according to package directions; spoon into prepared pan.

Combine pecans, oats, brown sugar, and, if desired, cinnamon; stir in butter. Stir in candy; sprinkle over batter.

Bake at 350° for 35 minutes. Cool and cut into squares.

Yield: 3 dozen.

WHITE CHOCOLATE BROWNIES

6 (1 1/4-ounce) white chocolate
    candy bars with almonds,
    divided
1/4 cup butter or margarine
2 large eggs
1/2 cup sugar
1 cup all-purpose flour
1/4 teaspoon baking powder
1/8 teaspoon salt
1 teaspoon vanilla extract
1/4 teaspoon almond extract
1 (1-ounce) square semisweet
    chocolate
1 teaspoon shortening

Melt 4 candy bars and butter in a heavy saucepan over low heat, stirring constantly. Set aside to cool.

Beat eggs at medium speed of an electric mixer until thick and pale; gradually add sugar, beating well.

Combine flour, baking powder, and salt; add to egg mixture, mixing well. Stir in cooled candy mixture and flavorings.

Coarsely chop remaining 2 candy bars, and stir into batter. Pour batter into a greased 8-inch square pan. Bake at 350° for 25 minutes or until lightly browned. Cool on a wire rack.

Combine semisweet chocolate and shortening in a small saucepan; cook over low heat, stirring until chocolate melts. Drizzle over brownies; chill until chocolate hardens. Cut into squares.

Yield: 16 brownies.

CHOCOLATE-NUT SUNDAE SQUARES

- ½ cup butter or margarine, softened
- ⅔ cup firmly packed brown sugar
- 1 egg
- 1 jar (10 ounces) maraschino cherries, drained and chopped, reserving ¼ cup liquid
- ½ teaspoon vanilla extract
- 1½ cups all-purpose flour
- ½ cup chocolate mix for milk
- ½ teaspoon baking powder
- 1 cup chopped pecans
- ⅓ cup semisweet chocolate chips
- ½ teaspoon vegetable shortening

Preheat oven to 350 degrees. In a large bowl, cream butter and brown sugar until fluffy. Add egg, reserved cherry liquid, and vanilla; beat until smooth.

Combine flour, chocolate mix, and baking powder in a small bowl. Add dry ingredients to creamed mixture; stir until a soft dough forms. Stir in pecans and cherries.

Line a 9-inch square baking pan with aluminum foil, extending foil over opposite sides of pan; grease foil. Spread mixture into prepared pan. Bake 20 to 25 minutes or until firm. Cool in pan 10 minutes. Lift from pan using ends of foil. Cool completely.

Melt chocolate chips and shortening in a small saucepan over low heat. Drizzle melted chocolate over baked mixture. Cut into 2-inch squares. Store in an airtight container.

Yield: about 16 squares.

EASY CHOCOLATE SAUCE

- 1 (14-ounce) can sweetened condensed milk
- 2 (1-ounce) squares unsweetened chocolate
- 2 tablespoons butter or margarine
  Dash of salt
- ½ teaspoon vanilla extract

Combine all ingredients in a heavy saucepan; cook over low heat, stirring constantly with a wire whisk, until chocolate melts and mixture is smooth. Serve warm sauce over ice cream.

Yield: 1⅝ cups.

CHOCOLATE SUBSTITUTIONS
- To substitute for 1 (1-ounce) square unsweetened chocolate: Use 3 tablespoons cocoa plus 1 tablespoon shortening.
- For 1 ounce semisweet chocolate: Use 1 ounce (about 3 tablespoons) semisweet chocolate morsels OR 1 (1-ounce) square unsweetened chocolate plus 1 tablespoon sugar.
- For a 4-ounce bar sweet baking chocolate: Use ¼ cup cocoa, ⅓ cup sugar, plus 3 tablespoons shortening.

ALL-AMERICAN POPCORN

Make separate recipes of red and blue popcorn; mix with 20 cups of plain popcorn.

    20 cups popped popcorn
     2 cups sugar
    1/2 cup butter or margarine
    1/2 cup light corn syrup
    1/4 teaspoon salt
     1 package (3 ounces) cherry or
         blueberry gelatin
         Red or blue paste food coloring

Preheat oven to 275 degrees. Place popcorn in a large greased roasting pan.

In a large heavy saucepan, combine sugar, butter, corn syrup, and salt. Stirring constantly, bring to a boil over medium heat; boil 5 minutes. Remove from heat. For red popcorn, stir in cherry gelatin and red food coloring; for blue popcorn, stir in blueberry gelatin and blue food coloring.

Pour sugar mixture over popcorn, stirring to coat. Bake 30 minutes, stirring every 10 minutes. Spread on ungreased aluminum foil to cool. Store in an airtight container.

Yield: about 22 cups flavored popcorn.

MEASURING INGREDIENTS

Liquid measuring cups have a rim above the measuring line to keep liquid ingredients from spilling. Nested measuring cups are used to measure dry ingredients, butter, shortening, and peanut butter. Measuring spoons are used for measuring both dry and liquid ingredients.

To measure flour or granulated sugar: Spoon ingredient into nested measuring cup and level off with a knife. Do not pack down.

To measure confectioners sugar: Sift sugar, spoon lightly into nested measuring cup, and level off with a knife.

To measure brown sugar: Pack into nested measuring cup and level off with a knife. Sugar should hold its shape when removed from cup.

To measure dry ingredients equaling less than 1/4 cup: Dip measuring spoon into ingredient and level off with a knife.

To measure butter, shortening, or peanut butter: Pack ingredient firmly into nested measuring cup and level off with a knife.

To measure liquids: Use a liquid measuring cup on a flat surface. Pour ingredient into cup and check measuring line at eye level.

To measure honey or syrup: For a more accurate measurement, lightly spray measuring cup or spoon with cooking spray before measuring so the liquid will release easily from cup or spoon.

METRIC EQUIVALENTS

The recipes that appear in this cookbook use the standard United States method for measuring liquid and dry or solid ingredients (teaspoons, tablespoons, and cups). The information on this chart is provided to help cooks outside the U.S. successfully use these recipes. All equivalents are approximate.

METRIC EQUIVALENTS FOR DIFFERENT TYPES OF INGREDIENTS

A standard cup measure of a dry or solid ingredient will vary in weight depending on the type of ingredient.
A standard cup of liquid is the same volume for any type of liquid. Use the following chart when converting standard cup measures to grams (weight) or milliliters (volume).

Standard Cup	Fine Powder	Grain	Granular	Liquid Solids	Liquid
	(ex. flour)	(ex. rice)	(ex. sugar)	(ex. butter)	(ex. milk)
1	140 g	150 g	190 g	200 g	240 ml
¾	105 g	113 g	143 g	150 g	180 ml
⅔	93 g	100 g	125 g	133 g	160 ml
½	70 g	75 g	95 g	100 g	120 ml
⅓	47 g	50 g	63 g	67 g	80 ml
¼	35 g	38 g	48 g	50 g	60 ml
⅛	18 g	19 g	24 g	25 g	30 ml

USEFUL EQUIVALENTS FOR LIQUID INGREDIENTS BY VOLUME

¼ tsp						=	1 ml	
½ tsp						=	2 ml	
1 tsp						=	5 ml	
3 tsp	=	1 tbls			=	½ fl oz	=	15 ml
		2 tbls	=	⅛ cup	=	1 fl oz	=	30 ml
		4 tbls	=	¼ cup	=	2 fl oz	=	60 ml
		5⅓ tbls	=	⅓ cup	=	3 fl oz	=	80 ml
		8 tbls	=	½ cup	=	4 fl oz	=	120 ml
		10⅔ tbls	=	⅔ cup	=	5 fl oz	=	160 ml
		12 tbls	=	¾ cup	=	6 fl oz	=	180 ml
		16 tbls	=	1 cup	=	8 fl oz	=	240 ml
1 pt			=	2 cups	=	16 fl oz	=	480 ml
1 qt			=	4 cups	=	32 fl oz	=	960 ml
						33 fl oz	=	1000 ml = 1 l

USEFUL EQUIVALENTS FOR DRY INGREDIENTS BY WEIGHT

(To convert ounces to grams, multiply the number of ounces by 30.)

1 oz	=	¹⁄₁₆ lb	=	30 g
4 oz	=	¼ lb	=	120 g
8 oz	=	½ lb	=	240 g
12 oz	=	¾ lb	=	360 g
16 oz	=	1 lb	=	480 g

USEFUL EQUIVALENTS FOR LENGTH

(To convert inches to centimeters, multiply the number of inches by 2.5.)

1 in					=	2.5 cm	
6 in	=	½ ft			=	15 cm	
12 in	=	1 ft			=	30 cm	
36 in	=	3 ft	=	1 yd	=	90 cm	
40 in					=	100 cm	= 1 m

USEFUL EQUIVALENTS FOR COOKING/OVEN TEMPERATURES

	Fahrenheit	Celsius	Gas Mark
Freeze Water	32° F	0° C	
Room Temperature	68° F	20° C	
Boil Water	212° F	100° C	
Bake	325° F	160° C	3
	350° F	180° C	4
	375° F	190° C	5
	400° F	200° C	6
	425° F	220° C	7
	450° F	230° C	8
Broil			Grill

OUR FAVORITE DESSERTS • RECIPE INDEX

OUR FAVORITE COOKIES • RECIPE INDEX

OUR FAVORITE GIFT MIXES • RECIPE INDEX

OUR FAVORITE SIMPLE SUPPERS • RECIPE INDEX

OUR FAVORITE PARTY FARE • RECIPE INDEX

OUR FAVORITE FAMILY FEASTS • RECIPE INDEX

HOORAY FOR QUICK MEALS • RECIPE INDEX

HOORAY FOR CHICKEN • RECIPE INDEX

HOORAY FOR SIDE DISHES • RECIPE INDEX

HOORAY FOR SALADS • RECIPE INDEX

HOORAY FOR DESSERTS • RECIPE INDEX

HOORAY FOR SWEETS • RECIPE INDEX

NOTES